Systems Analysis and Design

TENTH EDITION

Harry J. Rosenblatt

COURSE TECHNOLOGY
CENGAGE Learning®

SHELLY
CASHMAN
SERIES®

Australia • Brazil • Japan • Korea • Mexico • Singapore • Spain • United Kingdom • United States

COURSE TECHNOLOGY
CENGAGE Learning·

Systems Analysis and Design, Tenth Edition
Harry J. Rosenblatt

Editor-in-Chief: Marie Lee

Executive Editor: Kathleen McMahon

Associate Acquisitions Editor: Reed Curry

Product Manager: Caitlin Womersley

Associate Product Manager: Crystal Parenteau

Editorial Assistant: Sarah Ryan

Marketing Coordinator: Chris Walz

Senior Brand Manager: Robin LeFevre

Market Development Manager: Roy Rosa

Print Buyer: Julio Esperas

Content Project Manager: Divya Divakaran, PreMediaGlobal

Development Editor: Deb Kaufmann

Art Director: GEX Publishing Services

Interior and Text Design: Joel Sadagursky

Cover Design: Lisa Kuhn, Curio Press, LLC

Cover Photos: Tom Kates Photography

Production Management, Indexer, Proofreader, Photo Researcher, and Composition: PreMediaGlobal

For product information and technology assistance, contact us at
Cengage Learning Customer & Sales Support, 1-800-354-9706

For permission to use material from this text or product, submit all requests online at **cengage.com/permissions**
Further permissions questions can be emailed to **permissionrequest@cengage.com**

Design Elements
The magnifying glass icon appearing throughout the book is © benkworks/Shutterstock.com. The saw clip art appearing in Chapter 9 figures is © pichayasri/Shutterstock. The key icon appearing in Chapter 9 figures is © Kolopach/Shutterstock.

Library of Congress Control Number: 2012955551

ISBN-13: 978-1-285-17134-0

ISBN-10: 1-285-17134-9

Course Technology
20 Channel Center Street
Boston, MA 02210
USA

Cengage Learning is a leading provider of customized learning solutions with office locations around the globe, including Singapore, the United Kingdom, Australia, Mexico, Brazil, and Japan. Locate your local office at: **international.cengage.com/region**

Cengage Learning products are represented in Canada by Nelson Education, Ltd.

For your course and learning solutions, visit **www.cengage.com**

To learn more about Course Technology, visit **www.cengage.com/coursetechnology**

Purchase any of our products at your local college bookstore or at our preferred online store at **www.cengagebrain.com**

Printed in the United States of America
1 2 3 4 5 6 7 17 16 15 14 13

BRIEF CONTENTS

TABLE OF CONTENTS

Chapter 3

Managing Systems Projects

PHASE 2: SYSTEMS ANALYSIS

Chapter 4

Requirements Modeling

Chapter 5

Data and Process Modeling

Chapter 6

Object Modeling

Chapter 7

Development Strategies

PHASE 3: SYSTEMS DESIGN

Chapter 8

User Interface Design

Chapter 9

Data Design

Chapter 10

System Architecture

PHASE 4: SYSTEMS IMPLEMENTATION

Chapter 11

Managing Systems Implementation

PHASE 5: SYSTEMS SUPPORT AND SECURITY

Chapter 12

Managing Systems Support and Security

THE SYSTEMS ANALYST'S TOOLKIT

Toolkit Part A

Communication Tools

Toolkit Part B

CASE Tools

Toolkit Part C

Financial Analysis Tools

Toolkit Part D

Internet Resource Tools

PREFACE

The Shelly Cashman Series® offers the finest textbooks in computer education. We are proud that our previous editions of *Systems Analysis and Design* have been so well received by instructors and students. *Systems Analysis and Design, Tenth Edition* continues with the innovation, quality, and reliability you have come to expect from the Shelly Cashman Series.

Overview

Systems Analysis and Design, Tenth Edition includes exciting Video Learning Sessions, developed to maximize the learning experience. The Video Learning Sessions combined with the text offer an interactive, multimedia approach to information systems development. Many two- and four-year colleges and schools use this book in information systems, computer science, and e-commerce curriculums. The textbook emphasizes the role of the systems analyst in a dynamic, business-related environment.

Facing a challenging global marketplace, companies need strong IT resources to survive and compete effectively. Many of today's students will become the systems analysts, managers, and IT professionals of tomorrow. This textbook will help prepare them for those roles.

Using this book, students learn how to translate business requirements into information systems that support a company's short- and long-term objectives. Case studies and assignments teach analytical and problem-solving skills. Students learn about traditional structured analysis, object-oriented concepts, and agile methods. Extensive end-of-chapter exercises emphasize critical-thinking skills.

The *Tenth Edition* introduces several major new end-of-chapter features, including the Critical Thinking Challenge, a new set of Video Learning Session tasks, a new CASE Tool Workshop, and new Chapter Exercises. This edition also includes significant updates on topics such as cloud computing, Web 2.0, client/server architecture, e-commerce, wireless standards, and much more.

Objectives of This Textbook

Systems Analysis and Design, Tenth Edition is intended for a three credit-hour introductory systems analysis and design course. This textbook is designed to:

- Enhance critical thinking skills with the new Critical Thinking Challenge feature at the end of each chapter. The scenario-based tasks and sample answers help students develop perception, organization, analysis, problem-solving, and decision-making skills they can take to the workplace.

- Explain systems analysis and design using an appealing full-color format, numerous screen shots and illustrations, and an easy-to-read style that invites students to learn.

- Introduce project management concepts early in the systems development process, with a new chapter that explains project management tools and techniques.

- Challenge students with a Question of Ethics mini-case in each chapter that asks them to respond to real-life ethical issues in an IT environment.

- Provide multi-method coverage, including a comparison of structured, object-oriented, and agile systems development methods.

- Explain how IT supports business requirements in today's intensely competitive environment, and describe major IT developments and trends.

Video Learning Sessions

Eighteen multimedia Video Learning Sessions describe key systems analysis skills and concepts and provide students with a self-paced, interactive learning tool that reinforces the text. The sessions provide step-by-step explanations that are easy to follow and understand.

© craftvision/iStockphoto

- The new Training Tasks accompanying each Video Learning Session require soft skills and meta cognition where students must use what they have learned to create training materials for others.

- The **Your Turn** feature accompanying every Video Learning Session challenges students to apply their skills and check their work against sample answers. This hands-on practice can help students better handle actual assignments and tasks.

- The Video Learning Sessions offer a self-paced multimedia format that students can review at their convenience. Topics include concepts that students often struggle to understand. Especially in an online environment, a self-paced video can be a welcome learning partner for an individual student.

- Topics include DFDs, object-oriented analysis, functional decomposition diagrams, structure charts, data normalization, entity-relationship diagrams, decision tables, financial tools, and project management.

- Instructors may use the Video Learning Sessions as classroom presentations, distance-education support, student review tools, and exam preparation.

Other New and Updated Features in This Text

Systems Analysis and Design, Tenth Edition offers these exciting new and expanded features:

- New Critical Thinking Challenge feature helps students practice critical thinking skills, first by trying Practice Tasks and viewing sample answers, and then by completing the Challenge Tasks. These tasks can help students develop perception, organization, analysis, problem-solving, and decision-making skills that they will need in the workplace.

- New set of Video Learning Session Training Tasks provides added value for this key feature, and challenges students to develop training materials in a real-life context.

- New CASE Tool Workshop feature focuses on basic CASE skills that students can practice, using Visible Analyst® or another tool.

- New end-of-chapter content includes a major revision of Chapter Exercises, Apply Your Knowledge, and all Case Studies.

- New coverage of cloud computing, Web 2.0, client/server architecture, e-commerce, wireless standards, and much more.

- Updated Management Information Systems CourseMate Web site for *Systems Analysis and Design, Tenth Edition* available for a fully digital course solution. CourseMate provides one location for all interactive activities, Video Learning Sessions, and an interactive e-book. EngagementTracker provides the ability to assess student understanding of concepts through the interactive activities.

Organization of This Textbook

Systems Analysis and Design, Tenth Edition, contains 16 learning units in twelve chapters and a four-part Systems Analyst's Toolkit that teaches valuable cross-functional skills.

Chapter 1 – Introduction to Systems Analysis and Design Chapter 1 provides an up-to-date overview of IT issues, major trends, and various systems development approaches, including structured, object-oriented, and agile methods. The chapter emphasizes the important role of systems analysis and design in supporting business objectives.

Chapter 2 – Analyzing the Business Case Chapter 2 offers a business-related starting point for successful systems analysis. Topics include strategic planning, review of systems requests, how to conduct a feasibility study, and the steps in a preliminary investigation.

Chapter 3 – Managing Systems Projects Chapter 3 explains project management, cost estimating, and change control for information systems. This chapter includes hands-on skills that systems analysts can use to create Gantt charts and PERT charts.

Chapter 4 – Requirements Modeling Chapter 4 describes fact-finding techniques and team-based modeling methods, including JAD and RAD, that systems analysts use to model and document a new system.

Chapter 5 – Data and Process Modeling Chapter 5 explains how systems analysts create a logical model for the new system by using data flow diagrams and process description tools, including structured English, decision tables, and decision trees.

Chapter 6 – Object Modeling Chapter 6 explains object-oriented tools and techniques, including use case diagrams, class diagrams, sequence diagrams, state-transition diagrams, activity diagrams, and the Unified Modeling Language.

Chapter 7 – Development Strategies Chapter 7 focuses on software acquisition options, including outsourcing and offshore outsourcing options, application service providers, and other trends that view software as a service rather than a product.

Chapter 8 – User Interface Design Chapter 8 highlights output and report design, the interaction between humans and computers, including usability issues, graphical screen design, input issues, and data entry guidelines.

Chapter 9 – Data Design Chapter 9 describes data design terms, concepts, and skills including entity-relationship diagrams, cardinality, data normalization rules, data warehousing, data mining, a comparison of logical and physical records, and data control measures.

Chapter 10 – System Architecture Chapter 10 explains the elements of system architecture, with emphasis on RFID, ERP, supply chain management, client/server architecture, and network topology, including wireless networking standards and trends.

Chapter 11 – Managing Systems Implementation Chapter 11 includes coverage of application development and implementation topics, including structure charts, documentation techniques, system testing, user training, data conversion, changeover methods, and post-implementation evaluation.

Chapter 12 – Managing Systems Support and Security Chapter 12 describes user support, maintenance techniques, and factors that indicate the end of a system's useful life. This chapter explains IT security concepts, techniques, and tools, and specifically addresses six security levels: physical, network, application, file, user, and procedural security. Chapter 12 also describes risk management, data backup and disaster recovery, and explains future challenges and opportunities that IT professionals will face in a dynamic workplace.

Toolkit Part A – Communication Tools Part A of the Toolkit describes oral and written communication tools that can make a systems analyst more effective. Topics include guidelines for successful communications, tips for better readability, how to organize and plan a presentation, effective speaking techniques, and managing communication skills.

Toolkit Part B – CASE Tools Part B of the Toolkit focuses on computer-aided software engineering (CASE) tools that systems analysts use to document, model, and develop information systems. Examples of several popular CASE tools are provided, along with sample screens that show CASE tool features.

Toolkit Part C – Financial Analysis Tools Part C of the Toolkit explains various tools that systems analysts use to determine feasibility and evaluate the costs and benefits of an information system. Specific tools include payback analysis, return on investment (ROI), and net present value (NPV).

Toolkit Part D – Internet Resource Tools Part D of the Toolkit explains Internet-based information gathering strategies. Topics include search engines, subject directories, the invisible Web, advanced search techniques, Boolean logic and Venn diagrams. This Toolkit Part also discusses social networking, newsgroups, newsletters, blogs, podcasts, RSS feeds, Webinars, mailing lists, Web-based discussion groups, chat rooms, instant messaging, and online learning opportunities.

FOR THE STUDENT

The Shelly Cashman Series wants you to have a valuable learning experience that will provide the knowledge and skills you need to be successful. With that goal in mind, we have included many activities, games, and learning tools, that we hope you will find interesting, challenging, and enjoyable. For example, because a picture is worth a thou-sand words, each systems development phase begins with an eye-catching Dilbert© car-toon and a multi-color Gantt chart that provides a *"You are Here"* roadmap.

Chapter Learning Tools and How They Will Help You

Dilbert A Dilbert© cartoon introduces each systems development phase. If you've been in situations like these, the cartoon may be familiar. If not, you'll be prepared when they do happen.

Preview Case Each chapter begins with a Preview Case. Within each case, Tina and David show you how they develop a new system for a college bookstore. They discuss key points, and offer a realistic preview.

Toolkit Time These notes, appearing in the margins throughout the book, direct you to the Toolkit following Chapter 12, where you can find further information on certain topics. The Toolkit covers communications, CASE tools, financial analysis, and internet resources.

Case In Point Each chapter includes four brief cases that focus on key issues.

A Question of Ethics A realistic ethical issue is presented at the end of each chapter. These examples force you to examine your reactions and how you would respond to common workplace situations.

End-of-Chapter Exercises

Chapter Exercises

Chapter Exercises Your answers to the ten Questions will show that you understand the key points. Four Discussion Topics and four Projects offer opportunities to dig deeper and learn even more.

Apply Your Knowledge

Apply Your Knowledge Includes four mini-cases focusing on key concepts and skills from the chapter. The cases are brief and to the point, with four tasks for you to perform.

Case Studies

Case Studies Includes a Chapter Case, a Continuing Case, and a Capstone Case. You will work on one or more case studies and apply the skills and knowledge you learned in the chapter.

CASE Tool Workshop

CASE Tool Workshop In this hands-on feature, you will use a CASE tool. To perform the tasks, you need access to Visible Analyst ® or a similar tool.

MIS CourseMate Online Case Simulation Includes realistic emails, voice mails, and tasks. In this simulation, you act as an entry-level IT team member. You will work with your supervisor and help her develop a new information system.

Critical Thinking Challenge

MIS CourseMate Critical Thinking Challenge Allows students to focus on critical thinking skills while considering realistic scenarios and roles a systems analyst may face. You will perform Practice Tasks and check your answers, then work on Challenge Tasks that require critical thinking skills.

Video Learning Session
Payback Analysis

If you have an MIS CourseMate access code, you can launch interactive Video Learning Sessions to help you understand systems development concepts and practice your skills. You can watch the sessions on your computer or mobile device, and pause, rewind, or replay a video at any time. To log on to the MIS CourseMate site at **www.cengagebrain.com**, you must create a student account and then register this book.
    This session is about payback analysis. You'll learn how to calculate the payback period for a project and how to use a spreadsheet to determine a project's payback period.

© craftvision/iStockphoto

MIS CourseMate Video Learning Sessions Includes 18 Video Learning Sessions, complete with practice and training tasks. You will learn key skills and concepts by watching these streaming videos on your computer. You can pause, rewind, or replay at any time, and then perform Your Turn tasks to practice your skills.

Learn It Online

MIS CourseMate Learn It Online Includes Chapter Reinforcement Questions, Flash Cards, Practice Tests, and various games, such as Who Wants To Be a Computer Genius?, Wheel of Terms, and the Crossword Puzzle Challenge. You can use this feature to apply your knowledge and practice your skills.

Additional Support Tools

These additional tools can enhance your learning experience:

GLOSSARY/INDEX This edition of the textbook includes a glossary/index feature to assist your understanding of key terms and phrases, or to use as a quick reference tool.

MANAGEMENT INFORMATION SYSTEMS COURSEMATE MIS CourseMate with eBook for Systems Analysis and Design, Tenth Edition keeps today's students engaged and involved in the learning experience. MIS CourseMate includes an integrated, multimedia rich and interactive eBook, along with a variety of interactive learning tools, including quizzes and games, exercises, web links, videos, and other resources that specifically reinforce and build on the concepts presented in the chapter. These interactive activities are tracked within CourseMate's Engagement Tracker, making it easy to assess students' retention of concepts. All of these resources on the MIS CourseMate for Systems Analysis and Design enable students to become more comfortable using technology and help prepare students to use the Internet as a tool to enrich their lives. To sign in to MIS CourseMate **www.cengagebrain.com** you first must create a student account and then register this book, as described at www.cengage.com/ct/studentdownloads.

FOR THE INSTRUCTOR

The Shelly Cashman Series is dedicated to providing you all of the tools you need to make your class a success. Information on all supplementary materials is available through your Course Technology representative or by calling one of the following telephone numbers: Colleges, Universities, Continuing Education Departments, Post-Secondary Vocational Schools, Career Colleges, Business, Industry, Government, Trade, Retailer, Wholesaler, Library, and Resellers, call Cengage Learning at 800-354-9706; K-12 Schools, Secondary and Vocational Schools, Adult Education, and School Districts, call Cengage Learning at 800-354-9706. In Canada, call Nelson Cengage Learning at 800-268-2222.

Instructor Resources

The Instructor Resources for this textbook include both teaching and testing aids, and are available for download by logging in at login.cengage.com. The Instructor Resources include:

- **Instructor's Manual** Includes lecture notes summarizing the chapter sections, figures and boxed elements found in every chapter, teacher tips, classroom activities, lab activities, and quick quizzes in Microsoft Word files.
- **Syllabus** Easily customizable sample syllabus that covers policies, assignments, exams, and other course information. Also included is a Microsoft Project file used to create the five Phase Opener Gantt charts. An instructor can use this project file to create a visual syllabus that could include additional tasks, quizzes, and projects. The file also can be used to track class progress through the course. Instructors are welcome to distribute this file to students, and show them how to manage tasks, resources, and deadlines for team projects that might be assigned.
- **PowerPoint Presentations** A multimedia lecture presentation system provides slides for each chapter, based on chapter objectives.
- **Figure Files** Illustrations for every figure in the textbook in electronic form.
- **Solutions to Exercises** Includes solutions for end-of-chapter exercises, including Critical Thinking Challenge Practice and Challenge Task solutions, chapter reinforcement exercises, and extra case studies.

- **Test Bank & Test Engine** Test Banks include 112 questions for every chapter, and feature objective-based and critical thinking question types, page number references, and figure references when appropriate.

- **Additional Activities for Students** The forms that students can use to complete the Case Studies are included. Two additional case studies are also provided for every chapter, to be assigned as homework, extra credit, or assessment tools. Chapter Reinforcement Exercises, which are true/false, multiple-choice, and short answer questions that help students gain confidence in the material learned are included, as are the Your Turn Practice Tasks and sample solutions.

- **Additional Faculty Files** A copy of the powerful CASE tool, Visible Analyst — Student Edition, is provided for instructor evaluation. Several sample solutions to case study tasks also are included. To install this program, you follow a simple registration process that entitles you to use the software and obtain support. Detailed instructions are provided on the Instructor Companion Site. Also included are Word document versions of the e-mail and voice mail messages posted for students on the SCR Web site and the Interview Summaries for the New Century Case Study.

SOFTWARE BUNDLING OPPORTUNITIES *Systems Analysis and Design, Tenth Edition* can be bundled with several popular software programs:

- **Visible Analyst Student Edition** Whether you are designing e-business applications, developing a data warehouse, or integrating legacy systems with new enterprise applications, Visible Analyst is a valuable software based learning tool that helps students become more marketable with its advanced, affordable, and easy to use modeling capabilities. Visible Analyst was recently awarded the "Best Systems Analysis & Design Modeling Tool" by the Indian Education Ministry. Key users include: Business Analysts who analyze the organization and design of businesses or government departments and assess business models and their integration with technology; other professions that use systems analysis and design methods and techniques include Systems Analysts, Database Engineers, Computer Scientists, and Software Engineers. Visible Analyst is a separate software tool available individually as a Student Edition or as a University Edition with concurrent floating licenses for college or university computer labs. For more information about Visible Analyst, please visit: www.visible.com/Modeler/index.htm or contact sales@visible.com.

- **Microsoft Visio** The advanced diagramming tools of Visio 2010 help you simplify complexity with dynamic, data-driven visuals and new ways to share on the Web in real time. Start by building your diagram with professional-looking templates and modern, pre-drawn shapes. Then, easily link your diagram to popular data sources (such as Excel). You'll see data automatically refresh right within your diagram, reflected in vibrant visuals such as icons, symbols, colors, and bar graphs. Finally, with just a few clicks, publish your data-linked diagram to SharePoint, and provide access to others on the Web, even if they don't have Visio. Together, simplicity, data-driven shapes, and Web sharing make Visio 2010 one of the most powerful ways to see and understand important information.

- **Microsoft Project** Microsoft® Project 2010 delivers powerful, visually enhanced ways to effectively manage a wide range of projects and programs. From meeting crucial deadlines to selecting the right resources and empowering your teams, Project 2010 offers easier and more intuitive experiences to help you simply be more productive and realize amazing results.

AUTHOR'S NOTE

As an instructor and a longtime member of the Shelly Cashman Series team, I want this book to be student-friendly, easy to use, and focused on basic skills rather than the latest trend or silver bullet.

Our main goal is to help students learn how to perform systems analysis and design tasks. However, most entry-level IT positions are not filled on the basis of technical knowledge alone, because employers can teach new employees much of what they need to know. Instead, companies tend to seek highly motivated candidates with strong communication, interpersonal, and critical thinking skills. For that reason, the book offers many features and practice tasks that can help students develop "soft skills" that they can bring to the workplace.

To instructors who adopted this book, I know you had many other choices, and I sincerely appreciate your confidence. Together we can make a difference, and provide an outstanding learning experience for our students. Thank you.

ACKNOWLEDGMENTS

First and foremost, special thanks to Deb Kaufmann, our development editor. Deb's insight and suggestions were extremely valuable. Thanks also to Professor Tim Burns, who teaches at Ramapo College of New Jersey, and to Ron Savilla, my former student at Central Piedmont Community College and a senior network technician. Tim and Ron reviewed the prior edition, and their unique perspectives helped shape the new book.

Finally, sincere thanks to the instructors and students who offered feedback and comments. You said you wanted more interactive content and learning tools, updated end-of-chapter material, and several new features. We hope you will continue to offer suggestions, and we certainly will continue to listen carefully.

ABOUT OUR COVERS

The Shelly Cashman Series is continually updating our approach and content to reflect the way today's students learn and experience new technology. This focus on student success is reflected on our covers, which feature real students from the University of Rhode Island using the Shelly Cashman Series in their courses, and reflect the varied ages and backgrounds of the students learning with our books. When you use the Shelly Cashman Series, you can be assured that you are learning computer skills using the most effective courseware available.

PHASE | SYSTEMS PLANNING

DELIVERABLE
Preliminary investigation report

TOOLKIT SUPPORT
Communications and financial analysis tools

GOT MIS COURSEMATE?
Four Video Learning Sessions explain payback analysis and project management

As the Dilbert cartoon suggests, it is always a good idea to know whether a project fits the company's overall strategy. You will learn more about the relationship between systems projects and corporate strategies in the systems planning phase.

Systems planning is the first of five phases in the systems development life cycle. After an introduction to systems analysis and design, you will learn how systems projects get started, how to evaluate a project proposal to determine its feasibility, and how to use project management tools and techniques. The deliverable for this phase is the preliminary investigation report.

I

CHAPTER

Introduction to Systems Analysis and Design

Chapter 1 is the first of three chapters in the systems planning phase. This chapter describes the role of information technology in today's dynamic business environment. In this chapter, you will learn about the development of information systems, systems analysis and design concepts, and various systems development methods. This chapter also describes the role of the information technology department and its people.

INTRODUCTION

OBJECTIVES

When you finish this chapter, you will be able to:

- Describe the impact of information technology

- Define systems analysis and design and the role of a systems analyst

- Define an information system and describe its components

- Explain how to use business profiles and models

- Explain Internet business strategies and relationships, including B2C and B2B

- Identify various types of information systems and explain who uses them

- Distinguish among structured analysis, object-oriented analysis, and agile methods

- Explain the waterfall model, and how it has evolved

- Discuss the role of the information technology department and the systems analysts who work there

The headlines in Figure 1-1 offer dramatic examples of how information technology affects our society. Companies use information as a weapon in the battle to increase productivity, deliver quality products and services, maintain customer loyalty, and make sound decisions. In a global economy with intense competition, information technology can mean the difference between success and failure.

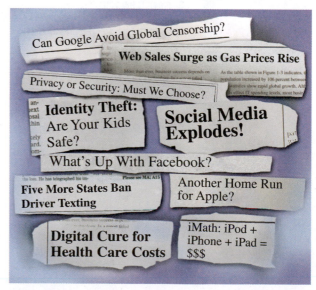

FIGURE 1-1 These headlines show the enormous impact of information technology on our lives.

© Cengage Learning 2014

PREVIEW CASE: Mountain View College Bookstore

Background: Mountain View College is located in New England. The school has grown rapidly and now has 8,000 students at three campuses, each with a branch bookstore. Wendy Lee, manager of college services, is responsible for all bookstore operations. Wendy wants a new information system that will increase efficiency and improve customer service.

As the case begins, Tina Allen, a systems analyst in the college's Information Technology department, is talking with David Conroe. David is majoring in information systems at Mountain View College and is earning credit toward his degree by working part-time as a student intern.

Participants:	Tina and David
Location:	Tina's office, 10 a.m., Monday morning, August 19, 2013
Project status:	Initial discussion
Discussion topics:	Basic systems development concepts

Tina: Welcome aboard, David.

David: *I'm glad to be here. What's on the agenda?*

Tina: Well, there's been some talk about a new bookstore information system. Wendy says nothing is definite yet, but she suggested that we should get ready.

David: *So we start by learning about the bookstore business?*

Tina: Yes, the best system in the world isn't worth much unless it supports business and information needs. But let's not get ahead of ourselves. First, we need to talk about business information systems in general. Then we'll build a business model so we can understand the specific operations and processes at the bookstore. We'll also discuss systems analysis and design tools and techniques. Let's start with an overview of information systems and their characteristics.

David: *That makes sense. What about the basic systems analysis techniques you mentioned?*

Tina: On this project, we'll use what's called a structured method, which is based on the concept of a systems development life cycle, or SDLC for short. I'll also explain object-oriented and agile methods, and you'll learn about modeling tools and techniques. We'll follow a set of basic system development guidelines as we go along.

David: *How does the SDLC work?*

Tina: The SDLC is like constructing a building. First, you would list specific objectives for the project. Then, you might hire an architect to create drawings that show the finished building. Later, you'd need detailed blueprints for the construction workers. When the building is done, you would check everything, turn it over to the new owners, and make sure they're happy with the results.

David: *And that's how we'll develop new information systems?*

Tina: It sure is. We'll use a program called Microsoft Project to create a list of tasks we can work on.

FIGURE 1-2 Typical introductory tasks for systems projects

© Cengage Learning 2014

© craftvision/iStockphoto

WHAT IS INFORMATION TECHNOLOGY?

Information technology (IT) refers to the combination of hardware, software, and services that people use to manage, communicate, and share information. Although fictitious, the bold headlines in Figure 1-1 show the huge impact of IT on our society.

More than ever, business success depends on information technology. IT is driving a new digital economy, where advances in hardware, software, and connectivity can provide enormous benefits to businesses and individuals. Although economic trends affect IT spending levels, most firms give IT budgets a high priority, in good times or bad. The reason is simple — during periods of growth, companies cannot afford to lag behind the IT curve. Conversely, when the economy slows down, firms often use IT to reduce operating costs and improve efficiency.

The following sections will give you a sense of IT history, an overview of systems analysis and design, and a description of the system analyst's role.

Welcome to the 21st Century: The IT Journey Continues

The history of IT is a fascinating study of human progress and achievement. We are dazzled by the latest and greatest technology, just as our parents and grandparents were astonished by the arrival of television, space flight, and personal computing. It is important for IT professionals, who live and work in this exciting world, to realize that each technology advance is part of a long-term process that often brings dramatic change, but never really ends. The story of IBM is a good example.

As its name suggests, International Business Machines was a major supplier of office equipment and typewriters long before the modern computer era. IBM's predecessor company was founded in 1896 by Herman Hollerith, who invented a card that identified characters by the location of punched holes. A deck of hundreds, or even thousands of these cards could store data that was easily sorted, queried, and printed by machines. This system sounds archaic today, but punch card technology was a huge advance that revolutionized the business world, and was in use into the 1960s and beyond. After a century of progress, IBM is now a global giant with a half-million employees, numerous patents, and more Nobel Prize winners than any other IT firm.

Figure 1-3 shows an employee clocking in with a punch card in 1953, and how an employee might clock in today, using a magnetic card linked to a corporate database. Perhaps students 60 years from now will view our current technology the same way we smile at punched cards. Meanwhile, welcome aboard — it will be an interesting ride!

Coming to work in 1953   **... and in 2013**

© ClassicStock / Alamy

© Cusp / SuperStock

FIGURE 1-3 How times have changed!

Systems Analysis and Design

Systems analysis and design is a step-by-step process for developing high-quality information systems. An **information system** combines technology, people, and data to provide support for business functions such as order processing, inventory control, human resources, accounting, and many more. Some information systems handle routine day-to-day tasks, while others can help managers make better decisions, spot marketplace trends, and reveal patterns that might be hidden in stored data.

Information systems typically are developed by talented people, including a mix of managers, users, network administrators, Web designers, programmers, and systems analysts. Capable IT professionals like these are always in demand, even in a slow economy. For example, notice how Dell reaches out to candidates on its Web site, as shown in Figure 1-4.

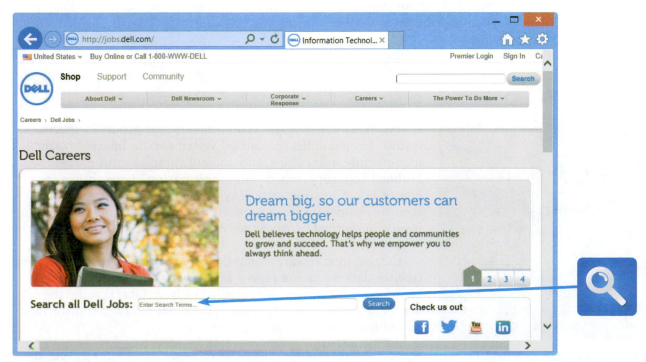

FIGURE 1-4 Dell is an example of a firm that invites potential candidates to search for jobs on its Web site.
© 2011 Dell

What Does a Systems Analyst Do?

A **systems analyst** is a valued member of the IT department team who helps plan, develop, and maintain information systems. Analysts must be excellent communicators with strong analytical and critical thinking skills. Because systems analysts transform business requirements into IT projects, they must be business-savvy as well as technically competent, and be equally comfortable with managers and programmers, who sometimes have different points of view, as Dilbert fans already know.

Most companies assign systems analysts to the IT department, but analysts also can report to a specific user area such as marketing, sales, or accounting. As a member of a functional team, an analyst is better able to understand the needs of that group and how IT supports the department's mission. Smaller companies often use consultants to perform systems analysis work on an as-needed basis.

On any given day, an analyst might be asked to document business processes, test hardware and software packages, design input screens, train users, and plan e-commerce Web sites. A systems analyst also manages IT projects, including tasks, resources, schedules, and costs. To keep managers and users informed, the analyst conducts meetings, delivers presentations, and writes memos, reports, and documentation.

To learn more about becoming a systems analyst, you should review the last section in this chapter, which lists typical skills and education requirements, certifications, career opportunities, and the impact of future IT trends on systems analysts.

CASE IN POINT 1.1: CLOUD NINE FINANCIAL ADVISORS

Cloud Nine provides its clients with a monthly newsletter that offers recommendations about stocks to buy or sell. Doug Layton, Cloud Nine's president, has asked your opinion on whether dot-com stocks might be good investments for the future. He specifically mentioned Google, eBay, Amazon.com, and Yahoo!, but he said you could suggest other companies. Doug wants you to do some Internet research to learn more about these Web-based companies and their future prospects. You can use a search engine, or start by visiting the Web sites of publications such as *Forbes, Fortune Magazine, Business Week,* or *The Wall Street Journal,* among others.

FIGURE 1-5 Consider the amazing technology that enabled the Hubbell telescope to capture this image.

INFORMATION SYSTEM COMPONENTS

A **system** is a set of related components that produces specific results. For example, specialized systems route Internet traffic, manufacture microchips, and control complex entities like the Hubbell Telescope, which took the amazing image shown in Figure 1-5. A **mission-critical system** is one that is vital to a company's operations. An order processing system, for example, is mission-critical because the company cannot do business without it.

Every system requires input data. For example, your computer receives data when you press a key or click a menu command. In an information system, **data** consists of basic facts that are the system's raw material. **Information** is data that has been transformed into output that is valuable to users.

An information system has five key components, as shown in Figure 1-6: hardware, software, data, processes, and people.

Hardware

Hardware consists of everything in the physical layer of the information system. For example, hardware can include servers, workstations, networks, telecommunications equipment, fiber-optic cables, mobile devices, scanners, digital capture devices, and other technology-based infrastructure. A large concentration of servers working together is called a **server farm**. As new technologies emerge, manufacturers race to market the innovations and reap the rewards.

Hardware purchasers today face a wide array of technology choices and decisions. In 1965, Gordon Moore, a cofounder of Intel, predicted that the number of transistors on an integrated circuit chip would double about every 24 months. His concept, called **Moore's Law**, has remained valid for almost 50 years. Fortunately, as hardware became more powerful, it also became much less expensive. Large businesses with thousands or millions of sales transactions require company-wide information systems and powerful servers, such as those shown in Figure 1-7.

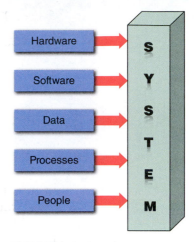

FIGURE 1-6 An information system needs these components.
© Cengage Learning 2014

Software

Software refers to the programs that control the hardware and produce the desired information or results. Software consists of system software and application software.

System software manages the hardware components, which can include a single workstation or a global network with many thousands of clients. Either the hardware manufacturer supplies the system software or a company purchases it from a vendor. Examples of system software include the operating system, security software that protects the computer from intrusion, device drivers that communicate with hardware such as printers, and utility programs that handle specific tasks such as data backup and disk management. System software also controls the flow of data, provides data security, and manages network operations. In today's interconnected business world, network software is vitally important.

FIGURE 1-7 Server farms provide the enormous power and speed that modern IT systems need.
© Joyfull/Shutterstock

Application software consists of programs that support day-to-day business functions and provide users with the information they need. Examples of company-wide applications, called **enterprise applications**, include order processing systems, payroll systems, and company communications networks. On a smaller scale, individual users can boost productivity with tools such as spreadsheets, presentation software, and database management systems.

Application software includes horizontal and vertical systems. A **horizontal system** is a system, such as an inventory or payroll application, that can be adapted for use in many different types of companies. A **vertical system** is designed to meet the unique requirements of a specific business or industry, such as a Web-based retailer, a medical practice, or an auto dealership.

Most companies use a mix of software that is acquired at various times. When planning an information system, a company must consider how a new system will interface with older systems, which are called **legacy systems**. For example, a new human resources system might need to exchange data with an legacy payroll application.

Data

Data is the raw material that an information system transforms into useful information. An information system can store data in various locations, called tables. By linking the tables, the system can display the specific information that the user needs — no more, and no less.

FIGURE 1-8   In a typical payroll system, data is stored in separate tables that are linked to form an overall database.

© Cengage Learning 2014

Figure 1-8 shows a payroll system that stores data in four separate tables. Notice that the linked tables work together to supply 19 different data items to the screen. A user can display any or all data items, and filter the data to fit defined limits. In this example, the user requested a list of employees who live in a certain city and worked more than 40 hours in the last pay period. Jane Doe's name was the first to display.

Processes

Processes describe the tasks and business functions that users, managers, and IT staff members perform to achieve specific results. Processes are the building blocks of an information system because they represent actual day-to-day business operations. To build a successful information system, analysts must understand business processes and document them carefully.

People

People who have an interest in an information system are called **stakeholders**. Stakeholders include the management group responsible for the system, the **users** (sometimes called end users) inside and outside the company who will interact with the system, and IT staff members, such as systems analysts, programmers, and network administrators who develop and support the system.

Each stakeholder group has a vital interest in the information system, but most experienced IT professionals agree that the success or failure of a system usually depends on whether it meets the needs of its users. For that reason, it is essential to understand user requirements and expectations throughout the development process.

BUSINESS IN THE 21ST CENTURY

To design successful systems, systems analysts must understand a company's business operations. Each situation is different. For example, a retail store, a medical practice, and a hotel chain all have unique information systems requirements. As the business world changes, systems analysts can expect to work in new kinds of companies that will require innovative IT solutions.

Business in the 21st century will be shaped by three major trends: rapidly increasing globalization, technology integration for seamless information access, and the rapid growth of cloud-based computing and services. All these trends will be Internet-centric, and driven by the immense power of the Web.

The Internet Model

Internet-based commerce is called **e-commerce (electronic commerce)** or **I-commerce (Internet commerce)**. Internet-based systems involve various hardware and software designs, but a typical model is a series of Web pages that provides a user interface, which communicates with database management software and a Web-based data server. As Internet-based commerce continues to grow, career opportunities will expand significantly for IT professionals such as Web designers, database developers, and systems analysts.

E-commerce includes two main sectors: **B2C (business-to-consumer)** and **B2B (business-to-business)**. Within these broad categories, competition is dynamic, extreme, and global. Every day brings new ideas, new players, and new ways to involve customers, suppliers, and hordes of social network participants. The following sections discuss this rapidly changing environment.

B2C (Business-to-Consumer)

Using the Internet, consumers can go online to purchase an enormous variety of products and services. This new shopping environment allows customers to do research, compare prices and features, check availability, arrange delivery, and choose payment methods in a single convenient session. Many companies, such as airlines, offer incentives for online transactions because Web-based processing costs are lower than traditional methods. By making flight information available online to last-minute travelers, some airlines also offer special discounts on seats that might otherwise go unfilled.

B2C commerce is changing traditional business models and creating new ones. For example, a common business model is a retail store that sells a product to a customer. To carry out that same transaction on the Internet, the company must develop an online store and deal with a totally different set of marketing, advertising, and profitability issues.

Some companies have found new ways to use established business models. For example, eBay.com has transformed a traditional auction concept into a popular and successful method of selling goods and services. Other retailers seek to enhance the online shopping experience by offering gift advisors, buying guides, how-to clinics, and similar features. In the e-commerce battles, the real winners are online consumers, who have more information, better choices, and the convenience of shopping at home.

B2B (Business-to-Business)

Although the business-to-consumer (B2C) sector is more familiar to retail customers, the volume of business-to-business (B2B) transactions is many times greater. Industry observers predict that B2B sales will increase sharply as more firms seek to improve efficiency and reduce costs.

Initially, electronic commerce between two companies used a data sharing arrangement called **electronic data interchange (EDI)**. EDI enabled computer-to-computer data transfer, usually over private telecommunications lines. Firms used EDI to plan production, adjust inventory levels, or stock up on raw materials using data from another company's information system. As B2B volume soared, company-to-company transactions migrated to the Internet, which offered standard protocols, universal availability, and low communication costs. The main advantage of the Web is that it offers seamless communication between different hardware and software environments, anywhere and anytime.

Because it allows companies to reach the global marketplace, B2B is especially important to smaller suppliers and customers who need instant information about prices and availability. In an approach that resembles an open marketplace, some B2B sites invite buyers, sellers, distributors, and manufacturers to offer products, submit specifications, and transact business.

Most large firms and government agencies use **supply chain management (SCM)** software. A **supply chain** refers to all the companies who provide materials, services, and functions needed to provide a product to a customer. For example, a Sherwin-Williams customer who buys a gallon of paint is at the end of a chain that includes the raw material sources, packaging suppliers, manufacturers, transporters, warehouses, and retail stores. Because SCM is complex and dynamic, specialized software helps businesses manage inventory levels, costs, alternate suppliers, and much more. Figure 1-9 shows a valuable overview of SCM issues that can be downloaded free from SAP, a world leader in corporate software solutions.

What's Next?

Traditionally, IT companies were identified as product-oriented or service-oriented. **Product-oriented** firms manufactured computers, routers, or microchips, while **service-oriented** companies included consultants, vendors, software developers, and service providers.

Today, those distinctions are gone. Most successful IT companies offer a mix of products, services, and support. Value-added services such as consulting, software, and technical support often are more profitable than hardware sales. In a striking example of this trend, IBM's 2011 annual report notes that software and services produced more than 80 percent of pre-tax income. Figure 1-10 shows the contrast: Over an 11-year period, hardware and financing profit remained flat, while software and services income more than tripled!

These days, with rising fuel prices and an eye on expenses, shopping at home is more popular than ever. The strongest players in this market are called Internet-dependent firms, because their primary business depends

SAP® SUPPLY CHAIN MANAGEMENT
YOUR INDUSTRY, YOUR BUSINESS, YOUR FUTURE

SAP Solution Overview
SAP Supply Chain Management

THE BEST-RUN BUSINESSES RUN SAP®   SAP

FIGURE 1-9 This free publication offers a valuable overview of SCM issues. You can download it at SAP's Web site.

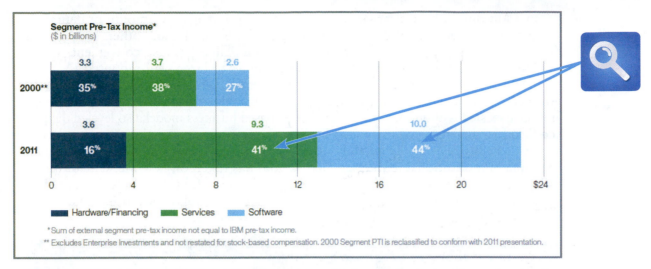

FIGURE 1-10 IBM's 2011 report shows a dramatic increase in key business segments such as software and services, compared to slow-growth profits from hardware sales and financing.

on the Internet rather than a traditional business channel. At the other end of the scale are traditional businesses, sometimes called brick-and-mortar companies because they conduct business primarily from physical locations. Although they have stores where customers can see and touch the products, most successful brick-and-mortar firms — such as Lowe's, Costco, Target, and Wal-Mart — have expanded their Web-based marketing channels to increase sales and serve customers better. This strategy combines the convenience of online shopping *and* the alternative of hands-on purchasing for those who prefer that option. Figure 1-11 shows several shopping and pickup options that Wal-Mart offers, so customers can choose the method they prefer.

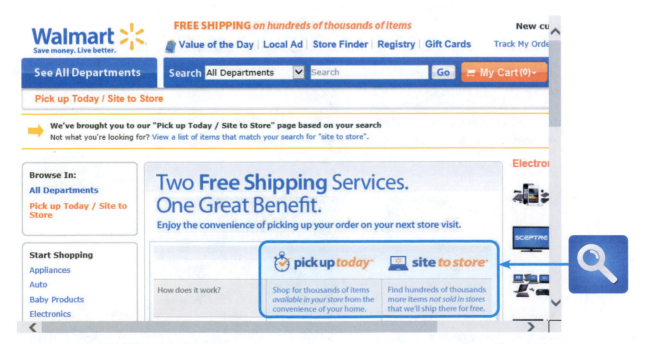

FIGURE 1-11 Wal-Mart enhances a customer's online experience by offering several shopping and pickup options, so customers can choose the method they prefer.

In addition to physical products, consumers also buy a huge amount of digital content. Firms such as Apple, Amazon, Kindle, Netflix, and many others are fighting for a share of this rapidly growing market. Digital delivery is fast, convenient, and can be consumed on everything from mobile phones to large wall-mounted TVs.

The Web makes it possible for businesses to operate 100% online, as virtual companies. Although we take this for granted today, giant companies such as Amazon and eBay could not have existed without the Internet. The Web-based business model also leveled the playing field for small firms, so that micro-businesses can reach out to a global marketplace.

Just as eBay revived the auction model, the discount coupon business is another example of a traditional marketing method that has taken on new life. One of the best examples is a firm called Groupon, which claims to find daily deals in more than 48 countries. If it knows where you are, Groupon will display local offers and bargains, such as the Boston-based ads shown in Figure 1-12.

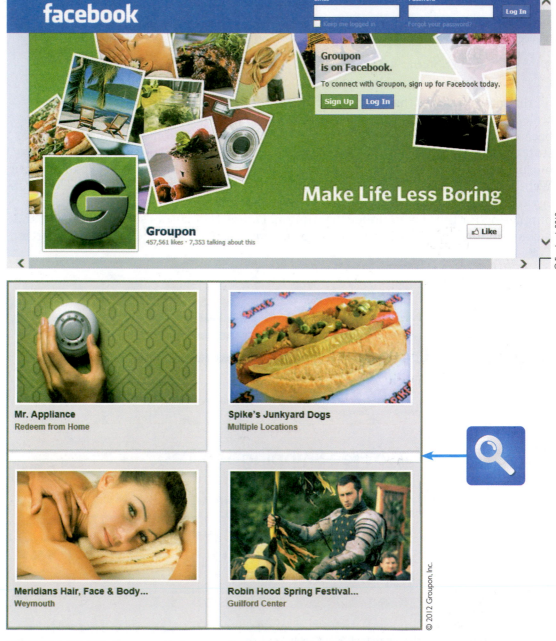

FIGURE I-12 This Groupon ad showcases local offers and bargains in the Boston area.

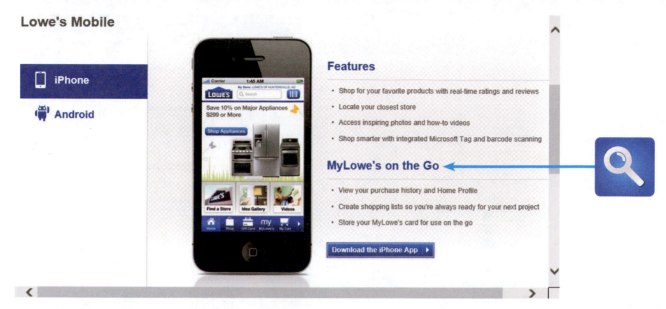

FIGURE 1-13 Lowe's offers a mobile app that customers can use to shop online.
© 2012 Lowe's

With an eye on Groupon's success, many observers predict a huge synergy between mobile computing and location-based marketing, where firms will use global positioning system (GPS) coordinates to tempt travelers with nearby bargains. The winners will be the firms that can offer consumers a portable shopping experience. For example, Figure 1-13 shows how Lowe's is encouraging its customers to download a mobile app that they can use on cell phones and other mobile devices. The MyLowe's on the Go® feature helps customers shop online, create shopping lists, and find local stores. By providing more options, the firm hopes to appeal to more customers.

MODELING BUSINESS OPERATIONS

Systems analysts use modeling to represent company operations and information needs. Business process modeling involves a business profile and a set of models that document business operations.

Business Profiles

A **business profile** is an overview of a company's mission, functions, organization, products, services, customers, suppliers, competitors, constraints, and future direction. Although much of this information is readily available, a systems analyst usually needs to do additional research and fact-finding. A business profile is the starting point for the modeling process.

Business Processes

A **business process** is a specific set of transactions, events, and results that can be described and documented. A **business process model (BPM)** graphically displays one or more business processes, such as handling an airline reservation, filling a product order, or updating a customer account. The sales order example in Figure 1-14 on the next page shows a simple model that includes an event, three processes, and a result.

> **🔧 TOOLKIT TIME**
>
> Business process modeling tools, which are described in Part B of the System's Analyst's Toolkit, can help you document and describe business operations. To learn more about these tools, turn to Part B of the four-part Toolkit that follows Chapter 12.

FIGURE 1-14 A simple business model might consist of an event, three processes, and a result.
© Cengage Learning 2014

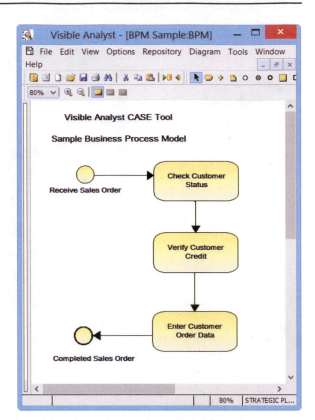

FIGURE 1-15 This sample uses business process modeling notation (BPMN) to represent the same events, processes, and workflow shown in Figure 1-14.
Screenshot used with permission from Visible Systems Corporation.

A rough sketch might be sufficient to document a simple business process. For complex models, analysts can choose computer-based tools that use **business process modeling notation (BPMN)**. BPMN includes standard shapes and symbols to represent events, processes, workflows, and more. To create BPMN models, you can use a multi purpose application such as Microsoft Visio or a CASE tool such as Visible Analyst. Notice that the Visible Analyst model in Figure 1-15 uses BPMN symbols to represent the same sales order process shown in Figure 1-14. Also note the drag-and-drop BPMN symbols that are displayed under the menu bar.

BUSINESS INFORMATION SYSTEMS

In the past, IT managers identified an information system based on its primary users. For example, administrative staff used *office systems*, operational people used *operational systems*, middle managers used *decision support systems*, and top managers used *executive information systems*.

Today, those traditional labels no longer apply. For example, all employees, including top managers, use office productivity systems to do their jobs. Similarly, operational users often require decision support systems to do their Jobs. As business changes, information use also changes, and now it makes more sense to identify a system by its functions and features, rather than by its users. A new set of system definitions includes enterprise computing systems, transaction processing systems, business support systems, knowledge management systems, and user productivity systems.

Enterprise Computing

Enterprise computing refers to information systems that support company-wide operations and data management requirements. Wal-Mart's inventory control system, Boeing's production control system, and Hilton Hotels' reservation system are examples of enterprise computing systems. The main objective of enterprise computing is to integrate a company's primary functions (such as production, sales, services, inventory control, and accounting) to improve efficiency, reduce costs, and help managers make key decisions. Enterprise computing also improves data security and reliability by imposing a company-wide framework for data access and storage.

In many large companies, applications called **enterprise resource planning (ERP)** systems provide cost-effective support for users and managers throughout the company. For example, a car rental company can use ERP to forecast customer demand for rental cars at hundreds of locations.

By providing a company-wide computing environment, many firms have been able to achieve dramatic cost reductions. Other companies have been disappointed in the time, money, and commitment necessary to implement ERP successfully. A potential disadvantage is that ERP systems generally impose an overall structure that might or might not match the way a company operates. ERP is described in more detail in Chapter 7, which discusses system development strategies.

Because of its growth and potential, many hardware and software vendors target the enterprise computing market and offer a wide array of products and services. For example, in Figure 1-16, Infor cites the Herman Miller furniture company as an example of a firm that used ERP to boost productivity.

Transaction Processing

Transaction processing (TP) systems process data generated by day-to-day business operations. Examples of TP systems include customer order processing, accounts receivable, and warranty claim processing.

TP systems perform a series of tasks whenever a specific transaction occurs. In the example shown in Figure 1-17, a TP system verifies the customer's data, checks the customer's credit status, checks the stock status, posts to accounts receivable, adjusts the inventory level, and updates the sales file. TP systems typically involve large

FIGURE 1-16   Infor cites Herman Miller Furniture as an example of an ERP solution that boosted productivity.
© Copyright 2012, Infor

FIGURE 1-17 A single sales transaction consists of six separate tasks, which the TP system processes as a group.

© Cengage Learning 2014

amounts of data and are mission-critical systems because the enterprise cannot function without them.

TP systems are efficient because they process a set of transaction-related commands as a group rather than individually. To protect data integrity, however, TP systems ensure that if any single element of a transaction fails, the system does not process the rest of the transaction.

Business Support

Business support systems provide job-related information support to users at all levels of a company. These systems can analyze transactional data, generate information needed to manage and control business processes, and provide information that leads to better decision making.

The earliest business computer systems replaced manual tasks, such as payroll processing. Companies soon realized that computers also could produce valuable information. The new systems were called **management information systems (MIS)** because managers were the primary users. Today, employees at *all* levels need information to perform their jobs, and they rely on information systems for that support.

A business support system can work hand in hand with a TP system. For example, when a company sells merchandise to a customer, a TP system records the sale, updates the customer's balance, and makes a deduction from inventory. A related business support system highlights slow- or fast-moving items, customers with past-due balances, and inventory levels that need adjustment.

To compete effectively, firms must collect production, sales, and shipping data and update the company-wide business support system immediately. The newest development in data acquisition is called **radio frequency identification (RFID)** technology, which uses high-frequency radio waves to track physical objects, such as the item shown in Figure 1-18. RFID's dramatic growth has been fueled by major retailers such as Wal-Mart, which requires its suppliers to add RFID tags to all items.

An important feature of a business support system is decision support capability. Decision support helps users make decisions by creating a computer model and applying a set of variables. For example, a truck fleet dispatcher might run a series of what-if scenarios to determine the impact of increased shipments or bad weather. Alternatively, a retailer might use what-if analysis to determine the price it must charge to increase profits by a specific amount while volume and costs remain unchanged.

Knowledge Management

Knowledge management systems use a large database called a **knowledge base** that allows users to find information by entering keywords or questions in normal English phrases. A knowledge management system uses **inference rules**, which are logical rules that identify data patterns and relationships.

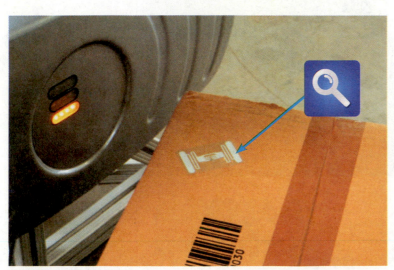

FIGURE 1-18 With an RFID tag, items can be tracked and monitored throughout the shipping process.

© nullplus/photos.com

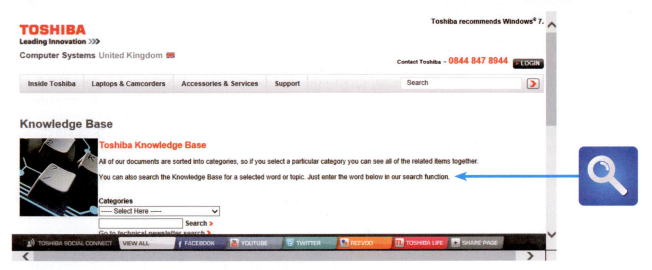

FIGURE 1-19 The interactive Toshiba Knowledge Base allows users to search for solutions.
© 2012 Toshiba Corporation

Figure 1-19 shows a knowledge management system that Toshiba maintains for its customers and users. After a user enters a symptom, problem, or question, Toshiba's Knowledge Base searches for a solution and displays the results.

User Productivity

Companies provide employees at all levels with technology that improves productivity. Examples of **user productivity systems** include e-mail, voice mail, fax, video and Web conferencing, word processing, automated calendars, database management, spreadsheets, desktop publishing, presentation graphics, company intranets, and integrated mobile computing systems. User productivity systems also include groupware. **Groupware** programs enable users to share data, collaborate on projects, and work in teams. Novell's GroupWise and Google Docs are two popular examples of groupware.

When companies first installed word processing systems, managers expected to reduce the number of employees as office efficiency increased. That did not happen, primarily because the basic nature of clerical work changed. With computers performing the repetitive work, office personnel were able to handle tasks that required more judgment, decision-making, and access to information.

Computer-based office work expanded rapidly as companies assigned more responsibility to employees at lower organizational levels. Relatively inexpensive hardware, powerful networks, corporate downsizing, and a move toward employee empowerment also contributed to this trend. Today, administrative assistants and company presidents alike are networked, use computer workstations, and share corporate data to perform their jobs.

Systems Integration

Most large companies require systems that combine transaction processing, business support, knowledge management, and user productivity features. For example, suppose an international customer makes a warranty claim. A customer service representative enters the claim into a TP system, which updates two other systems: a knowledge management system that tracks product problems and warranty activity, and a quality control system with decision support capabilities. A quality control engineer uses what-if analysis to determine if the firm should make product design changes to reduce warranty claims. In this example, a TP system is integrated with a knowledge management system and a business support system with decision support features.

WHAT INFORMATION DO USERS NEED?

Corporate organizational structure has changed considerably in recent years. In an effort to increase productivity, many companies reduced the number of management levels and delegated responsibility to operational personnel. Although modern organization charts tend to be flatter, an organizational hierarchy still exists in most firms.

A typical organizational model identifies business functions and organizational levels, as shown in Figure 1-20. Within the functional areas, operational personnel report to supervisors and team leaders. The next level includes middle managers and knowledge workers, who, in turn, report to top managers. In a corporate structure, the top managers report to a board of directors elected by the company's shareholders.

A systems analyst must understand the company's organizational model to recognize who is responsible for specific processes and decisions and to be aware of what information is required by whom.

Top Managers

Top managers develop long-range plans, called **strategic plans**, which define the company's overall mission and goals. To plot a future course, top managers ask questions such as "How much should the company invest in information technology?" or "How much will Internet sales grow in the next five years?" or "Should the company build new factories or contract out production functions?"

Strategic planning affects the company's future survival and growth, including long-term IT plans. Top managers focus on the overall business enterprise and use IT to set the company's course and direction. To develop a strategic plan, top managers also need information from outside the company, such as economic forecasts, technology trends, competitive threats, and governmental issues.

Middle Managers and Knowledge Workers

Just below the top management level, most companies have a layer of middle managers and knowledge workers. Middle managers provide direction, necessary resources, and performance feedback to supervisors and team leaders. Because they focus on a somewhat shorter

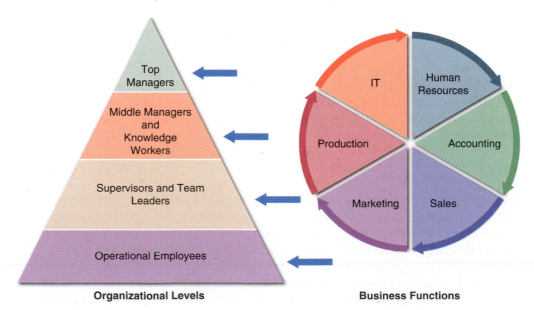

Organizational Levels   Business Functions

FIGURE 1-20 A typical organizational model identifies business functions and organizational levels.

© Cengage Learning 2014

time frame, middle managers need more detailed information than top managers, but somewhat less than supervisors who oversee day-to-day operations. For example, a middle manager might review a weekly sales summary for a three-state area, whereas a local sales team leader would need a daily report on customer sales at a single location.

In addition to middle managers, every company has people called knowledge workers. Knowledge workers include systems analysts, programmers, accountants, researchers, trainers, human resource specialists, and other professionals. Knowledge workers also use business support systems, knowledge management systems, and user productivity systems. Knowledge workers provide support for the organization's basic functions. Just as a military unit requires logistical support, a successful company needs knowledge workers to carry out its mission.

Supervisors and Team Leaders

Supervisors, often called team leaders, oversee operational employees and carry out day-to-day functions. They coordinate operational tasks and people, make necessary decisions, and ensure that the right tools, materials, and training are available. Like other managers, supervisors and team leaders need decision support information, knowledge management systems, and user productivity systems to carry out their responsibilities.

Operational Employees

Operational employees include users who rely on TP systems to enter and receive data they need to perform their jobs. In many companies, operational users also need information to handle tasks and make decisions that were assigned previously to supervisors. This trend, called **empowerment**, gives employees more responsibility and accountability. Many companies find that empowerment improves employee motivation and increases customer satisfaction.

SYSTEMS DEVELOPMENT TOOLS

In addition to understanding business operations, systems analysts must know how to use a variety of techniques, such as modeling, prototyping, and computer-aided systems engineering tools to plan, design, and implement information systems. Systems analysts work with these tools in a team environment, where input from users, managers, and IT staff contributes to the system design.

Modeling

Modeling produces a graphical representation of a concept or process that systems developers can analyze, test, and modify. A systems analyst can describe and simplify an information system by using a set of business, data, object, network, and process models.

A **business model** describes the information that a system must provide. Analysts also create models to represent data, objects, networks, and other system components. Although the models might appear to overlap, they actually work together to describe the same environment from different points of view.

System developers often use multipurpose charting tools such as Microsoft Visio to display business-related models. Visio is a popular tool that systems analysts can use to create business process diagrams, flowcharts, organization charts, network diagrams, floor plans, project timelines, and work flow diagrams, among others.

Figure 1-21 on the next page shows how you can drag and drop various symbols from the left pane into the drawing on the right, and connect them to show a business process.

You will learn about many types of models in this textbook, including data flow diagrams, object diagrams, and entity-relationship diagrams. Business process modeling is explained in more detail in Part B of the Systems Analyst's Toolkit.

TOOLKIT TIME

The CASE tools in Part B of the Systems Analyst's Toolkit can help you develop and maintain complex information systems. To learn more about these tools, turn to Part B of the four-part Toolkit that follows Chapter 12.

FIGURE 1-21 Microsoft Visio allows you to drag and drop various symbols and connect them to show a business process.

Prototyping

Prototyping tests system concepts and provides an opportunity to examine input, output, and user interfaces before final decisions are made. A **prototype** is an early working version of an information system. Just as an aircraft manufacturer tests a new design in a wind tunnel, systems analysts construct and study information system prototypes. A prototype can serve as an initial model that is used as a benchmark to evaluate the finished system, or the prototype itself can develop into the final version of the system. Either way, prototyping speeds up the development process significantly.

A possible disadvantage of prototyping is that important decisions might be made too early, before business or IT issues are understood thoroughly. A prototype based on careful fact-finding and modeling techniques, however, can be an extremely valuable tool.

Computer-Aided Systems Engineering (CASE) Tools

Computer-aided systems engineering (CASE), also called **computer-aided software engineering**, is a technique that uses powerful software, called **CASE tools**, to help systems analysts develop and maintain information systems. CASE tools provide an overall framework for systems development and support a wide variety of design methodologies, including structured analysis and object-oriented analysis.

Because CASE tools make it easier to build an information system, they boost IT productivity and improve the quality of the finished product. Part B of the Systems Analyst's Toolkit explains how analysts use CASE tools to create business profiles, build business models, and document complex processes. After developing a model, many CASE tools can generate program code, which speeds the implementation process. Figure 1-22 shows the Web site for Visible Systems Corporation, a leading vendor of CASE tools.

FIGURE 1-22 Visible Systems Corporation offers a wide array of software engineering tools, including Visible Analyst, a popular CASE tool.

SYSTEMS DEVELOPMENT METHODS

Many options exist for developing information systems, but the most popular alternatives are **structured analysis**, which is a traditional method that still is widely used, **object-oriented (O-O) analysis**, which is a more recent approach that many analysts prefer, and **agile methods**, also called **adaptive methods**, which include the latest trends in software development. Figure 1-23 provides an overview of the three methods, which are discussed in the following sections.

	STRUCTURED ANALYSIS	OBJECT-ORIENTED ANALYSIS	AGILE/ADAPTIVE METHODS
Description	Represents the system in terms of data and the processes that act upon that data. System development is organized into phases, with deliverables and milestones to measure progress. The waterfall model typically consists of five phases. Iteration is possible among the phases, as shown in Figure 1-25 on page 23.	Views the system in terms of objects that combine data and processes. The objects represent actual people, things, transactions, and events, as shown in Figure 1-26. Compared to structured analysis, O-O phases tend to be more interactive. Can use the waterfall model or the model that stresses greater iteration, as shown in Figure 1-27 on page 25.	Stresses intense team-based effort, as shown in Figure 1-28. Breaks development into cycles, or iterations that add functionality. Each cycle is designed, built, and tested in an ongoing process. Attempts to reduce major risks by incremental steps in short time intervals.
Modeling tools	Data flow diagrams (DFDs) and process descriptions, which are described in Chapter 5. Also, business process modeling, which is explained in Part B of the Systems Analyst's Toolkit.	Various object-oriented diagrams depict system actors, methods, and messages, which are described in Chapter 6. Also, business process modeling, which is explained in Part B of the Systems Analyst's Toolkit.	Tools that enhance communication, such as collaborative software, brainstorming, and whiteboards. Business process modeling, which is explained in Part B of the Systems Analyst's Toolkit, works well with agile methods.
Pros	Traditional method, which has been very popular over time. Relies heavily on written documentation. Frequent phase iteration can provide flexibility comparable with other methods. Well-suited to project management tools and techniques.	Integrates easily with object-oriented programming languages. Code is modular and reusable, which can reduce cost and development time. Easy to maintain and expand because new objects can be cloned using inherited properties.	Very flexible and efficient in dealing with change. Stresses team interaction and reflects a set of community-based values. Frequent deliverables constantly validate the project and reduce risk.
Cons	Changes can be costly, especially in later phases. Requirements are defined early, and can change during development. Users might not be able to describe their needs until they can see examples of features and functions.	Somewhat newer method might be less familiar to development team members. Interaction of objects and classes can be complex in larger systems.	Team members need a high level of technical and communications skills. Lack of structure and documentation can introduce risk factors. Overall project might be subject to scope change as user requirements change.

FIGURE 1-23 Comparison of structured, object-oriented, and agile/adaptive development methods.

Although most projects utilize one approach, it is not unusual for system developers to mix and match methods to gain a better perspective. In addition to these three main development methods, some organizations choose to develop their own in-house approaches or use techniques offered by software suppliers, CASE tool vendors, or consultants. Many alternatives exist, and IT experts agree that no one development method is best in all cases. An approach that works well for one project might have disadvantages or risks in another situation. The important thing is to understand the various methods and the strengths and weaknesses of each approach.

Regardless of the development strategy, people, tasks, timetables, and costs must be managed effectively. Complex projects can involve dozens of people, hundreds of tasks, and many thousands of dollars. **Project management** is the process of planning, scheduling, monitoring, controlling, and reporting upon the development of an information system. Chapter 3 describes project management tools and techniques in detail.

Structured Analysis

Structured analysis is a traditional systems development technique that is time-tested and easy to understand. Structured analysis uses a series of phases, called the **systems development life cycle (SDLC)**, to plan, analyze, design, implement, and support an information system. Although structured analysis evolved many years ago, it remains a popular systems development method. Structured analysis is based on an overall plan, similar to a blueprint for constructing a building, so it is called a predictive approach.

Structured analysis uses a set of process models to describe a system graphically. Because it focuses on processes that transform data into useful information, structured analysis is called a process-centered technique. In addition to modeling the processes, structured analysis also addresses data organization and structure, relational database design, and user interface issues.

A process model shows the data that flows in and out of system processes. Inside each process, input data is transformed by **business rules** that generate the output. Figure 1-24 shows a process model that was created with Visible Analyst, a popular software development tool. The model, which represents a school registration system,

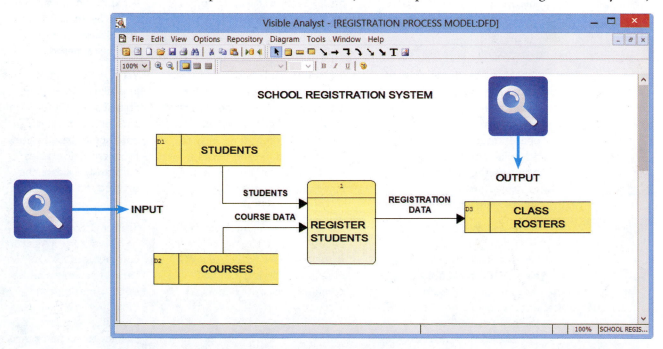

FIGURE 1-24 This Visible Analyst screen shows a process model for a school registration system. The REGISTER STUDENTS process accepts input data from two sources and transforms it into output data.

is a called a **data flow diagram (DFD)** because it uses various symbols and shapes to represent data flow, processing, and storage. You will learn more about DFDs in Chapter 5, and if you have MIS CourseMate, you can view three Video Learning Sessions that explain DFDs and how they are used as modeling tools.

Structured analysis uses the SDLC to plan and manage the systems development process. The SDLC describes activities and functions that all systems developers perform, regardless of which approach they use. In the **waterfall model**, the result of each phase is called a **deliverable**, which flows into the next phase.

Some analysts see a disadvantage in the built-in structure of the SDLC, because the waterfall model does not emphasize interactivity among the phases. This criticism can be valid if the SDLC phases are followed too rigidly. However, adjacent phases can and do interact, as shown by the circular arrows in Figure 1-25 and interaction among several phases is not uncommon. Used in this manner, the traditional model is not as different from agile methods as it might appear to be.

The SDLC model usually includes five steps, which are described in the following sections: systems planning, systems analysis, systems design, systems implementation, and systems support and security.

SYSTEMS PLANNING The systems planning phase usually begins with a formal request to the IT department, called a **systems request**, which describes problems or desired changes in an information system or a business process. In many companies, IT systems planning is an integral part of overall business planning. When managers and users develop their business plans, they usually include IT requirements that generate systems requests.

FIGURE 1-25 Development phases and deliverables are shown in the waterfall model. The circular symbols indicate interaction among the phases.

© Cengage Learning 2014

A systems request can come from a top manager, a planning team, a department head, or the IT department itself. The request can be very significant or relatively minor. A major request might involve a new information system or the upgrading of an existing system. In contrast, a minor request might ask for a new feature or a change to the user interface.

The purpose of this phase is to perform a **preliminary investigation** to evaluate an IT-related business opportunity or problem. The preliminary investigation is a critical step because the outcome will affect the entire development process. A key part of the preliminary investigation is a **feasibility study** that reviews anticipated costs and benefits and recommends a course of action based on operational, technical, economic, and time factors.

Suppose you are a systems analyst and you receive a request for a system change or improvement. Your first step is to determine whether it makes sense to launch a preliminary investigation at all. Often you will need to learn more about business operations before you can reach a conclusion. After an investigation, you might find that the information system functions properly, but users need more training. In some situations, you might recommend a business process review, rather than an IT solution. In other cases, you might conclude that a full-scale systems review is necessary. If the development process continues, the next step is the systems analysis phase.

SYSTEMS ANALYSIS The purpose of the **systems analysis phase** is to build a logical model of the new system. The first step is **requirements modeling**, where you investigate business processes and document what the new system must do to satisfy users.

Requirements modeling continues the investigation that began during the systems planning phase. To understand the system, you perform fact-finding using techniques such as interviews, surveys, document review, observation, and sampling. You use the fact-finding results to build business models, data and process models, and object models.

The deliverable for the systems analysis phase is the **system requirements document**. The system requirements document describes management and user requirements, costs and benefits, and outlines alternative development strategies.

SYSTEMS DESIGN   The purpose of the **systems design phase** is to create a physical model that will satisfy all documented requirements for the system. At this stage, you design the user interface and identify necessary outputs, inputs, and processes. In addition, you design internal and external controls, including computer-based and manual features to guarantee that the system will be reliable, accurate, maintainable, and secure. During the systems design phase, you also determine the application architecture, which programmers will use to transform the logical design into program modules and code.

The deliverable for this phase is the **system design specification**, which is presented to management and users for review and approval. Management and user involvement is critical to avoid any misunderstanding about what the new system will do, how it will do it, and what it will cost.

SYSTEMS IMPLEMENTATION   During the systems implementation phase, the new system is constructed. Whether the developers use structured analysis or O-O methods, the procedure is the same — programs are written, tested, and documented, and the system is installed. If the system was purchased as a package, systems analysts configure the software and perform any necessary modifications. The objective of the systems implementation phase is to deliver a completely functioning and documented information system. At the conclusion of this phase, the system is ready for use. Final preparations include converting data to the new system's files, training users, and performing the actual transition to the new system.

The systems implementation phase also includes an assessment, called a systems evaluation, to determine whether the system operates properly and if costs and benefits are within expectations.

SYSTEMS SUPPORT AND SECURITY   During the **systems support and security phase**, the IT staff maintains, enhances, and protects the system. Maintenance changes correct errors and adapt to changes in the environment, such as new tax rates. Enhancements provide new features and benefits. The objective during this phase is to maximize return on the IT investment. Security controls safeguard the system from both external and internal threats. A well-designed system must be secure, reliable, maintainable, and scalable. A **scalable design** can expand to meet new business requirements and volumes. Information systems development is always a work in progress. Business processes change rapidly, and most information systems need to be updated significantly or replaced after several years of operation.

Object-Oriented Analysis

Whereas structured analysis treats processes and data as separate components, object-oriented analysis combines data and the processes that act on the data into things called **objects**. Systems analysts use O-O to model real-world business processes and operations. The result is a set of software objects that represent actual people, things, transactions, and events. Using an O-O programming language, a programmer then writes the code that creates the objects.

An object is a member of a **class**, which is a collection of similar objects. Objects possess characteristics called **properties**, which the object inherits from its class or possesses on its own. As shown in Figure 1-26, the class called PERSON includes

INSTRUCTOR and STUDENT. Because the PERSON class has a property called Address, a STUDENT inherits the Address property. A STUDENT also has a property called Major that is not shared by other members of the PERSON class.

In O-O design, built-in processes called *methods* can change an object's properties. For example, in a Web-based catalog store, an ORDER object might have a property called STATUS that changes when a CUSTOMER object clicks to place, confirm, or cancel the order.

One object can send information to another object by using a message. A *message* requests specific behavior or information from another object. For example, an ORDER object might send a message to a CUSTOMER object that requests a shipping address. When it receives the message, the CUSTOMER object supplies the information. The ORDER object has the capability to send the message, and the CUSTOMER object knows what actions to perform when it receives the message. O-O analysis uses object models to represent data and behavior, and to show how objects affect other objects. By describing the objects and methods needed to support a business operation, a system developer can design reusable components that speed up system implementation and reduce development cost.

Object-oriented methods usually follow a series of analysis and design phases that are similar to the SDLC, although there is less agreement on the number of phases and their names. In an O-O model, the phases tend to be more interactive. Figure 1-27 shows a development model where planning, analysis, and design tasks interact to produce prototypes that can be tested and implemented. The result is an interactive model that can accurately depict real-world business processes.

O-O methodology is popular because it provides an easy transition to O-O programming languages such as Java, Smalltalk, C++, Python, and Perl. Chapter 6 covers O-O analysis and design, with a detailed description of O-O terms, concepts, tools, and techniques.

FIGURE 1-26 The PERSON class includes INSTRUCTOR and STUDENT objects, which have their own properties and inherited properties.

© Cengage Learning 2014

FIGURE 1-27 In a typical O-O development model, planning, analysis, and design tasks interact continuously to generate prototypes that can be tested.

© Cengage Learning 2014

Agile Methods

Development techniques change over time. For example, structured analysis is a traditional approach, and agile methods are the newest development. Structured analysis builds an overall plan for the information system, just as a contractor might use a blueprint for constructing a building. Agile methods, in contrast, attempt to develop a system incrementally, by building a series of prototypes and constantly adjusting them to user requirements. As the agile process continues, developers revise, extend, and merge earlier versions into the final product. An agile approach emphasizes continuous feedback, and each incremental step is affected by what was learned in the prior steps.

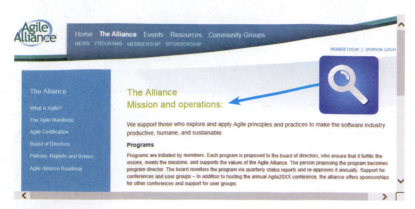

FIGURE 1-28 Agile methods have attracted a wide following and an entire community of users.
© 2012 Agile Alliance

Although relatively new to software development, the notion of **iterative** development can be traced back to Japanese auto firms that were able to boost productivity by using a flexible manufacturing system, where team-based effort and short-term milestones helped keep quality up and costs down. Agile methods have attracted a wide following and an entire community of users, as shown in Figure 1-28.

Agile methods typically use a **spiral model**, which represents a series of iterations, or revisions, based on user feedback. As the process continues, the final product gradually evolves. An agile approach requires intense interactivity between developers and individual users, and does not begin with an overall objective. Instead, the agile process determines the end result. Proponents of the spiral model believe that this approach reduces risks and speeds up software development.

Spiral models initially were suggested in the 1990s by Barry Boehm, a noted software engineering professor. He stated that each iteration, or phase, of the model must have a specific goal that is accepted, rejected, or changed by the user, or client. Thus, each iteration produces feedback and enhancements, which enable the team to reach the overall project goal. Typically, each iteration in a spiral model includes planning, risk analysis, engineering, and evaluation. The repeated iterations produce a series of prototypes, which evolve into the finished system. Notice that these phases resemble SDLC tasks, which also can be iterative.

Numerous other adaptive variations and related methods exist, and most IT developers expect this trend to continue in the future. Two examples are Scrum and Extreme Programming (XP), which are discussed in detail in Chapter 4, Requirements Modeling, and in Chapter 11, Application Development.

Although agile methods are becoming popular, analysts should recognize that these approaches have advantages and disadvantages. By their nature, agile methods can allow developers to be much more flexible and responsive, but can be riskier than more traditional methods. For example, without a detailed set of system requirements, certain features requested by some users might not be consistent with the company's larger game plan.

Other potential disadvantages of agile methods can include weak documentation, blurred lines of accountability, and too little emphasis on the larger business picture. Also, unless properly implemented, a long series of iterations might actually add to project cost and development time. The bottom line is that systems analysts should understand the pros and cons of any approach before selecting a development method for a specific project.

Other Development Methods

IT professionals know that the key to success is user input — before, during, and after a system is developed. Over time, many companies discovered that systems development teams composed of IT staff, users, and managers could complete their work more rapidly and produce better results. Two methodologies became popular: **joint application development (JAD)** and **rapid application development (RAD)**.

Both JAD and RAD use teams composed of users, managers, and IT staff. The difference is that JAD focuses on team-based fact-finding, which is only one phase of the development process, whereas RAD is more like a compressed version of the entire process. JAD, RAD, and agile methods are described in more detail in Chapter 4.

In addition to the methods described in this chapter, you might encounter other systems development techniques, and there are many to choose from. Two popular examples are IBM's Rational® software and the Microsoft Solutions Framework®.

Companies often choose to follow their own methodology. Using CASE tools, an IT team can apply a variety of techniques rather than being bound to a single, rigid methodology. As shown in Part B of the Systems Analyst's Toolkit, many CASE tools offer a complete set of analysis and modeling tools that support various methods and strategies. Regardless of the development model, it will be necessary to manage people, tasks, timetables, and expenses by using various project management tools and techniques.

> **🔧 TOOLKIT TIME**
>
> The CASE tools in Part B of the Systems Analyst's Toolkit can help you develop and maintain complex information systems. To learn more about these tools, turn to Part B of the four-part Toolkit that follows Chapter 12.

THE INFORMATION TECHNOLOGY DEPARTMENT

The IT department develops and maintains information systems. The structure of the IT department varies among companies, as does its name and placement within the organization. In a small firm, one person might handle all computer support activities and services, whereas a large corporation might require many people with specialized skills to provide information systems support. Figure 1-29 shows a typical IT organization in a company that has networked PCs, enterprise-wide databases, centralized processing, and Web-based operations.

The IT group provides **technical support**, which includes seven main functions: application development, systems support and security, user support, database administration, network administration, Web support, and quality assurance. These functions overlap considerably and often have different names in different companies.

FIGURE 1-29 Depending on its size, an IT department might have separate organizational units for these functions, or they might be combined into a smaller number of teams.

© Cengage Learning 2014

Application Development

The IT application development group typically provides leadership and overall guidance, but the systems themselves are developed by teams consisting of users, managers, and IT staff members. A popular model for information systems development is a project-oriented team using RAD or JAD, with IT professionals providing overall coordination, guidance, and technical support.

CASE IN POINT 1.2: GLOBAL HOTELS AND MOMMA'S MOTELS

Suppose you work in the IT department of Global Hotels, a multinational hotel chain. Global Hotels runs several specialized business support systems, including a guest reservations system that was developed in-house to meet the requirements of a large company with worldwide operations. Guests can make one-stop online reservations by visiting Global's Web site, which has links to all major travel industry sites.

Global Hotels just acquired Momma's, a regional chain of 20 motels in western Canada. Momma's uses a vertical reservations package suitable for small- to medium-sized businesses, and a generic accounting and finance package. Should Momma's use Global Hotels' information systems or continue with its own? In your answer, consider issues such as business profiles, business processes, system interactivity, EDI, e-commerce, and the characteristics of both information systems. What additional information would be helpful to you in making a recommendation?

Systems Support and Security

Systems support and security provides vital protection and maintenance services for system hardware and software, including enterprise computing systems, networks, transaction processing systems, and corporate IT infrastructure. The systems support and security group implements and monitors physical and electronic security hardware, software, and procedures. This group also installs and supports operating systems, telecommunications software, and centralized database management systems. In addition, systems support and security technicians provide technical assistance to other groups in the IT department. If a site has a large number of remote clients, the systems support group often includes a deployment team that installs and configures the workstations.

User Support

User support provides users with technical information, training, and productivity support. The user support function usually is called a **service desk** or **help desk (IC)**. A help desk's staff trains users and managers on application software such as e-mail, word processing spreadsheets, and graphics packages. User support specialists answer questions, troubleshoot problems, and serve as a clearinghouse for user problems and solutions.

Database Administration

Database administration involves data design, management, security, backup, and access. In small- and medium-sized companies, an IT support person performs those roles in addition to other duties. Regardless of company size, mission-critical database applications require continuous attention and technical support.

Network Administration

Business operations depend on networks that enable company-wide information systems. Network administration includes hardware and software maintenance, support, and security. In addition to controlling user access, network administrators install, configure, manage, monitor, and maintain network applications. Network administration is discussed in more detail in Chapter 10.

Web Support

Web support is a vital technical support function. Web support specialists design and construct Web pages, monitor traffic, manage hardware and software, and link Web-based applications to the company's information systems. Reliable, high-quality Web support is especially critical for companies engaged in e-commerce.

Quality Assurance (QA)

Many large IT departments also use a quality assurance (QA) team that reviews and tests all applications and systems changes to verify specifications and software quality standards. The QA team usually is a separate unit that reports directly to IT management.

CASE IN POINT 1.3: WHAT SHOULD LISA DO?

Lisa Jameson has two job offers. One is from Pembroke Boats, a boat manufacturer that employs 200 people in a small Ohio town. Pembroke does not have an IT department and wants her to create one. The job position is called information coordinator, but she would be the only IT person.

The other offer, which pays about $7,500 more annually, is from Albemarle Express, a nationwide trucking firm located in Detroit. At Albemarle Express, Lisa would be a programmer-analyst, with the promise that if she does well in her position, she eventually will move into a systems analyst position and work on new systems development. Lisa has heard a rumor that another company might acquire Albemarle Express, but that rumor has occurred before and nothing has ever happened. What should Lisa do, and why?

THE SYSTEMS ANALYST

A systems analyst investigates, analyzes, designs, develops, installs, evaluates, and maintains a company's information systems. To perform those tasks, a systems analyst constantly interacts with users and managers within and outside the company. The following sections describe a system analyst's role, knowledge, skills, education, certifications, and career opportunities.

Role

As you learned earlier in the chapter, a systems analyst helps develop IT systems that support business requirements. To succeed, analysts often must act as translators. For example, when they describe business processes to programmers, they must speak a language that programmers will understand clearly. Typically, the analyst builds a series of models, diagrams, decision tables, and uses other descriptive tools and techniques. Similarly, when communicating with managers, the analyst often must translate complex technical issues into words and images that nontechnical people can grasp. To do this, the analyst uses various presentation skills, models, and communication methods.

Analysts are often the company's best line of defense against an IT disaster — a system that is technically sound, but fails because it does not meet the needs of users and managers. When this occurs, poor communication is usually to blame. For an analyst, the most valuable skill is the ability to listen. An effective analyst will involve users in every step of the development process, and listen carefully to what they have to say. As the process continues, the analyst will seek feedback and comments from the users. This input can provide a valuable early warning system for projects that might otherwise go off the track.

> **⚙ TOOLKIT TIME**
>
> The communications tools in Part A of the Systems Analyst's Toolkit can help you develop better reports and presentations. To learn more about these tools, turn to Part A of the four-part Toolkit that follows Chapter 12.

The chapters on project management, modeling, and user interface design will be especially valuable to you as a user-focused analyst. In addition, the Systems Analyst's Toolkit that follows Chapter 12 includes many tools to help you with each of those important skills.

Knowledge, Skills, and Education

A successful systems analyst needs technical knowledge, oral and written communication skills, an understanding of business operations, and critical thinking skills. Educational requirements vary widely depending on the company and the position. In a rapidly changing IT marketplace, a systems analyst must manage his or her own career and have a plan for professional development.

TECHNICAL KNOWLEDGE   State-of-the-art knowledge is extremely important in a rapidly changing business and technical environment. The Internet offers numerous opportunities to update technical knowledge and skills. Many IT professionals go online to learn about technical developments, exchange experiences, and get answers to questions. For example, the ZDNet site shown in Figure 1-30 offers IT news, blogs, reviews, downloads, and more. Analysts also maintain their skills by attending training courses, both onsite and online. Networking with colleagues is another way to keep up with new developments, and membership in professional associations also is important.

FIGURE 1-30   ZDNet offers IT news, blogs, reviews, downloads, and more.
© 2012 CBS Interactive

COMMUNICATION SKILLS   A systems analyst needs strong oral and written communication skills, and the ability to interact with people at all levels, from operational staff to senior executives. Often, the analyst must work with people outside the company, such as software and hardware vendors, customers, and government officials. Analysts often coordinate IT project teams, where they use communication skills to guide and motivate team members.

BUSINESS SKILLS   A systems analyst works closely with managers, supervisors, and operational employees. To be effective, he or she must understand business operations and processes, communicate clearly, and translate business needs into requirements that can be understood by programmers and systems developers. A successful analyst is business-oriented, curious, comfortable with financial tools, and able to see the big picture. Chapter 2, Analyzing the Business Case, describes some basic concepts, including strategic planning, SWOT analysis, and feasibility tests. In addition, the Systems Analyst's Toolkit, which follows Chapter 12, explains communication and financial tools that can help analysts handle business-related tasks.

CRITICAL THINKING SKILLS   Although no standard definition exists, most educators agree that **critical thinking skills** include the ability to compare, classify, evaluate, recognize patterns, analyze cause-and-effect, and apply logic. Critical thinkers often use a *what-if* approach, and they have the ability to evaluate their own thinking and reasoning.

Critical thinking skills are valuable in the IT industry, where employers seek job candidates who can demonstrate these skills and bring them to the workplace. Figure 1-31 shows the Foundation for Critical Thinking site, which offers many resources to support the critical thinking community.

EDUCATION   Companies typically require systems analysts to have a college degree in information systems, computer science, or business, and some IT experience usually is required. For higher-level positions, many companies require an advanced degree. Sometimes, educational requirements can be waived if a candidate has significant experience, skills, or professional certifications. Part D of the Systems Analyst's Toolkit describes many valuable IT resources for personal and professional development.

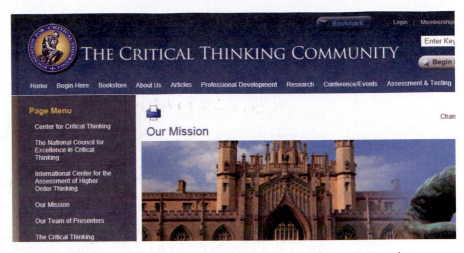

FIGURE 1-31   The Critical Thinking Community is a nonprofit organization that provides encouragement and resources for critical thinkers.
© 2011 Foundation for Critical Thinking

Certification

Many hardware and software companies offer certification for IT professionals. **Certification** verifies that an individual demonstrated a certain level of knowledge and skill on a standardized test. Certification is an excellent way for IT professionals to learn new skills and gain recognition for their efforts. Although certification does not guarantee competence or ability, many companies regard certification as an important credential for hiring or promotion. You can learn more about certification in Chapter 12, Managing Systems Support and Security, and by visiting the Web sites of individual companies such as Microsoft, Cisco Systems, Oracle, and Novell.

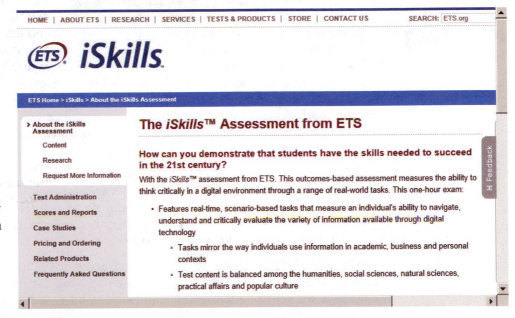

FIGURE 1-32   Employers like to hire people who can think logically and effectively. The Educational Testing Service (ETS) tests and certifies critical thinking skills using an interactive test with realistic scenarios.
© 2012 by Educational Testing Service

In addition to traditional hardware and software certifications, some firms are exploring ways to assess critical thinking skills, as shown in Figure 1-32. These skills include perception, organization, analysis, problem solving, and decision making. Whether or not formal certification is involved, these skills are extremely valuable to IT professionals and the employers who hire them.

Career Opportunities

The demand for systems analysts is expected to remain strong. Companies will need systems analysts to apply new information technology, and the explosion in e-commerce will fuel IT job growth. The systems analyst position is a challenging and rewarding one that can lead to a top management position. With an understanding of technical and business issues, a systems analyst has an unlimited horizon. Many companies have presidents and senior managers who started in IT departments as systems analysts.

The responsibilities of a systems analyst at a small firm are different from those at a large corporation. Would you be better off at a small or large company? Where will you find the best opportunity for experience and professional growth? Each person looks for different rewards in a job. What will be important to you?

JOB TITLES First, do not rely on job titles alone. Some positions are called systems analysts, but involve only programming or technical support. In other cases, systems analyst responsibilities are found in positions titled computer specialist, programmer, programmer/analyst, systems designer, software engineer, and various others. Be sure the responsibilities of the job are stated clearly when you consider a position.

COMPANY ORGANIZATION Find out all you can about the company and where the IT department fits in the organization chart. Where are IT functions performed, and by whom? A firm might have a central IT group, but decentralize the systems development function. This situation sometimes occurs in large conglomerates, where the parent company consolidates information that actually is developed and managed at the subsidiary level. Where would you rather work?

COMPANY SIZE If you like more variety, a smaller firm might suit you best. If you want to specialize, however, then consider a larger company with state-of-the-art systems. Although you might have more responsibility in a smaller company, the promotional opportunities and financial rewards often are greater in larger companies. You also might want to consider working as an independent consultant, either on your own or with others. Many consulting firms have been successful in offering their services to smaller business enterprises that do not have the expertise to handle systems development on their own.

SALARY, LOCATION, AND FUTURE GROWTH Finally, consider salary, location, and the company's prospects for future growth and success. Think about your impressions of the company and the people you met during your interviews. Most important, review your short- and long-term goals very carefully before deciding which position is best for you.

CORPORATE CULTURE In addition to having goals, methods, and information systems requirements, every firm has an underlying **corporate culture**. A corporate culture is the set of beliefs, rules, traditions, values, and attitudes that define a company and influence its way of doing business. To be successful, a systems analyst must understand the corporate culture and how it affects the way information is managed. Companies sometimes include statements about corporate culture in their mission statements, which are explained in Chapter 2.

A systems analyst must understand the firm's culture and find it comfortable. If the company encourages personal growth and empowerment, work is much more enjoyable. For example, consider the workplace described by IBM chairman Samuel J. Palmisano and President and CEO Virginia M. Rometty in Figure 1-33.

TOOLKIT TIME

The information technology resource tools in Part D of the Systems Analyst's Toolkit can help you obtain technical data, advance your career, and network with other IT professionals. To learn more about these tools, turn to Part D of the four-part Toolkit that follows Chapter 12.

CASE IN POINT 1.4: JUST-IN-TIME AIRFREIGHT, INC.

Suppose you are the IT director at Just-in-Time Airfreight, and you have received authorization to hire another systems analyst. This will be an entry-level position, and the person will assist senior systems analysts on various projects involving the reservations and the human resources systems. Using the information in this chapter, draft an ad that would appear in *The Wall Street Journal*, local newspapers, and online. You can get some ideas by visiting monster.com or a similar site. In your ad, be sure to list desired skills, experience, and educational requirements.

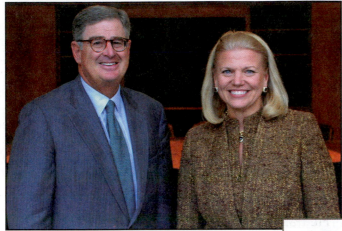

© JON IWATA/DPA /Landov

At this institution, an individual can actually change the world, can learn something new every day, can collaborate with some of the smartest people on the planet, can work in a progressive environment and can truly be a global citizen.

© IBM Corporation 1994, 2012

FIGURE 1-33   A corporate culture like IBM's is likely to attract, retain, and motivate the best and brightest people.

A QUESTION OF ETHICS

© faberfoto_it/iStockphoto

You are enjoying your job as a summer intern in the IT department of a local company. At lunch yesterday, several people were discussing ethical issues. You learned that some of them belong to IT organizations that have ethical codes to guide members and set professional standards. For example, Ann, your supervisor, belongs to the Association for Computing Machinery (ACM), which has over 100,000 members from more than 100 countries and a Web site at **acm.org.** Ann said that the ACM code of ethics is important to her, and would definitely influence her views. On the other hand, Jack, a senior programmer, believes that his own personal standards would be sufficient to guide him if ethical questions were to arise.

Because you are excited about your career as an IT professional, you decide to visit ACM's site at acm.org to examine the code of ethics and make up your own mind. After you do so, would you tend to agree more with Ann or with Jack?

CHAPTER SUMMARY

In this chapter, you learned that information technology (IT) refers to the combination of hardware, software, and services that people use to manage, communicate, and share information. Technology is changing rapidly, and IT professionals must prepare for the future. IT supports business operations, improves productivity, and helps managers make decisions. Systems analysis and design is the process of developing information systems that transform data into useful information, and systems analysts are IT team members who help plan, develop, and maintain information systems.

The essential components of an information system are hardware, software, data, processes, and people. Hardware consists of everything in the physical layer of the information system. Software consists of system software, which manages the hardware components, and application software, which supports day-to-day business operations. Data is the raw material that an information system transforms into useful information. Processes describe the tasks and functions that users, managers, and IT staff members perform. People who interact with a system include users, from both within and outside the company.

Most successful companies offer a mix of products, technical and financial services, consulting, and customer support. A rapidly growing business category is the Internet-dependent firm, which relies solely on Internet-based operations. E-commerce includes business-to-consumer (B2C) sales, and business-to-business (B2B) transactions that use Internet-based digital marketplaces or private electronic data interchange (EDI) systems.

A systems analyst starts with a business profile, which is an overview of company functions, and then he or she creates a series of business models that represent business processes, which describe specific transactions, events, tasks, and results. Analysts use business process modeling tools to document complex operations.

Based on their functions and features, business information systems are identified as enterprise computing systems, transaction processing systems, business support systems, knowledge management systems, or user productivity systems. In most companies, significant overlap and integration exists among the various types of information systems.

A typical organization structure includes top managers, middle managers and knowledge workers, supervisors and team leaders, and operational employees. Top managers develop strategic plans, which define an overall mission and goals. Middle managers provide direction, resources, and feedback to supervisors and team leaders. Knowledge workers include various professionals who function as support staff. Supervisors and team leaders oversee operational employees. Each organizational level has a different set of responsibilities and information needs.

Systems analysts use modeling, prototyping, and computer-aided systems engineering (CASE) tools. Modeling produces a graphical representation of a concept or process, whereas prototyping involves the creation of an early working model of the information or its components. A systems analyst uses CASE tools to perform various systems development tasks.

Three popular system development approaches are structured analysis, which is a traditional method that still is widely used, object-oriented analysis (O-O), which is a more recent approach that many analysts prefer, and agile methods, also called adaptive methods, which include the latest trends in software development.

Structured analysis uses a series of phases, called the systems development life cycle (SDLC) that usually is shown as a waterfall model. Structured analysis uses an overall plan, similar to a blueprint for constructing a building, so it is called a predictive approach. This method uses a set of process models to describe a system graphically, and also addresses data organization and structure, relational database design, and user interface issues.

Object-oriented analysis combines data and the processes that act on the data into things called objects that represent people, things, transactions, and events. Objects have characteristics called properties, built-in processes called methods, and can send information to other objects by using messages. Using an O-O programming language, a programmer then writes the code that creates the objects. Object-oriented methods usually follow a series of analysis and design phases similar to the SDLC, but the phases are more interactive.

Agile methods are the newest development approach, and attempt to develop a system incrementally by building a series of prototypes and constantly adjusting them to user requirements. Agile methods typically use a spiral model, which represents a series of iterations, or revisions, based on user feedback. The repeated iterations produce a series of prototypes, which evolve into the finished system.

Regardless of the development strategy, people, tasks, timetables, and costs must be managed effectively using project management tools and techniques, which are described in detail in Chapter 3.

Some firms choose to develop their own in-house methods or adopt techniques offered by software suppliers, CASE tool vendors, or consultants. Companies also use team-based strategies called joint application development (JAD) and rapid application development (RAD). JAD focuses on team-based fact-finding, whereas RAD is more like a compressed version of the entire process. JAD and RAD are described in more detail in Chapter 4.

The IT department develops, maintains, and operates a company's information systems. IT staff members provide technical support, including application development, systems support, user support, database administration, network administration, Web support, and quality assurance. These functions overlap considerably and often have different names in different companies.

In addition to technical knowledge, a systems analyst must understand the business, think critically, and communicate effectively. Valuable credentials such as certifications are available to systems analysts. A systems analyst's responsibilities depend on a company's organization, size, and culture. Systems analysts need to consider salary, location, and future growth potential when making a career decision.

Key Terms

adaptive methods *21*

agile methods *21*

application software *8*

B2B (business-to-business) *13*

B2C (business-to-consumer) *13*

business model *19*

business process *10*

business process model (BPM) *10*

business process modeling notation (BPMN) *10*

business profile *10*

business rules *22*

business support systems *16*

CASE tools *20*

certification *32*

class *24*

computer-aided software engineering (CASE) *20*

computer-aided systems engineering (CASE) *20*

corporate culture *33*

critical thinking skills *31*

data *7*

data flow diagram (DFD) *22*

deliverable *22*

e-commerce (electronic commerce) *13*

electronic data interchange (EDI) *14*

empowerment *19*

enterprise applications *8*

enterprise computing *15*

enterprise resource planning (ERP) *15*

feasibility study *23*

groupware *17*

hardware *8*

help desk *29*

horizontal system *8*

I-commerce (Internet commerce) *13*

inference rules *17*

information *7*

information system *7*

information technology (IT) *4*

iterative *25*

joint application development (JAD) *26*

knowledge base *17*

legacy systems *9*

management information systems (MIS) *16*

mission-critical system *7*

modeling *19*

Moore's Law *8*

object-oriented (O-O)
   analysis *21*

object *24*

preliminary investigation *23*

process *9*

product-oriented *11*

project management *22*

properties *24*

prototype *20*

radio frequency identification (RFID) *16*

rapid application development (RAD) *26*

requirements modeling *23*

scalable *24*

server farm *7*

service-oriented *11*

software *8*

spiral model *26*

stakeholders *10*

strategic plans *18*

structured analysis *21*

supply chain *10*

supply chain management (SCM) *14*

system *7*

system design specification *24*

system requirements document *24*

system software *8*

systems analysis and design *7*

systems analysis phase *23*

systems analyst *7*

systems design phase *24*

systems development life cycle (SDLC) *22*

systems implementation
   phase *24*

systems planning phase *23*

systems request *23*

systems support and security phase *24*

technical support *28*

transaction processing (TP) systems *15*

user productivity systems *17*

users *10*

vertical system *8*

waterfall model *22*

Chapter Exercises

Questions

1. What is information technology and why is it important? Suggest three fictitious headlines that might be added to Figure 1-1 on page 2.
2. Why would a systems analyst have to act as a translator? What groups might be involved?
3. Write a business profile for a large business in your town. You can use your imagination to supply details you might not know.
4. What strategies are Wal-Mart and Lowe's using to gain more online customers?
5. Identify the main components of an information system. What is a mission-critical system?
6. Compare enterprise computing systems to transaction processing systems. Provide three examples of each type of system.
7. What are the four organizational levels common to many businesses? Which level typically requires data that supports long-term strategic planning and the overall business enterprise? What level of worker might rely heavily on transaction processing systems?
8. Describe three systems development tools and three development methods.
9. What are the phases of the SDLC waterfall model? Who was Barry Boehm, and what did he have to say about spiral models?
10. Review the IBM history on page 4, and then consider the powerful statement shown in Figure 1-33 on page 33. Is there a connection between the two? Why or why not?

Discussion Topics

1. Some experts believe that the growth in e-commerce will cause states and local governments to lose tax revenue, unless Internet transactions are subject to sales tax. What is one argument that supports this view, and one that opposes it?
2. Are top managers likely to be more effective if they have IT experience? Why or why not?
3. Should the IT director report to the company president, or somewhere else? Does it matter?
4. Will online transactions eventually replace person-to-person contact? Why or why not?

Projects

1. Contact four people at your school who use information systems. List their positions, the systems they use, and the business functions they perform.
2. Research newspaper, business magazine articles, or the Web to find IT companies whose stock is traded publicly. Choose a company and *pretend* to buy $5,000 of its stock. Why did you choose that company? What is the current price per share? Report each week to your class.
3. Visit at least three Web sites to learn more about agile system development and spiral models. Prepare a list of the sites you visited and a summary of the results.
4. Explore the *Critical Thinking Community* Web site at **criticalthinking.org**. Identify three important topics currently being discussed, and describe your findings.

Apply Your Knowledge

The Apply Your Knowledge section contains four mini-cases. Each case describes a situation, explains your role, and asks you to apply what you learned in the chapter.

1 Hi-Volt Components

You are the IT manager at Hi-Voltage Components, a medium-sized firm that makes specialized circuit boards. Hi-Voltage's largest customer, Green Industries, recently installed a computerized purchasing system. If Hi-Voltage connects to the purchasing system, Green Industries will be able to submit purchase orders electronically. Although Hi-Voltage has a computerized accounting system, that system is not capable of handling EDI.

Tasks

1. What options does Hi-Voltage have for developing a system to connect with Green Industries' purchasing system?
2. What terms or concepts describe the proposed computer-to-computer relationship between Hi-Voltage and Green Industries?
3. Would Hi-Voltage's proposed new system be a transaction processing system? Why or why not?
4. Before Hi-Voltage makes a final decision, should the company consider an ERP system? Why or why not?

2 Systems Analyst Salaries

As part of your job search, you decide to find out more about salaries and qualifications for systems analysts in the area where you would like to work. To increase your knowledge, search the Internet to perform the following research:

Tasks

1. Find information about a career as a systems analyst.
2. Use the Internet to determine whether the Federal Bureau of Labor Statistics lists salary information for systems analysts. If so, summarize the information you find.
3. Find three online job postings for systems analysts. List the employers, the qualifications, and the salaries, if mentioned.
4. Visit **monster.com** and search for IT positions. Report your findings.

3 NewTech Interview

You have an interview for an IT position with NewTech, a large telecommunications company, and you want to learn more about the firm and its organizational structure. To prepare for the interview, you decide to review your knowledge about corporations, including the following questions:

Tasks

1. What are the four organizational levels in a typical company?
2. Go online and find three examples of retailers that offer both in-store and Web-based sales. What were the firms? Which one did you like best, and why?
3. What is empowerment? Provide two specific examples.
4. What types of information systems might a large company use? Would the same systems be found in a smaller firm? Why or why not?

4 Rainbow's End Interview

Your NewTech interview seemed to go well, but you did not get the job. During the meeting, the interviewer mentioned that NewTech uses structured analysis and relies heavily on modeling, prototyping, and CASE tools. Thinking back, you realize that you did not fully understand those terms. As you prepare for an interview with Rainbow's End, a large retail chain, you decide to review some IT terms and concepts. You want to be ready for the following questions:

Tasks

1. What are the differences between structured, O-O, and agile development methods? Which method do you think is best, and why?
2. What is a CASE tool and why is it important? What are two CASE tool examples?
3. What is business process modeling and how is it done?
4. What is prototyping and why is it important? What industries are likely to use prototyping?

Case Studies

Each chapter includes a Chapter Case, a Continuing Case, a Capstone Case, and an Online Case Simulation. You can learn more about the Online Case Simulation in the MIS CourseMate Features section.

Chapter Case: Hudson Kayak Adventures

Hudson Kayak Adventures (HKA) offers ecotours and kayak rentals along the Hudson River.

Background

Steve and Linda Lane are avid kayakers and amateur naturalists who spent many weekends exploring the Hudson River's numerous creeks and tributaries. Steve was a sales representative and Linda worked as a freelance Web designer. Two years ago, Steve's division was purchased by a rival company, which announced plans to move operations to another state.

Rather than relocate, the Lanes decided to launch HKA. They reasoned that Linda could continue her work, which would provide some income while Steve tried to build HKA into a profitable business. Steve and Linda are convinced that the ecotourism market will expand greatly, and they look forward to sharing their experience and knowledge with others who enjoy nature and kayaking.

Hudson Kayak Adventures advertises in regional magazines and maintains a Web site, which Linda designed. At this time, no other kayak rental firms operate within 20 miles of HKA's location. Customers say that the HKA site is attractive and informative, but the Lanes are not sure it is attracting new business.

So far, the Lanes' plan is working out well. HKA rents space at a nearby marina, where Linda runs the office and operates her Web design business. She also handles rentals when Steve is giving lessons or busy with a tour group. On summer weekends and holidays, Janet Jacobs, a local college student, handles telephone inquiries and reservations.

HKA's inventory includes 16 rental kayaks of various types, lengths, and capacities, eight car-top carriers, and a large assortment of accessories and safety equipment. Based on customer requests, Linda is considering adding a selection of books and videos about kayaking and ecotourism.

HKA has three main business segments: rentals, instruction, and guided tours. Most customers make advance reservations for scheduled tours and instruction sessions, but sometimes space is available for last-minute customers. Rentals are split evenly between reservations and walk-in customers.

Reservations are entered in a loose-leaf binder, with separate tabs for each business activity. Linda also created a Microsoft Access database to record reservations. When she has time, she enters the reservation date, the reservation details and kayak type, and the customer information into a table, which is sorted by reservation date. Each day, she prints a reservation list. For quick reference, Linda also displays kayak availability on a wall-mounted board with color-coded magnets that show the available or reserved status of each rental kayak. In addition to the database, Linda uses an inexpensive accounting package to keep HKA's books.

Although the HKA database handles the basic information, the Lanes have noticed some drawbacks. For example, reservations for guided tours or instruction sessions sometimes conflict with Steve's or Linda's availability. The Lanes also would like to get more information about rental patterns, customer profiles, advertising effectiveness, and future business opportunities. Steve and Linda have talked about updating the system, but they have been too busy to do so.

(continues)

Chapter Case: Hudson Kayak Adventures

Tasks

1. Develop a business profile for Hudson Kayak Adventures. Create a separate section for each of the following: HKA's business activities, organization, resources, customers, and potential for Web-based marketing.

2. List HKA's main functions and business processes. Draw a model of an HKA kayak rental, including possible events and results.

3. What types of information systems does HKA use? Do these systems support its current and future business objectives? Why or why not? What would you recommend?

4. From an object-oriented viewpoint, HKA treats kayaks as a class. Based on the background information provided, what are some properties of kayak objects?

Continuing Case: Personal Trainer, Inc.

Personal Trainer, Inc. owns and operates fitness centers in a dozen Midwestern cities. The centers have done well, and the company is planning an international expansion by opening a new "supercenter" in the Toronto area.

Background

Cassia Umi, president, heads Personal Trainer's management team. Three managers report to her at the firm's Chicago headquarters: Janet McDonald, manager, finance; Tai Tranh, manager, sales and marketing; and Reed Curry, manager, operations. The managers who run the 12 existing centers all report to Reed. Cassia wants the new supercenter to emphasize a wide variety of personal services and special programs for members. If the supercenter approach is successful, it will become the model for Personal Trainer's future growth. Cassia personally selected Gray Lewis, a manager with three years of fitness center experience, to run the new facility.

The new supercenter will feature a large exercise area with state-of-the-art equipment, a swimming pool, a sporting goods shop, a health food store, and a snack bar. In addition, the center will offer child care with special programs for various ages, a teen center, and a computer café. Cassia also wants members to have online access to customized training programs and progress reports.

Personal Trainer currently uses BumbleBee, a popular accounting package, to manage its receivables, payables, and general ledger. Membership lists and word processing are handled with Microsoft Office products.

Cassia believes the new supercenter will require additional data management capability, and she decided to hire Patterson and Wilder, an IT consulting firm, to help Personal Trainer develop an information system for the new operation. The firm assigned Susan Park, an experienced consultant, to work with the Personal Trainer team. Susan's first task was to learn more about business operations at the new center, so she requested a meeting with Gray. After some small talk, the discussion went like this:

Susan: Tell me about your plans for the new operation. I'm especially interested in what kind of information management you'll need.

Gray: Cassia thinks that we'll need more information support because of the size and complexity of the new operation. To tell the truth, I'm not so sure. We've had no problem with BumbleBee at the other centers, and I don't really want to reinvent the wheel.

Susan: Maybe we should start by looking at the similarities — and the differences — between the new center and the existing ones.

(continues)

Continuing Case: Personal Trainer, Inc.

Gray: Okay, let's do that. First of all, we offer the same basic services everywhere. That includes the exercise equipment, a pool, and, in most centers, a snack bar. Some centers also sell sporting goods, and one offers child care — but not child-fitness programs. It is true that we've never put all this together under one roof. And, I admit, we've never offered online access. To be honest, I'm not absolutely sure what Cassia has in mind when she talks about 24/7 Web-based access. One more feature — we plan to set up two levels of membership — let's call them silver and gold for now. Silver members can use all the basic services, but will pay additional fees for some special programs, such as child fitness. Gold members will have unlimited use of all services.

Susan: So, with all this going on, wouldn't an overall system make your job easier?

Gray: Yes, but I don't know where to start.

Susan: Gray, that's why I'm here. I'll work with you and the rest of the team to come up with a solution that supports your business.

Gray: Sounds good to me. When can we start?

Susan: Let's get together first thing tomorrow. Bring along an organization chart and think about how you plan to run the new facility. We'll try to build a model of the new operation so we can identify the business functions. When we know what the functions are, we'll know what kind of information is needed or generated by each function. That will be our starting point.

Tasks

1. Use the background information to create a business profile for Personal Trainer. Be sure to indicate areas where more information will be needed.

2. Each new supercenter service represents a business function, which is composed of one or more business processes. Using the background information and the conversation between Susan and Gray, list the business functions and the processes with each function.

3. Based on what you know, should Personal Trainer consider any of the following systems: ERP, transaction processing, business support, knowledge management, or user productivity? Why or why not?

4. What opportunities might Personal Trainer have for Web-based B2C transactions in the future? What about B2B?

Capstone Case: New Century Wellness Group

New Century Wellness Group offers a holistic approach to health care with an emphasis on preventive medicine as well as traditional medical care. In your role as an IT consultant, you will help New Century develop a new information system.

Background

Ten years ago, internal medicine specialists Timothy Jones and Dolores Garcia decided to combine their individual practices in Brea, California, to form New Century Wellness Group. They wanted to create a clinic that would concentrate on preventive medicine and fitness, as well as traditional medical care. New Century has competition from other health care providers, but no other clinic offers the same range of services.

New Century's practice has grown and now includes four primary care physicians, one nurse practitioner, four physical therapists, one registered nutritionist, eight nurses, and eight support staff people. The clinic currently has a patient base of 8,000 patients from 325 different employers, many of which provide insurance coverage for employee wellness and health maintenance. Currently, New Century accepts insurance plans from 25 licensed health insurance providers. New Century is also considering opening another location, near a new medical center.

(continues)

Capstone Case: New Century Wellness Group

Doctor Jones and Doctor Garcia recently decided that the practice needs a modern information system to support its business and health information management needs. The new system would replace a mix of paper-based and legacy systems. Dr. Jones asked you to design an information system that could support the clinic's current operations and future growth.

In your first meeting, Dr. Jones provided an overview of the clinic's business processes and staff members. He told you that Anita Davenport, who has been with New Century since its inception, is the office manager. She supervises the support staff of seven people. Fred Brown handles human resources and employee benefits. Corinne Summers reports directly to Fred and works with payroll, tax reporting, and profit distribution among the associates. Susan Gifford is responsible for the maintenance of patient medical records. Tom Capaletti handles accounts receivables and Tammy Alipio is the insurance billing specialist. Lisa Sung is responsible for managing appointments. Her duties include reminder calls to patients and preparing daily appointment lists. Carla Herrera is concerned primarily with ordering and organizing office and medical supplies.

After studying this information, you start to prepare for your next meeting with Dr. Jones.

Tasks

1. Use the background information to create a business profile for New Century, and indicate areas where more information will be needed. The profile should include an organization chart of the office staff. You can create the chart using Microsoft Word or a similar program, or you can draw it by hand. In Word 2010, click the Insert tab on the Ribbon, then Smart Art, then Organization Chart.

2. Identify six business processes that New Century performs, and explain who has primary responsibility for each process. Also describe what data is required and what information is generated by each process.

3. Based on what you know at this point, is it likely that you will recommend a transaction processing system, a business support system, or a user productivity system? What about an ERP system? Explain your reasons.

4. Describe the systems development method you plan to use, and explain the pros and cons of using this method.

CASE Tool Workshop

Systems analysts use CASE tools to help them plan, build, and maintain information systems. To learn more about CASE tools, turn to Part B of the Toolkit that follows Chapter 12. You can complete these tasks with the Visible Analyst® CASE tool, which is available with this textbook, or a similar tool.

Background

Suppose you are a part-time student assistant in the computer lab at your school. Janet Jacobs, the IT department chair, recently announced that a CASE tool will be installed on the lab network. Her decision was welcomed by many IT faculty members, who think it is important for students to learn about CASE tools and how to use them to complete assignments in MIS courses.

You have been asked to evaluate various CASE tools, and submit the results. Your initial tasks will be to provide an overview of the Visible Analyst® CASE tool, or a similar tool.

Tasks

1. Describe the user interface. Is it attractive and easy to use? Why or why not?
2. How do you open an existing project? How do you create a new project?

MIS CourseMate Features

If you have an MIS CourseMate access code, you can reinforce and extend your learning with premium content created for this textbook. For example, you can launch interactive Video Learning Sessions to help you understand systems development concepts and practice your skills. In addition, you can use MindTap Reader, which is a full, interactive, digital e-book.

MIS CourseMate also offers many learning features within each chapter, including an Online Case Simulation, a Critical Thinking Challenge, Video Learning Tasks, and a set of Learn It Online activities. To log on to the MIS CourseMate site at **www.cengagebrain.com**, you must create a student account and register this book.

Online Case Simulation: SCR Associates

Session I: Introduction

Overview

The SCR Associates case study is a Web-based simulation that allows you to practice your skills in a real-world environment. The firm offers IT consulting, solutions, and training. SCR plans to open a new high-tech training center, and needs to develop a Training Information Management System (TIMS) to support the center. You are a newly hired systems analyst reporting to Jesse Baker, systems group manager, and will help her develop the system.

The case study takes you to the SCR Web site, where you receive e-mail and voice mail messages from Jesse, obtain information from SCR's resource libraries, and perform various tasks. Jesse has high standards, but seems very fair. She made it clear that she expects your work to be accurate, thorough, and professional.

Before You Begin

To prepare for this work session, you should review the following topics:

- Overview of systems analysis and design
- Role of the systems analyst and the IT department

How Do I Use the Online Case Simulation?

- Read the preview, and review the Chapter 1 background material, if necessary.
- Visit the MIS CourseMate Web site at **www.cengagebrain.com**, locate the **SCR Case Simulation**, and click the **intranet** link. Enter your name and the password **sad10e**.
- When the opening screen displays, select this session. Then check your e-mail and voice mail, and start to work on your task list.

Preview: Session I

This is your second day at SCR. You spent most of yesterday filling out forms and learning your way around. You have a meeting this afternoon with Jesse Baker, your supervisor, so you have time to explore the SCR Web site. As you navigate the site, you are impressed with SCR's history, purpose, and values. You also see the strong emphasis that SCR puts on its relationships with clients. You are sure this will be a great opportunity, and you are eager to get started.

Critical Thinking Challenge

In addition to technical ability, IT professionals need critical thinking skills. These exercises can help you practice perception, organization, analysis, problem-solving, and decision-making skills that you can take to the workplace. You can visit **www.criticalthinking.org** to learn more about critical thinking and why it is so important.

Background

You are an intern in the IT department at Game Technology. You report to the IT director, Mike McGee. Mike assigned you to work with two systems analysts: Lauren Jacksina and Cathy Ross. Lauren and Cathy both report to Felesia Stukes, manager — IT development, who reports to Mike. Joe Turner, manager — IT operations, also reports to Mike. Dawn Rountree, database administrator, and Greg Wade, network administrator, report to Joe.

As an intern, you are expected to keep a journal to record your day-to-day experiences and what you are learning. This week, you will describe the systems development methods that the IT team uses, including structured analysis, object-oriented analysis, and agile approaches. Your journal should include a description of each method and its characteristics.

Practice Tasks

Visit the MIS CourseMate Web site at **www.cengagebrain.com**. Then navigate to the resources for this chapter and locate the **Critical Thinking Challenge** feature. You will complete two Practice Tasks, using what you learned in the chapter. Then you can check your answers to be sure you're ready for the Challenge Tasks.

Challenge Tasks

After you complete the Practice tasks, you learn about new developments at Game Technology.

Last Friday, a number of changes were announced, and you will need to update the organization chart. You also decide to include more information on development methods in your journal. To continue, navigate back to the **Critical Thinking Challenge** feature for this chapter, select the **Challenge Tasks**, and follow the instructions.

Video Learning Sessions

Video Learning Sessions can help you understand systems development concepts and practice your skills. In this scenario, you will help design a Video Learning Session for this chapter.

Before You Begin
To prepare for the tasks, review the chapter and list the main topics. Which ones did you find difficult to understand, and why? Can you think of other ways to explain the topics?

Training Tasks
Suppose the IT training manager wants to encourage team members to watch the Video Learning Sessions. She wants you to submit a proposal for a new session that would explain the key topics in this chapter.

1. Which topics would you choose?
2. What specific skills or concepts would you include in the session?
3. How would you present the material?
4. Describe at least three graphic images that you would include in the video session.

Learn It Online

In each chapter, you can use this feature to apply your knowledge and practice your skills. The exercises include Chapter Reinforcement Questions, Flash Cards, Practice Tests, and various games, such as *Who Wants To Be a Computer Genius?, Wheel of Terms, and the Crossword Puzzle Challenge.*

CHAPTER 2

Analyzing the Business Case

Chapter 2 explains how to analyze a business case. This chapter also explains why it is important to understand business operations and requirements, how IT projects support a company's overall strategic plan, how systems projects get started, and how systems analysts conduct a preliminary investigation and feasibility study.

INTRODUCTION

OBJECTIVES

When you finish this chapter, you will be able to:

- Explain the concept of a business case and how a business case affects an IT project

- Describe the strategic planning process and why it is important to the IT team

- Explain the purpose of a mission statement

- Conduct a SWOT analysis and describe the four factors involved

- Explain how the SDLC serves as a framework for systems development

- List reasons for systems projects and factors that affect such projects

- Describe systems requests and the role of the systems review committee

- Define operational, technical, economic, and schedule feasibility

- Describe the steps and the end product of a preliminary investigation

During the systems planning phase, the IT team reviews a proposal to determine if it presents a strong business case. The term **business case** refers to the reasons, or justification, for a proposal. To analyze the business case for a specific proposal, the analyst must consider the company's overall mission, objectives, and IT needs.

This chapter begins with a discussion of strategic planning because the IT team must understand and support the firm's long-term strategic goals.

Systems development typically starts with a systems request, followed by a preliminary investigation, which includes a feasibility study. You will learn how systems requests originate, how to evaluate a request, and how to conduct a preliminary investigation. You also will learn about fact-finding techniques that begin at this point and carry over into later development phases. Finally, you will examine the report to management, which concludes the systems planning phase.

If you have MIS CourseMate, you can view a Video Learning Session that explains a financial analysis tool called payback analysis.

PREVIEW CASE: Mountain View College Bookstore

Background: Wendy Lee, manager of college services at Mountain View College, wants a new information system that will improve efficiency and service at the three college bookstores.

In this part of the case, Tina Allen (systems analyst) and David Conroe (student intern) are talking about justification for the new system and the project's feasibility.

Participants:	Tina and David
Location:	Mountain View College cafeteria, Tuesday afternoon, September 3, 2013
Project status:	Tina has received a systems request from Wendy Lee for a new bookstore information system
Discussion topics:	Analysis of business justification and project feasibility

Tina: Hi, David. Ready to get started?

David: *Sure. What's our next step?*

Tina: Well, when we analyze a specific systems request, we need to see how the proposal fits into the overall picture at the college. In other words, we have to analyze the business case for the request.

David: *What's a business case?*

Tina: A business case is the justification for a project. A strong business case means that a proposal will add substantial value to the organization and support our strategic plan.

David: *What's a strategic plan?*

Tina: A strategic plan is like a road map. Without a plan, it's hard to know if you're heading in the right direction. Our plan starts with a mission statement, which reflects our purpose, vision, and values.

David: *I see what you mean. I read the mission statement this morning. It says that we will strive to be an efficient, customer-friendly bookstore that uses a mix of interpersonal skills and technology to serve our students and support the overall objectives of the college. That says a lot in just one sentence.*

Tina: It sure does. Now, let's get to the specifics. I just received a systems request from the college business manager. She wants us to develop a new information system for the bookstore.

David: *Do we have a green light to get started?*

Tina: Yes and no. Mountain View College doesn't have a formal procedure for evaluating IT requests, and we don't have a systems review committee. Maybe that's something we should consider for the future. Meanwhile, we need to conduct a preliminary investigation to see whether this request is feasible.

David: *What do you mean by "feasible"?*

Tina: To see if a systems request is feasible, we have to look at four separate yardsticks: operational feasibility, technical feasibility, economic feasibility, and schedule feasibility. If the request passes all the tests, we continue working on the system. Here's a task list to get us started:

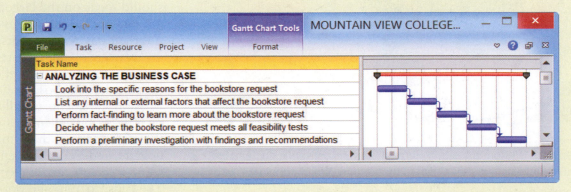

FIGURE 2-1 Typical business case analysis task list.

A FRAMEWORK FOR IT SYSTEMS DEVELOPMENT

If you could look into the future, you probably would see new industries, new products, and new services — all spurred by huge advances in technology. You also would see a surge in Internet commerce, a cloud computing explosion, and a new business environment that is global, dynamic, and incredibly challenging. To some firms, these changes will be very threatening. Other companies will see great opportunities and take advantage of them by creating strategic plans.

Strategic planning is the process of identifying long-term organizational goals, strategies, and resources. A strategic plan looks beyond day-to-day activities and focuses on a horizon that is three, five, ten, or more years in the future. A company requires information technology to support its strategic goals. Because the firm's IT group will be expected to deliver IT resources, IT managers must understand and participate in strategic planning. IT managers have to prepare for long-range needs, such as a new factory, even as they handle immediate problems, such as a logic bug in the payroll system. In most companies, the IT team reviews each IT-related proposal, project, and systems request to determine if it presents a strong business case, or justification.

The following sections provide an overview of strategic planning, a description of SWOT analysis, and a look at the changing role of the IT department.

Strategic Planning Overview

Why should a systems analyst be interested in strategic planning? The answer might be found in an old story about two stonecutters who were hard at work when a passerby asked them what they were doing. "I am cutting stones," said the first worker. The second worker replied, "I am building a cathedral."

So it is with information technology: One analyst might say, "I am using a CASE tool," while another might say, "I am helping the company succeed in a major new business venture." The difference is clear: Systems analysts should focus on the larger, strategic role of IT even as they carry out their day-to-day tasks.

Strategic planning starts with a **mission statement** that reflects the firm's vision, purpose, and values. Mission statements usually focus on long-term challenges and goals, the importance of the firm's stakeholders, and a commitment to the firm's role as a corporate citizen. The PepsiCo annual report for 2011 shown in Figure 2-2 is a typical example.

At PepsiCo, we believe being a responsible corporate citizen is not only the right thing to do, but the right thing to do for our business.

Performance with Purpose

At PepsiCo, "Performance with Purpose" means delivering sustainable growth by investing in a healthier future for people and our planet.

FIGURE 2-2 PepsiCo's annual report for 2011 refers to the firm's mission, vision, and values.
© PepsiCo, Inc.

With the mission statement as a backdrop, a firm develops shorter-term goals and objectives. For example, the company might establish one-year, three-year, and five-year goals for expanding market share. To achieve those goals, the company might develop a list of shorter-term objectives. If it wants to increase Web-based orders by 30% next year, a company might set quarterly objectives with monthly milestones. High-priority objectives are called critical success factors. A **critical success factor** is one that must be achieved to fulfill the company's mission.

Objectives also might include tactical plans, such as creating a new Web site and training a special customer support group to answer e-mail inquiries. Finally, the objectives translate into day-to-day business operations, supported by IT and other corporate resources. The outcome is a set of business results that affect company stakeholders. There is no standard process for strategic planning, but Figure 2-3 shows a typical example.

What Is SWOT Analysis?

The letters SWOT stand for strengths, weaknesses, opportunities, and threats. A **SWOT analysis** can focus on a specific product or project, an operating division, the entire company, or the mission statement itself. The overall aim is to avoid seeking goals that are unrealistic, unprofitable, or unachievable.

An enterprise SWOT analysis usually begins with these questions:

- What are our strengths, and how can we use them to achieve our business goals?

- What are our weaknesses, and how can we reduce or eliminate them?

- What are our opportunities, and how do we plan to take advantage of them?

- What are our threats, and how can we assess, manage, and respond to the possible risks?

A SWOT analysis examines a firm's technical, human, and financial resources. In Figure 2-4, the bulleted lists show samples of typical strengths, weaknesses, opportunities, and threats.

As the SWOT process continues, management reviews specific resources and business operations. For example, suppose that the company owns an important patent. A SWOT review for the patent might resemble Figure 2-5.

FIGURE 2-3 Strategic planning is a dynamic process that starts with a mission statement, which is shaped by the firm's purpose, vision, and values. The mission generates goals and objectives that produce business results.
© Cengage Learning 2014

FIGURE 2-4 A SWOT analysis might produce results similar to those shown here.
© Cengage Learning 2014

SWOT Analysis of a Corporate Patent

Strengths

- Our patent covers valuable technology that we can use in popular products.

Weaknesses

- Our patent has a limited life. When it expires, the technology will no longer be protected.

Patent

Opportunities

- We can use the technology in more products, license it to others, or seek more patents.

Threats

- A competitor might develop similar technology that does not legally infringe our patent.

FIGURE 2-5 This SWOT analysis example focuses on a specific asset, such as a company patent.
© Cengage Learning 2014

There is no standard approach to strategic planning. Some managers believe that a firm's mission statement should contain an inspirational message to its stakeholders. Others feel that unless a firm starts with a realistic SWOT assessment, it might develop a mission statement that is unachievable. The majority of companies view the strategic planning process as a dynamic interaction, similar to the diagram in Figure 2-3 on the previous page, where the company's mission statement reflects a long-term horizon, but sets forth goals that are achievable and consistent with real-world conditions.

CASE IN POINT 2.1: LO CARB MEALS

Lo Carb is a successful new company that has published several cookbooks and marketed its own line of low-carbohydrate meals. Joe Turner, Lo Carb's president, has asked your opinion. He wants to know whether a mission statement really is necessary. After you review the chapter material, write a brief memo with your views. Be sure to include good (and not-so-good) examples of actual mission statements that you find on the Web.

Strategic Planning for IT Projects

In the previous section, you learned about strategic planning at the enterprise level. But what about specific IT systems and projects? Should you use a similar approach to define and develop an information system? The answer is definitely yes! Experienced analysts know that planning is essential for IT project success, and must start as early as possible. Careful planning can help assure that:

- The project supports overall business strategy and operational needs.
- The project scope is well-defined and clearly stated.
- The project goals are realistic, achievable, and tied to specific statements, assumptions, constraints, factors, and other inputs.

The first step is to select a planning tool. Some developers stick to traditional text-based methods, using Microsoft Word tables to provide structure and clarity. Others prefer a spreadsheet, such as Microsoft Excel, because it is easy to display priorities and the relative importance of planning assumptions. However, the most effective approach is to use a CASE tool to define and document the overall environment. To understand why this is so, consider the following scenario and illustration:

You are a systems analyst in the IT department of a large hotel chain. Your task is to review the Visible Analyst CASE tool to see whether it would be helpful in planning a new marketing system. After you open the program, you navigate to the Help section for an overview, which is shown in Figure 2-6a.

Next, you create a sample project and enter an assumption about the target date for a new network, as shown in Figure 2-6b. You see that many types of planning statements are possible, including goals, objectives, and critical success factors, among others. Planning statements also can document strengths, weaknesses, opportunities, and threats, as shown in Figure 2-6c.

After entering the planning statement, you open the strategic planning screen and see the new statement displayed, as shown in Figure 2-6d. You can see that Visible Analyst has embedded the planning statement directly into the project, so it can be accessed at any point in the development process.

This example shows how a CASE tool can integrate various statements, entities, data elements, and graphical models into an overall structure. The result: more consistency, better quality, and much less effort for developers.

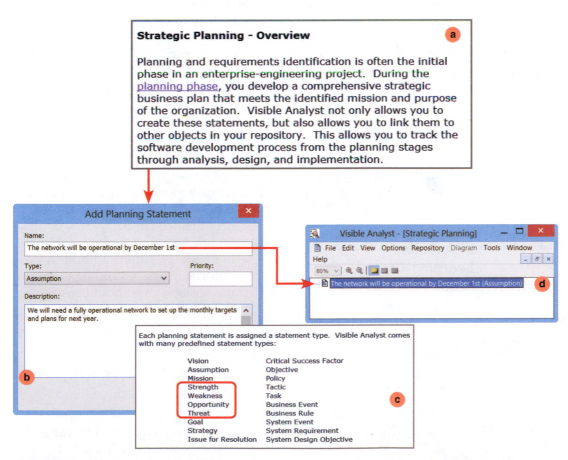

FIGURE 2-6 The Visible Analyst CASE tool supports strategic planning and allows a user to enter many kinds of planning statements. Notice the four SWOT categories highlighted in the list.

Screenshots used with permission from Visible Systems Corporation.

A New Role for the IT Department

Management and IT are linked closely, and remarkable changes have occurred in both areas. For example, in the 1990s a typical IT department handled *all* aspects of systems development and consulted users only when, and if, the department wanted user input. Today, systems development is much more team-oriented. New approaches to systems development, such as agile methods, joint application development (JAD), and rapid application development (RAD), typically involve groups of users, managers, and IT staff working together right from the start.

Although team-oriented development is the norm, some companies still see the role of the IT department as a gatekeeper, responsible for screening and evaluating systems requests. Should the IT department perform the initial evaluation, or should a cross-functional team do it? The answer probably depends on the company's size. In smaller companies or firms where only one person has IT skills, that person acts as a coordinator and consults closely with users and managers to evaluate systems requests. Larger firms are more likely to use an evaluation team or systems review committee.

CASE IN POINT 2.2: ATTAWAY AIRLINES, PART ONE

You are the IT director at Attaway Airlines, a small regional air carrier. You chair the company's systems review committee, and you currently are dealing with strong disagreements about two key projects. Dan Esposito, the marketing manager, says it is vital to have a new computerized reservation system that can provide better customer service and reduce operational costs. Molly Kinnon, vice president of finance, is equally adamant that a new accounting system is needed immediately because it will be very expensive to adjust the current system to new federal reporting requirements. Molly outranks Dan, and she is your boss. The next meeting, which promises to be a real showdown, is set for 9:00 a.m. tomorrow. How will you prepare for the meeting? What questions and issues should be discussed?

WHAT IS A BUSINESS CASE?

As mentioned earlier, the term *business case* refers to the reasons, or justification, for a proposal. A business case should be comprehensive, yet easy to understand. It should describe the project clearly, provide the justification to proceed, and estimate the project's financial impact. ProSci's BPR Online Learning Center, as shown in Figure 2-7, offers a Business Case Tutorial Series. According to ProSci, the business case should answer questions such as the following:

- Why are we doing this project?
- What is the project about?
- How does this solution address key business issues?
- How much will it cost and how long will it take?
- Will we suffer a productivity loss during the transition?

Welcome to the BPR Tutorial Series

Home - Bookstore - Tutorials - Best Practices

Send this page to a friend

BPR Online Learning Center
Sponsored by Prosci

**Business Case Tutorial Series
how to write an effective business case**

Module 1 - What is the Business Case

This tutorial series focuses on how to write a business case. This tutorial is taken from Prosci's Business Case Toolkit which includes a complete business case template, guidelines, exercises, worksheets and checklists for developing an effective business case. It follows the series dedicated to project planning and reengineering design.

FIGURE 2-7 ProSci's BPR Online Learning Center offers a Business Case Tutorial Series that focuses on how to write a business case.

- What is the return on investment and payback period?
- What are the risks of doing the project? What are the risks of *not* doing the project?
- How will we measure success?
- What alternatives exist?

INFORMATION SYSTEMS PROJECTS

This section discusses reasons for systems projects and the internal and external factors that affect systems projects. The section also includes a preview of project management, which is discussed in detail in Chapter 3.

Main Reasons for Systems Projects

The starting point for most projects is called a **systems request**, which is a formal way of asking for IT support. A systems request might propose enhancements for an existing system, the correction of problems, the replacement of an older system, or the development of an entirely new information system that is needed to support a company's current and future business needs.

As Figure 2-8 shows, the main reasons for systems requests are improved service to customers, better performance, support for new products and services, more information, stronger controls, and reduced cost.

TOOLKIT TIME

The Financial Analysis tools in Part C of the Systems Analyst's Toolkit can help you analyze project costs, benefits, and economic feasibility. To learn more about these tools, turn to Part C of the four-part Toolkit that follows Chapter 12.

FIGURE 2-8   Six main reasons for systems requests.
© Cengage Learning 2014

IMPROVED SERVICE   Systems requests often are aimed at improving service to customers or users within the company. Allowing mutual fund investors to check their account balances on a Web site, storing data on rental car customer preferences, or creating an online college registration system are examples that provide valuable services and increased customer satisfaction.

SUPPORT FOR NEW PRODUCTS AND SERVICES   New products and services often require new types or levels of IT support. For example, a software vendor might offer an automatic upgrade service for subscribers; or a package delivery company might add a special service for RFID-tagged shipments. In situations like these, it is most likely that additional IT support will be required. At the other end of the spectrum, product obsolescence can also be an important factor in IT planning. As new products enter the marketplace, vendors often announce that they will no longer provide support for older versions. A lack of vendor support would be an important consideration in deciding whether or not to upgrade.

BETTER PERFORMANCE   The current system might not meet performance requirements. For example, it might respond slowly to data inquiries at certain times, or it might be unable to support company growth. Performance limitations also result when a system that was designed for a specific hardware configuration becomes obsolete when new hardware is introduced.

MORE INFORMATION The system might produce information that is insufficient, incomplete, or unable to support the company's changing information needs. For example, a system that tracks customer orders might not be capable of analyzing and predicting marketing trends. In the face of intense competition and rapid product development cycles, managers need the best possible information to make major decisions on planning, designing, and marketing new products and services.

STRONGER CONTROLS A system must have effective controls to ensure that data is secure and accurate. Some common security controls include passwords, various levels of user access, and **encryption**, or coding data to keep it safe from unauthorized users. Hardware-based security controls include **biometric devices** that can identify a person by a retina scan or by mapping a facial pattern. One biometric tool scans hands, rather than faces. The technology uses infrared scanners that create images with thousands of measurements of hand and finger characteristics, as shown in Figure 2-9.

In addition to being secure, data also must be accurate. Controls should minimize data entry errors whenever possible. For example, if a user enters an invalid customer number, the order processing system should reject the entry immediately and prompt the user to enter a valid number. Data entry controls must be effective without being excessive. If a system requires users to confirm every item with an "Are you sure? Y/N" message, internal users and customers might complain that the system is not user-friendly.

FIGURE 2-9 Students at West Virginia University use a hand scanning device to identify themselves.
Courtesy of Ingersoll Rand Security Technologies

REDUCED COST The current system could be expensive to operate or maintain as a result of technical problems, design weaknesses, or the changing demands of the business. It might be possible to adapt the system to newer technology or upgrade it. On the other hand, cost-benefit analysis might show that a new system would be more cost effective and provide better support for long-term objectives.

CASE IN POINT 2.3: Trent College

Trent College is a private school in a small Maryland town. The college has outgrown its computerized registration system and is considering a new system. Althea Riddick, the college president, has asked you to list the reasons for systems projects, which are described on pages 55–56, and assign a relative weight to each reason, using a scale of 1–10, low to high. She said to use your best judgment, and support your conclusions in a brief memo to her. She also wants you to create a Microsoft Excel spreadsheet that will calculate the weighted values automatically for each reason.

Factors That Affect Systems Projects

Internal and external factors affect every business decision that a company makes, and IT projects are no exception. Figure 2-10 shows internal and external factors that shape corporate IT choices.

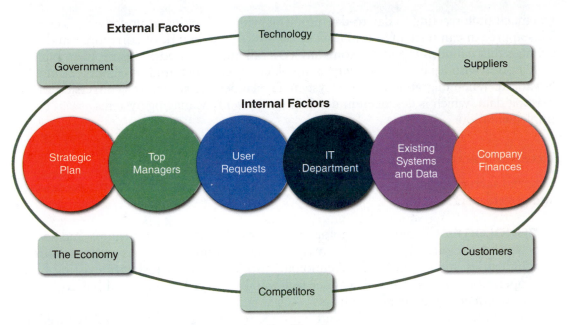

FIGURE 2-10 Internal and external factors that affect IT projects.
© Cengage Learning 2014

Internal Factors

Internal factors include the strategic plan, top managers, user requests, information technology department, and existing systems and data.

STRATEGIC PLAN   A company's strategic plan sets the overall direction for the firm and has an important impact on IT projects. Company goals and objectives that need IT support will generate systems requests and influence IT priorities. A strategic plan that stresses technology tends to create a favorable climate for IT projects that extends throughout the organization.

TOP MANAGERS   Because significant resources are required, top management usually initiates large-scale projects. Those decisions often result from strategic business goals that require new IT systems, more information for decision making, or better support for mission-critical information systems.

USER REQUESTS   As users rely more heavily on information systems to perform their jobs, they are likely to request even more IT services and support. For example, sales reps might request improvements to the company's Web site, a more powerful sales analysis report, a network to link all sales locations, or an online system that allows customers to obtain the status of their orders instantly. Or, users might not be satisfied with the current system because it is difficult to learn or lacks flexibility. They might want information systems support for business requirements that did not even exist when the system was developed.

INFORMATION TECHNOLOGY DEPARTMENT   Many systems project requests come from the IT department. IT staff members often make recommendations based on their knowledge of business operations and technology trends. IT proposals might be strictly technical matters, such as replacement of certain network components, or suggestions might be more business oriented, such as proposing a new reporting or data collection system.

EXISTING SYSTEMS AND DATA   Errors or problems in existing systems can trigger requests for systems projects. When dealing with older systems, analysts sometimes spend too much time reacting to day-to-day problems without looking at underlying causes. This approach can turn an information system into a patchwork of corrections and changes that cannot support the company's overall business needs. This problem typically occurs with legacy systems, which are older systems that are less technologically advanced. When migrating to a new system, IT planners must plan the conversion of existing data, which is described in detail in Chapter 11, Managing Systems Implementation.

External Factors

External factors include technology, suppliers, customers, competitors, the economy, and government.

TECHNOLOGY   Changing technology is a major force affecting business and society in general. For example, the rapid growth of telecommunications has created entire new industries and technologies. Technology also dramatically reshapes existing business operations. The success of scanner technology resulted in universal bar coding that now affects virtually all products.

Some industry experts predict that bar code technology will be overshadowed in the future by **electronic product code (EPC)** technology that uses RFID tags to identify and monitor the movement of each individual product, from the factory floor to the retail checkout counter.

FIGURE 2-11 Just-in-time (JIT) inventory systems rely on computer-to-computer data exchange to minimize unnecessary inventory.

© TEAL Electronics Corporation

SUPPLIERS   With the growth of electronic data interchange (EDI), relationships with suppliers are critically important. For example, an automobile company might require that suppliers code their parts in a certain manner to match the auto company's inventory control system. EDI also enables **just-in-time (JIT)** inventory systems, as shown in Figure 2-11, which rely on computer-to-computer data exchange to minimize unnecessary inventory. The purpose of a JIT system is to provide the right products at the right place at the right time.

CUSTOMERS   Customers are vitally important to any business. Information systems that interact with customers usually receive top priority. Many companies implement **customer relationship management (CRM)** systems that integrate all customer-related events and transactions, including marketing, sales, and customer service activities. Vendor-oriented CRM systems often interconnect with supply chain management (SCM) systems, which were discussed in Chapter 1. CRM components can provide automated responses to sales inquiries, Web-based order processing, and online inventory tracking. Because an efficient warehouse is just as important as a successful Web site, suppliers use *smart* forklifts that can read RFID tags or UPC numbers and transmit data to a CRM system, as shown in Figure 2-12.

Another RFID application is called **electronic proof of delivery (EPOD)**. Using EPOD, a supplier uses RFID tags on each crate, case, or shipping unit to create a digital shipping list. The customer receives the list and scans the incoming shipment. If a discrepancy is detected, it is reported and adjusted automatically. Because they would be expensive to investigate manually, small shipping inconsistencies might not otherwise be traced. This is an example of technology-related cost control.

COMPETITORS   Competition drives many information systems decisions. For example, if one cellular telephone provider offers a new type of digital service, other firms must match the plan in order to remain competitive. New product research and development, marketing, sales, and service all require IT support.

THE ECONOMY   Economic activity has a powerful influence on corporate information management. In a period of economic expansion, firms need to be ready with scalable systems that can handle additional volume and growth. Predicting the business cycle is not an exact science, and careful research and planning are important.

GOVERNMENT   Federal, state, and local government regulations directly affect the design of corporate information systems. For example, up-to-date IRS reporting requirements must be designed into a payroll package.

FIGURE 2-12   In an efficient warehouse, *smart* forklifts can read RFID tags or UPC numbers and transmit data to a CRM system.
Courtesy of Intermec Technologies

EVALUATION OF SYSTEMS REQUESTS

In most organizations, the IT department receives more systems requests than it can handle. Many organizations assign responsibility for evaluating systems requests to a group of key managers and users. Many companies call this group a **systems review committee** or a **computer resources committee**. Regardless of the name, the objective is to use the combined judgment and experience of several managers to evaluate systems projects.

Systems Request Forms

Many organizations use a special form for systems requests, similar to the online sample shown in Figure 2-13 on the next page. A properly designed form streamlines the request process and ensures consistency. The form must be easy to understand and include clear instructions. It should include enough space for all required information and should indicate what supporting documents are needed. Most companies use online systems request forms that users submit electronically.

When a systems request form is received, a systems analyst or IT manager examines it to determine what IT resources are required for the preliminary investigation. A designated person or a committee then decides whether to proceed with a preliminary investigation. Sometimes, a situation requires an immediate response. For example, if the problem involves a mission-critical system, an IT maintenance

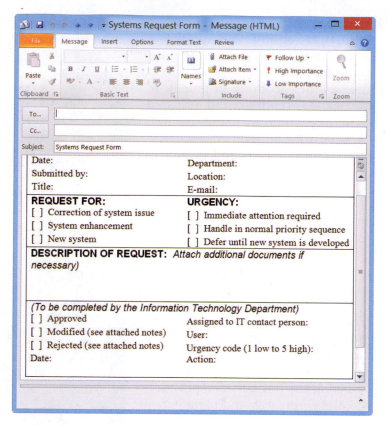

FIGURE 2-13 Example of an online systems request form.
© Cengage Learning 2014

team must restore normal operations ASAP. When the system is functioning properly, the team conducts a review and prepares a systems request to document the work that was performed.

Systems Review Committee

Most large companies use a systems review committee to evaluate systems requests. Instead of relying on a single individual, a committee approach provides a variety of experience and knowledge. With a broader viewpoint, a committee can establish priorities more effectively than an individual, and one person's bias is less likely to affect the decisions. A typical committee consists of the IT director and several managers from other departments. The IT director usually serves as a technical consultant to ensure that committee members are aware of crucial issues, problems, and opportunities.

Although a committee offers many advantages, some disadvantages exist. For example, action on requests must wait until the committee meets. To avoid delay, committee members typically use e-mail and teleconferencing to communicate. Another potential disadvantage of a committee is that members might favor projects requested by their own departments, and internal political differences could delay important decisions.

Many smaller companies rely on one person to evaluate system requests instead of a committee. If only one person has the necessary IT skills and experience, that person must consult closely with users and managers throughout the company to ensure that business and operational needs are considered carefully.

Whether one person or a committee is responsible, the goal is to evaluate the requests and set priorities. Suppose four requests must be reviewed:

- The marketing group wants to analyze current customer spending habits and forecast future trends.

- The technical support group wants a cellular link so service representatives can download technical data instantly.

- The accounting department wants to redesign customer statements and allow Internet access.

- The production staff wants an inventory control system that can exchange data with major suppliers.

Which projects should the firm pursue? What criteria should be applied? How should priorities be determined? To answer those questions, the individual or the committee must assess the feasibility of each request.

OVERVIEW OF FEASIBILITY

As you learned in Chapter 1, a systems request must pass several tests, called a feasibility study, to see whether it is worthwhile to proceed further. As shown in Figure 2-14, a feasibility study uses four main yardsticks to measure a proposal: operational feasibility, technical feasibility, **economic feasibility**, and schedule feasibility.

Sometimes a feasibility study is quite simple and can be done in a few hours. If the request involves a new system or a major change, however, extensive fact-finding and investigation are required.

How much effort should go into a feasibility study? That depends on the request. For example, if a department wants an existing report sorted in a different order, the analyst can decide quickly whether the request is feasible. On the other hand, a proposal by the marketing department for a new market research system to predict sales trends would require much more effort. In both cases, the systems analyst asks these important questions:

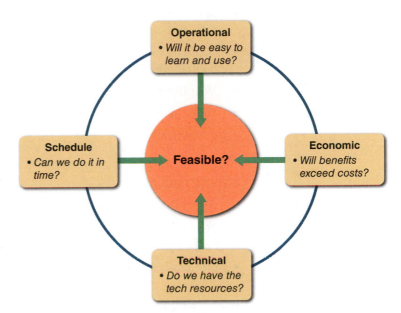

FIGURE 2-14 A feasibility study examines operational, technical, economic, and schedule factors.

© Cengage Learning 2014

- Is the proposal desirable in an operational sense? Is it a practical approach that will solve a problem or take advantage of an opportunity to achieve company goals?

- Is the proposal technically feasible? Are the necessary technical resources and people available for the project?

- Is the proposal economically desirable? What are the projected savings and costs? Are other intangible factors involved, such as customer satisfaction or company image? Is the problem worth solving, and will the request result in a sound business investment?

- Can the proposal be accomplished within an acceptable time frame?

To obtain more information about a systems request, you might perform initial fact-finding by studying organization charts, performing interviews, reviewing current documentation, observing operations, and surveying users. If the systems request is approved, more intensive fact-finding will continue during the systems analysis phase.

Operational Feasibility

Operational feasibility means that a proposed system will be used effectively after it has been developed. If users have difficulty with a new system, it will not produce the expected benefits. Organizational culture also can also affect operational feasibility. For instance, a system that works well in a highly structured workplace might be very unpopular in a more relaxed corporate culture. Operational feasibility is difficult to measure with precision, but must be studied very carefully. For example, the following questions would help predict a system's operational feasibility:

- Does management support the project? Do users support the project? Is the current system well liked and effectively used? Do users see the need for change?

- Will the new system result in a workforce reduction? If so, what will happen to affected employees?

- Will the new system require training for users? If so, is the company prepared to provide the necessary resources for training current employees?

- Will users be involved in planning the new system right from the start?

- Will the new system place any new demands on users or require any operating changes? For example, will any information be less accessible or produced less frequently? Will performance decline in any way? If so, will an overall gain to the organization outweigh individual losses?

- Will customers experience adverse effects in any way, either temporarily or permanently?

- Will any risk to the company's image or goodwill result?

- Does the development schedule conflict with other company priorities?

- Do legal or ethical issues need to be considered?

Technical Feasibility

Technical feasibility refers to the technical resources needed to develop, purchase, install, or operate the system. When assessing technical feasibility, an analyst must consider the following points:

- Does the company have the necessary hardware, software, and network resources? If not, can those resources be acquired without difficulty?

- Does the company have the needed technical expertise? If not, can it be acquired?

- Does the proposed platform have sufficient capacity for future needs? If not, can it be expanded?

- Will a prototype be required?

- Will the hardware and software environment be reliable? Will it integrate with other company information systems, both now and in the future? Will it interface properly with external systems operated by customers and suppliers?

- Will the combination of hardware and software supply adequate performance? Do clear expectations and performance specifications exist?

- Will the system be able to handle future transaction volume and company growth?

Economic Feasibility

Economic feasibility means that the projected benefits of the proposed system outweigh the estimated costs usually considered the **total cost of ownership (TCO)**, which includes ongoing support and maintenance costs, as well as acquisition costs. To determine TCO, the analyst must estimate costs in each of the following areas:

- People, including IT staff and users
- Hardware and equipment
- Software, including in-house development as well as purchases from vendors
- Formal and informal training, including peer-to-peer support
- Licenses and fees
- Consulting expenses
- Facility costs
- The estimated cost of not developing the system or postponing the project

Tangible costs, such as those listed above, usually can be measured in dollars. But **intangible costs** also must be considered. For example, low employee morale might not have an immediate dollar impact, but certainly will affect the company's performance.

In addition to costs, you need to assess tangible and intangible benefits to the company. The systems review committee will use those figures, along with your cost estimates, to decide whether to pursue the project beyond the preliminary investigation phase.

Tangible benefits are benefits that can be measured in dollars. Tangible benefits result from a decrease in expenses, an increase in revenues, or both. Examples of tangible benefits include the following:

- A new scheduling system that reduces overtime
- An online package tracking system that improves service and decreases the need for clerical staff
- A sophisticated inventory control system that cuts excess inventory and eliminates production delays

Intangible benefits are advantages that are difficult to measure in dollars but are important to the company. Examples of intangible benefits include the following:

- A user-friendly system that improves employee job satisfaction
- A sales tracking system that supplies better information for marketing decisions
- A new Web site that enhances the company's image

TOOLKIT TIME

The Financial Analysis tools in Part C of the Systems Analyst's Toolkit can help you analyze project costs, benefits, and economic feasibility. To learn more about these tools, turn to Part C of the four-part Toolkit that follows Chapter 12.

You also must consider the development timetable because some benefits might occur as soon as the system is operational, but others might not take place until later.

Schedule Feasibility

Schedule feasibility means that a project can be implemented in an acceptable time frame. When assessing schedule feasibility, a systems analyst must consider the interaction between time and costs. For example, speeding up a project schedule might make a project feasible, but much more expensive.

Other issues that relate to schedule feasibility include the following:

- Can the company or the IT team control the factors that affect schedule feasibility?
- Has management established a firm timetable for the project?
- What conditions must be satisfied during the development of the system?
- Will an accelerated schedule pose any risks? If so, are the risks acceptable?
- Will project management techniques be available to coordinate and control the project?
- Will a project manager be appointed?

Chapter 3 describes various project management tools and techniques.

EVALUATING FEASIBILITY

The first step in evaluating feasibility is to identify and weed out systems requests that are not feasible. For example, a request would not be feasible if it required hardware or software that the company already had rejected.

Even if the request is feasible, it might not be necessary. For example, a request for multiple versions of a report could require considerable design and programming effort. A better alternative might be to download the server data to a personal computer-based software package and show users how to produce their own reports. In this case, training users would be a better investment than producing reports for them.

Also keep in mind that systems requests that are not currently feasible can be resubmitted as new hardware, software, or expertise becomes available. Development costs might decrease, or the value of benefits might increase enough that a systems request eventually becomes feasible. Conversely, an initially feasible project can be rejected later.

As the project progresses, conditions often change. Acquisition costs might increase, and the project might become more expensive than anticipated. In addition, managers and users sometimes lose confidence in a project. For all those reasons, feasibility analysis is an ongoing task that must be performed throughout the systems development process.

SETTING PRIORITIES

After rejecting systems requests that are not feasible, the systems review committee must establish priorities for the remaining items. The highest priority goes to projects that provide the greatest benefit, at the lowest cost, in the shortest period of time. Many factors, however, influence project evaluation.

Factors That Affect Priority

When assessing a project's priority, a systems analyst should consider the following:

- Will the proposed system reduce costs? Where? When? How? How much?
- Will the system increase revenue for the company? Where? When? How? How much?

- Will the systems project result in more information or produce better results? How? Are the results measurable?

- Will the system serve customers better?

- Will the system serve the organization better?

- Can the project be implemented in a reasonable time period? How long will the results last?

- Are the necessary financial, human, and technical resources available?

Few projects will score high in all areas. Some proposals might not reduce costs but will provide important new features. Other systems might reduce operating costs substantially but require the purchase or lease of additional hardware. Some systems might be very desirable but require several years of development before producing significant benefits.

Whenever possible, the analyst should use tangible costs and benefits that can be measured in dollars. However, the proposal might involve intangible benefits, such as enhancing the organization's image, raising employee morale, or improving customer service. These examples would be harder to measure, but must also be considered.

Discretionary and Nondiscretionary Projects

Is the project absolutely necessary? Projects where management has a choice in implementing them are called **discretionary projects**. Projects where no choice exists are called **nondiscretionary projects**. Creating a new report for a user is an example of a discretionary project; adding a report required by a new federal law is an example of a nondiscretionary project.

If a particular project is not discretionary, is it really necessary for the systems review committee to evaluate it? Some people believe that waiting for committee approval delays critical nondiscretionary projects unnecessarily. Others believe that submitting all requests to the systems review keeps the committee aware of all projects that compete for IT resources. As a result, the committee can review priorities and create realistic schedules.

Many nondiscretionary projects are predictable. Examples include annual updates to payroll, tax percentages, or quarterly changes in reporting requirements for an insurance processing system. By planning ahead for predictable projects, the IT department manages its resources better and keeps the systems review committee fully informed without needing prior approval in every case.

CASE IN POINT 2.4: ATTAWAY AIRLINES, PART TWO

Back at Attaway Airlines, the morning meeting ended with no agreement between Dan Esposito and Molly Kinnon. In fact, a new issue arose. Molly now says that the new accounting system is entitled to the highest priority because the federal government soon will require the reporting of certain types of company-paid health insurance premiums. Because the current system will not handle this report, she insists that the entire accounting system is a nondiscretionary project. As you might expect, Dan is upset. Can part of a project be nondiscretionary? What issues need to be discussed? The committee meets again tomorrow, and the members will look to you, as the IT director, for guidance.

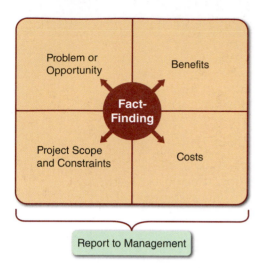

FIGURE 2-15 Model of a preliminary investigation. Notice the importance of fact-finding in each of the four areas.

© Cengage Learning 2014

1. Understand the problem or opportunity

2. Define the project scope and constraints

3. Perform fact-finding
   - Analyze organization charts
   - Review documentation
   - Observe operations
   - Conduct a user survey

4. Study usability, cost, benefit, and schedule data

5. Evaluate feasibility
   - Operational
   - Technical
   - Economic

6. Present recommendations to management

FIGURE 2-16 Six main steps in a typical preliminary investigation.

© Cengage Learning 2014

PRELIMINARY INVESTIGATION OVERVIEW

A systems analyst conducts a **preliminary investigation** to study the systems request and recommend specific action. After obtaining an authorization to proceed, the analyst interacts with managers and users, as shown in the model in Figure 2-15. The analyst gathers facts about the problem or opportunity, project scope and constraints, project benefits, and estimated development time and costs. The end product of the preliminary investigation is a report to management.

Interaction with Managers and Users

Before starting a preliminary investigation, it is important to let people know about the investigation and explain your role. You should meet with key managers, users, and IT staff to describe the project, explain your responsibilities, answer questions, and invite comments. Interactive communication with users starts at this point and continues throughout the development process.

A systems project often produces significant changes in company operations. Employees may be curious, concerned, or even opposed to those changes. It is not surprising to encounter some user resistance during a preliminary investigation. Employee attitudes and reactions are important and must be considered.

When interacting with users, you should be careful in your use of the word *problem* because it has a negative meaning. When you ask users about *problems*, some will stress current system limitations rather than desirable new features or enhancements. Instead of focusing on difficulties, you should question users about additional capability they would like to have. Using this approach, you highlight ways to improve the user's job, you get a better understanding of operations, and you build better, more positive relationships with users.

Planning the Preliminary Investigation

During a preliminary investigation, a systems analyst typically follows a series of steps, as shown in Figure 2-16. The exact procedure depends on the nature of the request, the size of the project, and the degree of urgency.

Step 1: Understand the Problem or Opportunity

If the systems request involves a new information system or a substantial change in an existing system, systems analysts might need to develop a business profile that describes business processes and functions, as explained in Chapter 1. Even where the request involves relatively minor changes or enhancements, you need to understand how those modifications will affect business operations and other information systems. Often a change in one system has an unexpected effect on another system. When you analyze a systems request, you need to determine which departments, users, and business processes are involved.

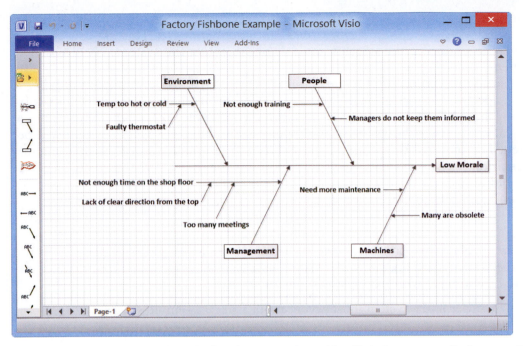

FIGURE 2-17 A fishbone diagram displays the causes of a problem. Typically, you must dig deeper to identify actual *causes* rather than just symptoms.
© Cengage Learning 2014

In many cases, the systems request does not reveal the underlying problem, but only a symptom. For example, a request to investigate mainframe processing delays might reveal improper scheduling practices rather than hardware problems. Similarly, a request for analysis of customer complaints might disclose a lack of sales representative training, rather than problems with the product.

A popular technique for investigating causes and effects is called a **fishbone diagram**, or **Ishikawa diagram**, as shown in Figure 2-17. A fishbone diagram is an analysis tool that represents the possible causes of a problem as a graphical outline. When using a fishbone diagram, an analyst first states the problem and draws a main bone with sub-bones that represent possible causes of the problem. In the example shown in Figure 2-17, the problem is *Low Morale*, and the analyst has identified four areas to investigate: *Environment, People, Management,* and *Machines*. In each area, the analyst identifies possible causes and draws them as horizontal sub-bones. For example, *Temp too hot or cold* is a possible cause in the *Environment* bone. For each cause, the analyst must dig deeper and ask the question: What could be causing *this* symptom to occur? For example, *why* is it too hot? If the answer is a *Faulty thermostat*, the analyst indicates this as a sub-bone to the *Temp too hot or cold* cause. In this manner, the analyst adds additional sub-bones to the diagram, until he or she uncovers root causes of a problem, rather than just the symptoms.

Step 2: Define the Project Scope and Constraints

Determining the **project scope** means defining the specific boundaries, or extent, of the project. For example, a statement that, *payroll is not being produced accurately* is very general, compared with the statement, *overtime pay is not being calculated correctly for production workers on the second shift at the Yorktown plant.* Similarly, the statement, *the project scope is to modify the accounts receivable system,* is not as specific as the statement, *the project scope is to allow customers to inquire online about account balances and recent transactions.*

Some analysts find it helpful to define project scope by creating a list with sections called *Must Do, Should Do, Could Do,* and *Won't Do.* This list can be reviewed later, during the systems analysis phase, when the systems requirements document is developed.

Projects with very general scope definitions are at risk of expanding gradually, without specific authorization, in a process called **project creep**. To avoid this problem, you should define project scope as clearly as possible. You might want to use a graphical model that shows the systems, people, and business processes that will be affected. The scope of the project also establishes the boundaries of the preliminary investigation itself. A systems analyst should limit the focus to the problem at hand and avoid unnecessary expenditure of time and money.

Along with defining the scope of the project, you need to identify any constraints on the system. A **constraint** is a requirement or condition that the system must satisfy or an outcome that the system must achieve. A constraint can involve hardware, software, time, policy, law, or cost. System constraints also define project scope. For example, if the system must operate with existing hardware, that is a constraint that affects potential solutions. Other examples of constraints are:

- The order entry system must accept input from 15 remote sites.
- The human resources information system must produce statistics on hiring practices.
- The new Web site must be operational by March 1.

When examining constraints, you should identify their characteristics, as follows.

PRESENT VERSUS FUTURE   Is the constraint something that must be met as soon as the system is developed or modified, or is the constraint necessary at some future time?

INTERNAL VERSUS EXTERNAL   Is the constraint due to a requirement within the organization, or does some external force, such as government regulation, impose it?

MANDATORY VERSUS DESIRABLE   Is the constraint mandatory? Is it absolutely essential to meet the constraint, or is it merely desirable?

Figure 2-18 shows five examples of constraints. Notice that each constraint has three characteristics, which are indicated by its position in the figure and by the symbol that represents the constraint, as follows:

- The constraint in Example A is present, external, and mandatory.
- The constraint in Example B is future, external, and mandatory.
- The constraint in Example C is present, internal, and desirable.
- The constraint in Example D is present, internal, and mandatory.
- The constraint in Example E is future, internal, and desirable.

Regardless of the type, all constraints should be identified as early as possible to avoid future problems and surprises. A clear definition of project scope and constraints avoids misunderstandings that arise when managers assume that the system will have a certain feature or support for a project, but later find that the feature is not included.

Step 3: Perform Fact-Finding

The objective of fact-finding is to gather data about project usability, costs, benefits, and schedules. Fact-finding involves various techniques, which are described below. Depending on what information is needed to investigate the systems request, fact-finding

Sample Constraints Shown by Timing, Type, and Urgency

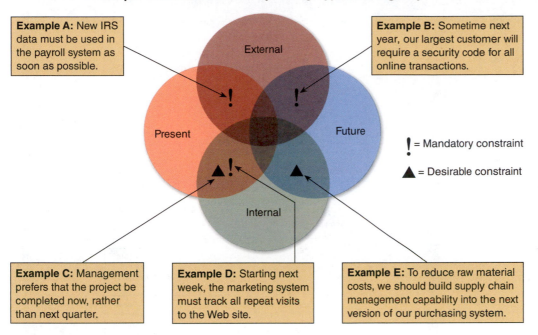

Example A: New IRS data must be used in the payroll system as soon as possible.

Example B: Sometime next year, our largest customer will require a security code for all online transactions.

! = Mandatory constraint

▲ = Desirable constraint

Example C: Management prefers that the project be completed now, rather than next quarter.

Example D: Starting next week, the marketing system must track all repeat visits to the Web site.

Example E: To reduce raw material costs, we should build supply chain management capability into the next version of our purchasing system.

FIGURE 2-18 Examples of various types of constraints.

© Cengage Learning 2014

might consume several hours, days, or weeks. For example, a change in a report format or data entry screen might require a single telephone call or e-mail message to a user, whereas a new inventory system would involve a series of interviews. During fact-finding, you might analyze organization charts, conduct interviews, review current documentation, observe operations, and carry out a user survey.

ANALYZE ORGANIZATION CHARTS   In many instances, you will not know the organizational structure of departments involved in the study. You should obtain organization charts to understand the functions and identify people you want to interview.

If organization charts are not available, or are out-of-date, you should obtain the necessary information from department personnel and construct your own charts, as shown in Figure 2-19 on the next page.

Even when charts are available, you should verify their accuracy. Keep in mind that an organization chart shows formal reporting relationships but not the informal alignment of a group, which also is important.

CONDUCT INTERVIEWS   The primary method of obtaining information during the preliminary investigation is the interview. The interviewing process involves a series of steps:

1. Determine the people to interview.
2. Establish objectives for the interview.
3. Develop interview questions.
4. Prepare for the interview.
5. Conduct the interview.
6. Document the interview.
7. Evaluate the interview.

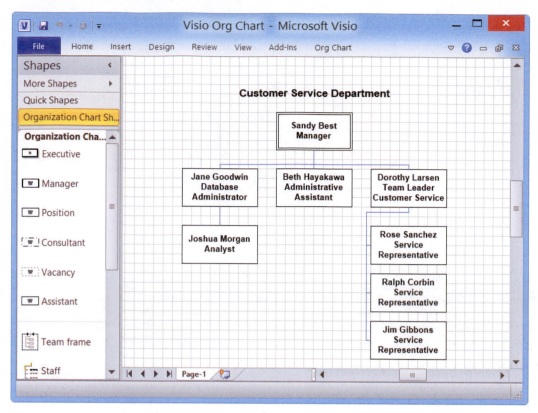

FIGURE 2-19 Microsoft Visio includes an organization chart drawing tool that allows a user to drag and drop various symbols.

© Cengage Learning 2014

These seven steps are discussed in detail in Chapter 4, which describes fact-finding techniques that occur during the systems analysis phase of the SDLC.

Remember that the purpose of the interview, and of the preliminary investigation itself, is to uncover facts, not to convince others that the project is justified. Your primary role in an interview is to ask effective questions and listen carefully. If you plan to talk to several people about the same topic, you should prepare a standard set of questions for all the interviews. Also be sure to include open-ended questions, such as "What else do you think I should know about the system?" or "Is there any other relevant information that we have not discussed?"

When conducting interviews during the preliminary investigation, you should interview managers and supervisors who have a broad knowledge of the system and can give you an overview of the business processes involved. Depending on the situation, you might talk to operational personnel to learn how the system functions on a day-to-day basis.

REVIEW DOCUMENTATION   Although interviews are an extremely important method of obtaining information, you also might want to investigate the current system documentation. The documentation might not be up to date, so you should check with users to confirm that you are receiving accurate and complete information.

OBSERVE OPERATIONS   Another fact-finding method is to observe the current system in operation, as shown in Figure 2-20. You might see how workers carry out typical tasks. You might choose to trace or follow the actual paths taken by input source documents or output reports. In addition to observing operations, you might want to sample the inputs or outputs of the system. Using sampling techniques described in Chapter 4, you can obtain valuable information about the nature and frequency of the problem.

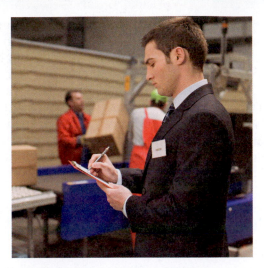

FIGURE 2-20 Sometimes, an analyst can get a better understanding of a system by watching actual operations.

© Jupiterimages/Getty Images

CONDUCT A USER SURVEY   Interviews can be time consuming. Sometimes you can obtain information from a larger group by conducting a user survey. In this case, you design a form that users complete and return to you for tabulation. A survey is not as flexible as a series of interviews, but it is less expensive, generally takes less time, and can involve a broad cross-section of people.

ANALYZE THE DATA   Systems analysts use many techniques to locate the source of a problem. For example, the **Pareto chart** is a widely used tool for visualizing issues that need attention. Named for a 19th century economist, a Pareto chart is drawn as a vertical bar graph, as shown in Figure 2-21. The bars, which represent various causes of a problem, are

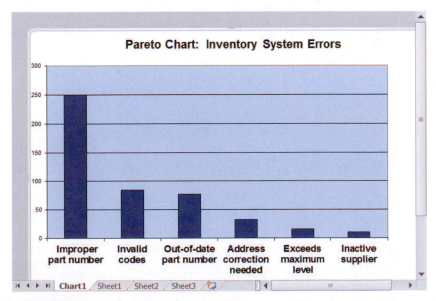

FIGURE 2-21 A Pareto chart displays the causes of a problem, in priority order, so an analyst can tackle the most important causes first. In this example, the part number issue would be the obvious starting point.

© Cengage Learning 2014

arranged in descending order, so the team can focus on the most important causes. In the example shown, a systems analyst might use a Pareto chart to learn more about the causes of inventory system problems, so that necessary improvements can be made.

The **XY chart**, sometimes called a **scatter diagram**, is another problem-solving tool. Often, an analyst looks for a correlation between two variables. For example, suppose you are getting complaints about network response time, and you want to determine the cause. You would try to identify variables, such as the number of users, to see whether there is a correlation, or pattern. Figure 2-22 shows two XY charts with data samples. The first chart sample would suggest that there is no correlation between the delays and the number of users, and you would look elsewhere

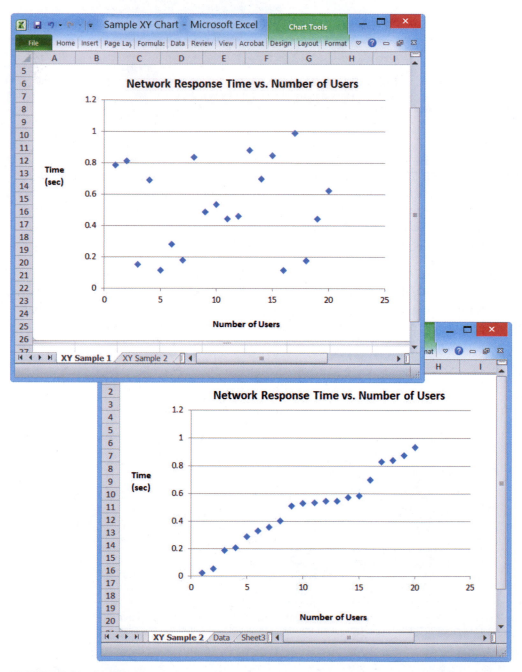

FIGURE 2-22 An XY chart shows correlation between variables, which is very important in problem-solving. Conversely, a *lack* of correlation suggests that the variables are independent, and that you should look elsewhere for the cause.

for the source of the problem. However, if the data resembles the second XY sample, it indicates a strong relationship between the number of users and the longer response times. That information would be extremely valuable in the problem-solving process.

Step 4: Analyze Project Usability, Cost, Benefit, and Schedule Data

During fact-finding, you gathered data about the project's predicted costs, anticipated benefits, and schedule issues that could affect implementation. Before you can evaluate feasibility, you must analyze this data carefully. If you conducted interviews or used surveys, you should tabulate the data to make it easier to understand. If you observed current operations, you should review the results and highlight key facts that will be useful in the feasibility analysis. If you gathered cost and benefit data, you should be able to prepare financial analysis and impact statements using spreadsheets and other decision-support tools.

Also, you should develop time and cost estimates for the requirements modeling tasks for the next SDLC phase, systems analysis. Specifically, you should consider the following:

- What information must you obtain, and how will you gather and analyze the information?

- Will you conduct interviews? How many people will you interview, and how much time will you need to meet with the people and summarize their responses?

- Will you conduct a survey? Who will be involved? How much time will it take people to complete it? How much time will it take to tabulate the results?

- How much will it cost to analyze the information and prepare a report with findings and recommendations?

Step 5: Evaluate Feasibility

You have analyzed the problem or opportunity, defined the project scope and constraints, and performed fact-finding to evaluate project usability, costs, benefits, and time constraints. Now you are ready to evaluate the project's feasibility. You should start by reviewing the answers to the questions listed on pages 61–65. Also consider the following guidelines:

OPERATIONAL FEASIBILITY   Your fact-finding should have included a review of user needs, requirements, and expectations. When you analyze this data, you should look for areas that might present problems for system users and how they might be resolved. Because operational feasibility means that a system will be used effectively, this is a vital area of concern.

TECHNICAL FEASIBILITY   The fact-finding data should identify the hardware, software, and network resources needed to develop, install, and operate the system. With this data, you can develop a checklist that will highlight technical costs and concerns, if any.

ECONOMIC FEASIBILITY   Using the fact-finding data, you can apply the financial analysis tools described in Part C of the Systems Analyst's Toolkit to assess feasibility. The cost-benefit data will be an important factor for management to consider. Also, a cost estimate for the project development team will be built into the project management plan.

SCHEDULE FEASIBILITY   The fact-finding data should include stakeholder expectations regarding acceptable timing and completion dates. As mentioned previously, often a trade-off exists between a project's schedule and its costs. For example, compressing a project schedule might be possible, but only if the budget is increased accordingly. The schedule data will be incorporated into the project plan in the form of task durations and milestones.

Step 6: Present Results and Recommendations to Management

At this stage, you have several alternatives. You might find that no action is necessary or that some other strategy, such as additional training, is needed. To solve a minor problem, you might implement a simple solution without performing further analysis. In other situations, you will recommend that the project proceed to the next development phase, which is systems analysis.

The final task in the preliminary investigation is to prepare a report to management, and possibly deliver a presentation, as shown in Figure 2-23. The report includes an evaluation of the systems request, an estimate of costs and benefits, and a **case for action**, which is a summary of the project request and a specific recommendation.

The format of a preliminary investigation report varies from one company to another. A typical report might consist of the following sections:

- *Introduction* — the first section is an overview of the report. The introduction contains a brief description of the system, the name of the person or group who performed the investigation, and the name of the person or group who initiated the investigation.

- *Systems Request Summary* — the summary describes the basis of the systems request.

- *Findings* — the findings section contains the results of your preliminary investigation, including a description of the project's scope, constraints, and feasibility.

- *Case for Action* — a summary of the project request and a specific recommendation. Management will make the final decision, but the IT department's input is an important factor.

- *Project Roles* — this section lists the people who will participate in the project, and describes each person's role.

- *Time and Cost Estimates* — this section describes the cost of acquiring and installing the system, and the total cost of ownership during the system's useful life. Intangible costs also should be noted.

- *Expected Benefits* — this section includes anticipated tangible and intangible benefits and a timetable that shows when they are to occur.

- *Appendix* — an appendix is included in the report if you need to attach supporting information. For example, you might list the interviews you conducted, the documentation you reviewed, and other sources for the information you obtained. You do not need to include detailed interview reports, but you should retain those documents to support your findings and for future reference.

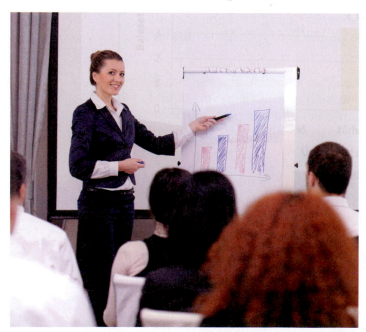

FIGURE 2-23 Oral presentations often are required during systems development, and systems analysts need to develop strong presentation skills.

© shock/Shutterstock

A QUESTION OF ETHICS

© faberfoto_it/iStockphoto

As a new systems analyst at Premier Financial Services, you are getting quite an education. You report to Mary, the IT manager, who also chairs the systems review committee. Several months ago, the committee rejected a request from Jack, the finance director, for an expensive new accounts payable system because the benefits did not appear to outweigh the costs.

Yesterday, Mary's boss called her in and asked her to reconsider Jack's request, and to persuade the other members to approve it. Mary wanted to discuss the merits of the request, but he cut her off rather abruptly. Mary happens to know that Jack and her boss are longtime friends.

Mary has confided in you. She is very uncomfortable about the meeting with her boss, and she believes that his request would undermine the integrity of the systems review process. Mary feels it would be unethical to grant preferred treatment just because a friendship is involved. She is thinking of submitting a request to step down as review committee chair, even though that might harm her career at the company.

Is this an ethical question, or just a matter of office politics? What would you say to Mary?

CHAPTER SUMMARY

Systems planning is the first phase of the systems development life cycle. Effective information systems help an organization support its business processes, carry out its mission, and serve its stakeholders. During strategic planning, a company examines its purpose, vision, and values and develops a mission statement, which leads to goals, objectives, day-to-day operations, and business results that affect company stakeholders. SWOT analysis examines strengths, weaknesses, opportunities, and threats. SWOT analysis can be used at the enterprise level and for individual projects.

During the systems planning phase, an analyst reviews the business case, which is the basis, or reason, for a proposed system. A business case should describe the project clearly, provide the justification to proceed, and estimate the project's financial impact.

Systems projects are initiated to improve performance, provide more information, reduce costs, strengthen controls, or provide better service. Various internal and external factors affect systems projects, such as user requests, top management directives, existing systems, the IT department, software and hardware vendors, technology, customers, competitors, the economy, and government.

During the preliminary investigation, the analyst evaluates the systems request and determines whether the project is feasible from an operational, technical, economic, and schedule standpoint. Analysts evaluate systems requests on the basis of their expected costs and benefits, both tangible and intangible.

The steps in the preliminary investigation are to understand the problem or opportunity; define the project scope and constraints; perform fact-finding; analyze project usability, cost, benefit, and schedule data; evaluate feasibility; and present results and recommendations to management. During the preliminary investigation, analysts often use investigative tools such as fishbone or Ishikawa diagrams, Pareto charts, and XY charts. The last task in a preliminary investigation is to prepare a report to management. The report must include an estimate of time, staffing requirements, costs, benefits, and expected results for the next phase of the SDLC.

Key Terms

Chapter Exercises

Questions

1. How does strategic planning influence day-to-day business operations? Why is it important for systems analysts to understand a company's strategic plan?
2. What is a SWOT analysis? Prepare a SWOT analysis of your school or your employer.
3. What is an effective way to assess user requests for additional features and functions?
4. What are four types of feasibility? Which type focuses on total cost of ownership? Which type is influenced primarily by users?
5. Describe the six steps in a typical preliminary investigation. Why should an analyst be careful when using the word *problem*?
6. What is project scope? What are constraints? Provide an example of a mandatory, external, future constraint. Also provide an example of a discretionary, internal, present constraint.
7. Identify and briefly describe five common fact-finding methods.
8. What fact-finding methods are well-suited for complex technical issues? Which might be appropriate for the pursuit of new, cutting-edge features?
9. What type of tool might a systems analyst use to identify a relationship between two variables? What tool is useful for identifying and prioritizing causes of problems?
10. What is a fishbone diagram, and why would you use one? Think of a problem you have experienced at school or work, and draw a sample fishbone diagram with at least two levels.

Discussion Topics

1. Suppose that the vice president of marketing asks you to write a program to create labels for a one-time advertising promotion. As IT manager, you know that the labels can be prepared more efficiently by exporting the data to a word processing program and using a mail merge feature. How would you handle this situation?
2. The vice president of accounting says to you, the IT director, "This request procedure takes too long. My people know what they are doing and their systems requests are necessary and important." She suggests that the IT department bypass the initial steps and immediately get to work on her requests. What would you say to her?
3. One of your coworkers says, "Mission statements are nice, but they really don't change things down here where the work gets done." How would you reply?
4. Would you continue to work for a company if you disagreed with the firm's mission statement? Why or why not?

Projects

1. Use the Internet to find two examples of corporate mission statements.
2. Many articles have been written on how to develop, understand, and evaluate a business case. Visit the Web sites for *TechRepublic, CIO,* or another IT magazine, and find an article that discusses business cases. Describe the article and what you learned from it.
3. Suppose you own a travel agency in a large city. You have many corporate clients, but growth has slowed somewhat. Some long-term employees are getting discouraged, but you feel that there might be a way to make technology work in your favor. Use your imagination and suggest at least one strength, weakness, opportunity, and threat that your business faces.
4. Write a mission statement and three goals for the travel agency described in Project 3.

Apply Your Knowledge

The Apply Your Knowledge section contains four mini-cases. Each case describes a situation, explains your role, and asks you to respond to questions by applying what you learned in the chapter.

1 Last Chance Securities

The IT director opened the department staff meeting today by saying, "I've got some good news and some bad news. The good news is that management approved the payroll system project this morning. The new system will reduce clerical time and errors, improve morale in the payroll department, and avoid possible fines and penalties for noncompliance. The bad news is that the system must be installed by January 1st in order to meet new federal reporting rules, all expenses from now on must be approved in advance, the system should have a modular design if possible, and the vice president of finance would like to announce the new system in a year-end report if it is ready by mid-December."

Tasks

1. Why is it important to define the project scope? How would you define the scope of the payroll project in this case?
2. Review each constraint and identify its characteristics: present versus future, internal versus external, and mandatory versus desirable.
3. What questions would you ask to determine the feasibility of this project?
4. Given the time constraints, could you shorten any of the typical steps in the preliminary investigation? Which ones? Explain your answer.

2 Way Out Bikes

The owner of Way Out Bikes asked you for advice about acquiring an information system for her business. The company specializes in helping customers select exactly the right bicycle for their needs and lifestyles. Way Out cannot compete on price with mass merchandisers, but it seeks to offer value and expertise for which customers are willing to pay. You ask the owner whether she has long-range plans for the company, and she replies that she has not really thought beyond a one-year time frame.

Tasks

1. Develop questions to ask Way Out's owner to help her conduct a SWOT analysis.
2. How could a mission statement help Way Out?
3. What are the critical success factors for Way Out?
4. What questions would you ask the owner to help her develop a business case for an information system?

The Monday IT Staff Meeting

Your boss, the IT manager, was ready to explode. "Why can't we get our priorities straight?" he fumed. "Here we go again, working on a low-value project, just because it's a favorite of the marketing group. I wish we could get away from departmental politics! I want you to draft a memo that proposes a systems review committee for this company. Explain the advantages, but don't step on anyone's toes!"

Tasks

1. Write a draft of the proposal explaining the advantages of a review committee, as your boss requested.
2. What would you tell your boss about the potential disadvantages of the committee approach and what are the alternatives?
3. What are some of the questions that are typically asked on a formal systems request form?
4. Explain how a company can systematically determine what project requests get approved and which ones do not. How can they prioritize the projects that are approved?

The Friday IT Staff Meeting

By the end of the week, things have quieted down. The IT staff discussed how to prioritize IT project requests, taking into account technical, operational, economic, and schedule feasibility. The group decided that a standard set of questions would be a good starting point.

Tasks

1. Provide three sample questions to determine whether a project has technical feasibility.
2. Provide three sample questions to determine whether a project has operational feasibility.
3. Provide three sample questions to determine whether a project has economic feasibility.
4. Provide three sample questions to determine whether a project has schedule feasibility.

Case Studies

Each chapter includes a Chapter Case, a Continuing Case, a Capstone Case, and an Online Case Simulation. You can learn more about the Online Case Simulation in the MIS CourseMate Features section.

Chapter Case: Town of Eden Bay

The town of Eden Bay owns and maintains a fleet of vehicles. You are a systems analyst reporting to Dawn, the town's IT manager.

Background

Eden Bay is a medium-sized municipality. The town has grown rapidly, and so has the demand for town services. Eden Bay currently owns 90 vehicles, which the town's equipment department maintains. The fleet includes police cars, sanitation trucks, fire trucks, and other vehicles assigned to town employees. The maintenance budget has risen sharply in recent years, and people are asking whether the town should continue to perform its own maintenance or outsource it to private firms.

This morning, Dawn called you into her office to discuss the situation. A summary of her comments follows:

Dawn (IT manager): When I came here two years ago, I was told that Eden Bay had a computerized information system for vehicle maintenance. What I found was a spreadsheet designed by a part-time employee as a quick answer to a complex problem. It's probably better than no system at all, but what we really need is a new information system to meet our current and future needs.

I want to develop a proposal for a new system. For now, let's call it RAVE, which stands for Repair Analysis for Vehicular Equipment. I met with the town manager, the equipment department, and several maintenance employees to understand their needs and concerns. I want you to start by reading the interview summaries I prepared.

Before You Begin

Review the following interview summaries from Marie (town manager), Martin (equipment department manager), Phil (maintenance supervisor), Alice (maintenance clerk), and Joe (mechanic):

Marie (town manager): Maintenance costs have risen 14 to 16% annually. I'm not sure that we have any real control over these costs. Some members of the town council think we should get out of the maintenance business and contract it out to a private firm. That might mean laying off current employees, and I'm not sure whether outsourcing is the right way to go.

Both the equipment department manager and the IT manager tell me that our current record-keeping system is outdated, and I wonder if a new information system would give us a better handle on the problem. My own view is that if there's a way we can become more efficient, we should continue to perform our own maintenance.

Dawn, our IT manager, tells me that she has developed a proposal for a maintenance information system. I plan to bring it up at the next council meeting.

Martin (equipment department manager): I hear a lot of criticism about the maintenance budget, but I'm doing the best I can. We operate from one budget year to the next, without a long-term plan. I belong to a professional association of fleet maintenance managers, and I know that we should be developing a strategic plan instead of juggling annual budget figures.

I'd like to build this department into a first-class organization. Our people are great, but they could use more technical training. Our shop and equipment are generally adequate for what we do, but we haven't kept up with some of the newer diagnostic equipment. We have a real problem in record keeping. Instead of a short-term solution, Eden Bay should have developed a maintenance information system years ago. Prior to taking this position, I was assistant maintenance manager in a medium-sized city, and they had developed a system that handled scheduling and cost analysis, in addition to day-to-day maintenance operations.

(continues)

Chapter Case: Town of Eden Bay

Phil (maintenance supervisor): I'm in the middle — I get pressure from above to cut costs, and I get complaints from below that management doesn't know what it's doing. One thing for sure — short-term solutions are not the answer. I hope they don't ask me to cut back on preventive maintenance. The last time we did that, we extended routine oil changes and servicing, and we ended up with even more repairs than we had previously.

My mechanics are capable people, and they're doing the best they can. One problem I see is that it's hard to pull up a history for a particular vehicle. We keep the data on a computer, but different people used different codes and procedures over the years, and the system probably needs a good overhaul.

Alice (maintenance clerk): I'm in charge of maintenance record keeping. We use a spreadsheet system that was designed by a part-time employee who is no longer around. Because we work on a monthly budget, the spreadsheet has a separate page for each month. When the year is over, we start a new set of monthly pages. The spreadsheet is supposed to record labor and parts used, and assign the cost to a specific vehicle, but it doesn't always work out that way.

I also use a notebook to keep track of vehicle mileage and scheduled service intervals, so I can let the department heads know when a vehicle needs to come in for service. I write up work orders for scheduled service or necessary repairs, but often a mechanic finds other problems and has to write up an additional charges form.

Each time a vehicle comes into the shop, I start a new row on the spreadsheet. I enter the vehicle number, mileage, and date. Then I enter the rest of the data into the columns for parts, labor hours, job code, shop supplies, and miscellaneous charges. At the end of the month, I calculate total costs from the spreadsheet, and we compare these with actual payroll and parts vouchers for the month. If the totals are close, everyone is happy. If not, we try to figure out what work didn't get reported and entered into the spreadsheet.

The labor codes also are a problem. Specific codes are assigned for certain types of shop labor, but these were changed three years ago when the new director arrived. Also, about half the labor can be coded, but the rest has to be entered manually — and there are no standards. Two mechanics might do the same job, and one records four specific tasks, while the other calls it a tune-up.

I know the mechanics don't like paperwork, but what can I do? I asked the IT manager if she could do anything to help, but she says that it isn't worthwhile to update the current system. She says she has heard some talk about developing a new information system specifically designed for vehicle fleet maintenance. It can't be soon enough for me.

Joe (mechanic): I love my job, but I hate the paperwork. We get a work order from the clerk for all scheduled maintenance, but if we find other problems, we have to handwrite an additional work ticket. Personally, I think some of these vehicles should be retired before they get too expensive to maintain.

I would hate to see the town contract out the maintenance. I've put in 17 years here, and I don't want to lose my job, but I know that some specialized repairs would be less expensive on the outside. Most of the mechanics realize this, but let management figure it out — they're the ones with the fancy computer system.

Tasks

1. Upon investigation, you learn that the town does not have a strategic plan or a mission statement. In your view, does this affect the current situation? Why or why not? Prepare a brief mission statement for Dawn to review.

2. Based on the fact statements provided, summarize the maintenance department's most important strengths, weaknesses, opportunities, and threats.

3. Describe the specific steps you will follow during a preliminary investigation, including any fact-finding techniques you will use. Be sure to include the tools mentioned in this chapter.

4. Compared to a profit-making company, is it more difficult or less difficult for a government entity to develop a strategic plan or mission statement? Explain your answer.

Continuing Case: Personal Trainer, Inc.

Personal Trainer, Inc. owns and operates fitness centers in a dozen Midwestern cities. The centers have done well, and the company is planning an international expansion by opening a new "supercenter" in the Toronto area. Personal Trainer's president, Cassia Umi, hired an IT consultant, Susan Park, to help develop an information system for the new facility. During the project, Susan will work closely with Gray Lewis, who will manage the new operation.

Background

At their initial meeting, Susan and Gray discussed some initial steps in planning an information system for the new facility. The next morning, they worked together on a business profile, drew an organization chart, discussed feasibility issues, and talked about various types of information systems that would provide the best support for the supercenter's operations. Their main objective was to carry out a preliminary investigation of the new system and report their recommendations to Personal Trainer's top managers.

After the working session with Gray, Susan returned to her office and reviewed her notes. She knew that Personal Trainer's president, Cassia Umi, wanted the supercenter to become a model for the company's future growth, but she did not remember any mention of an overall strategic plan for the company. Susan also wondered whether the firm had done a SWOT analysis or analyzed the internal and external factors that might affect an information system for the supercenter.

Because the new operation would be so important to the company, Susan believed that Personal Trainer should consider an enterprise resource planning strategy that could provide a company-wide framework for information management. After she finished compiling her notes, Susan listed several topics that might need more study and called Gray to arrange another meeting the following day.

Tasks

1. Review the fact statements in Chapter 1, and perform Internet research to find out as much as you can about fitness center operations. Using this background, conduct a SWOT analysis with at least three entries in each area.
2. Does the proposed system present a strong business case? Why or why not?
3. What fact-finding techniques should Susan and Gray consider during the preliminary investigation? Also develop a list of questions they should include in an employee survey.
4. For each type of feasibility, suggest two questions that will help Susan reach a determination.

Capstone Case: New Century Wellness Group

New Century Wellness Group offers a holistic approach to healthcare with an emphasis on preventive medicine as well as traditional medical care. In your role as an IT consultant, you will help New Century develop a new information system.

Background

New Century Wellness Group is interested in a new information system to support its business and health information management needs. The new system would replace a mix of paper-based and fragmented computer systems. Dr. Jones had previously asked you to work with him as a systems analyst and help the group develop an information system that will support current operations and future growth. You will explore the possibility of a business support system for the scheduling, billing, accounting, and payroll functions of the practice as well as a system to support the clinical applications of Electronic Medical Records (EMR), Computerized Provider Order Entry (CPOE), and a Clinical Decision Support System (CDSS).

At your next meeting, Dr. Jones explains what the practice partners have in mind in more detail. They are looking for a medical practice software solution that allows each office worker to conduct their job more efficiently. He explains to you what systems they are looking for from the perspective of a patient who comes into the office.

Lisa Sung schedules a patient's appointment and the patient comes into the office for the first time. On this appointment, an EMR is started for the patient that includes the patient's demographic information, medical history, and insurance information. A patient may be coming in to see any one of the healthcare providers, including a physician, nurse practitioner, physical therapists, or the nutritionist. These providers would enter any orders or prescriptions into the EMR with the CPOE system. The Providers who use the EMR and CPOE system are supported by the CDSS. Patients often schedule a follow-up appointment before leaving the practice office.

After a patient's visit, Susan Gifford, who maintains the patient medical records, reviews the records to ensure they are complete. Carla Herrera orders any supplies needed to replace items used by the patient.

Tammy Alipio begins billing the patient's insurance provider for services that were rendered to the patient. Tom Capaletti follows up on the billing to ensure the practice is getting paid for all claims. Dr. Jones also tells you that the system should also include modules to support Fred Brown and Corinne Summers in HR and payroll.

You explain to Dr. Jones that you would like to conduct a preliminary investigation that will give you the information you need to make recommendations about what system they should pursue. Dr. Jones agrees to your investigation and you set a follow-up appointment in one month.

Tasks

1. Health information management is a rapidly-growing sector that directly affects healthcare costs. Every specialized area has its own vocabulary, and health information management is no exception. Conduct an Internet search to learn about Electronic Medical Records (EMR), Computerized Provider Order Entry (CPOE), and a Clinical Decision Support System (CDSS). Describe your findings, using nontechnical language that is easy to understand.

2. You are planning a preliminary investigation of Dr. Jones's request. For each step, describe the steps you will take, the methods you will use, and the information you will seek. Also explain how you plan to define the project's scope and why this task is so important.

3. Based on what you know about New Century, conduct a feasibility study that includes operational, technical, economic, and schedule feasibility. Describe the results in detail, and explain how you reached your conclusions.

4. Prepare a brief preliminary investigation report for Dr. Jones. Before you begin this task, you should review the sample report in this chapter, and visit Part A of the Systems Analyst's Toolkit, which provides suggestions for oral and written presentations.

CASE Tool Workshop

Systems analysts use CASE tools to help them plan, build, and maintain information systems. To learn more about CASE tools, turn to Part B of the Toolkit that follows Chapter 12. You can complete these tasks with the Visible Analyst® CASE tool, which is available with this textbook, or a similar tool.

Background

As a part-time student assistant in the computer lab at your school, you have been asked to evaluate various CASE tools, and submit the results. You began with an overview of the user interface, and how to open existing projects and create new ones. As you continue your analysis, you decide to get some hands-on experience with the CASE tool you are using.

Tasks

1. Study the program's documentation, tutorials, glossary, and help menu to learn more about how the tool handles strategic planning. Prepare a summary of your findings, and be sure to include specific examples and screen shots.
2. Review the planning example and examine Figure 2-6 on page 53. In that scenario, a systems analyst for a large hotel chain wanted to determine whether the Visible Analyst CASE tool would be helpful in planning a new marketing system. Now, using the same example, create a sample project named HOTEL. Add at least seven sample planning statements, including an assumption, an objective, a critical success factor, strength, a weakness, an opportunity, and a threat. You should try to suggest realistic examples, and you can use your imagination freely.

MIS CourseMate Features

If you have an MIS CourseMate access code, you can reinforce and extend your learning with premium content created for this textbook. For example, you can launch interactive Video Learning Sessions to help you understand systems development concepts and practice your skills. In addition, you can use MindTap Reader, which is a full, interactive, digital e-book.

MIS CourseMate also offers many learning features within each chapter, including an Online Case Simulation, a Critical Thinking Challenge, Video Learning Tasks, and a set of Learn It Online activities. To log on to the MIS CourseMate site at **www.cengagebrain.com**, you must create a student account and register this book.

Online Case Simulation: SCR Associates

Session 2: Analyzing the Business Case

Overview

The SCR Associates case study is a Web-based simulation that allows you to practice your skills in a real-world environment. The firm offers IT consulting, solutions, and training. SCR plans to open a new high-tech training center and needs to develop a Training Information Management System (TIMS) to support the operation. You are a newly hired systems analyst reporting to Jesse Baker, systems group manager, and will help her develop the system.

The case study takes you to the SCR Web site, where you receive e-mail and voice mail messages from Jesse, obtain information from SCR's resource libraries, and perform various tasks. Jesse has high standards, but seems very fair. She made it clear that she expects your work to be accurate, thorough, and professional.

Before You Begin

To prepare for this work session, you should review the following topics:

- Mission statements
- Project scope
- Role of the system review committee

How Do I Use the Online Case Simulation?

- Read the preview, and review the Chapter 1 background material, if necessary.
- Visit the MIS CourseMate Web site at **www.cengagebrain.com**, locate the **SCR Case Simulation**, and click the **intranet** link. Enter your name and the password **sad10e**.
- When the opening screen displays, select this session. Then check your e-mail and voice mail, and start to work on your task list.

Preview: Session 2

During your orientation, you found your way around the office and had a chance to explore SCR's Web site and intranet. Now, after a week on the job, your supervisor, Jesse Baker, explained the new TIMS system and asked you to help her lead the systems development team. Jesse said that she has confidence in you and is looking forward to working with you.

Critical Thinking Challenge

In addition to technical ability, IT professionals need critical thinking skills. This feature can help you practice perception, organization, analysis, problem-solving, and decision-making skills that will be valuable in the workplace. You can visit **www.criticalthinking.org** to learn more about critical thinking and why it is so important.

Background

As an IT intern at Game Technology, you assist analysts with feasibility studies. The work often includes intense fact-finding and tight deadlines. You decide to add a new section to your journal to describe the four different types of feasibility. In your journal, you want to include a definition of each feasibility type, and a sample statement that would indicate a lack of feasibility. For example:

- The hardware has limited capacity for future needs.
- Our users will resist the new system because it is the third change in 18 months.
- The project will take too long to pay for itself.
- Development cannot begin until next year, which is too late.

You also want to learn more about project constraints. You know that constraints can be grouped into various categories, such as present versus future, internal versus external, and mandatory versus desirable. You plan to use a diagram like the one in Figure 2-19 on page 70 to show the constraints.

Practice Tasks

Visit the MIS CourseMate Web site at **www.cengagebrain.com**. Then navigate to the resources for this chapter and locate the **Critical Thinking Challenge** feature. You will complete two Practice Tasks, using what you learned in the chapter. Then you can check your answers to be sure you're ready for the Challenge Tasks.

Challenge Tasks

After you complete the Practice Tasks, you learn about new developments at Game Technology.

This morning you received a message from Marci Smith, the IT director. She is sending you a list of planning statements and she wants you to decide which type of feasibility applies. She also wants you to prepare a diagram that will show a list of constraints. To continue, navigate to the **Critical Thinking Challenge** feature for this chapter, select the **Challenge Tasks**, and follow the instructions.

Video Learning Sessions

The Video Learning Session for this chapter explains how to use a financial analysis tool called payback analysis. You'll learn how to calculate the payback period for a project and how to use a spreadsheet to determine a project's payback period.

© craftvision/iStockphoto

Before You Begin

To prepare for the tasks, you should review the following topics:

- Economic feasibility
- Total cost of ownership
- Preliminary investigation

How to Watch a Session

Go to the Management Information Systems CourseMate Web site at **www.cengagebrain.com**. Then navigate to the resources for this book, locate the **Video Learning Sessions**, and select a session. You can watch the session on your computer or mobile device, and pause, rewind, or replay a video at any time.

Practice Tasks

After each session, visit the **Your Turn** feature to perform the tasks and check your answers.

Training Tasks

Suppose the IT training manager wants to encourage team members to watch the Video Learning Sessions. To spark interest, she plans to post a set of VLS previews, which you will prepare. Each preview must include an overview of the session, a description of the main topics, and one or more screen examples from the video. To get you started, she provided a task list:

1. Select a Video Learning Session from this chapter. Launch the video and note the title, objectives, and total running time. Include this information in your preview.
2. Run though the session and find a segment that does a good job of explaining a specific skill or concept.
3. In the segment you selected, choose one or more specific screens and capture each screen image with the Windows Snipping Tool. To do this in Windows 7 or Windows Vista, click **Start,** and then type **Snipping Tool.** In Windows 8, you can display the **Start** menu, and then type **Snipping Tool.**
4. Paste the screen image into your preview and explain how it would help a viewer understand the topic. Also add your comments about the video, and why it would be important to an IT professional. Your preview should be well-organized and readable.

Learn It Online

In each chapter, you can use this feature to apply your knowledge and practice your skills. The exercises include Chapter Reinforcement Questions, Flash Cards, Practice Tests, and various games, such as *Who Wants To Be a Computer Genius?, Wheel of Terms,* and the *Crossword Puzzle Challenge.*

CHAPTER 3 Managing Systems Projects

Chapter 3 is the final chapter in the systems planning phase of the SDLC. In this chapter, you will learn about project management and how to plan, schedule, monitor, and report on IT projects.

INTRODUCTION

OBJECTIVES

When you finish this chapter, you will be able to:

- Explain project planning, scheduling, monitoring, and reporting

- Draw a project triangle that shows the relationship among project cost, scope, and time

- Describe work breakdown structures, task patterns, and critical path analysis

- Explain techniques for estimating task completion times and costs

- Describe various scheduling tools, including Gantt charts and PERT/CPM charts

- Analyze task dependencies, durations, start dates, and end dates

- Describe project management software and how it can assist you

- Discuss the importance of managing project risks

- Understand why projects sometimes fail

Chapter 3 explains project management for IT projects. You will learn about project planning, scheduling, monitoring, reporting, and the use of project management software. You will learn how to create a work breakdown structure, identify task patterns, and calculate a critical path. You will also learn how to use Gantt charts and PERT/CPM techniques to schedule and monitor projects. Finally, you will learn how to control and manage project changes as they occur.

In addition to the project management material in this chapter, you can visit the MIS CourseMate Web site for this book at **www.cengagebrain.com** and explore links in the SWL project management resources library.

If you have MIS CourseMate, you can view three Video Learning Sessions that explain work breakdown structures, task patterns, and how to calculate a project's critical path.

PREVIEW CASE: Mountain View College Bookstore

Background: Wendy Lee, manager of college services at Mountain View College, wants a new information system that will improve efficiency and customer service at the three college bookstores.

In this part of the case, Tina Allen, systems analyst, and David Conroe, student intern, are talking about project management tools and techniques.

Participants:	Tina and David
Location:	The college cafeteria, Wednesday afternoon, September 19, 2013
Discussion topics:	Project planning, Gantt charts, PERT/CPM charts, Microsoft Project software, project monitoring, and risk management techniques

Tina: Hi, David. Glad I ran into you. I'd like to talk with you about project management, which we'll be using as we plan and execute the bookstore information system project.

David: *Sure. I've read a little about project management, but I don't know the specifics.*

Tina: Well, we manage business and personal projects every day, but we don't always give it much thought. To manage large-scale IT projects, you need specific tools and techniques. You also need a project manager, who is responsible for planning, leading, organizing, and controlling all the tasks.

David: *I guess that's you?*

Tina: Sure is. No matter which tools you use, the idea is to break the project down into individual tasks, determine the order in which the tasks need to be performed, and figure out how long each task will take. With this information, you can use Gantt charts or PERT/CPM charts to schedule and manage the work.

David: *I've seen Gantt charts — they're the ones that look like horizontal bar charts?*

Tina: Right. In addition to Gantt charts, we'll use PERT/CPM charts, which look like network diagrams that show all the tasks, patterns, and calculations that we'll need. We'll learn how to create PERT/CPM charts manually, and we'll also experiment with Microsoft Project, which is a powerful project management tool.

David: *Anything else we need to know?*

Tina: Yes. After we have a specific plan, we need to monitor it carefully, report the progress, and employ a process called risk management. If you are ready, here's a task list to get us started:

FIGURE 3-1   Typical project management tasks.
© Cengage Learning 2014

FIGURE 3-2 Building construction and systems development projects both need careful management and monitoring.
© Peter Close/Shutterstock

FIGURE 3-3 A successful project must balance cost, scope, and time against a set of constraints. In this example, the project appears to be a success.
Scale image: © 3DProfi/Shutterstock.com; concept art © Cengage Learning 2014

OVERVIEW OF PROJECT MANAGEMENT

Whether you are developing an information system or working on a construction project like the one in Figure 3-2, the process is the same. The only difference is the nature of the project. **Project management** for IT professionals includes planning, scheduling, monitoring and controlling, and reporting on information system development.

What Shapes a Project?

A successful project must be completed on time, within budget, and deliver a quality product that satisfies users and meets requirements. Project management techniques can be used throughout the SDLC. System developers can initiate a formal project as early as the preliminary investigation stage, or later on, as analysis, design, and implementation activities occur.

Systems development projects tend to be dynamic and challenging. Figure 3-3 shows the typical balance between constraints, which you learned about in Chapter 2, and interactive elements such as project cost, scope, and time. In this example, it appears that the project will succeed.

What Is a Project Triangle?

Figure 3-4 shows a very simple example of a project triangle. The message is clear to all customers of the Busted Knuckle Garage: You must decide what is most important to you because the work is not going to be good *and* fast *and* cheap.

When it comes to project management, things are not quite so simple. You don't have to make all-or-nothing decisions like Busted Knuckle customers, but you do need to recognize that *any change in one leg of the triangle will affect the other two legs.* Figure 3-5 represents a common view of a **project triangle**, where the three legs are cost, scope, and time. The challenge is to find the optimal balance among these factors. How does a project manager do that? There is no standard answer, but most successful project managers rely on personal experience, communication ability, and resourcefulness. For example, if an extremely time-critical project starts to slip, the project manager might have to trim some features, seek approval for a budget increase, simplify the testing plan, or a combination of all three actions.

On its Web site, Microsoft offers an interesting suggestion for project managers who have a project at risk: Find the *stuck side* of the triangle. Microsoft states that in most projects, at least one side of the triangle is fixed, and you are not likely to change it. It might be a budget cast in stone, a scope that is inflexible, or a schedule driven by factors beyond the firm's control. Whichever side is fixed is probably critical to the project's success. You also need to identify the leg where the problem resides: cost, scope, or time. Microsoft suggests that if the problem is in the fixed leg, you should work on the other two legs. For example, if your project *must not* exceed the budget and it is starting to run over, you can adjust the schedule, or the scope, or both. However, if the problem is *not* related to the fixed leg, the adjustment might have to be in the remaining leg. So, if you are up against an inflexible budget (fixed leg) and the schedule is slipping (problem leg), you might have to adjust the project's scope (remaining leg). Explaining this situation to management is sometimes the most difficult task of all.

What Does a Project Manager Do?

Whether a project involves a new office building or an information system, good leadership is essential. In a systems project, the **project manager**, or **project leader**, usually is a senior systems analyst or an IT department manager if the project is large. An analyst or a programmer/analyst might manage smaller projects. In addition to the project manager, most large projects have a project coordinator. A **project coordinator** handles administrative responsibilities for the team and negotiates with users who might have conflicting requirements or want changes that would require additional time or expense. Project managers typically perform four activities, or functions: planning, scheduling, monitoring, and reporting.

- **Project planning** includes identifying all project tasks and estimating the completion time and cost of each.
- **Project scheduling** involves the creation of a specific timetable, usually in the form of charts that show tasks, task dependencies, and critical tasks that

FIGURE 3-4   The sign at this imaginary garage tells a familiar story. If you can't get everything you want, you have to make choices.
© Cengage Learning 2014

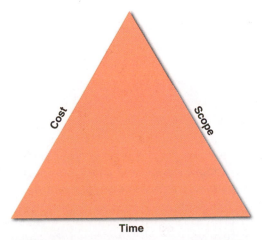

FIGURE 3-5   A typical project triangle includes cost, scope, and time.
© Cengage Learning 2014

might delay the project. Scheduling also involves selecting and staffing the project team and assigning specific tasks to team members. Project scheduling uses Gantt charts and PERT/CPM charts, which are explained in the following sections.

- **Project monitoring** requires guiding, supervising, and coordinating the project team's workload. The project manager must monitor the progress, evaluate the results, and take corrective action when necessary to control the project and stay on target.

- **Project reporting** includes regular progress reports to management, users, and the project team itself. Effective reporting requires strong communication skills and a sense of what others want and need to know about the project.

The following sections describe project planning and scheduling steps. You will learn how to create a work breakdown structure, identify task patterns, and calculate the project's critical path. If you have MIS CourseMate, you can view three Video Learning Sessions that will help you master these skills. You can view the sessions before, during, or after you study each step.

STEP 1: CREATE A WORK BREAKDOWN STRUCTURE

A **work breakdown structure (WBS)** involves breaking a project down into a series of smaller tasks. Before creating work breakdown structures, you should understand the two primary chart types: Gantt charts and PERT/CPM charts.

What Is a Gantt Chart?

Gantt charts were developed almost 100 years ago by Henry L. Gantt, a mechanical engineer and management consultant. His goal was to design a chart that could show planned and actual progress on a project. A **Gantt chart** is a horizontal bar chart that represents a set of tasks. For example, the Gantt chart in Figure 3-6 displays five tasks in a vertical array, with time shown on the horizontal axis. The position of the bar shows the planned starting and ending time of each task, and the length of the bar indicates its duration. On the horizontal axis, time can be shown as elapsed time from a fixed starting point, or as actual calendar dates. A Gantt chart also can simplify a complex project by combining several activities into a **task group** that contains subsidiary tasks. This allows a complex project to be viewed as a set of integrated modules.

© craftvision/iStockphoto

Video Learning Session
Work Breakdown Structures

If you have an MIS CourseMate access code, you can launch interactive Video Learning Sessions to help you understand systems development concepts and practice your skills. You can watch the sessions on your computer or mobile device, and pause, rewind, or replay a video at any time. To log on to the MIS CourseMate site at **www.cengagebrain.com**, you must create a student account and then register this book.

This session is about work breakdown structures. You'll learn what a work breakdown structure is and why it is important, how to create a work breakdown structure, and how to use Microsoft Project to display a work breakdown structure.

FIGURE 3-6   In this Gantt chart, notice the yellow bars that show the percentage of task completion.
Screenshot used with permission from Microsoft.

A Gantt chart can show task status by adding a contrasting color to the horizontal bars. For example, a vertical red arrow marks the current date in Figure 3-6. With a fixed reference point, it is easy to see that Task 1 is way behind schedule, Task 2 is only about 80 percent done and is running behind schedule, Task 3 should have started, but no work has been done, Task 4 actually is running ahead of schedule, and Task 5 will begin in several weeks.

Gantt charts can present an overview of the project's status, but they do not provide enough detailed information, which is necessary when managing a complex project. Most project managers find that PERT/CPM charts, which are discussed in the following section, are better tools for managing large projects.

What Is a PERT/CPM Chart?

The **Program Evaluation Review Technique (PERT)** was developed by the U.S. Navy to manage very complex projects, such as the construction of nuclear submarines. At approximately the same time, the **Critical Path Method (CPM)** was developed by private industry to meet similar project management needs. The distinction between the two methods has disappeared over time, and today the technique is called either PERT, CPM, or **PERT/CPM**. The textbook will use the term PERT chart.

PERT is a **bottom-up technique** because it analyzes a large, complex project as a series of individual tasks. To create a PERT chart, you first identify all the project tasks and estimate how much time each task will take to perform. Next, you must determine the logical order in which the tasks must be performed. For example, some tasks cannot start until other tasks have been completed. In other situations, several tasks can be performed at the same time.

Once you know the tasks, their durations, and the order in which they must be performed, you can calculate the time that it will take to complete the project. You also can identify the specific tasks that will be critical to the project's on-time completion. An example of a PERT chart, which Microsoft calls a **network diagram**, is shown in the lower screen in Figure 3-7 on the next page.

Which Type of Chart Is Better?

Although a Gantt chart offers a valuable snapshot view of the project, PERT charts are more useful for scheduling, monitoring, and controlling the actual work. With a PERT chart, a project manager can convert task start and finish times to actual dates by laying out the entire project on a calendar. Then, on any

FIGURE 3-7 The top screen shows a Gantt chart with six tasks. The PERT chart in the bottom screen displays an easy-to-follow task pattern for the same project. When the user mouses over the summary box for Task 5, the details become visible.

Screenshots used with permission from Microsoft.

given day, the manager can compare what *should* be happening with what *is* taking place, and react accordingly. Also, a PERT chart displays complex task patterns and relationships. This information is valuable to a manager who is trying to address high priority issues. PERT and Gantt charts are not mutually exclusive techniques, and project managers often use both methods.

Figure 3-7 shows both chart types. The top screen is a Gantt chart with six tasks. The PERT chart below it shows the same project, using a separate box for each task instead of a horizontal bar. Although they both show the task patterns and flow, the PERT chart boxes can provide more information, such as task duration, start date, finish date, and the names of resources assigned to the task. The PERT chart in Figure 3-7 would be too small to view

the actual details, which are shown in the expanded text box at the bottom of the figure. You will learn how to create PERT charts in a later section.

Identifying Tasks in a Work Breakdown Structure

A work breakdown structure must clearly identify each task and include an estimated duration. A **task**, or **activity**, is any work that has a beginning and an end and requires the use of company resources such as people, time, or money. Examples of tasks include conducting interviews, designing a report, selecting software, waiting for the delivery of equipment, or training users. Tasks are basic units of work that the project manager plans, schedules, and monitors — so they should be relatively small and manageable.

In addition to tasks, every project has events, or milestones. An **event**, or **milestone**, is a recognizable reference point that you can use to monitor progress. For example, an event might be the start of user training, the conversion of system data, or the completion of interviews. A milestone such as *Complete 50 percent of program testing* would not be useful information unless you could determine exactly when that event will occur.

Figure 3-8 shows tasks and events that might be involved in the creation, distribution, and tabulation of a questionnaire. Notice that the beginning and end of each task are marked by a recognizable event. If you tried to manage a project as one large task, it would be impossible. Instead, you break the project down into smaller tasks, creating a work breakdown structure (WBS). The first step in creating a WBS is to list all the tasks.

FIGURE 3-8 Using a questionnaire requires a series of tasks and events to track the progress. The illustration shows the relationship between the tasks and the events, or milestones, that mark the beginning and end of each task.

© Cengage Learning 2014

First version

First, reserve the meeting room. Then order the marketing materials and brief the managers. After the briefings, send out customer e-mails and burn sample DVDs. When the e-mails are sent and the DVDs are ready, load the new software. When the marketing materials have arrived and the software is ready, do a dress rehearsal.

Second version

First, *reserve the meeting room*. Then *order the marketing materials* and *brief the managers*. After the briefings, *send out customer e-mails* and *burn sample DVDs*. When the e-mails are sent and the DVDs are ready, *load the new software*. When the marketing materials have arrived and the software is ready, *do a dress rehearsal*.

Third version

- First, *reserve the meeting room*.
- Then *order the marketing materials* and *brief the managers*.
- After the briefings, *send out customer e-mails* and *burn sample DVDs*.
- When the e-mails are sent and the DVDs are ready, *load the new software*.
- When the marketing materials have arrived and the software is ready, *do a dress rehearsal*.

FIGURE 3-9 The three versions show how to transform a task statement into a list of specific tasks for a work breakdown structure.
© Cengage Learning 2014

Task No.	Description	Duration (Days)	Predecessor Tasks
1	Reserve the meeting room		
2	Order the marketing materials		
3	Brief the managers		
4	Send out customer e-mails		
5	Burn sample DVDs		
6	Load the new software		
7	Do a dress rehearsal		

FIGURE 3-10 In this table, columns have been added for task number, description, duration, and predecessor tasks, which must be completed before another task can start.
© Cengage Learning 2014

LISTING THE TASKS While this step sounds simple, it can be challenging because the tasks might be embedded in a document, such as the one shown in the first version of Figure 3-9. One trick is to start by highlighting the individual tasks, as shown in the second version. Adding bullets makes the tasks stand out more clearly, as shown in the third version. The next step is to number the tasks and create a table, similar to the one shown in Figure 3-10, with columns for task number, description, duration, and **predecessor tasks**, which must be completed before another task can start.

CASE IN POINT 3.1: PARALLEL SERVICES

The project management team at Parallel Services is having a debate about how to define tasks in the work breakdown structure (WBS). Ann, the project manager, wants to break tasks down into the smallest possible units. For example, she objected to a broad task statement called *Develop a training schedule*. Instead, she suggested three subtasks: (1) *Determine availability of training room*, (2) *Determine availability of attendees*, and (3) *Select specific dates and training times*.

Karen, another project team member, disagrees. She feels that the broader task statement is better because it allows more flexibility and will produce the same result. Karen says that if you break tasks into pieces that are too small, you risk overmanaging the work and spending more time on monitoring than actually performing the tasks. As a member of the team, would you tend to agree more with Ann or Karen? What are the pros and cons of each approach?

ESTIMATING TASK DURATION Task duration can be hours, days, or weeks — depending on the project. Because the following example uses days, the units of measurement are called person-days. A **person-day** represents the work that one person can complete in one day. This approach, however, can present some problems. For example, if it will take one person 20 days to perform a particular task, it might not be true that two people could complete the same task in 10 days or that 10 people could perform the task in two days. Some tasks can be divided evenly so it is possible to use different combinations of time and people, up to a point. For instance, if it takes two person-days to install the cables for a new local area network, one person might do the task in two days, two people in one day, or four people in half a day. In most systems analysis tasks, however, time and people are not interchangeable. If one analyst needs two hours to interview a user, two analysts also will need two hours to do the same interview.

Project managers often use a weighted formula for estimating the duration of each task. The project manager first makes three time estimates for each task: an optimistic, or **best-case estimate** (B), a **probable-case estimate** (P), and a pessimistic, or **worst-case estimate** (W). The manager then assigns a **weight**, which is an importance value, to each estimate. The weight can vary, but a common approach is to use a ratio of B = 1, P = 4, and W = 1. The expected task duration is calculated as follows:

$$\frac{(B+4P+W)}{6}$$

For example, a project manager might estimate that a file-conversion task could be completed in as few as 20 days or could take as many as 34 days, but most likely will require 24 days. Using the formula, the expected task duration is 25 days, calculated as follows:

$$\frac{(20+(4*24)+34)}{6} = 25$$

Factors Affecting Duration

When developing duration estimates, project managers consider four factors:

- Project size
- Human resources
- Experience with similar projects
- Constraints

PROJECT SIZE   You learned in Chapter 1 that information systems have various characteristics that affect their complexity and cost. In addition to considering those factors, a project manager must estimate the time required to complete each project phase. To develop accurate estimates, a project manager must identify all project tasks, from initial fact-finding to system implementation. Regardless of the systems development methodology used, the project manager must determine how much time will be needed to perform each task. In developing an estimate, the project manager must allow time for meetings, project reviews, training, and any other factors that could affect the productivity of the development team.

HUMAN RESOURCES   Companies must invest heavily in cutting-edge technology and Web-based systems to remain competitive in a connected world. In many areas, skilled IT professionals are in great demand, and firms must work hard to attract and retain the talent they need. A project manager must assemble and guide a development team that has the skill and experience to handle the project. If necessary, additional systems analysts or programmers must be hired or trained, and this must be accomplished within a specific time frame. After a project gets under way, the project manager must deal with turnover, job vacancies, and escalating salaries in the technology sector — all of which can affect whether the project can be completed on time and within budget.

EXPERIENCE WITH SIMILAR PROJECTS   A project manager can develop time and cost estimates based on the resources used for similar, previously developed information systems. The experience method works best for small- or medium-sized projects where the two systems are similar in size, basic content, and operating environment. In large systems with more variables, the estimates are less reliable.

In addition, you might not be able to use experience from projects that were developed in a different environment. For example, when you use a new Web-based database application, you might not have previous experience to measure in this environment. In this situation, you could design a prototype or pilot system to gain technical and cost estimating experience.

CONSTRAINTS   You learned in Chapter 2 that constraints are defined during the preliminary investigation. A constraint is a condition, restriction, or requirement that the system must satisfy. For example, a constraint might involve maximums for one or more resources, such as time, dollars, or people. A project manager must define system requirements that can be achieved realistically within the required constraints. In the absence of constraints, the project manager simply calculates the resources needed. However, if constraints are present, the project manager must adjust other resources or change the scope of the project. This approach is similar to the what-if analysis that is described in Chapter 12.

CASE IN POINT 3.2: SUNRISE SOFTWARE

A lively discussion is under way at Sunrise Software, where you are a project manager. The main question is whether the person-days concept has limitations. In other words, if a task will require 100 person-days, does it matter whether the work is performed by two people in 50 days, five people in 20 days, 10 people in 10 days, or some other combination that adds up to 100?

Programmers Paula and Ethan seem to think it doesn't matter. On the other hand, Hector, a systems analyst, says it is ridiculous to think that any combination would work. To support his point, he offers this extreme example: Could a task estimated at 100 person-days be accomplished by 100 people in one day?

Is Hector correct? If so, what are the limits in the people versus days equation? Taking the concept a step further, is there an *optimum* number of people to be assigned to a task? If so, how would that number be determined? You need to offer some guidance at the next project team meeting. What will you say?

Displaying the Work Breakdown Structure

After you enter the task durations, the work breakdown structure will look like Figure 3-11. If you are managing a complex project with many tasks, you can use task groups, just as you would in a Gantt chart, to simplify the list. If you are using Microsoft Project, the WBS might resemble Figure 3-12 on the next page.

Task No.	Description	Duration (Days)	Predecessor Tasks
1	Reserve the meeting room	1	
2	Order the marketing materials	9	
3	Brief the managers	2	
4	Send out customer e-mails	3	
5	Burn sample DVDs	3	
6	Load the new software	2	
7	Do a dress rehearsal	1	

FIGURE 3-11   Task durations have been added, and the WBS is complete except for predecessor task information. The predecessor tasks will determine task patterns and sequence of performance.

© Cengage Learning 2014

FIGURE 3-12   This Microsoft Project screen displays the same WBS, including task number, task name, duration, and predecessor tasks.

Video Learning Session
Task Patterns

If you have an MIS CourseMate access code, you can launch interactive Video Learning Sessions to help you understand systems development concepts and practice your skills. You can watch the sessions on your computer or mobile device, and pause, rewind, or replay a video at any time. To log on to the MIS CourseMate site at **www.cengagebrain.com**, you must create a student account and then register this book.

   This session is about task patterns. You'll learn what task patterns are and why are they are important, how to identify and use task patterns, and how to use Microsoft Project to show task patterns.

STEP 2: IDENTIFY TASK PATTERNS

Tasks in a work breakdown structure must be arranged in a logical sequence called a **task pattern**. This section will show you how to understand and create graphical models of these patterns.

What Are Task Patterns?

In any project, large or small, tasks depend on each other and must be performed in a sequence, not unlike the commands in a software program. Task patterns can involve dependent tasks, multiple successor tasks, and multiple predecessor tasks. In larger projects, these patterns can be very complex, and an analyst must study the logical flow carefully.

How Do I Use Task Boxes to Create a Model?

In a PERT/CPM chart, project tasks are shown as rectangular boxes, arranged in the sequence in which they must be performed. Each rectangular box, called a **task box**, has five sections, as shown in Figure 3-13. Each section of the task box contains important information about the task, including the Task Name, Task ID, Task Duration, Start Day/Date, and Finish Day/Date.

TASK BOX FORMAT	
Task Name	
Start Day/Date	Task ID
Finish Day/Date	Task Duration

FIGURE 3-13   Each section of the task box contains important information about the task, including the Task Name, Task ID, Task Duration, Start Day/Date, and Finish Day/Date.

TASK NAME   The **task name** should be brief and descriptive, but it does not have to be unique in the project. For example, a task named *Conduct Interviews* might occur in several phases of the project.

TASK ID   The **task ID** can be a number or code that provides unique identification.

TASK DURATION   The **duration** is the amount of time it will take to complete a task. All tasks must use the same time units, which can be hours, days, weeks, or months, depending on the project. An actual project starts on a specific date, but can also be measured from a point in time, such as *Day 1*.

START DAY/DATE   The **start day/date** is the time that a task is scheduled to begin. For example, suppose that a simple project has two tasks: Task 1 and Task 2. Also suppose that Task 2 cannot begin until Task 1 is finished. An analogy might be that you cannot run a program until you turn on your computer. If Task 1 begins on Day 1 and has a duration of three days, it will finish on Day 3. Because Task 2 cannot begin until Task 1 is completed, the start time for Task 2 is Day 4, which is the day *after* Task 1 is finished.

FINISH DAY/DATE   The **finish day/date** is the time that a task is scheduled to be completed. To calculate the finish day or date, you add the duration to the start day or date. When you do this, you must be very careful not to add too many days. For example, if a task starts on Day 10 and has a duration of 5 days, then the finish would be on Day 14 — *not* Day 15.

What Are the Main Types of Task Patterns?

A project is based on a pattern of tasks. In a large project the overall pattern would be quite complex, but it can be broken down into three basic patterns: dependent tasks, multiple successor tasks, and multiple predecessor tasks.

DEPENDENT TASKS   When tasks must be completed one after another, like the relay race shown in Figure 3-14, they are called **dependent tasks** because one depends on the other. For example, Figure 3-15 shows that Task 2 depends on Task 1, because Task 2 cannot start until Task 1 is completed. In this example, the finish time of Task 1, Day 5, controls the start date of Task 2, which is Day 6.

MULTIPLE SUCCESSOR TASKS   When several tasks can start at the same time, each is called a **concurrent task**. Often, two or more concurrent tasks depend on a single prior task, which is called a predecessor task. In this situation, each concurrent task is called a **successor task**. In the example shown in Figure 3-16 on the next page,

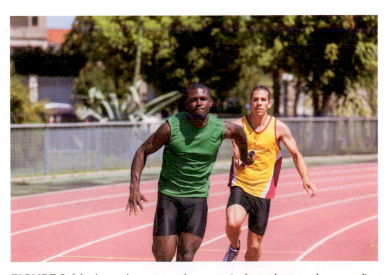

FIGURE 3-14   In a relay race, each runner is dependent on the preceding runner and cannot start until the earlier runner finishes.
© William Perugini/Shutterstock.com

EXAMPLE OF A DEPENDENT TASK			
Prepare Outline		Create Document	
Start: Day 1	ID: 1	Start: Day 6	ID: 2
Finish: Day 5	Dur: 5	Finish: Day 14	Dur: 9

FIGURE 3-15   This example of a dependent task shows that the finish time of Task 1, Day 5, controls the start date of Task 2, which is Day 6.
© Cengage Learning 2014

EXAMPLE OF MULTIPLE SUCCESSOR TASKS

FIGURE 3-16 This example of multiple successor tasks shows that the finish time for Task 1 determines the start time for both Tasks 2 and 3.

© Cengage Learning 2014

successor Tasks 2 and 3 both can begin as soon as Task 1 is finished. Notice that the finish time for Task 1 determines the start time for both Tasks 2 and 3. In other words, the earliest that Task 1 can finish is day 30, so day 31 is the earliest that Tasks 2 and 3 can start.

MULTIPLE PREDECESSOR TASKS

Suppose that a task requires two or more prior tasks to be completed before it can start. Figure 3-17 shows that example because Task 3 cannot begin until Tasks 1 and 2 are both completed. Since the two tasks might not finish at the same time, the longest (latest) predecessor task becomes the controlling factor. Notice that the start for Task 3 is Day 16, *not* Day 6. Why is this so? Because Task 3 depends on two predecessor tasks, Tasks 1 and 2, Task 3 cannot begin until the *later* of those tasks is complete. Therefore, the start time for a successor task must be the latest (largest) finish time for any of its preceding tasks. In the example shown, Task 1 ends on Day 15, while Task 2 ends on Day 5, so Task 1 controls the start time for Task 3.

How Do I Identify Task Patterns?

You can identify task patterns by looking carefully at the wording of the task statement. Words like *then*, *when*, or *and* are action words that signal a sequence of events. Here are three simple examples:

- *Do Task 1, **then** do Task 2* describes dependent tasks that must be completed one after the other.

- ***When** Task 2 is finished, start two tasks: Task 3 **and** Task 4* describes multiple successor tasks that can both start as soon as Task 2 is finished.

- ***When** Tasks 5 **and** 6 are done, start Task 7* indicates that Task 7 is a multiple predecessor task because it can't start until two or more previous tasks all are completed.

How Do I Work With Complex Task Patterns?

When several task patterns combine, you must study the facts very carefully to understand the logic and sequence. A project schedule will not be accurate if the underlying task pattern is incorrect. For example, consider the following three fact statements and the task patterns they represent. Examples of the task patterns are shown in Figures 3-18, 3-19, and 3-20.

EXAMPLE OF MULTIPLE PREDECESSOR TASKS

FIGURE 3-17 This example of multiple predecessor tasks shows that the start time for a successor task must be the latest (largest) finish time for any of its preceding tasks. In the example shown, Task 1 ends on Day 15, while Task 2 ends on Day 5, so Task 1 controls the start time for Task 3.

© Cengage Learning 2014

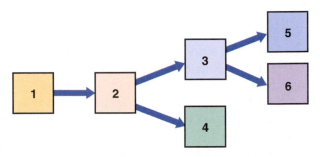

FIGURE 3-18   Dependent tasks.
© Cengage Learning 2014

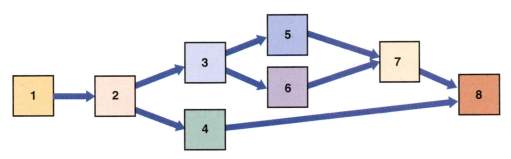

FIGURE 3-19   Dependent tasks and multiple successor tasks.
© Cengage Learning 2014

FIGURE 3-20   Dependent tasks, multiple successor tasks, and multiple predecessor tasks.
© Cengage Learning 2014

DEPENDENT TASKS   Perform Task 1. When Task 1 is complete, perform Task 2.

DEPENDENT TASKS AND MULTIPLE SUCCESSOR TASKS   Perform Task 1. When Task 1 is complete, perform Task 2. When Task 2 is finished, start two tasks: Task 3 and Task 4. When Task 3 is complete, start two more tasks: Task 5 and Task 6.

DEPENDENT TASKS, MULTIPLE SUCCESSOR TASKS, AND MULTIPLE PREDECESSOR TASKS   Perform Task 1. When Task 1 is complete, perform Task 2. When Task 2 is finished, start two Tasks: Task 3 and Task 4. When Task 3 is complete, start two more tasks: Task 5 and Task 6. When Tasks 5 and 6 are done, start Task 7. Then, when Tasks 4 and 7 are finished, perform Task 8.

Video Learning Session
Critical Path Analysis

If you have an MIS CourseMate access code, you can launch interactive Video Learning Sessions to help you understand systems development concepts and practice your skills. You can watch the sessions on your computer or mobile device, and pause, rewind, or replay a video at any time. To log on to the MIS CourseMate site at **www.cengagebrain.com**, you must create a student account and then register this book.

This session is about critical path analysis. You'll learn what a critical path is and why it is important, how to calculate task dates and identify the critical path, and how to use Microsoft Project to analyze and display the critical path.

© craftvision/iStockphoto

STEP 3: CALCULATE THE CRITICAL PATH

Task patterns determine the order in which the tasks are performed. Once the task sequence has been defined, a project manager can schedule the tasks and calculate the critical path.

What Is a Critical Path?

A **critical path** is a series of tasks which, if delayed, would affect the completion date of the overall project. If any task on the critical path falls behind schedule, the entire project will be delayed. For example, suppose that you invite Joan and Jim to your home for dinner. Joan arrives on time, but Jim arrives 30 minutes late. Jim's arrival is part of the critical path because you do not want to start without him, so the meal will be served 30 minutes later than originally planned.

Project managers always must be aware of the critical path, so they can respond quickly to keep the project on track. Microsoft Project and other project management software can highlight the series of tasks that form the critical path.

How Do I Calculate the Critical Path?

Figure 3-21 shows a training project with five tasks. Notice that the analyst has arranged the tasks and entered task names, IDs, and durations. First, you should review the task patterns. In this example, Task 1 is followed by Task 2, which is a dependent task. Task 2 has two successor tasks: Task 3 and Task 4. Tasks 3 and 4 are predecessor tasks for Task 5.

The next step is to determine start and finish dates, which will determine the critical path for the project. The following explanation will guide you through a step-by-step process. The result is shown in Figure 3-22.

- Task 1 starts on Day 1 and has a duration of 10 days, so the finish date is Day 10.

- Task 2, which is dependent on Task 1, can start on Day 11 — the day *after* Task 1 ends. With a duration of 30 days, Task 2 will end on Day 40.

- Tasks 3 and 4 are multiple successor tasks that can start after Task 2 is done. Task 2 ends on Day 40, so Tasks 3 and 4 *both* can start on Day 41. Task 3 has a duration of 5 days, and will end on Day 45. Task 4 has a duration of 25 days, and will not end until Day 65.

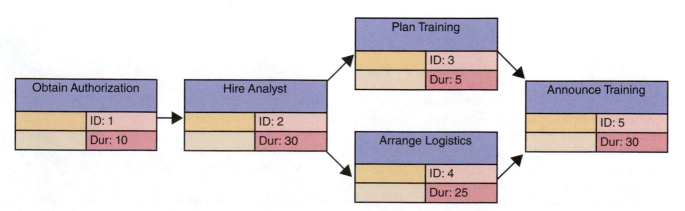

FIGURE 3-21 Example of a PERT/CPM chart with five tasks. Task 2 is a dependent task that has multiple successor tasks. Task 5 has multiple predecessor tasks. In this figure, the analyst has arranged the tasks and entered task names, IDs, and durations.

© Cengage Learning 2014

FIGURE 3-22   Now the analyst has entered the start and finish times, using the rules explained in this section. Notice that the overall project has a duration of 95 days.
© Cengage Learning 2014

- Task 5 depends on Tasks 3 and 4, which are multiple predecessors. Because Task 5 depends on *both* tasks, it cannot start until the later of the two tasks is complete. In this example, Task 3 ends earlier, but Task 4 will not be completed until Day 65, so Task 5 cannot start until Day 66.

Recall that the critical path is a series of tasks which, if delayed, would affect the final completion date of the overall project. In this example, Tasks 1 and 2 are the first tasks on the critical path. Now look at Task 5, which cannot start until both Tasks 3 and 4 are done. In this case, Task 4 is the controlling factor because Task 4 finishes on Day 65, which is 20 days later than Task 3, which is completed on Day 45. Therefore, the start date for Task 5 is determined by the finish date for Task 4. In contrast, Task 3 has slack time, and could be delayed up to 20 days without affecting Task 5. **Slack time** is the amount of time that the task could be late without pushing back the completion date of the entire project. Tasks 1, 2, 4, and 5 represent the critical path, which is highlighted with red arrows in Figure 3-22.

PROJECT MONITORING AND CONTROL

Regardless of whether the project was planned and scheduled with project management software or in some other manner, the project manager must keep track of the tasks and progress of team members, compare actual progress with the project plan, verify the completion of project milestones, and set standards and ensure that they are followed.

Monitoring and Control Techniques

To help ensure that quality standards are met, many project managers institute structured walk-throughs. A **structured walk-through** is a review of a project team member's work by other members of the team. Generally, systems analysts review the work of other systems analysts, and programmers review the work of other programmers, as a form of peer review. Structured walk-throughs take place throughout the SDLC and are called **design reviews**, **code reviews**, or **testing reviews**, depending on the phase in which they occur.

Maintaining a Schedule

Maintaining a project schedule can be challenging, and most projects run into at least some problems or delays. By monitoring and controlling the work, the project manager tries to anticipate problems, avoid them or minimize their impact, identify potential solutions, and select the best way to solve the problem.

The better the original plan, the easier it will be to control the project. If clear, verifiable milestones exist, it will be simple to determine if and when those targets are achieved. If enough milestones and frequent checkpoints exist, problems will be detected rapidly. A project that is planned and scheduled with PERT/CPM can be tracked and controlled using these same techniques. As work continues, the project manager revises the plan to record actual times for completed tasks and revises times for tasks that are not yet finished.

Project managers spend most of their time tracking the tasks along the critical path because delays in those tasks have the greatest potential to delay or jeopardize the project. Other tasks cannot be ignored, however. For example, suppose that a task not on the critical path takes too long and depletes the allotted slack time. At that point, the task actually becomes part of the critical path, and any further delay will push back the overall project.

REPORTING

Members of the project team regularly report their progress to the project manager, who in turn reports to management and users. As shown in Figure 3-23, the project manager collects, verifies, organizes, and evaluates the information he or she receives from the team. Then the manager decides which information needs to be passed along, prepares a summary that can be understood easily, adds comments and explanations if needed, and submits it to management and users.

Project Status Meetings

Project managers, like the one shown in Figure 3-24, schedule regular meetings to update the team and discuss project status, issues, problems, and opportunities. Although meetings can be time consuming, most project managers believe they are worth the effort. The sessions give team members an opportunity to share information, discuss common problems, and explain new techniques. The meetings also give the project manager an opportunity to seek input and conduct brainstorming sessions.

Project Status Reports

Before going further, you should read the *Question of Ethics* feature on page 119, which describes an interesting conflict at Final Four Industries. A project is in trouble, but the project manager is reluctant to report the problems. The case highlights important ethical issues that often arise in this situation.

> **🔧 TOOLKIT TIME**
>
> The Communication Tools in Part A of the Systems Analyst's Toolkit can help you develop better reports and presentations. To learn more about these tools, turn to Part A of the four-part Toolkit that follows Chapter 12.

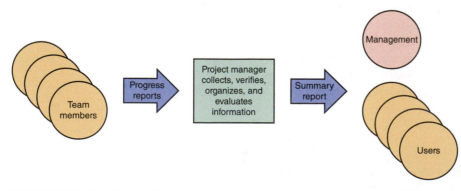

FIGURE 3-23 Members of the project team regularly report their progress to the project manager, who in turn reports to management and users.

© Cengage Learning 2014

FIGURE 3-24 Project managers schedule regular meetings to update the project team and discuss project status, issues, problems, and opportunities.

© Monkey Business Images/Shutterstock

A project manager must report regularly to his or her immediate supervisor, upper management, and users. Although a progress report might be given verbally to an immediate supervisor, reports to management and users usually are written. Gantt charts often are included in progress reports to show project status graphically. Deciding how to handle potential problems can be difficult. At what point should you inform management about the possibility of cost overruns, schedule delays, or technical problems? At one extreme is the overly cautious project manager who alerts management to every potential snag and slight delay. The danger here is that the manager loses credibility over a period of time, and management might ignore potentially serious situations. At the other extreme is the project manager who tries to handle all situations single-handedly and does not alert management until a problem is serious. By the time management learns of the problem, little time might remain in which to react or devise a solution.

A project manager's best course of action lies somewhere between the two extremes, but is probably closer to the first. If you are unsure of the consequences, you should be cautious and warn management about the possibility of a problem. When you report the situation, you also should explain what you are doing to handle and monitor the problem. If you believe the situation is beyond your control, you might want to suggest possible actions that management can take to resolve the situation. Most managers recognize that problems do occur on most projects; it is better to alert management sooner rather than later.

PROJECT MANAGEMENT EXAMPLES

You can use these examples to practice the skills you learned in this chapter. You will also see how you can use project management software to help you manage and display the tasks.

PERT/CPM Example

Figure 3-25 shows a work breakdown structure with 11 tasks. The example is more complex, but the same guidelines apply. Notice that each task has an ID, a description, a duration, and a reference to predecessor tasks, if any, which must be completed before the task can begin. Also notice that dependent tasks can have one predecessor task, or several. You construct a PERT/CPM chart from this task list in a two-step process:

STEP 1: DISPLAY THE TASKS AND TASK PATTERNS   In the first step, as shown in Figure 3-26 on the next page, you identify the tasks, determine task dependencies, and enter the task name, ID, and duration. Notice that this example includes dependent tasks, multiple successor tasks, and multiple predecessor tasks.

STEP 2: ENTER START AND FINISH TIMES
In the second step, as shown in Figure 3-27 on the next page, you enter the start and finish times by applying the guidelines in this section. For example, Task 1 has a one-day duration, so you enter the start and finish times for Task 1 as Day 1. Then you enter Day 2 as the start time for

Task No.	Description	Duration (Days)	Predecessor Tasks
1	Develop Plan	1	-
2	Assign Tasks	4	1
3	Obtain Hardware	17	1
4	Programming	70	2
5	Install Hardware	10	3
6	Program Test	30	4
7	Write User Manual	25	5
8	Convert Files	20	5
9	System Test	25	6
10	User Training	20	7, 8
11	User Test	25	9, 10

FIGURE 3-25   Example of a work breakdown structure listing 11 tasks, together with their descriptions, durations, and predecessor tasks.

FIGURE 3-26 To transform a task list into a PERT/CPM chart, you first enter the task name, ID, duration, and predecessors for each task. Notice that this example includes dependent tasks, tasks with multiple successors, and tasks with multiple predecessors.
© Cengage Learning 2014

successor Tasks 2 and 3. Continuing from left to right, you add the task duration for each task to its start time to determine its finish time. As you proceed, there are three important rules you must keep in mind:

- If a successor task has more than one predecessor task, use the *latest* finish time of the predecessor tasks to determine the start time for the successor task.

- If a predecessor task has more than one successor task, use the predecessor task's finish time to determine the start time for *all* successor tasks.

- Continuing from left to right, add the task duration for each task to its start time to determine and enter its finish time. Again, be very careful not to add too many days. For example, if a task starts on Day 10 and has a duration of 5 days, then the finish would be Day 14 — *not* Day 15.

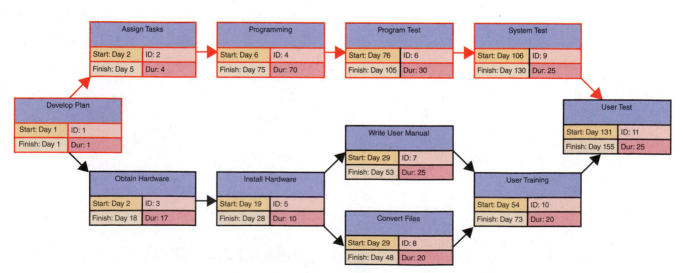

FIGURE 3-27 To complete the PERT/CPM chart, you apply the guidelines explained in this section. For example, Task 1 has a one-day duration, so you enter the start and finish for Task 1 as Day 1. Then you enter Day 2 as the start for successor Tasks 2 and 3.
© Cengage Learning 2014

When you enter all the start and finish times, you determine that the project will be completed on Day 155. Also, you note that Tasks 1, 2, 4, 6, 9, and 11 represent the critical path shown by the red arrows.

PROJECT MANAGEMENT SOFTWARE

Project managers use powerful software to help plan, schedule, monitor, and report on a project. Most programs offer features such as PERT/CPM, Gantt charts, resource scheduling, project calendars, and cost tracking. **Microsoft Project** is a full-featured program that holds the dominant share of the market. As shown in Figure 3-28, Microsoft offers online demos, trial versions, training, and tips.

When you use project management software, you follow a step-by-step process to develop a WBS, work with task patterns, and analyze the critical path. The main difference is that the software does most of the work for you, and enables you to manage much more effectively. The following sections explain how you could use Microsoft Project to handle the sample task summary for a preliminary investigation shown in Figure 3-29 on the next page.

WORK BREAKDOWN STRUCTURE   You already know how to create a work breakdown structure manually. If you are using Microsoft Project, the process is the same. You must identify the tasks, durations, and task patterns. You might have to

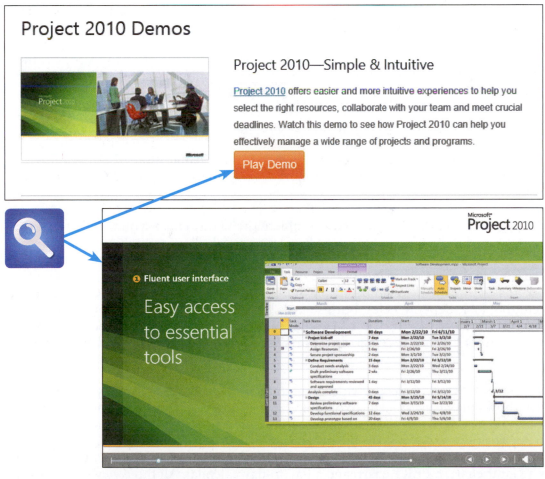

FIGURE 3-28   Microsoft invites prospective customers to view an extensive demo that showcases the features of Project 2010.

Screenshots used with permission from Microsoft.

Please study the following task summary:

- First, we need to spend one day studying potential problems or opportunities.

- Then, we will define the project scope and constraints. That will take two days.

- Next, we will analyze the organization charts. That will take one day.

- After we analyze the charts, four fact-finding tasks can start at once:

    ○ Observe operations (two days)

    ○ Conduct a user survey (three days)

    ○ Conduct interviews (two days)

    ○ Review documentation (one day)

- When all four fact-finding tasks are finished, we will spend one day evaluating feasibilty.

- Then we will spend one day presenting the results and recommendations to management.

FIGURE 3-29   A sample task summary for a preliminary investigation.
© Cengage Learning 2014

develop this information on your own, or you might work with a task summary like the one in Figure 3-29. Your goal is to document all tasks, dependencies, dates, and total project duration. Your first step is to create a Gantt chart showing the necessary information. As you enter each task in Microsoft Project, you also note the duration and the predecessor tasks, if any.

GANTT CHART   As you enter the tasks, the program automatically performs the calculations, detects the task patterns, and creates a Gantt chart. The chart consists of horizontal bars, connected with arrows that indicate task dependencies. If you select a typical work week, tasks will not be scheduled on Saturdays and Sundays. However, for a mission-critical project, you might create a 24/7 calendar. Whatever you specify, the program will handle the tasks accordingly. Microsoft Project offers numerous choices of display settings, formats, and calculation methods. To learn more about these features and much more, you can visit **www.microsoft.com/ project**.

NETWORK DIAGRAM   After you complete the Gantt chart, you decide to view the data in the form of a Microsoft Project network diagram, which is similar to a PERT chart. When you select the Network Diagram option on the View menu, you will see the project tasks, dependencies, and a start and finish date for each task. A network diagram displays the same information as the Gantt chart, including task dependencies, but use task boxes to include much more detail. Using Microsoft Project, you can assign each task to one or more people, assign budget targets, produce progress reports, and readjust schedules and deadlines as necessary.

CALENDAR VIEW   Calendar view is a good way to manage day-to-day activity. This view shows the tasks, similar to a PERT chart, as an overlay on the actual calendar. Because the critical path is highlighted in red, it is easy for a project manager to determine priorities at any point in time.

Suppose your manager wants to view the preliminary investigation in Figure 3-29 as a Gantt chart, a PERT chart, and a day-to-day calendar. All three views are shown in Figure 3-30. Each view shows the tasks, the timing, the dependencies, and the critical path. Notice that of the four tasks scheduled for September 25, only the user survey is on the critical path. If you were the project manager that day, what would be your primary concern?

Although Microsoft is the industry leader, other vendors offer project management software. Some products, such as GanttProject, are free **open source** programs that are supported by a community of users and developers. Compared to Microsoft Project, GanttProject is less powerful—but it is free, has a similar look and feel, and can open files created in Project, as shown in Figure 3-31 on the next page.

Gantt Chart View

PERT Chart View

Calendar View

FIGURE 3-30   Notice how each view displays the project and highlights the critical path. If you were the project manager on September 25, what would be your primary concern?

Screenshots used with permission from Microsoft.

FIGURE 3-31   GanttProject is a free, open source program. The lower screen shows a GanttProject file that was created originally in Microsoft Project. Notice the similar layout and design.
© 2003-2012 GanttProject Team

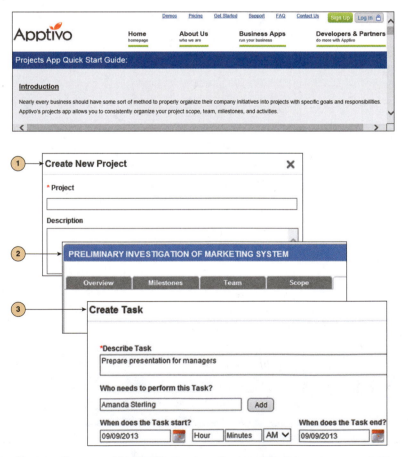

FIGURE 3-32   Apptivo offers several levels of business applications, including project management.
© 2012 Apptivo Inc.

Another interesting product is Apptivo, which is shown in Figure 3-32 on the previous page. Apptivo offers several levels of business applications, including project management. According to the company's Web site, the company's *Standard Plan* is free of charge with unlimited duration. Apptivo's approach is very different from Microsoft Project. In the three-step example shown in Figure 3-32, the user created a project, named it, and entered a task. Many customers use Apptivo in small- to medium-sized businesses.

Regardless of which software you use, these examples show that project management is dynamic and challenging. One significant advantage of integrated project management software is that it allows the project manager to adjust schedules, estimates, and resource assignments rapidly to response to real-world events.

CASE IN POINT 3.3: CENSUS 2010

Just before the 2010 census, the U.S. Commerce Department canceled a plan to acquire 500,000 handheld computers they had ordered to tabulate data. According to Commerce Secretary Carlos Gutierrez, costs had skyrocketed. He blamed the problem on "a lack of effective communications with one of our major suppliers."

Apparently, there was plenty of blame to go around. Secretary Gutierrez noted that the Census Bureau had submitted numerous technical changes to the vendor, Harris Corporation. This greatly increased the cost and the complexity of the devices. Gutierrez stated, "The Census Bureau was unaccustomed to working with an outside vendor on such a large contract." He also pointed out that the vendor had submitted an initial estimate of $36 million to operate a help desk to assist census-takers, but that figure had jumped to $217 million. "It was a bad estimate. I can't think of a better way to say it. Harris gave us the number. We accepted it. It was totally underestimated."

What can be learned from the failure of this project, and could it have been prevented? Suppose you were asked to head up a similar project. What would you do to prevent a similar outcome?

RISK MANAGEMENT

Every IT project involves risks that systems analysts and project managers must address. A **risk** is an event that could affect the project negatively. **Risk management** is the process of identifying, analyzing, anticipating, and monitoring risks to minimize their impact on the project.

Steps in Risk Management

The first step in risk management is to develop a specific plan. Although project management experts differ with regard to the number of steps or phases, a basic list would include the following tasks:

- *Develop a risk management plan.* A **risk management plan** includes a review of the project's scope, stakeholders, budget, schedule, and any other internal or external factors that might affect the project. The plan should define project roles and responsibilities, risk management methods and procedures, categories of risks, and contingency plans.

- *Identify the risks.* **Risk identification** lists each risk and assesses the likelihood that it could affect the project. The details would depend on the specific project, but most lists would include a means of identification, and a brief description of the risk, what might cause it to occur, who would be responsible for responding, and the potential impact of the risk.

FIGURE 3-33 You can use a Microsoft Excel XY chart type to display a risk matrix that shows risk probability and potential impact.
© Cengage Learning 2014

- *Analyze the risks.* This typically is a two-step process: Qualitative risk analysis and quantitative risk analysis. **Qualitative risk analysis** evaluates each risk by estimating the probability that it will occur and the degree of impact. Project managers can use a formula to weigh risk and impact values, or they can display the results in a two-axis grid. For example, a Microsoft Excel XY chart can be used to display the matrix, as shown in Figure 3-33. In the chart, notice the various combinations of risk and impact ratings for the five sample values. This tool can help a project manager focus on the most critical areas, where risk probability and potential impact are high.

The purpose of **quantitative risk analysis** is to understand the actual impact in terms of dollars, time, project scope, or quality. Quantitative risk analysis can involve a modeling process called what-if analysis, which allows a project manager to vary one or more element(s) in a model to measure the effect on other elements. This topic is discussed in more detail in Chapter 12, Managing Systems Support and Security.

- Create a risk response plan. A **risk response plan** is a proactive effort to anticipate a risk and describe an action plan to deal with it. An effective risk response plan can reduce the overall impact by triggering timely and appropriate action.

- Monitor risks. This activity is ongoing throughout the risk management process. It is important to conduct a continuous tracking process that can identify new risks, notice changes in existing risks, and update any other areas of the risk management plan.

Risk Management Software

Most project management software includes powerful features that allow a project manager to assign specific dates as constraints, align task dependencies, note external factors that might affect a task, track progress, and display tasks that are behind schedule.

The enterprise edition of Microsoft Project, Microsoft Project Server, has a built-in risk management capability that can be used for large, corporate-wide projects. Microsoft claims that the software can link risks with specific tasks and projects, specify probability and impact, assign ownership, and track progress to manage projects more efficiently. Microsoft's risk management model includes the following factors:

- Probability, which represents the likelihood that the risk will happen, expressed as a percentage

- Impact, which indicates the degree of adverse effect should the risk occur, on a scale of 1 to 10

- Cost, which indicates the potential financial impact of the risk

- Category, which specifies the risk type

- Description, which specifies the nature of the risk
- Mitigation plan, which identifies plans to control or limit the risk
- Contingency plan, which specifies actions to be taken if the risk occurs
- Trigger, which identifies a condition that would initiate the contingency plan

Armed with this information, the IT team can quantify the project's risks, just as they use financial analysis tools to quantify costs and benefits.

In addition to Microsoft, other vendors offer risk management software. For example, Intaver Institute offers an add-on risk management package that integrates with Microsoft Project, as shown in Figure 3-34. Notice that the color-coded matrix reflects risk probability and impact.

FIGURE 3-34 Intaver Institute offers an add-on risk management package for Microsoft Project. Notice that the color-coded matrix reflects risk probability and impact. Intaver's model is a much more complex version of the simple risk matrix shown in Figure 3-33, but the concept is basically the same.

© Intaver Institute Inc., 2002–2012

MANAGING FOR SUCCESS

To be successful, an information system must satisfy business requirements, stay within budget, be completed on time, and — most important of all — be managed effectively. When a project develops problems, the reasons typically involve business, budget, or schedule issues, as explained in the following sections. In addition to planning and managing the project, a project manager must be able to recognize problems and deal with them effectively.

Business Issues

The major objective of every system is to provide a solution to a business problem or opportunity. If the system does not do this, then it is a failure — regardless of positive reaction from users, acceptable budget performance, or timely delivery. When the information system does not meet business requirements, causes might include unidentified or unclear requirements, inadequately defined scope, imprecise targets, shortcuts or sloppy work during systems analysis, poor design choices, insufficient testing or inadequate testing procedures, and lack of change control procedures. Systems also fail because of changes in the organization's culture, funding, or objectives. A system that falls short of business needs also produces problems for users and reduces employee morale and productivity.

As you learned in Chapter 2, projects without clear scope definitions are risky because they tend to expand gradually, without specific authorization, in a process called **project creep**. However, even when a project is clearly described, it must be managed constantly.

Budget Issues

Cost overruns typically result from one or more of the following:

- Unrealistic estimates that are too optimistic or based on incomplete information
- Failure to develop an accurate forecast that considers all costs over the life of the project

- Poor monitoring of progress and slow response to early warning signs of problems
- Schedule delays due to factors that were not foreseen
- Human resource issues, including turnover, inadequate training, and motivation

Schedule Issues

Problems with timetables and project milestones can indicate a failure to recognize task dependencies, confusion between effort and progress, poor monitoring and control methods, personality conflicts among team members, or turnover of project personnel. The failure of an IT project also can be caused by poor project management techniques.

If the project manager fails to plan, staff, organize, supervise, communicate, motivate, evaluate, direct, and control properly, then the project is certain to fail. Even when factors outside his or her control contribute to the failure, the project manager is responsible for recognizing the early warning signs and handling them effectively.

CASE IN POINT 3.4: SPRING FORWARD PRODUCTS

After three years with the company, you recently were asked to manage several IT projects. You are confident that you have the technical skills you need, but you are concerned about morale at the company. There has been some downsizing, and many employees are worried about the future.

As a longtime fan of the Dilbert cartoon strip, you know that maintaining morale can be a real challenge. Your current project involves a team of a dozen people, several of whom remind you of Dilbert and his coworkers. What are some techniques that you might use to motivate the team and inspire its members? What are some things you might *not* want to do?

THE BOTTOM LINE

Project management is a challenging task. Project managers must be alert, technically competent, and highly resourceful. They also must be good communicators with strong human resource skills. Like the people shown in Figure 3-35, project managers can be proud when they handle a successful project that helps the company achieve its business objectives.

Unfortunately, projects can and do get derailed for a wide variety of reasons. When problems occur, the project manager's ability to handle the situation becomes the critical factor. When a project manager first recognizes that a project is in trouble, what options are available? Alternatives can include trimming the project requirements, adding to the project resources, delaying the project deadline, and improving management controls and procedures. Sometimes, when a project experiences delays or cost overruns, the system still can be delivered on time and within budget if several less critical requirements are trimmed. The system can be delivered to satisfy the most necessary requirements, and additional features can be added later as a part of a maintenance or enhancement project.

FIGURE 3-35 When a project is successful, the project management team has a right to be proud!

© Philip Date/Shutterstock.com

If a project is in trouble because of a lack of resources or organizational support, management might be willing to give the project more commitment and higher priority. For example, management might agree to add more people to a project that is behind schedule. Adding staff, however, will reduce the project's completion time only if the additional people can be integrated effectively into the development team. If team members lack experience with certain aspects of the required technology, temporary help might be obtained from IT consultants or part-time staff. Adding staff can mean training and orienting the new people, however. In some situations, adding more people to a project actually might increase the time necessary to complete the project because of a principle called **Brooks' Law**. This interesting concept was stated by Frederick Brooks, Jr., an IBM engineer, who observed that adding manpower to a late software project only makes it later. Brooks reached this conclusion when he saw that new workers on a project first had to be educated and instructed by existing employees whose own productivity was reduced accordingly.

A QUESTION OF ETHICS

© faberfoto_it/iStockphoto

"Better blow the whistle," says Roy, your friend and project teammate at Final Four Industries. "The project is out of control, and you know it!" "Maybe so," you respond, "But that's not my call — I'm not the project manager." What you don't say is that Stephanie, the project manager, feels like her career is on the line and she is reluctant to bring bad news to management at this time. She honestly believes that the project can catch up, and says that a bad report on a major project could result in bad publicity for the firm and frighten potential customers.

To be fair, the next management progress report is scheduled in three weeks. It is possible that the team could catch up, but you doubt it. You wonder if there is an ethical question here: Even though the report isn't due yet, should a significant problem be reported to management as soon as possible? You are concerned about the issue, and you decide to discuss it with Stephanie. What will you say to her?

CHAPTER SUMMARY

Project management is the process of planning, scheduling, monitoring, and reporting on the development of an information system. A successful project must be completed on time, within budget, and deliver a quality product that satisfies users and meets requirements. A project triangle shows three legs: project cost, scope, and time. A project manager must find the best balance among these elements because a change in any leg of the triangle will affect the other two legs. Project management techniques can be used throughout the SDLC.

Project managers are responsible for project planning, scheduling, monitoring, and reporting. Planning includes identifying all project tasks and estimating the completion time and cost of each. Project scheduling involves the creation of a specific timetable, usually in the form of charts that show tasks, task dependencies, and critical tasks that might delay the project. Project monitoring requires guiding, supervising, and coordinating the project team's workload. The project manager must monitor the progress, evaluate the results, and take corrective action when necessary to control the project and stay on target. Project reporting includes regular progress reports to management, users, and the project team itself. Effective reporting requires strong communication skills and a sense of what others want and need to know about the project.

Planning, scheduling, monitoring and reporting all take place within a larger project development framework, which includes three key steps: creating a work breakdown structure, identifying task patterns, and calculating the critical path.

A work breakdown structure must clearly identify each task and include an estimated duration. A task, or activity, is any work that has a beginning and an end and requires the use of company resources such as people, time, or money. Time and cost estimates for tasks usually are made in person-days. A person-day represents the work that one person can accomplish in one day. Estimating the time for project activities is more difficult with larger systems. Project managers must consider the project size and scope, IT resources, prior experience with similar projects or systems, and applicable constraints. In addition to tasks, every project has events, or milestones. An event, or milestone, is a recognizable reference point that you can use to monitor progress.

Task patterns establish the sequence of work in a project. Task patterns involve dependent tasks, multiple successor tasks, and multiple predecessor tasks. In larger projects, these patterns can be very complex.

A critical path is a series of tasks which, if delayed, would affect the completion date of the overall project. If any task on the critical path falls behind schedule, the entire project will be delayed. Tasks on the critical path cannot have slack time. To identify the critical path, you calculate the start and finish date for each task, which will determine the critical path for the project.

In project scheduling, the project manager develops a specific time for each task, based on available resources and whether or not the task is dependent on other predecessor tasks. The manager can use graphical tools such as Gantt charts and PERT charts to assist in the scheduling process.

A Gantt chart is a horizontal bar chart that represents the project schedule with time on the horizontal axis and tasks arranged vertically. It shows individual tasks and task groups, which include several tasks. In a Gantt chart, the length of the bar indicates the duration of the tasks. A Gantt chart can display progress, but does not show task dependency details or resource assignment unless the chart was created with a project management program that supports dependency linking and the entry of other information.

A PERT/CPM chart shows the project as a network diagram with tasks connected by arrows. Using a prescribed calculation method, the project manager uses a PERT chart to determine the overall duration of the project and provide specific information for each task, including the task IDs, their durations, start and finish times, and the order in which they must be performed. With this information, the manager can determine the critical path, which is the sequence of tasks that have no slack time and must be performed on schedule in order to meet the overall project deadline.

Most project managers use powerful software such as Microsoft Project to plan, schedule, and monitor projects. Project managers are responsible for risk management, which is the process of identifying, analyzing, anticipating, and monitoring risks to minimize their impact on the project.

In the end, every successful information system must support business requirements, stay within budget, and be completed on time. Sound project management involves the same skills as any other management. The project manager must be perceptive, analytical, well-organized, and a good communicator. If the project manager senses that the project is off-track, he or she must take immediate steps to diagnose and solve the problem. If the project manager fails to plan, staff, organize, supervise, communicate, motivate, evaluate, direct, and control properly, then the project is certain to fail. Even when factors outside his or her control contribute to the failure, the project manager is responsible for recognizing the early warning signs and handling them effectively.

Key Terms

activity *94*
best-case estimate *96*
bottom-up technique *93*
Brooks' Law *115*
code review *103*
concurrent task *99*
critical path *102*
Critical Path Method (CPM) *93*
dependent task *99*
design review *103*
duration *99*
event *94*
finish day/date *99*
Gantt chart *92*
gateway *124*
Microsoft Project *107*
milestone *94*
network diagram *93*
open source *109*
person-day *95*
PERT/CPM *93*
predecessor task *95*
probable-case estimate *96*
Program Evaluation Review Technique (PERT) *93*
project coordinator *91*
project creep *113*
project leader *91*
project management *90*

project manager *91*
project monitoring *92*
project planning *91*
project reporting *92*
project scheduling *91*
project triangle *90*
qualitative risk analysis *112*
quantitative risk analysis *112*
risk *111*
risk identification *111*
risk management *111*
risk management plan *111*
risk response plan *112*
slack time *103*
start day/date *99*
structured walk-through *103*
successor task *99*
task *94*
task box *98*
task group *92*
task ID *99*
task name *99*
task pattern *98*
testing review *103*
weight *96*
work breakdown structure (WBS) *92*
worst-case estimate *96*

Chapter Exercises

Questions

1. Write the script for a one-minute explanation of basic project management concepts.
2. What is a task? What is an event? What is a milestone?
3. What specific information do you need to create a work breakdown structure?
4. What are the three main task patterns? Provide an example of each.
5. Explain the differences between a Gantt chart and a PERT/CPM chart.
6. What formula can a project manager use to estimate task duration? Provide an example.
7. What is a common problem in calculating start and finish times? Provide an example.
8. Why is the critical path important? Why would a task be on the critical path?
9. Why is it important to deliver effective project reports and communications?
10. What is risk management, and why is it important? Provide an example.

Discussion Topics

1. In Poor Richard's Almanac, Benjamin Franklin penned the familiar lines: "For the want of a nail the shoe was lost, for the want of a shoe the horse was lost, for the want of a horse the rider was lost, for the want of a rider the battle was lost, for the want of a battle the kingdom was lost — and all for the want of a horseshoe nail." Looking at the outcome in hindsight, could project management concepts have avoided the loss of the kingdom? How?
2. Microsoft Project is powerful, but quite expensive. As a manager, how would you justify the purchase of this software?
3. Suppose you want to manage a small project, but you don't have access to project management software. Could you use a spreadsheet or database program instead? How?
4. Some managers believe that they have "seat of the pants" intuition and don't need project management tools. Does that make sense to you? Why or why not?

Projects

1. Think of all the tasks that you perform when you purchase a car. Include any research, decisions, or financial issues that relate to the purchase. Create a work breakdown structure that shows all the tasks, their estimated duration, and any predecessor tasks.
2. Perform Internet research to learn more about project risk management, and write a summary of the results. Be sure to search for a book titled *Waltzing with Bears: Managing Risk on Software Projects*, by Tom Demarco and Timothy Lister.
3. Go to the Apptivo site at **www.apptivo.com** and download the free project management application. Explore the program's features, and describe what you liked and didn't like.
4. Describe three personal experiences where project management would have helped you avoid a problem or take advantage of an opportunity. Be specific.

Apply Your Knowledge

The Apply Your Knowledge section contains four mini-cases. Each case describes a situation, explains your role, and asks you to respond to questions by applying what you learned in the chapter.

1 Forest Point Construction

At Forest Point Construction, your boss says that he can estimate the total project time based on his personal experience. You are trying to convince him that he should use project management techniques to handle a complex project.

To prove your point, you decide to use a simple example of a commercial steel building construction project, with eight steps. You create a hypothetical work breakdown structure, as follows:

- Prepare the site (3 days), and then set the building footers (3 days).
- Finish the foundation (5 days), and then assemble the building (3 days).
- When the building is assembled, start two tasks at once: finish the interior work (5 days) and set up an appointment for the final building inspection (15 days).
- When the interior work is done, start two more tasks at once: landscaping (7 days) and driveway paving (3 days).
- When the landscaping and driveway are done, do the painting (2 days).
- Finally, when the painting is done and the final inspection has occurred, arrange the sale (2 days).

Now you ask your boss to review the tasks, estimate the total time, and write the answer on a piece of paper. You look at the paper and see that his guess is wrong.

Tasks

1. What is the correct total time?
2. What is the critical path?
3. Create a Gantt chart that shows the WBS.
4. Create a PERT/CPM chart.

2 Crescent View High School Class

The computer science instructor at Crescent View High School asked you to visit his class and give a presentation about project management. You have just a few days to prepare, and you need to develop a presentation that describes project management tools and techniques. You can be creative, and you might want to include examples of actual projects that you know about. In any case, try to describe how projects are planned, scheduled, monitored, and reported upon. Your presentation should consist of five to seven slides with notes about what you are going to talk about that include the following:

Tasks

1. Prepare opening comments that give the class an overview of project management.
2. Provide the class with a glossary of the most important project management terms and definitions.
3. Think of a common event like buying a new home, and show the class how a project manager might handle the matter.
4. Create a short scenario with four to six tasks, some of which depend on each other. You can use the two preceding cases as a model. Develop a sample answer that you will show students after you give them a chance to analyze the tasks.

3 Brightstar Industries

You will lead a training session for new employees at Brightstar Industries. You must develop a specific schedule for the following tasks (the estimated duration is shown in parentheses):

- First, you need to contact the participants and explain their roles (1 day). Then you must obtain approval from their department managers (3 days).
- After you obtain the approval, two tasks can begin at the same time: you can arrange the meeting room (1 day) and prepare an agenda for the initial session (8 days).
- When the agenda is ready, you can start two more concurrent tasks: prepare the information packets (3 days) and create visual aids (6 days).
- When the meeting room is arranged and the information packets are ready, you can send out an e-mail to participants (1 day).
- Finally, after the e-mail is sent to participants and the visual aids are ready, you can conduct the JAD sessions (7 days).

Tasks

1. Prepare a list showing all tasks and their durations.
2. Analyze the fact situation carefully to determine which tasks are concurrent and which ones depend on other tasks.
3. Develop a PERT/CPM chart that shows the project. Use a format similar to Figure 3-27 on page 110. Use project management software if it is available.
4. What is the critical path for this project? How do you know?

4 Bayside Financial

At Bayside Financial, where you work as a project manager, you have been asked to conduct user training sessions for a new information system. You must develop a specific schedule for the tasks (the estimated task duration for each is shown in parentheses):

- First, confirm arrangements for the training facility you plan to use (3 days).
- After you have confirmed the training facility, two tasks can begin at the same time: you need to send an e-mail message to all department managers announcing the training sessions (1 day) and you can develop the training material (5 days).
- As soon as the training material is complete, you can work on two tasks at once: arrange to have copies of handout material printed (2 days) and develop a set of PowerPoint slides (5 days).
- When the PowerPoint slides are ready, you conduct a practice training session with the instructor who will assist you (2 days).
- Finally, when the practice session is over and the handout material is ready, you can conduct the user training sessions (4 days).

Tasks

1. Prepare a list showing all tasks and their durations.
2. Analyze the fact situation carefully to determine which tasks are concurrent and which ones are dependent on other tasks.
3. Create a PERT chart that shows the project. Use a format similar to Figure 3-27 on page 110. If project management software is available, use it to develop the chart.
4. What is the critical path for this project? How do you know?

Case Studies

Each chapter includes a Chapter Case, a Continuing Case, a Capstone Case, and an Online Case Simulation. You can learn more about the Online Case Simulation in the MIS CourseMate Features section.

Chapter Case: Town of Eden Bay (Part 2)

The town of Eden Bay owns and maintains a fleet of vehicles. You are a systems analyst reporting to Dawn, the town's IT manager.

Background

Eden Bay is a medium-sized municipality. The town has grown rapidly, and so has the demand for town services. Eden Bay currently owns 90 vehicles, which the town's equipment department maintains. The fleet includes police cars, sanitation trucks, fire trucks, and other vehicles assigned to town employees. The maintenance budget has risen sharply in recent years, and people are asking whether the town should continue to perform its own maintenance or outsource it to private firms.

In the first part of the case, you planned a preliminary investigation for a new information system that would cut costs and improve maintenance efficiency. Based on your investigation, Dawn wants to move forward, and she asked you to help her present a budget request at the next Town Council meeting. She suggested the following to-do list:

- First, double-check the cost and benefit data we will need for the proposal (3 days).
- Then, start two tasks at the same time: send an e-mail message to the Town Council requesting that the proposal be placed on the agenda (1 day), and develop the proposal itself, including all necessary documents and charts (5 days).
- As soon as the proposal is complete, start work on two tasks at once: print copies of handout material for the meeting (2 days) and develop a PowerPoint presentation (5 days).
- When the presentation is ready, conduct a rehearsal for the Council meeting. (2 days).
- Finally, when the rehearsal is done and the handout material is ready, help Dawn deliver the presentation. (1 day).

Tasks

1. Prepare a list showing all tasks and their durations.
2. Analyze the fact situation carefully to identify any tasks that are dependent on other tasks.
3. Create a PERT chart that shows the project. Use a format similar to Figure 3-27 on page 110. If project management software is available, use it to develop the chart.
4. What is the critical path for this project? How do you know?

Continuing Case: Personal Trainer, Inc.

Personal Trainer, Inc. owns and operates fitness centers in a dozen Midwestern cities. The centers have done well, and the company is planning an international expansion by opening a new "supercenter" in the Toronto area. Personal Trainer's president, Cassia Umi, hired an IT consultant, Susan Park, to help develop an information system for the new facility. During the project, Susan will work closely with Gray Lewis, who will manage the new operation.

Background

You are enjoying your job as a student intern at Personal Trainer. Last week, Susan asked you to help her plan the new information system project. Susan knows that you have completed several information systems courses at the local college, and that you have studied project management tools and techniques.

Specifically, she wants you to get ready for the next set of systems development tasks, which will be requirements modeling for the new system. Yesterday, Susan called you into her office to discuss the specific tasks she wants you to perform. After meeting with Susan, you sit down and review your notes. She wants you to treat the set of tasks as a project, and to use project management skills to plan the tasks.

Here is what she suggested to you as a work breakdown structure, including the duration she estimated for each task:

- First, you need to meet with fitness center managers at other Personal Trainer locations (5 days).
- After these meetings, you can conduct a series of interviews (5 days).
- When the interviews are complete, two tasks can begin at the same time: you can review company records (3 days) and observe business operations (8 days).
- When you have reviewed the records and observed business operations, you can analyze the BumbleBee accounting software (5 days) and study a sample of sales and billing transactions (2 days).
- After completing the analysis and studying the sales transactions, prepare a report for Susan (1 day)

You are excited about the opportunity to practice your skills, and you start to work on the following list.

Tasks

1. Create a table listing all tasks separately, with their duration.
2. Identify all dependent tasks, and indicate what predecessor tasks are required.
3. Construct a PERT/CPM chart similar to the one in Figure 3-27 on page 110. If you have access to Microsoft Project or other project management software, you can use it to help you create the chart.
4. Determine the overall duration of the project, and identify the critical path.

Capstone Case: New Century Wellness Group

New Century Wellness Group offers a holistic approach to healthcare with an emphasis on preventive medicine as well as traditional medical care. In your role as an IT consultant, you will help New Century develop a new information system.

Background

In the previous chapter, you conducted a preliminary investigation into New Century's request for a business support system and a medical practice support system. In your presentation to the partners, you explained that although they will communicate and share data, the two systems should be treated as separate IT projects. After discussing your recommendations, Dr. Jones and the partners decided to move forward with the business support system project and want you to describe the next steps.

Project Management

To ensure the quality, cost, and timeliness of the new system, you suggested that New Century use a project management approach. Dr. Jones agreed, and he wants you develop a brief presentation that will describe project management concepts and benefits. You realize that most of the partners do not have project management experience, and it is important to deliver a clear, informative presentation.

You plan to include an overview of project management, a step-by-step description of project planning, and an explanation of key terms. You also need to describe various types of task patterns, and show examples of Gantt and PERT/CPM charts.

Tasks

1. Create a Microsoft PowerPoint presentation to explain project management concepts and benefits.
2. Create a Microsoft Word handout with a list of all key project management terms, including a definition and an example for each term.
3. In your presentation, provide an example of an imaginary project with at least six tasks. Assign task durations and dependencies that include all types of task patterns. Create a Gantt chart that displays the project.
4. Use the Task 3 example to create a PERT/CPM chart.

CASE Tool Workshop

Systems analysts use CASE tools to help them plan, build, and maintain information systems. To learn more about CASE tools, turn to Part B of the Toolkit that follows Chapter 12. You can complete these tasks with the Visible Analyst® CASE tool, which is available with this textbook, or a similar tool.

Background

As a part-time student assistant in the computer lab at your school, you were asked to evaluate various CASE tools. So far, you completed an overview and created a sample project called HOTEL, which includes a number of planning statements. As you continue your analysis, you want to see how the CASE tool handles business process modeling (BPM). You also decide to examine the relationship between BPM and project management software.

Tasks

1. In business process modeling notation, a **gateway** is like a fork in the road, allowing the flow to go one way or another. You can learn more about gateways in the Visible Analyst Glossary feature.

    Suppose, in your software company, a key issue is whether a new product will be ready for release on June 1, or whether it will require further testing. If it is ready, *Release Tasks* can start. Otherwise, *Testing Tasks* must continue. Use Visible Analyst to create a simple business process model with a gateway that shows the two possible paths.

2. No modeling tool is perfect. For example, BPM easily shows gateways that depend on a condition, but most project management software does not have that built-in capability. Programmers can create macros or custom scripts to handle such situations, but that can be expensive and time-consuming. Some project managers have discovered that they can create an alternative task series by making certain tasks active or inactive, depending on a specific condition. In Microsoft Project help, search for information about *active tasks*, and write a summary of your research. Then create a PERT chart that shows the business process model you developed in Task 1.

MIS CourseMate Features

If you have an MIS CourseMate access code, you can reinforce and extend your learning with premium content created for this textbook. For example, you can launch interactive Video Learning Sessions to help you understand systems development concepts and practice your skills. In addition, you can use MindTap Reader, which is a full, interactive, digital e-book.

MIS CourseMate also offers many learning features within each chapter, including an Online Case Simulation, a Critical Thinking Challenge, Video Learning Tasks, and a set of Learn It Online activities. To log on to the MIS CourseMate site at **www.cengagebrain.com**, you must create a student account and register this book.

Online Case Simulation: SCR Associates

Session 3: Managing Systems Projects

Overview

The SCR Associates case study is a Web-based simulation that allows you to practice your skills in a real-world environment. The firm offers IT consulting, solutions, and training. SCR plans to open a new high-tech training center, and needs to develop a Training Information Management System (TIMS) to support the operation. You are a newly hired systems analyst reporting to Jesse Baker, systems group manager, and will help her develop the system.

The case study takes you to the SCR Web site, where you receive e-mail and voice mail messages from Jesse, obtain information from SCR's resource libraries, and perform various tasks. Jesse has high standards, but seems very fair. She made it clear that she expects your work to be accurate, thorough, and professional.

Before You Begin

To prepare for this work session, you should review the following topics:

- Task definitions, examples, and main types of patterns
- Calculating task start and finish dates
- The importance of the critical path

How Do I Use the Online Case Simulation?

- Read the preview, and review the Chapter 1 background material if necessary.
- Visit the MIS CourseMate Web site at **www.cengagebrain.com**, locate the **SCR Case Simulation**, and click the **intranet** link. Enter your name and the password **sad10e**.
- When the opening screen displays, select this session. Then check your e-mail and voice mail, and start to work on your task list.

Preview: Session 3

The TIMS system was approved by top management. Jesse Baker, systems group manager, wants you to help manage the project. She said it will be a great opportunity to learn more about project management and practice your skills, so you'll be able to handle a future project on your own. To make sure that you are prepared, you decide to study the project management material in your textbook and watch the Video Learning Sessions that explain project management terms, concepts, and skills.

Critical Thinking Challenge

In addition to technical ability, IT professionals need critical thinking skills. This feature can help you practice perception, organization, analysis, problem-solving, and decision-making skills that will be valuable in the workplace. You can visit **www.criticalthinking.org** to learn more about critical thinking and why it is so important.

Background

The IT group at Game Technology received approval to add a new entry-level systems analyst position. You will help set up the hiring timetable and create a task list to handle the interviewing logistics. After checking with several people in the IT department, you identified seven specific tasks, estimated their duration, and determined the order in which they should be performed. Now you need to create a work breakdown structure and a PERT chart that shows the task pattern and a critical path.

Practice Tasks

Visit the MIS CourseMate Web site at **www.cengagebrain.com.** Then navigate to the resources for this chapter and locate the **Critical Thinking Challenge** feature. You will complete two Practice Tasks, using what you learned in the chapter. Then you can check your answers to be sure you're ready for the Challenge Tasks.

Challenge Tasks

After you complete the Practice tasks, you learn about new developments at Game Technology.

Yesterday, the hiring committee made a job offer to Sharon Adams and she accepted. She will start her new job in three weeks. You need to set up an orientation day for her, including meetings with key people, an introduction to the IT team, lunch with the IT director, and several other appointments. To continue, navigate back to the **Critical Thinking Challenge** feature for this chapter, select the **Challenge Tasks,** and follow the instructions.

Video Learning Sessions

The Video Learning Sessions in this chapter explain how to use project management tools and techniques. You'll learn basic project management skills, including how to plan, organize, and monitor a systems project.

© craftvision/iStockphoto

Before You Begin

To prepare for the tasks, you should review the following topics:

- Work breakdown structures
- Identifying task patterns
- Calculating the critical path

How to Watch a Session

Go to the Management Information Systems CourseMate Web site at **www.cengagebrain.com.** Then navigate to the resources for this book, locate the **Video Learning Sessions,** and select a session. You can watch the session on your computer or mobile device, and pause, rewind, or replay a video at any time.

Practice Tasks

After each session, visit the **Your Turn** feature to perform the tasks and check your answers.

Training Tasks

Suppose the IT training manager wants to encourage team members to watch the Video Learning Sessions. To spark interest, she plans to post a set of VLS previews, which you will prepare. Each preview must include an overview of the session, a description of the main topics, and one or more screen examples from the video. To get you started, she provided a task list:

1. Select a Video Learning Session from this chapter. Launch the video and note the title, objectives, and total running time. Include this information in your preview.
2. Run though the session and find a segment that does a good job of explaining a specific skill or concept.
3. In the segment you selected, choose one or more specific screens and capture each screen image with the Windows Snipping Tool. To do this in Windows 7 or Windows Vista, click **Start,** and then type **Snipping Tool.** In Windows 8, you can display the **Start** menu, and then type **Snipping Tool.**
4. Paste the screen image into your preview and explain how it would help a viewer understand the topic. Also add your comments about the video, and why it would be important to an IT professional. Your preview should be well-organized and readable.

Learn It Online

In each chapter, you can use this feature to apply your knowledge and practice your skills. The exercises include Chapter Reinforcement Questions, Flash Cards, Practice Tests, and various games, such as *Who Wants To Be a Computer Genius?, Wheel of Terms, and the Crossword Puzzle Challenge.*

PHASE 2

SYSTEMS ANALYSIS

DELIVERABLE
System requirements document

TOOLKIT SUPPORT
Communication, CASE, and financial analysis tools

GOT MIS COURSEMATE?
Nine Video Learning Sessions explain modeling and financial analysis tools

As the Dilbert cartoon suggests, a successful project manager must determine the requirements before starting the design process, not the other way around. You will learn more about fact-finding and modeling system requirements in the systems analysis phase.

Systems analysis is the second of five phases in the systems development life cycle. In the previous phase, systems planning, you conducted a preliminary investigation to determine the project's feasibility. Now you will use requirements modeling, data and process modeling, and object modeling techniques to represent the new system. You also will consider various development strategies for the new system, and plan for the transition to systems design tasks. The deliverable for this phase is the system requirements document.

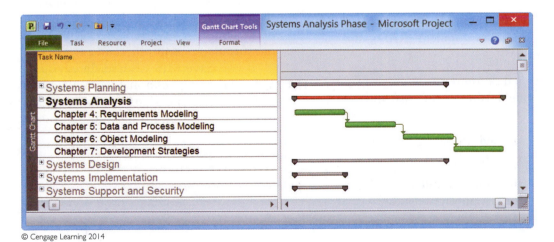

© Cengage Learning 2014

CHAPTER 4 Requirements Modeling

Chapter 4 is the first of four chapters in the systems analysis phase. This chapter describes the process of gathering facts about a systems project, preparing documentation, and creating models that will be used to design and develop the system.

INTRODUCTION

OBJECTIVES

When you finish this chapter, you will be able to:

- Describe systems analysis phase activities

- Explain joint application development (JAD), rapid application development (RAD), and agile methods

- Use a functional decomposition diagram (FDD) to model business functions and processes

- Describe the Unified Modeling Language (UML) and examples of UML diagrams

- List and describe system requirements, including outputs, inputs, processes, performance, and controls

- Explain the concept of scalability

- Use fact-finding techniques, including interviews, documentation review, observation, questionnaires, sampling, and research

- Define total cost of ownership (TCO)

- Conduct a successful interview

- Develop effective documentation methods to use during systems development

After an overview of the systems analysis phase, this chapter describes requirements modeling techniques and team-based methods that systems analysts use to visualize and document new systems. The chapter then discusses system requirements and fact-finding techniques, which include interviewing, documentation review, observation, surveys and questionnaires, sampling, and research.

If you have MIS CourseMate, you can view a Video Learning Session that explains how you can use a functional decomposition diagram (FDD) to model business functions and processes.

PREVIEW CASE: Mountain View College Bookstore

Background: Wendy Lee, manager of college services at Mountain View College, wants a new information system that will improve efficiency and customer service at the three college bookstores.

In this part of the case, Tina Allen (systems analyst) and David Conroe (student intern) are talking about requirements modeling tasks and concepts.

Participants:	Tina and David
Location:	Tina's office, Monday morning, October 1, 2013
Project status:	The project has advanced to the systems analysis phase; now, Tina and David will work on modeling, fact-finding, and the documentation they need for a requirements model
Discussion topics:	Modeling, team-based development strategies, fact-finding techniques, and documentation

Tina: Before we get started, let me tell you about a funny Dilbert© cartoon I saw this morning. It begins with Alice saying to a user "I can't design your software until you tell me **what** you want it to do." Instead of listing his requirements, he replies "What **can** it do?" At this point, she gets really mad, and says it can do **whatever** she designs it to do! In the final panel, he asks her, "Can you design it to tell me my requirements?"

David: *That's funny, but a little scary, too. Hope we don't run into a situation like that!*

Tina: Me, too. That's why we have to do a good job of creating a requirements model that will include all the outputs, inputs, processes, and controls. The model will consist of diagrams, charts, and documentation.

David: *How will we use the model?*

Tina: We'll study it carefully and review it frequently with system users.

David: *Who are the users?*

Tina: Users include bookstore staff, students, faculty members, and the college business office. External users might include textbook publishers and suppliers of bookstore merchandise. The main thing is to get input from each user group. Here's a task list to get us started:

Task Name
REQUIREMENTS MODELING
Review team-based fact-finding and development techniques
Learn to use the UML and functional decomposition diagrams
Develop a system requirements checklist with all required sections
Develop effective interviews, questionnaires, and sampling methods
Set up a requirements modeling documentation system

FIGURE 4-1   Typical requirements modeling task list.

© Cengage Learning 2014

Systems Analysis Phase Tasks

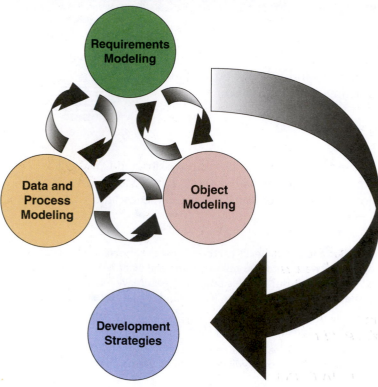

FIGURE 4-2 The systems analysis phase consists of requirements modeling, data and process modeling, object modeling, and consideration of development strategies. Notice that the systems analysis tasks are interactive, even though the waterfall model generally depicts sequential development.

© Cengage Learning 2014

SYSTEMS ANALYSIS PHASE OVERVIEW

The overall objective of the systems analysis phase is to understand the proposed project, ensure that it will support business requirements, and build a solid foundation for system development. In this phase, you use models and other documentation tools to visualize and describe the proposed system.

Systems Analysis Activities

The systems analysis phase includes the four main activities shown in Figure 4-2: requirements modeling, data and process modeling, object modeling, and consideration of development strategies.

Although the waterfall model shows sequential SDLC phases, it is not uncommon for several phases (or certain tasks within a phase) to interact during the development process, just as they would in an adaptive model. For example, this occurs whenever new facts are learned or system requirements change during the modeling process. Figure 4-2 shows typical interaction among the three modeling tasks: requirements modeling, data and process modeling, and object modeling.

REQUIREMENTS MODELING This chapter describes **requirements modeling**, which involves fact-finding to describe the current system and identification of the requirements for the new system, such as outputs, inputs, processes, performance, and security. **Outputs** refer to electronic or printed information produced by the system. **Inputs** refer to necessary data that enters the system, either manually or in an automated manner. **Processes** refer to the logical rules that are applied to transform the data into meaningful information. **Performance** refers to system characteristics such as speed, volume, capacity, availability, and reliability. **Security** refers to hardware, software, and procedural controls that safeguard and protect the system and its data from internal or external threats.

DATA AND PROCESS MODELING In Chapter 5, Data and Process Modeling, you will continue the modeling process by learning how to represent graphically system data and processes using traditional structured analysis techniques. As you learned in Chapter 1, structured analysis identifies the data flowing into a process, the business rules that transform the data, and the resulting output data flow.

OBJECT MODELING Chapter 6 discusses object modeling, which is another popular modeling technique. While structured analysis treats processes and data as separate components, object-oriented analysis (O-O) combines data and the processes that act on the data into things called objects. These objects represent actual people, things, transactions, and events that affect the system. During the system development process, analysts often use both modeling methods to gain as much information as possible.

DEVELOPMENT STRATEGIES In Chapter 7, Development Strategies, you will consider various development options and prepare for the transition to the systems design phase of the SDLC. You will learn about software trends, acquisition and development alternatives, outsourcing, and formally documenting requirements for the new system.

The deliverable, or end product, of the systems analysis phase is a **system requirements document,** which is an overall design for the new system. In addition, each activity within the systems analysis phase has an end product and one or more milestones. As you learned in Chapter 3, project managers use various tools and techniques to coordinate people, tasks, timetables, and budgets.

Systems Analysis Skills

You will need strong analytical and interpersonal skills to build an accurate model of the new system. Analytical skills enable you to identify a problem, evaluate the key elements, and develop a useful solution. Interpersonal skills are especially valuable to a systems analyst who must work with people at all organizational levels, balance conflicting needs of users, and communicate effectively.

Because information systems affect people throughout the company, you should consider team-oriented strategies as you begin the systems analysis phase.

Team-Based Techniques: JAD, RAD, and Agile Methods

The IT department's goal is to deliver the best possible information system, at the lowest possible cost, in the shortest possible time. To achieve the best results, system developers view users as partners in the development process. Greater user involvement usually results in better communication, faster development times, and more satisfied users.

The traditional model for systems development was an IT department that used structured analysis and consulted users only when their input or approval was needed. Although the IT staff still has a central role, and structured analysis remains a popular method of systems development, most IT managers invite system users to participate actively in various development tasks.

As you learned in Chapter 1, team-based approaches have been around for some time. A popular example is **joint application development (JAD),** which is a user-oriented technique for fact-finding and requirements modeling. Because it is not linked to a specific development methodology, systems developers use JAD whenever group input and interaction are desired.

Another popular user-oriented method is **rapid application development (RAD).** RAD resembles a condensed version of the entire SDLC, with users involved every step of the way. While JAD typically focuses only on fact-finding and requirements determination, RAD provides a fast-track approach to a full spectrum of system development tasks, including planning, design, construction, and implementation.

Finally, as you learned in Chapter 1, **agile methods** represent a recent trend that stresses intense interaction between system developers and users. JAD, RAD, and agile methods are discussed in the following sections.

JOINT APPLICATION DEVELOPMENT

Joint application development (JAD) is a popular fact-finding technique that brings users into the development process as active participants.

User Involvement

Users have a vital stake in an information system, and they should participate fully in the development process. Until recent years, the IT department usually had sole responsibility for systems development, and users had a relatively passive role. During the development process, the IT staff would collect information from users, define system requirements, and construct the new system. At various stages of the process, the IT staff might ask users to review the design, offer comments, and submit changes.

Today, users typically have a much more active role in systems development. IT professionals now recognize that successful systems must be user-oriented, and users need to be involved, formally or informally, at every stage of system development.

One popular strategy for user involvement is a JAD team approach, which involves a task force of users, managers, and IT professionals that works together to gather information, discuss business needs, and define the new system requirements.

JAD Participants and Roles

A JAD team usually meets over a period of days or weeks in a special conference room or at an off-site location. Either way, JAD participants should be insulated from the distraction of day-to-day operations. The objective is to analyze the existing system, obtain user input and expectations, and document user requirements for the new system.

The JAD group usually has a project leader, who needs strong interpersonal and organizational skills, and one or more members who document and record the results and decisions. Figure 4-3 describes typical JAD participants and their roles. IT staff members often serve as JAD project leaders, but that is not always the case. Systems analysts on the JAD team participate in discussions, ask questions, take notes, and provide support to the team. If CASE tools are available, analysts can develop models and enter documentation from the JAD session directly into the CASE tool.

A typical JAD session agenda is shown in Figure 4-4. The JAD process involves intensive effort by all team members. Because of the wide range of input and constant interaction among the participants, many companies believe that a JAD group produces the best possible definition of the new system.

JAD PARTICIPANT	ROLE
JAD project leader	Develops an agenda, acts as a facilitator, and leads the JAD session
Top management	Provides enterprise-level authorization and support for the project
Managers	Provide department-level support for the project and understanding of how the project must support business functions and requirements
Users	Provide operational-level input on current operations, desired changes, input and output requirements, user interface issues, and how the project will support day-to-day tasks
Systems analysts and other IT staff members	Provide technical assistance and resources for JAD team members on issues such as security, backup, hardware, software, and network capability
Recorder	Documents results of JAD sessions and works with systems analysts to build system models and develop CASE tool documentation

FIGURE 4-3 Typical JAD participants and roles.
© Cengage Learning 2014

Project leader	• Introduce all JAD team members • Discuss ground rules, goals, and objectives for the JAD sessions • Explain methods of documentation and use of CASE tools, if any
Top management (sometimes called the project owner or sponsor)	• Explain the reason for the project and express top management authorization and support
Project leader	• Provide overview of the current system and proposed project scope and constraints • Present outline of specific topics and issues to be investigated
Open discussion session, moderated by project leader	• Review the main business processes, tasks, user roles, input, and output • Identify specific areas of agreement or disagreement • Break team into smaller groups to study specific issues and assign group leaders
JAD team members working in smaller group sessions, supported by IT staff	• Discuss and document all system requirements • Develop models and prototypes
Group leaders	• Report on results and assigned tasks and topics • Present issues that should be addressed by the overall JAD team
Open discussion session, moderated by project leader	• Review reports from small group sessions • Reach consensus on main issues • Document all topics
Project leader	• Present overall recap of JAD session • Prepare report that will be sent to JAD team members

FIGURE 4-4 Typical agenda for a JAD session.
© Cengage Learning 2014

JAD Advantages and Disadvantages

Compared with traditional methods, JAD is more expensive and can be cumbersome if the group is too large relative to the size of the project. Many companies find, however, that JAD allows key users to participate effectively in the requirements modeling process. When users participate in the systems development process, they are more likely to feel a sense of ownership in the results, and support for the new system. When properly used, JAD can result in a more accurate statement of system requirements, a better understanding of common goals, and a stronger commitment to the success of the new system.

RAPID APPLICATION DEVELOPMENT

Rapid application development (RAD) is a team-based technique that speeds up information systems development and produces a functioning information system. Like JAD, RAD uses a group approach, but goes much further. While the end product of JAD is a requirements model, the end product of RAD is the new information system. RAD is a complete methodology, with a four-phase life cycle that parallels the traditional SDLC phases. Companies use RAD to reduce cost and development time, and increase the probability of success.

RAD relies heavily on prototyping and user involvement. The RAD process allows users to examine a working model as early as possible, determine if it meets their needs, and suggest necessary changes. Based on user input, the prototype is modified and the interactive process continues until the system is completely developed and users are satisfied. The project team uses CASE tools to build the prototypes and create a continuous stream of documentation.

RAD Phases and Activities

The RAD model consists of four phases: requirements planning, user design, construction, and cutover, as shown in Figure 4-5. Notice the continuous interaction between the user design and construction phases.

Requirements Planning Tasks
- Users, managers, and IT staff agree upon business needs, project scope, and systems requirements
- Obtain approval to continue

User Design Tasks
- Interact with users
- Build models and prototypes
- Conduct intensive JAD-type sessions

Construction Tasks
- Program and application development
- Coding
- Unit, integration, and system testing

Cutover Tasks
- Data conversion
- Full-scale testing
- System changeover
- User training

FIGURE 4-5 The four phases of the RAD model are requirements planning, user design, construction, and cutover. Notice the continuous interaction between the user design and construction phases.
© Cengage Learning 2014

REQUIREMENTS PLANNING The **requirements planning phase** combines elements of the systems planning and systems analysis phases of the SDLC. Users, managers, and IT staff members discuss and agree on business needs, project scope, constraints, and system requirements. The requirements planning phase ends when the team agrees on the key issues and obtains management authorization to continue.

USER DESIGN During the **user design phase**, users interact with systems analysts and develop models and prototypes that represent all system processes, outputs, and inputs. The RAD group or subgroups typically use a combination of JAD techniques and CASE tools to translate user needs into working models. User design is a continuous, interactive process that allows users to understand, modify, and eventually approve a working model of the system that meets their needs.

CONSTRUCTION   The **construction phase** focuses on program and application development tasks similar to the SDLC. In RAD, however, users continue to participate and still can suggest changes or improvements as actual screens or reports are developed.

CUTOVER   The **cutover phase** resembles the final tasks in the SDLC implementation phase, including data conversion, testing, changeover to the new system, and user training. Compared with traditional methods, the entire process is compressed. As a result, the new system is built, delivered, and placed in operation much sooner.

RAD Objectives

The main objective of all RAD approaches is to cut development time and expense by involving users in every phase of systems development. Because it is a continuous process, RAD allows the development team to make necessary modifications quickly, as the design evolves. In times of tight corporate budgets, it is especially important to limit the cost of changes that typically occur in a long, drawn-out development schedule.

   In addition to user involvement, a successful RAD team must have IT resources, skills, and management support. Because it is a dynamic, user-driven process, RAD is especially valuable when a company needs an information system to support a new business function. By obtaining user input from the beginning, RAD also helps a development team design a system that requires a highly interactive or complex user interface.

RAD Advantages and Disadvantages

RAD has advantages and disadvantages compared with traditional structured analysis methods. The primary advantage is that systems can be developed more quickly with significant cost savings. A disadvantage is that RAD stresses the mechanics of the system itself and does not emphasize the company's strategic business needs. The risk is that a system might work well in the short term, but the corporate and long-term objectives for the system might not be met. Another potential disadvantage is that the accelerated time cycle might allow less time to develop quality, consistency, and design standards. RAD can be an attractive alternative, however, if an organization understands the possible risks.

AGILE METHODS

In Chapter 1, you learned that agile methods attempt to develop a system incrementally, by building a series of prototypes and constantly adjusting them to user requirements. As the agile process continues, developers revise, extend, and merge earlier versions into the final product. An agile approach emphasizes continuous feedback, and each incremental step is affected by what was learned in the prior steps.

   As agile methods become more popular, a large community of agile-related software and services has evolved. For example, Visual Paradigm offers Agilian, which includes a set of agile modeling tools, as shown in Figure 4-6 on the next page. The Agilian modeling toolset includes support for many modeling tools, such as the Unified Modeling Language, entity-relationship diagrams, data flow diagrams, and business process modeling, among others. Agilian's interface is similar to the Zachman Framework, which is described later in this chapter.

   Some agile developers prefer not to use CASE tools at all, and rely instead on whiteboard displays and arrangements of movable sticky notes. This approach, they believe, reinforces the agile strategy: simple, rapid, flexible, and user-oriented.

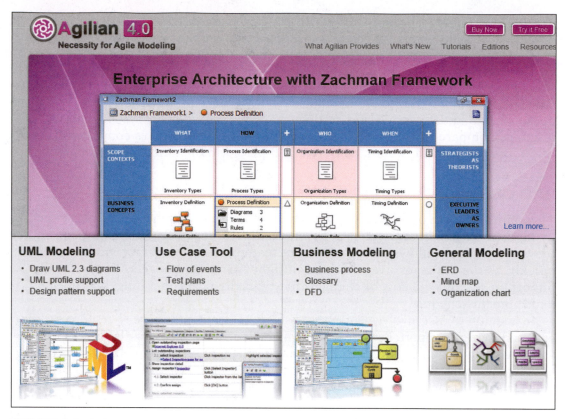

FIGURE 4-6   Agilian supports various modeling tools, such as the Unified Modeling Language, use cases, and business process modeling, among others.

© 1999–2011 by Visual Paradigm

Scrum is another agile approach. The name comes from the rugby term *scrum*, where team members lunge at each other to achieve their objectives, as shown in Figure 4-7. The systems development version of Scrum involves the same intense interaction, though it is more mental than physical. In a Scrum session, agile team members play specific roles, including colorful designations such as *pigs* or *chickens*. These roles are based on the old joke about the pig and chicken who discuss a restaurant where ham and eggs would be served. However, the pig declines, because that role would require a total commitment, while for the chicken, it would only be a contribution.

In the agile world, the *pigs* include the product owner, the facilitator, and the development team; while the *chickens* include users, other stakeholders, and managers. Scrum sessions have specific guidelines that emphasize time blocks, interaction, and team-based activities that result in deliverable software. An agile team uses a series of scrums to pause the action and allow the players to reset the game plan, which remains in effect until the next scrum.

Agile Method Advantages and Disadvantages

Agile, or adaptive, methods are very flexible and efficient in dealing with change. They are popular because they stress team interaction and reflect a set of community-based values. Also, frequent deliverables constantly validate the project and reduce risk.

However, some potential problems exist. For example, team members need a high level of technical and interpersonal skills. Also, a lack of structure and documentation can introduce risk factors. Finally, the overall project may be subject to significant change in scope as user requirements continue to evolve during the project.

FIGURE 4-7   In a rugby scrum, team members prepare to lunge at each other to achieve their objectives.
© fotograf.lv / Shutterstock.com

CASE IN POINT 4.1: NORTH HILLS COLLEGE

North Hills College has decided to implement a new registration system that will allow students to register online, as well as in person. As IT manager, you decide to set up a JAD session to help define the requirements for the new system. The North Hills organization is fairly typical, with administrative staff that includes a registrar, a student support and services team, a business office, an IT group, and a number of academic departments. Using this information, you start work on a plan to carry out the JAD session. Who would you invite to the session, and why? What would be your agenda for the session, and what would take place at each stage of the session?

MODELING TOOLS AND TECHNIQUES

Models help users, managers, and IT professionals understand the design of a system. Modeling involves graphical methods and nontechnical language that represent the system at various stages of development. During requirements modeling, you can use various tools to describe business processes, requirements, and user interaction with the system.

In Chapter 1, you learned about CASE tools that offer powerful modeling features. CASE tool modeling is discussed in detail in Part B of the Systems Analyst's Toolkit.

Systems analysts use modeling and fact-finding interactively — first they build fact-finding results into models, then they study the models to determine whether additional fact-finding is needed. To help them understand system requirements, analysts use functional decomposition diagrams, business process models, data flow diagrams, and Unified Modeling Language diagrams. Any of these diagrams can be created with CASE tools or stand-alone drawing tools if desired.

Video Learning Session
Functional Decomposition Diagrams

If you have an MIS CourseMate access code, you can launch interactive Video Learning Sessions to help you understand systems development concepts and practice your skills. You can watch the video on your computer or mobile device, and pause, rewind, or replay the session at any time. To log on to the MIS CourseMate site at **www.cengagebrain.com**, you must create a student account and then register this book.

This session is about functional decomposition diagrams (FDDs). You'll learn about FDDs and why they are important, how to use FDDs to model business function and processes, and how to use CASE tools to create FDDs.

© craftvision/iStockphoto

Functional Decomposition Diagrams

A **functional decomposition diagram (FDD)** is a top-down representation of a function or process. Using an FDD, an analyst can show business functions and break them down into lower-level functions and processes. Creating an FDD is similar to drawing an organization chart — you start at the top and work your way down. Figure 4-8 shows an FDD of a library system drawn with the Visible Analyst CASE tool. FDDs can be used at several stages of systems development. During

FIGURE 4-8 This Visible Analyst FDD shows a library system with five top-level functions. The Library Operations function includes two additional levels of processes and subprocesses.

Screenshot used with permission from Visible Systems Corporation.

requirements modeling, analysts use FDDs to model business functions and show how they are organized into lower-level processes. Those processes translate into program modules during application development.

Business Process Modeling

As you learned in Chapter 1, a **business process model (BPM)** describes one or more business processes, such as handling an airline reservation, filling a product order, or updating a customer account. During requirements modeling, analysts often create models that use a standard language called **business process modeling notation (BPMN)**. BPMN includes various shapes and symbols to represent events, processes, and workflows.

When you create a business process model using a CASE tool such as Visible Analyst, your diagram automatically becomes part of the overall model. In the example shown in Figure 4-9, using BPMN terminology, the overall diagram is called a **pool**, and the designated customer areas are called **swim lanes**. Integrating BPM into the CASE development process leads to faster results, fewer errors, and reduced cost. Part B of the Systems Analyst's Toolkit describes business process modeling in more detail.

FIGURE 4-9   Using the Visible Analyst CASE tool, an analyst can create a business process diagram. The overall diagram is called a pool, and the two separate customer areas are called swim lanes.
Screenshot used with permission from Visible Systems Corporation.

Data Flow Diagrams

Working from a functional decomposition diagram, analysts can create **data flow diagrams (DFDs)** to show how the system stores, processes, and transforms data. The DFD in Figure 4-10 describes adding and removing books, which is a function shown in the Library Management diagram in Figure 4-8. Notice that the two shapes in the DFD represent processes, each with various inputs and outputs. Additional levels of information and detail are depicted in other, related DFDs. Data and process modeling is described in detail in Chapter 5.

Unified Modeling Language

The **Unified Modeling Language (UML)** is a widely used method of visualizing and documenting software systems design. UML uses object-oriented design concepts, but it is independent of any specific programming language and can be used to describe business processes and requirements generally.

UML provides various graphical tools, such as use case diagrams and sequence diagrams. During requirements modeling, a systems analyst can utilize the UML to represent the information system from a user's viewpoint. Use case diagrams, sequence diagrams, and other UML

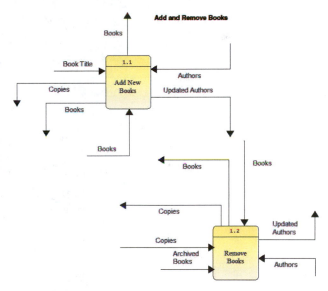

FIGURE 4-10   This Visible Analyst DFD shows how books are added and removed in a library system.
Screenshot used with permission from Visible Systems Corporation.

concepts are discussed in more detail in Chapter 6, along with other object-oriented analysis concepts. A brief description of each technique follows.

USE CASE DIAGRAMS   During requirements modeling, systems analysts and users work together to document requirements and model system functions. A **use case diagram** visually represents the interaction between users and the information system. In a use case diagram, the user becomes an **actor**, with a specific role that describes how he or she interacts with the system. Systems analysts can draw use case diagrams freehand or use CASE tools that integrate the use cases into the overall system design.

Figure 4-11 on the next page shows a simple use case diagram for a sales system where the actor is a customer and the use case involves a credit card validation that is performed by the system. Because use cases depict the system through the eyes of a user, common business language can be used to describe the transactions. For example,

FIGURE 4-11 This Visible Analyst use case diagram shows a sales system, where the actor is a customer and the use case is a credit card validation.
Screenshot used with permission from Visible Systems Corporation.

Name of Use Case:	Credit card validation process
Actor:	Customer
Description:	Describes the credit card validation process
Successful Completion:	1. Customer clicks the input selector and enters credit card number and expiration date 2. System verifies card 3. System sends authorization message
Alternative:	1. Customer clicks the input selector and enters credit card number and expiration date 2. System rejects card 3. System sends rejection message
Precondition:	Customer has selected at least one item and has proceeded to checkout area
Postcondition:	Credit card information has been validated Customer can continue with order
Assumptions:	None

FIGURE 4-12 This table documents the credit card validation use case shown in Figure 4-11.
© Cengage Learning 2014

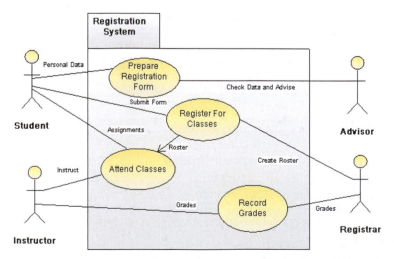

FIGURE 4-13 This Visible Analyst use case diagram shows a student records system.

Screenshot used with permission from Visible Systems Corporation.

Figure 4-12 shows a table that documents the credit card validation use case, and Figure 4-13 shows a student records system, with several use cases and actors.

SEQUENCE DIAGRAMS A sequence **diagram** shows the timing of interactions between objects as they occur. A systems analyst might use a sequence diagram to show all possible outcomes, or focus on a single scenario. Figure 4-14 shows a simple sequence diagram of a successful credit card validation. The interaction proceeds from top to bottom along a vertical time-line, while the horizontal arrows represent messages from one object to another.

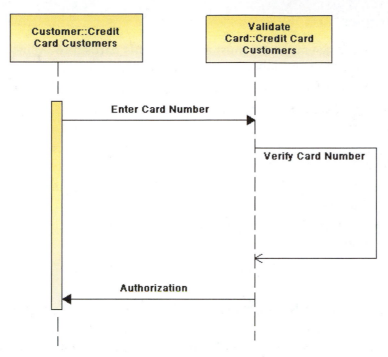

FIGURE 4-14   This Visible Analyst sequence diagram shows a credit card validation process.

Screenshot used with permission from Visible Systems Corporation.

SYSTEM REQUIREMENTS CHECKLIST

During requirements modeling, systems developers must identify and describe all system requirements. A **system requirement** is a characteristic or feature that must be included in an information system to satisfy business requirements and be acceptable to users. System requirements serve as benchmarks to measure the overall acceptability of the finished system.

System requirements fall into five general categories: outputs, inputs, processes, performance, and controls. Typical examples of system requirements for each category are listed below.

Output Examples

✓ The Web site must report online volume statistics every four hours, and hourly during peak periods.

✓ The inventory system must produce a daily report showing the part number, description, quantity on hand, quantity allocated, quantity available, and unit cost of all sorted by part number.

✓ The contact management system must generate a daily reminder list for all sales reps.

✓ The purchasing system must provide suppliers with up-to-date specifications.

✓ The sales tracking system must produce a daily fast-moving-item report, listing all products that exceed the forecasted sales volume grouped by style, color, size, and reorder status.

✓ The customer analysis system must produce a quarterly report that identifies changes in ordering patterns or trends with statistical comparisons to the previous four quarters.

Input Examples

✓ Manufacturing employees must swipe their ID cards into online data collection terminals that record labor costs and calculate production efficiency.

✓ The department head must enter overtime hours on a separate screen.

✓ Student grades must be entered on machine-scannable forms prepared by the instructor.

✓ Each input form must include date, time, product code, customer number, and quantity.

✓ Data entry screens must be uniform, except for background color, which can be changed by the user.

✓ A data entry person at the medical group must input patient services into the billing system.

Process Examples

✓ The student records system must calculate the GPA at the end of each semester.

✓ As the final step in year-end processing, the payroll system must update employee salaries, bonuses, and benefits and produce tax data required by the IRS.

✓ The warehouse distribution system must analyze daily orders and create a routing pattern for delivery trucks that maximizes efficiency and reduces unnecessary mileage.

✓ The human resources system must interface properly with the existing payroll system.

✓ The equipment rental system must not execute new rental transactions for customers who have overdue accounts.

✓ The prescription system must automatically generate an insurance claim form.

Performance Examples

✓ The system must support 25 users online simultaneously.

✓ Response time must not exceed four seconds.

✓ The system must be operational seven days a week, 365 days a year.

✓ The accounts receivable system must prepare customer statements by the third business day of the following month.

✓ The student records system must produce class lists within five hours after the end of registration.

✓ The online inventory control system must flag all low-stock items within one hour after the quantity falls below a predetermined minimum.

Control Examples

✓ The system must provide logon security at the operating system level and at the application level.

✓ An employee record must be added, changed, or deleted only by a member of the human resources department.

✓ The system must maintain separate levels of security for users and the system administrator.

✓ All transactions must have audit trails.

✓ The manager of the sales department must approve orders that exceed a customer's credit limit.

✓ The system must create an error log file that includes the error type, description, and time.

FUTURE GROWTH, COSTS, AND BENEFITS

In addition to the system requirements, systems analysts must consider scalability, which determines how a system will handle future growth and demands, and the total cost of ownership, which includes all future operational and support costs.

Scalability

Scalability refers to a system's ability to handle increased business volume and transactions in the future. Because it will have a longer useful life, a scalable system offers a better return on the initial investment.

To evaluate scalability, you need information about projected future volume for all outputs, inputs, and processes. For example, for a Web-based order processing system, you would need to know the maximum projected number of concurrent users, the periods of peak online activity, the number and types of data items required for each transaction, and the method of accessing and updating customer files.

Even to print customer statements, you need to know the number of active accounts and have a forecast for one, two, or five years because that information affects future hardware decisions. In addition, with realistic volume projections, you can provide reliable cost estimates for related expenses, such as postage and online charges.

Similarly, to ensure that a Web-based hotel reservation system is sufficiently scalable, you would need to project activity levels for several years of operation. For example, you might forecast the frequency of online queries about room availability and estimate the time required for each query and the average response time. With that information, you could estimate server transaction volume and network requirements.

Transaction volume has a significant impact on operating costs. When volume exceeds a system's limitations, maintenance costs increase sharply. Volume can change dramatically if a company expands or enters a new line of business. For example, a new Internet-based marketing effort might require an additional server and 24-hour technical support.

Data storage also is an important scalability issue. You need to determine how much data storage is required currently and predict future needs based on system activity and growth. Those requirements affect hardware, software, and network bandwidth needed to maintain system performance. You also must consider data retention requirements and determine whether data can be deleted or archived on a specific timetable.

Total Cost of Ownership

In addition to direct costs, systems developers must identify and document indirect expenses that contribute to the **total cost of ownership (TCO)**. TCO is especially important if the development team is assessing several alternatives. After considering the indirect costs, which are not always apparent, a system that seems inexpensive initially might actually turn out to be the most costly choice. One problem is that cost estimates tend to understate indirect costs such as user support and downtime productivity losses. Even if accurate figures are unavailable, systems analysts should try to identify indirect costs and include them in TCO estimates.

TOOLKIT TIME

The financial analysis tools in Part C of the Systems Analyst's Toolkit can help you analyze project costs, benefits, and economic feasibility. To learn more about these tools, turn to Part C of the four-part Toolkit that follows Chapter 12.

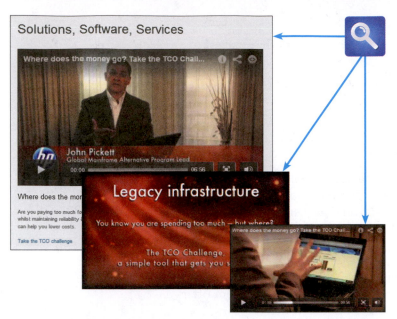

FIGURE 4-15 HP urges viewers to Take the TCO Challenge. Interested viewers can download a step-by-step TCO analysis that HP created.

© 2012 Hewlett-Packard Development Company, L.P.

Because cost control is so important, vendors often claim that their products or services will reduce TCO significantly. For example, HP reaches out to potential customers with online videos, like the one shown in Figure 4-15, in which HP urges *viewers to Take the TCO Challenge.* The video relates to legacy infrastructure costs, and asks a provocative question: *"You know you are spending too much – but where?"* To answer the question, interested viewers can download a step-by-step TCO analysis that HP created.

Microsoft has developed a method for measuring total costs and benefits, called **Rapid Economic Justification (REJ).** According to Microsoft, REJ is a framework to analyze and optimize IT investments. The basic REJ model shown in Figure 4-16 emphasizes business improvements that generate specific financial value.

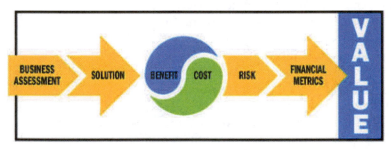

FIGURE 4-16 Microsoft claims that its Rapid Economic Justification (REJ) can help optimize IT investments.

Screenshot used with permission from Microsoft.

FACT-FINDING

Now that you understand the categories of system requirements, scalability, and TCO, the next step is to begin collecting information. Whether you are working on your own or as a member of a JAD team, during requirements modeling you will use various fact-finding techniques, including interviews, document review, observation, surveys and questionnaires, sampling, and research.

Fact-Finding Overview

Although software can help you to gather and analyze facts, no program actually performs fact-finding for you. First, you must identify the information you need. Typically, you begin by asking a series of questions, such as these:

- What business functions are supported by the current system?
- What strategic objectives and business requirements must be supported by the new system?
- What are the benefits and TCO of the proposed system?
- What transactions will the system process?
- What information do users and managers need from the system?
- Must the new system interface with legacy systems?

- What procedures could be eliminated by business process reengineering?
- What security issues exist?
- What risks are acceptable?
- What budget and timetable constraints will affect system development?

To obtain answers to these questions, you develop a fact-finding plan, which can involve another series of questions (*who, what, where, when,* and *how*), or use a more structured approach such as the Zachman Framework, which is explained in a following section. Either way, you will develop a strategy, carry out fact-finding techniques, document the results, and prepare a system requirements document, which is presented to management.

Who, What, Where, When, How, and Why?

Fact-finding involves answers to five familiar questions: *who, what, where, when,* and *how*. For each of those questions, you also must ask another very important question: *why*. Some examples of these questions are:

1. *Who?* Who performs each of the procedures within the system? Why? Are the correct people performing the activity? Could other people perform the tasks more effectively?

2. *What?* What is being done? What procedures are being followed? Why is that process necessary? Often, procedures are followed for many years and no one knows why. You should question why a procedure is being followed at all.

3. *Where?* Where are operations being performed? Why? Where could they be performed? Could they be performed more efficiently elsewhere?

4. *When?* When is a procedure performed? Why is it being performed at this time? Is this the best time?

5. *How?* How is a procedure performed? Why is it performed in that manner? Could it be performed better, more efficiently, or less expensively in some other manner?

There is a difference between asking what *is* being done and what *could* or *should* be done. The systems analyst first must understand the current situation. Only then can he or she tackle the question of what *should* be done. Figure 4-17 lists the basic questions and when they should be asked. Notice that the first two columns relate to the current system, but the third column focuses on the proposed system.

CURRENT SYSTEM		PROPOSED SYSTEM
Who does it?	Why does this person do it?	Who should do it?
What is done?	Why is it done?	What should be done?
Where is it done?	Why is it done there?	Where should it be done?
When is it done?	Why is it done then?	When should it be done?
How is it done?	Why is it done this way?	How should it be done?

FIGURE 4-17 Sample questions during requirements modeling as the focus shifts from the current system to the proposed system.

© Cengage Learning 2014

The Zachman Framework

In the 1980s, John Zachman observed how industries such as architecture and construction handled complex projects, and he suggested that the same ideas could be applied to information systems development. His concept, the **Zachman Framework for Enterprise Architecture**, is a model that asks the traditional fact-finding questions in a systems development context, as shown in Figure 4-18. The Zachman Framework is a popular approach, and the Visible Analyst CASE tool now includes a Zachman Framework interface that allows users to view a systems project from different perspectives and levels of detail. The Zachman Framework helps managers and users understand the model and ensures that overall business goals translate into successful IT projects.

FIGURE 4-18   Visible Analyst uses the Zachman Framework for Enterprise Architecture. The Zachman concept presents traditional fact-finding questions in a systems development context.
Screenshot used with permission from Visible Systems Corporation.

INTERVIEWS

Interviewing is an important fact-finding tool during the systems analysis phase. An **interview** is a planned meeting during which you obtain information from another person. You must have the skills needed to plan, conduct, document, and evaluate interviews successfully.

After you identify the information you need, as described earlier in the chapter, you can begin the interviewing process, which consists of seven steps for each interview:

1. Determine the people to interview.
2. Establish objectives for the interview.
3. Develop interview questions.
4. Prepare for the interview.
5. Conduct the interview.
6. Document the interview.
7. Evaluate the interview.

Step 1: Determine the People to Interview

To get an accurate picture, you must select the right people to interview and ask them the right questions. During the preliminary investigation, you talked mainly to middle managers or department heads. Now, during the systems analysis phase, you might need to interview people from all levels of the organization.

Although you can select your interview candidates from the formal organization charts that you reviewed earlier, you also must consider any informal structures that exist in the organization. Informal structures usually are based on interpersonal relationships and can develop from previous work assignments, physical proximity, unofficial procedures, or personal relationships such as the informal gathering shown in Figure 4-19. In an **informal structure**, some people have more influence or knowledge than appears on an organization chart. Your knowledge of the company's formal and informal structures helps you determine the people to interview during the systems analysis phase.

Should you interview several people at the same time? Group interviews can save time and provide an opportunity to observe interaction among the participants. Group interviews also can present problems. One person might dominate the conversation, even when questions are addressed specifically to others. Organization level also can present a problem because the presence of senior managers in an interview might prevent lower-level employees from expressing themselves candidly.

Step 2: Establish Objectives for the Interview

After deciding on the people to interview, you must establish objectives for the session. First, you should determine the general areas to be discussed, and then list the facts you want to gather. You also should try to solicit ideas, suggestions, and opinions during the interview.

The objectives of an interview depend on the role of the person being interviewed. Upper-level managers can provide the big picture and help you to understand the system as a whole. Specific details about operations and business processes are best learned from people who actually work with the system on a daily basis.

In the early stages of systems analysis, interviews usually are general. As the fact-finding process continues, however, the interviews focus more on specific topics. Interview objectives also vary at different stages of the investigation. By setting specific objectives, you create a framework that helps you decide what questions to ask and how to phrase the questions.

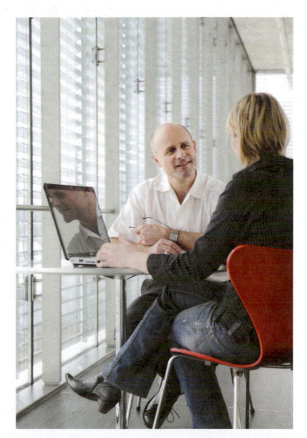

FIGURE 4-19 When setting up interviews, an analyst should look outside a formal organization chart to identify people who might provide valuable information.
© mammamart/iStockphoto

Step 3: Develop Interview Questions

Creating a standard list of interview questions helps to keep you on track and avoid unnecessary tangents. Also, if you interview several people who perform the same job, a standard question list allows you to compare their answers. Although you have a list of specific questions, you might decide to depart from it because an answer to one question leads to another topic that you want to pursue. That question or topic then should be included in a revised set of questions used to conduct future interviews. If the question proves to be extremely important, you may need to return to a previous interviewee to query him or her on the topic.

The interview should consist of several different kinds of questions: open-ended, closed-ended, or questions with a range of responses. When you phrase your questions, you should avoid **leading questions** that suggest or favor a particular reply. For example, rather than asking, "What advantages do you see in the proposed system?" you might ask, "Do you see any advantages in the proposed system?"

OPEN-ENDED QUESTIONS   **Open-ended questions** encourage spontaneous and unstructured responses. Such questions are useful when you want to understand a larger process or draw out the interviewee's opinions, attitudes, or suggestions. Here are some examples of open-ended questions: What are users saying about the new system? How is this task performed? Why do you perform the task that way? How are the checks reconciled? What added features would you like to have in the new billing system? Also, you can use an open-ended question to probe further by asking: Is there anything else you can tell me about this topic?

CLOSED-ENDED QUESTIONS   **Closed-ended questions** limit or restrict the response. You use closed-ended questions when you want information that is more specific or when you need to verify facts. Examples of closed-ended questions include the following: How many personal computers do you have in this department? Do you review the reports before they are sent out? How many hours of training does a clerk receive? Is the calculation procedure described in the manual? How many customers ordered products from the Web site last month?

RANGE-OF-RESPONSE QUESTIONS   **Range-of-response questions** are closed-ended questions that ask the person to evaluate something by providing limited answers to specific responses or on a numeric scale. This method makes it easier to tabulate the answers and interpret the results. Range-of-response questions might include these: On a scale of 1 to 10, with 1 the lowest and 10 the highest, how effective was your training? How would you rate the severity of the problem: low, medium, or high? Is the system shutdown something that occurs never, sometimes, often, usually, or always?

Step 4: Prepare for the Interview

After setting the objectives and developing the questions, you must prepare for the interview. Careful preparation is essential because an interview is an important meeting and not just a casual chat. When you schedule the interview, suggest a specific day and time and let the interviewee know how long you expect the meeting to last. It is also a good idea to send an e-mail or place a reminder call the day before the interview.

Remember that the interview is an interruption of the other person's routine, so you should limit the interview to no more than one hour. If business pressures force a postponement of the meeting, you should schedule another appointment as soon as it is convenient. Remember to keep department managers informed of your meetings with their staff members. Sending a message to each department manager listing your planned appointments is a good way to keep them informed. Figure 4-20 is an example of such a message.

You should send a list of topics to an interviewee several days before the meeting, especially when detailed information is needed, so the person can prepare for the interview and minimize the need for a follow-up meeting. Figure 4-21 shows a sample message that lists specific questions and confirms the date, time, location, purpose, and anticipated duration of the interview.

If you have questions about documents, ask the interviewee to have samples available at the meeting. Your advance memo should include a list of the documents you want to discuss, if you know what they are. Also, you can make a general request for documents, as the analyst did in her e-mail shown in Figure 4-21.

Two schools of thought exist about the best location for an interview. Some analysts believe that interviews should take place in the interviewee's office, whereas other analysts feel that a neutral location such as a conference room is better.

Supporters of interviews in the interviewee's office believe that is the best location because it makes the interviewee feel comfortable during the meeting. A second argument in favor of the interviewee's office is that the office is where he or she has the easiest access to supporting material that might be needed during the discussion. If you provide a complete list of topics in advance, however, the interviewee can bring the necessary items to a conference room or other location.

Supporters of neutral locations stress the importance of keeping interruptions to a minimum so both people can concentrate fully. In addition, an interview that is free of interruptions takes less time. If the meeting does take place in the interviewee's office, you should suggest tactfully that all calls be held until the conclusion of the interview.

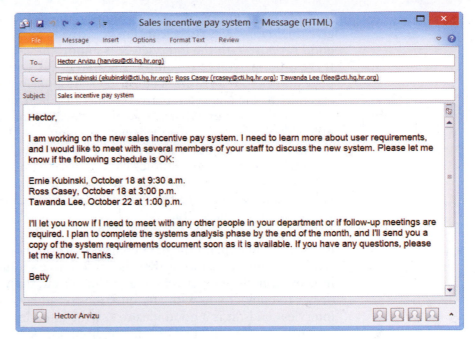

FIGURE 4-20 Sample message to a department head about interviews.
© Cengage Learning 2014

FIGURE 4-21 Sample message to confirm an interview.
© Cengage Learning 2014

Step 5: Conduct the Interview

After determining the people to interview, setting your objectives, and preparing the questions, you should develop a specific plan for the meeting. When conducting an interview, you should begin by introducing yourself, describing the project, and explaining your interview objectives.

During the interview, ask questions in the order in which you prepared them, and give the interviewee sufficient time to provide thoughtful answers. Establishing a good rapport with the interviewee is important, especially if this is your first meeting. If the other person feels comfortable and at ease, you probably will receive more complete and candid answers. Your primary responsibility during an interview is to listen carefully to the answers. Analysts sometimes hear only what they expect to hear. You must concentrate on what is said and notice any nonverbal communication that takes place. This process is called **engaged listening**.

After asking a question, allow the person enough time to think about the question and arrive at an answer. Studies have shown that the maximum pause during a conversation is usually three to five seconds. After that interval, one person will begin talking. You will need to be patient and practice your skills in many actual interview situations to be successful.

When you finish asking your questions, summarize the main points covered in the interview and explain the next course of action. For example, mention that you will send a follow-up memo or that the interviewee should get back to you with certain information. When you conclude the interview, thank the person and encourage him or her to contact you with any questions or additional comments. Also, when the interview ends, it is a good idea to ask the interviewee whether he or she can suggest any additional topics that should be discussed.

After an interview, you should summarize the session and seek a confirmation from the other person. By stating your understanding of the discussion, the interviewee can respond and correct you, if necessary. One approach is to rephrase the interviewee's answers. For example, you can say, "If I understand you correctly, you are saying that ..." and then reiterate the information given by the interviewee.

Step 6: Document the Interview

Although taking notes during an interview has both advantages and disadvantages, the accepted view is that note taking should be kept to a minimum. Although you should write down a few notes to jog your memory after the interview, you should avoid writing everything that is said. Too much writing distracts the other person and makes it harder to establish a good rapport.

After conducting the interview, you must record the information quickly. You should set aside time right after the meeting to record the facts and evaluate the information. For that reason, try not to schedule back-to-back interviews. Studies have shown that 50 percent of a conversation is forgotten within 30 minutes. You, therefore, should use your notes to record the facts immediately so you will not forget them. You can summarize the facts by preparing a narrative describing what took place or by recording the answers you received next to each question on your prepared question list.

Small, portable recorders are effective tools for interviews, but some people are uncomfortable when they are used. Before using a recorder, you should discuss its use with the interviewee. Assure the interviewee that you will erase the recording after you transcribe your notes and that you will stop anytime during the interview at his or her request. If you ask sensitive questions or the interviewee wants to answer a question without being recorded, explain that you will turn off the recorder for a period of time during the interview.

Instead of using a traditional recorder that calls attention to its presence, an interviewer can use built-in audio (or even video) recording features on a notebook or mobile device. Also, as the Documentation section on page 160 points out, an interviewer can use powerful information management software, such as Microsoft OneNote, to record the meeting, store the results, and create a searchable file for easy access.

Whether or not you record the meeting, you should listen carefully to the interviewee's responses so you can ask good follow-up questions. Otherwise, you might have to return for a second visit to ask the questions you missed the first time. Also, remember that each recorded interview takes twice the amount of time because you must listen to or view the recorded meeting again after conducting the interview itself.

After the meeting, send a memo to the interviewee expressing your appreciation for his or her time and cooperation. In the memo, you should note the date, time, location, purpose of the interview, and the main points you discussed so the interviewee has a written summary and can offer additions or corrections.

Step 7: Evaluate the Interview

In addition to recording the facts obtained in an interview, try to identify any possible biases. For example, an interviewee who tries to protect his or her own area or function might give incomplete answers or refrain from volunteering information. Or, an interviewee with strong opinions about the current or future system might distort the facts. Some interviewees might answer your questions in an attempt to be helpful even though they do not have the necessary experience to provide accurate information.

CASE IN POINT 4.2: DEEP RIVER COLLEGE

Deep River College is a two-year school in Southern California. Twice a year, the fund-raising office at Deep River mails requests for donations to the alumni. The staff uses a word processing program and a personal information database to create personalized letters. Data on past contributions and other alumni information, however, is stored manually. The dean, Alexandra Ali, recently submitted a systems request asking the college's IT department to develop a computerized alumni information system. The school does not have a formal systems review committee, and each department has an individual budget for information services.

Eddie Bateman, a systems analyst, performed a preliminary investigation and he concluded that the system met all the feasibility tests. After reading his report, Alexandra asked him to proceed with the systems analysis phase. Eddie has scheduled an interview with her, and he has asked you to help him prepare for the meeting. Specifically, he wants you to list all the topics he should cover during the interview. Eddie also wants you to prepare a list of specific questions that he should ask. Be sure to include open-ended, closed-ended, and range-of-response questions.

Unsuccessful Interviews

No matter how well you prepare for interviews, some are not successful. One of the main reasons could be that you and the interviewee did not get along well. Such a situation can be caused by several factors. For example, a misunderstanding or personality conflict could affect the interview negatively, or the interviewee might be afraid that the new system will eliminate or change his or her job.

In other cases, the interviewee might give only short or incomplete responses to your open-ended questions. If so, you should switch to closed-ended questions or questions with a range of responses, or try rephrasing your open-ended questions into those types of questions. If that still does not help, you should find a tactful way to conclude the meeting.

Continuing an unproductive interview is difficult. The interviewee could be more cooperative later, or you might find the information you seek elsewhere. If failure to obtain specific information will jeopardize the success of the project, inform your supervisor, who can help you decide what action to take. Your supervisor might contact the interviewee's supervisor, ask another systems analyst to interview the person, or find some other way to get the needed information.

CASE IN POINT 4.3: FastPak Overnight Package System

FastPak, the nation's fourth-largest overnight package system, is headquartered in Los Angeles, California. Jesse Evans is a systems analyst on an IT team that is studying ways to update FastPak's package tracking system. Jesse prepared well for her interview with Jason Tanya, FastPak's executive vice president. Mr. Tanya did not ask his assistant to hold his calls during the meeting, however. After several interruptions, Jesse tactfully suggested that she could come back another time, or perhaps that Mr. Tanya might ask his assistant to hold his calls. "No way," he replied. "I'm a very busy man and we'll just have to fit this in as we can, even if it takes all day." Jesse was unprepared for his response. What are her options? Is an analyst always in control of this kind of situation? Why or why not?

OTHER FACT-FINDING TECHNIQUES

In addition to interviewing, systems analysts use other fact-finding techniques, including document review, observation, questionnaires and surveys, sampling, and research. Such techniques are used before interviewing begins to obtain a good overview and to help develop better interview questions.

Document Review

Document review can help you understand how the current system is supposed to work. Remember that system documentation sometimes is out of date. Forms can change or be discontinued, and documented procedures often are modified or eliminated. You should obtain copies of actual forms and operating documents currently in use. You also should review blank copies of forms, as well as samples of actual completed forms. You usually can obtain document samples during interviews with the people who perform that procedure. If the system uses a software package, you should review the documentation for that software.

Observation

The **observation** of current operating procedures is another fact-finding technique. Seeing the system in action gives you additional perspective and a better understanding of system procedures. Personal observation also allows you to verify statements made in interviews and determine whether procedures really operate as they are described. Through observation, you might discover that neither the system documentation nor the interview statements are accurate.

Personal observation also can provide important advantages as the development process continues. For example, recommendations often are better accepted when they are based on personal observation of actual operations. Observation also can provide the knowledge needed to test or install future changes and can help build relationships with the users who will work with the new system.

Plan your observations in advance by preparing a checklist of specific tasks you want to observe and questions you want to ask. Consider the following issues when you prepare your list:

1. Ask sufficient questions to ensure that you have a complete understanding of the present system operation. A primary goal is to identify the methods of handling situations that are not covered by standard operating procedures. For example, what happens in a payroll system if an employee loses a time card? What is the procedure if an employee starts a shift 10 minutes late but then works 20 minutes overtime? Often, the rules for exceptions such as these are not written or formalized; therefore, you must try to document any procedures for handling exceptions.

2. Observe all the steps in a transaction and note the documents, inputs, outputs, and processes involved.

3. Examine each form, record, and report. Determine the purpose each item of information serves.

4. Consider each user who works with the system and the following questions: What information does that person receive from other people? What information does this person generate? How is the information communicated? How often do interruptions occur? How much downtime occurs? How much support does the user require, and who provides it?

5. Talk to the people who receive current reports to see whether the reports are complete, timely, accurate, and in a useful form. Ask whether information can be eliminated or improved and whether people would like to receive additional information.

As you observe people at work, as shown in Figure 4-22, consider a factor called the **Hawthorne Effect**. The name comes from a well-known study performed in the Hawthorne plant of the Western Electric Company in the 1920s. The purpose of the study was to determine how various changes in the work environment would affect employee productivity. The surprising result was that productivity improved during observation whether the conditions were made better or worse. Researchers concluded that productivity seemed to improve whenever the workers knew they were being observed.

Although some recent studies have raised questions about the original findings, you should be aware that observation can and does have an effect on normal operations. With this in mind, always give advance notice to the

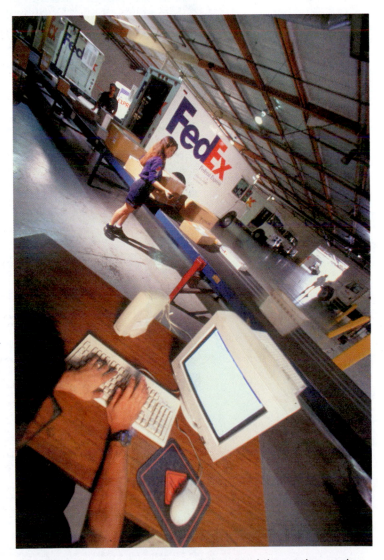

FIGURE 4-22 The Hawthorne study suggested that worker productivity improves during observation. Always consider the Hawthorne Effect when observing the operation of an existing system.

© Mark Richards/Photoedit

supervisor in that area. In some situations, it might be helpful to explain the purpose of your visit to the people being observed.

Questionnaires and Surveys

In projects where it is desirable to obtain input from a large number of people, a questionnaire can be a valuable tool. A **questionnaire**, also called a **survey**, is a document containing a number of standard questions that can be sent to many individuals.

Questionnaires can be used to obtain information about a wide range of topics, including workloads, reports received, volumes of transactions handled, job duties, difficulties, and opinions of how the job could be performed better or more efficiently. Figure 4-23 shows a sample questionnaire that includes several different question and response formats.

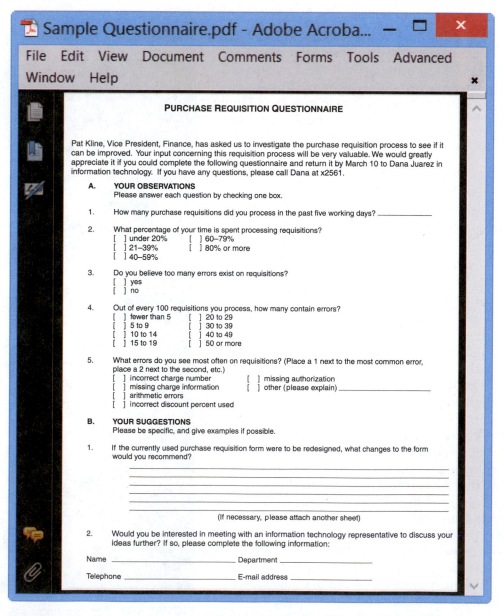

FIGURE 4-23 Online version of a sample questionnaire. Does it follow the suggested guidelines?

© Cengage Learning 2014

A typical questionnaire starts with a heading, which includes a title, a brief statement of purpose, the name and telephone number of the contact person, the deadline date for completion, and how and where to return the form. The heading usually is followed by general instructions that provide clear guidance on how to answer the questions. Headings also are used to introduce each main section or portion of the survey and include instructions when the type of question or response changes. A long questionnaire might end with a conclusion that thanks the participants and reminds them how to return the form.

What about the issue of anonymity? Should people be asked to sign the questionnaire, or is it better to allow anonymous responses? The answer depends on two questions. First, does an analyst really need to know who the respondents are in order to match or correlate information? For example, it might be important to know what percentage of users need a certain software feature, but specific usernames might not be relevant. Second, does the questionnaire include any sensitive or controversial topics? Many people do not want to be identified when answering a question such as "How well has your supervisor explained the system to you?" In such cases, anonymous responses might provide better information.

When designing a questionnaire, the most important rule of all is to make sure that your questions collect the right data in a form that you can use to further your fact-finding. Here are some additional ideas to keep in mind when designing your questionnaire:

- Keep the questionnaire brief and user-friendly.

- Provide clear instructions that will answer all anticipated questions.

- Arrange the questions in a logical order, going from simple to more complex topics.

- Phrase questions to avoid misunderstandings; use simple terms and wording.

- Try not to lead the response or use questions that give clues to expected answers.

- Limit the use of open-ended questions that are difficult to tabulate.

- Limit the use of questions that can raise concerns about job security or other negative issues.

- Include a section at the end of the questionnaire for general comments.

- Test the questionnaire whenever possible on a small test group before finalizing it and distributing to a large group.

A questionnaire can be a traditional paper form, or you can create a **fill-in form** and collect data on the Internet or a company intranet. For example, you can use Microsoft Word, as shown in Figure 4-24, to create form fields, including text boxes and drop-down lists where users can click selections. Before you publish the form, you should protect it so users can fill it in but cannot change the layout or design. Forms also can be automated, so if a user answers *no* to question three, he or she goes directly to question eight, where the form-filling resumes.

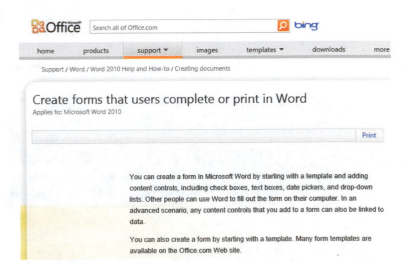

FIGURE 4-24 You can use Microsoft Word to create convenient fill-in forms that include data fields, text boxes, and drop-down lists. Before you publish a form, you should protect it so users can fill it in but cannot change the layout or design.

Screenshot used with permission from Microsoft.

Sampling

When studying an information system, you should collect examples of actual documents using a process called **sampling**. The samples might include records, reports, operational logs, data entry documents, complaint summaries, work requests, and various types of forms. Sampling techniques include systematic sampling, stratified sampling, and random sampling.

Suppose you have a list of 200 customers who complained about errors in their statements, and you want to review a representative sample of 20 customers. A **systematic sample** would select every tenth customer for review. If you want to ensure that the sample is balanced geographically, however, you could use a **stratified sample** to select five customers from each of four postal codes. Another example of stratified sampling is to select a certain percentage of transactions from each postal code, rather than a fixed number. Finally, a **random sample** selects any 20 customers.

The main objective of a sample is to ensure that it represents the overall population accurately. If you are analyzing inventory transactions, for example, you should select a sample of transactions that are typical of actual inventory operations and do not include unusual or unrelated examples. For instance, if a company performs special processing on the last business day of the month, that day is not a good time to sample *typical* daily operations. To be useful, a sample must be large enough to provide a fair representation of the overall data.

You also should consider sampling when using interviews or questionnaires. Rather than interviewing everyone or sending a questionnaire to the entire group, you can use a sample of participants. You must use sound sampling techniques to reflect the overall population and obtain an accurate picture.

Research

Research is another important fact-finding technique. Your research can include the Internet, IT magazines, and books to obtain background information, technical material, and news about industry trends and developments. In addition, you can attend professional meetings, seminars, and discussions with other IT professionals, which can be very helpful in problem solving.

The Internet is an extremely valuable resource. Part D of the Systems Analyst's Toolkit describes a variety of Internet resource tools. Using the Internet, you also can access information from federal and state governments, as well as from publishers, universities, and libraries around the world. Online forums and newsgroups are good resources for exchanging information with other professionals, seeking answers to questions, and monitoring discussions that are of interest to you.

All major hardware and software vendors maintain sites on the Web where you can obtain information about products and services offered by the company and send e-mail with specific questions to company representatives. In addition to contacting specific firms, you can access Web sites maintained by publishers and independent firms that provide links to hundreds of hardware and software vendors. For example, the InfoWorld site shown in Figure 4-25 is a one-stop information center where IT professionals can find information, share ideas, and keep posted on developments in technology. Notice that InfoWorld uses *channels* that make it easy to scan major IT topics.

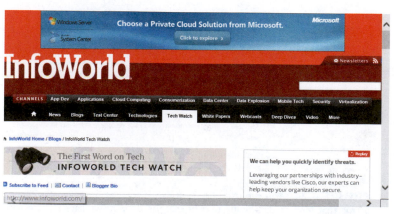

FIGURE 4-25 IT professionals can visit InfoWorld's site to find information, share ideas, and keep posted on technology developments.

Research also can involve a visit to a physical location, called a **site visit**, where the objective is to observe a system in use at another location. If you are studying your firm's human resources information system, for example, you might want to see how another company's system works. Site visits also are important when considering the purchase of a software package. If the software vendor suggests possible sites to visit, be aware that such sites might constitute a biased sample. A single site visit seldom gives you true pictures, so you should try to visit more than one installation.

Before a site visit such as the one shown in Figure 4-26, prepare just as you would for an interview. Contact the appropriate manager and explain the purpose of your visit. Decide what questions you will ask and what processes you will observe. During your visit, observe how the system works and note any problems or limitations. You also will want to learn about the support provided by the vendor, the quality of the system documentation, and so on.

FIGURE 4-26   A site visit provides an opportunity to observe a system in use.
© Image Source/Getty Images

Interviews versus Questionnaires

When you seek input from a large group, a questionnaire is a very useful tool. On the other hand, if you require detailed information from only a few people, then you probably should interview each person individually. Is it better to interview or use a questionnaire? Each situation is different, and you must consider the type of information, time constraints, and expense factors.

The interview is more familiar and personal than a questionnaire. People who are unwilling to put critical or controversial comments in writing might talk more freely in person. Moreover, during a face-to-face interview, you can react immediately to anything the interviewee says. If surprising or confusing statements are made, you can pursue the topic with additional questions. In addition, during a personal interview, you can watch for clues to help you determine if responses are knowledgeable and unbiased. Participation in interviews also can affect user attitudes because people who are asked for their opinions often view the project more favorably.

Interviewing, however, is a costly and time-consuming process. In addition to the meeting itself, both people must prepare, and the interviewer has to do follow-up work. When a number of interviews are planned, the total cost can be quite substantial. The personal interview usually is the most expensive fact-finding technique.

In contrast, a questionnaire gives many people the opportunity to provide input and suggestions. Questionnaire recipients can answer the questions at their convenience and do not have to set aside a block of time for an interview. If the questionnaire allows anonymous responses, people might offer more candid responses than they would in an interview.

Preparing a good questionnaire, however, like a good interview, requires skill and time. If a question is misinterpreted, you cannot clarify the meaning as you can in a face-to-face interview. Furthermore, unless questionnaires are designed well, recipients might view them as intrusive, time-consuming, and impersonal. As an analyst, you should select the technique that will work best in a particular situation.

Another popular method of obtaining input is called **brainstorming**, which refers to a small group discussion of a specific problem, opportunity, or issue. This technique encourages new ideas, allows team participation, and enables participants to build on each other's inputs and thoughts. Brainstorming can be structured or unstructured. In **structured brainstorming**, each participant speaks when it is his or her turn, or passes. In **unstructured brainstorming**, anyone can speak at any time. At some point, the results are recorded and made part of the fact-finding documentation process.

CASE IN POINT 4.4:   CYBERSTUFF

Ann Ellis is a systems analyst at CyberStuff, a large company that sells computer hardware and software via telephone, mail order, and the Internet. CyberStuff processes several thousand transactions per week on a three-shift operation and employs 50 full-time and 125 part-time employees. Lately, the billing department has experienced an increase in the number of customer complaints about incorrect bills. During the preliminary investigation, Ann learned that some CyberStuff representatives did not follow established order entry procedures. She feels that with more information, she might find a pattern and identify a solution for the problem.

Ann is not sure how to proceed. She came to you, her supervisor, with two separate questions. First, is a questionnaire the best approach, or would interviews be better? Second, whether she uses interviews, a questionnaire, or both techniques, should she select the participants at random, include an equal number of people from each shift, or use some other approach? As Ann's supervisor, what would you suggest, and why?

DOCUMENTATION

Keeping accurate records of interviews, facts, ideas, and observations is essential to successful systems development. The ability to manage information is the mark of a successful systems analyst and an important skill for all IT professionals.

The Need for Recording the Facts

As you gather information, the importance of a single item can be overlooked or complex system details can be forgotten. The basic rule is to write it down. You should document your work according to the following principles:

- Record information as soon as you obtain it.
- Use the simplest recording method possible.
- Record your findings in such a way that they can be understood by someone else.
- Organize your documentation so related material is located easily.

Often, systems analysts use special forms for describing a system, recording interviews, and summarizing documents. One type of documentation is a narrative list with simple statements about what is occurring, apparent problems, and suggestions for improvement. Other forms of documentation that are described in this chapter include data flow diagrams, flowcharts, sample forms, and screen captures.

Software Tools

Many software programs are available to help you record and document information. Some examples are described here.

CASE TOOLS   You can use CASE tools at every stage of systems development. This chapter contains several examples of CASE tools. Part B of the Systems Analyst's Toolkit describes other features and capabilities of CASE tools.

PRODUCTIVITY SOFTWARE   Productivity **software** includes word processing, spreadsheet, database management, presentation graphics, and collaboration software programs. Although Microsoft Office is the best-known set of productivity software programs, other vendors offer products in each of these categories.

Using word processing software such as Microsoft Word, you can create reports, summaries, tables, and forms. In addition to standard document preparation, the program can help you organize a presentation with templates, bookmarks, annotations, revision control, and an index. You can consult the program's Help system for more information about those and other features. You also can create fill-in forms to conduct surveys and questionnaires, as described earlier in this chapter.

Spreadsheet software, such as Microsoft Excel, can help you track and manage numeric data or financial information. You also can generate graphs and charts that display the data and show possible patterns, and you can use the statistical functions in a spreadsheet to tabulate and analyze questionnaire data. A graphical format often is used in quality control analysis because it highlights problems and their possible causes, and it is effective when presenting results to management. A common tool for showing the distribution of questionnaire or sampling results is a vertical bar chart called a **histogram**. Most spreadsheet programs can create histograms and other charts that can display data you have collected. Figure 4-27 displays a typical histogram that might have resulted from the questionnaire shown in Figure 4-23 on page 156.

Database management software allows you to document and organize fact-finding results such as events, observations, and data samples. You can use a database program such as Microsoft Access to manage the details of a complex project, create queries to retrieve specific information, and generate custom reports.

Presentation graphics software, such as Microsoft PowerPoint, is a powerful tool for organizing and developing your formal presentation. Presentation graphics programs enable you to create organization charts that can be used in a preliminary investigation and later during requirements modeling. These high-quality charts also can be included in written reports and management presentations.

Collaboration software is the latest weapon in the struggle to boost productivity. More than ever, people work in teams and use Web-based software such as Google Docs and Microsoft Web Apps to access data and share files. Google and others are

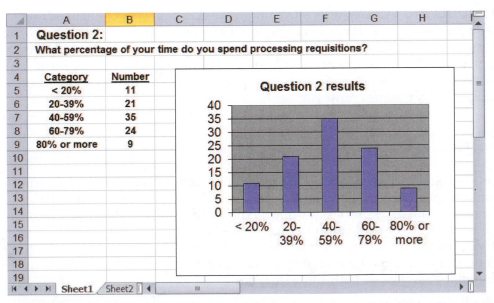

FIGURE 4-27   This histogram displays the results from Question 2 in the questionnaire shown in Figure 4-23 on page 156.

© Cengage Learning 2014

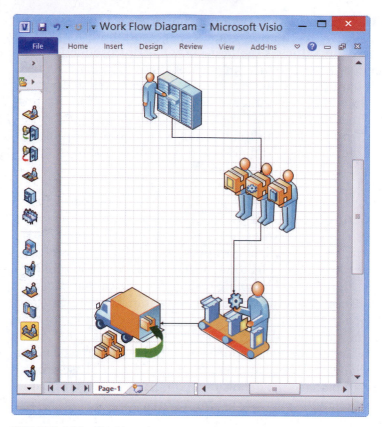

FIGURE 4-28   This Visio drawing uses drag-and-drop shapes to represent a business process.
© Cengage Learning 2014

betting that cloud computing will create a virtual workplace, where people will be able to interact in real time, with all the benefits of a traditional face-to-face workplace, but none of the limitations.

GRAPHIC MODELING SOFTWARE   Microsoft Visio is a popular graphic modeling tool that can produce a wide range of charts and diagrams. Visio includes a library of templates, stencils, and shapes. An analyst can use Visio to create many types of visual models, including business processes, flowcharts, network diagrams, organization charts, and many more. For example, in Figure 4-28, the analyst used drag-and-drop shapes to represent a business process.

INFORMATION MANAGEMENT SOFTWARE

Busy IT professionals need to manage email, text messages, personal contacts, meetings, appointments, deadlines, and much more. They also require powerful tools to capture, organize, and access project documentation and details. Although there is a substantial overlap, two broad categories have evolved: Software that is better-suited for handling personal data; and information management programs designed for the large amount of information generated by an IT project. The following sections describe popular examples of both software types.

- *Personal data management.* A **personal information manager** (PIM), such as Microsoft Outlook, includes a personal calendar, a to-do list with priorities and the capability to check off completed items, and powerful contact management features. Outlook can manage e-mail and appointments, and supports collaboration and team projects. Novell's GroupWise is another popular PIM, and a quick search on the Web will reveal many other options, including payware, shareware, and some free programs.

- *Project data management.* Although a PIM such as Microsoft Outlook can handle day-to-day activities, tasks, and schedules, it is not the best way to capture and organize large amounts of information. Instead, analysts use information management software such as Microsoft OneNote, which is a powerful, flexible tool that can handle many different types of input, including text, handwritten notes, images, audio and video recording, Web links, and much more. OneNote is included in most versions of the Office suite. In the example shown in Figure 4-29, the analyst is using OneNote to store fact-finding results, and has elected to make the notebook accessible on the Web. Notice that during the interview with Joy Brooks, the analyst used an audio recording tool.

Figure 4-30 shows another popular information manager called Evernote, which claims to have more than 20 million users. Evernote is available as a free download at *www.evernote.com*. In a January, 2012 *PC World* article, author Michelle Mastin compared the two programs. She noted that OneNote does a better job of handling multimedia content, adding free-form notes, and providing templates. However, in her view, Evernote is a better choice for entering basic text, and offers stronger cross-platform compatibility.

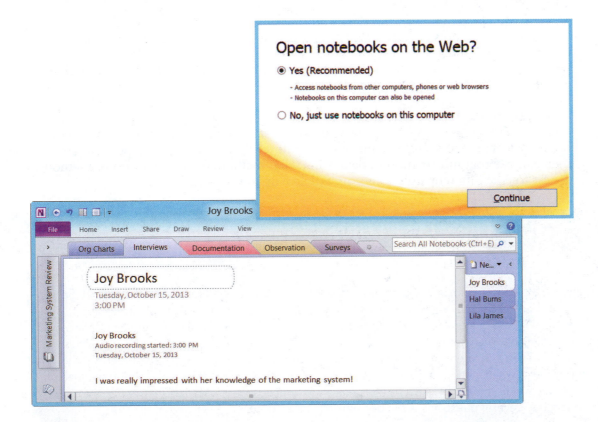

FIGURE 4-29   The analyst is using Microsoft OneNote to store fact-finding results and has elected to make the notebook accessible on the Web. During the interview with Joy Brooks, the analyst used an audio recording tool.

Screenshots used with permission from Microsoft.

FIGURE 4-30   Evernote offers a free version of its popular information management software.
© Evernote Corporation

PREVIEW OF LOGICAL MODELING

At the conclusion of requirements modeling, systems developers should have a clear understanding of business processes and system requirements. The next step is to construct a logical model of the system.

Data and process modeling, which is described in Chapter 5, uses a structured analysis approach. Structured analysis is a popular, traditional technique that describes the system in terms of data and the processes that act on that data.

An alternative to structured analysis modeling is object modeling, which is described in Chapter 6. Object modeling is a methodology that combines data and processes into things called objects that represent actual people, things, transactions, and events. Systems analysts use object models to visualize and document real-world business processes and operations.

IT professionals have differing views about systems development methodologies, and no universally accepted approach exists. By studying both structured analysis and object-oriented methods, you gain valuable knowledge, skills, and perspective. You then can use that information to determine what method, or combination of methods, is best for the different situations you will face in your career.

A QUESTION OF ETHICS

© faberfoto_it/iStockphoto

Your supervisor manages the corporate office where you work as a systems analyst. Several weeks ago, after hearing rumors of employee dissatisfaction, he asked you to create a survey for all IT employees. After the responses were returned and tabulated, he was disappointed to learn that many employees assigned low ratings to morale and management policies.

This morning he called you into his office and asked whether you could identify the departments that submitted the lowest ratings. No names were used on the individual survey forms. However, with a little analysis, you probably could identify the departments because several questions were department-related.

Now you are not sure how to respond. The expectation was that the survey would be anonymous. Even though no individuals would be identified, would it be ethical to reveal which departments sent in the low ratings? Would your supervisor's motives for wanting this information matter?

CHAPTER SUMMARY

The systems analysis phase includes three activities: requirements modeling, data and process modeling, and consideration of development strategies. The main objective is to understand the proposed project, ensure that it will support business requirements, and build a solid foundation for the systems design phase.

During requirements modeling, you identify the business-related requirements for the new information system, including outputs, inputs, processes, performance, and controls. You consider scalability to ensure that the system can support future growth and expansion. You also estimate total cost of ownership (TCO) to identify all costs, including indirect costs.

Popular team-based approaches include JAD, RAD, and agile methods. Joint application development (JAD) is a popular, team-based approach to fact-finding and requirements modeling. JAD involves an interactive group of users, managers, and IT professionals who participate in requirements modeling and develop a greater commitment to the project and to their common goals.

Rapid application development (RAD) is a team-based technique that speeds up information systems development and produces a functioning information system. RAD is a complete methodology, with a four-phase life cycle that parallels the traditional SDLC phases.

Agile methods attempt to develop a system incrementally, by building a series of prototypes and constantly adjusting them to user requirements.

Systems analysts use various tools and techniques to model system requirements. Unified Modeling Language (UML) is a widely used method of visualizing and documenting software design through the eyes of the business user. UML tools include use case diagrams and sequence diagrams to represent actors, their roles, and the sequence of transactions that occurs.

A functional decomposition diagram (FDD) is a model of business functions and processes. A CASE tool can generate a set of data flow diagrams directly from an FDD.

The fact-finding process includes interviewing, document review, observation, questionnaires, sampling, and research. Successful interviewing requires good planning and strong interpersonal and communication skills. The systems analyst must decide on the people to interview, set interview objectives, and prepare for, conduct, and analyze interviews. The analyst also might find it helpful to use one or more software tools during fact-finding.

Systems analysts should carefully record and document factual information as it is collected, and various software tools can help an analyst visualize and describe an information system. The chapter concluded with a preview of logical modeling. Data and process modeling is a structured analysis approach that views the system in terms of data and the processes that act on that data. Object modeling is an approach that views the system in terms of data and the processes that act on that data.

Key Terms

actor *141*

agile methods *133*

brainstorming *159*

business process model (BPM) *140*

business process modeling notation (BPMN) *140*

closed-ended questions *150*

construction phase *137*

cutover phase *137*

data flow diagram (DFD) *141*

document review *154*

engaged listening *152*

fill-in form *158*

functional decomposition diagram (FDD) *140*

Hawthorne Effect *155*

histogram *161*

informal structure *149*

inputs *132*

interview *148*

joint application development (JAD) *133*

leading questions *150*

observation *154*

open-ended questions *150*

outputs *132*

performance *132*

personal information manager (PIM) *162*

pool *141*

processes *132*

productivity software *161*

questionnaire *156*

random sample *158*

range-of-response questions *150*

rapid application development (RAD) *133*

Rapid Economic Justification (REJ) *146*

requirements modeling *132*

requirements planning phase *136*

research *158*

sampling *158*

scalability *145*

Scrum *138*

security *132*

sequence diagram *142*

site visit *159*

stratified sample *158*

structured brainstorming *159*

survey *156*

swim lanes *141*

system requirement *143*

system requirements document *133*

systematic sample *158*

total cost of ownership (TCO) *145*

Unified Modeling Language (UML) *141*

unstructured brainstorming *160*

use case diagram *141*

user design phase *136*

Zachman Framework for Enterprise Architecture *148*

Chapter Exercises

Questions

1. What five questions typically are used in fact-finding? What other question does the Zachman Framework include? Is the additional question important?
2. What is a systems requirement, and how are systems requirements classified?
3. What are JAD and RAD, and how do they differ from traditional fact-finding methods? What are the main advantages of team-based methods?
4. What is total cost of ownership (TCO)? What costs often are underestimated?
5. Provide three examples each of closed-ended, open-ended, and range-of-response questions.
6. What are three types of sampling? Which one would you use to analyze data input errors?
7. What is the Hawthorne Effect? Have you ever experienced it? When and where?
8. What is a functional decomposition diagram (FDD) and why would you use one? Explain how to create an FDD.
9. What are agile methods? Are they better than traditional methods? Why or why not?
10. To what three different audiences might you have to give a presentation? How would the presentation differ for each? Which one would be the most challenging for you?

Discussion Topics

1. A group meeting sometimes is suggested as a useful compromise between interviews and questionnaires. In a group meeting, a systems analyst meets with a number of users at one time. Discuss the advantages and disadvantages of group meetings.
2. JAD requires strong interpersonal and communication skills on the part of the systems analyst. Are those skills different from the ones that an analyst needs when conducting one-to-one interviews? Explain your answer.
3. Research the Internet, magazines, or textbooks to find examples of visual aids, including a bar chart, pie chart, line chart, table, diagram, and bulleted list. How effective was each example? Find at least one example that you could improve. Explain your choice.
4. Review Part A of the Systems Analyst's Toolkit, and then attend a speech or presentation and analyze its effectiveness. Consider the speaker's delivery and how he or she organized the material, used visual aids, and handled audience questions. Was the speech or presentation effective? How could it have been improved?

Projects

1. Design a questionnaire to learn what students think of the registration process at your school. Apply the guidelines you learned in this chapter.
2. Use Microsoft Word to design a simple fill-in form with at least five fields.
3. Create a functional decomposition diagram similar to the one in Figure 4-8 on page 140, but showing your school instead of the library example.
4. Use the Internet to find a site that contains current IT industry news, information, and links. Write a brief description of what you liked and didn't like.

Apply Your Knowledge

This section contains four mini-cases. Each case describes a situation, explains your role, and requires you to apply what you learned in the chapter.

1 Colonial Movers

You are the IT manager at a regional moving company that recently merged with a major competitor. The company president asked you to prepare requirements for a new information system to support the combined company.

Tasks

1. Should employees be involved in developing the new system? If so, what should be their role?
2. What types of system requirements will you focus on? Explain each one in detail.
3. You decide to conduct a series of JAD sessions. Prepare a memo to participants, and include a detailed plan.
4. What fact-finding methods could you use to collect information from employees at Colonial Movers? Suggest at least three methods, and explain the pros and cons of each.

2 General Hardware Products

Your boss, the IT director, wants you to explain FDDs, BPM, DFDs, and UML to a group of company managers and users who will serve on a systems development team for the new marketing system.

Tasks

1. Explain how an FDD can be used in requirements modeling.
2. Describe BPM and how it can be used.
3. Explain how DFDs can be used in requirements modeling.
4. Describe the UML and how it can be used during systems development.

3 **Zevo Chemical Company**

Zevo is currently reaching the end of the requirements modeling phase of a new inventory control system for their global company. As a systems analyst, you are asked to support this ongoing project.

Tasks

1. How would you explain scalability? How would you ensure that scalability has been considered in Zevo's requirements model?
2. How would you define total cost of ownership (TCO)? What costs should be included in a TCO estimate?
3. Explain why documentation is essential for Zevo's new system, and how documentation can be used during systems development.
4. What software tools could you use to develop, publish, and distribute Zevo's systems documentation?

4 **Westwood College**

The school is considering a new system to speed up the registration process. As a member of Westwood's IT team, you will interview stakeholders affected by the registration process.

Tasks

1. List all the registration system stakeholders. How is each group affected?
2. Interviews can be time-consuming and expensive. What are your specific goals, and how would you justify a series of interviews?
3. During the interviews, what types of questions will you use, and why? Develop at least five sample questions and explain how each question will help you achieve your objectives.
4. What are the advantages and disadvantages of open-ended, closed-ended, and range-of-response questions?

Case Studies

Each chapter includes a Chapter Case, a Continuing Case, a Capstone Case, and an Online Case Simulation. You can learn more about the Online Case Simulation in the MIS CourseMate Features section.

Chapter Case: Town of Eden Bay (Part 3)

The town of Eden Bay owns and maintains a fleet of vehicles. You are a systems analyst reporting to Dawn, the town's IT manager.

Background

In Chapter 2, you learned that the town's maintenance budget has risen sharply in recent years. Based on a preliminary investigation, the town has decided to develop a new information system to manage maintenance costs more effectively, instead of outsourcing it to private firms.

In Chapter 3, you helped plan the presentation to the Town Council for an initial budget request, which was approved. The new system will be named RAVE, which stands for Repair Analysis for Vehicular Equipment. Now Dawn wants you to perform additional fact-finding to document the specific requirements for the new system. She stressed that user input is absolutely critical at this stage.

Tasks

1. Review the interview summaries in Chapter 2. For each person (Marie, Martin, Phil, Alice, and Joe), develop three additional questions: an open-ended question, a closed-ended question, and a range-of-response question.
2. Based on what you know so far, list the requirements for the new system. You can use your imagination if necessary. Consider outputs, inputs, processes, performance, and controls. Include at least two examples for each category.
3. You decide to analyze a sample of vehicle records. What sampling methods are available to you? Which one should you use, and why?
4. Dawn thinks it would be a good idea to conduct a JAD session to perform additional fact-finding. Draft a message to the participants, with a brief explanation of JAD methods and a proposed agenda.

Continuing Case: Personal Trainer, Inc.

Personal Trainer, Inc. owns and operates fitness centers in a dozen Midwestern cities. The centers have done well, and the company is planning an international expansion by opening a new "supercenter" in the Toronto area. Personal Trainer's president, Cassia Umi, hired an IT consultant, Susan Park, to help develop an information system for the new facility. During the project, Susan will work closely with Gray Lewis, who will manage the new operation.

Background

During requirements modeling for the new system, Susan Park met with fitness center managers at several Personal Trainer locations. She conducted a series of interviews, reviewed company records, observed business operations, analyzed the BumbleBee accounting software, and studied a sample of sales and billing transactions. Susan's objective was to develop a list of system requirements for the proposed system.

(continues)

Continuing Case: Personal Trainer, Inc.

Fact-Finding Summary

- A typical center has 300–500 members, with two membership levels: full and limited. Full members have access to all activities. Limited members are restricted to activities they have selected, but they can participate in other activities by paying a usage fee. All members have charge privileges. Charges for merchandise and services are recorded on a charge slip, which is signed by the member.

- At the end of each day, cash sales and charges are entered into the BumbleBee accounting software, which runs on a computer workstation at each location. Daily cash receipts are deposited in a local bank and credited to the corporate Personal Trainer account. The BumbleBee program produces a daily activity report with a listing of all sales transactions.

- At the end of the month, the local manager uses BumbleBee to transmit an accounts receivable summary to the Personal Trainer headquarters in Chicago, where member statements are prepared and mailed. Members mail their payments to the Personal Trainer headquarters, where the payment is applied to the member account.

- The BumbleBee program stores basic member information, but does not include information about member preferences, activities, and history.

- Currently, the BumbleBee program produces one local report (the daily activity report) and three reports that are prepared at the headquarters location: a monthly member sales report, an exception report for inactive members and late payers, and a quarterly profit-and-loss report that shows a breakdown of revenue and costs for each separate activity.

During the interviews, Susan received a number of "wish list" comments from managers and staff members. For example, managers want more analytical features so they can spot trends and launch special promotions and temporary discounts. Managers also want better information about the profitability of specific business activities at their centers, instead of bottom-line totals.

Several managers want to offer computerized activity and wellness logs, fitness coaching for seniors, and various social networking options, including e-mail communications, fitness blogs, Facebook, and Twitter posts. Staff members want better ways to handle information about part-time instructors and trainers, and several people suggested using scannable ID cards to capture data.

Tasks

1. Draw a DFD that shows how data will be stored, processed, and transformed in the TIMS system.
2. Draw an FDD that shows the Personal Trainer's main functions. Also draw a use case diagram that represents the interaction between a user and the proposed TIMS system.
3. Using the information gathered during fact-finding, develop a requirements checklist that includes examples in each of the five main categories.
4. Gray is not familiar with the TCO concept. How should Susan explain it to him?

Capstone Case: New Century Wellness Group

New Century Wellness Group offers a holistic approach to healthcare with an emphasis on preventive medicine as well as traditional medical care. In your role as an IT consultant, you will help New Century develop a new information system.

Background

New Century asked you to perform a preliminary investigation for a new business support system. You had several meetings with Dr. Jones to discuss office records and accounting systems. Anita Davenport, New Century's office manager, participated in those meetings. You also completed a project management plan for New Century. Now, you are ready to develop a system requirements model.

In the preliminary investigation report, you recommended a detailed analysis of four key areas: patient scheduling, billing and accounts receivable, human resources, and payroll. Because these areas are highly interactive, you suggested that an integrated system would provide the greatest benefits. Dr. Jones and the partners agreed, but they also expressed interest in a medical practice support system and asked whether the business support system could be expanded. After research and analysis, you concluded that medical practice support should be a separate system to be considered in New Century's long-term strategic plans. Because future integration would be very important, the business support system design should be compatible with a future medical practice support system.

In your meetings with Dr. Jones and Anita, you stressed that IT projects are much more successful when users have a sense of ownership, and the best way to create that "buy-in" is to get them involved in the development process. In your view, joint application development would be ideal method to develop the new system, and everyone agrees. Your next task is to form a JAD team and conduct the requirements modeling process.

Tasks

1. Review the organization chart you prepared in Chapter 1 and determine who should be on the JAD team, and why. Also, how will you create a sense of team ownership from the start?

2. You may be given a standard set of interview summaries, or you may conduct role-play interviews. Either way, use the information to complete Tasks 3 and 4.

3. Develop a checklist that includes several requirements for system output, input, process, performance, and control.

4. Design a questionnaire to learn how New Century patients feel about insurance procedures and appointment scheduling. Your questionnaire should be designed for a sample group of patients, and should follow the suggestions in this chapter. After you complete the questionnaire, select a sampling method and explain your choice.

CASE Tool Workshop

Systems analysts use CASE tools to help them plan, build, and maintain information systems. To learn more about CASE tools, turn to Part B of the Toolkit that follows Chapter 12. You can complete these tasks with the Visible Analyst® CASE tool, which is available with this textbook, or a similar tool.

Background

As a part-time student assistant in the computer lab at your school, you were asked to evaluate various CASE tools and submit the results. You have completed an overview of the software and you got some hands-on experience. Now you want to try creating a functional decomposition diagram FDD) that will show business functions and processes.

Tasks

1. According to Visible Analyst, functional decomposition diagrams (FDDs) involve top-down business planning decisions, and should be the starting point for modeling business functions and processes. Visible states that "There is no rule that you must begin here, but some other things are easier if you do." Visit the Visible Analyst glossary function to learn what, specifically, might be easier. Report your findings in a memo.

2. Suppose you want to create an FDD of the functions at your school or your place of employment. Using Figure 4-8 on page 140 as a model, create a simple FDD with three top-level functions. For one of the functions, create two additional levels.

MIS CourseMate Features

If you have an MIS CourseMate access code, you can reinforce and extend your learning with premium content created for this textbook. For example, you can launch interactive Video Learning Sessions to help you understand systems development concepts and practice your skills. In addition, you can use MindTap Reader, which is a full, interactive, digital e-book.

MIS CourseMate also offers many learning features within each chapter, including an Online Case Simulation, a Critical Thinking Challenge, Video Learning Tasks, and a set of Learn It Online activities. To log on to the MIS CourseMate site at **www.cengagebrain.com**, you must create a student account and register this book.

Online Case Simulation: SCR Associates

Session 4: Requirements Modeling

Overview

The SCR Associates case study is a Web-based simulation that allows you to practice your skills in a real-world environment. The firm offers IT consulting, solutions, and training. SCR plans to open a new high-tech training center, and needs to develop a Training Information Management System (TIMS) to support the operation. You are a newly hired systems analyst reporting to Jesse Baker, systems group manager, and will help her develop the system.

The case study takes you to the SCR Web site, where you receive e-mail and voice mail messages from Jesse, obtain information from SCR's resource libraries, and perform various tasks. Jesse has high standards, but seems very fair. She made it clear that she expects your work to be accurate, thorough, and professional.

Before You Begin

To prepare for this work session, you should review the following topics:

- System requirements
- Functional decomposition diagrams

How Do I Use the Online Case Simulation?

- Read the preview, and review the Chapter 1 background material if necessary.
- Visit the MIS CourseMate Web site at **www.cengagebrain.com**, locate the **SCR Case Simulation**, and click the **intranet** link. Enter your name and the password **sad10e**.
- When the opening screen displays, select this session. Then check your e-mail and voice mail, and start to work on your task list.

Preview: Session 4

As you begin the requirements modeling process, you receive specific directions from your supervisor, Jesse Baker. She wants you to conduct a survey of former and prospective students, lead a JAD group session, and draft a list of system requirements based on the results of the JAD session. She also wants to see an FDD showing the main TIMS functions.

Critical Thinking Challenge

In addition to technical ability, IT professionals need critical thinking skills. This feature can help you practice perception, organization, analysis, problem-solving, and decision-making skills that will be valuable in the workplace. You can visit **www.criticalthinking.org** to learn more about critical thinking and why it is so important.

Background

As a leader in the game development field, Game Technology has many customers. The company wants to add a customer contact management feature to the sales system, and you will assist the IT team on this project. One of your first tasks is to interview users to find out what functions they want. When you have this information, you can construct a functional decomposition diagram (FDD) to list and organize the functions.

Before you talk to the users, you decide to practice your interviewing skills. Specifically, you want to use open-ended, closed-ended, and range-of-response questions. To test yourself, you ask a team member to develop the following sample questions for you to identify:

- Do you foresee any problems with this system?
- On a scale of one to five (high), how important is the project?
- Do you maintain current e-mail addresses for customers?
- Who is responsible for entering these records?
- What would be some benefits of the new feature?

During the interviews, you learned that most users want to start with an opening screen that allows them to look up a customer, add a customer, edit a customer, delete a customer, or get help. The Help option should allow them to search a knowledge base or contact the IT Help Desk. If they select the knowledge base option, they want to search by keyword or by topic. If they select the IT Help Desk, they want to have an e-mail or a telephone call-back option.

Practice Tasks

Visit the MIS CourseMate Web site at **www.cengagebrain.com**. Then navigate to the resources for this chapter and locate the **Critical Thinking Challenge** feature. You will complete two Practice Tasks, using what you learned in the chapter. Then you can check your answers to be sure you're ready for the Challenge Tasks.

Challenge Tasks

After you complete the Practice Tasks, you learn about new developments at Game Technology.

Although the interviews were successful, you need more detail. Specifically, you want more feedback about the user interface, built-in error checking, and reports that could be generated for users. Using these topics, or others you think would be relevant, prepare two samples of each type of question.

Also, your FDD was good, but users want you to add a Reports function to the opening screen. That option would allow users to list reports by name or by type. Users also would be able to view or print a report. If they select the Print option, they should be able to print the full report, the current page, or selected pages. To continue, navigate to the **Critical Thinking Challenge** feature for this chapter, select the **Challenge Tasks**, and follow the instructions.

Video Learning Sessions

The Video Learning Session in this chapter explains functional decomposition diagrams (FDDs). You'll learn about FDDs and why they are important, how to use FDDs to model business functions and processes, and how to use CASE tools to create FDDs.

© craftvision/iStockph

Before You Begin

To prepare for the tasks, you should review the following topics:

- Requirements modeling objectives
- Functional decomposition diagrams

How to Watch a Session

Go to the Management Information Systems CourseMate Web site at **www.cengagebrain.com**. Then navigate to the resources for this book, locate the **Video Learning Sessions**, and select a session. You can watch the session on your computer or mobile device, and pause, rewind, or replay a video at any time.

Practice Tasks

After each session, visit the **Your Turn** feature to perform the tasks and check your answers.

Training Tasks

Suppose the IT training manager wants to encourage team members to watch the Video Learning Sessions. To spark interest, she plans to post a set of VLS previews, which you will prepare. Each preview must include an overview of the session, a description of the main topics, and one or more screen examples from the video. To get you started, she provided a task list:

1. Select a Video Learning Session from this chapter. Launch the video and note the title, objectives, and total running time. Include this information in your preview.
2. Run though the session and find a segment that does a good job of explaining a specific skill or concept.
3. In the segment you selected, choose one or more specific screens and capture each screen image with the Windows Snipping Tool. To do this in Windows 7 or Windows Vista, click **Start**, and then type **Snipping Tool**. In Windows 8, you can display the **Start** menu, and then type **Snipping Tool**.
4. Paste the screen image into your preview and explain how it would help a viewer understand the topic. Also add your comments about the video, and why it would be important to an IT professional. Your preview should be well-organized and readable.

Learn It Online

In each chapter, you can use this feature to apply your knowledge and practice your skills. The exercises include Chapter Reinforcement Questions, Flash Cards, Practice Tests, and various games, such as *Who Wants To Be a Computer Genius?, Wheel of Terms, and the Crossword Puzzle Challenge.*

CHAPTER 5 Data and Process Modeling

Chapter 5 is the second of four chapters in the systems analysis phase of the SDLC. This chapter discusses data and process modeling techniques that analysts use to show how the system transforms data into useful information. The deliverable, or end product, of data and process modeling is a logical model that will support business operations and meet user needs.

INTRODUCTION

OBJECTIVES

When you finish this chapter, you will be able to:

- Describe data and process modeling concepts and tools, including data flow diagrams, a data dictionary, and process descriptions

- Describe the symbols used in data flow diagrams and explain the rules for their use

- Draw data flow diagrams in a sequence, from general to specific

- Explain how to level and balance a set of data flow diagrams

- Describe how a data dictionary is used and what it contains

- Use process description tools, including structured English, decision tables, and decision trees

- Describe the relationship between logical and physical models

During the requirements modeling process described in Chapter 4, you used fact-finding techniques to investigate the current system and identify user requirements. Now, in Chapters 5 and 6 you will use that information to develop a logical model of the proposed system and document the system requirements. A **logical model** shows *what* the system must do, regardless of how it will be implemented physically. Later, in the systems design phase, you build a **physical model** that describes *how* the system will be constructed. Data and process modeling involves three main tools: data flow diagrams, a data dictionary, and process descriptions.

If you have MIS CourseMate, you can view four Video Learning Sessions that explain how to work with DFD symbols and diagrams, how to create a context diagram, how to create a diagram 0 DFD, and how to use a decision table.

PREVIEW CASE: Mountain View College Bookstore

Background: Wendy Lee, manager of college services at Mountain View College, wants a new information system that will improve efficiency and customer service at the three college bookstores.

In this part of the case, Tina Allen (systems analyst) and David Conroe (student intern) are talking about data and process modeling tasks and concepts.

Participants: Tina and David
Location: Tina's office, Thursday afternoon, October 17, 2013
Project status: Tina and David are ready to develop a requirements model that will describe and document the proposed system
Discussion topics: Data flow diagrams, data dictionaries, and process description tools

Tina:	Hi, David. Any questions about the fact-finding we did?
David:	*Well, I found out that fact-finding is hard work.*
Tina:	Yes, but it was worth it. Look at what we learned — now we understand how the current system operates, and we know what users expect in the new system. This information will help us build a requirements model that we can present to Wendy and her staff.
David:	*What's the next step?*
Tina:	We need to draw a set of data flow diagrams, or DFDs for short.
David:	*Do we use a CASE tool to draw the DFDs?*
Tina:	We can draw the initial versions by hand and use a CASE tool to prepare the final diagrams.
David:	*What goes into a DFD?*
Tina:	DFDs use four basic symbols that represent processes, data flows, data stores, and entities. You'll learn about these as we go along. I'll also show you how we use techniques called leveling and balancing to develop accurate, consistent DFDs.
David:	*Apart from the diagrams, do we need to develop any other documentation?*
Tina:	Yes, we need to create a data dictionary and process descriptions. The data dictionary is an overall store-house of information about the system, and serves as a central clearinghouse for all documentation. We use process descriptions to explain the logical steps that each process performs. To create these descriptions, we use three tools: structured English statements, decision tables, and decision trees.
David:	*Sounds like a lot to do. Where do we begin?*
Tina:	Here's a task list to get us started:

FIGURE 5-1 Typical data and process modeling task list.
© Cengage Learning 2014

OVERVIEW OF DATA AND PROCESS MODELING TOOLS

TOOLKIT TIME

The CASE Tools in Part B of the Systems Analyst's Toolkit can help you document business functions and processes, develop graphical models, and provide an overall framework for information system development. To learn more about these tools, turn to Part B of the four-part Toolkit that follows Chapter 12.

Systems analysts use many graphical techniques to describe an information system. One popular method is to draw a set of data flow diagrams. A **data flow diagram (DFD)** uses various symbols to show how the system transforms input data into useful information. Other graphical tools include object models, which are explained in Chapter 6 (Object Modeling), and entity-relationship diagrams, which are described in Chapter 9 (Data Design).

DATA FLOW DIAGRAMS

In Part A of the Systems Analyst's Toolkit, you learn how to use visual aids to help explain a concept, as shown in Figure 5-2. Similarly, during the systems analysis phase, you learn how to create a visual model of the information system using a set of data flow diagrams.

A data flow diagram (DFD) shows how data moves through an information system but does not show program logic or processing steps. A set of DFDs provides a logical model that shows *what* the system does, not *how* it does it. That distinction is important because focusing on implementation issues at this point would restrict your search for the most effective system design.

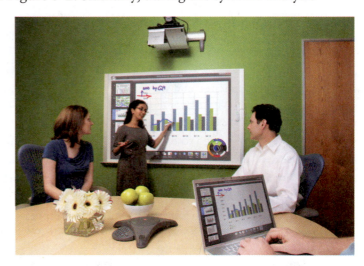

FIGURE 5-2 Systems analysts often use visual aids during presentations.
Courtesy of Luidia, Inc.

Video Learning Session
DFD Symbols and Diagrams

If you have an MIS CourseMate access code, you can launch interactive Video Learning Sessions to help you understand systems development concepts and practice your skills. You can watch the sessions on your computer or mobile device, and pause, rewind, or replay a video at any time. To log on to the MIS CourseMate site at **www.cengagebrain.com**, you must create a student account and then register this book.

This session is about DFD symbols and diagrams. You'll learn why DFDs are important modeling tools, how to use DFD symbols, and how you can use a CASE tool to create DFDs.

© craftvision/iStockphoto

DFD Symbols

DFDs use four basic symbols that represent processes, data flows, data stores, and entities. Several different versions of DFD symbols exist, but they all serve the same purpose. DFD examples in this textbook use the **Gane and Sarson** symbol set. Another popular symbol set is the **Yourdon** symbol set. Figure 5-3 shows examples of both versions. Symbols are referenced by using all capital letters for the symbol name.

PROCESS SYMBOL   A **process** receives input data and produces output that has a different content, form, or both. For instance, the process for calculating pay uses two inputs (pay rate and hours worked) to produce one output (total pay). Processes can be very simple or quite complex. In a typical company, processes might include calculating sales trends, filing online insurance claims, ordering inventory from a supplier's system, or verifying e-mail addresses for Web customers. Processes contain the **business logic**, also called **business rules**, that transform the data and produce the required results.

The symbol for a process is a rectangle with rounded corners. The name of the process appears inside the rectangle. The process name identifies a specific function and consists of a verb (and an adjective, if necessary) followed by a singular noun. Examples of process names are APPLY RENT PAYMENT, CALCULATE COMMISSION, ASSIGN FINAL GRADE, VERIFY ORDER, and FILL ORDER.

Processing details are not shown in a DFD. For example, you might have a process named DEPOSIT PAYMENT. The process symbol does not reveal the business logic for the DEPOSIT PAYMENT process. To document the logic, you create a process description, which is explained later in this chapter.

FIGURE 5-3   Data flow diagram symbols, symbol names, and examples of the Gane and Sarson and Yourdon symbol sets.
© Cengage Learning 2014

In DFDs, a process symbol can be referred to as a **black box**, because the inputs, outputs, and general functions of the process are known, but the underlying details and logic of the process are hidden. By showing processes as black boxes, an analyst can create DFDs that show how the system functions, but avoid unnecessary detail and clutter. When the analyst wishes to show additional levels of detail, he or she can zoom in on a process symbol and create a more in-depth DFD that shows the process's internal workings — which might reveal even more processes, data flows, and data stores. In this manner, the information system can be modeled as a series of increasingly detailed pictures.

FIGURE 5-4 Networks use various devices that act like *black boxes*. Cables carry data in and out, but internal operations are hidden inside the case.

© INSADCO Photography/Alamy

The network router shown in Figure 5-4 is an example of a black box. An observer can see cables that carry data into and out of the router, but the router's internal operations are not revealed — only the results are apparent.

DATA FLOW SYMBOL A **data flow** is a path for data to move from one part of the information system to another. A data flow in a DFD represents one or more data items. For example, a data flow could consist of a single data item (such as a student ID number) or it could include a set of data (such as a class roster with student ID numbers, names, and registration dates for a specific class). Although the DFD does not show the detailed contents of a data flow, that information is included in the data dictionary, which is described later in this chapter.

The symbol for a data flow is a line with a single or double arrowhead. The data flow name appears above, below, or alongside the line. A data flow name consists of a singular noun and an adjective, if needed. Examples of data flow names are DEPOSIT, INVOICE PAYMENT, STUDENT GRADE, ORDER, and COMMISSION. Exceptions to the singular name rule are data flow names, such as GRADING PARAMETERS, where a singular name could mislead you into thinking a single parameter or single item of data exists.

Figure 5-5 shows correct examples of data flow and process symbol connections. Because a process changes the data's content or form, at least one data flow must enter and one data flow must exit each process symbol, as they do in the CREATE INVOICE process.

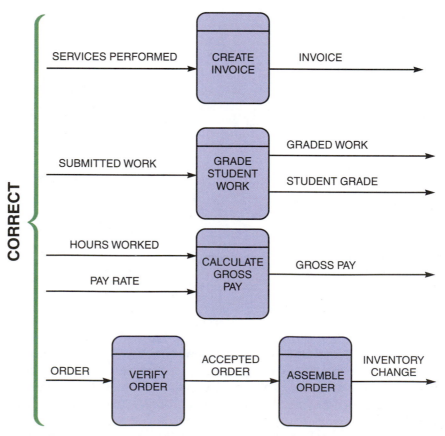

FIGURE 5-5 Examples of correct combinations of data flow and process symbols.

© Cengage Learning 2014

A process symbol can have more than one outgoing data flow, as shown in the GRADE STUDENT WORK process, or more than one incoming data flow, as shown in the CALCULATE GROSS PAY process. A process also can connect to any other symbol, including another process symbol, as shown by the connection between VERIFY ORDER and ASSEMBLE ORDER in Figure 5-5. A data flow, therefore, *must* have a process symbol on at least one end.

Figure 5-6 shows three data flow and process combinations that you must avoid:

- **Spontaneous generation.** The APPLY INSURANCE PREMIUM process, for instance, produces output, but has no input data flow. Because it has no input, the process is called a spontaneous generation process.

- **Black hole.** CALCULATE GROSS PAY is called a black hole process, which is a process that has input, but produces no output.

- **Gray hole.** A gray hole is a process that has at least one input and one output, but the input obviously is insufficient to generate the output shown. For example, a date of birth input is not sufficient to produce a final grade output in the CALCULATE GRADE process.

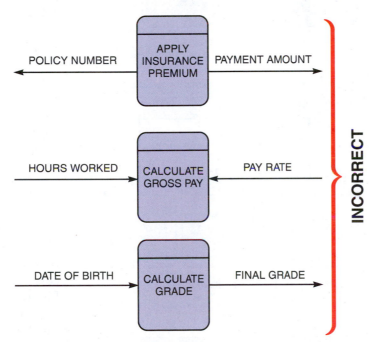

FIGURE 5-6 Examples of incorrect combinations of data flow and process symbols. APPLY INSURANCE PREMIUM has no input and is called a spontaneous generation process. CALCULATE GROSS PAY has no outputs and is called a black hole process. CALCULATE GRADE has an input that is obviously unable to produce the output. This process is called a gray hole.

© Cengage Learning 2014

Spontaneous generation, black holes, and gray holes are impossible logically in a DFD because a process must act on input, shown by an incoming data flow, and produce output, represented by an outgoing data flow.

DATA STORE SYMBOL   A **data store** is used in a DFD to represent data that the system stores because one or more processes need to use the data at a later time. For instance, instructors need to store student scores on tests and assignments during the semester so they can assign final grades at the end of the term. Similarly, a company stores employee salary and deduction data during the year in order to print W-2 forms with total earnings and deductions at the end of the year. A DFD does not show the detailed contents of a data store — the specific structure and data elements are defined in the data dictionary, which is discussed later in this chapter.

The physical characteristics of a data store are unimportant because you are concerned only with a logical model. Also, the length of time that the data is stored is unimportant — it can be a matter of seconds while a transaction is processed or a period of months while data is accumulated for year-end processing. What is important is that a process needs access to the data at some later time.

In a DFD, the Gane and Sarson symbol for a data store is a flat rectangle that is open on the right side and closed on the left side. The name of the data store appears between the lines and identifies the data it contains. A data store name is a plural name consisting of a noun and adjectives, if needed. Examples of data store names are STUDENTS, ACCOUNTS RECEIVABLE, PRODUCTS, DAILY PAYMENTS, PURCHASE ORDERS, OUTSTANDING CHECKS, INSURANCE POLICIES, and EMPLOYEES. Exceptions to the plural name rule are collective nouns that represent multiple occurrences of objects. For example, GRADEBOOK represents a group of students and their scores.

A data store must be connected to a process with a data flow. Figure 5-7 illustrates typical examples of data stores. In each case, the data store has at least one incoming and one outgoing data flow and is connected to a process symbol with a data flow.

Violations of the rule that a data store must have at least one incoming and one outgoing data flow are shown in Figure 5-8. In the first example, two data stores are connected incorrectly because no process is

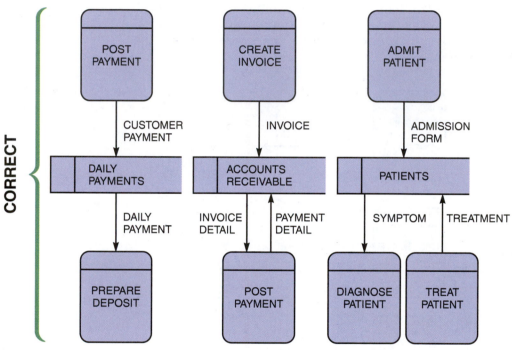

FIGURE 5-7 Examples of correct uses of data store symbols in a data flow diagram.
© Cengage Learning 2014

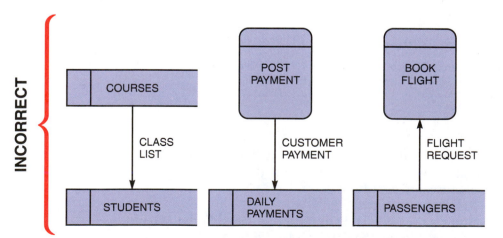

FIGURE 5-8 Examples of incorrect uses of data store symbols: Two data stores cannot be connected by a data flow without an intervening process, and each data store should have an outgoing and incoming data flow.
© Cengage Learning 2014

between them. Also, COURSES has no incoming data flow and STUDENTS has no outgoing data flow. In the second and third examples, the data stores lack either an outgoing or incoming data flow.

There is an exception to the requirement that a data store must have at least one incoming and one outgoing data flow. In some situations, a data store has no input data flow because it contains fixed reference data that is not updated by the system. For example, consider a data store called TAX TABLE, which contains withholding tax data that a company downloads from the Internal Revenue Service. When the company runs its payroll, the CALCULATE WITHHOLDING process accesses data from this data store. On a DFD, this would be represented as a one-way outgoing data flow from the TAX TABLE data store into the CALCULATE WITHHOLDING process.

ENTITY SYMBOL The symbol for an **entity** is a rectangle, which may be shaded to make it look three-dimensional. The name of the entity appears inside the symbol.

A DFD shows only external entities that provide data to the system or receive output from the system. A DFD shows the boundaries of the system and how the system interfaces with the outside world. For example, a customer entity submits an

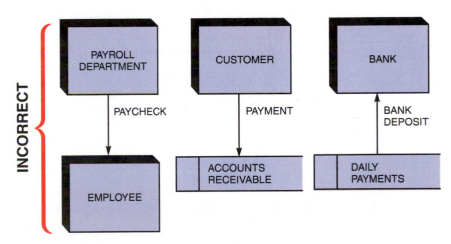

FIGURE 5-9 Examples of correct uses of external entities in a data flow diagram.
© Cengage Learning 2014

FIGURE 5-10 Examples of incorrect uses of external entities. An external entity must be connected by a data flow to a process, and not directly to a data store or to another external entity.
© Cengage Learning 2014

order to an order processing system. Other examples of entities include a patient who supplies data to a medical records system, a homeowner who receives a bill from a city property tax system, or an accounts payable system that receives data from the company's purchasing system.

DFD entities also are called **terminators** because they are data origins or final destinations. Systems analysts call an entity that supplies data to the system a **source**, and an entity that receives data from the system a **sink**. An entity name is the singular form of a department, outside organization, other information system, or person. An external entity can be a source or a sink or both, but each entity must be connected to a process by a data flow. Figures 5-9 and 5-10 show correct and incorrect examples of this rule.

With an understanding of the proper use of DFD symbols, you are ready to construct diagrams that use these symbols. Figure 5-11 on the next page shows a summary of the rules for using DFD symbols.

Correct and Incorrect Examples of Data Flows		
	Process to Process	✔
	Process to External Entity	✔
	Process to Data Store	✔
	External Entity to External Entity	✘
	External Entity to Data Store	✘
	Data Store to Data Store	✘

FIGURE 5-11   Examples of correct and incorrect uses of data flows.
© Cengage Learning 2014

CREATING A SET OF DFDs

During requirements modeling, you used interviews, questionnaires, and other techniques to gather facts about the system, and you learned how the various people, departments, data, and processes fit together to support business operations. Now you are ready to create a graphical model of the information system based on your fact-finding results.

To learn how to construct DFDs, you will use examples of two information systems. The first example is a grading system that instructors use to assign final grades based on the scores that students receive during the term. The second example is an order system that a company uses to enter orders and apply payments against a customer's balance. First, you will review a set of guidelines for drawing DFDs. Then you will learn how to apply these guidelines and create a set of DFDs using a three-step process.

Video Learning Session
DFD Context Diagrams

If you have an MIS CourseMate access code, you can launch interactive Video Learning Sessions to help you understand systems development concepts and practice your skills. You can watch the sessions on your computer or mobile device, and pause, rewind, or replay a video at any time. To log on to the MIS CourseMate site at **www.cengagebrain.com**, you must create a student account and then register this book.

This session is about DFD context diagrams, why they are important, how to construct a context diagram, and how you can use a CASE tool to create a context diagram.

© craftvision/iStockphoto

Guidelines for Drawing DFDs

When you draw a context diagram and other DFDs, you should follow several guidelines:

* Draw the context diagram so it fits on one page.
* Use the name of the information system as the process name in the context diagram. For example, the process name in Figure 5-12 is GRADING SYSTEM. Notice that the process name is the same as the system name. This is because

the context diagram shows the entire information system as if it were a single process. For processes in lower-level DFDs, you would use a verb followed by a descriptive noun, such as ESTABLISH GRADEBOOK, ASSIGN FINAL GRADE, or PRODUCE GRADE REPORT.

- Use unique names within each set of symbols. For instance, the diagram in Figure 5-12 shows only one entity named STUDENT and only one data flow named FINAL GRADE. Whenever you see the entity STUDENT on any other DFD in the grading system, you know that you are dealing with the same entity. Whenever the FINAL GRADE data flow appears, you know that you are dealing with the same data flow. The naming convention also applies to data stores.

- Do not cross lines. One way to achieve that goal is to restrict the number of symbols in any DFD. On lower-level diagrams with multiple processes, you should not have more than nine process symbols. Including more than nine symbols usually is a signal that your diagram is too complex and that you should reconsider your analysis. Another way to avoid crossing lines is to duplicate an entity or data store. When duplicating a symbol on a diagram, make sure to document the duplication to avoid possible confusion. A special notation, such as an asterisk, next to the symbol name and inside the duplicated symbols signifies that they are duplicated on the diagram.

- Provide a unique name and reference number for each process. Because it is the highest-level DFD, the context diagram contains process 0, which represents the entire information system, but does not show the internal workings. To describe the next level of detail inside process 0, you must create a DFD named diagram 0, which will reveal additional processes that must be named and numbered. As you continue to create lower-level DFDs, you assign unique names and reference numbers to all processes, until you complete the logical model.

- Obtain as much user input and feedback as possible. Your main objective is to ensure that the model is accurate, easy to understand, and meets the needs of its users.

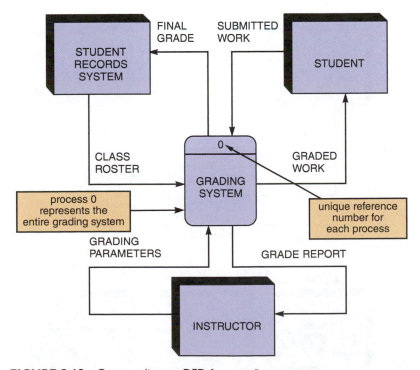

FIGURE 5-12 Context diagram DFD for a grading system.
© Cengage Learning 2014

Step 1: Draw a Context Diagram

The first step in constructing a set of DFDs is to draw a context diagram. A **context diagram** is a top-level view of an information system that shows the system's boundaries and scope. To draw a context diagram, you start by placing a single process symbol in the center of the page. The symbol represents the entire information system, and you identify it as **process** 0 (the numeral zero, and not the letter O). Then you place the system entities around the perimeter of the page and use data flows to connect the entities to the central process. Data stores are not shown in the context diagram because they are contained within the system and remain hidden until more detailed diagrams are created.

How do you know which entities and data flows to place in the context diagram? You begin by reviewing the system requirements to identify all external data sources and destinations. During that process, you identify the entities, the name and content of the data flows, and the direction of the data flows. If you do that carefully, and you did a good job of fact-finding in the previous stage, you should have no difficulty drawing the context diagram. Now review the following context diagram examples.

EXAMPLE: CONTEXT DIAGRAM FOR A GRADING SYSTEM   The context diagram for a grading system is shown in Figure 5-12. The GRADING SYSTEM process is at the center of the diagram. The three entities (STUDENT RECORDS SYSTEM, STUDENT, and INSTRUCTOR) are placed around the central process. Interaction among the central process and the entities involves six different data flows. The STUDENT RECORDS SYSTEM entity supplies data through the CLASS ROSTER data flow and receives data through the FINAL GRADE data flow. The STUDENT entity supplies data through the SUBMITTED WORK data flow and receives data through the GRADED WORK data flow. Finally, the INSTRUCTOR entity supplies data through the GRADING PARAMETERS data flow and receives data through the GRADE REPORT data flow.

EXAMPLE: CONTEXT DIAGRAM FOR AN ORDER SYSTEM   The context diagram for an order system is shown in Figure 5-13. Notice that the ORDER SYSTEM process is at the center of the diagram and five entities surround the process. Three of the

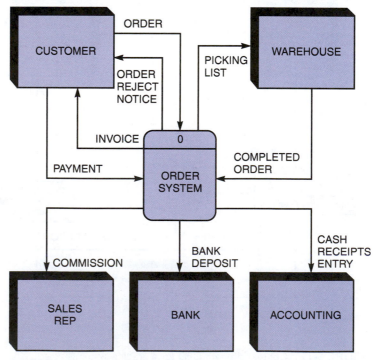

FIGURE 5-13   Context diagram DFD for an order system.
© Cengage Learning 2014

entities, SALES REP, BANK, and ACCOUNTING, have single incoming data flows for COMMISSION, BANK DEPOSIT, and CASH RECEIPTS ENTRY, respectively. The WAREHOUSE entity has one incoming data flow — PICKING LIST — that is, a report that shows the items ordered and their quantity, location, and sequence to pick from the warehouse. The WAREHOUSE entity has one outgoing data flow, COMPLETED ORDER. Finally, the CUSTOMER entity has two outgoing data flows, ORDER and PAYMENT, and two incoming data flows, ORDER REJECT NOTICE and INVOICE.

The context diagram for the order system appears more complex than the grading system because it has two more entities and three more data flows. What makes one system more complex than another is the number of components, the number of levels, and the degree of interaction among its processes, entities, data stores, and data flows.

Video Learning Session
DFD Diagram 0

If you have an MIS CourseMate access code, you can launch interactive Video Learning Sessions to help you understand systems development concepts and practice your skills. You can watch the sessions on your computer or mobile device, and pause, rewind, or replay a video at any time. To log on to the MIS CourseMate site at **www.cengagebrain.com**, you must create a student account and then register this book.

This session is about DFD diagram 0. You'll learn what a DFD diagram 0 is, how to create a diagram 0, and how you can use a CASE tool to create a DFD diagram 0.

© craftvision/iStockphoto

Step 2: Draw a Diagram 0 DFD

In the previous step, you learned that a context diagram provides the most general view of an information system and contains a single process symbol, which is like a black box. To show the detail inside the black box, you create DFD diagram 0. **Diagram 0** (the numeral zero, and not the letter O) zooms in on the system and shows major internal processes, data flows, and data stores. Diagram 0 also repeats the entities and data flows that appear in the context diagram. When you expand the context diagram into DFD diagram 0, you must retain all the connections that flow into and out of process 0.

The real-life scene in Figure 5-14 represents a complex manufacturing system with many interactive processes and data. In a large system such as this, each process in diagram 0 could represent a separate system

FIGURE 5-14   Complex manufacturing systems require many interactive processes and data sources.
© gerenme/iStockphoto

such as inventory, production control, and scheduling. Diagram 0 provides an overview of all the components that interact to form the overall system. Now review the following diagram 0 examples.

EXAMPLE: DIAGRAM 0 DFD FOR A GRADING SYSTEM   Figure 5-15 on the next page shows a context diagram at the top and diagram 0 beneath it. Notice that diagram 0 is an expansion of process 0. Also notice that the three same entities (STUDENT RECORDS SYSTEM, STUDENT, and INSTRUCTOR) and the same six data flows (FINAL GRADE,

Context Diagram for Grading System

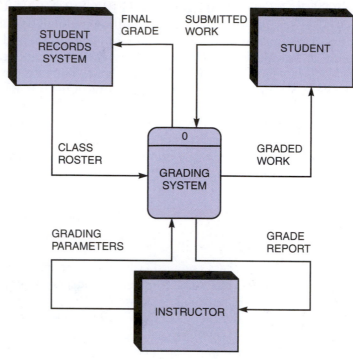

Diagram 0 for Grading System

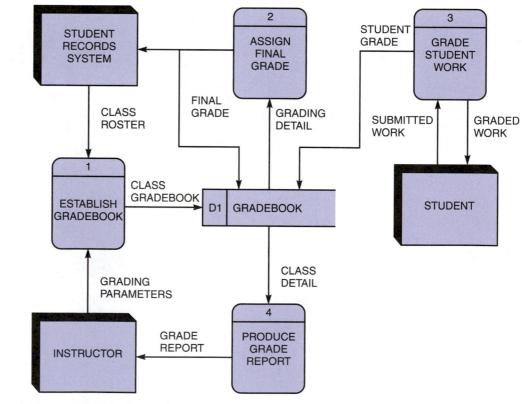

FIGURE 5-15   Context diagram and diagram 0 for the grading system.

CLASS ROSTER, SUBMITTED WORK, GRADED WORK, GRADING PARAMETERS, and GRADE REPORT) appear in both diagrams. In addition, diagram 0 expands process 0 to reveal four internal processes, one data store, and five additional data flows.

Notice that each process in diagram 0 has a reference number: ESTABLISH GRADEBOOK is 1, ASSIGN FINAL GRADE is 2, GRADE STUDENT WORK is 3, and PRODUCE GRADE REPORT is 4. These reference numbers are important because they identify a series of DFDs. If more detail were needed for ESTABLISH GRADEBOOK, for example, you would draw a diagram 1 because ESTABLISH GRADEBOOK is process 1.

The process numbers do not suggest that the processes are accomplished in a sequential order. Each process always is considered to be available, active, and awaiting data to be processed. If processes must be performed in a specific sequence, you document the information in the process descriptions (discussed later in this chapter), not in the DFD.

The FINAL GRADE data flow output from the ASSIGN FINAL GRADE process is a diverging data flow that becomes an input to the STUDENT RECORDS SYSTEM entity and to the GRADEBOOK data store. A **diverging data flow** is a data flow in which the same data travels to two or more different locations. In that situation, a diverging data flow is the best way to show the flow rather than showing two identical data flows, which could be misleading.

If the same data flows in both directions, you can use a double-headed arrow to connect the symbols. To identify specific data flows into and out of a symbol, however, you use separate data flow symbols with single arrowheads. For example, in Figure 5-15, the separate data flows (SUBMITTED WORK and GRADED WORK) go into and out of the GRADE STUDENT WORK process.

Because diagram 0 is an exploded version of process 0, it shows considerably more detail than the context diagram. You also can refer to diagram 0 as a partitioned or decomposed view of process 0. When you explode a DFD, the higher-level diagram is called the **parent diagram**, and the lower-level diagram is referred to as the **child diagram**. The grading system is simple enough that you do not need any additional DFDs to model the system. At that point, the four processes, the one data store, and the 10 data flows can be documented in the data dictionary.

When you create a set of DFDs for a system, you break the processing logic down into smaller units, called functional primitives, that programmers will use to develop code. A **functional primitive** is a process that consists of a single function that is not exploded further. For example, each of the four processes shown in the lower portion of Figure 5-15 is a functional primitive. You document the logic for a functional primitive by writing a process description in the data dictionary. Later, when the logical design is implemented as a physical system, programmers will transform each functional primitive into program code and modules that carry out the required steps. Deciding whether to explode a process further or determine that it is a functional primitive is a matter of experience, judgment, and interaction with programmers who must translate the logical design into code.

EXAMPLE: DIAGRAM 0 DFD FOR AN ORDER SYSTEM   Figure 5-16 on the next page shows the diagram 0 for an order system. Process 0 on the order system's context diagram is exploded to reveal three processes (FILL ORDER, CREATE INVOICE, and APPLY PAYMENT), one data store (ACCOUNTS RECEIVABLE), two additional data flows (INVOICE DETAIL and PAYMENT DETAIL), and one diverging data flow (INVOICE).

The following walkthrough explains the DFD shown in Figure 5-16:

1. A CUSTOMER submits an ORDER. Depending on the processing logic, the FILL ORDER process either sends an ORDER REJECT NOTICE back to the customer or sends a PICKING LIST to the WAREHOUSE.

2. A COMPLETED ORDER from the WAREHOUSE is input to the CREATE INVOICE process, which outputs an INVOICE to both the CUSTOMER process and the ACCOUNTS RECEIVABLE data store.

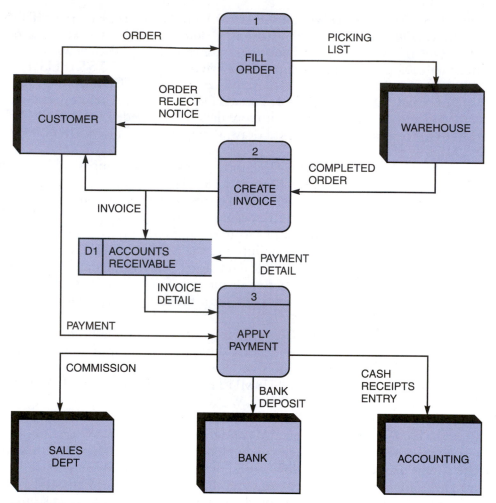

FIGURE 5-16   Diagram 0 DFD for the order system.
© Cengage Learning 2014

3. A CUSTOMER makes a PAYMENT that is processed by APPLY PAYMENT. APPLY PAYMENT requires INVOICE DETAIL input from the ACCOUNTS RECEIVABLE data store along with the PAYMENT. APPLY PAYMENT also outputs PAYMENT DETAIL back to the ACCOUNTS RECEIVABLE data store and outputs COMMISSION to the SALES DEPT, BANK DEPOSIT to the BANK, and CASH RECEIPTS ENTRY to ACCOUNTING.

The walkthrough of diagram 0 illustrates the basic requirements of the order system. To learn more, you would examine the detailed description of each separate process.

Step 3: Draw the Lower-Level Diagrams

This set of lower-level DFDs is based on the order system. To create lower-level diagrams, you must use leveling and balancing techniques. **Leveling** is the process of drawing a series of increasingly detailed diagrams, until all functional primitives are identified. **Balancing** maintains consistency among a set of DFDs by ensuring that input and output data flows align properly. Leveling and balancing are described in more detail in the following sections.

LEVELING EXAMPLES   Leveling uses a series of increasingly detailed DFDs to describe an information system. For example, a system might consist of dozens, or even hundreds, of separate processes. Using leveling, an analyst starts with an overall view, which is a context diagram with a single process symbol. Next, the analyst creates diagram 0, which shows more detail. The analyst continues to create lower-level

DFDs until all processes are identified as functional primitives, which represent single processing functions. More complex systems have more processes, and analysts must work through many levels to identify the functional primitives. Leveling also is called **exploding**, **partitioning**, or **decomposing**.

Figures 5-16 and 5-17 provide an example of leveling. Figure 5-16 shows diagram 0 for an order system, with the FILL ORDER process labeled as process 1. Now consider Figure 5-17, which provides an exploded view of the FILL ORDER process. Notice that FILL ORDER (process 1) actually consists of three processes: VERIFY ORDER (process 1.1), PREPARE REJECT NOTICE (process 1.2), and ASSEMBLE ORDER (process 1.3).

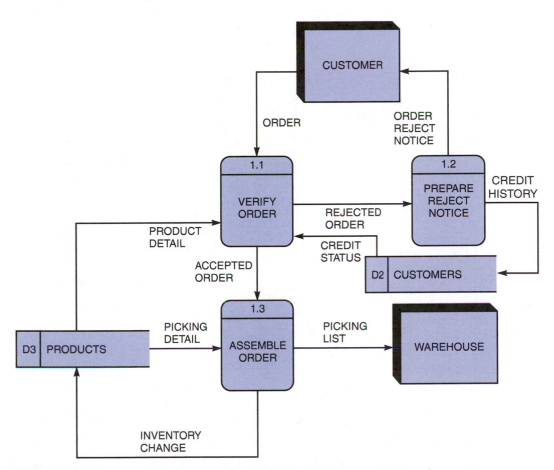

FIGURE 5-17   Diagram 1 DFD shows details of the FILL ORDER process in the order system.
© Cengage Learning 2014

As Figure 5-17 shows, all processes are numbered using a decimal notation consisting of the parent's reference number, a decimal point, and a sequence number within the new diagram. In Figure 5-17, the parent process of diagram 1 is process 1, so the processes in diagram 1 have reference numbers of 1.1, 1.2, and 1.3. If process 1.3, ASSEMBLE ORDER, is decomposed further, then it would appear in diagram 1.3 and the processes in diagram 1.3 would be numbered as 1.3.1, 1.3.2, 1.3.3, and so on. This numbering technique makes it easy to integrate and identify all DFDs.

When you compare Figures 5-16 and 5-17, you will notice that Figure 5-17 (the exploded FILL ORDER process) shows two data stores (CUSTOMER and PRODUCTS) that do not appear on Figure 5-16, which is the parent DFD. Why not? The answer is based on a simple rule: When drawing DFDs, you show a data store only when two or more processes use that data store. The CUSTOMER and PRODUCTS data stores were internal to the FILL ORDER process, so the analyst did not show them on diagram 0, which is the parent. When you explode the FILL ORDER process into diagram 1 DFD, however, you see that three processes (1.1, 1.2, and 1.3) interact with the two data stores, which now are shown.

Now compare Figure 5-17 (on the previous page) and Figure 5-18. Notice that Figure 5-18 shows the same data flows as Figure 5-17, but does not show the CUSTOMER and WAREHOUSE entities. Analysts often use this technique to simplify a DFD and reduce unnecessary clutter. Because the missing symbols appear on the parent DFD, you can refer to that diagram to identify the source or destination of the data flows.

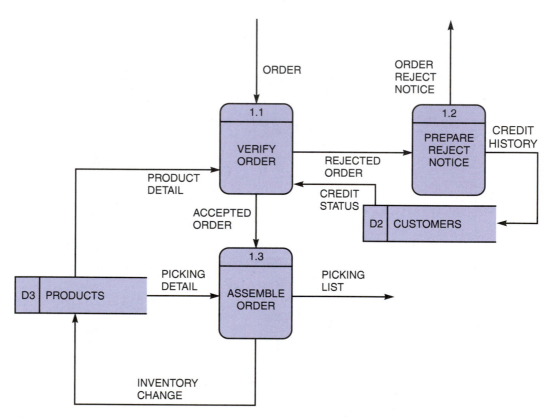

FIGURE 5-18   This diagram does not show the symbols that connect to data flows entering or leaving FILL ORDER on the context diagram.

© Cengage Learning 2014

BALANCING EXAMPLES   Balancing ensures that the input and output data flows of the parent DFD are maintained on the child DFD. For example, Figure 5-19 shows two DFDs: The order system diagram 0 is shown at the top of the figure, and the exploded diagram 3 DFD is shown at the bottom.

The two DFDs are balanced because the child diagram at the bottom has the same input and output flows as the parent process 3 shown at the top. To verify the balancing, notice that the parent process 3, APPLY PAYMENT, has one incoming data flow from an external entity, and three outgoing data flows to external entities. Now examine the child DFD, which is diagram 3. Now, ignore the internal data flows and count the data flows to and from external entities. You will see that the three processes maintain the same one incoming and three outgoing data flows as the parent process.

Order System Diagram 0 DFD

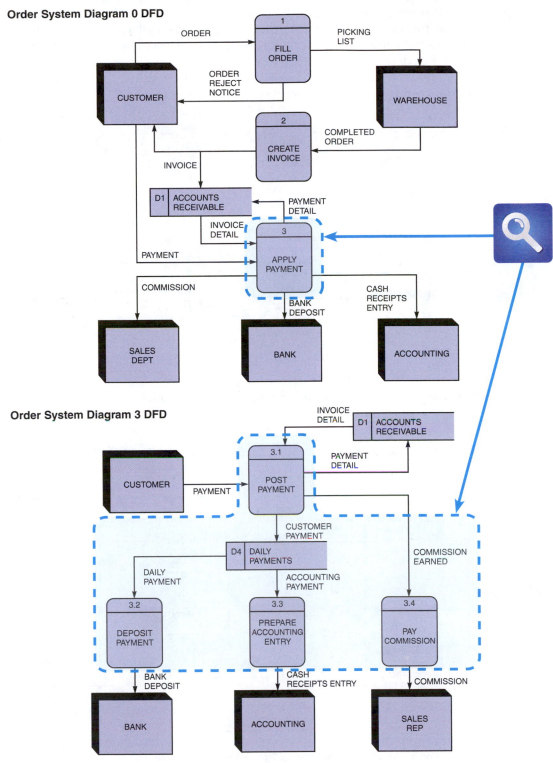

Order System Diagram 3 DFD

FIGURE 5-19   The order system diagram 0 is shown at the top of the figure, and exploded diagram 3 DFD (for the APPLY PAYMENT process) is shown at the bottom. The two DFDs are balanced because the child diagram at the bottom has the same input and output flows as the parent process 3 shown at the top.

© Cengage Learning 2014

Another example of balancing is shown in Figures 5-20 and 5-21 on the next page. The DFDs in these figures were created using Visible Analyst, a popular CASE tool.

Figure 5-20 shows a sample context diagram. The process 0 symbol has two input flows and two output flows. Notice that process 0 can be considered as a black box, with no internal detail shown. In Figure 5-21, process 0 (the parent DFD) is exploded into the next level of detail. Now three processes, two data stores, and four internal data flows are visible. Notice that the details of process 0 are shown inside a dashed line, just as if you could see inside the process.

FIGURE 5-20   Example of a parent DFD diagram, showing process 0 as a black box.
© Cengage Learning 2014

FIGURE 5-21   In the next level of detail, the process 0 black box reveals three processes, two data stores, and four internal data flows — all of which are shown inside the dashed line.
© Cengage Learning 2014

The DFDs in Figures 5-20 and 5-21 are balanced because the four data flows into and out of process 0 are maintained on the child DFD. The DFDs also are leveled because each internal process is numbered to show that it is a child of the parent process.

CASE IN POINT 5.1: BIG TEN UNIVERSITY

You are the IT director at Big Ten University. As part of a training program, you decide to draw a DFD that includes some obvious mistakes to see whether your newly hired junior analysts can find them. You came up with the diagram 0 DFD shown in Figure 5-22. Based on the rules explained in this chapter, how many problems should the analysts find?

FIGURE 5-22   What are the mistakes in this diagram 0 DFD?

© Cengage Learning 2014

DATA DICTIONARY

A set of DFDs produces a logical model of the system, but the details within those DFDs are documented separately in a data dictionary, which is the second component of structured analysis.

A **data dictionary,** or **data repository,** is a central storehouse of information about the system's data. An analyst uses the data dictionary to collect, document, and organize specific facts about the system, including the contents of data flows, data stores, entities, and processes. The data dictionary also defines and describes all data elements and meaningful combinations of data elements. A **data element,** also called a **data item** or **field,** is the smallest piece of data that has meaning within an information system. Examples of data elements are student grade, salary, Social Security number, account balance, and company name. Data elements are combined into **records,** also called **data structures.** A record is a meaningful combination of related data elements that is included in a data flow or retained in a data store. For example, an auto parts store inventory record might include part number, description, supplier code, minimum and maximum stock levels, cost, and list price.

Significant relationships exist among the items in a data dictionary. For example, data stores and data flows are based on data structures, which in turn are composed of data elements. Data flows are connected to data stores, entities, and processes. Accurately documenting these relationships is essential so the data dictionary is consistent with the DFDs. You can use CASE software to help you document the design.

TOOLKIT TIME

The CASE tools in Part B of the Systems Analyst's Toolkit can help you document business functions and processes. To learn more about these tools, turn to Part B of the four-part Toolkit that follows Chapter 12.

Using CASE Tools for Documentation

The more complex the system, the more difficult it is to maintain full and accurate documentation. Fortunately, modern CASE tools simplify the task. For example, in the Visible Analyst CASE tool, documentation automatically flows from the modeling diagrams into the central repository, along with information entered by the user. This section contains several examples of Visible Analyst screens that show the data repository and its contents.

A CASE repository ensures data consistency, which is especially important where multiple systems require the same data. In a large company, for example, the sales, accounting, and shipping systems all might use a data element called CUSTOMER NUMBER. Once the CUSTOMER NUMBER element has been defined in the repository, it can be accessed by other processes, data flows, and data stores. The result is that all systems across the enterprise can share data that is up to date and consistent. You will learn more about CASE tools in Part B of the Systems Analyst's Toolkit.

Documenting the Data Elements

You must document every data element in the data dictionary. Some analysts like to record their notes on online or manual forms. Others prefer to enter the information directly into a CASE tool. Several of the DFDs and data dictionary entries that appear in this chapter were created using a popular CASE tool called Visible Analyst. Although other CASE tools might use other terms or display the information differently, the objective is the same: to provide clear, comprehensive information about the data and processes that make up the system.

Figure 5-23 shows how the analyst used an online documentation form to record information for the SOCIAL SECURITY NUMBER data element. Notice that the figure caption identifies eight specific characteristics for this data element.

1. Online or manual documentation entries often indicate which system is involved. This is not necessary with a CASE tool because all information is stored in one file that is named for the system.
2. The data element has a standard label that provides consistency throughout the data dictionary.
3. The data element can have an alternative name, or alias.
4. This entry indicates that the data element consists of nine numeric characters.
5. Depending on the data element, strict limits might be placed on acceptable values.
6. The data comes from the employee's job application.
7. This entry indicates that only the payroll department has authority to update or change this data.
8. This entry indicates the individual or department responsible for entering and changing data.

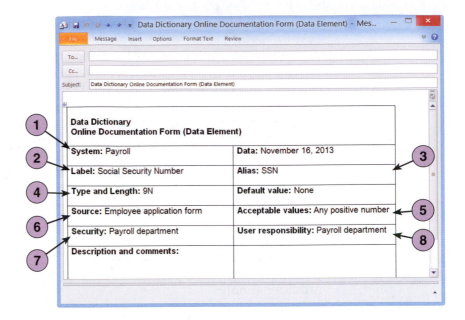

FIGURE 5-23 Using an online documentation form, the analyst has recorded information for a data element named SOCIAL SECURITY NUMBER. Later, the analyst will create a data dictionary entry using a CASE tool.

© Cengage Learning 2014

Figure 5-24 shows a sample screen that illustrates how the SOCIAL SECURITY NUMBER data element might be recorded in the Visible Analyst data dictionary.

Regardless of the terminology or method, the following attributes usually are recorded and described in the data dictionary:

Data element name or label. The data element's standard name, which should be meaningful to users.

Alias. Any name(s) other than the standard data element name; this alternate name is called an **alias**. For example, if you have a data element named CURRENT BALANCE, various users might refer to it by alternate names such as OUTSTANDING BALANCE, CUSTOMER BALANCE, RECEIVABLE BALANCE, or AMOUNT OWED.

Type and length. **Type** refers to whether the data element contains numeric, alphabetic, or character values. **Length** is the maximum number of characters for an alphabetic or character data element or the maximum number of digits and number of decimal positions for a numeric data element. In addition to text and numeric data, sounds and images also can be stored in digital form. In some systems, these binary data objects are managed and processed just as traditional data elements are. For example, an employee record might include a digitized photo image of the person.

Default value. The default value is the value for the data element if a value otherwise is not entered for it. For example, all new customers might have a default value of $500 for the CREDIT LIMIT data element.

FIGURE 5-24 A Visible Analyst screen describes the data element named SOCIAL SECURITY NUMBER. Notice that many of the items were entered from the online form shown in Figure 5-23.

Screenshot used with permission from Visible Systems Corporation.

Acceptable values. Specification of the data element's **domain**, which is the set of values permitted for the data element; these values either can be specifically listed or referenced in a table, or can be selected from a specified range of values. You also would indicate if a value for the data element is optional. Some data elements have additional **validity rules**. For example, an employee's salary must be within the range defined for the employee's job classification.

Source. The specification for the origination point for the data element's values. The source could be a specific form, a department or outside organization, another information system, or the result of a calculation.

Security. Identification for the individual or department that has access or update privileges for each data element. For example, only a credit manager has the authority to change a credit limit, while sales reps are authorized to access data in a read-only mode.

Responsible user(s). Identification of the user(s) responsible for entering and changing values for the data element.

Description and comments. This part of the documentation allows you to enter additional notes.

Documenting the Data Flows

In addition to documenting each data element, you must document all data flows in the data dictionary. Figure 5-25 shows a definition for a data flow named COMMISSION. The information on the manual form at the top was entered into the CASE tool data dictionary at the bottom of Figure 5-25.

Although terms can vary, the typical attributes are as follows:

Data flow name or label. The data flow name as it appears on the DFDs.

Description. Describes the data flow and its purpose.

Alternate name(s). Aliases for the DFD data flow name(s).

Origin. The DFD beginning, or source, for the data flow; the origin can be a process, a data store, or an entity.

Destination. The DFD ending point(s) for the data flow; the destination can be a process, a data store, or an entity.

Record. Each data flow represents a group of related data elements called a record or data structure. In most data dictionaries, records are defined separately from the data flows and data stores. When records are defined, more than one data flow or data store can use the same record, if necessary.

Volume and frequency. Describes the expected number of occurrences for the data flow per unit of time. For example, if a company has 300 employees, a TIME CARD data flow would involve 300 transactions and records each week as employees submit their work hour data.

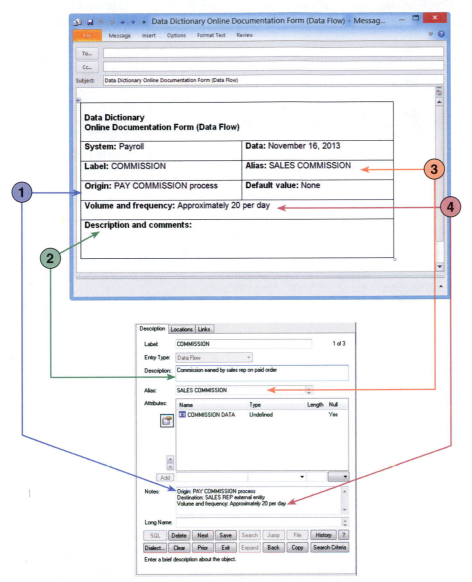

FIGURE 5-25   In the upper screen, an analyst has entered four items of information in an online documentation form. The lower screen shows the same four items entered into a Visible Analyst data dictionary form.

Screenshots used with permission from Visible Systems Corporation.

Documenting the Data Stores

You must document every DFD data store in the data dictionary. Figure 5-26 on the next page shows the definition of a data store named IN STOCK.

1. This data store has an alternative name, or alias.
2. For consistency, data flow names are standardized throughout the data dictionary.
3. It is important to document these estimates because they will affect design decisions in subsequent SDLC phases.

FIGURE 5-26   Visible Analyst screen that documents a data store named IN STOCK.

Screenshot used with permission from Visible Systems Corporation.

Typical characteristics of a data store are as follows:

Data store name or label. The data store name as it appears on the DFDs.

Description. Describes the data store and its purpose.

Alternate name(s). Aliases for the DFD data store name.

Attributes. Standard DFD names that enter or leave the data store.

Volume and frequency. Describes the estimated number of records in the data store and how frequently they are updated.

Documenting the Processes

You must document every process, as shown in Figure 5-27. Your documentation includes a description of the process's characteristics and, for functional primitives, a process description, which is a model that documents the processing steps and business logic.

The following are typical characteristics of a process:

Process name or label. The process name as it appears on the DFDs.

Description. A brief statement of the process's purpose.

Process number. A reference number that identifies the process and indicates relationships among various levels in the system.

Process description. This section includes the input and output data flows. For functional primitives, the process description also documents the processing steps and business logic. You will learn how to write process descriptions in the next section.

1. The process number identifies this process. Any sub-processes are numbered 1.1, 1.2, 1.3, and so on.
2. These data flows will be described specifically elsewhere in the data dictionary.

FIGURE 5-27   Visible Analyst screen that describes a process named VERIFY ORDER.

Screenshot used with permission from Visible Systems Corporation.

Documenting the Entities

By documenting all entities, the data dictionary can describe all external entities that interact with the system. Figure 5-28 shows a definition for an external entity named WAREHOUSE.

Typical characteristics of an entity include the following:

Entity name. The entity name as it appears on the DFDs.

Description. Describe the entity and its purpose.

Alternate name(s). Any aliases for the entity name.

Input data flows. The standard DFD names for the input data flows to the entity.

Output data flows. The standard DFD names for the data flows leaving the entity.

1. The external entity also can have an alternative name, or alias, if properly documented.
2. For consistency, these data flow names are standardized throughout the data dictionary.

FIGURE 5-28 Visible Analyst screen that documents an external entity named WAREHOUSE.

Screenshot used with permission from Visible Systems Corporation.

Documenting the Records

A record is a data structure that contains a set of related data elements that are stored and processed together. Data flows and data stores consist of records that you must document in the data dictionary. You define characteristics of each record, as shown in Figure 5-29.

Typical characteristics of a record include the following:

Record or data structure name. The record name as it appears in the related data flow and data store entries in the data dictionary.

Definition or description. A brief definition of the record.

Alternate name(s). Any aliases for the record name.

Attributes. A list of all the data elements included in the record. The data element names must match exactly what you entered in the data dictionary.

1. This data structure is named CREDIT STATUS.

2. The CREDIT STATUS data structure consists of two data elements: CUSTOMER NUMBER and CUSTOMER STATUS CODE.

FIGURE 5-29 Visible Analyst screen that documents a record, or data structure named CREDIT STATUS.

Screenshot used with permission from Visible Systems Corporation.

Data Dictionary Reports

The data dictionary serves as a central storehouse of documentation for an information system. A data dictionary is created when the system is developed, and is updated constantly as the system is implemented, operated, and maintained. In addition to describing each data element, data flow, data store, record, entity, and process, the data dictionary documents the relationships among these components. You can obtain many valuable reports from a data dictionary, including the following:

- An alphabetized list of all data elements by name
- A report describing each data element and indicating the user or department that is responsible for data entry, updating, or deletion
- A report of all data flows and data stores that use a particular data element
- Detailed reports showing all characteristics of data elements, records, data flows, processes, or any other selected item stored in the data dictionary

PROCESS DESCRIPTION TOOLS

A **process description** documents the details of a functional primitive, and represents a specific set of processing steps and business logic. Using a set of process description tools, you create a model that is accurate, complete, and concise. Typical process description tools include structured English, decision tables, and decision trees. When you analyze a functional primitive, you break the processing steps down into smaller units in a process called modular design.

It should be noted that this chapter deals with structured analysis, but the process description tools also can be used in object-oriented development, which is described in Chapter 6. You learned in Chapter 1 that O-O analysis combines data and the processes that act on the data into things called objects, that similar objects can be grouped together into classes, and that O-O processes are called methods. Although O-O programmers use different terminology, they create the same kind of modular coding structures, except that the processes, or methods, are stored inside the objects, rather than as separate components.

FIGURE 5-30 Sequence structure.
© Cengage Learning 2014

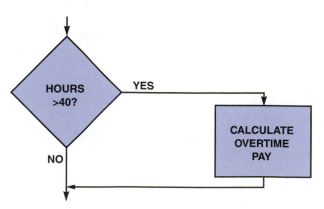

FIGURE 5-31 Selection structure.
© Cengage Learning 2014

Modular Design

Modular design is based on combinations of three **logical structures**, sometimes called **control structures**, which serve as building blocks for the process. Each logical structure must have a single entry and exit point. The three structures are called sequence, selection, and iteration. A rectangle represents a step or process, a diamond shape represents a condition or decision, and the logic follows the lines in the direction indicated by the arrows.

1. **Sequence.** The completion of steps in sequential order, one after another, as shown in Figure 5-30. One or more of the steps might represent a subprocess that contains additional logical structures.

2. **Selection.** The completion of one of two or more process steps based on the results of a test or condition. In the example shown in Figure 5-31, the system tests the input, and if the hours are greater than 40, it performs the CALCULATE OVERTIME PAY process.

3. **Iteration.** The completion of a process step that is repeated until a specific condition changes, as shown in Figure 5-32. An example of iteration is a process that continues to print paychecks until it reaches the end of the payroll file. Iteration also is called **looping**.

Sequence, selection, and iteration structures can be combined in various ways to describe processing logic.

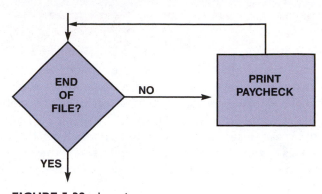

FIGURE 5-32   Iteration structure.
© Cengage Learning 2014

Structured English

Structured English is a subset of standard English that describes logical processes clearly and accurately. When you use structured English, you must conform to the following rules:

- Use only the three building blocks of sequence, selection, and iteration.

- Use indentation for readability.

- Use a limited vocabulary, including standard terms used in the data dictionary and specific words that describe the processing rules.

An example of structured English appears in Figure 5-33, which shows the VERIFY ORDER process that was illustrated earlier. Notice that the structured English version documents the actual logic that will be coded into the system. Structured English can help make your process descriptions accurate and understandable to users and system developers.

Structured English might look familiar to programming students because it resembles **pseudocode**, which is used in program design. Although the techniques are similar, the primary purpose of structured English is to describe the underlying business logic, while programmers, who are concerned with coding, mainly use pseudocode as a shorthand notation for the actual code.

Figure 5-34 shows another example of structured English. After you study the sales promotion policy, notice that the structured English version describes the processing logic that the system must apply. Following structured English rules ensures that your process descriptions are understandable to users who must confirm that the process is correct, as well as to other analysts and programmers who must design the information system from your descriptions.

FIGURE 5-33   The VERIFY ORDER process description includes logical rules and a structured English version of the policy. Notice the alignment and indentation of the logic statements.
Screenshot used with permission from Visible Systems Corporation.

Video Learning Session
Decision Tables

If you have an MIS CourseMate access code, you can launch interactive Video Learning Sessions to help you understand systems development concepts and practice your skills. You can watch the sessions on your computer or mobile device, and pause, rewind, or replay a video at any time. To log on to the MIS CourseMate site at **www.cengagebrain.com**, you must create a student account and then register this book.

This session is about decision tables, why they are important process description tools, how to create decision tables, and how to analyze conditions and outcomes in a decision table.

© craftvision/iStockphoto

Decision Tables

A **decision table** is a logical structure that shows every combination of conditions and outcomes. Analysts often use decision tables to describe a process and ensure that they have considered all possible situations. You can create decision tables using Microsoft PowerPoint, Word, or Excel.

TABLES WITH ONE CONDITION   If a process has a single condition, there only are two possibilities – *yes* or *no*. Either the condition is present or it is not, so there are only two rules. For example, to trigger an overtime calculation, the process condition might be: *Are the hours greater than 40?* If so, the calculation is made. Otherwise, it is not.

TABLES WITH TWO CONDITIONS   Suppose you want to create a decision table based on the Verify Order business process shown in Figure 5-34. When documenting a process, it is important to ensure that you list every possibility. In this example, the process description contains two conditions: product stock status and customer credit status. If *both* conditions are met, the order is accepted. Otherwise the order is rejected.

After you identify all the conditions and outcomes, you are ready to create a decision table similar to the one shown in Figure 5-35. To create the table, follow the four steps listed in the margin.

1. Place the name of the process in a heading at the top left.
2. Enter the conditions under the heading, with one condition per line, to represent the customer status and availability of products.
3. Enter all potential combinations of Y/N (for yes and no) for the conditions. Each column represents a numbered possibility called a rule.
4. Place an X in the action entries area for each rule to indicate whether to accept or reject the order.

VERIFY ORDER Business Process with Two Conditions

• An order will be accepted only if the product is in stock and the customer's credit status is OK.

• All other orders will be rejected.

FIGURE 5-34   The Verify Order business process has two conditions. For an order to be accepted, the product must be in stock and the customer must have an acceptable credit status.
© Cengage Learning 2014

VERIFY ORDER Process

	1	2	3	4
Credit status is OK	Y	Y	N	N
Product is in stock	Y	N	Y	N
Accept order	X			
Reject order		X	X	X

FIGURE 5-35   Example of a simple decision table showing the processing logic of the VERIFY ORDER process.
© Cengage Learning 2014

Notice that each condition has two possible values, so the number of rules doubles each time you add another condition. For example, one condition creates two rules, two conditions create four rules, three conditions create eight rules, and so on. In the two-condition example in Figure 5-35, four possibilities exist, but Rule 1 is the *only* combination that will accept an order.

TABLES WITH THREE CONDITIONS   Suppose the company now decides that the credit manager can waive the customer credit requirement, as shown in Figure 5-36. That creates a third condition, so there will be eight possible rules. The new decision table might resemble the one shown in Figure 5-37.

VERIFY ORDER Business Process with Three Conditions

- An order will be accepted only if the product is in stock and the customer's credit status is OK.

- The credit manager can waive the credit status requirement.

- All other orders will be rejected.

FIGURE 5-36   A third condition has been added to the Verify Order business process. For an order to be accepted, the product must be in stock and the customer must have an acceptable credit status. However, the credit manager now has the authority to waive the credit status requirement.
© Cengage Learning 2014

VERIFY ORDER Process with Credit Waiver (initial version)

	1	2	3	4	5	6	7	8
Credit status is OK	Y	Y	Y	Y	N	N	N	N
Product is in stock	Y	Y	N	N	Y	Y	N	N
Waiver from credit manager	Y	N	Y	N	Y	N	Y	N
Accept order	X	X			X			
Reject order			X	X		X	X	X

FIGURE 5-37   This table is based on the Verify Order conditions shown in Figure 5-36. With three conditions, there are eight possible combinations, or rules.
© Cengage Learning 2014

First, you must fill in the Y-N patterns, as shown in Figure 5-37. The best way to assure that all combinations appear is to use patterns like these. The first condition uses a pattern of Y-Y-Y-Y followed by N-N-N-N; the second condition uses a repeating Y-Y-N-N pattern; and the pattern in the third condition is a series of Y-Ns.

The next step is very important, regardless of the number of conditions. Each numbered column, or rule, represents a different set of conditions. You must analyze the logic carefully and show the outcome for each rule. Before going further, study the table in Figure 5-37 and be sure you understand the logical outcome for each of the eight rules.

When all the outcomes have been determined, you are ready to simplify the table. In a multicondition table, some rules might be duplicates, redundant, or unrealistic. To simplify the table, follow these steps:

1. Study each combination of conditions and outcomes. When you have rules with three conditions, only one or two of them may control the outcome, and the other conditions simply do not matter.

2. If you identify conditions that do not affect the outcome, mark them with dashes (-) as shown in the first table in Figure 5-38 on the next page.

3. Now combine and renumber the rules, as shown in the second table in Figure 5-38.

VERIFY ORDER Process with Credit Waiver (with rules marked for combination)

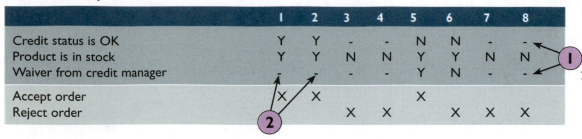

	1	2	3	4	5	6	7	8	
Credit status is OK	Y	Y	-	-	N	N	-	-	1. Because the product is not in stock, the other conditions do not matter.
Product is in stock	Y	Y	N	N	Y	Y	N	N	
Waiver from credit manager	-	-	-	-	Y	N	-	-	2. Because the other conditions are met, the waiver does not matter.
Accept order	X	X			X				
Reject order			X	X		X	X	X	

VERIFY ORDER Process with Credit Waiver (after rule combination and simplification)

	1 (COMBINES PREVIOUS 1, 2)	2 (PREVIOUS 5)	3 (PREVIOUS 6)	4 (COMBINES PREVIOUS 3, 4, 7, 8)
Credit status is OK	Y	N	N	-
Product is in stock	Y	Y	Y	N
Waiver from credit manager	-	Y	N	-
Accept order	X	X		
Reject order			X	X

FIGURE 5-38   In the first table, dashes have been added to indicate that a condition is not relevant. In the second version, rules have been combined. Notice that in final version, only four rules remain. These rules document the logic, and will be transformed into program code when the system is developed.

© Cengage Learning 2014

If you follow these steps, you will see that Rules 1 and 2 can be combined because credit status is OK in both rules, so the waiver would not matter. Rules 3, 4, 7, and 8 also can be combined because the product is not in stock, so other conditions do not matter. The result is that instead of eight possibilities, only four logical rules control the Verify Order process.

MULTIPLE OUTCOMES   In addition to multiple conditions, decision tables can have more than two possible outcomes. For example, the sales promotion policy shown in Figure 5-39 includes three conditions: Was the customer a preferred customer, did the customer order $1,000 or more, and did the customer use our company charge card? Based on these conditions, four possible actions can occur, as shown in the decision table in Figure 5-40.

SALES PROMOTION POLICY – Holiday Season, 2014

- Preferred customers who order $1,000 or more are entitled to a 5% discount, and an additional 5% discount if they use our charge card.

- Preferred customers who do not order $1,000 or more will receive a $25 bonus coupon.

- All other customers will receive a $5 bonus coupon.

FIGURE 5-39   A sales promotion policy with three conditions. Notice that the first statement contains two *separate* conditions – one for the 5% discount, and another for the additional discount.

© Cengage Learning 2014

Sales Promotion Policy (initial version)

	1	2	3	4	5	6	7	8
Preferred customer	Y	Y	Y	Y	N	N	N	N
Ordered $1,000 or more	Y	Y	N	N	Y	Y	N	N
Used our charge card	Y	N	Y	N	Y	N	Y	N
5% discount	X	X						
Additional 5% discount	X							
$25 bonus coupon			X	X				
$5 bonus coupon					X	X	X	X

FIGURE 5-40   This decision table is based on the sales promotion policy in Figure 5-39. This is the initial version of the table, before simplification.

© Cengage Learning 2014

As explained in the preceding section, most tables can be simplified, and this one is no exception. When you study the conditions and outcomes, you realize that:

- In Rule 1, all three conditions are met, so *both* 5% discounts apply.

- In Rule 2, a preferred customer orders $1,000 or more, but does not use our charge card, so only *one* 5% discount applies.

- Rules 3 and 4 can be combined into a single rule. Why? If preferred customers do not order $1,000 or more, it does not matter whether they use our charge card – either way, they only earn a $25 bonus coupon. Therefore, Rules 3 and 4 really are a single rule.

- Rules 5, 6, 7, and 8 also can be combined into a single rule – because if the person is *not* a preferred customer, he or she can *only* receive a $5 bonus coupon, and the other conditions simply do not matter. So, you insert a dash if a condition is irrelevant, as shown in Figure 5-41.

If you add dashes for rules that are not relevant, your table should resemble the one shown in Figure 5-41. When you combine and simplify the results, only four rules remain: Rule 1, Rule 2, Rule 3 (a combination of initial Rules 3 and 4), and Rule 4 (a combination of initial Rules 5, 6, 7, and 8).

Sales Promotion Policy (final version)

	1	2	3	4	5	6	7	8
Preferred customer	Y	Y	Y	Y	N	N	N	N
Ordered $1,000 or more	Y	Y	N	N	-	-	-	-
Used our charge card	Y	N	-	-	-	-	-	-
5% discount	X	X						
Additional 5% discount	X							
$25 bonus coupon			X	X				
$5 bonus coupon					X	X	X	X

FIGURE 5-41   In this version, dashes have been added to indicate that a condition is not relevant. At this point, it appears that several rules can be combined.

© Cengage Learning 2014

Decision tables often are the best way to describe a complex set of conditions. Many analysts use decision tables because they are easy to construct and understand, and programmers find it easy to work from a decision table when developing code.

CASE IN POINT 5.2:   Rock Solid Outfitters (Part 1)

Leah Jones is the IT manager at Rock Solid Outfitters, a medium-sized supplier of outdoor climbing and camping gear. Steve Allen, the marketing director, has asked Leah to develop a special Web-based promotion. As Steve described it to Leah, Rock Solid will provide free shipping for any customer who either completes an online survey form or signs up for the Rock Solid online newsletter. Additionally, if a customer completes the survey *and* signs up for the newsletter, Rock Solid will provide a $10 merchandise credit for orders of $100 or more. Leah has asked you to develop a decision table that will reflect the promotional rules that a programmer will use. She wants you to show all possibilities, and then to simplify the results to eliminate any combinations that would be unrealistic or redundant.

Decision Trees

A **decision tree** is a graphical representation of the conditions, actions, and rules found in a decision table. Decision trees show the logic structure in a horizontal form that resembles a tree with the roots at the left and the branches to the right. Like flowcharts, decision trees are useful ways to present the system to management. Decision trees and decision tables provide the same results, but in different forms. In many situations, a graphic is the most effective means of communication.

Figure 5-42 is based on the sales promotion policy shown in Figure 5-39 on page 208. A decision tree is read from left to right, with the conditions along the various branches and the actions at the far right. Because the example has two conditions with four resulting sets of actions, the example has four terminating branches at the right side of the tree.

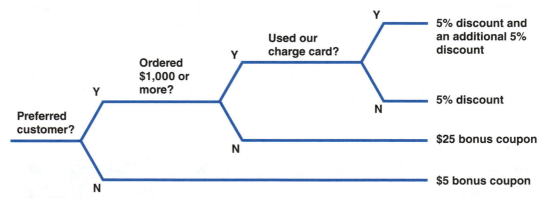

FIGURE 5-42   This example is based on the same Sales Promotion Policy shown in the decision tables in Figures 5-40 and 5-41 on the previous page. Like a decision table, a decision tree shows all combinations of conditions and outcomes. The main difference is the graphical format, which many viewers find easier to interpret.
© Cengage Learning 2014

Whether to use a decision table or a decision tree often is a matter of personal preference. A decision table might be a better way to handle complex combinations of conditions. On the other hand, a decision tree is an effective way to describe a relatively simple process.

CASE IN POINT 5.3:   Rock Solid Outfitters (Part 2)

Leah Jones, the IT manager at Rock Solid Outfitters, thinks you did a good job on the decision table task she assigned to you. Now she wants you to use the same data to develop a decision tree that will show all the possibilities for the Web-based promotion described in Part 1 of the case. She also wants you to discuss the pros and cons of decisions tables versus decision trees.

LOGICAL VERSUS PHYSICAL MODELS

While structured analysis tools are used to develop a logical model for a new information system, such tools also can be used to develop physical models of an information system. A physical model shows how the system's requirements are implemented. During the systems design phase, you create a physical model of the new information system that follows from the logical model and involves operational tasks and techniques.

Sequence of Models

What is the relationship between logical and physical models? Think back to the beginning of the systems analysis phase when you were trying to understand the existing system. Rather than starting with a logical model, you first studied the physical operations of the existing system to understand how the current tasks were carried out. Many systems analysts create a physical model of the current system and then develop a logical model of the current system before tackling a logical model of the new system. Performing that extra step allows them to understand the current system better.

Four-Model Approach

Many analysts follow a **four-model approach,** which means that they develop a physical model of the current system, a logical model of the current system, a logical model of the new system, and a physical model of the new system. The major benefit of the four-model approach is that it gives you a clear picture of current system functions before you make any modifications or improvements. That is important because mistakes made early in systems development will affect later SDLC phases and can result in unhappy users and additional costs. Taking additional steps to avoid these potentially costly mistakes can prove to be well worth the effort. Another advantage is that the requirements of a new information system often are quite similar to those of the current information system, especially where the proposal is based on new computer technology rather than a large number of new requirements. Adapting the current system logical model to the new system logical model in these cases is a straightforward process.

The only disadvantage of the four-model approach is the added time and cost needed to develop a logical and physical model of the current system. Most projects have very tight schedules that might not allow time to create the current system models. Additionally, users and managers want to see progress on the new system — they are much less concerned about documenting the current system. As a systems analyst, you must stress the importance of careful documentation and resist the pressure to hurry the development process at the risk of creating serious problems later.

CASE IN POINT 5.4:   TIP TOP STAFFING

Tip Top Staffing supplies employees to hundreds of IT firms that require specialized skills for specific projects. Systems analysts Lisa Nuevo and Bill Goodman are working on the logical model of Tip Top's billing and records system, using DFDs, a data dictionary, and process descriptions. At some point while working on the logical model of the system, Lisa felt that some improvements should be made in the data forms that Tip Top uses to obtain information about job applicants. Was the subject of improving the forms a physical implementation issue? Is Lisa going off on a tangent by considering *how* something will be done, instead of sticking to *what* will be done?

A QUESTION OF ETHICS

© faberfoto_it/iStockphoto

This is your first week in your new job at Safety Zone, a leading producer of IT modeling software. Your prior experience with a smaller competitor gave you an edge in landing the job, and you are excited about joining a larger company in the same field.

So far, all is going well and you are getting used to the new routine. However, you are concerned about one issue. In your initial meeting with the IT manager, she seemed very interested in the details of your prior position, and some of her questions made you a little uncomfortable. She did not actually ask you to reveal any proprietary information, but she made it clear that Safety Zone likes to know as much as possible about its competitors.

Thinking about it some more, you try to draw a line between information that is OK to discuss, and topics such as software specifics or strategy that should be considered private. This is the first time you have ever been in a situation like this. How will you handle it?

CHAPTER SUMMARY

During data and process modeling, a systems analyst develops graphical models to show how the system transforms data into useful information. The end product of data and process modeling is a logical model that will support business operations and meet user needs. Data and process modeling involves three main tools: data flow diagrams, a data dictionary, and process descriptions.

Data flow diagrams (DFDs) graphically show the movement and transformation of data in the information system. DFDs use four symbols: The process symbol transforms data; the data flow symbol shows data movement; the data store symbol shows data at rest; and the external entity symbol represents someone or something connected to the information system. Various rules and techniques are used to name, number, arrange, and annotate the set of DFDs to make them consistent and understandable.

A set of DFDs is like a pyramid with the context diagram at the top. The context diagram represents the information system's scope and its external connections but not its internal workings. Diagram 0 displays the information system's major processes, data stores, and data flows and is the exploded version of the context diagram's process symbol, which represents the entire information system. Lower-level DFDs show additional detail of the information system through the leveling technique of numbering and partitioning. Leveling continues until you reach the functional primitive processes, which are not decomposed further and are documented with process descriptions. All diagrams must be balanced to ensure their consistency and accuracy.

The data dictionary is the central documentation tool for structured analysis. All data elements, data flows, data stores, processes, entities, and records are documented in the data dictionary. Consolidating documentation in one location allows you to verify the information system's accuracy and consistency more easily and generate a variety of useful reports.

Each functional primitive process is documented using structured English, decision tables, and decision trees. Structured English uses a subset of standard English that defines each process with combinations of the basic building blocks of sequence, selection, and iteration. You also can document the logic by using decision tables or decision trees.

Structured analysis tools can be used to develop a logical model during one systems analysis phase, and a physical model during the systems design phase. Many analysts use a four-model approach, which involves a physical model of the current system, a logical model of the current system, a logical model of the new system, and a physical model of the new system.

Key Terms

alias *199*
balancing *192*
black box *181*
black hole *183*
business logic *181*
business rules *181*
child diagram *191*
context diagram *188*
control structures *204*
data dictionary *197*
data element *197*
data flow *182*
data flow diagram (DFD) *180*
data item *197*
data repository *197*
data store *183*
data structures *197*
decision table *206*
decision tree *210*
decomposing *193*
diagram 0 *189*
diverging data flow *191*
domain *200*
entity *185*
exploding *193*
field *197*
four-model approach *211*
functional primitive *191*

Gane and Sarson *180*
gray hole *183*
iteration *205*
length *199*
leveling *192*
logical model *178*
logical structures *204*
looping *205*
modular design *204*
parent diagram *191*
partitioning *193*
physical model *178*
process *181*
process 0 *188*
process description *204*
pseudocode *205*
records *197*
selection *204*
sequence *204*
sink *185*
source *185*
spontaneous generation *183*
structured English *205*
terminators *185*
type *199*
validity rules *200*
Yourdon *180*

Chapter Exercises

Questions

1. Describe data and process modeling concepts and tools.
2. Explain the differences between Gane and Sarson and Yourdon symbols. Provide examples of symbols that represent processes, data flows, data stores, and entities.
3. What is the difference between a context diagram and diagram 0? Which symbol is *not* used in a context diagram?
4. How would you *explode* DFDs?
5. Describe a data dictionary and list the types of information it contains.
6. How would you level DFDs?
7. How would you balance DFDs?
8. What is the purpose of decision tables? How do you create them?
9. Why would a manager prefer a decision tree instead of a decision table?
10. What is structured English?

Discussion Topics

1. Suppose you were assigned to develop a logical model of the registration system at a school or college. Would you be better off using a top-down approach, or would a bottom-up strategy be better? What would influence your decision?
2. Some systems analysts find it better to start with a decision table, and then construct a decision tree. Others believe it is easier to do it in the reverse order. Which do you prefer? Why?
3. A systems analyst attended a weeklong workshop on structured analysis. When she returned to her job, she told her boss that structured analysis was not worth the time to learn and use on the job. Her view was that it was too academic and had too much new terminology to be useful. Do you agree? Why or why not?
4. This chapter describes a *black box* concept that allows more detail to be shown as a process is exploded. Can the concept be applied in business management generally, or is it limited to information systems design? Provide some reasons and examples.

Projects

1. Draw a context diagram and a diagram 0 DFD that represents the information system at a typical library.
2. On the Internet, locate at least three firms that offer CASE tools as shareware or free, public domain software. Describe what you found.
3. Create a decision table with three conditions. You can make one up, or use a scenario from everyday life. Either way, be sure to show all possible outcomes.
4. The data flow symbols shown on page 181 were designed by Ed Yourdon, a well-known IT author, lecturer, and consultant. Many IT professionals consider him to be among the most influential men and women in the software field. Learn more about Mr. Yourdon by visiting his Web site at **www.yourdon.com**, and write a brief review of his work.

Apply Your Knowledge

This section contains four mini-cases. Each case describes a situation, explains your role, and requires you to apply what you learned in the chapter.

1 Globe Consulting

You are a senior systems analyst at Globe Consulting, a growing IT consulting firm. You are leading the development team for a major client. You need to explain data and process modeling to your two newly hired junior analysts (Michelle and Aidan) before meeting with the client tomorrow afternoon.

Tasks

1. Describe the rules for creating DFDs.
2. What are the data flow and process combinations that must be avoided when creating a DFD?
3. Explain what a diagram 0 is and how it is used.
4. Ask Michelle and Aidan to review the order system context diagram on page 188, and compare it with the order system diagram 0 DFD on page 192. Then ask them to answer the following questions: (a) How many external entities are shown in each diagram? (b) In each diagram, how many data flows connect to the external entities? (c) How many processes are identified in the diagram 0 DFD? (d) Could the data store have been shown in the context diagram? Why or why not?

2 Kitchen Gadgets

Kitchen Gadgets sells a line of high-quality kitchen utensils and gadgets. When customers place orders on the company's Web site or through electronic data interchange (EDI), the system checks to see if the items are in stock, issues a status message to the customer, and generates a shipping order to the warehouse, which fills the order. When the order is shipped, the customer is billed. The system also produces various reports.

Tasks

1. List four elements used in DFDs, draw the symbols, and explain how they are used.
2. Draw a context diagram for the order system.
3. Draw a diagram 0 DFD for the order system.
4. Explain the importance of leveling and balancing.

3 **Big State University**

The Big State University course catalog reads as follows: "To enroll in MIS 260, which is an advanced course, a student must complete two prerequisites: MIS 120 and MIS 222. A student who completes either one of these prerequisites and obtains the instructor's permission, however, will be allowed to take MIS 260."

Tasks

1. Create a decision table that describes the Big State University course catalog regarding eligibility for MIS 260. Show all possible rules.
2. Simplify the table you just created. Describe the results.
3. Draw a simplified decision tree to represent the Big State University catalog. Describe the results.
4. Why might you use a decision tree rather than a decision table?

4 **Fresh-Mart Grocery**

Fresh-Mart Grocery is a regional grocery chain that is developing an information system to monitor inventory levels, product sales, and merchandise turnover. As products are sold in stores, they need to be replaced by shipments from the distribution centers. The IT manager wants you to document a process called BALANCE that determines whether extra product inventory is needed in a particular store. The BALANCE process is to be used in a just-in-time inventory system that automatically orders products and routes them to various stores for sale. A store manager can override the automatic BALANCE process if he or she so desires to get more product into a store.

Tasks

1. Create a decision table that describes the movement of inventory.
2. Draw a decision tree that describes the merchandise inventory management process.
3. Name four attributes that you can use to define a data flow in the grocery inventory information system.
4. Name four attributes that you can use to define a data store in the grocery inventory information system.

Case Studies

Each chapter includes a Chapter Case, a Continuing Case, a Capstone Case, and an Online Case Simulation. You can learn more about the Online Case Simulation in the MIS CourseMate Features section.

Chapter Case: College Driver Insurance

College Driver Insurance offers discounted auto insurance to college students.

Background

The company uses several factors to set discounts, as follows:

- A student who has taken a safe driver course earns a 5% discount.
- A student with a clean record (no tickets or accidents in the last three years) earns a 5% discount.
- A student who is 23 or older earns a 5% discount.
- A student who meets all three conditions (has taken a safe driver course *and* has a clean record *and* is 23) earns an additional bonus discount of 5%.

Tasks

1. Create a decision table that describes the discount rules.
2. Simplify the table you just created. Describe the results.
3. Draw a simplified decision tree that shows the discount rules.
4. What are the pros and cons of using a decision table versus a decision tree?

Continuing Case: Personal Trainer, Inc.

Personal Trainer, Inc. owns and operates fitness centers in a dozen Midwestern cities. The centers have done well, and the company is planning an international expansion by opening a new "supercenter" in the Toronto area. Personal Trainer's president, Cassia Umi, hired an IT consultant, Susan Park, to help develop an information system for the new facility. During the project, Susan will work closely with Gray Lewis, who will manage the new operation.

Background

Susan Park has completed a preliminary investigation and performed the fact-finding tasks that were described in Chapters 2 and 4. Now, she will use the results to develop a logical model of the proposed information system.

Tasks

Before you perform the following tasks, you should review the information provided in Chapters 2 and 4 of the case.

1. Prepare a context diagram for the new system.
2. Prepare a diagram 0 DFD for the new system.
3. Write a brief memo that explains at least five attributes that you can use to define a process in the order system.
4. Write a brief memo that explains at least five attributes that you can use to define an entity in the order system.

Capstone Case: New Century Wellness Group

New Century Wellness Group offers a holistic approach to healthcare with an emphasis on preventive medicine as well as traditional medical care. In your role as an IT consultant, you will help New Century develop a new information system.

Background

You began the systems analysis phase by conducting interviews, reviewing existing reports, and observing office operations. (Your instructor may provide you with a sample set of interview summaries.)

The New Century medical team performs services and medical procedures, which are coded according to the American Medical Association's Current Procedure Terminology (CPT). CPT codes consist of five numeric digits and a two-digit suffix, and most insurance payers require the codes to be included with billing information.

The new system must be able to handle the new ICD-10 procedure coding system, which will be required by the Centers for Medicare & Medicaid Services (CMS) beginning October 1, 2014. ICD-10 codes consist of seven alphanumeric characters, which can be electronically transmitted and received. New Century's information system must interface with 25 California health insurance providers. The new system represents an opportunity for significant cost saving for New Century, and more convenience for patients, who will be able to go online to update medical information, schedule appointments, and request medical records.

During your fact-finding, you learned that the clinic requires various reports, as follows:

- Daily appointment list for each provider. The list shows all scheduled appointment times, patient names, and services to be performed, including the procedure code and description.

- Daily report call list, which shows the patients who are to be reminded of their next day's appointments. The call list includes the patient name, telephone number, appointment time, and provider name.

- Weekly provider report that lists each of the providers and the weekly charges generated, plus a month-to-date (MTD) and a year-to-date (YTD) summary as well as profit distribution data for the partners.

- Monthly patient statement, which includes the statement date, head of household name and address, previous month's balance, total household charges MTD, total payments MTD, and the current balance. The bottom section of the statement shows activity for the month in date order. For each service performed, a line shows the patient's name, the service date, the procedure code and description, and the charge. The statement also shows the date and amount of all payments and insurance claims. When an insurance payment is received, the source and amount are noted on the form. If the claim is denied or only partially paid, a code is used to explain the reason. A running balance appears at the far right of each activity line.

- Weekly Insurance Company Report.

- Monthly Claim Status Summary.

In addition to these reports, the office staff would like automated e-mail and text messaging capability for sending reminders to patients when it is time to schedule an appointment. Data also needs to be maintained on employers who participate in employee wellness programs. This information can be used for marketing purposes throughout the year. Finally, the new system needs to track employee schedules, attendance, vacation time, and paid time off.

Now you are ready to organize the facts and prepare a system requirements document that represents a logical model of the proposed system. Your tools will include DFDs, a data dictionary, and process descriptions.

Capstone Case: New Century Wellness Group

Tasks

1. Prepare a context diagram for New Century's information system.
2. Prepare a diagram 0 DFD for New Century. Be sure to show numbered processes for handling appointment processing, payment and insurance processing, report processing, and records maintenance. Also, prepare lower-level DFDs for each numbered process.
3. Prepare a list of data stores and data flows needed for the system. Under each data store, list the data elements required.
4. Prepare a data dictionary entry and process description for one of the system's functional primitives.

CASE Tool Workshop

Systems analysts use CASE tools to help them plan, build, and maintain information systems. To learn more about CASE tools, turn to Part B of the Toolkit that follows Chapter 12. You can complete these tasks with the Visible Analyst® CASE tool, which is available with this textbook, or a similar tool.

Background

You decided to start a mobile auto detailing service that will visit customers at their homes or businesses, and use traditional, high-quality hand washing and waxing methods. In addition to retail customers, several auto dealers have expressed interest in your services, and you are eager to get started. You plan to hire college students as technicians, train and supply them, and offer them a share of the profits as an incentive.

Your friend, who is an IT major, offered to help you set up an information system by customizing several Microsoft Office applications to meet your needs. She suggested that you prepare an initial context diagram and a DFD diagram 0, and not to be too concerned about the details — just the main entities, data flows, and data stores. Thinking it over, you know that you will have employees, retail customers, auto dealer accounts, one or more suppliers, and your local bank, where you plan to set up a business checking account to handle the business. You also plan to keep track of customers, employee information, profit-sharing data, and an operations log, among other things.

Tasks

1. Create a context diagram from the new business. It is okay to use your imagination with respect to data flows that you envision.
2. Create a diagram 0 that includes at least three processes and two data stores that would be typical in a small business of this kind. You can use your imagination with respect to the processes and data stores that might be needed.

MIS CourseMate Features

If you have an MIS CourseMate access code, you can reinforce and extend your learning with premium content created for this textbook. For example, you can launch interactive Video Learning Sessions to help you understand systems development concepts and practice your skills. In addition, you can use MindTap Reader, which is a full, interactive, digital e-book.

MIS CourseMate also offers many learning features within each chapter, including an Online Case Simulation, a Critical Thinking Challenge, Video Learning Tasks, and a set of Learn It Online activities. To log on to the MIS CourseMate site at **www.cengagebrain.com**, you must create a student account and register this book.

Online Case Simulation: SCR Associates

Session 5: Data and Process Modeling

Overview

The SCR Associates case study is a Web-based simulation that allows you to practice your skills in a real-world environment. The firm offers IT consulting, solutions, and training. SCR plans to open a new high-tech training center, and needs to develop a Training Information Management System (TIMS) to support the operation. You are a newly hired systems analyst reporting to Jesse Baker, systems group manager, and will help her develop the system.

The case study takes you to the SCR Web site, where you receive e-mail and voice mail messages from Jesse, obtain information from SCR's resource libraries, and perform various tasks. Jesse has high standards, but seems very fair. She made it clear that she expects your work to be accurate, thorough, and professional.

Before You Begin

To prepare for this work session, you should review the following topics:

- DFD symbols and diagrams
- DFD context diagrams
- DFD diagram 0
- Decision tables

How Do I Use the Online Case Simulation?

- Read the preview, and review the Chapter 1 background material, if necessary.
- Visit the MIS CourseMate Web site at **www.cengagebrain.com**, locate the **SCR Case Simulation**, and click the **intranet** link. Enter your name and the password **sad10e**.
- When the opening screen displays, select this session. Then check your e-mail and voice mail, and start to work on your task list.

Preview: Session 5

You recently completed requirements modeling tasks for the new Training Information Management System (TIMS). Now you are ready to begin data and process modeling, which will produce a logical model of the new system. You will create DFDs, develop a data dictionary, and use decision tables and decision trees.

Critical Thinking Challenge

In addition to technical ability, IT professionals need critical thinking skills. This feature can help you practice perception, organization, analysis, problem-solving, and decision-making skills that will be valuable in the workplace. You can visit **www.criticalthinking.org** to learn more about critical thinking and why it is so important.

Background

The IT team at Game Technology is moving forward with the new Customer Contact Care information system, or C^3. Your next assignment is to develop a set of data flow diagrams (DFDs). To be sure you can handle the tasks, you decide to review Chapter 5 of your systems analysis textbook. Based on your requirements model, you know that the new C^3 system will have three external entities, with the following data flows:

Entity	Data Flow from the Entity	Data Flow to the Entity
Customer	Contact Information	Sales Specials
Sales Records System	Customer Sales History	None
Marketing Rep	Suggested Contact Plan	Sales Feedback

The C^3 system also will have three processes (**Analyze Customer Data, Analyze Sales History,** and **Manage Contact Plan**), a data store (**Customer Profile**), and the following data flows:

Data Flow	From	To
Contact Information	Customer entity	Analyze Customer Data process
Sales Specials	Manage Contact Plan process	Customer entity
Customer Sales History	Sales Records System entity	Analyze Sales History process
Suggested Contact Plan	Marketing Rep entity	Develop Contact Plan process
Sales Feedback	Analyze Sales History process	Marketing Rep entity
Customer Data (two-way)	Analyze Customer Data process	Customer Profile data store
Customer Data (two-way)	Customer Profile data store	Analyze Customer Data process
Profile Data	Customer Profile data store	Manage Contact Plan process
Sales Data	Analyze Sales History process	Customer Profile data store

Practice Tasks

Visit the MIS CourseMate Web site at **www.cengagebrain.com**. Then navigate to the resources for this chapter and locate the **Critical Thinking Challenge** feature. You will complete two Practice Tasks, using what you learned in the chapter. Then you can check your answers to be sure you're ready for the Challenge Tasks.

Challenge Tasks

After you complete the Practice Tasks, you learn about new developments at Game Technology.

Your context diagram and DFD diagram 0 were accurate, but there have been some design changes. Management wants to connect the external Accounts Receivable System directly to the C^3 system as a fourth entity. A two-way data flow called AR Data will connect this entity to the C^3 system. Inside the C^3 system, AR Data will connect to the Analyze Sales History process. Also, another new two-way data flow called Billing Data will connect to the Analyze Sales History process and the Customer Profile data store. To continue, navigate to the **Critical Thinking Challenge** feature for this chapter, select the **Challenge Tasks,** and follow the instructions.

Video Learning Sessions

The Video Learning Sessions in this chapter explain data and process modeling and decision tables. You'll learn about DFD symbols and diagrams, DFD context diagrams, and DFD diagram 0. You'll also learn how decision tables can provide a graphical model of business process logic.

Before You Begin

To prepare for the tasks, you should review the following topics:

- DFD symbols and diagrams
- DFD context diagrams

How to Watch a Session

Go to the Management Information Systems CourseMate Web site at **www.cengagebrain.com**. Then navigate to the resources for this book, locate the **Video Learning Sessions**, and select a session. You can watch the session on your computer or mobile device, and pause, rewind, or replay a video at any time.

Practice Tasks

After each session, visit the **Your Turn** feature to perform the tasks and check your answers.

Training Tasks

Suppose the IT training manager wants to encourage team members to watch the Video Learning Sessions. To spark interest, she plans to post a set of VLS previews, which you will prepare. Each preview must include an overview of the session, a description of the main topics, and one or more screen examples from the video. To get you started, she provided a task list:

1. Select a Video Learning Session from this chapter. Launch the video and note the title, objectives, and total running time. Include this information in your preview.
2. Run though the session and find a segment that does a good job of explaining a specific skill or concept.
3. In the segment you selected, choose one or more specific screens and capture each screen image with the Windows Snipping Tool. To do this in Windows 7 or Windows Vista, click **Start**, and then type **Snipping Tool**. In Windows 8, you can display the **Start** menu, and then type **Snipping Tool**.
4. Paste the screen image into your preview and explain how it would help a viewer understand the topic. Also add your comments about the video, and why it would be important to an IT professional. Your preview should be well-organized and readable.

Learn It Online

In each chapter, you can use this feature to apply your knowledge and practice your skills. The exercises include Chapter Reinforcement Questions, Flash Cards, Practice Tests, and various games, such as *Who Wants To Be a Computer Genius?, Wheel of Terms, and the Crossword Puzzle Challenge.*

CHAPTER 6 Object Modeling

Chapter 6 is the third of four chapters in the systems analysis phase of the SDLC. This chapter discusses object modeling techniques that analysts use to create a logical model. In addition to structured analysis, object-oriented analysis is another way to represent and design an information system.

INTRODUCTION

OBJECTIVES

When you finish this chapter, you will be able to:

- Explain how object-oriented analysis can be used to describe an information system
- Define object modeling terms and concepts, including objects, attributes, methods, messages, classes, and instances
- Explain relationships among objects and the concept of inheritance
- Draw an object relationship diagram
- Describe Unified Modeling Language (UML) tools and techniques, including use cases, use case diagrams, class diagrams, sequence diagrams, state transition diagrams, and activity diagrams
- Explain the advantages of using CASE tools in developing the object model
- Explain how to organize an object model

In Chapter 5, you learned how to use structured analysis techniques to develop a data and process model of the proposed system. Now, in Chapter 6, you learn about object-oriented analysis, which is another way to view and model system requirements. In this chapter, you use object-oriented techniques to document, analyze, and model the information system. In Chapter 7, which concludes the systems analysis phase, you will evaluate alternatives, develop the system requirements document, and prepare for the systems design phase of the SDLC.

If you have MIS CourseMate, you can view two Video Learning Sessions that explain object-oriented modeling terms and diagrams.

PREVIEW CASE: Mountain View College Bookstore

Background: Wendy Lee, manager of college services at Mountain View College, wants a new information system that will improve efficiency and customer service at the three college bookstores.

   In this part of the case, Tina Allen (systems analyst) and David Conroe (student intern) are talking about object-oriented concepts, tools, and techniques.

Participants: Tina and David
Location: Mountain View College Cafeteria, Friday afternoon, November 1, 2013
Project status: Tina and David have completed data and processing modeling, and are discussing object-oriented techniques that they can use to develop an object model of the new system
Discussion topics: Object-oriented concepts, tools, and techniques

Tina: Hi, David. I want to chat with you about object-oriented analysis before we finish the systems analysis phase. Would this be a good time to talk?

David: *Sure. I know that object-oriented analysis is another way of viewing the system, but I don't know much about it.*

Tina: Well, object-oriented analysis describes an information system by identifying things called objects. An object represents a real person, place, event, or transaction. For example, in the bookstore, when a student purchases a textbook, the student is an object, the textbook is an object, and the purchase transaction itself is an object.

David: *That sounds a little like the entities we identify in structured analysis.*

Tina: Yes, but there's a major difference! In structured analysis we treat data and the processes that affect the data separately. Objects, on the other hand, contain the data *and* the processes, called methods, that can add, modify, or change the data. To make it even more interesting, one object can send a message to another object to request some action or response. For example, a driver object adjusts the cruise control, which sends one or more messages to the car object telling it to maintain a steady speed.

David: *I get it. So objects can be people, things, or events?*

Tina: Yes. To show how the system works, we use a special modeling language called the UML. We even show human actors as stick figures that interact with business functions called use cases.

David: *I'd like to give it a try.*

Tina: No problem. Although we'll still use structured analysis, it will be interesting to model the system in object-oriented terms. Let's get started on our task list:

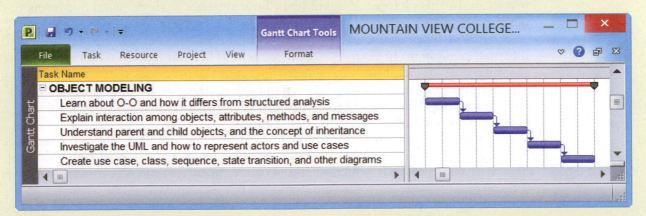

FIGURE 6-1 Typical object modeling task list.

© Cengage Learning 2014

OVERVIEW OF OBJECT-ORIENTED ANALYSIS

As you learned in Chapter 1, the most popular systems development options are structured analysis, object-oriented analysis (O-O), and agile methods, also called adaptive methods. The table in Figure 1-23 on page 21 shows the three alternatives and describes some pros and cons for each approach. As the table indicates, O-O methodology is popular because it integrates easily with object-oriented programming languages such as Java, Smalltalk, VB.Net, Python, and Perl. Programmers also like O-O code because it is modular, reusable, and easy to maintain.

Object-oriented (O-O) analysis describes an information system by identifying things called objects. An **object** represents a real person, place, event, or transaction. For example, when a patient makes an appointment to see a doctor, the patient is an object, the doctor is an object, and the appointment itself is an object.

Object-oriented analysis is a popular approach that sees a system from the viewpoint of the objects themselves as they function and interact. The end product of object-oriented analysis is an **object model**, which represents the information system in terms of objects and object-oriented concepts.

© craftvision/iStockphoto

Video Learning Session
Object-Oriented Terms and Concepts

If you have an MIS CourseMate access code, you can launch interactive Video Learning Sessions to help you understand systems development concepts and practice your skills. You can watch the sessions on your computer or mobile device, and pause, rewind, or replay a video at any time. To log on to the MIS CourseMate site at **www.cengagebrain.com**, you must create a student account and then register this book.

This session is about object-oriented terms and concepts. You'll learn basic object modeling terms and concepts, how to use symbols to create object models, and how you can use a CASE tool to create object models.

Object-Oriented Terms and Concepts

In Chapter 4, you learned that the **Unified Modeling Language (UML)** is a widely used method of visualizing and documenting an information system. In this chapter, you use the UML to develop object models. Your first step is to understand basic object-oriented terms, including objects, attributes, methods, messages, classes, and instances. In this chapter, you will learn how systems analysts use those terms to describe an information system.

An object represents a person, place, event, or transaction that is significant to the information system. In Chapter 5, you created DFDs that treated data and processes separately. An object, however, includes data *and* the processes that affect that data. For example, a customer object has a name, an address, an account number, and a current balance. Customer objects also can perform specific tasks, such as placing an order, paying a bill, and changing their address.

An object has certain **attributes,** which are characteristics that describe the object. For example, if you own a car, it has attributes such as make, model, and color. An object also has **methods,** which are tasks or functions that the object performs when it receives a **message,** or command, to do so. For example, your car performs a method called OPERATE WIPERS when you send a message with the wiper control, and it can APPLY BRAKES when you send a message by pressing the brake pedal. Figure 6-2 shows examples of attributes, messages, and methods for a car object.

A **class** is a group of similar objects. For example, Ford Fiestas belong to a class called CAR. An **instance** is a specific member of a class. *Your* 2013 Ford Fiesta for example, is an instance of the CAR class. At an auto dealership, like the one shown in

Figure 6-3, you might observe many instances of the CAR class, the TRUCK class, the MINIVAN class, and the SPORT UTILITY VEHICLE class, among others. Although the term "object" usually refers to a particular instance, systems analysts sometimes use the term to refer to a class of objects. Usually the meaning is understood from the context and the way the term is used.

Objects

Consider how the UML describes a family with parents and children. The UML represents an object as a rectangle with the object name at the top, followed by the object's attributes and methods.

Figure 6-4 shows a PARENT object with certain attributes such as name, age, sex, and hair color. If there are two parents, then there are two instances of the PARENT object. The PARENT object can perform methods, such as reading a bedtime story, driving the car pool van, or preparing a school lunch. When a PARENT object receives a message, it performs an action, or method.

For example, the message GOOD NIGHT from a child might tell the PARENT object to read a bedtime story, while the message DRIVE from another parent signals that it is the PARENT object's turn to drive in the car pool.

Continuing with the family example, the CHILD object in Figure 6-5 possesses the same attributes as the PARENT

The DRIVER object

... can send messages

... to the CAR object

... which performs the requested methods

FIGURE 6-2 Objects have attributes, can send and receive messages, and perform actions called methods.

© Vaju Ariel/Shutterstock.com; © Norph/Shutterstock.com; © Boykov/Shutterstock.com

FIGURE 6-3 At an auto dealership, you can observe the CAR class, the TRUCK class, the MINIVAN class, and the SPORT UTILITY VEHICLE class.

© carroteater/Shutterstock.com

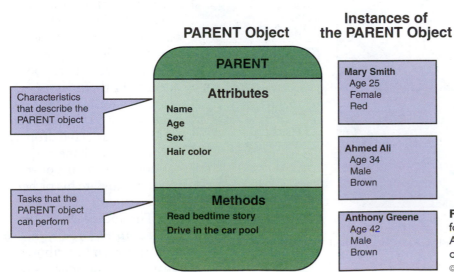

FIGURE 6-4 The PARENT object includes four attributes and two methods. Mary Smith, Ahmed Ali, and Anthony Greene are instances of the PARENT object.

© Cengage Learning 2014

FIGURE 6-5 The CHILD object includes five attributes and five methods. James Smith, Amelia Ali, and Misty Greene are instances of the CHILD object.

© Cengage Learning 2014

object and an additional attribute that shows the number of siblings. A CHILD object performs certain methods, such as picking up toys, eating dinner, playing, cooperating, and getting ready for bed. To signal the CHILD object to perform those tasks, a parent can send certain messages that the CHILD object will understand. For example, the DINNER'S READY message tells a CHILD object to come to the table, while the SHARE WITH YOUR BROTHER/SISTER message tells a CHILD object to cooperate with other CHILD objects.

The family also might have a DOG object, as shown in Figure 6-6. That object can have attributes such as name, breed, age, color, sex, and favorite food. The DOG object can perform methods such as wagging its tail, eating, fetching, and sleeping. The message GOOD DOG, when directed to the DOG object, signals it to wag its tail. Similarly, the DINNER'S READY message signals the DOG object to run to its food bowl.

Now consider an example of a fitness center, as shown in Figure 6-7, and the objects that interact with the fitness center's enrollment system. A typical fitness center might have students, instructors, fitness-class schedules, and a registration process.

STUDENT and INSTRUCTOR objects are shown in Figure 6-8. Each STUDENT object has the following attributes: student number, name, address, telephone, date of birth, fitness record, and status. In addition, a STUDENT can add a fitness-class; drop a fitness-class; change an address, telephone, or status; and update his or her fitness record.

The INSTRUCTOR object in Figure 6-8 has the following attributes: instructor number,

FIGURE 6-6 The DOG object includes six attributes and four methods. Buddy, Annie, and Megan are instances of the DOG object.

© Cengage Learning 2014

name, address, telephone, fitness-classes taught, availability, private lesson fee, and status. An INSTRUCTOR object can teach a fitness-class, and change his or her availability, address, telephone, private lesson fee, or status.

The FITNESS-CLASS SCHEDULE object shown in Figure 6-9 on the next page includes data about fitness classes, including fitness-class number, date, time, type, location, instructor number, and maximum enrollment. The FITNESS-CLASS SCHEDULE object includes the methods that can add or delete a fitness class, or change a fitness-class date, time, instructor, location, or enrollment.

The REGISTRATION RECORD object shown in Figure 6-10 on the next page includes the student number, fitness-class number, registration date, fee, and status. The REGISTRATION RECORD object includes methods to add a REGISTRATION instance when a student enrolls, or drop a REGISTRATION instance if the fitness class is canceled or for nonpayment. Notice that if a student registers for three fitness classes, the result is three instances of the REGISTRATION RECORD object. The REGISTRATION RECORD object also includes a method of notifying students and instructors of information.

Attributes

If objects are similar to nouns, attributes are similar to adjectives that describe the characteristics of an object. How many attributes are needed? The answer depends on the business requirements of the information system and its users. Even a relatively simple object, such as an inventory item, might have a part number, description, supplier, quantity on hand, minimum stock level, maximum stock level, reorder time, and so on. Some objects might have a few attributes; others might have dozens.

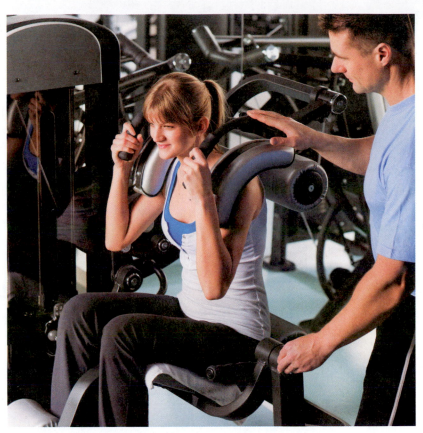

FIGURE 6-7 A typical fitness center might have students, instructors, fitness-class schedules, and a registration process.

© CandyBox Images/Shutterstock.com

STUDENT Object	**INSTRUCTOR Object**
STUDENT	**INSTRUCTOR**
Attributes	**Attributes**
Student number	Instructor number
Name	Name
Address	Address
Telephone	Telephone
Date of birth	Fitness-classes taught
Fitness record	Availability
Status	Private lesson fee
	Status
Methods	**Methods**
Add fitness-class	Teach fitness-class
Drop fitness-class	Change availability
Change address	Change address
Change telephone	Change telephone
Change status	Change private lesson fee
Update fitness record	Change status

FIGURE 6-8 The STUDENT object includes seven attributes and six methods. The INSTRUCTOR object includes eight attributes and six methods.

© Cengage Learning 2014

FITNESS-CLASS SCHEDULE Object

FITNESS-CLASS SCHEDULE

Attributes
Fitness-class number
Date
Time
Type
Location
Instructor number
Maximum enrollment

Methods
Add fitness-class
Delete fitness-class
Change date
Change time
Change instructor
Change location
Change enrollment

FIGURE 6-9 The FITNESS-CLASS SCHEDULE object includes seven attributes and seven methods.

© Cengage Learning 2014

REGISTRATION RECORD Object

REGISTRATION RECORD

Attributes
Student number
Fitness-class number
Registration date
Fee
Status

Methods
Add student
Drop student
Notify instructor of add
Notify instructor of drop
Notify all of fitness-class cancellations

FIGURE 6-10 The REGISTRATION RECORD object includes five attributes and five methods.

© Cengage Learning 2014

Systems analysts define an object's attributes during the systems design process. In an object-oriented system, objects can inherit, or acquire, certain attributes from other objects. When you learn about relationships between objects and classes, you will understand how that occurs.

Objects can have a specific attribute called a **state**. The state of an object is an adjective that describes the object's current status. For example, depending on the state, a student can be a future student, a current student, or a past student. Similarly, a bank account can be active, inactive, closed, or frozen.

Methods

A method defines specific tasks that an object can perform. Just as objects are similar to nouns and attributes are similar to adjectives, methods resemble verbs that describe *what* and *how* an object does something.

Consider a server who prepares fries in a fast-food restaurant, as shown in Figure 6-11. A systems analyst might describe the operation as a method called MORE FRIES, as shown in Figure 6-12. The MORE FRIES method includes the steps required to heat the oil, fill the fry basket with frozen potato strips, lower it into the hot oil, check for readiness, remove the basket when ready and drain the oil, pour the fries into a warming tray, and add salt.

FIGURE 6-11 In a fast-food restaurant, preparing more fries is a common task.

© Jeff Baker/Getty Images

FIGURE 6-12 The MORE FRIES method requires the server to perform seven specific steps.
© Cengage Learning 2014

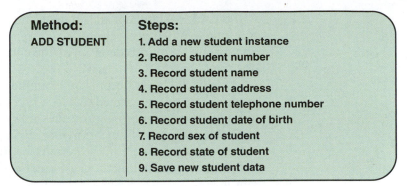

FIGURE 6-13 In the fitness center example, the ADD STUDENT method requires the STUDENT object to perform nine specific steps.
© Cengage Learning 2014

Figure 6-13 shows another example of a method. At the fitness center, an ADD STUDENT method adds a new instance of the STUDENT class. Notice that nine steps are required to add the new instance and record the necessary data.

Messages

A message is a command that tells an object to perform a certain method. For example, the message ADD STUDENT directs the STUDENT class to add a STUDENT instance. The STUDENT class understands that it should add the student number, name, and other data about that student, as shown in Figure 6-14. Similarly, a message named DELETE STUDENT tells the STUDENT class to delete a STUDENT instance.

The same message to two different objects can produce different results. The concept that a message gives different meanings to different objects is called **polymorphism**. For example, in Figure 6-15, the message GOOD NIGHT signals the PARENT object to read a bedtime story, but the same message to the DOG object tells the dog to sleep. The GOOD NIGHT message to the CHILD object signals it to get ready for bed.

You can view an object as a **black box**, because a message to the object triggers changes within the object

FIGURE 6-14 The message ADD STUDENT signals the STUDENT class to perform the ADD STUDENT method. The message DELETE STUDENT signals the STUDENT class to perform the DELETE STUDENT method.
© Cengage Learning 2014

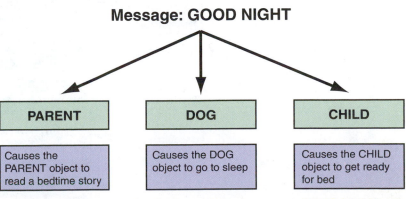

FIGURE 6-15 In an example of polymorphism, the message GOOD NIGHT produces different results, depending on which object receives it.
© Cengage Learning 2014

without specifying how the changes must be carried out. A gas pump is an example of a black box. When you select the economy grade at a pump, you do not need to think about how the pump determines the correct price and selects the right fuel, as long as it does so properly.

The black box concept is an example of **encapsulation,** which means that all data and methods are self-contained. A black box does not want or need outside interference. By limiting access to internal processes, an object prevents its internal code from being altered by another object or process. Encapsulation allows objects to be used as modular components anywhere in the system, because objects send and receive messages but do not alter the internal methods of other objects.

Object-oriented designs typically are implemented with object-oriented programming languages. A major advantage of O-O designs is that systems analysts can save time and avoid errors by using modular objects, and programmers can translate the designs into code, working with reusable program modules that have been tested and verified. For example, in Figure 6-16, an INSTRUCTOR object sends an ENTER GRADE message to an instance of the STUDENT RECORD class. Notice that the INSTRUCTOR object and STUDENT RECORD class could be reused, with minor modifications, in other school information systems where many of the attributes and methods would be similar.

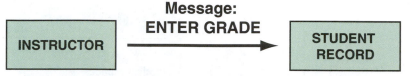

FIGURE 6-16 In a school information system, an INSTRUCTOR object sends an ENTER GRADE message to an instance of the STUDENT RECORD class.

© Cengage Learning 2014

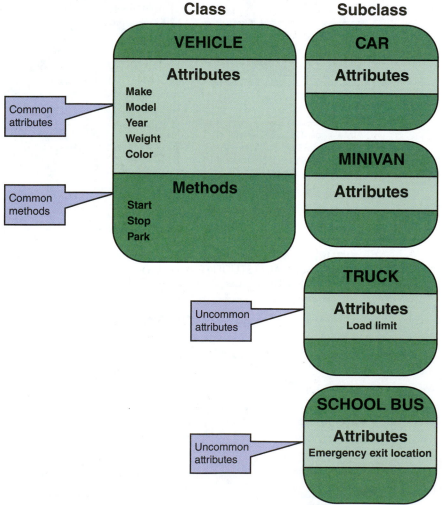

Classes

An object belongs to a group or category called a class. All objects within a class share common attributes and methods, so a class is like a blueprint, or template for all the objects within the class. Objects within a class can be grouped into **subclasses,** which are more specific categories within a class. For example, TRUCK objects represent a subclass within the VEHICLE class, along with other subclasses called CAR, MINIVAN, and SCHOOL BUS, as shown in Figure 6-17. Notice that all four subclasses share common traits of the VEHICLE class, such as make, model, year, weight, and color. Each subclass also can possess traits

FIGURE 6-17 The VEHICLE class includes common attributes and methods. CAR, TRUCK, MINIVAN, and SCHOOL BUS are instances of the VEHICLE class.

© Cengage Learning 2014

that are uncommon, such as a load limit for the TRUCK or an emergency exit location for the SCHOOL BUS.

In the fitness center example shown in Figure 6-18, INSTRUCTOR objects represent a subclass within the EMPLOYEE class. The EMPLOYEE class also can contain MANAGER and OFFICE STAFF subclasses, because a manager and staff members are employees. All INSTRUCTOR, MANAGER, and OFFICE STAFF objects contain similar information (such as employee name, title, and pay rate) and perform similar tasks (such as getting hired and changing an address or telephone number).

A class can belong to a more general category called a **superclass**. For example, a NOVEL class belongs to a superclass called BOOK, because all novels are books in this example. The NOVEL class can have subclasses called HARDCOVER and PAPERBACK. Similarly, as shown in Figure 6-19, the EMPLOYEE class belongs to the PERSON superclass, because every employee is a person, and the INSTRUCTOR class is a subclass of EMPLOYEE.

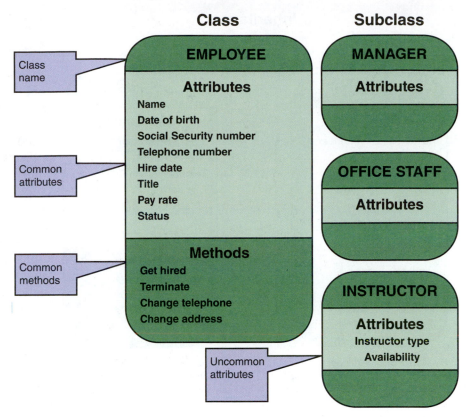

FIGURE 6-18 The fitness center EMPLOYEE class includes common attributes and methods. INSTRUCTOR, MANAGER, and OFFICE STAFF are subclasses within the EMPLOYEE class.

© Cengage Learning 2014

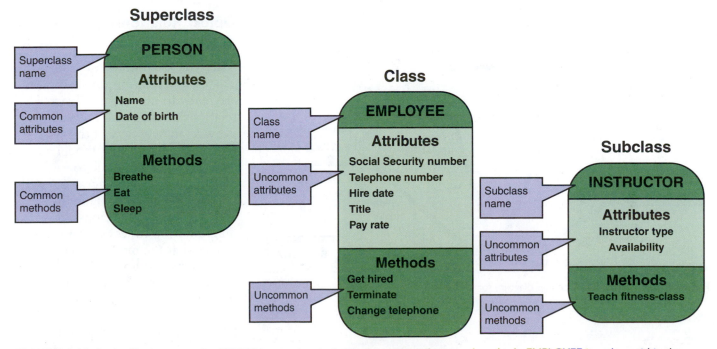

FIGURE 6-19 At the fitness center, the PERSON superclass includes common attributes and methods. EMPLOYEE is a class within the PERSON superclass. INSTRUCTOR is a subclass within the EMPLOYEE class.

© Cengage Learning 2014

Inheritance

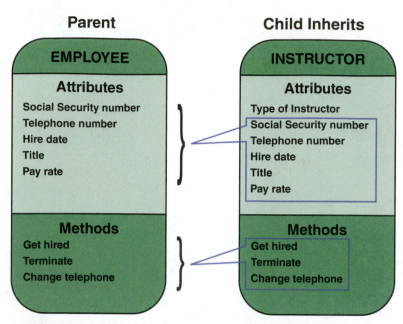

FIGURE 6-20 An inheritance relationship exists between the INSTRUCTOR and EMPLOYEE objects. The INSTRUCTOR (child) object inherits characteristics from the EMPLOYEE (parent) class and can have additional attributes of its own.

© Cengage Learning 2014

RELATIONSHIPS AMONG OBJECTS AND CLASSES

Relationships enable objects to communicate and interact as they perform business functions and transactions required by the system. Relationships describe what objects need to know about each other, how objects respond to changes in other objects, and the effects of membership in classes, superclasses, and subclasses. Some relationships are stronger than others (just as a relationship between family members is stronger than one between casual acquaintances). The strongest relationship is called inheritance. **Inheritance** enables an object, called a **child**, to derive one or more of its attributes from another object, called a **parent**. In the example in Figure 6-20, the INSTRUCTOR object (child) inherits many traits from the EMPLOYEE object (parent), including SOCIAL SECURITY NUMBER, TELEPHONE NUMBER, and HIRE DATE. The INSTRUCTOR object also can possess additional attributes, such as TYPE OF INSTRUCTOR. Because all employees share certain attributes, those attributes are assumed through inheritance and do not need to be repeated in the INSTRUCTOR object.

Object Relationship Diagram

After you identify the objects, classes, and relationships, you are ready to prepare an object relationship diagram that will provide an overview of the system. You will use that model as a guide as you continue to develop additional diagrams and documentation. Figure 6-21 shows an object relationship diagram for a fitness center. Notice that the model shows the objects and how they interact to perform business functions and transactions.

FIGURE 6-21 Object relationship diagram for the fitness center.

© Cengage Learning 2014

OBJECT MODELING WITH THE UNIFIED MODELING LANGUAGE

Just as structured analysis uses DFDs to model data and processes, systems analysts use the Unified Modeling Language (UML) to describe object-oriented systems.

In Chapter 4, you learned that the UML is a popular technique for documenting and modeling a system. The UML uses a set of symbols to represent graphically the various components and relationships within a system. Although the UML can be used for business process modeling and requirements modeling, it mainly is used to support object-oriented system analysis and to develop object models.

© craftvision/iStockphoto

Video Learning Session
Object-Oriented Diagrams and Models

If you have an MIS CourseMate access code, you can launch interactive Video Learning Sessions to help you understand systems development concepts and practice your skills. You can watch the sessions on your computer or mobile device, and pause, rewind, or replay a video at any time. To log on to the MIS CourseMate site at **www.cengagebrain.com**, you must create a student account and then register this book.

This session is about object-oriented diagrams and models. You'll learn how to create various types of object diagrams, including use-case, class, sequence, state-transition, and activity diagrams, and how you can use a CASE tool to create object models.

Use Case Modeling

A **use case** represents the steps in a specific business function or process. An external entity, called an **actor**, initiates a use case by requesting the system to perform a function or process. For example, in a medical office system, a PATIENT (actor) can MAKE APPOINTMENT (use case), as shown in Figure 6-22.

Notice that the UML symbol for a use case is an oval with a label that describes the action or event. The actor is shown as a stick figure, with a label that identifies the actor's role. The line from the actor to the use case is called an association, because it links a particular actor to a use case. Figure 6-23 shows use case examples of a passenger making an airline reservation, a customer placing an order, and a bus dispatcher changing a student's pickup address.

Use cases also can interact with other use cases. When the outcome of one use case is incorporated by another use case, we say that the second case *uses* the first case. The UML indicates the relationship with an arrow

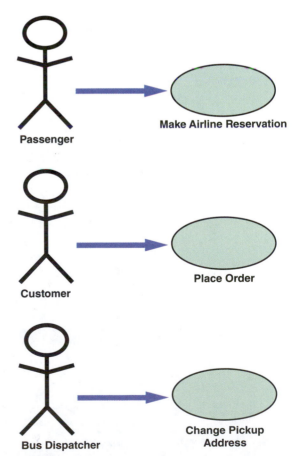

FIGURE 6-23 Three use case examples. The UML symbol for a use case is an oval. The actor is shown as a stick figure.
© Cengage Learning 2014

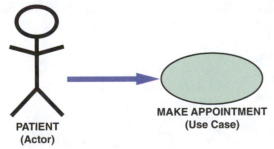

FIGURE 6-22 In a medical office system, a PATIENT (actor) can MAKE APPOINTMENT (use case).
© Cengage Learning 2014

that *points at* the use case being used. Figure 6-24 shows an example where a student adds a fitness class and PRODUCE FITNESS-CLASS ROSTER *uses* the results of ADD FITNESS-CLASS to generate a new fitness-class roster. Similarly, if an instructor changes his or her availability, UPDATE INSTRUCTOR INFORMATION *uses* the CHANGE AVAILABILITY use case to update the instructor's information.

To create use cases, you start by reviewing the information that you gathered during the requirements modeling phase. Your objective is to identify the actors and the functions or transactions they initiate. For each use case, you also develop a **use case description** in the form of a table. A use case description documents the name of the use case, the actor, a description of the use case, a step-by-step list of the tasks and actions required for successful completion, a description of alternative courses of action, preconditions, postconditions, and assumptions. Figure 6-25 shows an example of the ADD NEW STUDENT use case.

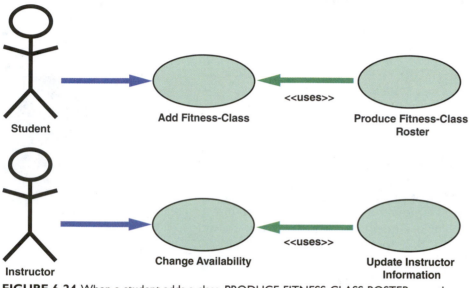

FIGURE 6-24 When a student adds a class, PRODUCE FITNESS-CLASS ROSTER uses the results of ADD CLASS to generate a new class roster. When an instructor changes his or her availability, UPDATE INSTRUCTOR INFORMATION uses the CHANGE AVAILABILITY use case to update the instructor's information.

© Cengage Learning 2014

ADD NEW STUDENT Use Case

Add New Student

Name:	Add New Student
Actor:	Student/Manager
Description:	Describes the process used to add a student to a fitness-class
Successful completion:	1. Manager checks FITNESS-CLASS SCHEDULE object for availability 2. Manager notifies student 3. Fitness-class is open and student pays fee 4. Manager registers student
Alternative:	1. Manager checks FITNESS-CLASS SCHEDULE object for availability 2. Fitness-class is full 3. Manager notifies student
Precondition:	Student requests fitness-class
Postcondition:	Student is enrolled in fitness-class and fees have been paid
Assumptions:	None

FIGURE 6-25 The ADD NEW STUDENT use case description documents the process used to add a current student into an existing class.

© Cengage Learning 2014

When you identify use cases, try to group all the related transactions into a single use case. For example, when a hotel customer reserves a room, the reservation system blocks a room, updates the occupancy forecast, and sends the customer a confirmation. Those events are all part of a single use case called RESERVE ROOM, and the specific actions are step-by-step tasks within the use case.

CASE IN POINT 6.1: HILLTOP MOTORS

You were hired by Hilltop Motors as a consultant to help the company plan a new information system. Hilltop is an old-line dealership, and the prior owner was slow to change. A new management team has taken over, and they are eager to develop a first-class system. Right now, you are reviewing the service department, which is going though a major expansion. You decide to create a model of the service department in the form of a use case diagram. The main actors in the service operation are customers, service writers who prepare work orders and invoices, and mechanics who perform the work. You are meeting with the management team tomorrow morning. Create a draft of the diagram to present to them.

Use Case Diagrams

A **use case diagram** is a visual summary of several related use cases within a system or subsystem. Consider a typical auto service department, as shown in Figure 6-26. The service department involves customers, service writers who prepare work orders and invoices, and mechanics who perform the work. Figure 6-27 on the next page shows a possible use case diagram for the auto service department.

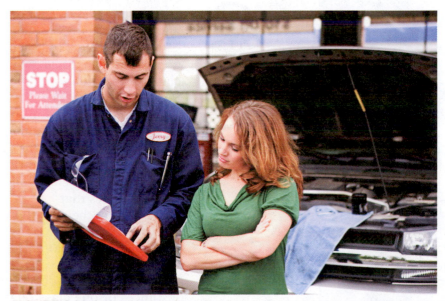

FIGURE 6-26 A typical auto service department might involve customers, service writers who prepare work orders, and mechanics who perform the work.
©Sean Locke/iStockphoto

Use Case Diagram: Auto Service Department

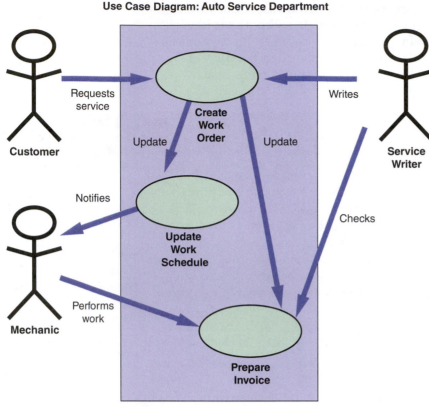

FIGURE 6-27 A use case diagram to handle work at an auto service department.
© Cengage Learning 2014

Use Case Diagram: Create Bus Route

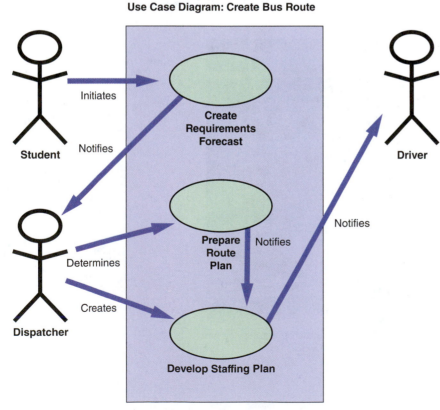

FIGURE 6-28 A use case diagram to create a school bus route.
© Cengage Learning 2014

When you create a use case diagram, the first step is to identify the system boundary, which is represented by a rectangle. The **system boundary** shows what is included in the system (inside the rectangle) and what is not included in the system (outside the rectangle). After you identify the system boundary, you place the use cases on the diagram, add the actors, and show the relationships. Figure 6-28 shows a use case diagram for a school bus system that creates a new bus route.

Class Diagrams

A **class diagram** shows the object classes and relationships involved in a use case. Like a DFD, a class diagram is a logical model, which evolves into a physical model and finally becomes a functioning information system. In structured analysis, entities, data stores, and processes are transformed into data structures and program code. Similarly, class diagrams evolve into code modules, data objects, and other system components.

In a class diagram, each class appears as a rectangle, with the class name at the top, followed by the class's attributes and methods. Lines show relationships between classes and have labels identifying the action that relates the two classes. To create a class diagram, you review the use case and identify the classes that participate in the underlying business process.

The class diagram also includes a concept called **cardinality**, which describes how instances of one class relate to instances of another class. For example, an employee might have earned no vacation days or one vacation day or many vacation days. Similarly, an employee might have no spouse or one spouse. Figure 6-29 shows various UML notations and cardinality examples. Notice that in Figure 6-29, the first column shows a UML notation symbol that identifies the relationship shown in the second column. The third column provides a typical example of the relationship, which is described in the last column. In the first row of the figure, the UML notation *0..** identifies a *zero or many* relation. The example is that an employee can have no payroll deductions or many deductions.

UML Notation	Nature of the Relationship	Example		Description
0..*	Zero or many	Employee —1—	Payroll Deduction 0..*	An employee can have no payroll deductions or many deductions.
0..1	Zero or one	Employee —1—	Spouse 0..1	An employee can have no spouse or one spouse.
1	One and only one	Office Manager —1—	Sales Office 1	An office manager manages one and only one office.
1..*	One or many	Order —1—	Item Ordered 1..*	One order can include one or many items ordered.

FIGURE 6-29 Examples of UML notations that indicate the nature of the relationship between instances of one class and instances of another class.

© Cengage Learning 2014

You will learn more about cardinality in Chapter 9, which discusses data design.

Figure 6-30 shows a class diagram for a sales order use case. Notice that the sales office has one sales manager who can have anywhere from zero to many sales reps. Each sales rep can have anywhere from zero to many customers, but each customer has only one sales rep.

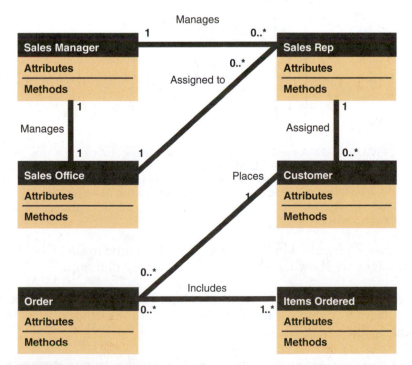

FIGURE 6-30 Class diagram for a sales order use case (attributes and methods omitted for clarity).

© Cengage Learning 2014

CASE IN POINT 6.2: Train the Trainer, Inc.

Train the Trainer develops seminars and workshops for corporate training managers, who in turn train their employees. Your job at Train the Trainer is to put together the actual training materials. Right now, you are up against a deadline. The new object modeling seminar has a chapter on cardinality, and the client wants you to come up with at least three more examples for each of the four cardinality categories listed in Figure 6-29 on the previous page. The four categories are *zero or many*, *zero or one*, *one and only one*, and *one or many*. Even though you are under pressure, you are determined to use examples that are realistic and familiar to the students. What examples will you submit?

Sequence Diagrams

A **sequence diagram** is a dynamic model of a use case, showing the interaction among classes during a specified time period. A sequence diagram graphically documents the use case by showing the classes, the messages, and the timing of the messages. Sequence diagrams include symbols that represent classes, lifelines, messages, and focuses. These symbols are shown in Figure 6-31.

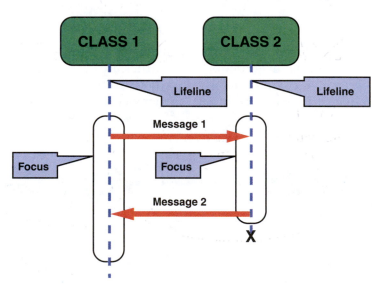

FIGURE 6-31 A sequence diagram with two classes. Notice the X that indicates the end of the CLASS 2 lifeline. Also notice that each message is represented by a line with a label that describes the message, and that each class has a focus that shows the period when messages are sent or received.

© Cengage Learning 2014

CLASSES A class is identified by a rectangle with the name inside. Classes that send or receive messages are shown at the top of the sequence diagram.

LIFELINES A lifeline is identified by a dashed line. The **lifeline** represents the time during which the object above it is able to interact with the other objects in the use case. An X marks the end of the lifeline.

MESSAGES A message is identified by a line showing direction that runs between two objects. The label shows the name of the message and can include additional information about the contents.

FOCUSES A focus is identified by a narrow vertical shape that covers the lifeline. The **focus** indicates when an object sends or receives a message.

The fitness center example shown in Figure 6-32 shows a sequence diagram for the ADD NEW STUDENT use case. Notice that the vertical position of each message indicates the timing of the message.

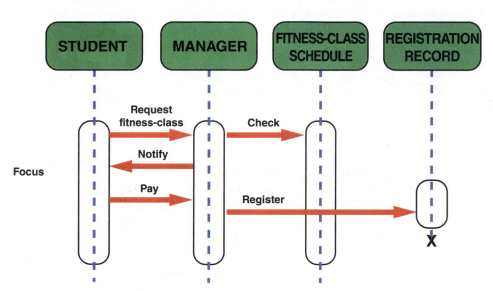

FIGURE 6-32 The sequence diagram for the ADD NEW STUDENT use case. The use case description for ADD NEW STUDENT is shown in Figure 6-25 on page 240.

© Cengage Learning 2014

State Transition Diagrams

Earlier in this chapter you learned that state refers to an object's current status. A **state transition diagram** shows how an object changes from one state to another, depending on events that affect the object. All possible states must be documented in the state transition diagram, as shown in Figure 6-33. A bank account, for example, could be opened as a NEW account, change to an ACTIVE or EXISTING account, and eventually become a CLOSED or FORMER account. Another possible state for a bank account could be FROZEN, if the account's assets are legally attached.

In a state transition diagram, the states appear as rounded rectangles with the state names inside. The small circle to the left is the initial state, or the point where the object first interacts with the system. Reading from left to right, the lines show direction and describe the action or event that causes a transition from one state to another. The circle at the right with a hollow border is the final state.

FIGURE 6-33 An example of a state transition diagram for a bank account.

© Cengage Learning 2014

Activity Diagrams

An **activity diagram** resembles a horizontal flowchart that shows the actions and events as they occur. Activity diagrams show the order in which the actions take place and identify the outcomes. Figure 6-34 shows an activity diagram for a cash withdrawal at an ATM machine. Notice that the customer initiates the activity by inserting an ATM card and requesting cash. Activity diagrams also can display multiple use cases in the form of a grid, where classes are shown as vertical bars and actions appear as horizontal arrows.

FIGURE 6-34 An activity diagram shows the actions and events involved in withdrawing cash from an ATM machine.
© Cengage Learning 2014

Sequence diagrams, state transition diagrams, and activity diagrams are dynamic modeling tools that can help a systems analyst understand how objects behave and interact with the system.

CASE IN POINT 6.3: TRAVELBIZ

Jack Forester and Lisa Turner are systems analysts in the IT department of TravelBiz, a nationwide travel agency that specializes in business travel. TravelBiz has decided to expand into the vacation travel market by launching a new business division called TravelFun. The IT director assigned Jack and Lisa to create a flexible, efficient information system for the new division. Jack wants to use traditional analysis and modeling techniques for the project. Lisa, on the other hand, wants to use an object-oriented methodology. Which approach would you suggest and why?

Business Process Modeling

In addition to sequence diagrams and activity diagrams, you can use **business process modeling (BPM)** to represent the people, events, and interaction in a system. BPM initially was discussed in Chapter 3 as a requirements modeling tool, but you can use it anytime during the systems development process. BPM works well with object modeling, because both methods focus on the actors and the way they behave.

Figure 6-35 shows the Bizagi Modeler site, where you can download free BPM software that includes video tutorials, support forums, and templates. In a typical BPM diagram, the outside rectangle is called a **pool**, and designated **swim lanes** show specific actions and events. The swim lanes can interact when certain events occur, as shown in Figure 6-35, where a decision in Lane 1 interacts with the flow in Lane 2.

FIGURE 6-35 The Bizagi Modeler site offers free BPM software that uses a swimming pool and swim lanes to represent interactive business processes and events

© 2012–Bizagi

The bottom image in Figure 6-35 shows a template for an internal help desk. The template, which shows swim lanes for employees and Help Desk staff, is one of many supplied by Bizagi.

CASE Tools

Object modeling requires many types of diagrams to represent the proposed system. Creating the diagrams by hand is time consuming and tedious, so systems analysts rely on CASE tools to speed up the process and provide an overall framework for documenting the system components. In addition, CASE tools ensure consistency and provide common links so that once objects are described and used in one part of the design, they can be reused multiple times without further effort.

ORGANIZING THE OBJECT MODEL

In this chapter, you learned how to use object-oriented tools and techniques to build a logical model of the information system. Now you are ready to organize your diagrams and documentation so the object model is easily read and understood. If you used a CASE tool to develop the design, much of this work will be performed automatically by the CASE software.

There are many ways to proceed with the task of organizing the object model, and experience will be your best teacher. After you identify the system's objects, classes, and relationships, you should develop an object relationship diagram that provides an overview of the system. If you do not use a CASE-generated model, each diagram or object definition should be supported by clear, relevant documentation that can be accessed easily by anyone who reviews the object model. For example, you should organize your use cases and use case diagrams so they can be linked to the appropriate class, state transition, sequence, and activity diagrams. Your diagrams and documentation are the foundation for the system's design, so accuracy is important. Remember that it is much easier to repair a diagram now than to change the software later.

CASE IN POINT 6.4:   CYBER ASSOCIATES

One of your responsibilities at Cyber Associates, an IT consulting firm, is to assign new systems analysts to various tasks and projects. Some of the senior people believe that inexperienced analysts should start with object-oriented techniques, which are easier to learn and apply. Others think that an analyst should learn structured analysis first, and then proceed to object-oriented skills. What is your viewpoint, and why?

A QUESTION OF ETHICS

© faberfoto_it/iStockphoto

Last month, your company launched a peer review process for IT projects. At the end of each project, team members rate the performance of the overall team, and his or her co-workers individually. The stated goal was to obtain honest, peer-based feedback. Unfortunately, like many good ideas, there was a downside. Although the input is anonymous, the results are submitted to the entire team. Some members, including you, are uncomfortable with the new process because it could encourage cliques and actually undermine a team-based culture. Others see it as an opportunity for honest input.

One team member, who is a close friend of yours, is not very popular with her team-mates. To make matters worse, she recently had some personal problems that affected her work, and she is worried that her ratings will be quite negative. She has not specifically asked you about your feedback, but you know she is hoping for a favorable review from you. Even though her work was not great, you don't want to see her get hurt by a process that you yourself are not comfortable with.

Is this a question of ethics versus friendship? Would it be wrong to tilt the scales in her favor just a bit?

CHAPTER SUMMARY

This chapter introduces object modeling, which is a popular technique that describes a system in terms of objects. Objects represent real people, places, events, and transactions. Unlike structured analysis, which treats data and processes separately, objects include data and processes that can affect the data. During the implementation process, systems analysts and programmers transform objects into program code modules that can be optimized, tested, and reused as often as necessary.

Object-oriented terms include classes, attributes, instances, messages, and methods. Classes include objects that have similar attributes, or characteristics. Individual members of a class are called object instances. Objects within a class can be grouped into subclasses, which are more specific categories within the class. A class also can belong to a more general category called a superclass.

Objects can send messages, or commands, that require other objects to perform certain methods, or tasks. The concept that a message gives different meanings to different objects is called polymorphism. An object resembles a black box, with encapsulated, or self-contained, data and methods. The strongest relationship between objects is inheritance.

After you identify the objects, classes, and relationships, you prepare an object relationship diagram that shows the objects and how they interact to perform business functions and transactions.

The Unified Modeling Language (UML) is a widely used method of visualizing and documenting an information system. UML techniques include use cases, use case diagrams, class diagrams, sequence diagrams, state transition diagrams, and activity diagrams.

A use case describes a business situation initiated by an actor, who interacts with the information system. Each use case represents a specific transaction, or scenario. A use case diagram is a visual summary of related use cases within a system or subsystem. A class diagram represents a detailed view of a single use case, showing the classes that participate in the underlying business transaction, and the relationship among class instances, which is called cardinality. A sequence diagram is a dynamic model of a use case, showing the interaction among classes during a specified time period. Sequence diagrams include lifelines, messages, and focuses. A state transition diagram shows how an object changes from one state to another, depending on events that affect the object. An activity diagram resembles a horizontal flowchart that shows actions and events as they occur in a system.

CASE tools provide an overall framework for system documentation. CASE tools can speed up the development process, ensure consistency, and provide common links that enable objects to be reused.

At the end of the object modeling process, you organize your use cases and use case diagrams and create class, sequence, state transition, and activity diagrams.

In addition to object models, you can use business process modeling (BPM) to represent the people, events, and interaction in a system. BPM uses a swimming pool concept to represent interactive business processes and events, which are shown as swim lanes in the pool.

Key Terms

activity diagram *242*

actor *235*

attributes *226*

black box *231*

business process modeling (BPM) *242*

cardinality *238*

child *234*

class *226*

class diagram *238*

encapsulation *232*

focus *241*

inheritance *234*

instance *226*

lifeline *240*

message *226*

methods *226*

object *226*

object model *226*

object-oriented (O-O) analysis *226*

parent *234*

polymorphism *231*

pool *242*

relationships *234*

sequence diagram *240*

state *230*

state transition diagram *241*

subclass *232*

superclass *233*

swim lane *242*

system boundary *238*

Unified Modeling Language (UML) *226*

use case *235*

use case description *236*

use case diagram *237*

Chapter Exercises

Questions

1. What is object-oriented analysis, and what are some advantages of this method?
2. Define an object, and provide three examples.
3. Define an attribute, and provide three examples.
4. Define a method, and provide three examples.
5. Define encapsulation, and explain how it is used in object-oriented analysis.
6. Define polymorphism, and provide three examples.
7. Define a class, subclass, and superclass, and provide three examples of each.
8. Define an actor, and provide three examples.
9. Define a use case and a use case diagram, and prepare a sample of each.
10. Define the term *black box*, and explain why it is an important concept in object-oriented analysis. Can you think of other black boxes that you use in everyday life?

Discussion Topics

1. The chapter mentioned that systems analysts and programmers transform objects into program code modules. Modular design is a very popular concept in many industries. What other modular design examples can you suggest?
2. You are an IT consultant, and you are asked to create a new system for a small real estate brokerage firm. You have no experience with object-oriented approach, and you decide to try it. How will you begin? How will the tasks differ from structured analysis?
3. You are creating a system for a bowling alley to manage information about its leagues. During the modeling process, you create a state transition diagram for an object called *League Bowlers*. What are the possible states of a league bowler, and what happens to a bowler who quits the league and rejoins the following season?
4. A debate is raging at the IT consulting firm where you work. Some staff members believe that it is harder for experienced analysts to learn object-modeling techniques, because the analysts are accustomed to thinking about data and processes as separate entities. Others believe that solid analytical skills are easily transferable and do not see a problem in crossing over to the newer approach. What do you think, and why?

Projects

1. Write a brief history of the UML, and prepare a presentation on the subject.
2. Contact the IT staff at your school or at a local business to learn they use object-oriented programming languages. If so, determine what languages and versions are used, how long they have been in use, and why they were selected.
3. Perform a Web search for the exact phrase "*object-oriented systems analysis*". How many hits did you get? Provide three examples.
4. Prepare a report on at least three CASE tools that provide UML support.

Apply Your Knowledge

This section contains four mini-cases. Each case describes a situation, explains your role, and requires you to apply what you learned in the chapter.

1 Osceola Auto Parts

Osceola Auto Parts is an independent auto parts dealer that sells auto parts, runs tests on customers' cars, and delivers parts and tools to mechanic shops around town.

Tasks

1. Identify possible actors and use cases involved in Osceola's business functions.
2. Create a use case diagram for Osceola's operations.
3. Select one of the use cases and create a class diagram.
4. Create a sequence diagram for the use case you selected.

2 Area Transit Authority

The Area Transit Authority (ATA) is a rural public transportation company. ATA operates a fleet of 25 buses that serve approximately 1,000 riders each day. The bus operation involves 10 regular routes, plus routes for special events. The ATA employs 20 full-time drivers and 10 to 15 part-time drivers. A dispatcher coordinates the staffing and routes and relays messages to drivers regarding traffic information and special passenger pick-up arrangements.

Tasks

1. Identify possible actors and use cases involved in ATA's bus operations.
2. Create a use case diagram for the bus system.
3. Create a sequence diagram for the use case you selected.
4. Create a state transition diagram that describes typical passenger states and how they change based on specific actions and events.

Oakwood Community College Registration

Oakwood Community College has a student registration process similar to the one at your school. The administration asked you, as IT director, to develop a new system that would be more user-friendly. Your first task is to create an object-oriented model of the current system. You can use your school's registration process as the basis for the model.

Tasks

1. List possible objects in the registration system, including their attributes and methods.
2. Identify possible use cases and actors.
3. Create a use case diagram that shows how students register.
4. Create a state transition diagram that describes typical student states and how they change based on specific actions and events.

Oakwood Community College Library

The library staff at Oakwood Community College works hard to satisfy students and faculty. One of library's main goals is to use new technology whenever possible to enhance service and efficiency. The collection is updated constantly, and faculty members often request new books to support current courses and research needs. Students and faculty can visit the library to use on-site resources, including some materials that cannot be checked out. In addition, the library maintains extensive online resources. The head librarian wants you to develop an object-oriented model for a new library information system that would be user-friendly and cost-effective. You can use your schools library as a model, and you are free to use your imagination.

Tasks

1. List possible objects in the library operation, including their attributes and methods.
2. Identify possible use cases and actors.
3. Select one of the use cases and create a sequence diagram.
4. Create an object relationship diagram that provides an overview of the system, including how books are requested by faculty and checked out to students.

Case Studies

Each chapter includes a Chapter Case, a Continuing Case, a Capstone Case, and an Online Case Simulation. You can learn more about the Online Case Simulation in the MIS CourseMate Features section.

Chapter Case: Campus Bikes

Campus Bikes is a popular bicycle shop located near a major university. The business has grown and the owner, Mark Turner, wants to install an up-to-date computer system to handle all business functions.

Background

Campus Bikes sells several brands of new bikes, including everything from high-end racing models to beach cruisers. In addition to sales of new bikes and accessories, Mark's service department is always busy. The staff includes Mark himself, a bookkeeper, two part-time sales reps, a full-time mechanic, and several part-time service helpers who assemble bikes.

Before opening the shop three years ago, Mark worked for many years in his father's auto dealership, Turner Motors, and he learned all about the automobile business. In the bike shop, he runs a similar operation, but on a much smaller scale. For example, sales orders are recorded on pre-printed forms, and service requests are written up just as they would be in an auto service department.

Mark's customers find him fair and reasonable. He likes to say that the main difference between his business and a big-box retailer is that he knows his customers and will do whatever it takes to keep them happy.

You work at the college as a lab assistant in the computer information department. You earned a computer science degree at a two-year school, and you recently decided to work toward your four-degree. The computer lab manager, Jill, often suggests that local businesses contact you for help in troubleshooting IT issues.

This morning, you received a call from Mark, who wants to hire you as a consultant to help plan a system for Campus Bikes. You learned that Jill had referred him, and you are excited to have this opportunity. It probably didn't hurt that both you and Jill had bought bikes from Mark, and already knew him. After spending several weekends talking with Mark and the staff, you are ready to start. You decide to use an object-oriented approach that will be easy to understand.

Tasks

1. List possible objects in the new bike shop system, including their attributes and methods.
2. Identify at least three possible use cases and actors.
3. Create a use case diagram that shows how service requests are handled.
4. Create a state transition diagram that describes typical customer states and how they change based on specific actions and events.

Continuing Case: Personal Trainer, Inc.

Personal Trainer, Inc. owns and operates fitness centers in a dozen Midwestern cities. The centers have done well, and the company is planning an international expansion by opening a new "supercenter" in the Toronto area. Personal Trainer's president, Cassia Umi, hired an IT consultant, Susan Park, to help develop an information system for the new facility. During the project, Susan will work closely with Gray Lewis, who will manage the new operation.

(continues)

Continuing Case: Personal Trainer, Inc.

Background

Working as an IT consultant for Personal Trainer, Susan Park used data and process modeling tools to create a logical model of the proposed information system. Now she wants to build an object-oriented view of the system using O-O tools and techniques. Before you perform the following tasks, you should review the information and background in Chapters 1 and 2, and the fact-finding summary of the case provided in Chapter 4.

Tasks

1. Identify possible actors and use cases involved in Personal Trainer's operations.
2. Create an object relationship diagram for the Personal Trainer information system.
3. Create a use case diagram for the system.
4. Select one of the use cases and create a sequence diagram and a state transition diagram.

Capstone Case: New Century Wellness Group

New Century Wellness Group offers a holistic approach to healthcare with an emphasis on preventive medicine as well as traditional medical care. In your role as an IT consultant, you will help New Century develop a new information system.

Background

You began the systems analysis phase at New Century by completing a series of interviews, reviewing existing reports, and observing office operations. Then, in Chapter 5, you acquired more information and developed a set of DFDs, process descriptions, and a data dictionary.

The next step in the SDLC is to perform an object-oriented analysis of the new system. Before you begin, go back and review the organization chart and processes list from Chapter 1, and the diagrams data store list from Chapter 5. Then complete the following tasks.

Tasks

1. Identify possible use cases and actors, and create a use case diagram for the New Century Wellness Group system.
2. Select one of the use cases and create a class diagram.
3. Create a sequence diagram for the use case that you selected.
4. Create a state transition diagram that describes typical patient states and how they change based on specific actions and events.

CASE Tool Workshop

Systems analysts use CASE tools to help them plan, build, and maintain information systems. To learn more about CASE tools, turn to Part B of the Toolkit that follows Chapter 12. You can complete these tasks with the Visible Analyst® CASE tool, which is available with this textbook, or a similar tool.

Background

In the previous chapter, you created a data and process model for a new business venture. You plan to operate a mobile auto detailing service that will visit customers at their homes or businesses, and offer traditional, high-quality hand washing and waxing. In addition to retail customers, several auto dealers have expressed interest in your services, and you are eager to get started. You will hire college students as technicians, train and supply them, and offer them a share of the profits as an incentive.

Your friend, who is an IT major, offered to help you set up an information system by customizing several Microsoft Office applications to meet your needs. In addition to the data and process model you created, she recommended that you prepare an object model. She suggested that you focus on the main actors and events, and that it was OK to use your imagination.

Thinking it over, you know that you will have employees, retail customers, auto dealer accounts, one or more suppliers, and your local bank, where you plan to set up a business checking account. You also plan to keep track of customers, employee information, profit-sharing data, and an operations log.

Tasks

1. List possible objects in the new business, including their attributes and methods, and create a use case diagram that shows how an on-site service request would be handled.
2. Create a sequence diagram that models the on-site service request mentioned in Task 1.

MIS CourseMate Features

If you have an MIS CourseMate access code, you can reinforce and extend your learning with premium content created for this textbook. For example, you can launch interactive Video Learning Sessions to help you understand systems development concepts and practice your skills. In addition, you can use MindTap Reader, which is a full, interactive, digital e-book.

MIS CourseMate also offers many learning features within each chapter, including an Online Case Simulation, a Critical Thinking Challenge, Video Learning Tasks, and a set of Learn It Online activities. To log on to the MIS CourseMate site at **www.cengagebrain.com**, you must create a student account and register this book.

Online Case Simulation: SCR Associates

Session 6: Object Modeling

Overview

The SCR Associates case study is a Web-based simulation that allows you to practice your skills in a real-world environment. The firm offers IT consulting, solutions and training. SCR plans to open a new high-tech training center, and needs to develop a Training Information Management System (TIMS) to support the center. You are a newly hired systems analyst reporting to Jesse Baker, systems group manager, and will help her develop the system.

The case study takes you to the SCR Web site, where you receive e-mail and voice mail messages from Jesse, obtain information from SCR's resource libraries, and perform various tasks. Jesse has high standards, but seems very fair. She made it clear that she expects your work to be accurate, thorough, and professional.

Before You Begin

To prepare for this work session, you should review the following topics:

- Use case, class, sequence, and state-transition diagrams

How Do I Use the Online Case Simulation?

- Read the preview, and review the Chapter 1 background material if necessary.
- Visit the MIS CourseMate Web site at **www.cengagebrain.com**, locate the **SCR Case Simulation**, and click the **intranet** link. Enter your name and the password **sad10e**.
- When the opening screen displays, select this session. Then check your e-mail and voice mail, and start to work on your task list.

Preview: Session 6

In the last session, you used data and process modeling techniques to develop a logical model of the new system. Now you will apply your object modeling skills to create various diagrams and documentation for the new TIMS system. You will review the background material and develop an object-oriented model that includes several types of diagrams.

Critical Thinking Challenge

In addition to technical ability, IT professionals need critical thinking skills. This feature can help you practice perception, organization, analysis, problem-solving, and decision-making skills that will be valuable in the workplace. You can visit **www.criticalthinking.org** to learn more about critical thinking and why it is so important.

Background

The IT team at Game Technology prepared DFDs for the new C^3 system. You will help the team develop a set of object models. The C^3 system model will include use cases that represent various business processes. The customer and sales rep entities will be actors, with these methods:

Entity	Methods
Customer	• Request product information • Place order • Respond to Web promotion • Sign up on game blog
Sales Rep	• Initiate sales call to customer • Respond to customer inquiry • Follow up after prior order • Follow up after prior information request

You also learned that customer categories are based on specific conditions, as shown:

Category	Conditions
Potential	Has not placed an order in the last 24 months, but *has* responded to a Web promotion *or* requested product information *or* signed up on our game blog
Active	Has placed at least one order in the last 24 months
Preferred	Has placed at least three orders in the last 24 months
Former	An Active or Preferred customer with no orders in the last 24 months

Practice Tasks

Visit the MIS CourseMate Web site at **www.cengagebrain.com.** Then navigate to the resources for this chapter and locate the **Critical Thinking Challenge** feature. You will complete two Practice Tasks, using what you learned in the chapter. Then you can check your answers to be sure you're ready for the Challenge Tasks.

Challenge Tasks

After you complete the Practice Tasks, you learn about new developments at Game Technology.

The marketing group added a new data analyst position to provide IT support. The new person will track customer response times, prepare contact management plans for sales reps, and develop customer satisfaction surveys. Marketing also decided to update customer categories. The **Potential** and **Former** categories are not affected. The new categories are **Silver**, which replaces the **Active** category; **Gold**, which replaces the **Preferred** category; and **Platinum**, which includes any customer whose orders total at least $1,000 in the last 24 months. To continue, navigate to the **Critical Thinking Challenge** feature for this chapter, select the **Challenge Tasks,** and follow the instructions.

Video Learning Sessions

The Video Learning Sessions in this chapter explain how to create object-oriented models to plan, document, and design an information system.

Before You Begin

To prepare for the tasks, you should review the following topics:

- Object-oriented terms and concepts
- Object modeling tools and techniques

How to Watch a Session

Go to the Management Information Systems CourseMate Web site at www.cengagebrain.com. Then navigate to the resources for this book, locate the **Video Learning Sessions**, and select a session. You can watch the session on your computer or mobile device, and pause, rewind, or replay a video at any time.

Practice Tasks

After each session, visit the **Your Turn** feature to perform the tasks and check your answers.

Training Tasks

Suppose the IT training manager wants to encourage team members to watch the Video Learning Sessions. To spark interest, she plans to post a set of VLS previews, which you will prepare. Each preview must include an overview of the session, a description of the main topics, and one or more screen examples from the video. To get you started, she provided a task list:

1. Select a Video Learning Session from this chapter. Launch the video and note the title, objectives, and total running time. Include this information in your preview.
2. Run though the session and find a segment that does a good job of explaining a specific skill or concept.
3. In the segment you selected, choose one or more specific screens and capture each screen image with the Windows Snipping Tool. To do this in Windows 7 or Windows Vista, click **Start**, and then type **Snipping Tool**. In Windows 8, you can display the **Start** menu, and then type **Snipping Tool**.
4. Paste the screen image into your preview and explain how it would help a viewer understand the topic. Also add your comments about the video, and why it would be important to an IT professional. Your preview should be well-organized and readable.

Learn It Online

In each chapter, you can use this feature to apply your knowledge and practice your skills. The exercises include Chapter Reinforcement Questions, Flash Cards, Practice Tests, and various games, such as *Who Wants To Be a Computer Genius?*, *Wheel of Terms*, and the *Crossword Puzzle Challenge*.

© craftvision/iStockph

CHAPTER 7 Development Strategies

Chapter 7 is the final chapter in the systems analysis phase of the SDLC. This chapter describes software trends, acquisition and development strategies, traditional versus Web-based development, outsourcing versus in-house development, the system requirements document, prototyping, and preparing for the transition to the next SDLC phase — systems design.

INTRODUCTION

OBJECTIVES

When you finish this chapter, you will be able to:

- Describe the concept of Software as a Service
- Define Web 2.0 and cloud computing
- Explain software acquisition alternatives, including traditional and Web-based software development strategies
- Describe software outsourcing options, including offshore outsourcing and the role of service providers
- Explain advantages and disadvantages of in-house software development
- Discuss cost-benefit analysis and financial analysis tools
- Describe a request for proposal (RFP) and a request for quotation (RFQ)
- Describe the system requirements document
- Explain the transition from systems analysis to systems design

The main objective of the systems analysis phase is to build a logical model of the new information system. In Chapters 4, 5, and 6, you learned about requirements modeling, data and process modeling, and object modeling. Chapter 7 describes the remaining activities in the systems analysis phase, which include evaluation of alternative solutions, preparation of the system requirements document, and presentation of the system requirements document to management. The chapter also explains the transition to systems design.

If you have MIS CourseMate, you can view two Video Learning Sessions that explain return on investment (ROI) and net present value (NPV) financial analysis.

PREVIEW CASE: Mountain View College Bookstore

Background: Wendy Lee, manager of college services at Mountain View College, wants a new information system that will improve efficiency and customer service at the three college bookstores.

In this part of the case, Tina Allen (systems analyst) and David Conroe (student intern) are talking about development strategies for the new system.

Participants:	Tina and David
Location:	Tina's office, Wednesday morning, November 13, 2013
Project status:	Tina and David developed a logical model that includes data flow diagrams, a data dictionary, and process descriptions. They also created an object model. Now they are ready to discuss development strategies for the new bookstore system.
Discussion topics:	Web-based versus traditional development, cost-benefit analysis, the steps in purchasing a software package, and the transition to systems design.

Tina: Good morning, David. Are you ready for the next step?

David: *Sure. Now that we have a logical model of the bookstore system, what comes next?*

Tina: We're at a transition point between the logical design, which describes what the new system will do, and the physical design phase, which describes how it will be done, including the user interface and physical components. Before we start the physical design, we have to study various systems development options and make a recommendation to Wendy.

David: *What are the options?*

Tina: Well, some large organizations use Web-based systems hosted by outside vendors who supply and maintain the software. In a sense, the customer rents the application. I checked with our IT director, and she feels we're not ready for that approach. She wants us to implement a system on the college network and migrate to a Web-based system later. That brings us to the next set of questions.

David: *Such as?*

Tina: We need to consider our role in the development process. We can build the system ourselves, which is called in-house development. Or we can purchase a software package, which might need some degree of modification to meet our needs. Or we could consider outsourcing options, including hiring an IT consultant to help with development tasks. Either way, we need to do a cost-benefit study.

David: *What about the transition from logical to physical design that you mentioned?*

Tina: The idea is to take our logical design, which is similar to an architect's proposal, and translate it into a physical design, which is more like a working blueprint. If we decide to develop the system in-house, we'll start work on the design. If we decide to purchase a package, we'll follow a series of steps that will help us select the best product. Here's a task list to get us started:

FIGURE 7-1 Typical development strategies task list.

© Cengage Learning 2014

DEVELOPMENT STRATEGIES OVERVIEW

Just a few years ago, a typical company either developed software itself, purchased a software package (which might need some modification), or hired consultants or outside resources to perform the work. Today, a company has many more choices, including application service providers, Web-hosted software options, and firms that offer a variety of enterprise-wide software solutions.

Selecting the best development path is an important decision that requires companies to consider three key topics: the impact of the Internet, software outsourcing options, and in-house software development alternatives. These topics are reviewed in the following sections.

THE IMPACT OF THE INTERNET

The Internet has triggered enormous changes in business methods and operations, and software acquisition is no exception. This section examines a trend that views Software as a Service, the changing marketplace for software, and how Web-based development compares to traditional methods. The section concludes with a description of Internet-related trends, including Web 2.0 and cloud computing.

Software as a Service

In the traditional model, software vendors develop and sell application packages to customers. Typically, customers purchase licenses that give them the right to use the software under the terms of the license agreement. Although this model still accounts for most software acquisition, a new model, called **Software as a Service (SaaS)**, is changing the picture dramatically.

SaaS is a model of software deployment where an application is hosted as a service provided to customers over the Internet. SaaS reduces the customer's need for software maintenance, operation, and support.

In a highly competitive marketplace, major vendors constantly strive to deliver new and better solutions. For example, Microsoft claims that its SaaS platform offers the best solution and business value. Microsoft also promotes a broader vision, called Software + Services. The term refers to Microsoft's strategy for cloud computing, which integrates software applications, platforms and infrastructure. Figure 7-2 shows Accenture's view that SaaS offers great potential benefits. Accenture invites visitors to download a paper that describes the specific topics listed in the figure.

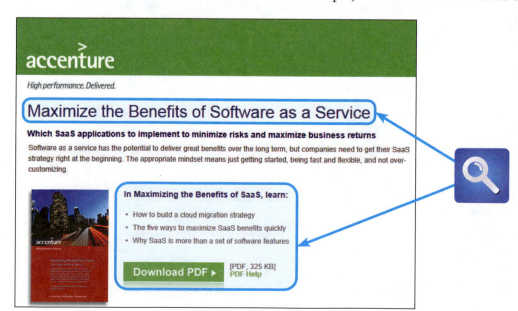

FIGURE 7-2 Accenture stresses the main benefits of SaaS deployment.

FIGURE 7-3 The Web Host Industry Review (WHIR) is a clearinghouse for SaaS information.
© 2012 iNET Interactive.

The Web Host Industry Review shown in Figure 7-3 is an online source of information about SaaS products, trends, and events. In a published report, the Review quoted a Gartner, Inc. prediction that worldwide SaaS revenue will reach $14.5 billion in 2012, which is a 17.9 percent increase from 2011, and that by 2015, SaaS revenue will grow to $22.1 billion.

Traditional vs. Web-Based Systems Development

As a systems analyst, you must consider whether development will take place in a Web-centric framework, or in a traditional environment. This section provides an overview of some of the similarities and differences.

In an Internet-based system, the Web becomes an integral part of the application, rather than just a communication channel, and systems analysts need new application development tools and solutions to handle the new systems. Two major Web-based development environments are Microsoft's **.NET** and IBM's **WebSphere,** which are shown in Figure 7-4.

FIGURE 7-4 Microsoft's .NET and IBM's WebSphere are comprehensive software development environments.
©IBM Corporation 1994, 2012 and ©2012 Microsoft Corporation

Microsoft regards .NET as a platform-independent software environment. IBM describes WebSphere as a set of products specifically designed to support e-business applications across multiple computing platforms.

Although there is a major trend toward Web-based architecture, many firms rely on traditional systems, either because they are legacy applications that are not easily replaced, or because they do not require a Web component to satisfy user needs. If you need to choose, you should consider some key differences between traditional and Web-based system development. Building the application in a Web-based environment can offer greater benefits, and sometimes greater risks, compared to a traditional environment. The following sections list some characteristics of traditional versus Web-based development.

TRADITIONAL DEVELOPMENT In a traditional systems development environment:

- Systems design is influenced by compatibility issues, including existing hardware and software platforms and legacy system requirements.

- Systems are designed to run on local and wide-area company networks.

- Systems often utilize Internet links and resources, but Web-based features are treated as enhancements rather than core elements of the design.

- Development typically follows one of three main paths: in-house development, purchase of a software package with possible modification, or use of outside consultants.

- Scalability can be affected by network limitations and constraints.

- Many applications require substantial desktop computing power and resources.

- Security issues usually are less complex than with Web-based systems, because the system operates on a private company network, rather than the Internet.

WEB-BASED DEVELOPMENT In a Web-based systems development environment:

- Systems are developed and delivered in an Internet-based framework such as .NET or WebSphere.

- Internet-based development treats the Web *as* the platform, rather than just a communication channel.

- Web-based systems are easily scalable, and can run on multiple hardware environments.

- Large firms tend to deploy Web-based systems as enterprise-wide software solutions for applications such as customer relationship management, order processing, and materials management.

- Web-based software treats the software application as a service that is less dependent on desktop computing power and resources.

- When companies acquire Web-based software as a *service* rather than a *product* they purchase, they can limit in-house involvement to a minimum and have the vendor install, configure, and maintain the system by paying agreed-upon fees.

- Web-based software usually requires additional layers, called **middleware**, to communicate with existing software and legacy systems.

Evolving Trends: Web 2.0 and Cloud Computing

In the constantly changing world of IT, no area is more dynamic than Internet technology. Two examples of evolving trends are Web 2.0 and cloud computing. Systems analysts should be aware of these concepts and consider them as they plan large-scale systems. Web 2.0 and cloud computing are discussed in more detail in Chapter 10, System Architecture.

Many IT professionals use the term **Web 2.0** to describe a second generation of the Web that enables people to collaborate, interact, and share information much more effectively. This new environment is based on continuously available user applications rather than static HTML Web pages, without limitations regarding the number of users or how they access, modify, and exchange data. The Web 2.0 environment enhances interactive experiences, including wikis and blogs, and social-networking applications such as Twitter, LinkedIn, and Facebook.

The term **cloud computing** refers to the cloud symbol that indicates a network or the Internet. Some industry leaders predict that cloud computing will offer an overall online software and data environment supported by supercomputer technology. If so, cloud computing would be an ultimate form of SaaS, delivering services and data to users who would need only an Internet connection and a browser. However, as the *InfoWorld* article shown in Figure 7-5 points out, no standard definition of cloud computing exists, and the concept means different things to different people.

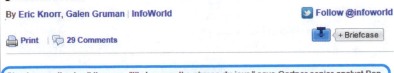

What cloud computing really means

The next big trend sounds nebulous, but it's not so fuzzy when you view the value proposition from the perspective of IT professionals

By Eric Knorr, Galen Gruman | InfoWorld   Follow @infoworld

🖨 Print | 💬 29 Comments   + Briefcase

Cloud computing is all the rage. "It's become the phrase du jour," says Gartner senior analyst Ben Pring, echoing many of his peers. The problem is that (as with Web 2.0) everyone seems to have a different definition.

As a metaphor for the Internet, "the cloud" is a familiar cliché, but when combined with "computing," the meaning gets bigger and fuzzier. Some analysts and vendors define cloud computing narrowly as an updated version of utility computing: basically virtual servers available over the Internet. Others go very broad, arguing anything you consume outside the firewall is "in the cloud," including conventional outsourcing.

FIGURE 7-5 Cloud computing holds the promise of a new generation of powerful Web applications and services. This is an evolving technology, and at this point, the term means different things to different people.

©1994–2012 Infoworld, Inc./Eric Knorr/Galen Gruman

OUTSOURCING

Outsourcing is the transfer of information systems development, operation, or maintenance to an outside firm that provides these services, for a fee, on a temporary or long-term basis. Outsourcing can refer to relatively minor programming tasks, renting software from a service provider, outsourcing a basic business process (often called **business process outsourcing,** or **BPO**), or handling a company's entire IT function. Numerous firms and organizations offer information about outsourcing topics and issues. For example, the Outsourcing Center site at *www.outsourcing-center.com* provides free research, case studies, database directories, market intelligence, and updates on trends and best practices in outsourcing as a strategic business solution.

The Growth of Outsourcing

Traditionally, firms outsourced IT tasks as a way of controlling costs and dealing with rapid technological change. While those reasons still are valid, outsourcing has become part of an overall IT strategy for many organizations. The outsourcing trend also has affected software vendors, who have adjusted their marketing accordingly. For example, Oracle Corporation offers a service called Oracle On Demand, which provides e-business applications, as shown in Figure 7-6. Oracle also cites data that shows that businesses spend up to 80% of their IT budgets maintaining existing software and systems, which forces IT managers "... to spend time managing tedious upgrades instead of revenue-generating IT projects."

A firm that offers outsourcing solutions is called a **service provider.** Some service providers concentrate on specific software applications; others offer business services such as order processing and customer billing. Still others offer enterprise-wide software

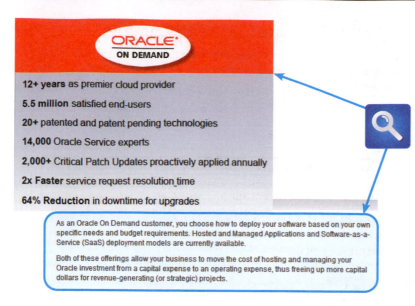

FIGURE 7-6 Oracle Corporation offers a fixed-fee outsourcing plan called Oracle On Demand.

© 2011, Oracle

solutions that integrate and manage functions such as accounting, manufacturing, and inventory control.

Two popular outsourcing options involve application service providers and firms that offer Internet business services. These terms are explained in the following sections.

APPLICATION SERVICE PROVIDERS An **application service provider (ASP)** is a firm that delivers a software application, or access to an application, by charging a usage or subscription fee. An ASP provides more than a license to use the software; it *rents* an operational package to the customer. ASPs typically provide commercially available software such as databases and accounting packages. If a company uses an ASP to supply a data management package, for example, the company does not have to design, develop, implement, or maintain the package. ASPs represent a rapidly growing trend, using the Internet as the primary delivery channel.

INTERNET BUSINESS SERVICES Some firms offer **Internet business services (IBS)**, which provide powerful Web-based support for transactions such as order processing, billing, and customer relationship management. Another term for IBS is **managed hosting**, because system operations are managed by the outside firm, or host.

An IBS solution is attractive to customers because it offers online data center support, mainframe computing power for mission-critical functions, and universal access via the Internet. Many firms, such as Rackspace, compete in the managed hosting market, as shown in Figure 7-7.

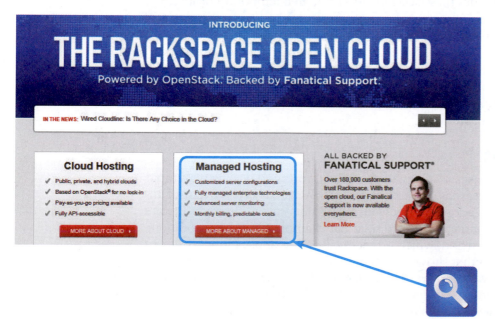

FIGURE 7-7 Rackspace Corporation offers multi-platform managed hosting and IBS services.

©2012 Rackspace, US Inc.

Outsourcing Fees

Firms that offer Software as a Service, rather than a product, have developed fee structures that are based on how the application is used by customers during a specific time period. Several models exist, including fixed fee, subscription, and usage or transaction. A **fixed fee model** uses a set fee based on a specified level of service and user support. An example of a fixed fee model is Oracle's On Demand service. A **subscription model** has a variable fee based on the number of users or workstations that have access to the application. Finally, a **usage model** or **transaction model** charges a variable fee based on the volume of transactions or operations performed by the application.

When a company considers outsourcing, it should estimate usage characteristics to determine which fee structure would be most desirable, and then attempt to negotiate a service provider contract based on that model.

Outsourcing Issues and Concerns

When a company decides to outsource IT functions, it takes an important step that can affect the firm's resources, operations, and profitability. Mission-critical IT systems should be outsourced only if the result is a cost-attractive, reliable, business solution that fits the company's long-term business strategy and involves an acceptable level of risk. Moving IT work overseas raises even more issues, including potential concerns about control, culture, communication, and security.

In addition to long-term strategic consequences, outsourcing also can raise some concerns. For example, a company must turn over sensitive data to an external service provider and trust the provider to maintain security, confidentiality, and quality. Also, before outsourcing, a company must carefully review issues relating to insurance, potential liability, licensing and information ownership, warranties, and disaster recovery.

Most important, a company considering outsourcing must realize that the solution can be only as good as the outsourcing firm that provides the service. A dynamic economy can give rise to business failures and uncertainty about the future. In this climate, it is especially important to review the history and financial condition of an outsourcing firm before making a commitment.

Mergers and acquisitions also can affect outsourcing clients. For example, after their merger, Compaq and Hewlett-Packard restructured and streamlined the products and services offered by the new company. Even with large, financially healthy firms such as these, a merger or acquisition can have some impact on clients and customers. If stability is important, an outsourcing client should consider these issues.

Outsourcing can be especially attractive to a company whose volume fluctuates widely, such as a defense contractor. In other situations, a company might decide to outsource application development tasks to an IT consulting firm if the company lacks the time or expertise to handle the work on its own. Outsourcing relieves a company of the responsibility of adding IT staff in busy times and downsizing when the workload lightens. A major disadvantage of outsourcing is that it raises employee concerns about job security. Talented IT people usually prefer positions where the firm is committed to in-house IT development — if they do not feel secure, they might decide to work directly for the service provider.

Offshore Outsourcing

Offshore outsourcing, or **global outsourcing**, refers to the practice of shifting IT development, support, and operations to other countries. In a trend similar to the outflow of manufacturing jobs over a several-decade period, many firms are sending IT work overseas at an increasing rate.

For example, Dartmouth professor Matthew Slaughter has noted that IT work will move offshore even faster than manufacturing, because it is easier to ship work across networks and telephone lines and put consultants on airplanes than it is to ship bulky raw materials, build factories, and deal with tariffs and transportation issues. Several years ago, the IT consulting firm Gartner, Inc., accurately forecast the steady growth of offshore outsourcing, and predicted that outsourcing would evolve from labor-intensive maintenance and support to higher-level systems development and software design.

In addition to exporting IT jobs, many large multinational firms, including Microsoft and IBM, have opened technical centers in India and other countries. Some observers believe that India might gain as many as 2 million IT jobs in the next decade.

The main reason for offshore outsourcing is the same as domestic outsourcing: lower bottom-line costs. Offshore outsourcing, however, involves some unique risks and concerns. For example, workers, customers, and shareholders in some companies have protested this trend, and have raised public awareness of possible economic impact. Even more important, offshore outsourcing involves unique concerns regarding project control, security issues, disparate cultures, and effective communication with critical functions that might be located halfway around the globe.

CASE IN POINT 7.1: TURNKEY SERVICES

Turnkey Services is an application service provider that offers payroll and tax preparation services for hundreds of businesses in the Midwest. The firm is considering a major expansion into accounting and financial services, and is looking into the possibility of supporting this move by hiring IT subcontractors in several foreign countries. Peter Belmont, Turnkey's president, has asked you to help him reach a decision. Specifically, he wants you to cite the pros and cons of offshore outsourcing. He expects you to perform Internet research on this topic, and he wants you to present your views at a meeting of Turnkey managers next week.

IN-HOUSE SOFTWARE DEVELOPMENT OPTIONS

In addition to numerous outsourcing options, a company can choose to develop its own systems, or purchase, possibly customize, and implement a software package. These development alternatives are shown in Figure 7-8. Although many factors influence this decision, the most important consideration is the total cost of ownership (TCO), which was explained in Chapter 4. In addition to these options, companies also develop user applications designed around commercial software packages, such as Microsoft Office, to improve user productivity and efficiency.

Make or Buy Decision

The choice between developing versus purchasing software often is called a **make or buy,** or **build or buy** decision. The company's IT department makes, builds, and develops **in-house software.** A **software package** is obtained from a vendor or application service provider.

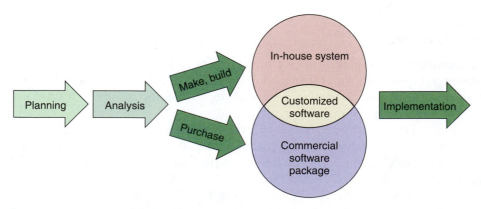

FIGURE 7-8 Instead of outsourcing, a company can choose to develop a system in-house, or purchase and possibly customize a commercial package.

© Cengage Learning 2014

The package might be a standard commercial program or a customized package designed specifically for the purchaser. Companies that develop software for sale are called **software vendors**. A firm that enhances a commercial package by adding custom features and configuring it for a particular industry is called a **value-added reseller (VAR)**.

Software packages are available for every type of business activity. A software package that can be used by many different types of organizations is called a **horizontal application**. An accounting package is a good example of a horizontal application because it can be utilized by many different businesses, or separate divisions that exist in large, diversified companies.

In contrast, a software package developed to handle information requirements for a specific type of business is called a **vertical application**. For example, organizations with special system requirements include colleges, banks, hospitals, insurance companies, construction companies, real estate firms, and airlines. Figure 7-9 shows guests checking in at a hotel, and a typical restaurant touch screen. Both companies need vertical applications to handle their unique business requirements, but often use horizontal applications for basic business needs, such as payroll processing and accounts payable.

Of the in-house software acquisition options — developing a system, buying a software package, or customizing a software package — each has advantages, disadvantages, and cost considerations, as shown in Figure 7-10 on the next page. These software acquisition options are described in detail in the following sections.

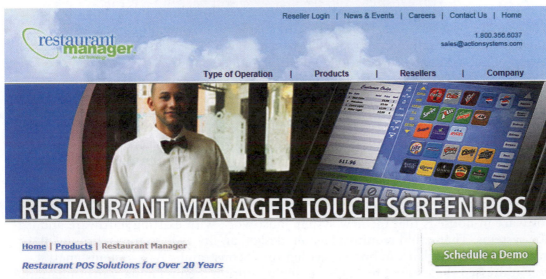

FIGURE 7-9 Hotel chains and restaurants both need vertical applications to support their unique business requirements.

©Andresr/Shutterstock.com (top), © 2012 by Action Systems, Inc. (bottom)

REASONS FOR IN-HOUSE DEVELOPMENT	REASONS FOR PURCHASING A SOFTWARE PACKAGE
Satisfy unique business requirements	Lower costs
Minimize changes in business procedures and policies	Requires less time to implement
Meet constraints of existing systems	Proven reliability and performance benchmarks
Meet constraints of existing technology	Requires less technical development staff
Develop internal resources and capabilities	Future upgrades provided by the vendor
Satisfy unique security requirements	Obtain input from other companies

FIGURE 7-10 Companies consider various factors when comparing in-house development with the purchase of a software package.

© Cengage Learning 2014

Developing Software In-House

With an enormous variety of software packages available to handle horizontal and vertical business operations, why would a firm choose to develop its own software? Typically, companies choose in-house development to satisfy unique business requirements, to minimize changes in business procedures and policies, to meet constraints of existing systems and existing technology, and to develop internal resources and capabilities.

SATISFY UNIQUE BUSINESS REQUIREMENTS Companies often decide to develop software in-house because no commercially available software package can meet their unique business requirements. A college, for example, needs a course scheduling system based on curriculum requirements, student demand, classroom space, and available instructors. A package delivery company needs a system to identify the best combination of routes and loading patterns for the company's fleet of delivery trucks. If existing software packages cannot handle those requirements, then in-house developed software might be the only choice.

MINIMIZE CHANGES IN BUSINESS PROCEDURES AND POLICIES A company also might choose to develop its own software if available packages will require changes in current business operations or processes. Installing a new software package almost always requires some degree of change in how a company does business; however, if the installation of a purchased package will be too disruptive, the organization might decide to develop its own software instead.

MEET CONSTRAINTS OF EXISTING SYSTEMS Any new software installed must work with existing systems. For example, if a new budgeting system must interface with an existing accounting system, finding a software package that works correctly with the existing accounting system might prove difficult. If so, a company could develop its own software to ensure that the new system will interface with the old system.

MEET CONSTRAINTS OF EXISTING TECHNOLOGY Another reason to develop software in-house is that the new system must work with existing hardware and legacy systems. That could require a custom design, an upgrade to the environment, or in-house software that can operate within those constraints. As a systems analyst, you addressed the issue of technical feasibility during the preliminary investigation. Now, in the systems analysis phase, you must determine whether in-house software development is the best overall solution.

DEVELOP INTERNAL RESOURCES AND CAPABILITIES By designing a system in-house, companies can develop and train an IT staff that understands the organization's business functions and information support needs. Many firms feel that in-house IT resources and capabilities provide a competitive advantage because an in-house team can respond quickly when business problems or opportunities arise. For example, if a company lacks internal resources, it must depend on an outside firm for vital business support. Also, outsourcing options might be attractive, but a series of short-term solutions would not necessarily translate into lower TCO over the long term. Top managers often feel more comfortable with an internal IT team to provide overall guidance and long-term stability. In-house development also allows a firm to leverage the skill set of the IT team, which is already on board and being compensated.

Purchasing a Software Package

If a company decides not to outsource, a commercially available software package might be an attractive alternative to developing its own software. Advantages of purchasing a software package over developing software in-house include lower costs, less time to implement a system, proven reliability and performance benchmarks, less technical development staff, future upgrades that are provided by the vendor, and the ability to obtain input from other companies who already have implemented the software.

LOWER COSTS Because many companies use software packages, software vendors spread the development costs over many customers. Compared with software developed in-house, a software package almost always is less expensive, particularly in terms of initial investment. However, even though the initial cost is less, purchased software can involve expenses caused by business disruption, changing business processes, and retraining employees.

REQUIRES LESS TIME TO IMPLEMENT When you purchase a package, it already has been designed, programmed, tested, and documented. The in-house time normally spent on those tasks, therefore, is eliminated. Of course, you still must install the software and integrate it into your systems environment, which can take a significant amount of time. Also, even though implementation is quicker, TOC can be higher due to added training expenses and software modifications.

PROVEN RELIABILITY AND PERFORMANCE BENCHMARKS If the package has been on the market for any length of time, any major problems probably have been detected already and corrected by the vendor. If the product is popular, it almost certainly has been rated and evaluated by independent reviewers.

REQUIRES LESS TECHNICAL DEVELOPMENT STAFF Companies that use commercial software packages often are able to reduce the number of programmers and systems analysts on the IT staff. Using commercial software also means that the IT staff can concentrate on systems whose requirements cannot be satisfied by software packages.

FUTURE UPGRADES PROVIDED BY THE VENDOR Software vendors regularly upgrade software packages by adding improvements and enhancements to create a new version or release. A new release of a software package, for example, can include drivers to support a new laser printer or a new type of data storage technology. In many cases, the vendor receives input and suggestions from current users when planning future upgrades.

INPUT FROM OTHER COMPANIES Using a commercial software package means that you can contact users in other companies to obtain their input and impressions. You might be able to try the package or make a site visit to observe the system in operation before making a final decision.

Customizing a Software Package

If the standard version of a software product does not satisfy a company's requirements, the firm can consider adapting the package to meet its needs. Three ways to customize a software package are:

1. You can purchase a basic package that vendors will customize to suit your needs. Many vendors offer basic packages in a standard version with add-on components that are configured individually. A vendor offers options when the standard application will not satisfy all customers. A human resources information system is a typical example, because each company handles employee compensation and benefits differently. If you need assistance in making a determination, firms such as Ideas International offer services to help you select and configure a system, as shown in Figure 7-11.

2. You can negotiate directly with the software vendor to make enhancements to meet your needs by paying for the changes.

3. You can purchase the package and make your own modifications, if this is permissible under the terms of the software license. A disadvantage of this approach is that systems analysts and programmers might be unfamiliar with the software and will need time to learn the package and make the modifications correctly.

Additionally, some advantages of purchasing a standard package disappear if the product must be customized. If the vendor does the customizing, the modified package probably will cost more and take longer to obtain. Another issue is future support: Although vendors regularly upgrade their standard software packages, they might not upgrade a customized version. In addition, if the modifications are done by the company purchasing the software, when a new release of the package becomes available, the company might have to modify the new version on its own, because the vendor will not support modifications installed by the customer.

Industrial strength comparisons

Ideas International's online products are backed up by expert industry analysts that can also deliver specialized advisory and consulting services. Our team of research analysts includes some of the most highly regarded specialists in the areas of enterprise servers, virtualization, enterprise storage, system software, and infrastructure services.

End users can depend on IDEAS Custom Consulting Services to provide tailored insight into vendor offerings, product strategies, pricing, and discounting. Users can leverage this information to make better technology purchase decisions and get help with:

  ✔ RFP tender evaluation
  ✔ Market requirements analyses
  ✔ Strategic advice on IT infrastructure choices

FIGURE 7-11 Firms such as Ideas International offer services to help customers select and configure a system.

Creating User Applications

Business requirements sometimes can be fulfilled by a user application, rather than a formal information system or commercial package. User applications are examples of user productivity systems, which were discussed in Chapter 1.

A **user application** utilizes standard business software, such as Microsoft Word or Microsoft Excel, which has been configured in a specific manner to enhance user productivity. For example, to help a sales rep respond rapidly to customer price requests, an IT support person can set up a form letter with links to a spreadsheet that calculates incentives and discounts. In addition to configuring the software, the IT staff can create a **user interface**, which includes screens, commands, controls, and features that enable users to interact more effectively with the application. User interface design is described in Chapter 8.

In some situations, user applications offer a simple, low-cost solution. Most IT departments have a backlog of projects, and IT solutions for individuals or small groups do not always receive a high priority. At the same time, application software is more powerful, flexible, and user friendly than ever. Companies such as Microsoft and Corel offer software suites and integrated applications that can exchange data with programs that include tutorials, wizards, and Help features to guide less experienced users who know what they need to do but do not know how to make it happen.

Many companies empower lower-level employees by providing more access to data and more powerful data management tools. The main objective is to allow lower-level employees more access to the data they require to perform their jobs, with no intervention from the IT department. This can be accomplished by creating effective user interfaces for company-wide applications such as accounting, inventory, and sales systems. Another technique is to customize standard productivity software, such as Microsoft Word or Microsoft Excel, to create user applications. In either case, empowerment makes the IT department more productive because it can spend less time responding to the daily concerns and data needs of users and more time on high-impact systems development projects that support strategic business goals.

Empowerment reduces costs and makes good business sense, but companies that adopt this approach must provide the technical support that empowered users require. In most large and medium-sized companies, a **service desk**, or **information center (IC)**, within the IT department is responsible for providing user support. The service desk offers services such as hotline assistance, training, and guidance to users who need technical help.

Once they learn an application, many users can perform tasks that once required a programmer. Some user applications have powerful **screen generators** and **report generators** that allow users to design their own data entry forms and reports. For example, as shown in Figure 7-12 on the next page, Microsoft Access includes a Form Wizard and a Report Wizard, which are menu-driven tools that can create screen forms and reports. These design tools allow users to design specific input and output views that meet their operational needs — with little or no assistance required from the IT staff.

Users typically require spreadsheets, database management programs, and other software packages to meet their information needs. If user applications access corporate data, you must provide appropriate controls to ensure data security and integrity. For example, some files should be hidden totally from view; others should have **read-only properties** so users can view, but not change, the data.

THE SYSTEMS ANALYST'S ROLE

At some point in the systems development process, the company must decide whether to use an outsourcing option, develop software in-house, acquire a software package, develop user applications, or select some combination of these solutions. The decision will affect the remaining SDLC phases and your involvement as a systems analyst. The decision to develop software in-house, for example, will require more participation from the systems analyst than outsourcing or choosing a commercial package. Management usually makes a determination after receiving written recommendations from the IT staff and a formal presentation, which is described later in this chapter.

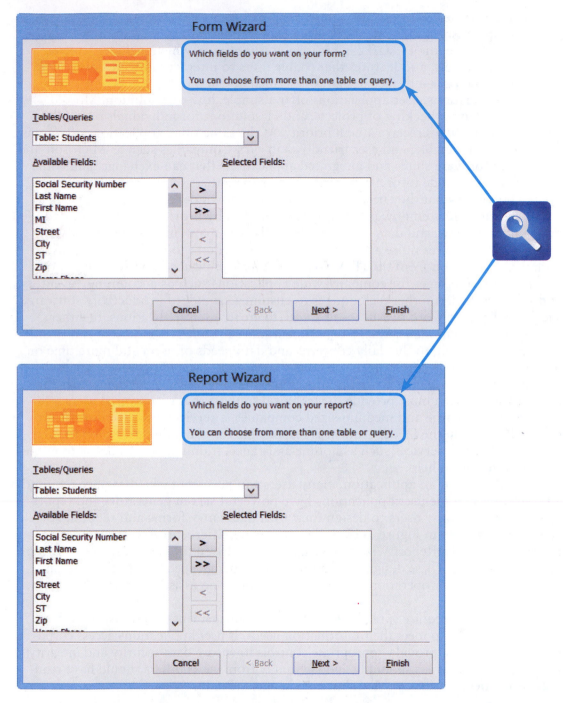

FIGURE 7-12 Microsoft Access includes Form Wizard and Report Wizard tools that ask a series of questions, and then create the form or report.
Screenshots used with permission from Microsoft.

Even a single system can use a mix of software alternatives. For example, a company might purchase a standard software package to process its payroll, and then develop its own software to handle the interface between the payroll package and the company's in-house manufacturing cost analysis system.

The evaluation and selection of alternatives is not a simple process. The objective is to obtain the product with the lowest total cost of ownership, but actual cost and performance can be difficult to forecast. With a large number of choices, how do you select the best alternative?

When selecting hardware and software, systems analysts often work as an **evaluation and selection team**. A team approach ensures that critical factors are not overlooked and that a sound choice is made. The evaluation and selection team also must include users, who will participate in the selection process and feel a sense of ownership in the new system.

The primary objective of the evaluation and selection team is to eliminate system alternatives that will not meet requirements, rank the alternatives that are feasible, and present the viable alternatives to management for a final decision. The process begins with a careful study of the costs and benefits of each alternative, as explained in the following section.

CASE IN POINT 7.2: STERLING ASSOCIATES

Joan Sterling is CEO and principal stockholder of Sterling Associates, which specializes in advising clients on IT projects and information systems development. Joan is creating a brochure for prospective new clients. She wants you to develop a section that describes payback analysis, ROI, and NPV in simple terms, and mentions the pros and cons of each financial analysis tool. She suggested that you start by viewing the Video Learning Sessions on financial analysis tools, and reviewing the material in Part C of the Systems Analyst's Toolkit.

ANALYZING COST AND BENEFITS

Financial analysis tools have been around for a long time. From the abacus to the slide rule shown in Figure 7-13, people have always sought easier ways to work with numbers. This section describes cost and benefit analysis, and explains popular tools that can help you analyze an IT project.

In Chapter 2, you learned that economic feasibility is one of the four feasibility measurements that are made during the preliminary investigation of a systems request. Now, at the end of the systems analysis phase of the SDLC, you must apply financial analysis tools and techniques to evaluate development strategies and decide how the project will move forward. Part C of the Systems Analyst's Toolkit describes three popular tools, which are payback analysis, return on investment (ROI), and net present value (NPV). These tools, and oth-

FIGURE 7-13 The slide rule was invented in the 17th century. The device uses logarithms to handle calculations. Engineers and scientists used slide rules into the 1950s and beyond.
© Laborant/Shutterstock.com

ers, can be used to determine total cost of ownership (TCO), which was described in Chapter 4. At this stage, you will identify specific systems development strategies and choose a course of action. For example, a company might find that its total cost of ownership will be higher if it develops a system in-house, compared with outsourcing the project or using an ASP.

An accurate forecast of TCO is critical, because nearly 80% of total costs occur *after* the purchase of the hardware and software, according to Gartner, Inc. An IT department can develop its own TCO estimates, or use TCO calculation tools offered by vendors. For example, as shown in Figure 7-14 on the next page, HP offers an online TCO calculator that includes a questionnaire and a graphical display of results. HP also provides videos, white papers, and other resources for visitors to its site who want to learn more about TCO.

Video Learning Session
Return on Investment (ROI)

If you have an MIS CourseMate access code, you can launch interactive Video Learning Sessions to help you understand systems development concepts and practice your skills. You can watch the sessions on your computer or mobile device, and pause, rewind, or replay a video at any time. To log on to the MIS CourseMate site at **www.cengagebrain.com**, you must create a student account and then register this book.

This session is about return on investment (ROI) analysis. You'll learn how to calculate the ROI for a project and how to use a spreadsheet to determine a project's ROI.

© craftvision/iStockphoto

FIGURE 7-14 HO offers a free online TCO calculator, and many resources to help viewers learn more about TCO.
©2012 Hewlett-Packard Development Company, L.P.

Financial Analysis Tools

Part C of the Systems Analyst's Toolkit explains how to use three main cost analysis tools: payback analysis, return on investment (ROI), and net present value (NPV). **Payback analysis** determines how long it takes an information system to pay for itself through reduced costs and increased benefits. **Return on investment (ROI)** is a percentage rate that compares the total net benefits (the return) received from a project to the total costs (the investment) of the project. The **net present value (NPV)** of a project is the total value of the benefits minus the total value of the costs, with both costs and benefits adjusted to reflect the point in time at which they occur.

Video Learning Session
Net Present Value (NPV)

If you have an MIS CourseMate access code, you can launch interactive Video Learning Sessions to help you understand systems development concepts and practice your skills. You can watch the sessions on your computer or mobile device, and pause, rewind, or replay a video at any time. To log on to the MIS CourseMate site at **www.cengagebrain.com**, you must create a student account and then register this book.

This session is about net present value (NPV) analysis. You'll learn how to calculate the NPV for a project and how to use a spreadsheet to determine a project's NPV.

© craftvision/iStockphoto

Cost-Benefit Analysis Checklist

In Chapter 2, you learned how to use the payback analysis tool during the preliminary investigation to help determine whether a project is economically feasible. Now, you will use all the financial analysis tools to evaluate various development strategies. The best way to apply the tools is to develop a cost-benefit checklist with the following steps:

- List each development strategy being considered.
- Identify all costs and benefits for each alternative. Be sure to indicate when costs will be incurred and benefits realized.

- Consider future growth and the need for scalability.
- Include support costs for hardware and software.
- Analyze various software licensing options, including fixed fees and formulas based on the number of users or transactions.
- Apply the financial analysis tools to each alternative.
- Study the results and prepare a report to management.

THE SOFTWARE ACQUISITION PROCESS

Although each situation is different, the following section describes a typical example of the issues and tasks involved in software acquisition.

Step 1: Evaluate the Information System Requirements

Based on your analysis of the system requirements, you must identify the system's key features; consider network and Web-related issues; estimate volume and future growth; specify any hardware, software, or personnel constraints; and prepare a request for proposal or quotation.

IDENTIFY KEY FEATURES Whether you are considering in-house development or outsourcing options, you must develop a clear, detailed list of features that can serve as an overall specification for the system. Using the data you gathered during fact-finding, which was discussed in Chapter 4, you must list all system requirements and critical features. This information will be included in the system requirements document, which is the end product of the SDLC systems analysis phase.

CONSIDER NETWORK AND WEB-RELATED ISSUES As you evaluate the system requirements, you must consider network and Web-related issues. You must decide whether the system will run on a network, the Internet, or a company intranet, and build these requirements into the design. Also, you must determine whether the system will exchange data with vendor or customer systems, and ensure that the system will be compatible.

ESTIMATE VOLUME AND FUTURE GROWTH You need to know the current volume of transactions and forecast future growth. Figure 7-15 shows volume estimates

Online Order Processing System Estimated Activity During Next 12-Month Period

	CURRENT LEVEL	FUTURE GROWTH (based on existing procedures)	FUTURE GROWTH (assuming new Web site is operational)
Customers	36,500	40,150	63,875
Daily Orders	1,435	1,579	2,811
Daily Order Lines	7,715	7,893	12,556
Sales Reps	29	32	12
Order Processing Support Staff	2	4	3
Products	600	650	900

FIGURE 7-15 Volume estimates for an order processing system showing current activity levels and two forecasts: one based on the existing order processing procedures and another that assumes a new Web site is operational.

for an order processing system. In addition to current levels, the figure displays two forecasts, one based on the existing order processing procedures and another that assumes a new Web site is operational.

A comparison of the two forecasts shows that the Web site will generate more new customers, process almost 80% more orders, and substantially reduce the need for sales reps and support staff. If you are considering in-house development, you must make sure that your software and hardware can handle future transaction volumes and data storage requirements. Conversely, if you are considering outsourcing, volume and usage data is essential to analyze ASP fee structures and develop cost estimates for outsourcing options.

SPECIFY HARDWARE, SOFTWARE, OR PERSONNEL CONSTRAINTS You must determine whether existing hardware, software, or personnel issues will affect the acquisition decision. For example, if the firm has a large number of legacy systems or if an ERP strategy has been adopted, these factors will have an impact on the decision. Also, you must investigate the company's policy regarding outsourcing IT functions, and whether outsourcing is part of a long-term strategy. With regard to personnel issues, you must define in-house staffing requirements to develop, acquire, implement, and maintain the system — and determine whether the company is willing to commit to those staffing levels versus an outsourcing option.

PREPARE A REQUEST FOR PROPOSAL OR QUOTATION To obtain the information you need to make a decision, you should prepare a request for proposal or a request for quotation. The two documents are similar but used in different situations, based on whether or not you have selected a specific software product.

A **request for proposal (RFP)** is a document that describes your company, lists the IT services or products you need, and specifies the features you require. An RFP helps ensure that your organization's business needs will be met. An RFP also spells out the service and support levels you require. Based on the RFP, vendors can decide if they have a product that will meet your needs. RFPs vary in size and complexity, just like the systems they describe. An RFP for a large system can contain dozens of pages with unique requirements and features. You can use an RFP to designate some features as essential and others as desirable. An RFP also requests specific pricing and payment terms.

Figure 7-16 shows an example of a ready-made RFP template offered by Infotivity Technologies. Notice that the vendor can choose from a range of responses, and also add comments.

When you evaluate several responses to an RFP, you might find it helpful to use an evaluation model. An **evaluation model** is a technique that uses a common yardstick to measure and compare vendor ratings.

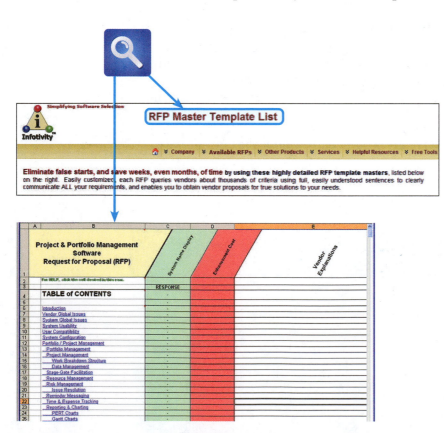

FIGURE 7-16 Infotivity Technologies offers a ready-made RFP template that allows a wide range of reponses and comments.
© 1993–2010 Infotivity Technologies, Inc.

Figure 7-17 shows two evaluation models for a network project. The evaluation model at the top of the figure simply lists the key elements and each vendor's score. The model at the bottom of the figure adds a weight factor. In this example, each element receives a rating based on its relative importance. Although the initial scores are the same in both models, notice that vendor A has the highest point total in the top example, but vendor C emerges as the best in the weighted model.

No standard method exists for assigning the weight factors. Each firm will have its own approach, which might be tailored to fit a specific situation. An analyst usually obtains as much input as possible, then circulates proposed values for further comment and, hopefully, a consensus.

Evaluation models can be used throughout the SDLC, and you will find them a valuable tool. You can use a spreadsheet program to build an evaluation model, experiment with different weighting factors, and graph the results.

A **request for quotation (RFQ)** is more specific than an RFP. When you use an RFQ, you already know the specific product or service you want and you need to obtain price quotations or bids. RFQs can involve outright purchase or a variety of leasing options and can include maintenance or technical support terms. Some vendors even provide convenient RFP or RFQ forms on their Web sites. RFPs and RFP or RFQs have the same objective: to obtain vendor replies that are clear, comparable, and responsive so you can make a well-informed selection decision.

Unweighted Evaluation Model for a Network Project

Instructions: Rate each vendor on a scale from 1 (low) to 10 (high), then add vendor scores to calculate total points.			
	VENDOR A	**VENDOR B**	**VENDOR C**
Price	6	5	9
Completion Date	2	5	8
Layout/Design	8	8	5
References	10	6	3
TOTAL POINTS	26	24	25

Weighted Evaluation Model for a Network Project

Instructions: Rate each vendor on a scale from 1 (low) to 10 (high), then multiply the vendor's score by the weight factor. Add vendor scores to calculate total points.			
	WEIGHT FACTOR	**VENDOR A**	**VENDOR B**	**VENDOR C**
Price	25	6 * 25 = 150	5 * 25 = 125	9 * 25 = 225
Completion Date	25	2 * 25 = 50	5 * 25 = 125	8 * 25 = 200
Layout/Design	35	8 * 35 = 280	8 * 35 = 280	5 * 35 = 175
References	15	10 * 15 = 150	6 * 15 = 90	3 * 15 = 45
TOTAL POINTS	100	630	620	645

FIGURE 7-17 The three vendors have the same initial ratings, but the two evaluation models produce different results. In the unweighted model at the top of the figure, vendor A has the highest total points. However, after applying weight factors, vendor C is the winner, as shown in the model at the bottom of the figure.

Step 2: Identify Potential Vendors or Outsourcing Options

The next step is to identify potential vendors or outsourcing providers. The Internet is a primary marketplace for all IT products and services, and you can find descriptive information on the Web about all major products and acquisition alternatives.

If you need to locate vertical applications for specific industries, you can research industry trade journals or Web sites to find reviews for industry-specific software. Industry trade groups often can direct you to companies that offer specific software solutions.

Another approach is to work with a consulting firm. Many IT consultants offer specialized services that help companies select software packages. A major advantage of using a consultant is that you can tap into broad experience that is difficult for any one company to acquire. Consultants can be located by contacting professional organizations or industry sources, or simply by searching the Internet. Using a consultant involves additional expense but can prevent even more costly mistakes.

No matter what topics interest you, there are sure to be one or more **forums**, or **newsgroups**, where people gather to meet, offer support, and exchange ideas. Forums can be hosted by private or public entities, or reside in a larger communities such as Google Groups, or Yahoo Groups, which allow users to join existing groups or start their own. You can search the Web for forums that interest you, or you can visit the sites of specific companies, such as Microsoft, that provide a valuable source of information for IT professionals, including blogs, technical chats, forums, RSS feeds, Webcasts, and other resources, as shown in Figure 7-18.

Step 3: Evaluate the Alternatives

After identifying the alternatives, you must select the one that best fits the company's needs. You should obtain information about the options from as many sources as possible, including vendor presentations and literature, product documentation, trade

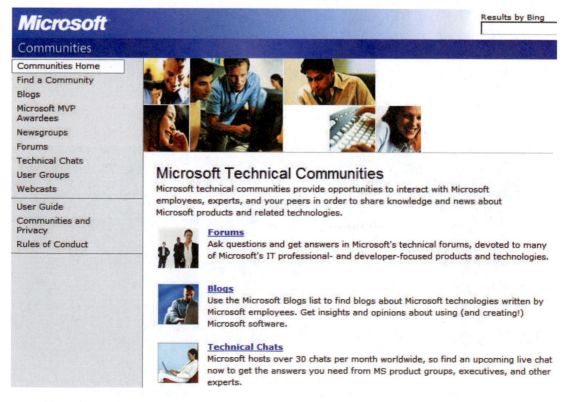

FIGURE 7-18 Microsoft Communities is an excellent resource for IT professionals.

Screenshot used with permission from Microsoft.

publications, and companies that perform software testing and evaluation. To learn more about particular software packages, search the Internet using keywords that describe the application. Web sites maintained by consultants and software publishers often include product references and links to vendors. As part of the evaluation process, you should try to obtain information from existing users, test the application, and benchmark the package.

EXISTING USERS You can contact existing users to obtain feedback and learn about their experiences. For large-scale software packages, ASPs and vendors typically supply user references. User references are important because you need to know whether the software package has worked well for companies like yours. Be aware that some vendors limit their reference lists to satisfied clients, so you can expect mostly positive feedback from those firms.

APPLICATION TESTING If a software package is one of the options, find out if it is possible for users in your organization to try the product. For horizontal applications or small systems, using a demo copy to enter a few sample transactions could be an acceptable test. For vertical applications or large systems, a team of IT staff and users might need several days or weeks to perform tests.

BENCHMARKING To determine whether a package can handle a certain transaction volume efficiently, you can perform a benchmark test. A **benchmark** measures the time a package takes to process a certain number of transactions. For example, a benchmark test can measure the time needed to post 1,000 sales transactions.

If you use benchmarks, remember that a benchmark test is conducted in a controlled environment, which might not resemble the actual day-to-day situation at your company. Although benchmarking cannot predict your specific results, benchmark testing is a good way to measure relative performance of two or more competing products in a standard environment.

Many IT publications publish regular reviews of individual packages, including benchmark tests, and often have annual surveys covering various categories of software. Some of the publications shown in Figure 7-19 also offer online versions and additional Web-based features, search capability, and IT links.

You also can obtain information from independent firms that benchmark various software packages and sell comparative analyses of the results, as shown in Figure 7-20 on the next page. The Transaction Processing Performance Council (TPC) is an example of a non-profit organization that publishes standards and reports for its members and the general public.

Finally, you should match each package against the RFP features and rank the choices. If some features are more important than others, give them a higher weight using an evaluation model similar to the one shown in Figure 7-17 on page 281.

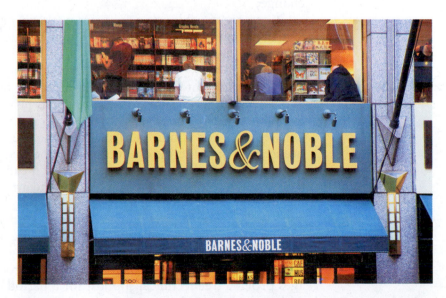

FIGURE 7-19 Many IT publications test and review software packages. Although an enormous amount of information is available on the Web, many IT professionals enjoy reading traditional magazines.

FIGURE 7-20 The Transaction Processing Performance Council is a nonprofit organization that publishes standards and reports for its members and the general public.
©2001–2012 TPC

Step 4: Perform Cost-Benefit Analysis

Review the suggestions in this chapter and in Part C of the Systems Analyst's Toolkit, and develop a spreadsheet to identify and calculate TCO for each option you are considering. Be sure to include all costs, using the volume forecasts you prepared. If you are considering outsourcing options, carefully study the alternative fee structure models described earlier. If possible, prepare charts to show the results graphically, and build in what-if capability so you can gauge the impact if one or more variables change.

If you are considering a software package, be sure to consider acquisition options. When you purchase software, what you are buying is a **software license** that gives you the right to use the software under certain terms and conditions. For example, the license could allow you to use the software only on a single computer, a specified number of computers, a network, or an entire site, depending on the terms of the agreement. Other license restrictions could prohibit you from making the software available to others or modifying the program. For desktop applications, software license terms and conditions usually cannot be modified. For large-scale systems, license agreement terms often can be negotiated.

Also consider user support issues, which can account for a significant part of TCO. If you select an outsourcing alternative, the arrangement probably will include certain technical support and maintenance. If you choose in-house development, you must consider the cost of providing these services on your own. If you purchase a software package, consider a supplemental **maintenance agreement**, which offers additional support and assistance from the vendor. The agreement might provide full support for a period of time or list specific charges for particular services. Some software packages provide free technical support for a period of time. Afterward, support is offered with a charge per occurrence, or per minute or hour of technical support time. Some software vendors contact registered owners whenever a new release is available and usually offer the new release at a reduced price.

Step 5: Prepare a Recommendation

You should prepare a recommendation that evaluates and describes the alternatives, together with the costs, benefits, advantages, and disadvantages of each option. At this point, you may be required to submit a formal system requirements document and deliver a presentation. You should review the suggestions for presenting written proposals and oral presentations in Part A of the Systems Analyst's Toolkit. Additional suggestions about preparing the system requirements document and the management presentation are contained in the following section.

Step 6: Implement the Solution

Implementation tasks will depend on the solution selected. In-house options will require more time and effort than outsourcing alternatives. For large systems or network installations, the process can require considerable time and effort. Your installation strategy should be planned well in advance, especially if any disruption of normal business operations is expected. If the software package is customized, then the task will be more complex and difficult.

Before the new software becomes operational, you must complete all implementation steps, including loading, configuring, and testing the software; training users; and converting data files to the new system's format. Chapter 11 discusses implementation strategies and techniques in more detail.

CASE IN POINT 7.3: Doug's Sporting Goods

Doug's Sporting Goods sells hiking and camping supplies. The company has grown considerably in the last two years. Doug Sawyer, the company's founder and president, wants to develop a customer order entry system and hired your IT consulting firm to advise him about software alternatives. Doug is leaning toward in-house development because he does not want to depend on outside vendors and suppliers for technical support and upgrades. Doug also says that he is not interested in selling on the Web, but that could change in the future.

Doug wants to meet with you tomorrow to make a decision. What will you say to Doug at the meeting?

COMPLETION OF SYSTEMS ANALYSIS TASKS

To complete the systems analysis phase, you must prepare the system requirements document and your presentation to management.

System Requirements Document

The **system requirements document,** or **software requirements specification,** contains the requirements for the new system, describes the alternatives that were considered, and makes a specific recommendation to management. This important document is the starting point for measuring the performance, accuracy, and completeness of the finished system before entering the systems design phase.

The system requirements document is like a contract that identifies what the system developers must deliver to users. Recall that system requirements are identified during the fact-finding process, and a system requirements checklist is created at that time. Various examples of system requirements are listed on pages 147–149 in

Chapter 4. You should write the system requirements document in language that users can understand so they can offer input, suggest improvements, and approve the final version.

Because the system requirements document can be lengthy, you should format and organize it so it is easy to read and use. The system requirements document should include a cover page and a detailed table of contents. You also can add an index and a glossary of terms to make the document easier to use. The content of the system requirements document will depend on the company and the complexity of the system.

Presentation to Management

The presentation to management at the end of the systems analysis phase is one of the most critical milestones in the systems development process. At this point, managers make key decisions that affect the future development of the system.

Prior to a management presentation, you might give two other presentations: one to the principal individuals in the IT department to keep them posted, and another presentation to users to answer their questions and invite feedback. The system requirements document is the basis for all three presentations, and you should distribute the document (or a summary) in advance so the recipients can review it.

When preparing your presentation, you should review the suggestions in Part A of the Systems Analyst's Toolkit, which will help you design and deliver a successful presentation. If you plan a slide presentation, you should review the Toolkit guidelines for effective presentations. In addition to the techniques found in the Toolkit, also keep the following suggestions in mind:

- Begin your presentation with a brief overview of the purpose and primary objectives of the system project, the objectives of this presentation, and what decisions need to be made.

- Summarize the primary viable alternatives. For each alternative, describe the costs, advantages, and disadvantages.

- Explain why the evaluation and selection team chose the recommended alternative.

- Allow time for discussion and for questions and answers.

- Obtain a final decision from management or agree on a timetable for the next step in the process.

The object of the management presentation is to obtain approval for the development of the system and to gain management's full support, including necessary financial resources. Management probably will choose one of five alternatives: develop an in-house system, modify a current system, purchase or customize a software package, perform additional systems analysis work, or stop all further work. Depending on their decision, your next task as a systems analyst will be one of the following:

1. Implement an outsourcing alternative. If outsourcing is selected, you will work with representatives of the service provider to achieve a smooth transition to the new environment.

2. Develop an in-house system. Begin systems design tasks, as described in Chapters 8, 9, and 10.

3. Purchase or customize a software package. Negotiate the purchase terms with the software vendor for management approval. Then, if the package will be used without modification, you can begin planning the systems implementation phase. If you must make modifications to the package, your next step is to start

the systems design phase. If the vendor will make the modifications, then your next step is to start planning the testing and documentation of the modifications as part of the systems implementation phase, which is described in Chapter 11.

4. Perform additional systems analysis work. Management might want you to investigate certain alternatives further, explore alternatives not examined, develop a prototype, reduce the project scope because of cost constraints, or expand the project scope based on new developments. If necessary, you will perform the additional work and schedule a follow-up presentation.

5. Stop all further work. The decision might be based on your recommendation, a shift in priorities or costs, or for other reasons. Whatever the reason, if that is management's decision, then you have no additional tasks for the project other than to file all your research in a logical location so it can be retrieved if the project is reopened in the future.

After the presentation and management decision, you will begin a transition to the systems design phase of the SDLC. If you are developing an in-house system or modifying a package, you will build a model of the proposed system and start designing the user interface, output, input, and data structures.

TRANSITION TO SYSTEMS DESIGN

In a traditional SDLC environment, systems design usually started when the systems analysis phase was done. Using the system requirements specification as a blueprint, developers transformed the logical design into a working model that could be tested, reviewed by users, and implemented. Today, the process is much more dynamic. In general, systems development is faster, more flexible, and more user-oriented. The introduction of adaptive methods such as agile development and extreme programming has changed the landscape significantly. Depending on the project, system developers often blend traditional and cutting-edge development methods, because what works in one situation might not work in another.

This textbook discusses systems analysis in Chapters 4, 5, 6, and 7, and systems design in Chapters 8, 9, and 10. However, in a typical IT workplace, all these tasks — and more — are integrated and managed together.

This section discusses preparation for systems design and the relationship between logical and physical design.

Preparing for Systems Design

Regardless of the development method, systems design requires accurate documentation. Traditionally, a system requirements document provided detailed specifications for output, input, data, processes, and whatever else was needed. Although agile methods do not require a particular form of documentation, a successful development team must understand and record user requirements as they evolve during the project.

Logical and Physical Design

A **logical design** defines *what* must take place, not *how* it will be accomplished. Logical designs do not address the actual methods of implementation. In contrast, a **physical design** is like a set of blueprints for the actual construction of a building. Typically, a physical design describes the actual processes of entering, verifying, and storing data; the physical layout of data files and sorting procedures, the format of reports, and so on. Because logical and physical designs are related so closely, good systems design is impossible without careful, accurate systems analysis. For example, you might return to fact-finding if you discover that you overlooked an important issue, if users have significant new needs, or if legal or governmental requirements change.

CASE IN POINT 7.4: DOWNTOWN!

Downtown! is a rapidly growing Web-based retailer with about 100 management and technical support employees at its headquarters office in Florida. Mary Estrada, the firm's IT manager, is planning a new information system that will give users better access to sales and marketing data and trends. She has a concern, however. She knows that users often request reports but use only a small portion of the data. In many offices she sees inboxes filled with printed reports gathering dust. Mary asked for your opinion: What if new system users could design most of their own reports without assistance from the IT staff, by using a powerful, user-friendly report writer program? Do you think they would request as many reports or the same types of reports? What are the pros and cons of giving users total control over output?

A QUESTION OF ETHICS

© faberfoto_it/iStockphoto

Sally works as a junior analyst for a medium-sized IT consulting firm. Her manager, Bob, has asked her to draft a response to an RFP from a large company that is seeking IT consulting services in connection with a new accounting system.

As Sally worked on the RFP, she noticed a specific question about her firm's recent experience on this type of system. To the best of her knowledge, the firm has only worked on one other accounting project in the last three years. When Bob saw Sally's draft response, he was upset about the way she answered the question. "You don't have to be quite that candid," he said. "Even though we only had one *formal* project, we do have several people who worked on accounting systems before they came here."

"Yes," Sally replied, "But that isn't what the question is asking." As he left her office, Bob's final comment was, "If we want that job, we'll have to come up with a better answer." Thinking about it, Sally isn't comfortable with anything but a straight answer. Is this an ethical question? What are Sally's options?

CHAPTER SUMMARY

This chapter describes system development strategies, and he preparation and presentation of the system requirements document.

An important trend that views Software as a Service (SaaS), rather than a product, has created new software acquisition options. Systems analysts must consider Web-based development environments such as .NET and WebSphere, and various outsourcing options, including application service providers and Internet business services. Application service providers (ASPs) charge subscription fees for providing application software packages. Internet business services (IBSs) offer powerful Web-based servers, software hosting, and IT support services to customers.

Traditional systems must function in various hardware and software environments, be compatible with legacy systems, and operate within the constraints of company networks and desktop computing capability. Such systems utilize Internet links and resources as enhancements. In contrast, Internet-based systems treat the Web *as* the platform, rather than just a communication channel. Many large companies use Web-based systems to handle enterprise-wide applications. Compared to traditional systems, Web-based systems are more scalable, less dependent on specific hardware and software, and more adaptable to outsourcing the operation and support of a software application.

The new Web generation is called Web 2.0, and it is fueling the expansion of information sharing, user collaboration, and social-networking applications such as Twitter, LinkedIn, and Facebook. Another development, called cloud computing because of the commonly used cloud symbol for the Internet, describes an overall online software and data environment, powered by supercomputer technology, that is the ultimate form of Software as a Service.

If a company chooses to handle its own software development needs, it can create in-house systems, or purchase (and possibly customize) commercially available software packages from a software vendor or value-added reseller (VAR).

Compared with developing an in-house system, an existing commercial software package can be an attractive alternative, because a package generally costs less, takes less time to implement, has a proven track record, and is upgraded frequently. In-house development or customizing a software package might be the best choice when a standard software package cannot meet specific business requirements or constraints. In addition to customizing software packages, companies can create user applications based on standard software that has been specially configured to enhance user productivity.

The systems analyst's role in the software development process depends on the specific development strategy. In-house development requires much more involvement than outsourcing or choosing a commercial package.

The most important factor in choosing a development strategy is total cost of ownership (TCO). Financial analysis tools include payback analysis, which determines how long it takes for a system to pay for itself through reduced costs and increased benefits; return on investment (ROI), which compares a project's total return with its total costs; and net present value (NPV), which analyzes the value of a project by adjusting costs and benefits to reflect the time that they occur.

The process of acquiring software involves a series of steps: evaluate the system requirements, consider network and Web-related issues, identify potential software vendors or outsourcing options, evaluate the alternatives, perform cost-benefit analysis, prepare a recommendation, and implement the solution. During software acquisition, a company can use a request for proposal (RFP) or a request for quotation (RFQ). An RFP invites vendors to respond to a list of system requirements and features; an RFQ seeks bids for a specific product or service.

The system requirements document is the deliverable, or end product, of the systems analysis phase. The document details all system requirements and constraints, recommends the best solution, and provides cost and time estimates for future development work. The system requirements document is the basis for the management presentation. At this point, the firm might decide to develop an in-house system, modify the current system, purchase or customize a software package, perform additional systems analysis work, or stop all further work.

Key Terms

application service provider (ASP) 264
benchmark 279
build or buy 266
business process outsourcing (BPO) 263
cloud computing 263
evaluation and selection team 273
evaluation model 276
fixed fee model 264
forum 278
global outsourcing 265
horizontal application 267
in-house software 266
information center (IC) 271
Internet business services (IBS) 264
logical design 283
maintenance agreement 280
make or buy 266
managed hosting 264
middleware 262
.NET 261
net present value (NPV) 274
newsgroup 278
offshore outsourcing 265
outsourcing 265

payback analysis 274
physical design 283
report generator 271
request for proposal (RFP) 276
request for quotation (RFQ) 277
return on investment (ROI) 274
screen generator 271
service desk 271
service provider 263
Software as a Service (SaaS) 260
software license 280
software package 266
software requirements specification 281
software vendor 267
subscription model 264
system requirements document 281
transaction model 265
usage model 265
user application 270
user interface 271
value-added reseller (VAR) 267
vertical application 267
Web 2.0 263
WebSphere 261

Chapter Exercises

Questions

1. Describe the concept of software as a service rather than a product. Is this an important trend? Why or why not?
2. Explain the difference between horizontal and vertical application software. Suggest two examples of each type.
3. What are three typical reasons why companies develop their own information systems?
4. What are user applications? Suggest three examples that could boost user productivity.
5. What are main steps in the software acquisition process?
6. What is an RFP, and how does it differ from an RFQ?
7. What is the purpose of a benchmark test? Suggest at least two examples of benchmarks.
8. What is an evaluation model? How would you create a weighted evaluation model?
9. What decisions might management reach at the end of the systems analysis phase, and what would be the next step in each case?
10. Explain the relationship between logical and physical design.

Discussion Topics

1. As more companies outsource systems development, will there be less need for in-house systems analysts? Why or why not?
2. Suppose you tried to explain the concept of weighted evaluation models to a manager, and she responded by asking, "So, how do you set the weight factors? Is it just a subjective guess?" How would you reply?
3. Select a specific vertical application to investigate. Visit local computer stores and use the Internet to determine what software packages are available. Describe the features of two packages.
4. Select a specific horizontal application to investigate. Visit local computer stores and use the Internet to determine what software packages are available. Describe the features of two packages.

Projects

1. Various firms and organizations offer IT benchmarking. Locate an example on the Internet, and describe its services.
2. Turn to Part C of the Systems Analyst's Toolkit and review the concept of net present value (NPV). Determine the NPV for the following: An information system will cost $95,000 to implement over a one-year period and will produce no savings during that year. When the system goes online, the company will save $30,000 during the first year of operation. For the next four years, the savings will be $20,000 per year. Assuming a 12% discount rate, what is the NPV of the system?
3. Visit the IT department at your school or at a local company and determine whether the systems were developed in-house or purchased. If packages were acquired, find out what customizing was done, if any. Write a brief memo describing the results.
4. To create user applications as described in this chapter, systems analysts often use macros. Learn more about macros by using the Help feature in Microsoft Word, and suggest three tasks that might be performed by macros.

Apply Your Knowledge

This section contains four mini-cases. Each case describes a situation, explains your role, and requires you to apply what you learned in the chapter.

1 Sandy Shores Time Shares

Sandy Shores Time Shares is one of the largest time-sharing and rental brokers for vacation cottages along the North Carolina coast. After 10 successful years of matching up owners and renters, Sandy Shores decided to acquire a computerized reservation and booking system. Tim Burns, the owner of Sandy Shores, read an article about software packages, and he asked you, as an IT consultant, for your advice.

Tasks

1. Would the new reservation and booking system be a horizontal or a vertical application? Explain your answer.
2. What software development and acquisition strategies should Sandy Shores consider?
3. Conduct an Internet search for online reservation systems, software, and services that Sandy Shores might consider. Describe your findings.
4. As a systems analyst, what would your role be in helping Sandy Shores develop a new system? Would the acquisition strategy affect your role? Why or why not?

2 Atrium Bio-Medical Supply, Inc.

Atrium Bio-Medical Supply is a medium sized regional supplier of medical and laboratory equipment. Since starting the company 12 years ago, Victoria Dawn has built Atrium into a competitive supply company across several metro areas, but her growth potential is limited because the firm does not have an integrated sales and logistics system. Victoria asked you to evaluate Atrium's options for acquiring a new system.

Tasks

1. What options does Atrium have for acquiring a new system?
2. What are the pros and cons of in-house development versus purchasing a system?
3. If the decision is made to purchase a new system, what are three options for customizing the software?
4. Based on Part C of the Systems Analyst's Toolkit, what financial analysis tools should you use to evaluate the software acquisition options for Atrium? Explain how you would apply each of the tools.

3 **Leading Edge Climbing Equipment**

Leading Edge Climbing Equipment is a retail rock climbing equipment vendor that is planning to install a new order entry and transaction processing system. As Leading Edge's IT manager, you are preparing for a follow-up meeting to confirm the owner's decision to move forward with the system.

Tasks

1. In deciding on your proposal, what options do the owners have?
2. If the owners decide to purchase or customize a software package, what steps will you take?
3. Explain the difference between logical and physical design.
4. Describe the steps typically performed in systems design.

 IT News and Views

You are a staff writer at IT News and Views, a popular online newsletter aimed at IT professionals. Your editor has asked you to prepare a special report for next week's edition. Specifically, she wants you to research the subject of software outsourcing, and other significant trends that might affect software development in the future. She wants you to cite specific sources for your information, including current IT employment statistics and employment forecasts from the U.S. Bureau of Labor Statistics.

Tasks

1. Search for information about software outsourcing generally, using the search techniques described in Part D of the Systems Analyst's Toolkit.
2. Visit the Bureau of Labor Statistics site at **www.bls.gov** and search for information about employment trends affecting systems analysts, computer programmers, and software engineers.
3. Does the Bureau of Labor Statistics offer any comments or insights into the subject of outsourcing generally? What conclusions does it reach?
4. In your report, comment on whether the offshore outsourcing of IT jobs is just another step in the progression that began with manufacturing jobs, or represents a whole new trend. Be sure to cite Web research sources and your own reasons.

Case Studies

Each chapter includes a Chapter Case, a Continuing Case, a Capstone Case, and an Online Case Simulation. You can learn more about the Online Case Simulation in the MIS CourseMate Features section.

Chapter Case: Campus Bikes (Part 2)

In Chapter 6, you learned that Campus Bikes is a popular bicycle shop located near a major university. The shop sells several brands of new bikes, including everything from high-end racing models to beach cruisers. In addition to sales of new bikes and accessories, Mark's service department is always busy. The staff includes Mark himself, a bookkeeper, two part-time sales reps, a full-time mechanic, and several part-time service helpers who assemble bikes.

Background

Until now, the owner, Mark Turner, kept the business records on his personal computer. He created a simple database to keep track of inventory, but it is not always up-to-date. He also developed spreadsheets to track expenses and payroll. The business has grown and Mark wants to install a new computer system to handle all business functions.

You are a lab assistant in the computer information department at the college. You earned a computer science degree at a two-year school, and you recently decided to work toward your four-year degree. Mark recently asked you to help him plan a system for Campus Bikes. You used an object-oriented approach to create a model of the business functions and actors involved.

Now Mark wants you to do a "make or buy" analysis. Specifically, you will look into the pros and cons of in-house development versus purchase of a software package. Your research indicates that the most popular bike shop package is offered by a vendor called BikeData.

In your last meeting, Mark said that tangible savings for a new system would be hard to measure, but improved customer care, better service department records, and increased productivity are expected. Mark estimates that these benefits will add up to about $3,000 per year, whether the system is developed in-house, or purchased from BikeData.

You decide to compare relative costs to establish a total cost of ownership (TOC) over the useful life of the system. Based on your research, you put together the following summary:

Costs for Option A: Develop In-house

- The system will have a six-year useful life, be very flexible, and easiest to maintain.
- It will cost $15,000 to develop, install, and configure the system, and $1,000 to load existing data.
- Mark and the bookkeeper can handle day-to-day support with no added expense.

Costs for Option B: Purchase BikeData Software Package

- This is a vertical package with a four-year useful life.
- The software is less flexible than an in-house system and some customizing will be needed.
- It will cost $8,000 to purchase, $1,500 to install and configure, $2,500 to load existing data, and $1,000 additional hardware will be needed
- Support is free for the first year, then there is a $2,000 annual fee

Benefits for Both Options: $3,000 per year

Tasks

1. Prepare a detailed list of pros and cons of in-house versus software purchase.
2. Calculate ROI for both options.
3. Calculate NPV for both options. Use an 8% discount factor.
4. Create a PowerPoint presentation for Mark showing the results of your analysis, including recommendations and reasons.

Continuing Case: Personal Trainer, Inc.

Personal Trainer, Inc. owns and operates fitness centers in a dozen Midwestern cities. The centers have done well, and the company is planning an international expansion by opening a new "supercenter" in the Toronto area. Personal Trainer's president, Cassia Umi, hired an IT consultant, Susan Park, to help develop an information system for the new facility. During the project, Susan will work closely with Gray Lewis, who will manage the new operation.

Background

During data and process modeling, Susan Park developed a logical model of the proposed system. She drew an entity-relationship diagram and constructed a set of leveled and balanced DFDs. Now Susan is ready to consider various development strategies for the new system. She will investigate traditional and Web-based approaches and weigh the pros and cons of in-house development versus other alternatives. Before you begin, you should review the background information and facts contained in Chapters 2, 4, and 5 of the case study.

Tasks

1. What options does Personal Trainer have for developing a new system? What are some specific issues and options that Susan should consider in making a decision?
2. Susan has been asked to prepare a system requirements document and deliver a presentation to the management team. What should be the main elements of the system requirements document?
3. Based on the suggestions in Part A of the Systems Analyst's Toolkit, what visual aids should Susan use during her presentation?
4. Susan wants to prepare a presentation that will calculate the total cost of ownership for the system. What financial analysis tools are available to her, and what are the advantages (and possible disadvantages) of each tool?

Capstone Case: New Century Wellness Group

New Century Wellness Group offers a holistic approach to healthcare with an emphasis on preventive medicine as well as traditional medical care. In your role as an IT consultant, you will help New Century develop a new information system.

Background

Based on your earlier recommendations, New Century decided to continue the systems development process for a new information system. Now, at the end of the systems analysis phase, you are ready to prepare a system requirements document and give a presentation to the New Century associates. Many of the proposed system's advantages were described during the fact-finding process. Those include smoother operation, better efficiency, and more user-friendly procedures for patients and New Century staff.

You also must examine tangible costs and benefits to determine the economic feasibility of several alternatives. If New Century decides to go ahead with the development process, the main options are to develop the system in-house or purchase a vertical package and configure it to meet New Century's needs. You have studied those choices and put together some preliminary figures.

You know that New Century's current workload requires six hours of office staff overtime per week at a base rate of $15 per hour. In addition, based on current projections, New Century will need to add another full-time clerical position in about six months. Neither the overtime nor the additional job will be needed if New Century implements the new system. The current manual system also causes an average of three errors per day, and each error takes about 20 minutes to correct. The new system should eliminate those errors.

(continues)

Capstone Case: New Century Wellness Group

You estimate that by working full-time you could complete the project in about 12 weeks. Your consulting rate, which New Century agreed to, is $35 per hour. If you design the new system as a database application, you can expect to spend about $2,500 for a networked commercial package. After the system is operational and the staff is trained, New Century should be able to handle routine maintenance tasks without your assistance.

As an alternative to in-house development, a vertical software package is available for about $12,000. The vendor offers a lease-purchase package of $4,000 down, followed by two annual installments of $4,000 each. If New Century buys the package, it would take you about four weeks to install, configure, and test it, working full-time. The vendor provides free support during the first year of operation, but then New Century must sign a technical support agreement at an annual cost of $600. Although the package contains many of the features that New Century wants, most of the reports are pre-designed and it would be difficult to modify their layouts.

No matter which approach is selected, New Century probably will need you to provide about 10 hours of initial training and support each week for the first three months of operation. After the new system is operational, it will need routine maintenance, file backups, and updating. These tasks will require about four hours per week and can be performed by a clinic staff member. In both cases, the necessary hardware and network installation will cost about $12,500.

In your view, the useful life of the system will be about five years, including the year in which the system becomes operational.

You are scheduled to deliver a presentation to New Century next week, and you will submit a system requirements document at that time. To prepare yourself, you reviewed the skills described in Part A of the Systems Analyst's Toolkit, and you listed tips to remember, as follows:

Presentation Tips

- Use suitable visual aids.
- Use presentation software, if possible.
- Distribute handouts before, during, or after the presentation.
- Follow the guidelines in Part A of the Systems Analyst's Toolkit.
- Keep your presentation to 30 minutes, including 5 minutes for questions.

System Requirements Document Tips

- Follow the guidelines in Part A of the Systems Analyst's Toolkit.
- Include charts, graphs, or other helpful visual information in the document. Also include other material to help the audience understand the new system and decide on the next step.
- Spell check and carefully proofread the entire document.
- For readability, try to keep the Flesch Reading Ease score above 60, and aim for a Flesch-Kincaid Grade Level of 8.0 to 9.0.

Tasks

1. Provide an overview of the proposed system, including costs and benefits, with an explanation of the various cost-benefit types and categories.
2. Develop an economic feasibility analysis, using payback analysis, ROI, and present value (assume a discount rate of 10%).
3. Prepare a context diagram and diagram 0 for the new system.
4. Provide a brief explanation of the various alternatives that should be investigated if development continues, including in-house development and any other possible strategies.

CASE Tool Workshop

Systems analysts use CASE tools to help them plan, build, and maintain information systems. To learn more about CASE tools, turn to Part B of the Toolkit that follows Chapter 12. You can complete these tasks with the Visible Analyst® CASE tool, which is available with this textbook, or a similar tool.

Background

Suppose your company wants to create a logical model of a proposed information system, and then decide whether to develop the system in-house and purchase a software package. You have been asked to use a CASE tool to construct the model.

Tasks

1. After you perform fact-finding, you begin to work on the model. What diagrams will you create, and why? Will you use DFDs, object models, or both? Will you create an entity-relationship diagram? Explain your answers.
2. Most CASE tools can generate program code directly from diagrams and a central repository, and some tools are able to export the repository to a database management program, where the design can be implemented. Since you don't know whether the new system will be developed in-house, it would be helpful to know more about this in advance. Perform research on the CASE tool you are using to learn what code-generation and export features are available, and describe your findings.

MIS CourseMate Features

If you have an MIS CourseMate access code, you can reinforce and extend your learning with premium content created for this textbook. For example, you can launch interactive Video Learning Sessions to help you understand systems development concepts and practice your skills. In addition, you can use MindTap Reader, which is a full, interactive, digital e-book.

MIS CourseMate also offers many learning features within each chapter, including an Online Case Simulation, a Critical Thinking Challenge, Video Learning Tasks, and a set of Learn It Online activities. To log on to the MIS CourseMate site at **www.cengagebrain.com**, you must create a student account and register this book.

Online Case Simulation: SCR Associates

Session 7: Development Strategies

Overview

The SCR Associates case study is a Web-based simulation that allows you to practice your skills in a real-world environment. The firm offers IT consulting, solutions and training. SCR plans to open a new high-tech training center, and needs to develop a Training Information Management System (TIMS) to support the operation. You are a newly hired systems analyst reporting to Jesse Baker, systems group manager, and will help her develop the system.

The case study takes you to the SCR Web site, where you receive e-mail and voice mail messages from Jesse, obtain information from SCR's resource libraries, and perform various tasks. Jesse has high standards, but seems very fair. She made it clear that she expects your work to be accurate, thorough, and professional.

Before You Begin

To prepare for this work session, you should review the following topics:

* Cost-benefit analysis
* Pros and cons of in-house development

How Do I Use the Online Case Simulation?

* Read the preview, and review the Chapter 1 background material if necessary.
* Visit the MIS CourseMate Web site at **www.cengagebrain.com**, locate the **SCR Case Simulation**, and click the **intranet** link. Enter your name and the password **sad10e**.
* When the opening screen displays, select this session. Then check your e-mail and voice mail, and start to work on your task list.

Preview: Session 7

As you consider various development strategies for the TIMS system, you receive specific directions from your supervisor, Jesse Baker. She wants you to determine whether vertical software packages exist for TIMS, and she wants you to explore outsourcing options for the new system. She also expects you to conduct a cost-benefit analysis of developing TIMS in-house, and she wants your input on outsourcing and prototyping. She suggested that you check the SCR data library for more information.

Critical Thinking Challenge

In addition to technical ability, IT professionals need critical thinking skills. This feature can help you practice perception, organization, analysis, problem-solving, and decision-making skills that will be valuable in the workplace. You can visit **www.criticalthinking.org** to learn more about critical thinking and why it is so important.

Background

You are helping the IT team at Game Technology study several software acquisition options for their Customer Contact Care system (C^3). First, you review Chapter 7 of your systems analysis textbook and the material on financial analysis tools, including the Video Learning Sessions. The IT team is considering two commercial software packages and an in-house development option, as follows:

Option	Description	Costs	Benefits
Software Solutions, Inc.	Software package Four-year useful life Less flexible than in-house system Some customizing needed	$8,000 to purchase $1,500 to install and configure $2,500 to load existing data $1,000 additional hardware needed $2,000 annual support fee after first year free	$9,000/yr through positive customer response. Cannot predict other specific savings. Increased sales, improved customer care, and better productivity are expected.
CRM Corp.	Software package Five-year useful life Less flexible than in-house system Moderate customizing needed Runs slower than other options	$7,000 to purchase $2,500 to install and configure $2,000 to load existing data $4,000 additional hardware needed $1,200 annual support fee in all five years	Same as above
Develop C^3 system in-house	In-house system Six-year useful life, can use our software and hardware Easiest to update and maintain	$15,000 to develop, install, and configure $1,000 to load existing data Existing staff can handle support	Same as above

Practice Tasks

Visit the MIS CourseMate Web site at **www.cengagebrain.com**. Then navigate to the resources for this chapter and locate the **Critical Thinking Challenge** feature. You will complete two Practice Tasks, using what you learned in the chapter. Then you can check your answers to be sure you're ready for the Challenge Tasks.

Challenge Tasks

After you complete the Practice Tasks, you learn about new developments at Game Technology.

The Game Technology team liked your work, and asked you to perform some additional tasks. To continue, navigate to the **Critical Thinking Challenge** feature for this chapter, select the **Challenge Tasks,** and follow the instructions.

Video Learning Sessions

The Video Learning Sessions in this chapter explain return on investment (ROI) and net present value (NPV).

© craftvision/iStockph

Before You Begin

To prepare for the tasks, you should review the following topics:

- Cost-benefit analysis
- Pros and cons of each financial analysis tool

How to Watch a Session

Go to the Management Information Systems CourseMate Web site at www.cengagebrain.com. Then navigate to the resources for this book, locate the **Video Learning Sessions,** and select a session. You can watch the session on your computer or mobile device, and pause, rewind, or replay a video at any time.

Practice Tasks

After each session, visit the **Your Turn** feature to perform the tasks and check your answers.

Training Tasks

Suppose the IT training manager wants to encourage team members to watch the Video Learning Sessions. To spark interest, she plans to post a set of VLS previews, which you will prepare. Each preview must include an overview of the session, a description of the main topics, and one or more screen examples from the video. To get you started, she provided a task list:

1. Select a Video Learning Session from this chapter. Launch the video and note the title, objectives, and total running time. Include this information in your preview.
2. Run though the session and find a segment that does a good job of explaining a specific skill or concept.
3. In the segment you selected, choose one or more specific screens and capture each screen image with the Windows Snipping Tool. To do this in Windows 7 or Windows Vista, click **Start,** and then type **Snipping Tool.** In Windows 8, you can display the **Start** menu, and then type **Snipping Tool.**
4. Paste the screen image into your preview and explain how it would help a viewer understand the topic. Also add your comments about the video, and why it would be important to an IT professional. Your preview should be well-organized and readable.

Learn It Onlines

In each chapter, you can use this feature to apply your knowledge and practice your skills. The exercises include Chapter Reinforcement Questions, Flash Cards, Practice Tests, and various games, such as *Who Wants To Be a Computer Genius?, Wheel of Terms,* and the *Crossword Puzzle Challenge.*

DELIVERABLE
System design specification

TOOLKIT SUPPORT
Communication and CASE tools

GOT MIS COURSEMATE?
Four Video Learning Sessions explain
ERDs and data normalization

As the Dilbert cartoon suggests, you should understand a problem before you decide that a database is the solution. You will learn more about systems design topics, including database design, in the systems design phase.

Systems design is the third of five phases in the systems development life cycle. In the previous phase, systems analysis, you developed a logical model of the new system. Now you will work on a physical design that will meet the specifications described in the system requirements document. Your tasks will include user interface design, data design, and system architecture. The deliverable for this phase is the system design specification.

© Cengage Learning 2014

CHAPTER 8 User Interface Design

Chapter 8 is the first of three chapters in the systems design phase of the SDLC. This chapter explains how to design an effective user interface, and how to handle data security and control issues. The chapter stresses the importance of user feedback and involvement in all design decisions.

INTRODUCTION

OBJECTIVES

When you finish this chapter, you will be able to:

- Explain the concept of user interface design and human-computer interaction, including basic principles of user-centered design

- Explain how experienced interface designers perform their tasks

- Describe rules for successful interface design

- Discuss input and output technology issues

- Design effective source documents and forms

- Explain printed output guidelines

- Describe output and input controls and security

- Explain modular design and prototyping techniques

User interface design is the first task in the systems design phase of the SDLC. Designing the interface is extremely important because everyone wants a system that is easy to learn and use.

After discussing the user interface, human-computer interaction, and interface design rules, the chapter describes output, data security and control issues, prototyping, and the next steps in the systems design process.

PREVIEW CASE: Mountain View College Bookstore

Background: Wendy Lee, manager of college services at Mountain View College, wants a new information system that will improve efficiency and customer service at the three college bookstores.

In this part of the case, Tina Allen (systems analyst) and David Conroe (student intern) are talking about user interface design issues.

Participants:	Tina and David
Location:	Mountain View College Cafeteria, Monday afternoon, November 25, 2013
Project status:	Tina and David have examined development strategies for the new bookstore system. After performing cost-benefit analysis, they recommended in-house development of the new bookstore system. Now they are ready to begin the systems design phase by working on user interface design for the new system.
Discussion topics:	User interface design concepts and principles

Tina: Hi, David. Ready to start work on user interface design?

David: *Sure. Will we start with output because it's important to users?*

Tina: Output is very important, but the *most* important issue for users is the interface itself. For example, is it easy to learn? Is it easy to work with? We'll try to design everything — output, input, and all the other elements — from a user's point of view.

David: *How do we do that?*

Tina: Well, many sources of information about effective design concepts and principles are available. We'll study those, and then ask our own users for their input and suggestions.

David: *What about input and data entry?*

Tina: Good question. You've heard the old saying, "garbage in, garbage out." User interface principles apply to user input generally, but repetitive data entry deserves special attention. We need to create screen forms that are logical and easy to understand, as well as input masks and data entry validation rules. We also need to review any source documents that will be filled in manually.

David: *Anything else?*

Tina: Yes. The bookstore system probably will have some confidential data regarding budgets and markup policies, so we'll have to consider security and control issues. If you're ready, here's a task list to get us started:

FIGURE 8-1   Typical user interface design tasks.

© Cengage Learning 2014

SYSTEMS DESIGN PHASE OVERVIEW

Because the components of a system are interdependent, the design phase is not a series of clearly defined steps. Although you might start in one area, you could find yourself working with several different elements at the same time. For example, a decision to change a report format might require changes in data design or input screens. Your design checklist will include the user interface, input and output procedures, data design, and system architecture. At the end of this phase, you will prepare a systems design specification and deliver a presentation to management.

The goal of **systems design** is to build a system that is effective, reliable, and maintainable.

- A system is reliable if it handles input errors, processing errors, hardware failures, or human mistakes. A good design will anticipate errors, detect them as early as possible, make it easy to correct them, and prevent them from damaging the system itself.

- A system is maintainable if it is flexible, scalable, and easily modified. Changes might be needed to correct problems, adapt to user requirements, or take advantage of new technology.

- A system is effective if it supports business requirements and meets user needs.

Although each project is different, the following basic principles usually apply.

Will It Succeed?

A system might have advanced technology and powerful features, but the *real* test is whether users like it and feel that it meets their needs. Here are some suggestions for successful design:

- **Think like a user.** Carefully examine any point where users provide input or receive output. The user interface must be easy to learn. Input processes should be easy to follow, intuitive, and forgiving of errors. Predesigned output should be attractive and easy to understand, with an appropriate level of detail.

- **Anticipate future needs.** Consider a parts inventory database that contains a one-character field for *category,* such as electrical, mechanical, or hydraulic. The design works well, but what if the company decides to break these overall groups down into more specific segments? A better design would anticipate possible expansion to two or more characters. For example, in 1999, there was widespread concern about what was called the **Y2K issue** because many older programs used only two characters to store the year, and might not recognize the start of a new century.

- **Provide flexibility.** Suppose that a user wants a screen display of all customer balances that exceed $5,000 in an accounts receivable system. How should you design that feature? The program could be coded to check customer balances against a fixed value of 5000, which is a simple solution for both the programmer and the user because no extra keystrokes are required to produce the display. However, that approach is inflexible. A better approach would be to let the user enter the amount. Or you could start with a **default value** that displays automatically. Users can press ENTER to accept the value, or type in another value. Often the best design strategy is to offer several alternatives, so users can decide what will work best for them.

- **Manage data effectively.** In addition to its effect on users, data management impacts company efficiency, productivity, and security. To reduce input errors, the system should enter and verify data as soon as possible, and each data item should have a specific type, such as alphabetic, numeric, or alphanumeric, and a range of acceptable values.

It is important to collect input data as close to its source as possible. For instance, using barcode scanners rather than manual forms on a warehouse freight dock, or having salespeople use tablets to record orders rather than filling in source documents. The easiest, most accurate, and least expensive data input strategy is automated data capture, such as the RFID scanner shown in Figure 8-2.

In an efficient design, data is entered only once. For example, if input data for a payroll system also is needed for a human resources system, you can either design an interface to transfer data automatically, or create a central data storage area that both systems can access. In Chapter 9, you will learn about normalization, which is a set of rules that can help you avoid data design problems. A secure system also includes **audit trails** that can log every instance of data entry and changes. For example, the system should record when a customer's credit limit was set, by whom, and any other information necessary to construct the history of a transaction.

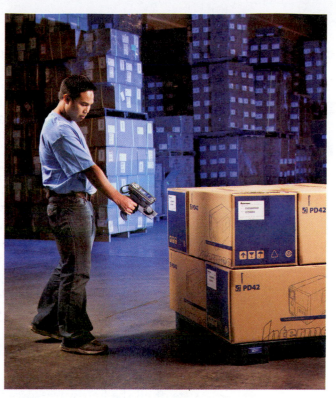

FIGURE 8-2   Automated data entry methods, such as the RFID scanner shown above, reduce input errors and improve employee productivity.

Courtesy of Intermec Technologies

CHAPTER OVERVIEW

Traditionally, a chapter on user interface design started with a discussion of output because output is what users touched, viewed, and needed to do their jobs. Today, the entire focus has shifted, for several important reasons:

- Users can design their own output. System designers are more aware of user needs and desires. A system can maintain data integrity and still allow users to view, sort, filter, and examine data in any way that helps them do their jobs. Years ago, the MIS department made those choices and users had little or no say in the matter. Today, successful applications are designed quite differently — the system developer identifies user needs, and then creates a design that will satisfy users *and* meet corporate requirements.

- Centralized IT departments no longer produce reams of printed reports. Those reports, called **greenbar reports** because of their appearance, often gathered dust while sitting on top of file cabinets. While a few examples might persist, the overwhelming trend has been to customer-designed output. The customer might be an individual user, or a community of users, such as a department. As Chapter 4 pointed out, the IT team must understand user requirements before creating a solution. That also was the message in the Dilbert cartoon on page 129.

- The user interface itself has evolved into a two-way channel, with powerful output capability, and most user information needs can be met with screen-generated data, which a user can print, view, or save. Well into the 1980s and beyond, a user interface was a blank character-based screen, which might or might not offer menu choices. If a user entered a command improperly, the system responded with an error message, which frustrated users and stifled productivity. Many hardware-centric vendors did not understand the importance of the user interface and its implications.

Apple was a pioneer in user interface development, introducing the **graphical user interface (GUI)**, complete with mouse and screen icons, in the early 1980s. At that point, not many companies were ready for this concept. When software giant Microsoft finally jumped on the GUI bandwagon with its Windows® operating system, the corporate doors swung open, and everyone from managers on down said "How did we ever do without this?"

The user interface will continue to evolve, and it is difficult to predict the future. Advanced technology will support the evolution, but the *real* driving force will be user empowerment, which results in employee satisfaction, increased productivity, and bottom-line savings for a company.

WHAT IS A USER INTERFACE?

A **user interface (UI)** describes how users interact with a computer system, and consists of all the hardware, software, screens, menus, functions, output, and features that affect two-way communications between the user and the computer. The UI is the key to **usability**, which includes user satisfaction, support for business functions, and system effectiveness.

Figure 8-3 suggests an interesting viewpoint that interface designers should keep in mind: Industry leader IBM believes that the best interfaces are the ones that users do not even notice — they make sense because they do what users expect them to do.

When developing older systems, analysts typically designed all the printed and screen output first, then worked on the inputs necessary to produce the results. Often, the user interface mainly consisted of **process-control** screens that allowed the user to send commands to the system. That approach worked well with traditional systems that simply transformed input data into structured output.

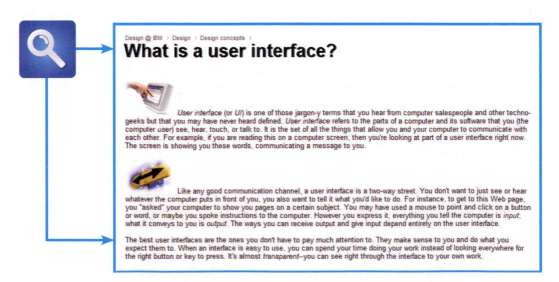

FIGURE 8-3 According to IBM, the best user interfaces are the ones you don't really notice.

As information management evolved from centralized data processing to dynamic, enterprise-wide systems, the primary focus also shifted — from the IT department to the users themselves. The IT group became a supplier of information technology, rather than a supplier of information. Today, the main focus is on users within and outside the company, how they communicate with the information system, and how the system supports the firm's business operations.

In a **user-centered** system, the distinction blurs between input, output, and the interface itself. Most users work with a varied mix of input, screen output, and data queries as they perform their day-to-day job functions. Because all those tasks require interaction with the computer system, the user interface is a vital element in the systems design phase.

User interface design requires an understanding of human-computer interaction and user-centered design principles, which are discussed in the next section.

Human-Computer Interaction

A user interface is based on basic principles of human-computer interaction. **Human-computer interaction (HCI)** describes the relationship between computers and people who use them to perform their jobs, like the worker shown in Figure 8-4. HCI concepts apply to everything from smartphones to global networks. In its broadest sense, a user interface includes all the communications and instructions necessary to enter input to the system and to obtain output in the form of screen displays or printed reports.

Early user interfaces involved users typing complex commands on a keyboard, which displayed as green text on a black screen. Then came the graphical user interface (GUI), which was a huge improvement because it used icons, graphical objects, and pointing devices. Today, designers strive to translate user behavior, needs, and desires into an interface that users don't really notice. As IBM points out in Figure 8-3, the best user interfaces are "*almost transparent* — you can see right though the interface to your own work." In other words, a **transparent interface** does not distract the user and calls no attention to itself.

As a systems analyst, you will design user interfaces for in-house–developed software and customize interfaces for various commercial packages and user productivity applications. Your main objective is to create a user-friendly design that is easy to learn and use.

Industry leaders Microsoft and IBM both devote considerable resources to user interface research. Figure 8-5 on the next page describes Microsoft's Redmond labs, where engineers observe volunteers who participate in software usability studies. Notice that the site invites visitors to watch an interesting video about Microsoft User Research.

Because HCI has a major impact on user productivity, it gets lots of attention — especially where multi-million dollar issues are concerned. For example, consider the article by Elizabeth Gardner in *Health Data Management*, which is shown in Figure 8-6 on the next page. The title tells the story, which involves government incentives for medical providers who use the new **electronic health records (EHRs)**. However, many physicians feel that EHR software is difficult to use and does not meet their needs.

FIGURE 8-4 HCI is essential to employee productivity, whether the work is done in a traditional office setting, or on a construction site like the one shown here.

© Goodluz/Shutterstock.com

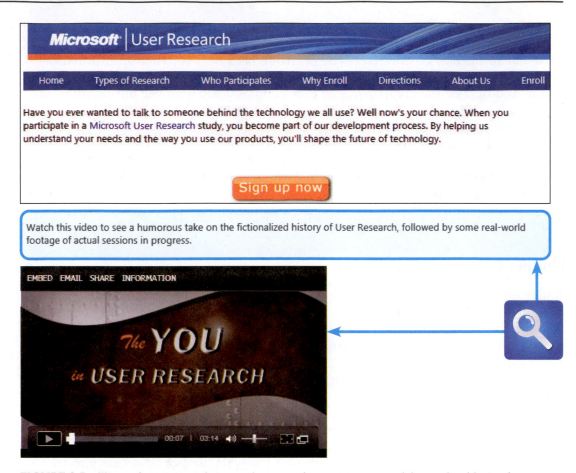

FIGURE 8-5   Microsoft engineers observe volunteers who participate in usability studies. Notice the invitation to watch a video about Microsoft User Research.

Screenshots used with permission from Microsoft.

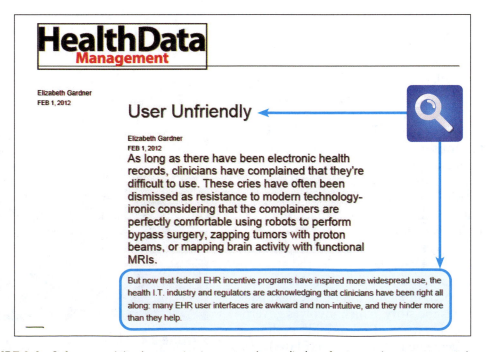

FIGURE 8-6   Software usability has a major impact on the medical profession, and not everyone is happy about it.

© 2012 Health Data Management and SourceMedia, Inc.

In her article, Ms. Gardner points out that physicians often multi task, answering a question about one patient while writing a prescription for another, and EHR software was not designed around that type of workflow.

The article also mentions Dr. Scott Finley, who consults on usability issues for the U.S. Department of Veterans' Affairs and other agencies. Dr. Finley says that EHRs were designed to do a good job of gathering structured analytical data, but that approach does not promote usability. Dr. Finley says, *The data capture process needs to be judged on its own merits. It's easier to make it hard than to make it easy.* Perhaps all systems analysts and UI designers should reflect on the implications of his comment.

CASE IN POINT 8.1: CASUAL OBSERVER SOFTWARE

Casual Observer Software's main product is a program that monitors and analyzes user keystrokes and mouse clicks to learn more about the way employees use their computer systems. The problem is that some users feel this is an unwarranted intrusion into their privacy, and they prefer not to be observed. Some even fear that the data would be used for other reasons, including performance appraisal. You are a consultant who has been hired by a client firm that is trying to decide whether or not to use this software.

Before you advise the client, go back and review the Microsoft usability lab shown in Figure 8-5, where the users being studied in the Redmond labs were willing participants. Then, refer to Chapter 4, Requirements Modeling, page 155, and consider the Hawthorne Effect, which suggests that employees might behave differently when they know they are being observed. Finally, think about the ethical issues that might be involved in this situation. What will you advise your client, and why?

SEVEN HABITS OF SUCCESSFUL INTERFACE DESIGNERS

Although IT professionals have different views about interface design, most would agree that good design depends on seven basic principles, which are described in the following sections.

Understand the Business

The interface designer must understand the underlying business functions and how the system supports individual, departmental, and enterprise goals. The overall objective is to design an interface that helps users to perform their jobs. A good starting point might be to analyze a functional decomposition diagram (FDD). As you learned in Chapter 4, an FDD is a graphical representation of business functions that starts with major functions, and then breaks them down into several levels of detail. An FDD can provide a checklist of user tasks that you must include in the interface design.

Maximize Graphical Effectiveness

Studies show that people learn better visually. The immense popularity of Apple Mac OS and Microsoft Windows is largely the result of their graphical user interfaces that are easy to learn and use. A well-designed interface can help users learn a new system rapidly and be more productive. Also, in a graphical environment, a user can display and work with multiple windows on a single screen and transfer data between programs. If the interface supports data entry, it must follow the guidelines for data entry screen design that are discussed later in this chapter.

Think Like a User

A systems analyst should understand user experience, knowledge, and skill levels. If a wide range of capability exists, the interface should be flexible enough to accommodate novices as well as experienced users.

To develop a user-centered interface, the designer must learn to think like a user and see the system through a user's eyes. The interface should use terms and metaphors that are familiar to users. Users are likely to have real-world experience with many other machines and devices that provide feedback, such as automobiles, ATMs, and microwave ovens. Based on that experience, users will expect useful, understandable feedback from a computer system.

Use Models and Prototypes

From a user's viewpoint, the interface is the most critical part of the system design because it is where he or she interacts with the system — perhaps for many hours each day. It is essential to construct models and prototypes for user approval. An interface designer should obtain as much feedback as possible, as early as possible. You can present initial screen designs to users in the form of a **storyboard,** which is a sketch that shows the general screen layout and design. The storyboard can be created with software or drawn freehand. Users must test all aspects of the interface design and provide feedback to the designers. User input can be obtained in interviews, via questionnaires, and by observation. Interface designers also can obtain data, called **usability metrics,** by using software that can record and measure user interaction with the system.

Focus on Usability

The user interface should include all tasks, commands, and communications between users and the information system. The opening screen should show the main options (Figure 8-7 is an illustration). Each screen option leads to another screen, with more options. The objective is to offer a reasonable number of choices that a user easily can comprehend. Too many options on one screen can confuse a user — but too few options increase the number of submenu levels and complicate the navigation process. Often, an effective strategy is to present the most common choice as a default but allow the user to select other options.

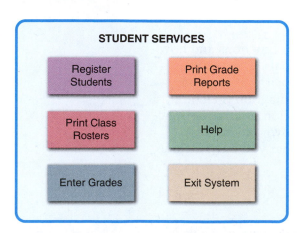

STUDENT SERVICES

Register Students

Print Grade Reports

Print Class Rosters

Help

Enter Grades

Exit System

FIGURE 8-7 The opening screen displays the main options for a student registration system. A user can click an option to see lower-level actions and menu choices.

© Cengage Learning 2014

Invite Feedback

Even after the system is operational, it is important to monitor system usage and solicit user suggestions. You can determine if system features are being used as intended by observing and surveying users. Sometimes, full-scale operations highlight problems that were not apparent when the prototype was tested. Based on user feedback, Help screens might need revision and design changes to allow the system to reach its full potential.

Document Everything

You should document all screen designs for later use by programmers. If you are using a CASE tool or screen generator, number the screen designs and save them in a hierarchy similar to a menu tree. User-approved sketches and storyboards also can be used to document the user interface.

By applying basic user-centered design principles, a systems analyst can plan, design, and deliver a successful user interface.

A HANDBOOK FOR USER INTERFACE DESIGN

What follows is a set of suggestions for user interface design, based on the author's experience and observation. There is some overlap because many of the main rules share common elements.

Although there is no standard approach to interface design, these rules will get you started. Perhaps the *most* important rule is that you don't have to follow all of these recommendations — the best interface is the one that works best for your users.

RULE 1: Create an Interface That Is Easy to Learn and Use

1.1 Focus on system design objectives, rather than calling attention to the interface.

1.2 Create a design that is easy to understand and remember. Maintain a common design in all modules of the interface, including the use of color, screen placements, fonts, and the overall "look and feel."

1.3 Provide commands, actions, and system responses that are consistent and predictable.

1.4 Allow users to correct errors easily.

1.5 Clearly label all controls, buttons, and icons.

1.6 Select familiar images that users can understand, and provide on-screen instructions that are logical, concise, and clear. For example, the top screen in Figure 8-8 shows four control buttons, but none of them has an obvious meaning. In the bottom screen, the first five messages provide little or no information. The last message is the only one that is easy to understand.

1.7 Show all commands in a list of menu items, but dim any commands that are not available to the user.

1.8 Make it easy to navigate or return to any level in the menu structure.

RULE 2: Enhance User Productivity

The interface is where a user interacts with the system, so it can have a dramatic effect on productivity. If the interface empowers a user and enables him or her to handle more complex tasks, the user becomes more productive. Conversely, if the interface is difficult to work with, productivity declines.

FIGURE 8-8   In the example at the top, the icons do not have a clear message. In the Help text examples at the bottom, only one message is understandable. The others would frustrate and annoy most users.

© Cengage Learning 2014

2.1   Organize tasks, commands, and functions in groups that resemble actual business operations. You should group functions and submenu items in a multilevel menu hierarchy, or tree, that is logical and reflects how users typically perform the tasks. Figure 8-9 shows an example of a menu hierarchy for an order tracking system.

2.2   Create alphabetical menu lists or place the selections used frequently at the top of the menu list. No universally accepted approach to menu item placement exists. The best strategy is to design a prototype and obtain feedback from users. Some applications even allow menus to show recently used commands first. Some users like that feature, but others find it distracting. The best approach is to offer a choice, and let users decide.

2.3   Provide shortcuts for experienced users so they can avoid multiple menu levels. You can create shortcuts using hot keys that allow a user to press the Alt key + the underlined letter of a command.

2.4   Use default values if the majority of values in a field are the same. For example, if 90% of the firm's customers live in Albuquerque, use *Albuquerque* as the default value in the City field.

2.5   Use a duplicate value function that enables users to insert the value from the same field in the previous record, but allow users to turn this feature on or off as they prefer.

2.6   Provide a fast-find feature that displays a list of possible values as soon as users enter the first few letters.

2.7   If available, consider a **natural language** feature that allows users to type commands or requests in normal text phrases. For example, many applications allow users to request Help by typing a question into a dialog box. The software then uses natural language technology to retrieve a list of topics that match the request. Natural language technology is used in speech recognition systems, text-to-speech synthesizers, automated voice response systems, Web search engines, text editors, and language instruction materials.

RULE 3: Provide Users with Help and Feedback

This is one of the most important rules because it has a high impact on users. Never allow Help to slow a user down. Instead, make Help easy to find, but not around when you users don't need it.

Customer Order Tracking System

FIGURE 8-9   This menu hierarchy shows tasks, commands, and functions organized into logical groups and sequences. The structure resembles a functional decomposition diagram (FDD), which is a model of business functions and processes.

3.1   Ensure that help is always available on demand. Help screens should provide information about menu choices, procedures, shortcuts, and errors.

3.2   Provide user-selected help and context-sensitive help. **User-selected** help displays information when the user requests it. By making appropriate choices through the menus and submenus, the user eventually reaches a screen with the desired information. Figure 8-10 shows the main Help screen for the student registration system. **Context-sensitive** help offers assistance for the task in progress. Figure 8-11 shows a Help dialog box that is displayed if a user requests help while entering data into the ADVISOR ASSIGNED field. Clicking the Close button returns the user to the current task.

FIGURE 8-10   The main Help screen for a student registration system.
© Cengage Learning 2014

3.3   Provide a direct route for users to return to the point from where help was requested. Title every help screen to identify the topic, and keep help text simple and concise. Insert blank lines between paragraphs to make Help easier to read, and provide examples where appropriate.

3.4   Include contact information, such as a telephone extension or e-mail address if a department or help desk is responsible for assisting users.

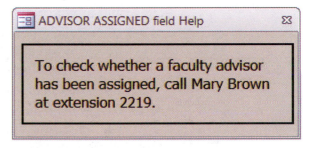

FIGURE 8-11   A context-sensitive dialog box displays if a user requests help while entering data into the ADVISOR ASSIGNED field. Clicking the Close button returns the user to the task.
© Cengage Learning 2014

3.5   Require user confirmation before data deletion *(Are you sure?)* and provide a method of recovering data that is deleted inadvertently. Build in safeguards that prevent critical data from being changed or erased.

3.6   Provide an Undo key or a menu choice that allows the user to eradicate the results of the most recent command or action.

3.7   When a user-entered command contains an error, highlight the erroneous part and allow the user to make the correction without retyping the entire command.

3.8   Use hypertext links to assist users as they navigate help topics.

3.9   Display messages at a logical place on the screen, and be consistent.

3.10 Alert users to lengthy processing times or delays. Give users an on-screen progress report, especially if the delay is lengthy.

3.11 Allow messages to remain on the screen long enough for users to read them. In some cases, the screen should display messages until the user takes some action.

3.12 Let the user know whether the task or operation was successful or not. For example, use messages such as *Update completed, All transactions have been posted,* or *The ID Number was not found.*

3.13 Provide a text explanation if you use an icon or image on a control button. This helps the user to identify the control button when moving the mouse pointer over the icon or image.

3.14 Use messages that are specific, understandable, and professional. Avoid messages that are cute, cryptic, or vague, such as: *ERROR — You have entered an unacceptable value*, or *Error DE-4-16. Better examples are:*

- *Enter a number from 1 (low) to 5 (high)*
- *Customer number must be numeric*
- *Please re-enter a numeric value*
- *Call the Accounting Department, Ext. 239 for assistance*

RULE 4: Create an Attractive Layout and Design

This is a subjective area because reasonable people can differ on what is attractive. You should consider color, layout, and ease of use. You might create some screen mock-ups and menu trees and try them out on users to get their input. If in doubt, err on the side of doing a bit less. Although you might love blinking messages, they might not be the best choice for your interface design. Also try to avoid too many fonts, styles, and sizes, which can be distracting. Each separate style should communicate *something* — a different level of detail, another topic, mandatory versus optional actions, and so on.

4.1 Use appropriate colors to highlight different areas of the screen; avoid gaudy and bright colors.

4.2 Use special effects sparingly. For example, animation and sound might be effective in some situations, but too many special effects can be distracting and annoying to a user, especially if he or she must view them repeatedly.

4.3 Use hyperlinks that allow users to navigate to related topics.

4.4 Group related objects and information. Visualize the screen the way a user will see it, and simulate the tasks that the user will perform.

4.5 Screen density is important. Keep screen displays uncluttered, with enough white space to create an attractive, readable design.

4.6 Display titles, messages, and instructions in a consistent manner and in the same general locations on all screens.

4.7 Use consistent terminology. For example, do not use the terms delete, cancel, and erase to indicate the same action. Similarly, the same sound always should signal the same event.

4.8 Ensure that commands always will have the same effect. For example, if the BACK control button returns a user to the prior screen, the BACK command always should perform that function throughout the application.

4.9 Ensure that similar mouse actions will produce the same results throughout the application. The results of pointing, clicking, and double-clicking should be consistent and predictable.

4.10 When the user enters data that completely fills the field, do not move automatically to the next field. Instead, require the user to confirm the entry by pressing the Enter key or Tab key at the end of every fill-in field.

4.11 Remember that users are accustomed to a pattern of red = stop, yellow = caution, and green = go. Stick to that pattern and use it when appropriate to reinforce on-screen instructions.

4.12 Provide a keystroke alternative for each menu command, with easy-to-remember letters, such as File, Exit, and Help.

4.13 Use familiar commands if possible, such as Cut, Copy, and Paste.

4.14 Provide a Windows look and feel in your interface design if users are familiar with Windows-based applications.

4.15 Avoid complex terms and technical jargon; instead, select terms that come from everyday business processes and the vocabulary of a typical user.

RULE 5: Enhance the Interface

A designer can include many features, such as menu bars, toolbars, dialog boxes, text boxes, toggle buttons, list boxes, scroll bars, drop-down list boxes, option buttons, check boxes, command buttons, and calendar controls, among others. Screen design requires a sense of aesthetics as well as technical skills. You should obtain user feedback early and often as the design process continues.

5.1 The opening screen is especially important because it introduces the application and allows users to view the primary options. The starting point can be a **switchboard** with well-placed command buttons that allow users to navigate the system. Figure 8-12 shows the switchboard and a data entry screen for a project management system. Notice the drop-down list box that allows users to enter a status code by clicking a selection.

FIGURE 8-12 An example of a switchboard and data entry screen for a project management system.

© Cengage Learning 2014

5.2   Use a **command button** to initiate an action such as printing a form or re-
        questing help. For example, when a user clicks the Find Student command
        button in Figure 8-13, a dialog box opens with instructions.

5.3   If you are using a software package, check to see if it allows you to create cus-
        tomized **menu bars** and toolbars. If so, consider these options.

5.4   Add a shortcut feature that lets a user select a menu command either by click-
        ing the desired choice or by pressing the Alt key + the underlined letter. Some
        forms also use a **toolbar** that contains icons or buttons that represent short-
        cuts for executing common commands.

5.5   If variable input data is needed, provide a **dialog box** that explains what is
        required.

5.6   A **toggle button** makes it easy to show on or off status — clicking the toggle
        button switches to the other state.

5.7   Use **list boxes** that display the available choices. If the list does not fit in the
        box, a **scroll bar** allows the user to move through the available choices. Also,
        be sure to provide another way to enter data that does not align with a spe-
        cific list choice.

5.8   Use an **option button**, or **radio button**, to control user choices. For example,
        if the user can select only one option, display a suitable message *(Choose one
        item)*, but if there is no restriction, display a different message *(Choose all
        that apply)*. Use a black dot to show selected options.

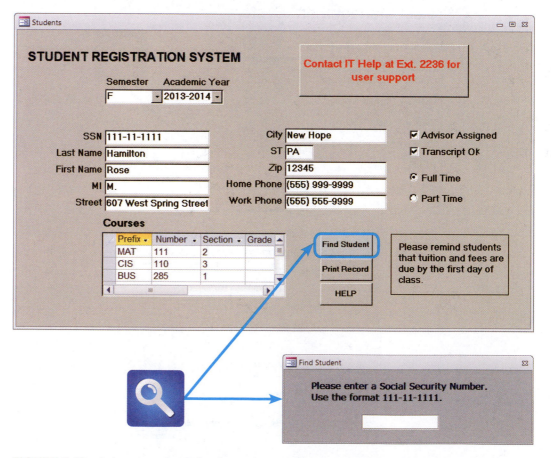

FIGURE 8-13   A data entry screen for the student registration system. This screen uses several design
features that are described in the text. When a user clicks the Find Student command button, a dialog box is
displayed with instructions.

5.9   If you use **check boxes** to select one or more choices from a group, show the choices with a checkmark or an X.

5.10   When dates must be entered, use a **calendar control** that allows the user to select a date that the system will use as a field value.

RULE 6: Focus on Data Entry Screens

Data entry is especially important because it is in the job description of so many users.

6.1   Whenever possible, use a data entry method called **form filling,** where a blank form that duplicates or resembles the source document is completed on the screen.

6.2   Restrict user access to screen locations where data is entered. For example, when the screen in Figure 8-14 appears, the system should position the insertion point in the first data entry location. After the operator enters a Customer ID, the insertion point should move automatically to the entry location for the next field (Item). A user should be able to position the insertion point only in places where data is entered on the form.

6.3   Provide a way to leave the data entry screen at any time without entering the current record. This feature is not available in the screen shown in Figure 8-14, but is provided in the enhanced version of the same screen shown in Figure 8-15 on the next page. Notice that the new version has command buttons that provide flexibility and allow the user to perform various functions. For example, clicking the Cancel Order button cancels the current order and moves the insertion point back to the beginning of the form.

6.4   Provide a descriptive caption for every field, and show the user where to enter the data and the required or maximum field size. Typically, white boxes show the location and length of each field. Other methods used to indicate field locations are video highlighting, underscores, special symbols, or a combination of these features.

■ Generated by the system   ■ Entered by the user   ■ Retrieved or calculated by the system

FIGURE 8-14   In this data screen for customer orders, the system generates an order number and logs the current date and time. The user enters a customer ID. If the entry is valid, the system displays the customer name so the user can verify it. The user then enters the item and quantity. Note that the description, price, extended price, total price, sales tax, and grand total are retrieved automatically or calculated by the system.

© Cengage Learning 2014

FIGURE 8-15   This is an enhanced version of the data entry screen shown in Figure 8-14. The new version has command buttons that allow the user to perform various functions.
© Cengage Learning 2014

6.5 Provide a means for users to move among fields on the form in a standard order or in any order they choose. For example, when a user opens the form shown in Figure 8-15, the insertion point automatically will be in the first field. After the user fills in each field and confirms the entry, the insertion point moves to the next field, in a predetermined order. In a graphical user interface (GUI), the user can override the standard field order and select field locations using the mouse or arrow keys.

6.6 Allow users to add, change, delete, and view records. Figure 8-15 helps users enter orders, find items, and find customers. After the user enters a customer code, the form displays current values for all appropriate fields. Then the operator can view the data, make changes, enter the order, or cancel the order. Messages such as: Apply these changes? (Y/N) or Delete this record? (Y/N) should require users to confirm the actions. Highlighting the letter N as a default response will avoid problems if the user presses the Enter key by mistake.

6.7 Design the screen form layout to match the layout of the source document. If the source document fields start at the top of the form and run down in a column, the input screen should use the same design.

6.8 Display a sample format if a user must enter values in a field in a specific format. For example, provide an on-screen instruction to let users know that the date format is MMDDYY, and provide an example if the user must enter separators, such as slashes.

6.9 In addition to the sample format in the preceding rule, it might be better to use an **input mask,** which is a template or pattern that restricts data entry and prevents errors. Microsoft Access provides standard input masks for fields such as dates, telephone numbers, postal codes, and Social Security numbers. In addition, you can create custom input masks, as shown in Figure 8-16. Notice that a mask

FIGURE 8-16   Microsoft Access 2010 provides various input masks for dates, phone numbers, and postal codes, among others. In addition, it is easy to create a custom mask using the characters shown here.

can have a specific format. For example, if a user enters text in lowercase letters, the input mask >L<???????????? will capitalize the first letter automatically.

6.10 Require an ending keystroke for every field. Pressing the Enter key or the Tab key should signify the end of a field entry. Avoid a design that moves automatically to the next item when the field is full. The latter approach requires an ending keystroke only when the data entered is less than the maximum field length. It is confusing to use two different data entry procedures.

6.11 Do not require users to type leading zeroes for numeric fields. For example, if a three-digit project number is 045, the operator should be able to type 45 instead of 045 before pressing the Enter key. An exception to that rule might occur when entering a date, where a leading zero is needed to identify single-digit months or days, such as 06-04-2013.

6.12 Do not require users to type trailing zeroes for numbers that include decimals. For example, when a user types a value of 98, the system should interpret the value as 98.00 if the field has been formatted to include numbers with two decimal places. The decimal point is needed only to indicate nonzero decimal places, such as 98.76.

6.13 Display default values so operators can press the Enter key to accept the suggested value. If the default value is not appropriate, the operator can change it.

6.14 Use a default value when a field value will be constant for successive records or throughout the data entry session. For example, if records are input in order by date, the date used in the first transaction should be used as the default date until a new date is entered, at which time the new date becomes the default value.

6.15 Display a list of acceptable values for fields, and provide meaningful error messages if the user enters an unacceptable value. An even better method, which was described under Rule 5: Enhance the Interface, is to provide a drop-down list box containing acceptable values that allows the user to select a value by clicking.

6.16 Provide users with an opportunity to confirm the accuracy of input data before entering it by displaying a message such as, Add this record? (Y/N). A positive response (Y) adds the record, clears the entry fields, and positions the insertion point in the first field so the user can input another record. If the response is negative (N), the current record is not added and the user can correct the errors.

RULE 7: Use Validation Rules

Reducing input errors improves data quality. One way to reduce input errors is to eliminate unnecessary data entry. For example, a user cannot misspell a customer name if it is not entered, or is entered automatically based on the user entering the customer ID. Similarly, an outdated item price cannot be used if the item price is retrieved from a master file instead of being entered manually. The best defense against incorrect data is to identify and correct errors before they enter the system by using data validation rules, as shown in Figure 8-17. A **data validation rule** improves input quality by testing the data and rejecting any entry that fails to meet specified conditions. In your design, you can include at least eight types of data validation rules.

7.1 A **sequence check** can be used when the data must be in some predetermined sequence. If the user must enter work orders in numerical sequence, for example, then an out-of-sequence order number indicates an error, or if the user must enter transactions chronologically, then a transaction with an out-of-sequence date indicates an error.

FIGURE 8-17   Validation rules can improve data quality by requiring the input to meet specific requirements or conditions.

Screenshots used with permission from Microsoft.

7.2   An **existence check** can apply to mandatory data items. For example, if an employee record requires a Social Security number, an existence check would not allow the user to save the record until he or she enters a suitable value in the Social Security number field.

7.3   A **data type check** can test to ensure that a data item fits the required data type. For example, a numeric field must have only numbers or numeric symbols, and an alphabetic field can contain only the characters A through Z (or a through z).

7.4   A **range check** can be used to verify that data items fall between a specified minimum and maximum value. The daily hours worked by an employee, for example, must fall within the range of 0 to 24. When the validation check involves a minimum or a maximum value, but not both, it is called a **limit check**. Checking that a payment amount is greater than zero, but not specifying a maximum value, is an example of a limit check.

7.5   A **reasonableness check** identifies values that are questionable, but not *necessarily* wrong. For example, input payment values of $.05 and $5,000,000.00 both pass a simple limit check for a payment value greater than zero, and yet both values could be errors. Similarly, a daily hours worked value of 24 passes a 0 to 24 range check; however, the value seems unusual, and the system should verify it using a reasonableness check.

7.6   A **validity check** can be used for data items that must have certain values. For example, if an inventory system has 20 valid item classes, then any input item that does not match one of the valid classes will fail the check. Verifying that a customer number on an order matches a customer number in the customer file is another type of validity check. Because the value entered must refer to another value, that type of check also is called *referential integrity,* which is explained in Chapter 9, Data Design. Another validity check might verify that a new customer number does not match a number already stored in the customer master file.

7.7   A **combination check** is performed on two or more fields to ensure that they are consistent or reasonable when considered together. Even though all the fields involved in a combination check might pass their individual validation checks, the combination of the field values might be inconsistent or unreasonable. For example, if an order input for 30 units of a particular item has an input discount rate applicable only for purchases of 100 or more units, then the combination is invalid; either the input order quantity or the input discount rate is incorrect.

7.8   **Batch controls** are totals used to verify batch input. Batch controls might check data items such as record counts and numeric field totals. For example, before entering a batch of orders, a user might calculate the total number of orders and the sum of all the order quantities. When the batch of orders is entered, the order system also calculates the same two totals. If the system totals do not match the input totals, then a data entry error has occurred. Unlike the other validation checks, batch controls do not identify specific errors. For example, if the sum of all the order quantities does not match the batch control total, you know only that one or more orders in that batch were entered incorrectly or not input. The batch control totals often are called **hash totals** because they are not meaningful numbers themselves, but are useful for comparison purposes.

RULE 8: Reduce Input Volume

This is the final rule, but in some ways it should be the first because it affects all the rest. When you reduce input volume, you avoid unnecessary labor costs, get the data into the system more quickly, and decrease the number of errors. You should start by reducing the number of data items required for each transaction.

8.1   Input necessary data only. Do not input a data item unless it is needed by the system. A completed order form, for example, might contain the name of the clerk who took the order. If that data is not needed by the system, the user should not enter it.

8.2   Do not input data that the user can retrieve from system files or calculate from other data. In the order system example shown in Figure 8-15 on page 314, the system generates an order number and logs the current date and time. Then the user enters a customer ID. If the entry is valid, the system displays the customer name so the user can verify it. The user then enters the item and quantity. Note that the description, price, extended price, total price, sales tax, and grand total are retrieved automatically or calculated by the system.

8.3   Do not input constant data. If orders are in batches with the same date, then a user should enter the order date only once for the first order in the batch. If orders are entered online, then the user can retrieve the order date automatically using the current system date.

8.4   Use codes. Codes are shorter than the data they represent, and coded input can reduce data entry time. You will learn more about various types of codes in Chapter 9, Data Design.

CASE IN POINT 8.2:   BOOLEAN TOYS

When should a systems analyst decide a design issue, and when should users be allowed to select what works best for them? The field of ergonomics is concerned with improving the work environment and studying how users interact with their environment.

Suppose you are a systems analyst studying the order processing system at Boolean Toys, a fast-growing developer of software for preschool children. You know that many data entry users have complained about the input screens. Some users would prefer to rearrange the order of the fields; others would like to change the background color on their screens; still others want shortcuts that would allow them to avoid a series of introductory screens.

What if Boolean's users could customize their own data entry screens without assistance from the IT staff by using a menu-driven utility program? What would be the pros and cons of such an approach?

SOURCE DOCUMENT AND FORM DESIGN

No matter how data enters an information system, the quality of the output is only as good as the quality of the input. The term **garbage in, garbage out (GIGO),** is familiar to IT professionals, who know that the best time to avoid problems is when the data is entered. The main objective is to ensure the quality, accuracy, and timeliness of input data. Unfortunately, the dream of a "paperless office" has never been realized. Even with RFID technology and automated data capture, we still enter data on source documents and forms, and instead of a human-computer interface, systems analysts must deal with the challenge of a human-paper interface.

A **source document** collects input data, triggers or authorizes an input action, and provides a record of the original transaction. During the input design stage, you develop source documents that are easy to complete and use for data entry. Source documents generally are paper-based, but also can be provided online. Either way, the design considerations are the same.

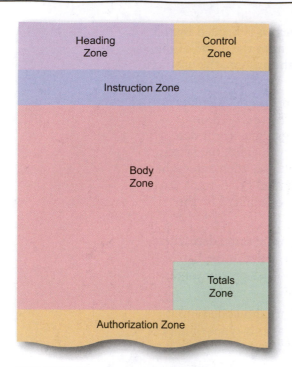

FIGURE 8-18   Source document zones.
© Cengage Learning 2014

Consider a time when you struggled to complete a poorly designed form. You might have encountered insufficient space, confusing instructions, or poor organization, all symptoms of incorrect **form layout**.

Good form layout makes the form easy to complete and provides enough space, both vertically and horizontally, for users to enter the data. A form should indicate data entry positions clearly using blank lines or boxes and descriptive captions. Also consider using check boxes whenever possible, so users can select choices easily. However, be sure to include an option for any input that does not match a specific check box.

The placement of information on a form also is important. Source documents typically include most of the zones shown in Figure 8-18. The **heading zone** usually contains the company name or logo and the title and number of the form. The **control zone** contains codes, identification information, numbers, and dates that are used for storing completed forms. The **instruction zone** contains instructions for completing the form. The main part of the form, called the **body zone**, usually takes up at least half of the space on the form and contains captions and areas for entering variable data. If totals are included on the form, they appear in the **totals zone**. Finally, the **authorization zone** contains any required signatures.

Information should flow on a form from left to right and top to bottom to match the way users read documents naturally. That layout makes the form easy to use for the individual who completes the form, and for users who enter data into the system using the completed form.

The same user-friendly design principles also apply to printed forms such as invoices and monthly statements, except that heading information usually is preprinted. You should make column headings short but descriptive, avoid nonstandard abbreviations, and use reasonable spacing between columns for better readability.

The order and placement of printed fields should be logical, and totals should be identified clearly. When designing a preprinted form, you should contact the form's vendor for advice on paper sizes, type styles and sizes, paper and ink colors, field placement, and other important form details. Your goal is to design a form that is attractive, readable, and effective.

Layout and design also are important on Web-based forms, and you can find many resources that will help you design efficient, user-friendly forms. For example, Luke Wroblewski, a well-known author and consultant, maintains a Web site at *www.lukew .com*. His site offers valuable suggestions, guidelines, and examples of Web-based forms.

PRINTED OUTPUT

Before designing printed output, ask yourself several questions:

- Why is this being delivered as printed output, rather than screen-based information, with an option for users to view, print, or save as needed?
- Who wants the information, why is it needed, and how will it be used?
- What specific information will be included?
- Will the printed output be designed for a specific device?
- When and how will the information be delivered, and how often must it be updated?
- Do security or confidentiality issues exist? How will they be managed?

The design process should not begin until you have answered the questions. Some information probably was gathered during the systems analysis phase. To complete your understanding, you should meet with users to find out exactly what kind of output *they* are requesting. You can use prototypes and mock-ups to obtain feedback throughout the design process.

Overview of Report Design

Although many organizations strive to reduce the flow of paper and printed reports, few firms have been able to eliminate printed output totally. Because they are portable, printed reports are convenient, and even necessary in some situations. Many users find it handy to view screen output, then print the information they need for a discussion or business meeting. Printed output also is used in **turnaround documents**, which are output documents that are later entered back into the same or another information system. In some areas, your telephone or utility bill, for example, might be a turnaround document printed by the company's billing system. When you return the required portion of the bill with your check, the bill is scanned into the company's accounts receivable system to record the payment accurately.

Designers use a variety of styles, fonts, and images to produce reports that are attractive and user friendly. Whether printed or viewed on-screen, reports must be easy to read and well organized. Rightly or wrongly, some managers judge an entire project by the quality of the reports they receive.

Database programs such as Microsoft Access include a variety of report design tools, including a Report Wizard, which is a menu-driven feature that designers can use to create reports quickly and easily. Microsoft Access also provides a comprehensive guide to designing reports, as shown in Figure 8-19.

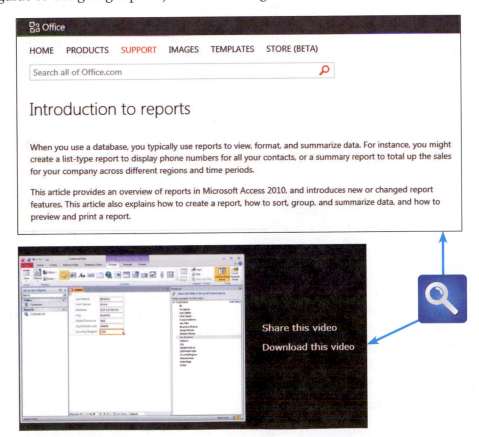

FIGURE 8-19   Microsoft offers suggestions, tips, and a video that can help you design better forms and reports.

Screenshots used with permission from Microsoft.

Although the vast majority of reports are designed graphically, some systems still produce one or more **character-based reports** that use a character set with fixed spacing. Printing character-based reports on high-speed impact printers is a fast, inexpensive method for producing large-scale reports, such as payroll or inventory reports, or registration rosters at a school. This is especially true if multiple copies are required.

Types of Reports

To be useful, a report must include the information that a user needs. From a user's point of view, a report with too little information is of no value. Too much information, however, can make a report confusing and difficult to understand. When designing reports, the essential goal is to match the report to the user's specific information needs. Depending on their job functions, users might need one or more of the reports described in the following sections.

DETAIL REPORTS A **detail report** produces one or more lines of output for each record processed. Because it contains one or more lines for each record, a detail report can be quite lengthy. Consider, for example, a large auto parts business. If the firm stocks 3,000 parts, then the detail report would include 3,000 detail lines on approximately 50 printed pages. A user who wants to locate any part in short supply has to examine 3,000 detail lines to find the critical items. A better alternative might be an exception report.

EXCEPTION REPORTS An **exception report** displays only those records that meet a specific condition or conditions. Exception reports are useful when the user wants information only on records that might require action, but does not need to know the details. For example, a credit manager might use an exception report to identify only those customers with past-due accounts, or a customer service manager might want a report on all packages that were not delivered within a specified time period.

SUMMARY REPORTS Upper-level managers often want to see total figures and do not need supporting details. A sales manager, for example, might want to know total sales for each sales representative, but not want a detail report listing every sale made by them. In that case, a **summary report** is appropriate. Similarly, a personnel manager might need to know the total regular and overtime hours worked by employees in each store but might not be interested in the number of hours worked by each employee.

User Involvement

Users should approve all report designs in advance. The best approach is to prepare a sample report, called a **mock-up**, or prototype, for users to review. The sample should include typical field values and contain enough records to show all the design features. Depending on the type of printed output, you can create a Microsoft Word document or use a report generator to create mock-up reports.

Report Design Principles

Printed reports must be attractive, professional, and easy to read. For example, a well-designed report should provide totals and subtotals for numeric fields. In the report shown in Figure 8-20, notice that when the value of a control field, such as Store Number, changes, a **control break** occurs. A control break usually causes specific actions, such as printing subtotals for a group of records. That type of detail report is called a **control break report**. To produce a control break report, the records must be arranged, or sorted, in **control field order**.

Good report design requires effort and attention to detail. To produce a well-designed report, the analyst must consider design features such as report headers and footers, page headers and footers, column headings and alignment, column spacing, field order, and grouping of detail lines.

REPORT HEADERS AND FOOTERS Every report should have a report header and a report footer. The **report header**, which appears at the beginning of the report, identifies the report, and contains the report title, date, and other necessary information. The **report footer**, which appears at the end of the report, can include grand totals for numeric fields and other end-of-report information, as shown in Figure 8-20.

PAGE HEADERS AND FOOTERS Every page should include a **page header**, which appears at the top of the page and includes the column headings that identify the data. The headings should be short but descriptive. Avoid abbreviations unless you

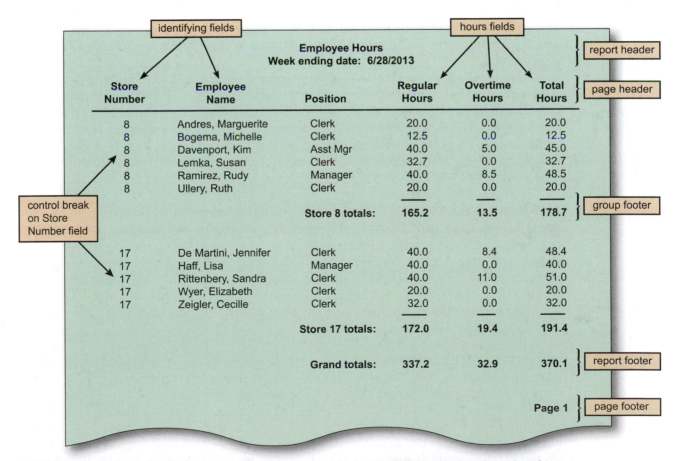

FIGURE 8-20 The Employee Hours report is a detail report with control breaks, subtotals, and grand totals. Notice that a report header identifies the report, a page header contains column headings, a group footer contains subtotals for each store, a report footer contains grand totals, and a page footer identifies the page number.

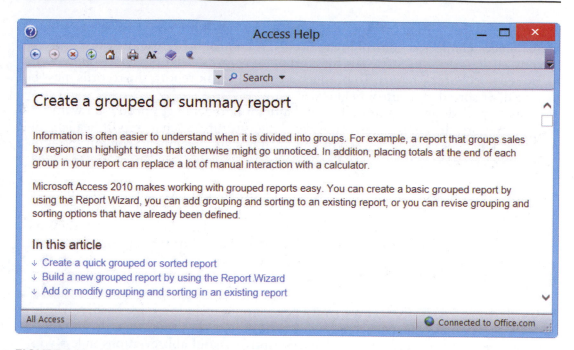

FIGURE 8-21   Microsoft Access includes an easy-to-use tool for grouping data.
Screenshot used with permission from Microsoft.

know that users will understand them clearly. Either a page header or a **page footer**, which appears at the bottom of the page, is used to display the report title and the page number.

Database programs such as Microsoft Access make it easy to create groups and subgroups based on particular fields. You also can have the report calculate and display totals, averages, record counts, and other data for any group or subgroup. For example, in a large company, you might want to see total sales and number of sales broken down by product within each of the 50 states. The screen shown in Figure 8-21 is an Access Help screen that refers to a step-by-step process for creating multilevel grouping.

REPEATING FIELDS   Report design is an art, not a science. User involvement is essential, but users often don't know what they want without seeing samples. For example, consider the issue of repeating fields. The sample report in Figure 8-20 repeats the store number on every row. Is that a good thing? The best advice is to ask users what they think and be guided accordingly. A similar issue exists with regard to the overtime hours column. Is it better to print the zero overtime data, or only print actual hours, so the data stands out clearly? Again, the best answer is usually the one that works best for users.

CONSISTENT DESIGN   Look and feel are important to users, so reports should be uniform and consistent. When a system produces multiple reports, each report should share common design elements. For example, the date and page numbers should print in the same place on each report page. Abbreviations used in reports also should be consistent. For example, when indicating a numeric value, it is confusing for one report to use #, another *NO*, and a third *NUM*. Items in a report also should be consistent. If one report displays the inventory location as a shelf number column followed by a bin number column, that same layout should be used on all inventory location reports.

CASE IN POINT 8.3: Lazy Eddie

Lynn Jennings is the IT manager at Lazy Eddie, a chain that specializes in beanbag chairs and recliners. She asked Jan Lauten, a senior systems analyst, to review the large number of printed reports that are distributed to Lazy Eddie's 35 store managers. "Jan, I just can't believe that our people really read all of those reports," Lynn said. "We constantly add new reports, and we never seem to eliminate the old ones. Sometimes I think all we're doing is keeping the paper companies in business!" Jan replied, "I agree, but what can we do? The managers say they want the reports, but I always see them stacked on top of file cabinets. I've never seen anyone read a report."

"I have an idea," Lynn said. "I want you to come up with a procedure that requires users to review and justify their information needs to see if they really use the reports we send them. You could design a form that asks if the information still is required, and why. Try to get users to decide if a report is worth the cost of producing it. Do you think you can do it?"

"Sure I can," Jan replied. When Jan returned to her office, she wondered where to begin. What advice would you give to Jan?

CASE IN POINT 8.4:   Trustworthy Insurance Company

Trustworthy Insurance maintains its headquarters in a large Midwestern city. Right now, a debate is raging in the IT department. Several analysts want to use standard, company-wide desktop screen layouts and icons. Others want to allow users to set up their screens any way they choose. Those who argue for standardization point out that Trustworthy employs a number of part-time employees, who fill in for employees on vacation. Without a standard interface, these people would have to reorient to every workstation, and the proponents of standardization claim that would reduce productivity and increase costs. Those opposed to standardization believe that employees are most productive when they have control over their workplace, including the ability to design an interface they feel is attractive, even if no one else does.

You are on a committee that was charged with resolving this issue, and yours is the tie-breaking vote. What will you decide, and why?

TECHNOLOGY ISSUES

Unlike early innovations such as the mouse and the inkjet printer, most technology advances today affect both output *and* input. In a very real sense, output and input have become interdependent, as they are in a user interface, and it is difficult to cite examples of changes in one that would not cause, or at least encourage, changes in the other. For example, new touch-screen input technology generates output that must be properly designed and sized for a particular device, which might be a smartphone, a tablet, or a 23-inch desktop monitor.

The following sections discuss output and input technology separately, but interface designers should always be alert to the possible opportunities, or potential problems, of input/output linkage.

Output Technology

Although business information systems still provide most output as screen displays and printed matter, technology is having an enormous impact on how people communicate and obtain information. This trend is especially important to firms that use information technology to lower their costs, improve employee productivity, and communicate effectively with their customers.

In addition to screen output and printed matter, output can be delivered in many ways. The system requirements document probably identified user output needs. Now, in the systems design phase, you will create the actual forms, reports, documents, and other types of output that might be accessed from workstations, notebooks, tablets, smartphones, and other devices. Also, you must consider how the information will be used, stored, and retrieved. The following subsections explain various output types and technologies.

INTERNET-BASED INFORMATION DELIVERY   Millions of firms use the Internet to reach new customers and markets around the world. To support the explosive growth in e-commerce, Web designers must provide user-friendly screen interfaces that display output and accept input from customers. For example, a business can link its inventory system to its Web site so the output from the inventory system is displayed as an online catalog. Customers visiting the site can review the items, obtain current prices, and check product availability.

Another example of Web-based output is a system that provides customized responses to product or technical questions. When a user enters a product inquiry or requests technical support, the system responds with appropriate information from an on-site knowledge base. Web-based delivery allows users to download a universe of files and documents to support their information needs. For example, the Web provides consumers with instant access to brochures, product manuals, and parts lists; while prospective home buyers can obtain instant quotes on mortgages, insurance, and other financial services.

To reach prospective customers and investors, companies also use a live or prerecorded **Webcast,** which is an audio or video media file distributed over the Internet. Radio and TV stations also use this technique to broadcast program material to their audiences.

TOOLKIT TIME

The Communication Tools in Part A of the Systems Analyst's Toolkit can help you communicate effectively with e-mail and other written communications. To learn more about these tools, turn to Part A of the four-part Toolkit that follows Chapter 12.

E-MAIL   E-mail is an essential means of internal and external business communication. Employees send and receive e-mail on local or wide area networks, including the Internet. Companies send new product information to customers via e-mail, and financial services companies use e-mail messages to confirm online stock trades. Employees use e-mail to exchange documents, data, and schedules and to share business-related information they need to perform their jobs. In many firms, e-mail has virtually replaced traditional memos and printed correspondence.

BLOGS   Web-based logs, called **blogs,** are another form of Web-based output. Because blogs are journals written from a particular point of view, they not only deliver facts to Web readers, but also provide opinions. Blogs are useful for posting news, reviewing current events, and promoting products.

INSTANT MESSAGING   This popular form of communication is another way for individuals and companies to communicate effectively over the Internet. Although some users feel that it can be a distraction, others like the constant flow of communication, especially as a team member in a collaborative situation.

WIRELESS DEVICES   Messages and data can be transmitted to a wide array of mobile devices, including tablet computers, smartphones, and similar wireless products that combine portable computing power, multimedia capability, and Internet access.

DIGITAL AUDIO, IMAGES, AND VIDEO   Sounds, images, and video clips can be captured, stored in digital format, and transmitted as output to users who can reproduce the content.

Audio or video output can be attached to an e-mail message or inserted as a clip in a Microsoft Word document. Businesses also use automated systems to handle voice transactions and provide information to customers. For example, using a telephone keypad, a customer can confirm an airline seat assignment, check a credit card balance, or determine the current price of a mutual fund.

If a picture is worth a thousand words, then digital images and video clips certainly are high-value output types that offer a whole new dimension. For example, an insurance adjuster with a digital camera phone can take a picture, submit the image via a wireless device, and receive immediate authorization to pay a claim on the spot. If images are a valuable form of output, video clips are even better in some situations. For example, video clips provide online virtual tours that allow realtors to show off the best features of homes they are marketing. The user can zoom in or out, and rotate the image in any direction.

PODCASTS   A **podcast** is a specially formatted digital audio file that can be downloaded by Internet users from a variety of content providers. Many firms use podcasts as sales and marketing tools, and to communicate with their own employees. Using software such as iTunes, you can receive a podcast, launch the file on your computer, and store it on your portable player. Podcasts can include images, sounds, and video.

AUTOMATED FACSIMILE SYSTEMS   An **automated facsimile** or **faxback** system allows a customer to request a fax using e-mail, via the company Web site, or by telephone. The response is transmitted in a matter of seconds back to the user's fax machine. Although most users prefer to download documents from the Web, many organizations, including the U.S. Department of Transportation, still offer an automated faxback service as another way to provide immediate response 24 hours a day.

COMPUTER OUTPUT TO MICROFILM (COM)   Computer output to microfilm (COM) is often used by large firms to scan and store images of original documents to provide high-quality records management and archiving. COM systems are especially important for legal reasons, or where it is necessary to display a signature, date stamp, or other visual features of a document.

COMPUTER OUTPUT TO DIGITAL MEDIA   This process is used when many paper documents must be scanned, stored in digital format, and retrieved quickly. For example, if an insurance company stores thousands of paper application forms, special software can treat the documents as data and extract information from a particular column or area on the form. Digital storage media can include magnetic tape, CDs, DVDs, and high-density laser disks.

SPECIALIZED FORMS OF OUTPUT   An incredibly diverse marketplace requires many forms of specialized output and devices. For example:

- Portable, Web-connected devices that can run multiple apps, handle multimedia output, and provide powerful, multipurpose communication for users
- Retail point-of-sale terminals that handle computer-based credit card transactions, print receipts, and update inventory records
- Automatic teller machines (ATMs) that can process bank transactions and print deposit and withdrawal slips
- Special-purpose printers that can produce labels, employee ID cards, driver's licenses, gasoline pump receipts, and, in some states, lottery tickets
- Plotters that can produce high-quality images such as blueprints, maps, and electronic circuit diagrams
- Electronic detection of data embedded in credit cards, bank cards, and employee identification cards

Input Technology

Input technology has changed dramatically in recent years. In addition to traditional devices and methods, there has been a rapid expansion of new hardware and ways to capture and enter data into a system, some of which are shown in Figure 8-22. Businesses are using the new technology to speed up the input process, reduce costs, and capture data in new forms, such as the digital signature shown in Figure 8-23.

INPUT TECHNOLOGY		
Traditional	**Evolving**	**Emerging**
Keyboard	Body motion detection	Brain-Computer Interface (BCI)
Mouse	Advanced voice recognition	Neural networks
Pointing devices	Biological feedback	Artificial intelligence (AI)
Microphone	Embedded magnetic data	Advanced motion sensors
OCR (optical character recognition)	RFID	Two-way satellite interface
MICR (magnetic ink character recognition)	Advanced optical recognition	Virtual environments
Graphic input devices	Physical adaptation devices	3-D technology

FIGURE 8-22 Input devices can be very traditional, or based on the latest technology.
© Cengage Learning 2014

Input methods should be cost-efficient, timely, and as simple as possible. Systems analysts study transactions and business operations to determine how and when data should enter the system. Usually, the first decision is whether to use batch or online input methods. Each method has advantages and disadvantages, and the systems analyst must consider the following factors.

BATCH INPUT Using **batch input**, data entry usually is performed on a specified time schedule, such as daily, weekly, monthly, or longer. For example, batch input occurs when a payroll department collects time cards at the end of the week and enters the data as a **batch**. Another example is a school that enters all grades for the academic term in a batch.

ONLINE INPUT Although batch input is used in specific situations, most business activity requires **online data entry**. The online method offers major advantages, including the immediate validation and availability of data. A popular online input method is **source data automation**, which combines online data entry and automated data capture using input devices such as **RFID tags** or **magnetic data strips**. Source data automation is fast and accurate, and minimizes human involvement in the translation process.

FIGURE 8-23 When a customer's signature is stored in digital form, it becomes input to the information system.
© tirc83/iStockphoto.com

Many large companies use a combination of source data automation and a powerful communication network to manage global operations instantly. Some common examples of source data automation are:

- Businesses that use point-of-sale (POS) terminals equipped with bar code scanners and magnetic swipe scanners to input credit card data.
- Automatic teller machines (ATMs) that read data strips on bank cards.
- Factory employees who use magnetic ID cards to clock on and off specific jobs so the company can track production costs accurately.
- Hospitals that imprint bar codes on patient identification bracelets and use portable scanners when gathering data on patient treatment and medication.
- Retail stores that use portable bar code scanners to log new shipments and update inventory data.
- Libraries that use handheld scanners to read optical strips on books.

TRADE-OFFS Although online input offers many advantages, it does have some disadvantages. For example, unless source data automation is used, manual data entry is slower and more expensive than batch input because it is performed at the time the transaction occurs and often done when computer demand is at its highest.

The decision to use batch or online input depends on business requirements. For example, hotel reservations must be entered and processed immediately, but hotels can enter their monthly performance figures in a batch. In fact, some input occurs naturally in batches. A cable TV provider, for example, receives customer payments in batches when the mail arrives.

SECURITY AND CONTROL ISSUES

A company must do everything in its power to protect its data. This includes not only the firm's own information, but that of its customers, employees, and suppliers. Most assets have a value, but corporate data is priceless because without safe, secure, accurate data, a company cannot function.

The following sections discuss output and input data security and control.

Output Security and Control

Output must be accurate, complete, current, and secure. Companies use various **output control** methods to maintain output integrity and security. For example, every report should include an appropriate title, report number or code, printing date, and time period covered. Reports should have pages that are numbered consecutively, identified as *Page nn of nn*, and the end of the report should be labeled clearly. Control totals and record counts should be reconciled against input totals and counts. Reports should be selected at random for a thorough check of correctness and completeness. All processing errors or interruptions must be logged so they can be analyzed.

Output security protects privacy rights and shields the organization's proprietary data from theft or unauthorized access. To ensure output security, you must perform several important tasks. First, limit the number of printed copies and use a tracking procedure to account for each copy. When printed output is distributed from a central location, you should use specific procedures to ensure that the output is delivered to authorized recipients only. That is especially true when reports contain sensitive information, such as payroll data. All sensitive reports should be stored in secure areas. All pages of confidential reports should be labeled appropriately.

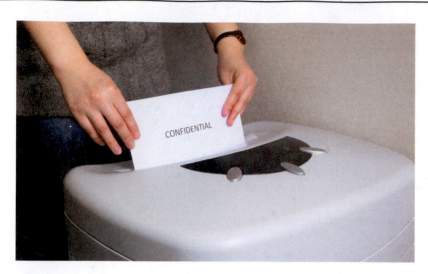

FIGURE 8-24   To maintain output security, it is important to shred sensitive material.

© Cupertino/Shutterstock.com

As shown in Figure 8-24, it is important to shred sensitive reports, out-of-date reports, and output from aborted print runs. Blank check forms must be stored in a secure location and be inventoried regularly to verify that no forms are missing. If signature stamps are used, they must be stored in a secure location away from the forms storage location.

In most organizations, the IT department is responsible for output control and security measures. Systems analysts must be concerned with security issues as they design, implement, and support information systems. Whenever possible, security should be designed into the system by using passwords, shielding sensitive data, and controlling user access. Physical security always will be necessary, especially in the case of printed output that is tangible and can be viewed and handled easily.

Enterprise-wide data access creates a whole new set of security and control issues. Many firms have responded to those concerns by installing diskless workstations. A **diskless workstation** is a network terminal that supports a full-featured user interface, but limits the printing or copying of data, except to certain network resources that can be monitored and controlled. This concept worked well with terminals that had limited hardware and software features.

However, over time, the number of removable media devices has expanded greatly, along with a wide variety of physical interfaces such as USB, FireWire, and PCMCIA, as well as wireless interfaces such as Wi-Fi and Bluetooth. A popular security solution is the use of a network-based application, often called a **port protector**, that controls access to and from workstation interfaces.

Input Security and Control

Input control includes the necessary measures to ensure that input data is correct, complete, and secure. You must focus on input control during every phase of input design, starting with source documents that promote data accuracy and quality. When a batch input method is used, the computer can produce an input log file that identifies and documents the data entered.

Every piece of information should be traceable back to the input data that produced it. That means that you must provide an **audit trail** that records the source of each data item and when it entered the system. In addition to recording the original source, an audit trail must show how and when data is accessed or changed, and by whom. All those actions must be logged in an audit trail file and monitored carefully.

A company must have procedures for handling source documents to ensure that data is not lost before it enters the system. All source documents that originate from outside the organization should be logged when they are received. Whenever source documents pass between departments, the transfer should be recorded.

Data security policies and procedures protect data from loss or damage, which is a vital goal in every organization. If the safeguards are not 100% effective, data recovery utilities should be able to restore lost or damaged data. Once data is entered, the company should store source documents in a safe location for some specified length of time. The company should have a **records retention policy** that meets all legal requirements and business needs.

Audit trail files and reports should be stored and saved. Then, if a data file is damaged, you can use the information to reconstruct the lost data. Data security also involves protecting data from unauthorized access. System sign-on procedures should prevent unauthorized individuals from entering the system, and users should change their passwords regularly. Having several levels of access also is advisable. For example, a data entry person might be allowed to *view* a credit limit, but not *change* it. Sensitive data can be **encrypted**, or coded, in a process called **encryption**, so only users with decoding software can read it.

WHERE DO WE GO FROM HERE?

The systems design phase begins with user interface design, followed by chapters on data design and system architecture. At this point, you should keep in mind that the deeper you go in the systems design process, the more expensive it will be to make changes and correct mistakes. You must be sure that you are aligned with users, and be alert for any changes or modifications that would affect your timetable or development costs. Two strategies that will help avoid major problems are a modular design approach and the use of prototyping. The following sections discuss these topics.

Modular Design

- In a **modular design**, you create individual components, called **modules**, which connect to a higher-level program or process. In a structured design, each module represents a specific process, which is shown on a DFD and documented in a process description. If you are using an object-oriented design, as described in Chapter 6, object classes are represented by code modules. You will learn more about modular design in Chapter 11, which describes systems implementation.

- You should try to design modules that perform a single function. Independent modules provide greater flexibility because they can be developed and tested individually, and then combined or reused later in the development process. Modular design is especially important in designing large-scale systems because separate teams of analysts and programmers can work on different areas and then integrate the results.

Prototyping

Prototyping produces an early, rapidly constructed working version of the proposed information system, called a **prototype**. Prototyping, which involves a repetitive sequence of analysis, design, modeling, and testing, is a common technique that can be used to design anything from a new home to a computer network. For example, engineers use a prototype to evaluate an aircraft design before production begins, as shown in the wind tunnel testing in Figure 8-25 on the next page.

User input and feedback is essential at every stage of the systems development process. Prototyping allows users to examine a model that accurately represents system outputs, inputs, interfaces, and processes. Users can "test-drive" the model in a risk-free environment and either approve it or request changes. In some situations, the prototype evolves into the final version of the information system. In other cases, the prototype is intended only to validate user requirements and is discarded afterward.

FIGURE 8-25 Wind tunnel testing is a typical example of prototyping.
Courtesy of NASA

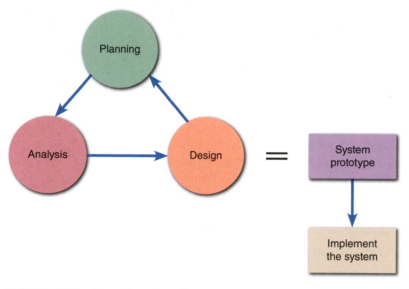

FIGURE 8-26 The end product of system prototyping is a working model of the information system, ready for implementation.
© Cengage Learning 2014

Perhaps the most intense form of prototyping occurs when agile methods are used. As you learned in Chapter 1, agile methods build a system by creating a series of prototypes and constantly adjusting them to user requirements. As the agile process continues, developers revise, extend, and merge earlier versions into the final product. An agile approach emphasizes continuous feedback, and each incremental step is affected by what was learned in the prior steps.

Systems analysts generally use two prototyping methods, system prototyping and design prototyping.

SYSTEM PROTOTYPING System prototyping produces a full-featured, working model of the information system. A system prototype that meets all requirements is ready for implementation, as shown in Figure 8-26. Because the model is "on track" for implementation, it is especially important to obtain user feedback, and to be sure that the prototype meets all requirements of users and management.

DESIGN PROTOTYPING Systems analysts also use prototyping to verify user requirements, after which the prototype is discarded and implementation continues, as shown in Figure 8-27. The approach is called **design prototyping**, or **throwaway prototyping**. In this case, the prototyping objectives are more limited, but no less important. The end product of design prototyping is a user-approved model that documents and benchmarks the features of the finished system. Design prototyping makes it possible to capture user input and approval while continuing to develop the system within the framework of the SDLC. Systems analysts typically use design prototyping as they construct outputs, inputs, and user interfaces.

TRADE-OFFS Prototyping offers many benefits, including the following:

- Users and systems developers can avoid misunderstandings.
- System developers can create accurate specifications for the finished system based on the prototype.
- Managers can evaluate a working model more effectively than a paper specification.
- Systems analysts can use a prototype to develop testing and training procedures before the finished system is available.
- Prototyping reduces the risk and potential financial exposure that occur when a finished system fails to support business needs.

Although most systems analysts believe that the advantages of prototyping far outweigh any disadvantages, you should consider the following potential problems:

- The rapid pace of development can create quality problems, which are not discovered until the finished system is operational.

- Other system requirements, such as reliability and maintainability, cannot be tested adequately using a prototype.

- In very complex systems, the prototype can become unwieldy and difficult to manage.

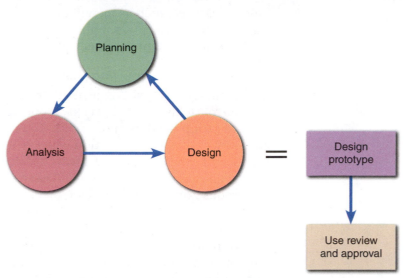

FIGURE 8-27 The end product of design prototyping is a user-approved model that documents and benchmarks the features of the finished system.
© Cengage Learning 2014

A QUESTION OF ETHICS

© faberfoto_it/iStockphoto

Jacob thought that he did a good job of designing the company's tech support Web page, but Emily, his supervisor, isn't so sure. She is concerned that Jacob's design is very similar to a page used by the company's major competitor, and she asked him whether he had used any HTML code from that site in his design. Although Jacob didn't copy any of the code, he did examine it in his Web browser to see how they handled some design issues.

Emily asked Jacob to investigate Web page copyright issues and report back to her. In his research, he learned that outright copying would be a copyright violation, but merely viewing other sites to get design ideas would be permissible. What is not so clear is the gray area in the middle. Jacob asked you, as a friend, for your opinion on this question: Even if no actual copying is involved, are there ethical constraints on how far you should go in using the creative work of others? How would you answer Jacob?

CHAPTER SUMMARY

The purpose of systems design is to create a physical model of the system that satisfies the design requirements that were defined during the systems analysis phase. The chapter began with a discussion of user interface design and human-computer interaction (HCI) concepts. A graphical user interface (GUI) uses visual objects and techniques that allow users to communicate effectively with the system. User-centered design principles include: understanding the business, maximizing graphic effectiveness, thinking like a user, using models and prototypes, focusing on usability, inviting feedback, and documenting everything.

When you design the interface itself, you should try to make it transparent; create an interface that is easy to learn and use; enhance user productivity; make it easy to obtain help or correct errors; minimize input data problems; provide feedback; create an attractive layout and design; and use familiar terms and images. You also can add control features, such as menu bars, toolbars, drop-down list boxes, dialog boxes, toggle buttons, list boxes, option buttons, check boxes, and command buttons. Controls are placed on a main switchboard, which is like a graphical version of a main menu.

The chapter described various types of printed reports, including detail, exception, and summary reports. You learned about the features and sections of reports, including control fields, control breaks, report headers and footers, page headers and footers, and group headers and footers. You also learned about other types of output, such as Web-based information delivery, audio output, instant messaging, podcasts, e-mail, and other specialized forms of output.

The discussion of input design began with a description of source documents and the various zones in a document, including the heading zone, the control zone, the instruction zone, the body zone, the totals zone, and the authorization zone. The discussion of data entry screen design explained the use of input masks and validation rules to reduce data errors. Input masks are like templates that only permit certain combinations of characters, and data validation rules can provide checks to ensure that inappropriate data is prevented from entering the system. These checks can include data sequence, existence, range and limit, reasonableness, and validity, among others.

You also learned about batch and online input methods, input media and procedures, and input volume. Input methods include data capture and data entry. Data capture, which may be automated, involves identifying and recording source data. Data entry involves converting source data into a computer-readable form and entering it into the system. New technology offers optical and voice recognition systems, biological feedback devices, motion sensors, and a variety of graphical input devices.

Finally, you learned about security and control. Output control includes physical protection of data and reports, and control of unauthorized ports or devices that can extract data from the system. Input controls include audit trails, encryption, password security, data security, and the creation of access levels to limit persons authorized to view or use data.

Key Terms

Chapter Exercises

Questions

1. Provide an overview of the systems design phase.
2. Explain IBM's view of user interface design.
3. Describe the habits of successful interface designers.
4. List the eight main rules for user interface design. How would you rank them in order of importance? Explain your answer.
5. How has input technology changed in recent years? Provide examples of traditional, evolving, and emerging input technology.
6. What are input masks? What are validation rules? Why are they important?
7. What is the difference between a detail report, a summary report, and an exception report?
8. What are the main principles of source document design?
9. Provide suggestions for reducing input volume.
10. Describe modular design, and explain the two main prototyping methods.

Discussion Topics

1. Some systems analysts maintain that source documents are unnecessary. They say that all input can be entered directly into the system, without wasting time in an intermediate step. Do you agree? Can you think of any situations where source documents are essential?
2. Some systems analysts argue, "Give users what they ask for. If they want lots of reports and reams of data, then that is what you should provide. Otherwise, they will feel that you are trying to tell them how to do their jobs." Others say, "Systems analysts should let users know what information can be obtained from the system. If you listen to users, you'll never get anywhere because they really don't know what they want and don't understand information systems." What do you think of these arguments?
3. Suppose your network support company employs 75 technicians who travel constantly and work at customer sites. Your task is to design an information system that provides technical data and information to the field team. What types of output and information delivery would you suggest for the system?
4. A user interface can be quite restrictive. For example, the interface design might not allow a user to exit to a Windows desktop or to log on to the Internet. Should a user interface include such restrictions? Why or why not?

Projects

1. Visit the administrative office at your school or a local company. Ask to see examples of input screens. Analyze the design and appearance of each screen, and try to identify at least one possible improvement.
2. Search the Web to find an especially good example of a user interface that includes guidelines in this chapter. Document your research and discuss it with your class.
3. Review Figure 8-6 on page 304 and the accompanying text about EHR usability. During 2012, The U.S. Department of Health and Human Services launched an initiative to focus on this issue, with more input from medical professionals. Research the current status of EHR usability, and describe all noteworthy developments.
4. Suggest at least two good examples and two bad examples of source document design.

Apply Your Knowledge

This section contains four mini-cases. Each case describes a situation, explains your role, and requires you to apply what you learned in the chapter.

1 Able Communications

Able Communications is a leading cable service provider in a metropolitan area. The new customer billing system has caused an increase in complaints. Zoe Valine, the office manager, asked you to investigate the situation. After interviewing data entry operators and observing the online data input process, you are fairly certain that most errors occur when data is entered.

Tasks

1. Write a brief memo to Zoe explaining the importance of data validation during the input process.
2. Suggest at least three specific data validation checks that might help reduce input errors.
3. Would a batch input system offer any advantages? Write a brief memo to Zoe stating your views.
4. Suppose that Able Communications is predicting 25% annual growth, on a current base of 90,000 customers. If the growth pattern holds, how many customers will Able have in three years? If it takes about 12 minutes to enter a new customer into the system, how many additional data entry operators will be needed to handle the growth next year? Assume that an operator works about 2,000 hours per year. Also assume a 30% annual attrition rate for existing customers.

2 Global Earth Mortgages

Global Earth Mortgages is a mortgage lender that makes home loans and resells the loans to investors. To resell loans, strict legal guidelines must be followed. Global Earth want to develop a Web-based loan application system based on these guidelines. Because legal compliance is critical to Global Earth's business, you decided to create a prototype that users can test before the final design is implemented. You will be meeting new week with Joanie James, Global Earth's president, and you need to prepare for the meeting.

Tasks

1. What is a prototype and why is it an important tool for system designers?
2. Explain two different ways that Global Earth might use prototypes.
3. What are some of the advantages and disadvantages of prototyping?
4. In addition to the wind tunnel shown in Figure 8-25 on page 332, think of at least three other products that would be good candidates for prototyping.

3 **Mountain High RV Sales**

Mountain High RV Sales offers new and used recreational vehicles and campers. The company has a dealer network, but also maintains a Web site where prospective buyers and sellers can browse through the inventory of new and used vehicles. Mountain High has grown, and needs a new information system to manage the inventory, dealer operations, and information about prospective customers. Reed Perry, the owner, asked you to design sample computer screens and reports that the new system might produce.

Tasks

1. Design a switchboard that includes the main information management functions that Mountain High might need. Create a storyboard with a design layout that allows customers to perform the following functions: Obtain information about new RVs and campers, obtain information about used vehicles, send an inquiry e-mail to Mountain High, learn more about the company, or review links to other RV camping-related sites.
2. Prospective buyers might want to search for RVs and campers by features, size, price range, or manufacturer. Develop a screen design that would permit those choices.
3. Suggest reports that might be useful to Mountain High's management.
4. Suggest the general layout for a Web-based source document that prospective sellers could use to describe their RVs and campers. The information should include key features, manufacturer, year, length, asking price, and a field to upload photos.

4 *Terrier News*

Terrier News is a monthly newsletter devoted to various breeds of terriers and topics of interest to terrier owners and breeders. Annie West, the editor and publisher, asked you to help her design a system to enter and manage the hundreds of classified ads that *Terrier News* publishes. Some ads are for dogs wanted; some are for dogs for sale; and some offer products and services.

Tasks

1. Design a suitable source document for ads that are telephoned or mailed in.
2. Explain user-centered design principles in a brief memo to Annie.
3. Suggest at least four user interface design guidelines for the new system.
4. Suggest several types of controls that might be used on a switchboard you plan to design. Explain why you chose each control, and create a storyboard that shows the switchboard layout.

Case Studies

Each chapter includes a Chapter Case, a Continuing Case, a Capstone Case, and an Online Case Simulation. You can learn more about the Online Case Simulation in the MIS CourseMate Features section.

Chapter Case: Tools 4 U

Tools 4 U is a tool rental company that reaches out to people with little or no experience. The firm has a staff of technicians to help customers select the right tools, show them how to use the tools, and provide 24/7 support.

Background

The company is working on an online system to manage its growing business. The company asked you to help design the user interface.

Tasks

1. Design a data entry screen for entering new members.
2. Design an online tool rental screen. You can use your imagination, but be sure to apply the principles discussed in this chapter.
3. Suggest at least three data validation rules that might help reduce input errors for the system.
4. Design a screen for managers, with weekly and monthly data on rentals, new customers, late charges, and anything else you think a store manager might want to review. Be sure to include numeric activity and dollar totals.

Continuing Case: Personal Trainer, Inc.

Personal Trainer, Inc. owns and operates fitness centers in a dozen Midwestern cities. The centers have done well, and the company is planning an international expansion by opening a new "supercenter" in the Toronto area. Personal Trainer's president, Cassia Umi, hired an IT consultant, Susan Park, to help develop an information system for the new facility. During the project, Susan will work closely with Gray Lewis, who will manage the new operation.

Background

Following the decision to use an in-house team to develop a design prototype, Susan began to work on the physical design for Personal Trainer's new information system. At this stage, she is ready to begin working with Gray on the output and user interface design. Together, Susan and Gray will seek to develop a user-centered design that is easy to learn and use. Personal Trainer users will include managers, fitness instructors, support staff, and members themselves.

Tasks

1. For the prototype user interface, design a switchboard that leads from main sections to subsections of related system tasks. The main sections may include member information, registration, payments, fitness instructors, and any other top-level sections necessary for Personal Trainer's system. Subsections may include account information, class registration, schedules, and class rosters. Prepare storyboards that show the proposed screens, including at least two sublevel tasks for each action.

(continues)

Continuing Case: Personal Trainer, Inc.

2. Members need to be able to register for classes online. Follow the guidelines and suggestions in this chapter, and design an online class registration screen form.

3. In addition to being available online, members can register for fitness classes through the mail or by dropping off a mail-in form. Follow the guidelines and suggestions in this chapter, and design a paper source document.

4. Personal Trainer is very concerned about the security and protection of the information they collect in the new information system. Prepare a memo to Gray and Personal Trainer's staff that explains the input and output security controls that will be built into the new systems and the policies that will enforce these controls.

Capstone Case: New Century Wellness Group

New Century Wellness Group offers a holistic approach to healthcare with an emphasis on preventive medicine as well as traditional medical care. In your role as an IT consultant, you will help New Century develop a new information system.

Background

Based on your presentation to New Century's partners, they decided to move forward with in-house development of a new business support system.

They liked the idea of a vertical software package, but they want to be able to customize the user interface because New Century's business functions are more varied. However, it is very important that the new system allow future integration with vertical packages such as electronic health records, computerized provider order entry, and a clinical decision support system.

Using the information you gained in the systems planning and analysis phases of the SDLC, you sit down to begin designing the user interface of the New Century's business support system. Before you begin, you decide to review the case studies, DFDs, and object-oriented diagrams you prepared in Chapters 5 and 6.

Tasks

1. Using the guidelines and suggestions in this chapter, design a user interface. Draw storyboards, then use Microsoft Access or another form-designing application to create the screens.

2. Determine the data required for a new patient. Design an input source document that will be used to capture the patient's data and a data entry screen to enter the information into the system.

3. What control features will you use in the input screens to aid in data entry? Give a specific example of how you will use at least eight different control features in the design of the user interface.

4. In addition to printed reports, what other output technologies could be used by New Century?

CASE Tool Workshop

Systems analysts use CASE tools to help them plan, build, and maintain information systems. To learn more about CASE tools, turn to Part B of the Toolkit that follows Chapter 12. You can complete these tasks with the Visible Analyst® CASE tool, which is available with this textbook, or a similar tool.

Background

Suppose you work for an IT consulting firm that specializes in user interface design. One of the firm's clients is a CASE tool vendor. Before releasing the next version of its tool, the vendor wants your firm to analyze the user interface and offer suggestions about improving it if possible.

Tasks

1. Study the user interface in Visible Analyst or another CASE tool, consider the guidelines described in this chapter, and prepare a detailed recommendation for interface design changes, if any. Be sure to explain your reasons, and the results you hope to achieve.

2. Assume that the client agreed to all your recommendations, but the improved version will not be available for six months. In the interim, the client wants you to write step-by-step guidelines to help users navigate the existing interface. Select a user interface feature that definitely needs improvement, and write a brief set of tips and user-friendly suggestions.

MIS CourseMate Features

If you have an MIS CourseMate access code, you can reinforce and extend your learning with premium content created for this textbook. For example, you can launch interactive Video Learning Sessions to help you understand systems development concepts and practice your skills. In addition, you can use MindTap Reader, which is a full, interactive, digital e-book.

MIS CourseMate also offers many learning features within each chapter, including an Online Case Simulation, a Critical Thinking Challenge, Video Learning Session Tasks, and a set of Learn It Online activities. To log on to the MIS CourseMate site at **www.cengagebrain.com**, you must create a student account and register this book.

Online Case Simulation: SCR Associates

Session 8: User Interface Design

Overview

The SCR Associates case study is a Web-based simulation that allows you to practice your skills in a real-world environment. The firm offers IT consulting, solutions, and training. SCR plans to open a new high-tech training center, and needs to develop a Training Information Management System (TIMS) to support the center. You are a newly hired systems analyst reporting to Jesse Baker, systems group manager, and will help her develop the system.

    The case study takes you to the SCR Web site, where you receive e-mail and voice mail messages from Jesse, obtain information from SCR's resource libraries, and perform various tasks. Jesse has high standards, but seems very fair. She made it clear that she expects your work to be accurate, thorough, and professional.

Before You Begin

To prepare for this work session, you should review the following topics:

- Human-computer interaction (HCI)
- Rules for successful interface design

How Do I Use the Online Case Simulation?

- Read the preview, and review the Chapter 1 background material, if necessary.
- Visit the MIS CourseMate Web site at **www.cengagebrain.com**, locate the **SCR Case Simulation**, and click the **intranet** link. Enter your name and the password **sad10e.**
- When the opening screen displays, select this session. Then check your e-mail and voice mail, and start to work on your task list.

Preview: Session 8

Now that the overall data design is complete, Jesse Baker wants you to work on user interface design. You will consider user needs, and apply principles of human-computer interaction to build a user-centered interface that is easy to learn and use. You also will consider input masks, data validation checks, source documents, and printed reports.

Critical Thinking Challenge

In addition to technical ability, IT professionals need critical thinking skills. This feature can help you practice perception, organization, analysis, problem-solving, and decision-making skills that will be valuable in the workplace. You can visit **www.criticalthinking.org** to learn more about critical thinking and why it is so important.

Background

This week, the IT team is working on user interface design for the new C^3 system. One goal is to reduce input errors by using validation rules and input masks. The team leader has assigned you to do research and develop a recommendation. To perform these tasks, you must navigate to the Microsoft Access Help area, where you will see examples of validation rules and input masks.

Based on requirements modeling, you know that the new C^3 system will store personal data about customers, their buying habits, and their interests. To reduce errors, the C^3 user interface will use various input masks. Here are five sample data items, with descriptions and examples:

Data Item	Description	Examples
First Name	Must start with a capital letter followed by at least one, and up to nine more lowercase letters.	Li Stephanie
Middle Initial	May have up to one capital letter, or none.	J
Last Name	Must start with a capital letter followed by at least one, and up to 11 more lowercase letters.	Steinbrenner Ho
Category	Must start with two capital letters followed by two digits.	AB12 XY01
Postal Code	Must have five digits, and may be followed by a hyphen and four more digits.	12345 12345-9999

In addition to input masks, the team leader wants you to learn about validation rules. Specifically, she wants you to go back to the Microsoft Access Help area and review the explanation of validation rules and the examples.

Practice Tasks

Visit the MIS CourseMate Web site at **www.cengagebrain.com**. Then navigate to the resources for this chapter and locate the **Critical Thinking Challenge** feature. You will complete two Practice Tasks, using what you learned in the chapter. Then you can check your answers to be sure you're ready for the Challenge Tasks.

Challenge Tasks

After you complete the Practice Tasks, you learn about new developments at Game Technology. Now that you are familiar with input masks and validation rules, your team leader wants you to review two more data items. To continue, navigate to the **Critical Thinking Challenge** feature for this chapter, select the **Challenge Tasks**, and follow the instructions.

Video Learning Sessions

Video Learning Sessions can help you understand systems development concepts and practice your skills. In this scenario, you will help design a Video Learning Session for this chapter.

© craftvision/iStockph

Before You Begin

Review the chapter and list the main topics. Which ones did you find difficult to understand, and why? Can you think of other ways to explain the topics?

Training Tasks

Suppose the IT training manager wants to encourage team members to watch the Video Learning Sessions. She wants you to submit a proposal for a new session that would explain the key topics in this chapter.

1. Which topics would you choose?
2. What specific skills or concepts would you include in the session?
3. How would you present the material?
4. Describe at least three graphic images that you would include in the video session.

Learn It Online

In each chapter, you can use this feature to apply your knowledge and practice your skills. The exercises include Chapter Reinforcement Questions, Flash Cards, Practice Tests, and various games, such as *Who Wants To Be a Computer Genius?*, *Wheel of Terms,* and the *Crossword Puzzle Challenge.*

CHAPTER 9 Data Design

Chapter 9 is the second of three chapters in the systems design phase of the SDLC. In this chapter, you will focus on data design skills that are necessary to construct the physical model of the information system.

INTRODUCTION

OBJECTIVES

When you finish this chapter, you will be able to:

- Explain file-oriented systems and how they differ from database management systems
- Explain data design terminology, including entities, fields, common fields, records, files, tables, and key fields
- Describe data relationships, draw an entity-relationship diagram, define cardinality, and use cardinality notation
- Explain the concept of normalization
- Explain the importance of codes and describe various coding schemes
- Explain data warehousing and data mining
- Differentiate between logical and physical storage and records
- Explain data control measures

During the systems analysis phase, you created a logical model of the system. Now, you must decide how data will be organized, stored, and managed. These are important issues that affect data quality and consistency.

This chapter begins with a review of data design concepts and terminology, then discusses file-based systems and database systems, including Web-based databases. You will learn how to create entity-relationship diagrams that show the relationships among data elements, and you will learn how to use normalization concepts. You also will learn about using codes to represent data items. The chapter concludes with a discussion of data storage and access issues, including data warehousing and data mining, physical design, logical and physical records, data storage formats, and data control.

If you have MIS CourseMate, you can view four Video Learning Sessions that explain entity-relationship diagrams and data normalization rules.

PREVIEW CASE: Mountain View College Bookstore

Background: Wendy Lee, manager of college services at Mountain View College, wants a new information system that will improve efficiency and customer service at the three college bookstores.

In this part of the case, Tina Allen (systems analyst) and David Conroe (student intern) are talking about data design issues.

Participants: Tina and David
Location: Tina's office, Thursday morning, December 5, 2013
Project status: Tina and David have completed their user interface design tasks and are ready to work on data design for the new system
Discussion topics: Data design terms and concepts, cardinality, relational databases, normalization, Web-based design, codes, and physical design issues

Tina: Good morning, David. Now that we have a logical model of the bookstore information system, we're ready for the next step. We have to select an overall data design strategy. I think we should start by looking at a relational database, rather than a file processing design.

David: *What are the pros and cons?*

Tina: Well, in some situations file processing systems are better, especially when you have to process large numbers of records in a sequence. But in our case, I think a relational database would be more powerful and flexible.

David: *I know what a database is, but what do you mean by the term* relational?

Tina: In a relational database, all the entities — the individual people, places, events, and transactions — are stored in separate locations called tables, which are related or linked together. That means you have to enter an item of data only once, and you can access all the data items just as if they were all stored in a single location.

David: *That makes sense. How do we decide what data goes where?*

Tina: We'll start by creating an entity-relationship diagram. Then we'll develop a set of table designs that follow a set of rules called normalization.

David: *I've heard that term before. Aren't there several different levels of normalization, called normal forms?*

Tina: Yes, and we want our data to be in what's called third normal form, which is what most business-related systems use. We also will consider using various codes to represent data items.

David: *I know that we decided to build the system to run on the college network and then migrate to a Web-based system in the future. But shouldn't we use a design that will make it easy to migrate to the Web?*

Tina: Yes, and a relational database will be the most flexible approach.

David: *Sounds good. Any other issues?*

Tina: Well, we need to consider some physical design issues, too. Here's a task list to get us started:

FIGURE 9-1 Typical data design task list.

© Cengage Learning 2014

DATA DESIGN CONCEPTS

Systems analysts must understand basic data design concepts, including data structures and the evolution of the relational database model.

Data Structures

A **data structure** is a framework for organizing, storing, and managing data. Data structures consist of files or tables that interact in various ways. Each **file** or **table** contains data about people, places, things, or events. For example, one file or table might contain data about customers, and other files or tables might store data about products, orders, suppliers, or employees. Many older, legacy systems were called file-oriented. Over time, the modern relational database became a standard model for systems developers. The following example of an auto service shop will compare the two concepts.

Mario and Danica: A Data Design Example

Figure 9-2 shows an auto shop mechanic at work. Imagine two shops that are very similar, but use two different information system designs. Let's call them Mario's Auto Shop and Danica's Auto Shop. Mario uses two file-oriented systems, while Danica uses a database management system.

FIGURE 9-2   In the example shown here, data about the mechanic, the customer, and the brake job might be stored in a file-oriented system or in a database system.
© Shutterstock/Lisa F. Young

MARIO'S AUTO SHOP   Mario relies on two **file-oriented systems**, sometimes called **file processing systems**, to manage his business. The two systems store data in separate files that are not connected or linked. Figure 9-3 shows Mario's file-oriented systems:

- The MECHANIC SYSTEM uses the MECHANIC file to store data about shop employees
- The JOB SYSTEM uses the JOB file to store data about work performed at the shop.

Unfortunately, using two separate systems means that some data is stored in two different places, and the data might or might not be consistent. For example, three data items (Mechanic No, Name, and Pay Rate) are stored in both files. This redundancy is a major disadvantage of file-oriented systems because it threatens data quality and integrity. In fact, Figure 9-3 includes a typical discrepancy. Can you spot it?

DANICA'S AUTO SHOP   Danica uses a database management system (DBMS) with two separate tables that are joined, so they act like one large table, as shown in Figure 9-4. In Danica's SHOP OPERATIONS SYSTEM, the tables are linked by the Mechanic No field, which is called a **common field** because it connects the tables. Notice that except for the common field, no other data items are duplicated. The DBMS design, also called a **relational database** or **relational model**, was introduced in the 1970s and continues to be the dominant approach for organizing, storing, and managing business data.

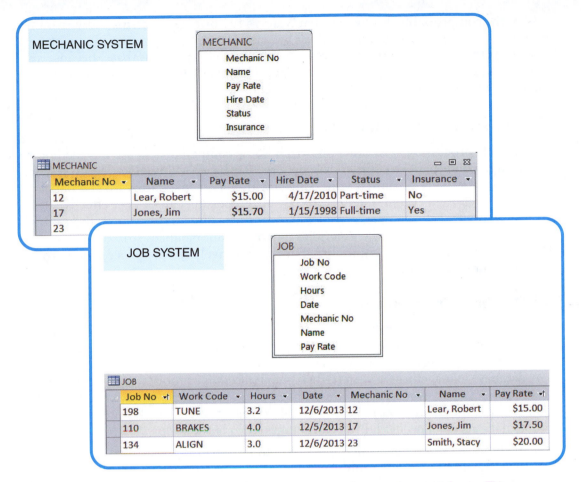

FIGURE 9-3   Mario's shop uses two separate systems, so certain data must be entered twice. This redundancy is inefficient, and can produce data errors.

© Cengage Learning 2014

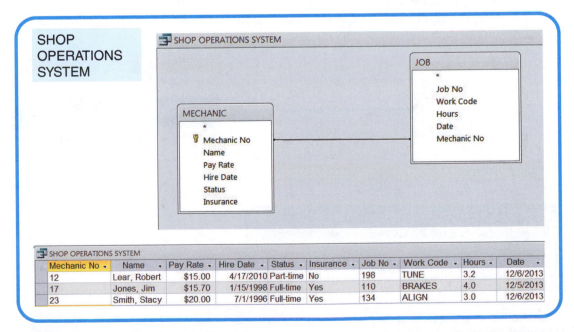

FIGURE 9-4   Danica's SHOP OPERATIONS SYSTEM uses a database design, which avoids duplication. The data can be viewed as if it were one large table, regardless of where the data is stored physically.

© Cengage Learning 2014

By now, you probably discovered that Mario's file-oriented systems show two different pay rates for Jim Jones, most likely because of a data entry error in one of them. That type of error could not occur in Danica's relational database, because an employee's pay rate is stored in only one place. However, DBMSs are not immune to data entry problems, which are discussed in detail later in this chapter.

Is File Processing Still Important?

Although file processing is an older approach, some companies still use this method to handle large volumes of structured data on a regular basis. Many older legacy systems utilized file processing because it worked well with mainframe hardware and batch input. Although it has very limited use today, file processing can be cost-effective in certain situations. For example, consider a credit card company that posts thousands of daily transactions from a TRANSACTIONS file to account balances stored in a CUSTOMERS file, as shown in Figure 9-5. For that relatively simple process, file processing might be an option.

The Database Environment

A database provides an overall framework that avoids data redundancy and supports a real-time, dynamic environment. Figure 9-6 shows a company-wide database that supports four separate information systems.

A **database management system (DBMS)** is a collection of tools, features, and interfaces that enables users to add, update, manage, access, and analyze data. From a user's point of view, the main advantage of a DBMS is that it offers timely, interactive, and flexible data access. Specific DBMS advantages include the following:

- **Scalability**, which means that a system can be expanded, modified, or downsized easily to meet the rapidly changing needs of a business enterprise. For example, if a company decides to add data about secondary suppliers of material it uses, a new table can be added to the relational database and linked with a common field.

- **Economy of scale.** Database design allows better utilization of hardware. If a company maintains an enterprise-wide database, processing is less expensive using

FIGURE 9-5 A credit card company that posts thousands of daily transactions might consider a file processing option.

© Cengage Learning 2014

powerful servers and communication networks. The inherent efficiency of high-volume processing on larger computers is called **economy of scale**.

- Enterprise-wide application. Typically, a DBMS is managed by a person called a **database administrator (DBA)**, who assesses overall requirements and maintains the database for the benefit of the entire organization rather than a single department or user. Database systems can support enterprise-wide applications more effectively than file processing systems.

- Stronger standards. Effective database administration helps ensure that standards for data names, formats, and documentation are followed uniformly throughout the organization.

- Better security. The DBA can define authorization procedures to ensure that only legitimate users can access the database and can allow different users to have different levels of access. Most DBMSs provide sophisticated security support.

- Data independence. Systems that interact with a DBMS are relatively independent of how the physical data is maintained. That design provides the DBA flexibility to alter data structures without modifying information systems that use the data.

FIGURE 9-6 In this example, a sales database can support four separate business systems.

© Cengage Learning 2014

Although the trend is toward enterprise-wide database design, many companies still use a combination of centralized DBMSs and smaller, department-level database systems. Why is this so? Most large businesses view data as a company-wide resource that must be accessible to users throughout the company. At the same time, other factors encourage a decentralized design, including network expense; a reluctance to move away from smaller, more flexible systems; and a realization that enterprise-wide DBMSs can be highly complex and expensive to maintain. The compromise, in many cases, is a client/server design, where processing is shared among several computers. Client/server systems are described in detail in Chapter 10. As with many design decisions, the best solution depends on the individual circumstances.

DBMS COMPONENTS

A DBMS provides an interface between a database and users who need to access the data. Although users are concerned primarily with an easy-to-use interface and support for their business requirements, a systems analyst must understand all of the components of a DBMS. In addition to interfaces for users, database administrators, and related systems, a DBMS also has a data manipulation language, a schema and subschemas, and a physical data repository, as shown in Figure 9-7.

Interfaces for Users, Database Administrators, and Related Systems

When users, database administrators, and related information systems request data and services, the DBMS processes the request, manipulates the data, and provides a response.

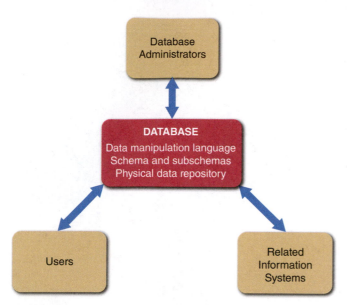

FIGURE 9-7 In addition to interfaces for users, database administrators, and related information systems, a DBMS also has a data manipulation language, a schema and subschemas, and a physical data repository.

© Cengage Learning 2014

USERS Users typically work with predefined queries and switchboard commands, but also use query languages to access stored data. A **query language** allows a user to specify a task without specifying how the task will be accomplished. Some query languages use natural language commands that resemble ordinary English sentences. With a **query by example (QBE)** language, the user provides an example of the data requested. Many database programs also generate **SQL (Structured Query Language)**, which is a language that allows client workstations to communicate with servers and mainframe computers. Figure 9-8 shows a QBE request for all Lime Squeeze or Blue Candy 2013 Ford Fiestas with power moonroof. The QBE request generates the SQL commands shown at the bottom of Figure 9-8.

DATABASE ADMINISTRATORS A DBA is responsible for DBMS management and support. DBAs are concerned with data security and integrity, preventing unauthorized access, providing backup

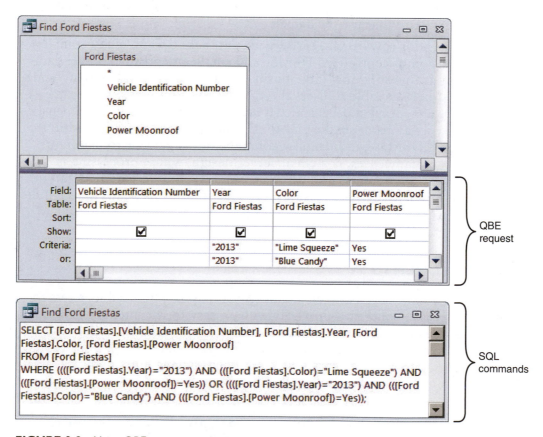

FIGURE 9-8 Using QBE, a user can display all 2013 Ford Fiestas that have a power moonroof and are either Lime Squeeze or Blue Candy color.

© Cengage Learning 2014

and recovery, audit trails, maintaining the database, and supporting user needs. Most DBMSs provide utility programs to assist the DBA in creating and updating data structures, collecting and reporting patterns of database usage, and detecting and reporting database irregularities.

RELATED INFORMATION SYSTEMS A DBMS can support several related information systems that provide input to, and require specific data from, the DBMS. Unlike a user interface, no human intervention is required for two-way communication between the DBMS and the related systems.

Data Manipulation Language

A **data manipulation language (DML)** controls database operations, including storing, retrieving, updating, and deleting data. Most commercial DBMSs, such as Oracle and IBM's DB/2, use a DML. Some database products, such as Microsoft Access, also provide an easy-to-use graphical environment that enables users to control operations with menu-driven commands.

Schema

The complete definition of a database, including descriptions of all fields, tables, and relationships, is called a **schema**. You also can define one or more subschemas. A **subschema** is a view of the database used by one or more systems or users. A subschema defines only those portions of the database that a particular system or user needs or is allowed to access. For example, to protect individual privacy, you might not want to allow a project management system to retrieve employee pay rates. In that case, the project management system subschema would not include the pay rate field. Database designers also use subschemas to restrict the level of access permitted. For example, specific users, systems, or locations might be permitted to create, retrieve, update, or delete data, depending on their needs and the company's security policies.

Physical Data Repository

In Chapter 5, you learned about a data dictionary, which describes all data elements included in the logical design. At this stage of the systems development process, the data dictionary is transformed into a physical data repository, which also contains the schema and subschemas. The physical repository might be centralized, or it might be distributed at several locations. In addition, the stored data might be managed by a single DBMS, or several systems. To resolve potential database connectivity and access problems, companies use ODBC-compliant software that enables communication among various systems and DBMSs. **ODBC**, which stands for **open database connectivity**, is an industry-standard protocol that makes it possible for software from different vendors to interact and exchange data. ODBC uses SQL statements that the DBMS understands and can execute, similar to the ones shown in Figure 9-7. Another common standard is called **JDBC**, or **Java database connectivity**. JDBC enables Java applications to exchange data with any database that uses SQL statements and is JDBC-compliant.

You will learn more about physical design issues in Chapter 10, which discusses system architecture, and in Chapter 11, which discusses system implementation and data conversion.

WEB-BASED DATA DESIGN

The following sections discuss characteristics of Web-based design, connecting to the Web, and online data security.

Overview

Figure 9-9 lists some major characteristics of Web-based data design. In a Web-based design, the Internet serves as the front end, or interface, for the database management system. Internet technology provides enormous power and flexibility because the system is not tied to any specific combination of hardware and software. Access to the database requires only a Web browser and an Internet connection. Web-based systems are popular because they offer ease of access, cost-effectiveness, and world-wide connectivity — all of which are vital to companies that must compete in a global economy.

Connecting to the Web

To access data in a Web-based system, the database must be connected to the Internet or intranet. The database and the Internet speak two different languages, however. Databases are created and managed by using various languages and commands that have nothing to do with HTML, which is the language of the Web. The objective is to connect the database to the Web and enable data to be viewed and updated.

CHARACTERISTIC	EXPLANATION
Global access	The Internet enables worldwide access, using existing infrastructure and standard telecommunications protocols.
Ease of use	Web browsers provide a familiar interface that is user-friendly and easily learned.
Multiple platforms	Web-based design is not dependent on a specific combination of hardware or software. All that is required is a browser and an Internet connection.
Cost effectiveness	Initial investment is relatively low because the Internet serves as the communication network. Users require only a browser, and Web-based systems do not require powerful workstations. Flexibility is high because numerous outsourcing options exist for development, hosting, maintenance, and system support.
Security issues	Security is a universal issue, but Internet connectivity raises special concerns. These can be addressed with a combination of good design, software that can protect the system and detect intrusion, stringent rules for passwords and user identification, and vigilant users and managers.
Adaptability issues	The Internet offers many advantages in terms of access, connectivity, and flexibility. Migrating a traditional database design to the Web, however, can require design modification, additional software, and some added expense.

FIGURE 9-9 Web-based design characteristics include global access, ease of use, multiple platforms, cost effectiveness, security issues, and adaptability issues. In a Web-based design, the Internet serves as the front end, or interface, for the database management system. Access to the database requires only a Web browser and an Internet connection.

© Cengage Learning 2014

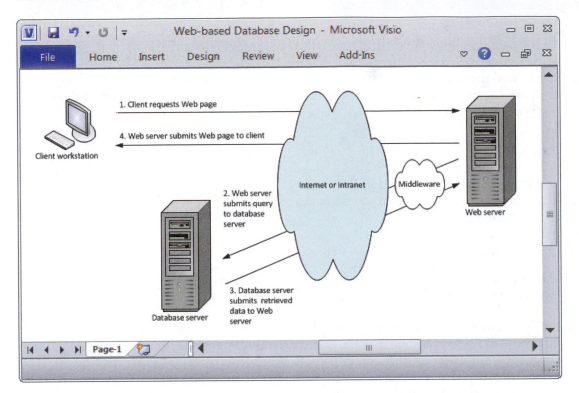

FIGURE 9-10   When a client workstation requests a Web page (1), the Web server uses middleware to generate a data query to the database server (2). The database server responds (3), and middleware translates the retrieved data into an HTML page that can be sent by the Web server and displayed by the user's browser (4).

© Cengage Learning 2014

To bridge the gap, it is necessary to use **middleware**, which is software that integrates different applications and allows them to exchange data. Middleware can interpret client requests in HTML form and translate the requests into commands that the database can execute. When the database responds to the commands, middleware translates the results into HTML pages that can be displayed by the user's browser, as shown in Figure 9-10. Notice that the four steps in the process can take place using the Internet or a company intranet as the communications channel.

The Middleware Resource Center shown in Figure 9-11 offers definitions, examples, and links to middleware topics. Middleware is discussed in more detail in Chapter 10.

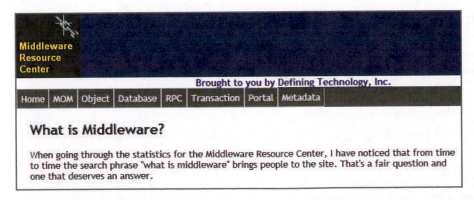

FIGURE 9-11   The Middleware Resource Center shown is a good starting point to learn more about middleware. The site offers an interesting answer to the question shown here.

© 1997–2008, Defining Technology, Inc.

Data Security

Web-based data must be secure, yet easily accessible to authorized users. To achieve this goal, well-designed systems provide security at three levels: the database itself, the Web server, and the telecommunication links that connect the components of the system.

Data security is discussed in this chapter and in Chapter 12, Managing System Support and Security.

DATA DESIGN TERMS

Using the concepts discussed in the previous section, a systems analyst can select a design approach and begin to construct the system. The first step is to understand data design terminology.

Definitions

Data design terms include entity, table, file, field, record, tuple, and key field. These terms are explained in the following sections.

ENTITY An **entity** is a person, place, thing, or event for which data is collected and maintained. For example, an online sales system may include entities named CUSTOMER, ORDER, PRODUCT, and SUPPLIER. When you prepared DFDs during the systems analysis phase, you identified various entities and data stores. Now you will consider the relationships among the entities.

TABLE OR FILE Data is organized into tables or files. A **table**, or file, contains a set of related records that store data about a specific entity. Tables and files are shown as two-dimensional structures that consist of vertical columns and horizontal rows. Each column represents a field, or characteristic of the entity, and each row represents a record, which is an individual instance, or occurrence of the entity. For example, if a company has 10,000 customers, the CUSTOMER table will include 10,000 records, each representing a specific customer.

Although they can have different meanings in a specific context, the terms *table* and *file* often can be used interchangeably.

FIELD A **field**, also called an **attribute**, is a single characteristic or fact about an entity. For example, a CUSTOMER entity might include the Customer ID, First Name, Last Name, Address, City, State, Postal Code, and E-mail Address.

A **common field** is an attribute that appears in more than one entity. Common fields can be used to link entities in various types of relationships.

RECORD A **record**, also called a **tuple** (rhymes with couple), is a set of related fields that describes one instance, or occurrence, of an entity, such as one customer, one order, or one product. A record might have one or dozens of fields, depending on what information is needed.

Key Fields

During the systems design phase, you use **key fields** to organize, access, and maintain data structures. The four types of keys are primary keys, candidate keys, foreign keys, and secondary keys.

PRIMARY KEY A **primary key** is a field or combination of fields that uniquely and minimally identifies a particular member of an entity. For example, in a customer table the customer number is a unique primary key because no two customers can have the same customer number. That key also is minimal because it contains no information beyond what is needed to identify the customer. In a CUSTOMER table, a Customer ID might be used as a unique primary key. Customer ID is an example of a primary key based on a single field.

A primary key also can be composed of two or more fields. For example, if a student registers for three courses, his or her student number will appear in three records in the registration system. If one of those courses has 20 students, 20 separate records will exist for that course number — one record for each student who registered.

In the registration file, neither the student number nor the course ID is unique, so neither field can be a primary key. To identify a specific student in a specific course, the primary key must be a combination of student number and course ID. In that case, the primary key is called a **combination key**. A combination key also can be called a **composite key**, a **concatenated key**, or a **multivalued key**.

Figure 9-12 on the next page shows four different tables: STUDENT, ADVISOR, COURSE, and GRADE. Three of these tables have single-field primary keys. Notice that in the GRADE table, however, the primary key is a combination of two fields: STUDENT NUMBER and COURSE NUMBER.

CANDIDATE KEY Sometimes you have a choice of fields or field combinations to use as the primary key. Any field that could serve as a primary key is called a **candidate key**. For example, if every employee has a unique employee number, then you could use either the employee number or the Social Security number as a primary key. Because you can designate only one field as a primary key, you should select the field that contains the least amount of data and is the easiest to use. Any field that is not a primary key or a candidate key is called a **nonkey field**.

The primary keys shown in Figure 9-12 also are candidate keys. Another candidate key is the COURSE-DESCRIPTION field in the COURSE table. What about the OFFICE field in the ADVISOR table? It could not be a candidate key because more than one advisor might share the same office.

FOREIGN KEY Recall that a common field exists in more than one table and can be used to form a relationship, or link, between the tables. For example, in Figure 9-12, the ADVISOR NUMBER field appears in both the STUDENT table and the ADVISOR table and joins the tables together. Notice that ADVISOR NUMBER is a primary key in the ADVISOR table, where it uniquely identifies each advisor, and is a foreign key in the STUDENT table. A **foreign key** is a field in one table that must match a primary key value in another table in order to establish the relationship between the two tables.

Unlike a primary key, a foreign key need not be unique. For example, Carlton Smith has advisor number 49. The value 49 must be a unique value in the ADVISOR table because it is the primary key, but 49 can appear any number of times in the STUDENT table, where the advisor number serves as a foreign key.

Figure 9-12 also shows how two foreign keys can serve as a composite primary key in another table. Consider the GRADE table at the bottom of the figure. The two fields that form the primary key for the GRADE table are both foreign keys: the STUDENT NUMBER field, which must match a student number in the STUDENT table, and the COURSE NUMBER field, which must match one of the course IDs in the COURSE table.

How can these two foreign keys serve as a primary key in the GRADE table? When you study the table, you will notice that student numbers and course IDs can appear any number of times, but the *combination* of a specific student and a specific course

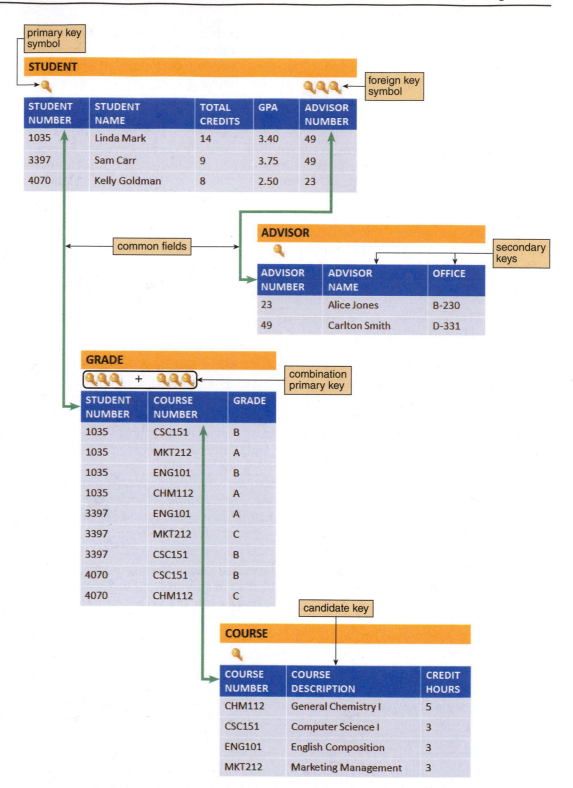

FIGURE 9-12   Examples of common fields, primary keys, candidate keys, foreign keys, and secondary keys.
© Cengage Learning 2014

occurs only once. For example, student 1035 appears four times and course CSC151 appears three times — but there is only *one* combined instance of student 1035 *and* course CSC151. Because the combination of the specific student (1035) and the specific course (CSC151) is unique, it ensures that the grade (B) will be assigned to the proper student in the proper course.

SECONDARY KEY A **secondary key** is a field or combination of fields that can be used to access or retrieve records. Secondary key values are not unique. For example, if you need to access records for only those customers in a specific postal code, you would use the postal code field as a secondary key. Secondary keys also can be used to sort or display records in a certain order. For example, you could use the GPA field in a STUDENT file to display records for all students in grade point order.

The need for a secondary key arises because a table can have only one primary key. In a CUSTOMER file, the CUSTOMER NUMBER is the primary key, so it must be unique. You might know a customer's name, but not the customer's number. For example, you might want to access a customer named James Morgan, but you do not know his customer number. If you search the table using the CUSTOMER NAME field as a secondary key, you can retrieve the records for all customers named James Morgan and then select the correct one.

In Figure 9-12, student name and advisor names are identified as secondary keys, but other fields also could be used. For example, to find all students who have a particular advisor, you could use the ADVISOR NUMBER field in the STUDENT table as a secondary key.

Referential Integrity

Validity checks can help avoid data input errors. One type of validity check, called **referential integrity**, is a set of rules that avoids data inconsistency and quality problems. In a relational database, referential integrity means that a foreign key value cannot be entered in one table unless it matches an existing primary key in another table. For example, referential integrity would prevent you from entering a customer order in an order table unless that customer already exists in the customer table. Without referential integrity, you might have an order called an **orphan**, because it had no related customer.

In the example shown in Figure 9-12, referential integrity will not allow a user to enter an advisor number (foreign key value) in the STUDENT table unless a valid advisor number (primary key value) already exists in the ADVISOR table.

Referential integrity also can prevent the deletion of a record if the record has a primary key that matches foreign keys in another table. For example, suppose that an advisor resigns to accept a position at another school. You cannot delete the advisor from the ADVISOR table while records in the STUDENT table still refer to that advisor number. Otherwise, the STUDENT records would be orphans. To avoid the problem, students must be reassigned to other advisors by changing the value in the ADVISOR NUMBER field; then the advisor record can be deleted.

When creating a relational database, you can build referential integrity into the design. Figure 9-13 on the next page shows a Microsoft Access screen that identifies a common field and allows the user to enforce referential integrity rules.

Video Learning Session
Entity-Relationship Diagrams

If you have an MIS CourseMate access code, you can launch interactive Video Learning Sessions to help you understand systems development concepts and practice your skills. You can watch the sessions on your computer or mobile device, and pause, rewind, or replay a video at any time. To log on to the MIS CourseMate site at **www.cengagebrain.com**, you must create a student account and then register this book.

This session is about entity-relationship diagrams (ERDs). You'll learn what an ERD is and why it is important, how to create an ERD, and how to use a CASE tool to create ERDs.

FIGURE 9-13   Microsoft Access allows a user to specify that referential integrity rules will be enforced in a relational database design.

Screenshots used with permission from Microsoft.

ENTITY-RELATIONSHIP DIAGRAMS

Recall that an entity is a person, place, thing, or event for which data is collected and maintained. For example, entities might be customers, sales regions, products, or orders.

An information system must recognize the relationships among entities. For example, a CUSTOMER entity can have several instances of an ORDER entity, and an EMPLOYEE entity can have one instance, or none, of a SPOUSE entity.

An **entity-relationship diagram** (ERD) is a model that shows the logical relationships and interaction among system entities. An ERD provides an overall view of the system and a blueprint for creating the physical data structures.

Drawing an ERD

The first step is to list the entities that you identified during the systems analysis phase and to consider the nature of the relationships that link them. At this stage, you can use a simplified method to show the relationships between entities.

Although there are different ways to draw ERDs, a popular method is to represent entities as rectangles and relationships as diamond shapes. The entity rectangles are labeled with singular nouns, and the relationship diamonds are labeled with verbs, usually in a top-to-bottom and left-to-right fashion. For example, in Figure 9-14, a DOCTOR entity *treats* a PATIENT entity. Unlike data flow diagrams, entity-relationship diagrams depict relationships, not data or information flows.

FIGURE 9-14   In an entity-relationship diagram, entities are labeled with singular nouns and relationships are labeled with verbs. The relationship is interpreted as a simple English sentence.

© Cengage Learning 2014

Types of Relationships

Three types of relationships can exist between entities: one-to-one, one-to-many, and many-to-many.

A **one-to-one relationship**, abbreviated **1:1**, exists when exactly one of the second entity occurs for each instance of the first entity. Figure 9-15 shows examples of several 1:1 relationships. A number 1 is placed alongside each of the two connecting lines to indicate the 1:1 relationship.

A **one-to-many relationship**, abbreviated **1:M**, exists when one occurrence of the first entity can relate to many instances of the second entity, but each instance of the second entity can associate with only one instance of the first entity. For example, the relationship between DEPARTMENT and EMPLOYEE is one-to-many: One department can have many employees, but each employee works in only one department at a time. Figure 9-16 shows several 1:M relationships. The line connecting the *many* entity is labeled with the letter M, and the number 1 labels the other connecting line. How many is *many*? The first 1:M relationship shown in Figure 9-16 shows the entities INDIVIDUAL and AUTOMOBILE. One individual might own five automobiles, or one, or none. Thus, *many* can mean any number, including zero.

A **many-to-many relationship**, abbreviated **M:N**, exists when one instance of the first entity can relate to many instances of the second entity, and one instance of the second entity can relate to many instances of the first entity. The relationship between STUDENT and CLASS, for example, is many-to-many — one student can take many classes, and one class can have many students enrolled. Figure 9-17 on the next page shows several M:N entity-relationships. One of the connecting lines is labeled with the letter M, and the letter N labels the other connection.

Notice that an M:N relationship is different from 1:1 or 1:M relationships because the event or transaction that links the two entities is actually a third entity, called an **associative entity**, that has its own characteristics. In the first example in Figure 9-17, the ENROLLS IN symbol represents a REGISTRATION entity that records each instance of a specific student enrolling in a specific course. Similarly, the RESERVES SEAT ON symbol represents a RESERVATION entity that records each instance of a specific passenger reserving a seat on a specific flight. In the third example, the LISTS symbol represents an ORDER LINE entity that records each instance of a specific product listed in a specific customer order.

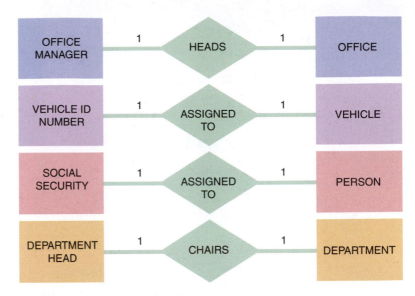

FIGURE 9-15   Examples of one-to-one (1:1) relationships.
© Cengage Learning 2014

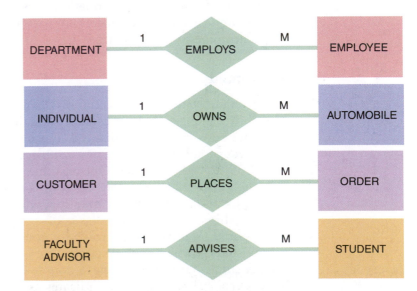

FIGURE 9-16   Examples of one-to-many (1:M) relationships.
© Cengage Learning 2014

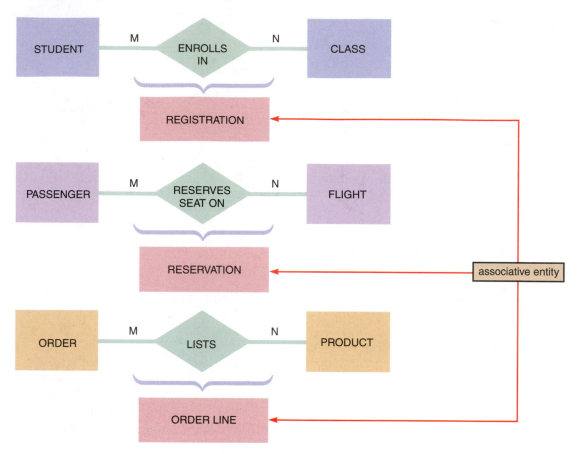

FIGURE 9-17 Examples of many-to-many (M:N) relationships. Notice that the event or transaction that links the two entities is an associative entity with its own set of attributes and characteristics.
© Cengage Learning 2014

Figure 9-18 shows an ERD for a sales system. Notice the various entities and relationships shown in the figure, including the associative entity named ORDER LINE. The detailed nature of these relationships is called cardinality. As an analyst, you must understand cardinality in order to create a data design that accurately reflects all relationships among system entities.

Cardinality

After an analyst draws an initial ERD, he or she must define the relationships in more detail by using a technique called cardinality. **Cardinality** describes the numeric relationship between two entities and shows how instances of one entity relate to instances of another entity. For example, consider the relationship between two entities: CUSTOMER and ORDER. One customer can have one order, many orders, or none, but each order must have one and only one customer. An analyst can model this interaction by adding **cardinality notation**, which uses special symbols to represent the relationship.

A common method of cardinality notation is called **crow's foot notation** because of the shapes, which include circles, bars, and symbols, that indicate various possibilities. A single bar indicates one, a double bar indicates one and only one, a circle indicates zero, and a crow's foot indicates many. Figure 9-19 shows various cardinality symbols, their meanings, and the UML representations of the relationships. As you learned in Chapter 4, the **Unified Modeling Language (UML)** is a widely used method of visualizing and documenting software systems design.

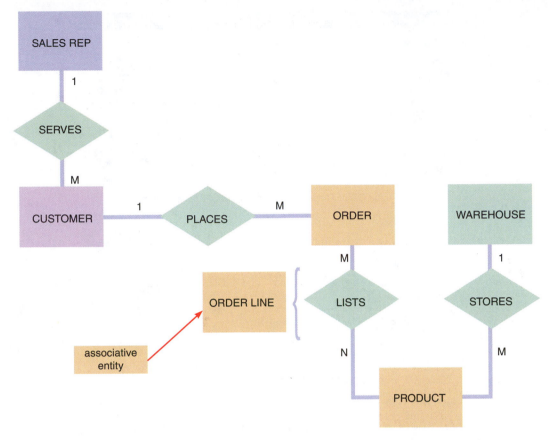

FIGURE 9-18 An entity-relationship diagram for SALES REP, CUSTOMER, ORDER, PRODUCT, and WAREHOUSE. Notice that the ORDER and PRODUCT entities are joined by an associative entity named ORDER LINE.

© Cengage Learning 2014

In Figure 9-20 on the next page, four examples of cardinality notation are shown. In the first example, one and only one CUSTOMER can place anywhere from zero to many of the ORDER entity. In the second example, one and only one ORDER can include one ITEM ORDERED or many. In the third example, one and only one EMPLOYEE can have one SPOUSE or none. In the fourth example, one EMPLOYEE, or many employees, or none, can be assigned to one PROJECT, or many projects, or none.

Most CASE products support the drawing of ERDs from entities in the data repository. Figure 9-21 shows part of a library system ERD drawn using the Visible Analyst CASE tool. Notice that crow's foot notation is used to show the nature of the relationships, which are described in both directions.

Now that you understand database elements and their relationships, you can start designing tables. The first step is the normalization of your table designs, which is described next.

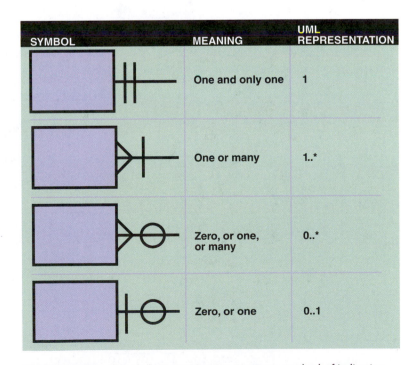

SYMBOL	MEANING	UML REPRESENTATION
	One and only one	1
	One or many	1..*
	Zero, or one, or many	0..*
	Zero, or one	0..1

FIGURE 9-19 Crow's foot notation is a common method of indicating cardinality. The four examples show how you can use various symbols to describe the relationships between entities.

© Cengage Learning 2014

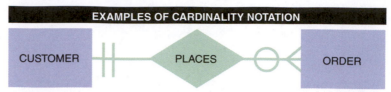

One and only one CUSTOMER can place anywhere from zero to many of the ORDER entity.

One and only one ORDER can include one ITEM ORDERED or many.

One and only one EMPLOYEE can have one SPOUSE or NONE.

One EMPLOYEE, or many employees, or none, can be assigned to one PROJECT, or many projects, or none.

FIGURE 9-20   In the first example of cardinality notation, one and only one CUSTOMER can place anywhere from zero to many of the ORDER entity. In the second example, one and only one ORDER can include one ITEM ORDERED or many. In the third example, one and only one EMPLOYEE can have one SPOUSE or none. In the fourth example, one EMPLOYEE, or many employees, or none, can be assigned to one PROJECT, or many projects, or none.

© Cengage Learning 2014

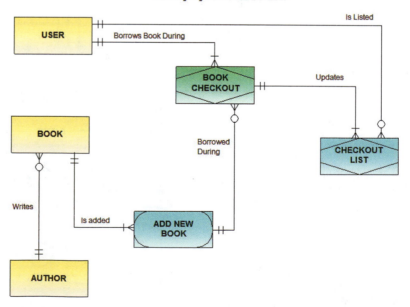

FIGURE 9-21   An ERD for a library system drawn with Visible Analyst. Notice that crow's foot notation has been used and relationships are described in both directions.

© Cengage Learning 2014

DATA NORMALIZATION

Normalization is the process of creating table designs by assigning specific fields
or attributes to each table in the database. A **table design** specifies the fields and
identifies the primary key in a particular table or file. Working with a set of initial
table designs, you use normalization to develop an overall database design that is
simple, flexible, and free of data redundancy. Normalization involves applying a set
of rules that can help you identify and correct inherent problems and complexities in
your table designs. The concept of normalization is based on the work of Edgar
Codd, a British computer scientist who formulated the basic principles of relational
database design.

The normalization process typically involves four stages: unnormalized design,
first normal form, second normal form, and third normal form. The three normal
forms constitute a progression in which third normal form represents the best
design. Most business-related databases must be designed in third normal form.

Standard Notation Format

The best way to learn about data design is to use examples, and standard notation
format is no exception. The following sections will use the example of an ORDER
system, but the same principles would apply to any situation.

Designing tables is easier if you use a **standard notation format** to show a table's
structure, fields, and primary key. The standard notation format in the following
examples starts with the name of the table, followed by a parenthetical expression
that contains the field names separated by commas. The primary key field(s) is
underlined, like this:

NAME (FIELD 1, FIELD 2, FIELD 3)

During data design, you must be able to recognize a repeating group of fields. A
repeating group is a set of one or more fields that can occur any number of times in a
single record, with each occurrence having different values.

A typical example of a repeating group is shown in Figure 9-22 on the next page.
If a company used written source documents to record orders, they might look like
this. As Figure 9-22 shows, two orders contain multiple items, which constitute
repeating groups within the same order number. Notice that in addition to the order
number and date, the records with multiple products contain repetitions of the product number, description, number ordered, supplier number, supplier name, and ISO
status. You can think of a repeating group as a set of child (subsidiary) records contained within the parent (main) record.

A table design that contains a repeating group is called **unnormalized**. The standard notation method for representing an unnormalized design is to enclose the

FIGURE 9-22   In the ORDER table design, two orders have repeating groups that contain several products. ORDER is the primary key for the ORDER table, and PRODUCT NUMBER serves as a primary key for the repeating group. Because it contains repeating groups, the ORDER table is unnormalized.
© Cengage Learning 2014

repeating group of fields within a second set of parentheses. An example of an unnormalized table would look like this:

NAME (<u>FIELD 1</u>, FIELD 2, FIELD 3, (REPEATING FIELD 1, REPEATING FIELD 2))

Now review the unnormalized ORDER table design shown in Figure 9-22. Following the notation guidelines, you can describe the design as follows:

ORDER (<u>ORDER</u>, DATE, (<u>PRODUCT NUMBER</u>, DESCRIPTION, NUMBER ORDERED, SUPPLIER NUMBER, SUPPLIER NAME, ISO))

The notation indicates that the ORDER table design contains eight fields, which are listed within the outer parentheses. The ORDER field is underlined to show that it is the primary key. The PRODUCT NUMBER, DESCRIPTION, NUMBER ORDERED, SUPPLIER NUMBER, SUPPLIER NAME, and ISO and NUMBER ORDERED fields are enclosed within an inner set of parentheses to indicate that they are fields within a repeating group. Notice that PRODUCT NUMBER also is underlined because it acts as the primary key of the repeating group. If a customer orders three different products in one order, then six fields must be repeated for each product, as shown in Figure 9-22.

Video Learning Session
First Normal Form

If you have an MIS CourseMate access code, you can launch interactive Video Learning Sessions to help you understand systems development concepts and practice your skills. You can watch the sessions on your computer or mobile device, and pause, rewind, or replay a video at any time. To log on to the MIS CourseMate site at **www.cengagebrain.com**, you must create a student account and then register this book.

This is the first of three Video Learning Sessions about data normalization. In this session, you'll learn how to transform unnormalized data into first normal form (1NF).

© craftvision/iStockphoto

First Normal Form

A table is in **first normal form (1NF)** if it does not contain a repeating group. To convert an unnormalized design to 1NF, you must expand the table's primary key to include the primary key of the repeating group.

For example, in the ORDER table shown in Figure 9-22, the repeating group consists of six fields: PRODUCT NUMBER, DESCRIPTION, NUMBER ORDERED, SUPPLIER NUMBER, SUPPLIER NAME, and ISO. Of the three fields, only PRODUCT NUMBER can be a primary key because it uniquely identifies each instance of the repeating group. The DESCRIPTION cannot be a primary key because it might or might not be unique. For example, a company might sell a large number of parts with the same descriptive name, such as *washer*, relying on a coded part number to identify uniquely each washer size.

When you expand the primary key of the ORDER table to include PRODUCT NUMBER, you eliminate the repeating group and the ORDER table is now in 1NF, as shown:

ORDER (<u>ORDER</u>, DATE, <u>PRODUCT NUMBER</u>, DESCRIPTION,
  NUMBER ORDERED, SUPPLIER NUMBER, SUPPLIER NAME, ISO)

Figure 9-23 shows the ORDER table in 1NF. Notice that when you eliminate the repeating group, additional records emerge — one for each combination of a specific order and a specific product. The result is more records, but a greatly simplified design. In the new version, the repeating group for order number 86223 has become three separate records, and the repeating group for order number 86390 has become two separate records. Therefore, when a table is in 1NF, each record stores data about a single instance of a specific order and a specific product.

Also notice that the 1NF design shown in Figure 9-23 has a combination primary key. The primary key of the 1NF design cannot be the ORDER field alone, because the order number does not uniquely identify each product in a multiple-item order. Similarly, PRODUCT NUMBER cannot be the primary key, because it appears more than once if several orders include the same product. Because each record must reflect a

in 1NF, the primary key is a **unique** combination of a specific ORDER and a specific PRODUCT NUMBER

ORDER in 1NF

ORDER	DATE	PRODUCT NUMBER	DESCRIPTION	NUMBER ORDERED	SUPPLIER NUMBER	SUPPLIER NAME	ISO
86223	9-13-2013	304	Blue gadget	7	A-602	Acme	Yes
86223	9-13-2013	633	Assembly	1	J-995	Jones	No
86223	9-13-2013	684	Super gizmo	4	C-876	Cabot	Yes
86390	9-14-2013	128	Steel widget	12	A-602	Acme	Yes
86390	9-14-2013	304	Blue gadget	3	A-602	Acme	Yes
86467	9-15-2013	304	Blue gadget	144	A-602	Acme	Yes

in 1NF
• There are no repeating groups
• The primary key is a **unique** combination of two foreign key values: ORDER and PRODUCT NUMBER
• All fields depend on the primary key, but some fields do not depend on the **whole** key — only part of it

FIGURE 9-23   The ORDER table as it appears in 1NF. The repeating groups have been eliminated. Notice that the repeating group for order 86223 has become three separate records, and the repeating group for order 86390 has become two separate records. The 1NF primary key is a combination of ORDER and PRODUCT NUMBER, which uniquely identifies each record.

specific product in a specific order, you need *both* fields, ORDER and PRODUCT NUMBER, to identify a single record uniquely. Therefore, the primary key is the *combination* of two fields: ORDER and PRODUCT NUMBER.

Video Learning Session
Second Normal Form

If you have an MIS CourseMate access code, you can launch interactive Video Learning Sessions to help you understand systems development concepts and practice your skills. You can watch the sessions on your computer or mobile device, and pause, rewind, or replay a video at any time. To log on to the MIS CourseMate site at **www.cengagebrain.com**, you must create a student account and then register this book.

This is the second of three Video Learning Sessions about data normalization. In this session, you'll learn how to transform data from first normal form (1NF) to second normal form (2NF).

© craftvision/iStockphoto

Second Normal Form

To understand second normal form (2NF), you must understand the concept of functional dependence. For example, *Field A* is **functionally dependent** on *Field B* if the value of *Field A* depends on *Field B*. For example, in Figure 9-23, the DATE value is functionally dependent on the ORDER, because for a specific order number, there can be only one date. In contrast, a product description is *not* dependent on the order number. For a particular order number, there might be several product descriptions — one for each item ordered.

A table design is in **second normal form (2NF)** if it is in 1NF *and* if all fields that are not part of the primary key are functionally dependent on the *entire* primary key. If any field in a 1NF table depends on only one of the fields in a combination primary key, then the table is not in 2NF.

Notice that if a 1NF design has a primary key that consists of only one field, the problem of partial dependence does not arise — because the entire primary key is a single field. Therefore, a 1NF table with a single-field primary key is automatically in 2NF.

Now reexamine the 1NF design for the ORDER table shown in Figure 9-23 on the previous page:

ORDER (<u>ORDER</u>, DATE, <u>PRODUCT NUMBER</u>, DESCRIPTION,
 NUMBER ORDERED, SUPPLIER NUMBER, SUPPLIER NAME, ISO)

Recall that the primary key is the combination of the order number and the product number. The NUMBER ORDERED field depends on the *entire* primary key because NUMBER ORDERED refers to a specific product number *and* a specific order number. In contrast, the DATE field depends on the order number, which is only a part of the primary key. Similarly, the DESCRIPTION field depends on the product number, which also is only a part of the primary key. Because some fields are not dependent on the *entire* primary key, the design is not in 2NF.

A standard process exists for converting a table from 1NF to 2NF. The objective is to break the original table into two or more new tables and reassign the fields so that each nonkey field will depend on the entire primary key in its table. To accomplish this, you follow these steps:

1. First, create and name a separate table for each field in the existing primary key. For example, in Figure 9-23, the ORDER table's primary key has two fields, ORDER and PRODUCT NUMBER, so you must create two tables. The ellipsis (. . .) indicates that fields will be assigned later. The result is:

    ORDER (<u>ORDER</u>, . . .)
    PRODUCT (<u>PRODUCT NUMBER</u>, . . .)

2. Next, create a new table for each possible combination of the original primary key fields. In the Figure 9-23 example, you would create and name a new table with a combination primary key of ORDER and PRODUCT NUMBER. This table describes individual lines in an order, so it is named ORDER LINE, as shown:

> ORDER LINE (<u>ORDER</u>, <u>PRODUCT NUMBER</u>)

3. Finally, study the three tables and place each field with its appropriate primary key, which is the minimal key on which it functionally depends. When you finish placing all the fields, remove any table that did not have any additional fields assigned to it. The remaining tables are the 2NF version of your original table. The three tables can be shown as:

> ORDER (<u>ORDER</u>, DATE)
> PRODUCT (<u>PRODUCT NUMBER</u>, DESCRIPTION, SUPPLIER NUMBER, SUPPLIER NAME, ISO)
> ORDER LINE (<u>ORDER</u>, <u>PRODUCT NUMBER</u>)

Figure 9-24 shows the 2NF table designs. By following the steps, you have converted the original 1NF table into three 2NF tables.

Why is it important to move from 1NF to 2NF? Four kinds of problems are found with 1NF designs that do not exist in 2NF:

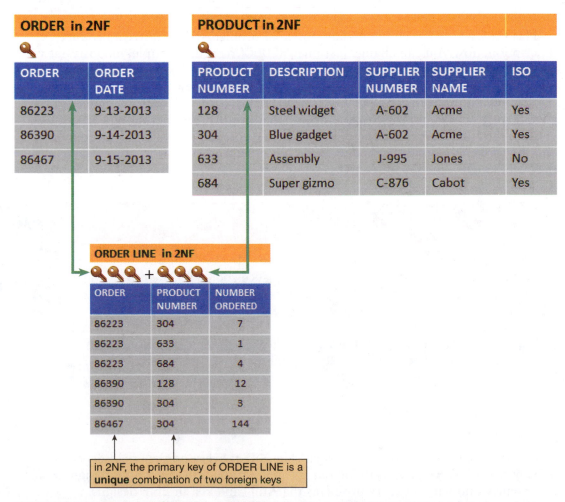

ORDER in 2NF

ORDER	ORDER DATE
86223	9-13-2013
86390	9-14-2013
86467	9-15-2013

PRODUCT in 2NF

PRODUCT NUMBER	DESCRIPTION	SUPPLIER NUMBER	SUPPLIER NAME	ISO
128	Steel widget	A-602	Acme	Yes
304	Blue gadget	A-602	Acme	Yes
633	Assembly	J-995	Jones	No
684	Super gizmo	C-876	Cabot	Yes

ORDER LINE in 2NF

ORDER	PRODUCT NUMBER	NUMBER ORDERED
86223	304	7
86223	633	1
86223	684	4
86390	128	12
86390	304	3
86467	304	144

In 2NF, the primary key of ORDER LINE is a **unique** combination of two foreign keys

FIGURE 9-24   ORDER, PRODUCT, and ORDER LINE tables in 2NF. All fields are functionally dependent on the primary key.

- Consider the work necessary to change a particular product's description. Suppose 500 current orders exist for product number 304. Changing the product description involves modifying 500 records for product number 304. Updating all 500 records would be cumbersome and expensive.

- 1NF tables can contain inconsistent data. Because someone must enter the product description in each record, nothing prevents product number 304 from having different product descriptions in different records. In fact, if product number 304 appears in a large number of order records, some of the matching product descriptions might be inaccurate or improperly spelled. Even the presence or absence of a hyphen in the orders for *All-purpose gadget* would create consistency problems. If a data entry person must enter a term such as *IO1 Queue Controller* numerous times, it certainly is possible that some inconsistency will result.

- Adding a new product is a problem. Because the primary key must include an order number and a product number, you need values for both fields in order to add a record. What value do you use for the order number when you want to add a new product that has not been ordered by any customer? You could use a dummy order number, and then replace it with a real order number when the product is ordered to solve the problem, but that solution also creates difficulties.

- Deleting a product is a problem. If all the related records are deleted once an order is filled and paid for, what happens if you delete the only record that contains product number 633? The information about that product number and its description is lost.

Has the 2NF design eliminated all potential problems? To change a product description, now you can change just one PRODUCT record. Multiple, inconsistent values for the product description are impossible because the description appears in only one location. To add a new product, you simply create a new PRODUCT record, instead of creating a dummy order record. When you remove the last ORDER LINE record for a particular product number, you do not lose that product number and its description because the PRODUCT record still exists. The four potential problems are eliminated, and the three 2NF designs are superior to both the original unnormalized table and the 1NF design.

Video Learning Session
Third Normal Form

If you have an MIS CourseMate access code, you can launch interactive Video Learning Sessions to help you understand systems development concepts and practice your skills. You can watch the sessions on your computer or mobile device, and pause, rewind, or replay a video at any time. To log on to the MIS CourseMate site at **www.cengagebrain.com**, you must create a student account and then register this book.

This is the third of three Video Learning Sessions about data normalization. In this session, you'll learn how to transform from second normal form (2NF) to third normal form (3NF).

© craftvision/iStockphoto

Third Normal Form

A popular rule of thumb is that a design is in 3NF if every nonkey field depends on *the key, the whole key, and nothing but the key*. As you will see, a 3NF design avoids redundancy and data integrity problems that still can exist in 2NF designs.

Continuing the ORDER example, now review the PRODUCT table design in Figure 9-25:

PRODUCT (<u>PRODUCT NUMBER</u>, DESCRIPTION, SUPPLIER NUMBER, SUPPLIER NAME, ISO)

FIGURE 9-25 When the PRODUCT table is transformed from 2NF to 3F, the result is two separate tables: PRODUCT and SUPPLIER. Note that in 3NF, all fields depend on the key, the whole key, and nothing but the key!
© Cengage Learning 2014

The PRODUCT table is in 1NF because it has no repeating groups. The table also is in 2NF because the primary key is a single field. But the table still has four potential problems:

- To change a supplier name, you must change every record in which that name appears. With hundreds, or even thousands of records, the process would be slow, expensive, and subject to input errors.

- The 2NF design allows a supplier to have a different name or ISO status in different records.

- Because the supplier name is included in the ORDER table, you must create a dummy ORDER record to add a new supplier who has not yet been received any orders.

- Finally, if you delete all the orders for a supplier, you will lose that supplier's number and name.

Those potential problems are caused because the design is not in 3NF. A table design is in **third normal form (3NF)** if it is in 2NF and if no nonkey field is dependent on another nonkey field. Remember that a nonkey field is a field that is not a candidate key for the primary key.

The PRODUCT table at the top of Figure 9-25 is not in 3NF because two nonkey fields, SUPPLIER NAME and ISO, both depend on another nonkey field, SUPPLIER NUMBER.

FIGURE 9-26 A faculty advisor, who represents an entity, can advise many students, each of whom can register for one or many courses.

© Shutterstock/Auremar

To convert the table to 3NF, you must remove all fields from the 2NF table that depend on another nonkey field and place them in a new table that uses the nonkey field as a primary key. In the PRODUCT example, you must remove SUPPLIER NAME and ISO, and place them into a new table that uses SUPPLIER NUMBER as the primary key. As shown in Figure 9-25, third normal form divides the 2NF version into two separate 3NF tables:

PRODUCT (<u>PRODUCT NUMBER</u>, DESCRIPTION, SUPPLIER NUMBER)

SUPPLIER (<u>SUPPLIER NUMBER</u>, SUPPLIER NAME, ISO)

TWO REAL-WORLD EXAMPLES

The best way to learn about normalization is to apply the rules to a situation you understand. This section presents two different scenarios: first a school and then a technical service company. If you follow a step-by step process, you can create data designs that are efficient, maintainable, and error-resistant.

Example 1: Crossroads College

Consider the familiar situation in Figure 9-26, which depicts several entities in the Crossroads College advising system: ADVISOR, COURSE, and STUDENT. The relationships among the three entities are shown in the ERD in Figure 9-27. The following sections discuss normalization rules for these three entities.

Before you start the normalization process, you notice that the STUDENT table contains fields that relate to the ADVISOR and COURSE entities, so you decide to begin with the initial design for the STUDENT table, which is shown in Figure 9-28. Notice that the table design includes the student number, student name, total credits taken, grade point average (GPA), advisor number, advisor name, and, for every course the student has taken, the course number, course description, number of credits, and grade received.

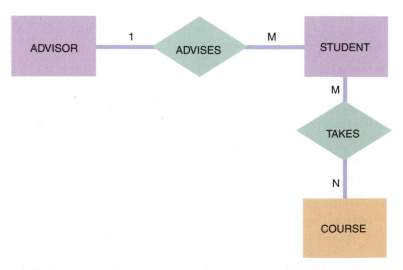

FIGURE 9-27 An initial entity-relationship diagram for ADVISOR, STUDENT, and COURSE.

© Cengage Learning 2014

STUDENT (Unnormalized)

STUDENT NUMBER	STUDENT NAME	TOTAL CREDITS	GPA	ADVISOR NUMBER	ADVISOR NAME	OFFICE	COURSE NUMBER	CREDIT HOURS	GRADE
1035	Linda	47	3.60	49	Smith	B212	CSC151	4	B
							MKT212	3	A
							ENG101	3	B
							CHM112	4	A
							BUS105	2	A
3397	Sam	29	3.00	49	Smith	B212	ENG101	3	A
							MKT212	3	C
							CSC151	4	B
4070	Kelly	14	2.90	23	Jones	C333	CSC151	4	B
							CHM112	4	C
							ENG101	3	C
							BUS105	2	C

FIGURE 9-28   The STUDENT table is unnormalized because it contains a repeating group that represents the courses each student has taken.

© Cengage Learning 2014

The STUDENT table in Figure 9-28 is unnormalized because it has a repeating group. The STUDENT table design can be written as:

STUDENT (<u>STUDENT NUMBER</u>, STUDENT NAME, TOTAL
   CREDITS, GPA, ADVISOR NUMBER, ADVISOR NAME,
   OFFICE, (<u>COURSE NUMBER</u>, CREDIT HOURS, GRADE))

To convert the STUDENT record to 1NF, you must expand the primary key to include the key of the repeating group, producing:

STUDENT (<u>STUDENT NUMBER,</u> STUDENT NAME, TOTAL
   CREDITS, GPA, ADVISOR NUMBER, ADVISOR NAME,
   OFFICE, <u>COURSE NUMBER</u>, CREDIT HOURS, GRADE)

Figure 9-29 on the next page shows the 1NF version of the sample STUDENT data. Do any of the fields in the 1NF STUDENT table depend on only a portion of the primary key? The student name, total credits, GPA, advisor number, and advisor name all relate only to the student number and have no relationship to the course number. The course description depends on the course number, but not on the student number. Only the GRADE field depends on the entire primary key.

Following the 1NF – 2NF conversion process described earlier, you would create a new table for each field and combination of fields in the primary key, and place the other fields with their appropriate key. The result is:

STUDENT (<u>STUDENT NUMBER</u>, STUDENT NAME, TOTAL CREDITS, GPA,
   ADVISOR NUMBER, ADVISOR NAME, OFFICE)

COURSE (<u>COURSE NUMBER</u>, CREDIT HOURS)

GRADE (<u>STUDENT NUMBER</u>, COURSE NUMBER, GRADE)

You now have converted the original 1NF STUDENT table to three tables, all in 2NF. In each table, every nonkey field depends on the entire primary key.

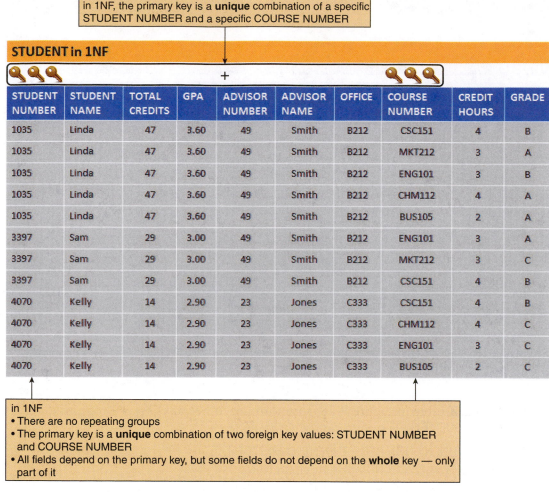

in 1NF, the primary key is a **unique** combination of a specific STUDENT NUMBER and a specific COURSE NUMBER

STUDENT in 1NF

STUDENT NUMBER	STUDENT NAME	TOTAL CREDITS	GPA	ADVISOR NUMBER	ADVISOR NAME	OFFICE	COURSE NUMBER	CREDIT HOURS	GRADE
1035	Linda	47	3.60	49	Smith	B212	CSC151	4	B
1035	Linda	47	3.60	49	Smith	B212	MKT212	3	A
1035	Linda	47	3.60	49	Smith	B212	ENG101	3	B
1035	Linda	47	3.60	49	Smith	B212	CHM112	4	A
1035	Linda	47	3.60	49	Smith	B212	BUS105	2	A
3397	Sam	29	3.00	49	Smith	B212	ENG101	3	A
3397	Sam	29	3.00	49	Smith	B212	MKT212	3	C
3397	Sam	29	3.00	49	Smith	B212	CSC151	4	B
4070	Kelly	14	2.90	23	Jones	C333	CSC151	4	B
4070	Kelly	14	2.90	23	Jones	C333	CHM112	4	C
4070	Kelly	14	2.90	23	Jones	C333	ENG101	3	C
4070	Kelly	14	2.90	23	Jones	C333	BUS105	2	C

in 1NF
• There are no repeating groups
• The primary key is a **unique** combination of two foreign key values: STUDENT NUMBER and COURSE NUMBER
• All fields depend on the primary key, but some fields do not depend on the **whole** key — only part of it

FIGURE 9-29   The STUDENT table in 1NF. Notice that the primary key has been expanded to include STUDENT NUMBER and COURSE NUMBER.

© Cengage Learning 2014

Figure 9-30 shows the 2NF STUDENT, COURSE, and GRADE designs and sample data. Are all three tables STUDENT in 3NF? The COURSE and GRADE tables are in 3NF. STUDENT is not in 3NF, however, because the ADVISOR NAME and OFFICE fields depend on the ADVISOR NUMBER field, which is not part of the STUDENT primary key. To convert STUDENT to 3NF, you remove the ADVISOR NAME and OFFICE fields from the STUDENT table and place them into a table with ADVISOR NUMBER as the primary key.

Figure 9-31 on page 376 shows the 3NF versions of the sample data for STUDENT, ADVISOR, COURSE, and GRADE. The final 3NF design is:

STUDENT (<u>STUDENT NUMBER</u>, STUDENT NAME, TOTAL CREDITS, GPA, ADVISOR NUMBER)

ADVISOR (<u>ADVISOR NUMBER</u>, ADVISOR NAME, OFFICE)

COURSE (<u>COURSE NUMBER</u>, CREDIT HOURS)

GRADE (<u>STUDENT NUMBER</u>, <u>COURSE NUMBER</u>, GRADE)

Figure 9-32 on page 376 shows the complete ERD after normalization. Now there are four entities: STUDENT, ADVISOR, COURSE, and GRADE, which is an associative entity. If you go back to Figure 9-27 on page 372, which was drawn before you identified GRADE as an entity, you can see that the M:N relationship between STUDENT and COURSE has been converted into two 1:M relationships: one relationship between STUDENT and GRADE and the other relationship between COURSE and GRADE.

FIGURE 9-30   The STUDENT, COURSE, and GRADE tables in 2NF. Notice that all fields are functionally dependent on the entire primary key of their respective tables.

© Cengage Learning 2014

To create 3NF designs, you must understand the nature of first, second, and third normal forms. In your work as a systems analyst, you will encounter designs that are much more complex than the examples in this chapter. You also should know that normal forms beyond 3NF exist, but they rarely are used in business-oriented systems.

FIGURE 9-31   STUDENT, ADVISOR, COURSE, and GRADE tables in 3NF. When the STUDENT table is transformed from 2NF to 3NF, the result is two tables: STUDENT and ADVISOR.

© Cengage Learning 2014

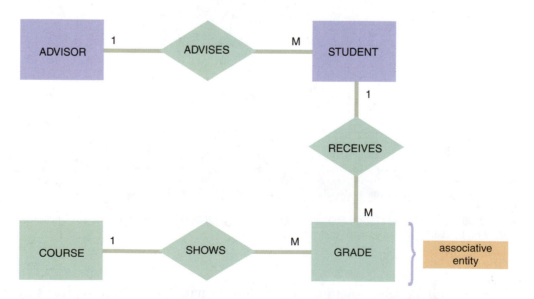

FIGURE 9-32   The entity-relationship diagram for STUDENT, ADVISOR, and COURSE after normalization. The GRADE entity was identified during the normalization process. GRADE is an associative entity that links the STUDENT and COURSE tables.

© Cengage Learning 2014

CASE IN POINT 9.2: CYBERTOYS

You handle administrative support for CyberToys, a small chain that sells computer hardware and software and specializes in personal service. The company has four stores located at malls and is planning more. Each store has a manager, a technician, and between one and four sales reps.

Bruce and Marcia Berns, the owners, want to create a personnel records database, and they asked you to review a table that Marcia designed. She suggested fields for store number, location, store telephone, manager name, and manager home telephone. She also wants fields for technician name and technician home telephone and fields for up to four sales rep names and sales rep home telephones.

Draw Marcia's suggested design and analyze it using the normalization concepts you learned in the chapter. What do you think of Marcia's design and why? What would you propose?

Example 2: Magic Maintenance

Magic Maintenance provides on-site service for electronic equipment. Figure 9-33 shows the overall database design that such a firm might use. If you study the figure carefully, you will see examples of many concepts described earlier. The database consists of seven separate tables, all joined by common fields so they form an integral data structure.

Figure 9-34 on the next page shows even more detail, including sample data, primary keys, and common fields. Notice that the entities include customers, technicians,

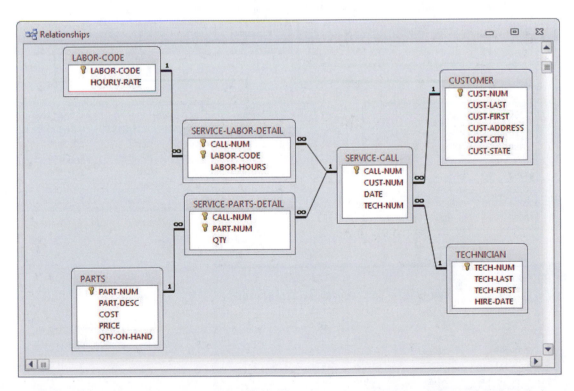

FIGURE 9-33   A relational database design for a computer service company uses common fields to link the tables and form an overall data structure. Notice the one-to-many notation symbols, and the primary keys, which are indicated with gold-colored key symbols.

© Cengage Learning 2014

CASE IN POINT 9.3: DOTCOM TOOLS

DotCom Tools operates a small business that specializes in hard-to-find woodworking tools. The firm advertises in various woodworking magazines, and currently accepts mail and telephone orders. DotCom is planning a Web site that will be the firm's primary sales channel. The site will feature an online catalog, powerful search capabilities, and links to woodworking information and resources.

DotCom has asked you, an IT consultant, whether a set of codes would be advantageous and if so, what codes you would suggest. Provide at least two choices for a customer code and at least two choices for a product code. Be sure to describe your choices and provide some specific examples. Also include an explanation of why you selected these particular codes and what advantages they might offer.

FIGURE 9-34 Sample data, primary keys, and common fields for the database shown in Figure 9-33. The design is in 3NF. Notice that all nonkey fields functionally depend on a primary key, the whole primary key, and nothing but the primary key.

© Cengage Learning 2014

service calls, and parts. Other tables store data about labor and parts that are used on specific service calls. Also notice that all tables use a single field as a primary key, except the SERVICE-LABOR-DETAIL and SERVICE-PARTS-DETAIL tables, where the primary key requires a combination of two fields to uniquely identify each record.

WORKING WITH A RELATIONAL DATABASE

To understand the power and flexibility of a relational database, try the following exercise. Suppose you work in IT, and the sales team needs answers to three specific questions. The data might be stored physically in seven tables. You know how to create Microsoft Access queries, but to learn more about database logic and design, you decide to study Figure 9-34, and then pretend to tell the database how to find the answers, step by step. The questions are shown in Figures 9-35, 9-36, and 9-37 on this page and the next page.

Question 1

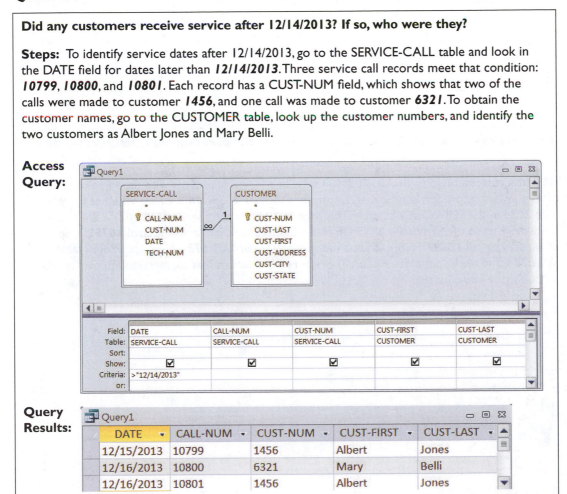

Did any customers receive service after 12/14/2013? If so, who were they?

Steps: To identify service dates after 12/14/2013, go to the SERVICE-CALL table and look in the DATE field for dates later than *12/14/2013*. Three service call records meet that condition: *10799*, *10800*, and *10801*. Each record has a CUST-NUM field, which shows that two of the calls were made to customer *1456*, and one call was made to customer *6321*. To obtain the customer names, go to the CUSTOMER table, look up the customer numbers, and identify the two customers as Albert Jones and Mary Belli.

FIGURE 9-35   Question 1.

© Cengage Learning 2014

Question 2

> **Did technician Marie Johnson put in more than six hours of labor on any service calls? If so, which ones?**
>
> **Steps:** To locate Marie Johnson, find her name in the TECHNICIAN table and locate her technician number, which is **21**. Then, go to the SERVICE-CALL table and seek matching values of **21** in the TECH-NUM field. Marie's two service calls are shown as call numbers **10798** and **10800**. Finally, go to the SERVICE-LABOR-DETAIL table and use those two values to see if either service call showed more than six hours of labor. In the example, only service call **10798** meets the conditions.
>
> **Access Query:**
>
>
>
> **Query Results:**
>
> | TECH-FIRST | TECH-LAST | TECH-NUM | CALL-NUM | LABOR-HOURS |
> |------------|-----------|----------|----------|-------------|
> | Marie | Johnson | 21 | 10798 | 5.0 |

FIGURE 9-36 Question 2.
© Cengage Learning 2014

Question 3

> **Were any parts used on service calls in Washington? If so, what were the part numbers, descriptions, and quantities?**
>
> **Steps:** To identify Washington customers, go to the CUSTOMER table and locate all records with the value of **WA** in the CUST-STATE field. This shows a record for Juan Gonzalez, customer number **2836**. Next, to see whether he received service, look for the value **2836** in the SERVICE-CALL table. This produces one record: service call **10797**. Then, to find out what, if any, parts were used, go to the SERVICE-PARTS-DETAIL table, and look for service record **10797**. It appears part **AB-6784** was used on service call **10797**. Finally, to get a description for part **AB-6784**, go to the PARTS table, look for part number **AB-6784**, and retrieve the description. The final result indicates that six meters with part number **AB-6784** were sold to Washington customers.
>
> **Access Query:**
>
>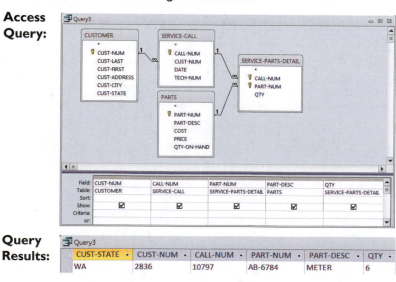
>
> **Query Results:**
>
> | CUST-STATE | CUST-NUM | CALL-NUM | PART-NUM | PART-DESC | QTY |
> |------------|----------|----------|----------|-----------|-----|
> | WA | 2836 | 10797 | AB-6784 | METER | 6 |

FIGURE 9-37 Question 3.
© Cengage Learning 2014

SHOULD YOU USE CODES?

A **code** is a set of letters or numbers that represents a data item. Codes can be used to simplify output, input, and data formats.

Overview of Codes

Because codes can represent data, you encounter them constantly in everyday life. Student numbers, for example, are unique codes to identify students in a school registration system. Three students with the name John Turner might be enrolled at your school, but *only* one is student number 268960.

Your postal code is another common example. A nine-digit postal code contains a lot of information. For example, the first digit identifies one of ten main geographical areas in the United States. The combination of the next three digits identifies a major city or major distribution point. The fifth digit identifies an individual post office, an area within a city, or a specific delivery unit. The last four digits identify a post office box or a specific street address.

For example, consider the postal code 27906-2624 shown in Figure 9-38. The first digit, 2, indicates a broad geographical area in the eastern United States. The digits, 790, indicate Elizabeth City, North Carolina. The fifth digit, 6, identifies the post office that serves the College of the Albemarle. The last four digits, 2624, identify the post office box for the college.

Codes can be used in many ways. Because codes are shorter than the data they represent, they save storage space and costs, reduce data transmission time, and decrease data entry time. Codes also can be used to reveal or conceal information. The last two digits of a seven-digit part number, for example, might represent the supplier number, or the maximum discount that a salesperson can offer.

Finally, codes can reduce data input errors in situations when the coded data is easier to remember and enter than the original source data, when only certain valid codes are allowed, and when something within the code itself can provide immediate verification that the entry is correct.

Types of Codes

Companies use many different coding methods. Because information system users must work with coded data, the codes should be easy to learn and apply. If you plan to create new codes or change existing ones, you should obtain comments and feedback from users. The following section describes seven common coding methods.

1. **Sequence codes** are numbers or letters assigned in a specific order. Sequence codes contain no additional information other than an indication of order of entry into the system. For example, a human resource system issues consecutive

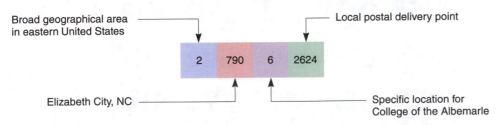

FIGURE 9-38   A postal code is an example of a significant digit code that uses groups and subgroups to store data.

© Cengage Learning 2014

employee numbers to identify employees. Because the codes are assigned in the order in which employees are hired, you can use the code to see that employee number 584 was hired after employee number 433. The code, however, does not indicate the starting date of either person's employment.

2. **Block sequence codes** use blocks of numbers for different classifications. College course numbers usually are assigned using a block sequence code. 100-level courses, such as Chemistry 110 and Mathematics 125, are freshman-level courses, whereas course numbers in the 200s indicate sophomore-level courses. Within a particular block, the sequence of numbers can have some additional meaning, such as when English 151 is the prerequisite for English 152.

3. **Alphabetic codes** use alphabet letters to distinguish one item from another based on a category, an abbreviation, or an easy-to-remember value, called a mnemonic code. Many classification codes fit more than one of the following definitions:

   a) **Category codes** identify a group of related items. For example, a local department store uses a two-character category code to identify the department in which a product is sold: GN for gardening supplies, HW for hardware, and EL for electronics.

   b) **Abbreviation codes** are alphabetic abbreviations. For example, standard state codes include NY for New York, ME for Maine, and MN for Minnesota. Some abbreviation codes are called **mnemonic codes** because they use a specific combination of letters that are easy to remember. Many three-character airport codes such as those pictured in Figure 9-39 are mnemonic codes, such as DEN for Denver, and MIA for Miami. However, some airport codes are not mnemonic, such as ORD (O'Hare) or MCO (Orlando). In Figure 9-39, how many airports can you identify?

4. **Significant digit codes** distinguish items by using a series of subgroups of digits. Postal codes, for example, are significant digit codes. Other such codes include inventory location codes that consist of a two-digit warehouse code, followed by a one-digit floor number code, a two-digit section code, a one-digit aisle number, and a two-digit bin number code. Figure 9-40 illustrates the inventory

FIGURE 9-39 This image shows abbreviations for the world's 30 busiest airports. How many can you identify?

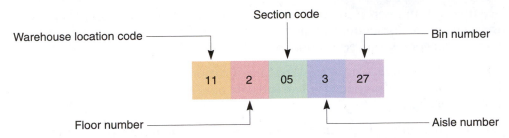

FIGURE 9-40   Sample of a code that uses significant digits to pinpoint the location of an inventory item.

© Cengage Learning 2014

location code 11205327. What looks like a large eight-digit number is actually five separate numbers, each of which has significance.

5. **Derivation codes** combine data from different item attributes, or characteristics. Most magazine subscription codes are derivation codes. For example, one popular magazine uses a subscriber's five-digit postal code, followed by the first, third, and fourth letters of the subscriber's last name, the last two digits of the subscriber's house number, and the first, third, and fourth letters of the subscriber's street name. A sample is shown in Figure 9-41.

FIGURE 9-41   A magazine subscriber code is derived from various parts of the name and address.

© Cengage Learning 2014

6. **Cipher codes** use a keyword to encode a number. A retail store, for example, might use a 10-letter word, such as CAMPGROUND, to code wholesale prices, where the letter C represents 1, A represents 2, and so on. Thus, the code, GRAND, indicates that the store paid $562.90 for the item.

7. **Action codes** indicate what action is to be taken with an associated item. For example, a student records program might prompt a user to enter or click an action code such as D (to display a record), A (to add a record), and X (to exit the program).

Designing Codes

Here are some code design suggestions:

1. Keep codes concise. Do not create codes that are longer than necessary. For example, if you need a code to identify each of 250 customers, you will not need a six-digit code.

2. Allow for expansion. A coding scheme must allow for reasonable growth in the number of assigned codes. If the company currently has eight warehouses, you should not use a one-digit code for the warehouse number. If three more warehouses are added, the code must be increased to two digits or changed to a character code in order to identify each location. The rule also applies to using a single letter as a character code because you might need more than 26 data items in the future. Of course, you can add more characters, which is just what the airline industry has done. Most airlines now use six-character codes that allow millions of combinations.

3. Keep codes stable. Changes in codes can cause consistency problems and require data updates. During the changeover period, you will have to change all the stored occurrences of a particular code and all documents containing the old code as users switch to the new code. Usually, both the old and new codes

are used for an interim period, and special procedures are required to handle the two codes. For example, when telephone area codes change, you can use either area code for a certain time period.

4. Make codes unique. Codes used for identification purposes must be unique to have meaning. If the code HW can indicate hardware or houseware, the code is not very useful.

5. Use sortable codes. If products with three-digit codes in the 100s or the 300s are of one type, while products with codes in the 200s are a different type, a simple sort will not group all the products of one type together. In addition, be careful that single-digit character codes will sort properly with double-digit codes — in some cases you must add a leading zero (01, 02, 03, and so on) to ensure that codes sort correctly.

6. Use a simple structure. Do not code some part numbers with two letters, a hyphen, and one digit, and others with one letter, a hyphen, and two digits. Avoid allowing both letters and numbers to occupy the same positions within a code because some of those are easily confused. This situation might be a good place to use an input mask to assure that the correct data type is entered.

7. Avoid confusion. It is easy to confuse the number zero (0) and the uppercase letter O, or the number one (1) with the lowercase letter L (l) or uppercase letter I. For example, the five-character code 5Z081 easily can be misread as 5Z08l, or 52081.

8. Make codes meaningful. Codes should be easy to remember, user-friendly, convenient, and easy to interpret. Using SW as a code for the southwest sales region, for example, has far more meaning than the code 14. Using ENG as the code for the English department is easier to interpret and remember than either XVA or 132.

9. Use a code for a single purpose. Do not use a code to classify unrelated attributes. For example, if you use a single code to identify the combination of an employee's department *and* the employee's insurance plan type, users will have difficulty identifying all the subscribers of a particular plan, or all the workers in a particular department, or both. A separate code for each separate characteristic makes much more sense.

10. Keep codes consistent. For example, if the payroll system already is using two-digit codes for departments, do not create a new, different coding scheme for the personnel system. If the two systems already are using different coding schemes, try to establish a consistent coding scheme.

DATA STORAGE AND ACCESS

Data storage and access involve strategic business tools, such as data warehousing and data mining software, as well as logical and physical storage issues, selection of data storage formats, and special considerations regarding storage of date fields.

Tools and Techniques

Companies use data warehousing and data mining as strategic tools to help manage the huge quantities of data they need for business operations and decisions. A large number of software vendors compete for business in this fast-growing IT sector.

DATA WAREHOUSING Large firms maintain many databases, which might or might not be linked together into an overall structure. To provide rapid access to this information, companies use software packages that organize and store data in special configurations called data warehouses. A **data warehouse** is an integrated collection of data that can include seemingly unrelated information, no matter where it is stored in the company. Because it can link various information systems and databases, a data warehouse provides an enterprise-wide view to support management analysis and decision making.

A data warehouse allows users to specify certain **dimensions**, or characteristics. By selecting values for each characteristic, a user can obtain multidimensional information from the stored data. For example, in a typical company, most data is generated by transaction-based systems, such as order processing systems, inventory systems, and payroll systems. If a user wants to identify the customer on sales order 34071, he or she can retrieve the data easily from the order processing system by entering an order number.

On the other hand, suppose that a user wants to see November, 2013 sales results for Sally Brown, the sales rep assigned to Jo-Mar Industries. The data is stored in two different systems: the sales information system and the human resources information system, as shown in Figure 9-42. Without a data warehouse, it would be difficult for a user to extract data that spans several information systems and time frames. Rather than accessing separate systems, a data warehouse stores transaction data in a format that allows users to retrieve and analyze the data easily.

FIGURE 9-42 A data warehouse stores data from several systems. By selecting data dimensions, a user can retrieve specific information without having to know how or where the data is stored.

© Cengage Learning 2014

While a data warehouse typically spans the entire enterprise, many firms prefer to use a **data mart**, which is designed to serve the needs of a specific department, such as sales, marketing, or finance. Each data mart includes only the data that users in that department require to perform their jobs. There are pros and cons to both approaches, and the best solution usually depends on the specific situation.

Regardless of the overall approach, storing large quantities of data is like building a house — it doesn't just happen. A well-constructed data warehouse needs an architecture that includes detailed planning and specifications.

DATA MINING **Data mining** software looks for meaningful data patterns and relationships. For example, data mining software could help a consumer products firm identify potential customers based on their prior purchases. Information about customer behavior is valuable, but data mining also raises serious ethical and privacy issues, such as the example in the Question of Ethics feature on page 391. Figure 9-43 on the next page shows North Carolina State University's Ethics in Computing site, which offers many articles and research papers on this subject.

The enormous growth in e-commerce has focused attention on data mining as a marketing tool. In an article in *New Architect*, a Web-based magazine, Dan R. Greening noted that Web hosts typically possess a lot of information about visitors,

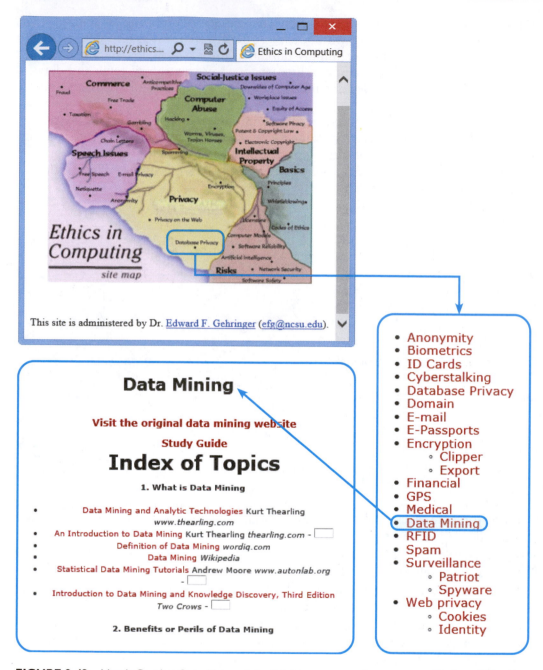

FIGURE 9-43 North Carolina State University's clickable map can take you to a collection of IT ethics issues. Here, the map points to the data mining area.

Courtesy of Dr. Edward F. Gehringer/NC State University/Designed by Lisa Fiedor

but most of it is of little value. His article mentions that smart marketers and business analysts are using data mining techniques, which he describes as "machine learning algorithms that find buried patterns in databases, and report or act on those findings." He concludes by saying that "The great advantage of Web marketing is that you can measure visitor interactions more effectively than in brick-and-mortar stores or direct mail. Data mining works best when you have clear, measurable goals." Some of the goals he suggests are:

- Increase the number of pages viewed per session
- Increase the number of referred customers

- Reduce **clicks to close**, which means average page views to accomplish a purchase or obtain desired information
- Increase checkouts per visit
- Increase average profit per checkout

This type of data gathering is sometimes called **clickstream storage**. Armed with this information, a skillful Web designer could build a profile of typical new customers, returning customers, and customers who browse but do not buy. Although this information would be very valuable to the retailer, clickstream storage could raise serious legal and privacy issues if an unscrupulous firm sought to link a customer's Web behavior to a specific name or e-mail address, and then sell or otherwise misuse the information.

Because it can detect patterns and trends in large amounts of data, data mining is a valuable tool for managers. The popular Wikipedia site contains an interesting example of data mining. According to the Wikipedia article, a hypothetical chain of supermarkets performed a detailed analysis of purchases, and found that beer and diapers were often purchased together. Without attempting to explain this correlation, the obvious tactic for a retailer would be to display these items in the same area of the store. Wikipedia states that this data mining technique is often called **market basket analysis**.

Logical versus Physical Storage

It is important to understand the difference between logical storage and physical storage. **Logical storage** refers to data that a user can view, understand, and access, regardless of how or where that information actually is organized or stored. In contrast, **physical storage** is strictly hardware-related because it involves the process of reading and writing binary data to physical media such as a hard drive, CD-ROM, or network-based storage device. For example, portions of a document might be stored in different physical locations on a hard drive, but the user sees the document as a single logical entity on the computer screen.

Logical storage consists of alphabetic and numeric **characters**, such as the letter *A* or the number 9. As you learned earlier in this chapter, a set of related characters forms a field, which describes a single characteristic, or attribute, of a person, place, thing, or event. A field also is called a **data element** or a **data item**.

When designing fields, you should provide space for the largest values that can be anticipated, without allocating unnecessarily large storage capacities that will not be used. For example, suppose you are designing a customer order entry system for a firm with 800 customers. It would be a mistake to limit the customer number field to three, or even four characters. Instead, you might consider a five-character field with leading zeros that could store customer numbers from *00001* to *99999*.

You also might consider a mix of alphabetic and numeric characters, which many people find easier to view and use. Alphabetic characters expand the storage capacity because there are 26 possible values for each character position. Most airlines now use six alphabetic characters as a record locator, which has over 300 million possible values.

A **logical record** is a set of field values that describes a single person, place, thing, or event. For example, a logical customer record contains specific field values for a single customer, including the customer number, name, address, telephone number, credit limit, and so on. Application programs see a logical record as a group of related fields, regardless of how or where the data is stored physically.

The term *record* usually refers to a logical record. Whenever an application program issues a read or write command, the operating system supplies one logical record to the program or accepts one logical record from the program. The physical data might be stored on one or more servers, in the same building or thousands of miles away, but all the application program sees is the logical record — the physical storage location is irrelevant.

Data Coding

Computers represent data as **bits**, or **binary digits**, that have only two possible values: 1 and 0. A computer understands a group of bits as a digital code that can be transmitted, received, and stored. Computers use various data coding and storage schemes, such as EBCDIC, ASCII, and binary. A more recent coding standard called Unicode also is popular. Also, the storage of dates raises some design issues that must be considered.

EBCDIC, ASCII, AND BINARY   EBCDIC (pronounced EB-see-dik), which stands for Extended Binary Coded Decimal Interchange Code, is a coding method used on mainframe computers and high-capacity servers. **ASCII** (pronounced ASK-ee), which stands for American Standard Code for Information Interchange, is a coding method used on most personal computers. EBCDIC and ASCII both require eight bits, or one **byte**, for each character. For example, the name Ann requires three bytes of storage, the number *12,345* requires five bytes of storage, and the number *1,234,567,890* requires ten bytes of storage.

Compared with character-based formats, a **binary storage format** offers a more efficient storage method because it represents numbers as actual binary values, rather than as coded numeric digits. For example, an **integer format** uses only 16 bits, or two bytes, to represent the number *12,345* in binary form. A **long integer format** uses 32 bits, or four bytes, to represent the number *1,234,567,890* in binary form.

UNICODE   **Unicode** is a more recent coding standard that uses two bytes per character, rather than one. This expanded scheme enables Unicode to represent more than 65,000 unique, multilingual characters. Why is this important? Consider the challenge of running a multinational information system, or developing a program that will be sold in Asia, Europe, and North America. Because it supports virtually all languages, Unicode has become a global standard.

Traditionally, domestic software firms developed a product in English, then translated the program into one or more languages. This process was expensive, slow, and error-prone. In contrast, Unicode creates translatable content right from the start. Today, most popular operating systems support Unicode, and the Unicode Consortium maintains standards and support, as shown in Figure 9-44. Although Unicode has many advantages, it also has some disadvantages. In fact, because of its size and certain typographical issues, Microsoft recommends that you use its Arial Unicode font ". . . only when you can't use multiple fonts tuned for different writing systems."

FIGURE 9-44   Unicode is an international coding format that represents characters as integers, using 16 bits per character. The Unicode Consortium maintains standards and support for Unicode.
© 1991–2012 Unicode, Inc.

STORING DATES What is the best way to store dates? The answer depends on how the dates will be displayed and whether they will be used in calculations.

At the beginning of the 21st century, many firms that used only two digits to represent the year were faced with a major problem called the **Y2K issue**. Based on that experience, most date formats now are based on the model established by the **International Organization for Standardization (ISO)**, which requires a format of four digits for the year, two for the month, and two for the day (YYYYMMDD). A date stored in that format can be sorted easily and used in comparisons. If a date in ISO form is larger than another date in the same form, then the first date is later. For example, 20130927 (September 27, 2013) is later than 20120713 (July 13, 2012).

But, what if dates must be used in calculations? For example, if a manufacturing order placed on June 23 takes three weeks to complete, when will the order be ready? If a payment due on August 13 is not paid until April 27 of the following year, exactly how late is the payment and how much interest is owed? In these situations, it is easier to use absolute dates.

An **absolute date** is the total number of days from some specific base date. To calculate the number of days between two absolute dates, you subtract one date from the other. For example, if the base date is January 1, 1900, then September 27, 2013, has an absolute date value of 41554. Similarly, July 13, 2012, has an absolute date of 41103. If you subtract the earlier date value from the later one, the result is 441 days. You can use a spreadsheet to determine and display absolute dates easily, as shown in Figure 9-45.

FIGURE 9-45 Microsoft Excel uses absolute dates in calculations. In this example, September 27, 2013, is displayed as 41544, and July 13, 2012, is displayed as 41103. The difference between the dates is 441 days.

Screenshot used with permission from Microsoft.

DATA CONTROL

Just as it is important to secure the physical part of the system, as shown in Figure 9-46, file and database control must include all measures necessary to ensure that data storage is correct, complete, and secure. File and database control also is related to input and output techniques discussed earlier.

FIGURE 9-46 In addition to network monitoring, system security includes access codes, data encryption, passwords, and audit trails.

iStockphoto.com/DenGuy

A well-designed DBMS must provide built-in control and security features, including subschemas, passwords, encryption, audit trail files, and backup and recovery procedures to maintain data. Your main responsibility is to ensure that the DBMS features are used properly.

Earlier in this chapter, you learned that a subschema can be used to provide a limited view of the database to a specific user, or level of users. Limiting access to files and databases is the most common way of protecting stored data. Users must furnish a proper **user ID** and **password** to access a file or database. Different privileges, also called **permissions,** can be associated with different users, so some employees can be limited to read-only access, while other users might be allowed to update or delete data. For highly sensitive data, additional access codes can be established that restrict specific records or fields within records. Stored data also can be encrypted to prevent unauthorized access. **Encryption** is the process of converting readable data into unreadable characters to prevent unauthorized access to the data.

All system files and databases must be backed up regularly and a series of **backup** copies must be retained for a specified period of time. In the event of a file catastrophe, **recovery procedures** can be used to restore the file or database to its current state at the time of the last backup. **Audit log files,** which record details of all accesses and changes to the file or database, can be used to recover changes made since the last backup. You also can include **audit fields,** which are special fields within data records to provide additional control or security information. Typical audit fields include the date the record was created or modified, the name of the user who performed the action, and the number of times the record has been accessed.

CASE IN POINT 9.4: SOCCERMOM

SoccerMom Company sells a patented seat that spectators can take to youth soccer games. The seat folds so it is small enough to fit in the glove box of most vehicles. The company operates a factory in Kansas and also contracts its manufacturing projects to small firms in Canada and Mexico.

An unusual problem has occurred for this small multinational company: People are getting confused about dates in internal memos, purchase orders, and e-mail. Towson Hopkins handles all IT functions for SoccerMom. When he designed the company's database, he was not aware that the format for dates in Canada and Mexico was different from the format used in the United States. For example, in Canada and Mexico, the notation 7/1/13 indicates January 7, 2013, whereas in the United States the same notation indicates July 1, 2013. Although it seems like a small point, the date confusion has resulted in several order cancellations.

Towson has asked for your advice. You could suggest writing a simple program to convert the dates automatically or designing a switchboard command that would allow users to select a date format as data is entered. You realize, however, that SoccerMom might want to do business in other countries in the future. What would be the best course of action? Should SoccerMom adapt to the standard of each country, or should it maintain a single international format? What are the arguments for each option?

A QUESTION OF ETHICS

© faberfoto_it/iStockphoto

Olivia is the database manager at Tip Top Toys, a relatively small division of Worldwide Enterprises. Worldwide has nine other divisions, which include insurance, healthcare products, and financial planning services, to name a few.

Riccardo, corporate marketing director for Worldwide, has requested Tip Top's customer shopping data to target people who might be likely to purchase items or services from other Worldwide divisions. Olivia is not totally comfortable with this, and pointed out Tip Top's Web privacy policy, which states that "Tip Top Toys, a division of Worldwide Enterprises, will not share personal data with other companies without a customer's consent."

Riccardo replied that the statement only applies to outside companies — not other Worldwide divisions. He said he checked with the corporate legal department, and they agreed. Emily responded "Even if it is legally OK, it's not the *right* thing to do. Many people take our statement to mean that their data does not leave Tip Top. At the very least, we should give customers a choice, and share the data only with their consent."

Do you agree with Olivia? Why or why not?

CHAPTER SUMMARY

In this chapter, you continued your study of the systems design phase of the SDLC. You learned that files and tables contain data about people, places, things, or events that affect the information system. File-oriented systems, also called file processing systems, manage data stored in separate.

A database consists of linked tables that form an overall data structure. A database management system (DBMS) is a collection of tools, features, and interfaces that enable users to add, update, manage, access, and analyze data in a database.

DBMS designs are more powerful and flexible than traditional file-oriented systems. A database environment offers scalability, support for organization-wide access, economy of scale, data sharing among user groups, balancing of conflicting user requirements, enforcement of standards, controlled redundancy, effective security, flexibility, better programmer productivity, and data independence. Large-scale databases are complex and require extensive security and backup/recovery features.

DBMS components include interfaces for users, database administrators, and related systems; a data manipulation language; a schema; and a physical data repository. Other data management techniques include data warehousing, which stores data in an easily accessible form for user access, and data mining, which looks for meaningful patterns and relationships among data. Data mining also includes clickstream storage, which records how users interact with a site, and market basket analysis, which can identify product relationships and consumer buying patterns.

In an information system, an entity is a person, place, thing, or event for which data is collected and maintained. A field, or attribute, is a single characteristic of an entity. A record, or tuple, is a set of related fields that describes one instance of an entity. Data is stored in files (in a file-oriented system) and tables (in a database environment).

A primary key is the field or field combination that uniquely and minimally identifies a specific record; a candidate key is any field that could serve as a primary key. A foreign key is a field or field combination that must match the primary key of another file or table. A secondary key is a field or field combination used as the basis for sorting or retrieving records.

An entity-relationship diagram (ERD) is a graphic representation of all system entities and the relationships among them. The ERD is based on entities and data stores in DFDs prepared during the systems analysis phase. The three basic relationships represented in an ERD are one-to-one (1:1), one-to-many (1:M), and many-to-many (M:N). In a M:N relationship, the two entities are linked by an associative entity.

The relationship between two entities also is referred to as cardinality. A common form of cardinality notation is called crow's foot notation, which uses various symbols to describe the characteristics of the relationship.

Normalization is a process for avoiding problems in data design. A first normal form (1NF) record has no repeating groups. A record is in second normal form (2NF) if it is in 1NF and all nonkey fields depend on the entire primary key. A record is in third normal form (3NF) if it is in 2NF and if no field depends on a nonkey field.

Data design tasks include creating an initial ERD; assigning data elements to an entity; normalizing all table designs; and completing the data dictionary entries for files, records, and data elements.

You learned that a code is a set of letters or numbers used to represent data in a system. By using codes, you can speed up data entry, reduce data storage space, and reduce transmission time. Codes also can be used to reveal or to conceal information. The main types of codes are sequence codes, block sequence codes, classification codes, alphabetic codes (including category codes, abbreviation codes, and mnemonic codes), significant digit codes, derivation codes, cipher codes, and action codes.

Logical storage is information seen through a user's eyes, regardless of how or where that information actually is organized or stored. Physical storage is hardware-related and involves reading and writing binary data to physical media. A logical record is a related set of field values that describes a single person, place, thing, or event. Data storage formats include EBCDIC, ASCII, binary, and Unicode. Dates can be stored in several formats, including ISO and absolute format.

File and database control measures include limiting access to the data, data encryption, backup/recovery procedures, audit-trail files, and internal audit fields.

Key Terms

Chapter Exercises

Questions

1. In the auto shop examples on page 348, what are some problems that might arise in Mario's system? Why won't Danica run into the same problems? Provide specific examples in your answer.
2. What is a DBMS? Briefly describe the components of a DBMS.
3. Describe a primary key, candidate key, secondary key, foreign key, and a combination key. Use your imagination to provide an example of each key that is *not* in the textbook.
4. What are entity-relationship diagrams and how are they used? What symbol is used for a relationship? What is an associative entity? Provide an example.
5. What is cardinality, and what symbols do you use in the crow's foot notation method?
6. What are data warehousing and data mining? How do businesses use these tools?
7. What is an unnormalized design, and how do you convert an unnormalized design to 1NF? In your answer, refer to specific pages and figures in this chapter.
8. How would you define second normal form? How do you convert a 1NF design to 2NF? In your answer, refer to specific pages and figures in this chapter.
9. How would you define third normal form? How do you convert a 2NF design to 3NF? In your answer, refer to specific pages and figures in this chapter.
10. How would a specific date, such as April 27, 2015, be represented as an absolute date?

Discussion Topics

1. Are there ethical issues to consider when planning a database? For example, should sensitive personal data (such as medical information) be stored in the same DBMS that manages employee salary and benefits data? Why or why not?
2. Suggest three typical business situations where referential integrity avoids data problems.
3. Consider an automobile dealership with three locations. Data fields exist for stock number, vehicle identification number, make, model, year, color, and invoice cost. Identify the possible candidate keys, the likely primary key, a probable foreign key, and potential secondary keys.
4. Do we use lots of codes in our personal and business lives? How many can your class name?

Projects

1. Search the Internet to find information about date formats. Determine whether the date format used in the United States is the most common format.
2. Visit the IT department at your school or at a local business and determine how the organization uses database management systems. Describe your findings in a memo.
3. Use Microsoft Access or similar database software to create a DBMS for the imaginary company called TopText Publishing, which is described in Case In Point 9.1 on page 365. Add several sample records to each table and report to the class on your progress.
4. Visit the bookstore at your school or in your area. Interview the manager or store employees to learn more about the business and the entities that are involved in bookstore operations. Remember that an entity is a person, place, thing, or event that affects an information system. Draw an ERD, including cardinality, that describes the bookstore's operations.

Apply Your Knowledge

This section contains four mini-cases. Each case describes a situation, explains your role, and requires you to apply what you learned in the chapter.

1 CM Builders

CM Builders is a regional building contractor specializing in multifamily residential buildings, including condominiums, townhomes, and apartments. Charles Manville, the owner, hired you as an IT consultant to design a new relational database system for his business. As a small business owner, Charles is very involved in the operation of his business and wants to know more about the new computer system. How would you respond to Charles when he asks the following questions? Try to use terms that most business owners would understand clearly.

Tasks

1. Charles asks you, "What is an entity, a table, a field, and a record?" He also wants to know the difference between primary key, candidate keys, foreign keys, secondary keys, and combination keys.
2. After looking at the ERD you developed, Charles asks you to explain the crow's foot notation symbols he sees on the diagram.
3. Charles says that he has heard of data normalization, but does not understand it. He wants you to explain it to him.
4. Charles also wants to know what kind of codes you plan to use. How would you answer him? Before you make a final decision about codes, are there any questions that you might want to ask Charles? Explain your answer.

2 Parrot Palace

Parrot Palace works with TV and movie producers who need birds that can perform special tricks, such as playing dead, reciting poetry, ladder climbs, and various other tricks. Parrot Palace has about 50 birds and a list of 20 tricks from which to choose. Each bird can perform one or more tricks, and many tricks can be performed by more than one bird. When a bird learns a new trick, the trainer assigns a skill level. Some customers insist on using birds that score a 10, which is the highest skill level. As an IT consultant, you have been asked to suggest 3NF table designs. You are fairly certain that a M:N relationship exists between birds and tricks.

Tasks

1. Draw an ERD for the Parrot Palace information system.
2. Indicate cardinality.
3. Identify all fields you plan to include in the birds and tricks tables. For example, in the bird table, you might want species, size, age, name, and so on. In the tricks table, you might want the trick name and description. You will need to assign a primary key in each table. *Hint:* Before you begin, review some database design samples in this chapter. You might spot a similar situation that requires an associative entity that you can use as a pattern. In addition, remember that numeric values work well in primary key fields.
4. Create 3NF table designs.

3   **Winfield Public Transit Authority**

Winfield is a small city with a population of 22,000. Until now, Winfield was served by a bus route from a nearby city. The Winfield City Council has held a bond sale to fund the purchase of several buses to serve three routes in Winfield and neighboring areas. As the city's IT director, you have been asked to set up an information system for the new Transportation Authority. Assume that multiple buses will run on each route.

Tasks

1. Draw an ERD for the Winfield Public Transit Authority system.
2. Indicate cardinality.
3. Identify all fields you plan to include in the tables.
4. Create 3NF table designs.

4   **Working Shoes**

Working Shoes is a multistate shoe store that offers an extensive selection of casual and dress shoes designed for men and women who work on their feet. Working Shoes plans to launch a new Web site, and the company wants to develop a new set of product codes. Currently, 250 different products exist, with the possibility of adding more in the future. Shoes and many accessories come in various sizes, styles, and colors. The marketing manager asked you to develop an individualized product code that can identify a specific item and its characteristics. Your initial reaction is that it can be done, but the code might be fairly complex. Back in your office, you give the matter some thought.

Tasks

1. Design a code scheme that will meet the marketing manager's stated requirements.
2. Write a brief memo to the marketing manager suggesting at least one alternative to the code she proposed, and state your reasons.
3. Suggest a code scheme that will identify each Working Shoes customer.
4. Suggest a code scheme that will identify each specific order.

Case Studies

Each chapter includes a Chapter Case, a Continuing Case, a Capstone Case, and an Online Case Simulation. You can learn more about the Online Case Simulation in the MIS CourseMate Features section.

Chapter Case: Scenic Routes

Scenic Routes operates a bus company that specializes in travelling on secondary roads, rather than Interstate highways. Their slogan is: "It Takes a Little Longer, But It's Scenic." The firm needs to update its passenger reservation system.

Background

Data items must include reservation number, Route Number, Date, Origin, Destinations, Departure Time, Arrival Time, Passenger Name, and Seat Number. For example, Route 97 leaves Monroe, VA, daily at 8:00 A.M. and arrives in Spencer, VA, 100 miles away, at 11:00 A.M. Scenic wants to use an alphabetic reservation code, similar to the codes that airlines use.

Tasks

1. Identify the entities and their relationships. Then create an ERD for the reservations system.
2. Create 3NF table designs for the system.
3. For each of the entities identified, design tables and identify the possible candidate keys, the primary key, a probable foreign key, and potential secondary keys.
4. Use sample data to populate the fields for three records.

Continuing Case: Personal Trainer, Inc.

Personal Trainer, Inc. owns and operates fitness centers in a dozen Midwestern cities. The centers have done well, and the company is planning an international expansion by opening a new "supercenter" in the Toronto area. Personal Trainer's president, Cassia Umi, hired an IT consultant, Susan Park, to help develop an information system for the new facility. During the project, Susan will work closely with Gray Lewis, who will manage the new operation.

Background

After evaluating various development strategies, Susan prepared a system requirements document and submitted her recommendations to Cassia Umi, Personal Trainer's president. During her presentation, Susan discussed in-house development and outsourcing options. She did not feel that a commercial software package would meet Personal Trainer's needs.

Based on her research, Susan felt it would be premature to select a development strategy at this time. Instead, she recommended to Cassia that an in-house team should develop a design prototype, using a relational database as a model. Susan said that the prototype would have two main objectives: It would represent a user-approved model of the new system, and it would identify all systems entities and the relationships among them. Susan explained that it would be better to design the basic system first, and then address other issues, including Web enhancements and implementation options. She proposed a three-step plan: data design, user interface design, and application architecture. She explained that systems analysts refer to this as the systems design phase of a development project.

Cassia agreed with Susan's recommendation, and asked her to go forward with the plan.

(continues)

Continuing Case: Personal Trainer, Inc.

Tasks

1. In your discussion of the systems design phase, you mentioned normalization to Cassia. She would like you to explain the basics of normalization in plain English to help her understand the data design tasks.

2. Review the Personal Trainer fact-finding summary in Chapter 4 and draw an ERD with cardinality notation. Assume that system entities include members, classes, merchandise, and fitness instructors.

3. Design tables in 3NF. As you create the database, include various codes for at least three of the fields.

4. Use sample data to populate the fields for at least three records in each table.

Capstone Case: New Century Wellness Group

New Century Wellness Group offers a holistic approach to healthcare with an emphasis on preventive medicine as well as traditional medical care. In your role as an IT consultant, you will help New Century develop a new information system.

Background

After completing the user interface, input, and output design for the new information system, you will now focus on the data design of the DBMS that will support the system. Begin by reviewing the DFDs that you prepared in Chapter 5 and the object models that you created in Chapter 6.

Tasks

1. Create an initial ERD for the new system that contains at least eight entities.

2. Analyze each relationship to determine if it is 1:1, 1:M, or M:N.

3. Normalize your designs for all tables to ensure they are 3NF, and verify that all primary, secondary, and foreign keys are identified properly. Update your ERD to reflect any changes.

4. Review the Data Dictionary you created in Chapter 5 and double-check all data dictionary entries. Make sure that the entries for data stores, records, and data elements are documented completely and correctly. Determine what codes, if any, will be used and be sure they are documented in the data dictionary.

CASE Tool Workshop

Systems analysts use CASE tools to help them plan, build, and maintain information systems. To learn more about CASE tools, turn to Part B of the Toolkit that follows Chapter 12. You can complete these tasks with the Visible Analyst® CASE tool, which is available with this textbook, or a similar tool.

Background

At your school, your capstone systems analysis project is due very soon. Your instructor assigned student teams to develop an information system proposal for Danica's Auto Shop, which is shown in Figure 9-4 on page 349. The Microsoft Access screen in Figure 9-4 shows two tables: one for MECHANICS and the other for JOBS. The two tables represent entities, and are linked by a common field called Mechanic No.

   You are a member of a three-person team, and your job is to prepare an ERD and design a relational database for Danica with all tables in third normal form (3NF). Based on what you learned in this chapter, you have a feeling that an associative entity will be needed in the ERD.

Tasks

1. Before you start on the capstone project, you decide to hone your ERD skills by drawing your own version of the ERD shown in Figure 9-21 on page 364. You don't have to be precise — it's just a practice task.

2. Now, using Visible Analyst®, or another CASE tool, create an ERD that shows the two main entities in Danica's shop, and the relationship between them. Add an associative entity if necessary, similar to the examples shown on pages 362 and 376.

MIS CourseMate Features

If you have an MIS CourseMate access code, you can reinforce and extend your learning with premium content created for this textbook. For example, you can launch interactive Video Learning Sessions to help you understand systems development concepts and practice your skills. In addition, you can use MindTap Reader, which is a full, interactive, digital e-book.

MIS CourseMate also offers many learning features within each chapter, including an Online Case Simulation, a Critical Thinking Challenge, Video Learning Session Tasks, and a set of Learn It Online activities. To log on to the MIS CourseMate site at **www.cengagebrain.com**, you must create a student account and register this book.

Online Case Simulation: SCR Associates

Session 9: Data Design

Overview

The SCR Associates case study is a Web-based simulation that allows you to practice your skills in a real-world environment. The firm offers IT consulting, solutions, and training. SCR plans to open a new high-tech training center, and needs to develop a Training Information Management System (TIMS) to support the center. You are a newly hired systems analyst reporting to Jesse Baker, systems group manager, and will help her develop the system.

The case study takes you to the SCR Web site, where you receive e-mail and voice mail messages from Jesse, obtain information from SCR's resource libraries, and perform various tasks. Jesse has high standards, but seems very fair. She made it clear that she expects your work to be accurate, thorough, and professional.

Before You Begin

To prepare for this work session, you should review the following topics:

- Cardinality
- Entity-relationship diagrams (ERDs)
- Associative entities
- Normalization

How Do I Use the Online Case Simulation?

- Read the preview, and review the Chapter 1 background material, if necessary.
- Visit the MIS CourseMate Web site at **www.cengagebrain.com**, locate the **SCR Case Simulation,** and click the **intranet** link. Enter your name and the password **sad10e.**
- When the opening screen is displayed, select this session. Then check your e-mail and voice mail, and start to work on your task list.

Preview: Session 9

Your supervisor, Jesse Baker, asked you to begin working on data design tasks for the new information system, which will be implemented as a relational database. You will need to identify the entities, draw an ERD, design the tables, and add sample data to each table.

Critical Thinking Challenge

In addition to technical ability, IT professionals need critical thinking skills. This feature can help you practice perception, organization, analysis, problem-solving, and decision-making skills that will be valuable in the workplace. You can visit **www.criticalthinking.org** to learn more about critical thinking and why it is so important.

Background

This week, the IT team at Game Technology is working on database design and codes. Your job is to develop a recommendation for keeping track of individual games and their authors. You will be expected to create an ERD and table designs. Here is what you know so far:

- Every game has a product ID, name, version number, category code, and category description.
- Every author has an author ID, name, mailing address, and e-mail address.
- An individual author can develop one or more games.
- A game also can be developed by several authors. In this case, each author receives a specific percentage of the royalty that the game earns.

This information must be stored in the database. Your plan is to develop an overall design, list all the individual data items, and then include them as fields in the tables you create. Your design must be in the form of an ERD that shows all the entities, including any associative entities, and their relationships. Also, all table designs must be in third normal form (3NF).

The IT team also discussed data codes. You read somewhere that six-letter codes can have over 300 million unique combinations, but you don't know the exact number. Your friend, a math major, said that you could figure out the answer on your own, and she gave you a hint by saying it was 26 to the sixth power.

Practice Tasks

Visit the MIS CourseMate Web site at **www.cengagebrain.com.** Then navigate to the resources for this chapter and locate the **Critical Thinking Challenge** feature. You will complete two Practice Tasks, using what you learned in the chapter. Then you can check your answers to be sure you're ready for the Challenge Tasks.

Challenge Tasks

After you complete the Practice Tasks, you learn about new developments at Game Technology.

Your recommended design ran into a snag. The team leader said it wasn't bad, but it did not go far enough. The specific comment was that it was not in third normal form. Also, the team finally decided on a code for the customer ID field, which is a primary key. The code will be a combination code, with four letters followed by four digits. The letters would be the first four letters of the customer's last name, which might make it easier for customers to remember. To continue, navigate to the **Critical Thinking Challenge** feature for this chapter, select the **Challenge Tasks,** and follow the instructions.

Video Learning Sessions

The Video Learning Sessions in this chapter explain entity-relationship diagrams (ERDs) and data normalization rules.

Before You Begin

To prepare for the tasks, you should review the following topics:

- ERDs
- Cardinality
- Normal forms

How to Watch a Session

Go to the Management Information Systems CourseMate Web site at **www.cengagebrain.com.** Then navigate to the resources for this book, locate the **Video Learning Sessions,** and select a session. You can watch the session on your computer or mobile device, and pause, rewind, or replay a video at any time.

Practice Tasks

After each session, visit the **Your Turn** feature to perform the tasks and check your answers.

Training Tasks

Suppose the IT training manager wants to encourage team members to watch the Video Learning Sessions. To spark interest, she plans to post a set of VLS previews, which you will prepare. Each preview must include an overview of the session, a description of the main topics, and one or more screen examples from the video. To get you started, she provided a task list:

1. Select a Video Learning Session from this chapter. Launch the video and note the title, objectives, and total running time. Include this information in your preview.
2. Run though the session and find a segment that does a good job of explaining a specific skill or concept.
3. In the segment you selected, choose one or more specific screens and capture each screen image with the Windows Snipping Tool. To do this in Windows 7 or Windows Vista, click **Start**, and then type **Snipping Tool**. In Windows 8, you can display the **Start** menu, and then type **Snipping Tool**.
4. Paste the screen image into your preview and explain how it would help a viewer understand the topic. Also add your comments about the video, and why it would be important to an IT professional. Your preview should be well-organized and readable.

Learn It Online

In each chapter, you can use this feature to apply your knowledge and practice your skills. The exercises include Chapter Reinforcement Questions, Flash Cards, Practice Tests, and various games, such as *Who Wants To Be a Computer Genius?, Wheel of Terms,* and the *Crossword Puzzle Challenge.*

CHAPTER 10 System Architecture

Chapter 10 is the final chapter in the systems design phase of the SDLC. This chapter describes system architecture, which translates the logical design of an information system into a physical blueprint. As you plan the system architecture, you will learn about servers, clients, processing methods, networks, and related issues.

INTRODUCTION

OBJECTIVES

When you finish this chapter, you will be able to:

- Provide a checklist of issues to consider when selecting a system architecture

- Trace the evolution of system architecture from mainframes to current designs

- Explain client/server architecture, including tiers, cost-benefit issues, and performance

- Compare in-house e-commerce development with packaged solutions and service providers

- Discuss the impact of cloud computing and Web 2.0

- Define network topology, including hierarchical, bus, ring, star, and mesh models

- Describe wireless networking, including wireless standards, topologies, and trends

- Describe the system design specification

At this point in the SDLC, your objective is to determine an overall architecture to implement the information system. You learned in Chapter 1 that an information system requires hardware, software, data, procedures, and people to accomplish a specific set of functions. An effective system combines those elements into an architecture, or design, that is flexible, cost-effective, technically sound, and able to support the information needs of the business. This chapter covers a wide range of topics that support the overall system design, just as a plan for a new home would include a foundation plan, building methods, wiring and plumbing diagrams, traffic flows, and costs.

System architecture translates the logical design of an information system into a physical structure that includes hardware, software, network support, processing methods, and security. The end product of the systems design phase is the system design specification. If this document is approved, the next step is systems implementation.

PREVIEW CASE: Mountain View College Bookstore

Background: Wendy Lee, manager of college services at Mountain View College, wants a new information system that will improve efficiency and customer service at the three college bookstores.

In this part of the case, Tina Allen (systems analyst) and David Conroe (student intern) are talking about system architecture issues.

Participants:	Tina and David
Location:	Mountain View College cafeteria, Thursday afternoon, January 9, 2014
Project status:	The team completed user interface and data design work. The last step in the systems design phase is to consider a system architecture for the bookstore system.
Discussion topics:	System architecture checklist, client/server architecture, processing methods, and network issues

Tina: Hi, David. Did you enjoy the holiday break?

David: *I sure did. Now I'm ready to get back to work.*

Tina: Good. As the last step in the systems design phase of the SDLC, we need to study the physical structure, or architecture, of the bookstore system. Our checklist includes our college's organization and culture, enterprise resource planning, total cost of ownership, scalability, Web integration, legacy systems, processing methods, security issues, and portals that could affect the system design.

David: *So, where do we start?*

Tina: Well, the bookstore interfaces with many publishers and vendors, so we'll consider supply chain management, which is part of enterprise resource planning, or ERP for short.

David: *What happens after we finish the checklist?*

Tina: Then we'll define a client/server architecture. As I see it, the bookstore client workstations will share the processing with a server in the IT department. Also, we may need to look at middleware software to connect the new system with existing legacy systems, such as the college accounting system.

David: *Anything else?*

Tina: Yes. We need to select a network plan, or topology, so we'll know how to plan the physical cabling and connections — or possibly use wireless technology. When we're done, we'll submit a system design specification for approval.

David: *Sounds good to me.*

Tina: Good. Here's a task list to get us started:

FIGURE 10-1   Typical system architecture tasks.
© Cengage Learning 2014

ARCHITECTURE CHECKLIST

Just as an architect begins a project with a list of the owner's requirements, a systems analyst must approach system architecture with an overall checklist. Before making a decision, the analyst must consider several issues that will affect the architecture choice:

- Corporate organization and culture
- Enterprise resource planning (ERP)
- Initial and total cost of ownership (TCO)
- Scalability
- Web integration
- Legacy system interface requirements
- Processing options
- Security issues
- Corporate portals

Corporate Organization and Culture

To be successful, an information system must perform well in a company's organization and culture. For example, consider two large bicycle brands, Green Bikes and Blue Bikes. Each firm has three operating divisions: an Asian subsidiary that manufactures the bicycles, a factory in Los Angeles that produces bike accessories and clothing, and a plant in Canada that makes bike carriers, racks, and custom trailers.

On the surface, the two firms are similar, but they have very different organizations and corporate cultures. Green Bikes is highly centralized, and oversees day-to-day operations from its Los Angeles office. Blue Bikes also has a Los Angeles executive office, but allows its three business units to operate separately, with minimal corporate oversight. Both firms are successful, and it is unlikely that their managerial styles will change anytime soon.

Suppose you were a consultant, and both firms asked you to suggest an IT architecture that would boost productivity and reduce costs. How would corporate organization and culture issues affect your recommendation? There is no easy answer to that question. The best approach probably would be to study day-to-day business functions, talk to users at all levels, and focus on operational feasibility issues, just as you did earlier in the development process.

Enterprise Resource Planning (ERP)

Many companies use **enterprise resource planning (ERP)** software, which was described in Chapter 1. The objective of ERP is to establish a company-wide strategy for using IT that includes a specific architecture, standards for data, processing, network, and user interface design. A main advantage of ERP is that it describes a specific hardware and software environment, also called a **platform**, that ensures connectivity and easy integration of future systems, including in-house software and commercial packages.

Even though ERP has been very popular, some argue that it is outdated because of major advances in technology. For example, in her *CIO Magazine* article shown in Figure 10-2, author Karen Goulart calls ERP an "old workhorse." She suggests that ERP's future success depends on integrating new technologies such as mobility and cloud computing, among others. In other words, an ERP designer might have to bring enterprise data, anytime, anywhere, to a smart phone in a sales rep's pocket.

Many companies are extending internal ERP systems to their suppliers and customers, using a concept called **supply chain management (SCM)**. For example, in a totally integrated supply chain system, a customer order could cause a manufacturing system to schedule a work order, which in turn triggers a call for more parts from one or more suppliers. In a dynamic, highly competitive economy, SCM can help companies achieve faster response, better customer service, and lower operating costs.

FIGURE 10-2   Is ERP outdated, or will it still be around? Author Karen Goulart says that ERP's future success depends on integrating new technology, such as mobility and cloud computing.
© 2007–2012, TechTarget

Microsoft offers an enterprise solution called Microsoft Dynamics, as shown in Figure 10-3 on the next page. The interesting "test drive" video provides a scenario-based preview of how the software can integrate financial management, customer relationship management (CRM), supply chain management (SCM), and business metrics.

CASE IN POINT 10.1:   ABC Systems

You are a systems analyst at ABC Systems, a fast-growing IT consulting firm that provides a wide range of services to companies that want to establish e-commerce operations. During the last 18 months, ABC acquired two smaller firms and set up a new division that specializes in supply chain management. Aligning ABC's internal systems was quite a challenge, and top management was not especially happy with the integration cost or the timetable. To avoid future problems, you have decided to suggest an ERP strategy, and you plan to present your views at the staff meeting tomorrow. ABC's management team is very informal and prefers a loose, flexible style of management. How will you persuade them that ERP is the way to go?

Initial Cost and TCO

You learned earlier about the importance of considering economic feasibility and TCO during systems planning and analysis. TCO includes tangible purchases, fees, and contracts called *hard* costs. However, additional *soft* costs of management, support, training, and downtime are just as important, but more difficult to measure.

Firms such as Micromation, which is shown in Figure 10-4 on page 409, offer specialized TCO analysis, benchmarks, and consulting. As the Micromation chart shows, user-related costs represent a very large slice of the total pie.

A TCO analysis should include the the following questions.

- If in-house development was selected as the best alternative initially, is it still the best choice? Is the necessary technical expertise available, and does the original cost estimate appear realistic?

- If a specific package was chosen initially, is it still the best choice? Are newer versions or competitive products available? Have any changes occurred in pricing or support?

- Have any new types of outsourcing become available?

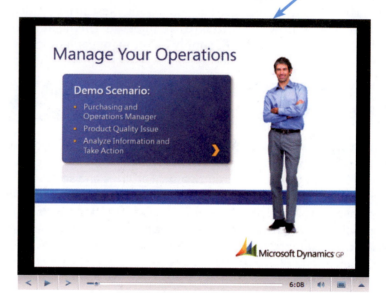

FIGURE 10-3   Microsoft invites you to watch or take a scenario-based test drive of its Microsoft Dynamics product.

Screenshots used with permission from Microsoft.

- Have any economic, governmental, or regulatory events occurred that could affect the proposed project?

- Have any significant technical developments occurred that could affect the proposed project?

- Have any major assumptions changed since the company made the build versus buy decision?

- Are there any merger or acquisition issues to consider, whereby the company might require compatibility with a specific environment?

- Have any new trends occurred in the marketplace? Are new products or technologies on the verge of being introduced?

- Have you updated the original TCO estimate? If so, are there any significant differences?

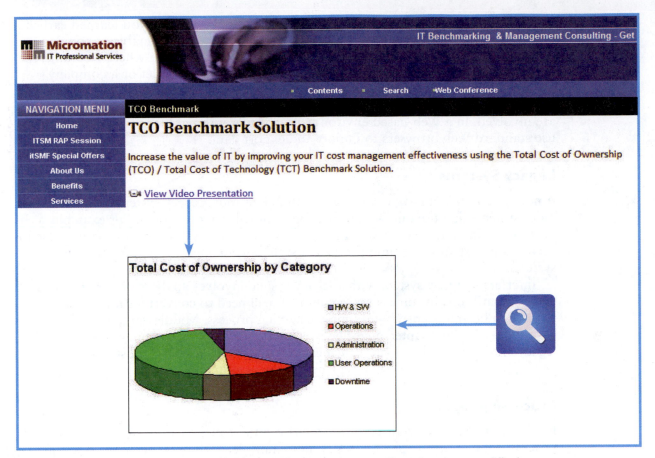

FIGURE 10-4 The Micromation site suggests that *soft* costs are very significant, but are more difficult to measure.
© 2012 Micromation

The answers to these questions might affect the initial cost and TCO for the proposed system. You should review system requirements and alternatives now, before proceeding to design the system architecture.

Scalability

A network is composed of individual nodes. A **node** represents a physical device, wired or wireless, that can send, receive, or manage network data. For example, nodes can be servers, workstations, shared printers, mass storage devices, wireless access points, or mobile computers.

Scalability, also called **extensibility**, refers to a system's ability to expand, change, or downsize easily to meet the changing needs of a business enterprise. Scalability is especially important in implementing systems that are volume-related, such as transaction processing systems. A scalable system is necessary to support a dynamic, growing business. For example, a scalable network could handle anywhere from a few dozen nodes to thousands of nodes, and a scalable DBMS could support the acquisition of an entire new sales division. When investing large amounts of money in a project, management is especially concerned about scalability issues that could affect the system's life expectancy.

Web Integration

An information system includes **applications**, which are programs that handle the input, manage the processing logic, and provide the required output. The systems analyst must know if a new application will be part of an e-commerce strategy and the degree of integration with other Web-based components. As you learned earlier, a **Web-centric** architecture follows Internet design protocols and enables a company to integrate the new application into its e-commerce strategy. Even where e-commerce is not involved, a Web-centric application can run on the Internet or a company intranet or extranet. A Web-based application avoids many of the connectivity and compatibility problems that typically arise when different hardware environments are involved. In a Web-based environment, a firm's external business partners can use standard Web browsers to import and export data.

Legacy Systems

A new system might have to interface with one or more **legacy systems**, which are older systems that use outdated technology, but still are functional. For example, a new marketing information system might need to report sales data to a server-based accounting system and obtain product cost data from a legacy manufacturing system.

Interfacing a new system with a legacy system involves analysis of data formats and compatibility. In some cases, a company will need to convert legacy file data, which can be an expensive and time-consuming process. Middleware, which is discussed later in this chapter, might be needed to pass data between new systems and legacy systems. Finally, to select the best architecture, the analyst must know if the new application eventually will replace the legacy system.

Processing Options

In planning the architecture, designers also must consider how the system will process data — online or in batches. For example, a high-capacity transaction processing system, such as an order entry system, requires more network, processing, and data storage resources than a monthly billing system that handles data in batches. Also, if the system must operate online, 24 hours a day and seven days a week (24/7), provision must be made for backup and speedy recovery in the event of system failure.

The characteristics of online and batch processing methods are described later in this chapter, with examples of each type.

Security Issues

From the password protection shown in Figure 10-5 to complex intrusion detection systems, security threats and defenses are a major concern to a systems ana-

lyst. As the physical design is translated into specific hardware and software, the analyst must consider security issues and determine how the company will address them. Security is especially important when data or processing is performed at remote locations, rather than at a centralized facility. In mission-critical systems, security issues will have a major impact on system architecture and design.

Web-based systems introduce additional security concerns, as critical data must be protected in the Internet environment. Also, firms that use e-commerce applications must assure customers that their personal data is safe and secure. System security concepts and strategies are discussed in detail in Chapter 12, Managing Systems Support and Security.

FIGURE 10-5 User IDs and passwords are important elements of system security.

Corporate Portals

Depending on the system, the planned architecture might include a corporate portal. A **portal** is an entrance to a multifunction Web site. After entering a portal, a user can navigate to a destination using various tools and features provided by the portal designer. A **corporate portal** can provide access for customers, employees, suppliers, and the public. A well-designed portal can integrate with various other systems and provide a consistent look and feel.

SYSTEM ARCHITECTURE: THEN AND NOW

Every business information system must carry out three main functions:

- Manage applications that perform the processing logic.

- Handle data storage and access.

- Provide an interface that allows users to interact with the system.

Depending on the architecture, the three functions are performed on a server, on a client, or are divided between the server and the client. As you plan the design, you must determine where the functions will be carried out and the advantages and disadvantages of each design approach.

Mainframe Architecture

A **server** is a computer that supplies data, processing services, or other support to one or more computers, called **clients**. The earliest servers were mainframe computers, and a system design where the server performs *all* the processing sometimes is described as **mainframe architecture**. Although the actual server does not have to be a mainframe, the term mainframe architecture typically describes a multiuser environment where the server is significantly more powerful than the clients. A systems analyst should know the history of mainframe architecture to understand the server's role in modern system design.

In the 1960s, mainframe architecture was the *only* choice. In addition to centralized data processing, the earliest systems performed all data input and output at a central location, often called a data processing center. Physical data was delivered or transmitted in some manner to the data processing center, where it was entered into the system. Users in the organization had no input or output capability, except for printed reports that were distributed by a corporate IT department.

As network technology advanced, companies installed terminals at remote locations, so that users could enter and access data from anywhere in the organization, regardless of where the centralized computer was located. A terminal included a keyboard and display screen to handle input and output, but lacked independent processing capability. In a centralized design, as shown in Figure 10-6, the remote user's keystrokes are transmitted from his or her terminal to the mainframe, which responds by sending screen output back to the user's screen.

Today, mainframe architecture still is used in industries that require large amounts of processing that can be done at a central location. For example, a bank might use mainframe servers to update customer balances each night. In a blend of old and new technology, an Internet-based retail operation might use mainframe architecture at a customer service center that fulfills its online sales as shown in Figure 10-7 on the next page.

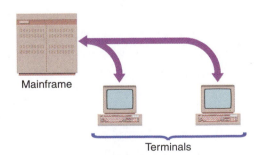

Mainframe

Terminals

FIGURE 10-6   In a centralized design, the remote user's keystrokes are transmitted to the mainframe, which responds by sending screen output back to the user's screen.

© Cengage Learning 2014

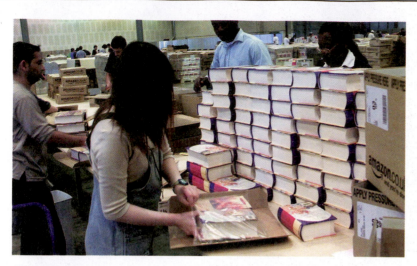

FIGURE 10-7   Internet-based retail operations such as Amazon.com use customer service centers to fulfill online sales.

© Bloomberg via Getty Images

Impact of the Personal Computer

When PC technology exploded in the 1990s, powerful microcomputers quickly appeared on corporate desktops. Users found that they could run their own word processing, spreadsheet, and database applications, without assistance from the IT group, in a mode called stand-alone computing. Before long, companies linked the stand-alone computers into networks that enabled the user clients to exchange data and perform local processing.

When an individual user works in stand-alone mode, the workstation performs all the functions of a server by storing, accessing, and processing data, as well as providing a user interface. Although stand-alone PCs improved employee productivity and allowed users to perform tasks that previously required IT department assistance, stand-alone computing was inefficient and expensive. Even worse, maintaining data on individual workstations raised major concerns about data security, integrity, and consistency. Without a central storage location, it was impossible to protect and back up valuable business data, and companies were exposed to enormous risks. In some cases, users who were frustrated by a lack of support and services from the IT department created and managed their own databases. In addition to security concerns, this led to data inconsistency and unreliability.

Network Evolution

As technology became available, companies resolved the problems of stand-alone computing by joining clients into a **local area network (LAN)** that allows sharing of data and hardware resources, as shown in Figure 10-8. One or more LANs, in turn, can connect to a centralized server. Further advances in technology made it possible to create powerful networks that could use satellite links, high-speed fiber-optic lines, or the Internet to share data.

A **wide area network (WAN)** spans long distances and can connect LANs that are continents apart, as shown in Figure 10-9. When a user accesses data on a LAN or WAN, the network is **transparent** because a user sees the data as if it were stored on his or her own workstation. Company-wide systems that connect one or more LANs or WANs are called **distributed systems**. The capabilities of a distributed system depend on the power and capacity of the underlying data communication network. Compared to mainframe architecture, distributed systems increase concerns about data security and integrity because many individual clients require access to perform processing.

FIGURE 10-8   A LAN allows sharing of data and hardware, such as printers and scanners.

© Cengage Learning 2014

CLIENT/SERVER DESIGNS

Today's interconnected world requires an information architecture that spans the entire enterprise. Whether you are dealing with a departmental network or a multinational corporation, as a systems analyst you will work with a distributed computing strategy called client/server architecture.

Overview

Although no standard definition exists, the term **client/server architecture** generally refers to systems that divide processing between one or more networked clients and a central server. In a typical client/server system, the client handles the entire user interface, including data entry, data query, and screen presentation logic. The server stores the data and provides data access and database management functions. Application logic is divided in some manner between the server and the clients. In a client/server interaction, the client submits a request for information from the server, which carries out the operation and responds to the client. As shown in Figure 10-10 the data file is not transferred from the server to the client — only the request and the result are transmitted across the network. To fulfill a request from a client, the server might contact other servers for data or processing support, but that process is transparent to the client. The analogy can be made to a restaurant where the customer gives an order to a server, who relays the request to a cook, who actually prepares the meal.

Figure 10-11 on the next page lists some major differences between client/server and traditional mainframe systems. Many early client/server systems did not produce expected savings because few clear standards existed, and development costs often were higher than anticipated. Implementation was expensive because clients needed powerful hardware and software to handle shared processing tasks. In addition, many companies had an installed base of data, called **legacy data**, which was difficult to access and transport to a client/server environment.

FIGURE 10-9   A WAN can connect many LANs and link users who are continents apart.
© Cengage Learning 2014

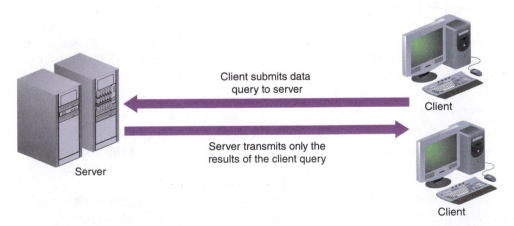

FIGURE 10-10   In a client/server design, data is stored and usually processed on the server.
© Cengage Learning 2014

Comparison of Client/Server and Mainframe Systems		
Characteristics	**Client/Server**	**Mainframe**
Basic architecture	Very flexible	Very rigid
Application development	Flexible Fast Object-oriented	Highly structured Slow Traditional
User environment	PC-based GUI Empowers the user Improves productivity	Uses terminals Text interface Constrains the user Limited options
Security and control features	Decentralized Difficult to control	Centralized Easier to control
Processing options	Can be shared and configured in any form desired	Cannot be modified
Data storage options	Can be distributed to place data closer to users	All data is stored centrally
Hardware/software integration	Very flexible Multivendor model	Very rigid Single proprietary vendor

FIGURE 10-11 Comparison of the characteristics of client/server and mainframe systems.

© Cengage Learning 2014

As large-scale networks grew more powerful, client/server systems became more cost-effective. Many companies invested in client/server systems to achieve a unique combination of computing power, flexibility, and support for changing business operations. Today, client/server architecture is the dominant form of systems design, using Internet protocols and network models such as the ones described on pages 426–430. As businesses form new alliances with customers and suppliers, the client/server concept continues to expand to include clients and servers outside the organization.

Cloud computing, which is discussed later in this chapter, is seen by some observers as an entirely new concept. Others see it as the ultimate form of client/server architecture, where Internet-based computing becomes the *server* part of client/server and handles processing tasks, while the Internet itself becomes the platform that replaces traditional networks. The bottom line is that it doesn't matter whether cloud computing is part of a client/server evolution, or a whole new way of thinking about computing. Either way, successful systems must support business requirements, and system architecture is an important step in the systems development process.

The Client's Role

The client/server relationship must specify how the processing will be divided between the client and the server. A **fat client**, also called a **thick client**, design locates all or most of the application processing logic at the client. A **thin client** design locates all or most of the processing logic at the server. What are the advantages and disadvantages of each design? Most IT experts agree that thin client designs provide better performance, because program code resides on the server, near the data. In contrast, a fat client handles more of the processing and must access and update the data more often. Compared with maintaining a central server, fat client TCO also is higher, because of initial hardware and software requirements and the ongoing expense of supporting and updating remote client computers. A fat client design, however, is simpler and less expensive to develop, because the architecture resembles traditional file server designs where all processing is performed at the client. Figure 10-12 compares the characteristics of fat and thin clients.

Client/Server Tiers

Early client/server designs were called two-tier designs. In a **two-tier** design, the user interface resides on the client, all data resides on the server, and the application logic can run either on the server or on the client, or be divided between the client and the server.

More recently, another form of client/server design, called a three-tier design, has become popular. In a **three-tier** design, the user interface runs on the client and the data is stored on the server, just as with a two-tier design. A three-tier design also has a middle layer between the client and server that processes the client requests and

Characteristic	Fat Client	Thin Client
Network traffic	Higher, because the fat client must communicate more often with the server to access data and update processing results	Lower, because most interaction between code and data takes place at the server
Performance	Slower, because more network traffic is required	Faster, because less network traffic is required
Initial cost	Higher, because more powerful hardware is required	Lower, because workstation hardware requirements are not as stringent
Maintenance cost	Higher, because more program code resides on the client	Lower, because most program code resides on the central server
Ease of development	Easier, because systems resemble traditional file-server designs where all processing was performed at the client	More difficult, because developers must optimize the division of processing logic

FIGURE 10-12   Characteristics of fat and thin clients.

© Cengage Learning 2014

translates them into data access commands that can be understood and carried out by the server, as shown in Figure 10-13. You can think of the middle layer as an **application server**, because it provides the **application logic**, or **business logic**, required by the system. Three-tier designs also are called **n-tier** designs, to indicate that some designs use more than one intermediate layer.

The advantage of the application logic layer is that a three-tier design enhances overall performance by reducing the data server's workload. The separate application logic layer also relieves clients of complex processing tasks. Because it can run on a minicomputer that is much more powerful than the typical client workstations, the middle layer is more efficient and cost-effective in large-scale systems. Figure 10-14 on the next page shows where the data, the application logic, and the user interface are located on various architectures. In a client/server system, the tiers communicate using software called middleware, which is described in the following section.

FIGURE 10-13   Characteristics of two-tier versus three-tier client/server design.

© Cengage Learning 2014

Architecture		Data	Application Logic	User Interface
Central data processing center	Server	X	X	X
	Client			
Central server with remote terminals	Server	X	X	
	Client			X
Stand-alone client	Server			
	Client	X	X	X
Two-tier client/server	Server	X	X	
	Client		X	X
Three-tier client/server	Data server	X		
	Application server		X	
	Client			X

FIGURE 10-14 The location of the data, the application logic, and the user interface depend on the type of architecture.

© Cengage Learning 2014

Middleware

A recent Internet search for the phrase "What is Middleware" returned 80,500 sites. Unfortunately, the term *middleware* means different things to different people. So, what is middleware?

In a multi-tier system, special software called **middleware** enables the tiers to communicate and pass data back and forth. Here are some other definitions you might encounter:

- Middleware offers an interface to connect software and hardware.

- Middleware can integrate legacy systems and Web-based applications. For example, when a user enters a customer number on a Web form, middleware can update a legacy accounting system.

- Middleware is like glue that holds different applications together.

- Middleware represents the slash in the term *client/server*.

- Middleware resembles the plumbing system in your home: it connects important objects in a way that requires little or attention.

The bottom line is that a hard and fast definition isn't all that important. If you grasp the concept of middleware, you'll be able to handle the development tools and learn the techniques required in your IT environment.

Cost-Benefit Issues

To support business requirements, information systems need to be scalable, powerful, and flexible. For most companies, client/server systems offer the best combination of features to meet those needs. Whether a business is expanding or downsizing, client/server systems enable the firm to scale the system in a rapidly changing environment. As the size of the business changes, it is easier to adjust the number of clients and the processing functions they perform than it is to alter the capability of a large-scale central server.

Client/server computing also allows companies to transfer applications from expensive mainframes to less-expensive client platforms. In addition, using common languages such as SQL, clients and servers can communicate across multiple platforms. That difference is important because many businesses have substantial investments in a variety of hardware and software environments.

Finally, client/server systems reduce network load and improve response times. For example, consider a user at a company headquarters who wants information about total sales figures. In a client/server system, the server locates the data, performs the necessary processing, and responds immediately to the client's request. The data retrieval and processing functions are transparent to the client because they are done on the server, not the client.

Performance Issues

While it provides many advantages, client/server architecture does involve performance issues that relate to the separation of server-based data and networked clients that must access the data.

Consider the difference between client/server design and a centralized environment, where a server-based program issues a command that is executed by the server's own CPU. Processing speed is enhanced because program instructions and data both travel on an internal system bus, which moves data more efficiently than an external network.

In contrast to the centralized system, a client/server design separates applications and data. Networked clients submit data requests to the server, which responds by sending data back to the clients. When the number of clients and the demand for services increases beyond a certain level, network capacity becomes a constraint, and system performance declines dramatically.

In the article shown in Figure 10-15, IBM states that the performance characteristics of a client/server system are not the same as a centralized processing environment. Client/server response times increase gradually as more requests are made, but then rise dramatically when the system nears its capacity. This point is called the **knee of the curve**, because it marks a sharp decline in the system's speed and efficiency. To deliver and maintain acceptable performance, system developers must anticipate the number of users, network traffic, server size and location, and design a client/server architecture that can support current and future business needs.

What is the answer to enhancing client/server performance? According to IBM, client/server systems must be designed so the client contacts the server only when necessary and makes as few trips as possible.

Another issue that affects client/server performance is data storage. Just as processing can be done at various places, data can be stored in more than one location using a **distributed database management system (DDBMS)**.

Using a DDBMS offers several advantages: Data stored closer to users can reduce network traffic; the system is scalable, so new data sites can be added without reworking the system design; and with data stored in various locations, the system is less likely to experience a catastrophic failure. A potential disadvantage of distributed data storage involves data security. It can be more difficult to maintain controls and standards when data is stored in various locations. In addition, the architecture of a DDBMS is more complex and difficult to manage. From a system design standpoint, the challenge is that companies often want it both ways — they want the control that comes with centralization *and* the flexibility associated with decentralization.

FIGURE 10-15   According to IBM, client/server response times increase gradually, and then rise dramatically when the system nears its capacity. That point is referred to as *the knee of the curve.*
© Copyright IBM Corporation 1994, 2012.

THE IMPACT OF THE INTERNET

The Internet has had an enormous impact on system architecture. The Internet has become more than a communication channel — many IT observers see it as a fundamentally different environment for system development.

Recall that in a traditional client/server system, the client handles the user interface, as shown in Figure 10-14 on the previous page, and the server (or servers in a multi-tier system) handles the data and application logic. In a sense, part of the system runs on the client, part on the server. In contrast, in an Internet-based architecture, in addition to data and application logic, the entire user interface is provided by the Web server in the form of HTML documents that are displayed by the client's browser. Shifting the responsibility for the interface from the client to the server simplifies data transmission and results in lower hardware cost and complexity.

The advantages of Internet-based architecture have changed fundamental ideas about how computer systems should be designed, and we are moving rapidly to a total online environment. At the same time, millions of people are using Web-based collaboration and social networking applications to accomplish tasks that used to be done in person, over the phone, or by more traditional Internet channels. The following sections examine cloud computing and Web 2.0. It is important to understand these trends, which are shaping the IT industry's future.

Cloud Computing

Cloud computing refers to the cloud symbol that often is used to represent the Internet. The cloud computing concept envisions a *cloud* of remote computers that provide a total online software and data environment that is hosted by third parties.

Company	Flagship Product
Amazon	EC2 (Elastic Computing)
ATT	Synaptic Hosting
Cisco	UCS (Unified Computing System)
Google	AppEngine
HP	HP CloudSystem
IBM	Blue Cloud
Microsoft	Azure
Oracle	Oracle Cloud
Rackspace	OpenStack

Cloud

Web Server

For example, a user's computer does not perform processing or computing tasks — the cloud does. This concept is in contrast to today's computing model, which is based on networks that strategically distribute processing and data across the enterprise. In a sense, the cloud of computers acts as one giant computer that performs tasks for users.

Figure 10-16 shows users connected to the cloud, which performs the computing work. Instead of requiring specific hardware and software on the user's computer, cloud computing spreads the workload to powerful remote systems that are part of the cloud. The user appears to be working on a local system, but all computing is actually performed in the cloud. No updates or maintenance are required of the user, and there are no compatibility issues.

Cloud computing effectively eliminates compatibility issues, because the Internet itself is the platform. This architecture also provides **scaling on demand**, which matches resources to needs at any given time. For example, during peak loads, additional cloud servers might come on line automatically to support the workload.

Cloud computing is an ideal platform for powerful Software as a Service (SaaS) applications. As you learned in Chapter 7, SaaS is a popular deployment method where software is not purchased but is paid for as a service, much like one pays for electricity or cable TV each month. In

FIGURE 10-16 The explosive growth of cloud computing has attracted many firms that fight hard for market share.

© Cengage Learning 2014

this architecture, updates and changes to services can be easily made by service providers without involving the users.

Even though cloud computing has tremendous advantages, some concerns exist. First, cloud computing requires significantly more **bandwidth** (the amount of data that can be transferred in a fixed time period) than traditional client/server networks. Second, because cloud computing is Internet-based, if a user's Internet connection becomes unavailable, he or she will be unable to access any cloud-based services. In addition, there are security concerns associated with sending large amounts of data over the Internet, as well as concerns about storing it securely. Finally, there is the issue of control. Because a service provider hosts the resources and manages data storage and access, the provider has complete control of the system. Many firms are wary of handing over control of mission-critical data and systems to a third-party provider.

Future technology advances will make cloud computing even more feasible, desirable, and secure. As the IT industry moves toward a Web-based architecture, cloud computing will be marketed aggressively and growth will be rapid. Figure 10-16 lists some of the major players in the cloud market. Although the list will change from month to month, or week to week, one thing will not change: cloud computing will be a cornerstone of IT growth in the coming decade.

Web 2.0

The shift to Internet-based collaboration has been so powerful and compelling that it has been named **Web 2.0**. Web 2.0 is not a reference to a more technically advanced version of the current Web. Rather, Web 2.0 envisions a second generation of the Web that will enable people to collaborate, interact, and share information more dynamically.

Leading Web 2.0 author Tim O'Reilly has suggested that the strong interest in Web 2.0 is driven by the concept of the *Internet as a platform*. O'Reilly sees future Web 2.0 applications delivering software as a continuous service with no limitations on the number of users that can connect or how users can consume, modify, and exchange data.

Social networking sites, such as Facebook, Twitter, and LinkedIn are seeing explosive growth in the Web 2.0 environment. Another form of social collaboration is called a wiki. A **wiki** is a Web-based repository of information that anyone can access, contribute to, or modify. In a sense, a wiki represents the collective knowledge of a group of people. One of the best-known wikis is Wikipedia.org, but smaller-scale wikis are growing rapidly at businesses, schools, and other organizations that want to compile and share information.

One of the goals of Web 2.0 is to enhance creativity, interaction, and shared ideas. In this regard, the Web 2.0 concept resembles the agile development process and the open-source software movement. Web 2.0 communities and services are based on a body of data created by users. As users collaborate, new layers of information are added in an overall environment known as the **Internet operating system**. These layers can contain text, sound bytes, images, and video clips that are shared with the user community.

E-COMMERCE ARCHITECTURE

The huge expansion of Web-based commerce is reshaping the IT landscape. Internet business solutions must be efficient, reliable, and cost-effective. When planning an e-commerce architecture, analysts can examine in-house development, packaged solutions, and service providers. The following sections discuss these options.

Guidelines for In-house E-commerce Site Development
Analyze the company's business needs and develop a clear statement of your goals. Consider the experience of other companies with similar projects.
Obtain input from users who understand the business and technology issues involved in the project. Plan for future growth, but aim for ease of use.
Determine whether the IT staff has the necessary skills and experience to implement the project. Consider training, additional resources, and the use of consultants if necessary.
Consider integration requirements for existing legacy systems or enterprise resource planning. Select a physical infrastructure carefully, so it will support the application, now and later.
Develop the project in modular form so users can test and approve the functional elements as you go along.
Connect the application to existing in-house systems and verify interactivity.
Test every aspect of the site exhaustively. Consider a preliminary rollout to a pilot group to obtain feedback before a full launch.

FIGURE 10-17 Guidelines for companies developing e-commerce strategies.
© Cengage Learning 2014

In-House Solutions

In Chapter 7, you learned how to analyze advantages and disadvantages of in-house development versus purchasing a software package. The same basic principles apply to system design.

If you decide to proceed with an in-house solution, you must have an overall plan to help achieve your goals. How should you begin? Figure 10-17 offers guidelines for companies developing e-commerce strategies. An in-house solution usually requires a greater initial investment, but provides more flexibility for a company that must adapt quickly in a dynamic e-commerce environment. By working in-house, a company has more freedom to integrate with customers and suppliers and is less dependent on vendor-specific solutions.

For smaller companies, the decision about in-house Web development is even more critical, because this approach will require financial resources and management attention that many small companies might be unable or unwilling to commit. An in-house strategy, however, can provide valuable benefits, including the following:

- A unique Web site, with a look and feel consistent with the company's other marketing efforts
- Complete control over the organization of the site, the number of pages, and the size of the files
- A scalable structure to handle increases in sales and product offerings in the future
- More flexibility to modify and manage the site as the company changes
- The opportunity to integrate the firm's Web-based business systems with its other information systems, creating the potential for more savings and better customer service

Whether a firm uses an in-house or a packaged design, the decision about Web hosting is a separate issue. Although internal hosting has some advantages, such as greater control and security, the expense would be much greater, especially for a small- to medium-sized firm.

CASE IN POINT 10.2: SMALL POTATOES, INC.

Small Potatoes is a family-operated seed business that has grown rapidly. Small Potatoes specializes in supplying home gardeners with the finest seeds and gardening supplies. Until now, the firm has done all its business by placing ads in gardening and health magazines, and taking orders using a toll-free telephone number.

Now, the family has decided to establish a Web site and sell online, but there is some disagreement about the best way to proceed. Some say it would be better to develop the site on their own, and Betty Lou Jones, a recent computer science graduate, believes she can handle the task. Others, including Sam Jones, Betty's grandfather, feel it would be better to outsource the site and focus on the business itself. Suppose the family asked for your opinion. What would you say? What additional questions would you ask?

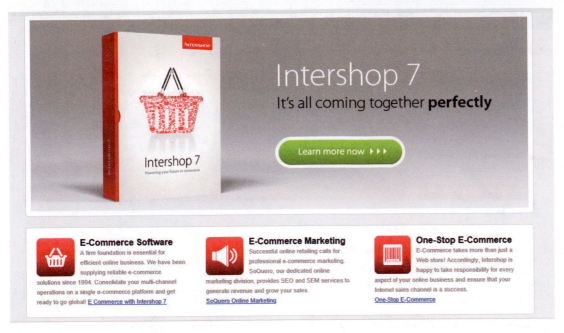

FIGURE 10-18   Intershop offers software solutions for smaller companies that want to get an e-business up and running quickly.

Packaged Solutions

If a small company is reluctant to take on the challenge and complexity of developing an Internet commerce site in-house, an alternative can be a packaged solution. This is true even for medium- to large-sized firms. Many vendors, including Microsoft and Intershop, offer turnkey systems for companies that want to get an e-business up and running quickly, as shown in Figure 10-18.

For large-scale systems that must integrate with existing applications, packaged solutions might be less attractive.

Service Providers

Another alternative is to use an application service provider (ASP). As explained in Chapter 7, an ASP provides applications, or access to applications, by charging a usage or subscription fee. Today, many ASPs offer full-scale Internet business services for companies that decide to outsource those functions.

Another service provider option is managed hosting, which also was discussed in Chapter 7. As shown in Figure 10-19 on the next page, a solution provider such as Rackspace can host and maintain a corporate Web site. Rackspace states that its customers will "never have to implement, update, troubleshoot, patch, monitor, administer, backup data, or worry again."

A systems analyst confronts a bewildering array of products and strategies when implementing Internet-based systems. A good starting point might be to consider the experience of other companies in the same industry. Many firms offer the names of clients and customers, along with their success stories. Although this information might or might not be reliable, it can provide valuable knowledge regarding a vendor's products and services.

PROCESSING METHODS

In selecting an architecture, the systems analyst must determine which transactions will be handled online, and what functions, if any, can be carried out using a batch processing method.

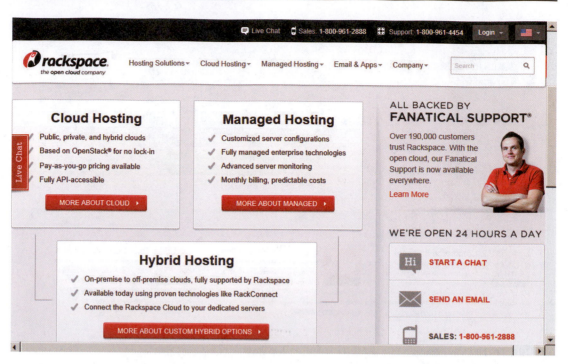

FIGURE 10-19 Rackspace offers managed hosting and a variety of cloud-based services.
© 2012 Rackspace, US Inc.

Online Processing

Early computer systems were designed to handle data records as a group, or *batch*. Few, if any systems use that model today. However, even the most advanced online systems must perform maintenance, post large quantities of data during off-hours when network traffic is low, and carry out housekeeping tasks just as their legacy computer ancestors did. This section will discuss the online processing capability that is at the core of powerful, modern systems, and the following section will describe the evolution of batch processing.

An **online system** handles transactions when and where they occur and provides output directly to users. Because it is interactive, online processing avoids delays and allows a constant dialog between the user and the system.

An airline reservations system is a familiar example of online processing. When an online customer visits the airline's Web site, he or she can enter the origin, destination, travel dates, and travel times. The system searches a database and responds by displaying available flights, times, and prices. The customer can make a reservation, enter a name, address, credit card information, and other required data and the system creates the reservation, assigns a seat, and updates the flight database immediately.

Online processing also can be used with file-oriented systems. Figure 10-20 shows what happens when a customer uses an ATM to inquire about an account balance. After the ATM verifies the customer's card and password, the customer enters the request (Step 1). Then, the system accesses the account master file using the account number as the primary key and retrieves the customer's record (Step 2). The system verifies the account number and displays the balance (Step 3). Data is retrieved and the system transmits the current balance to the ATM, which prints it for the customer. Online processing systems have four typical characteristics:

1. The system processes transactions completely when and where they occur.

2. Users interact directly with the information system.

3. Users can access data randomly.

4. The information system must be available whenever necessary to support business functions.

Batch Processing: Still With Us After All These Years

Batch processing means that data is managed in groups, or batches. That was an acceptable choice in the 1960s, and for most firms, it was the *only* choice. Today, all businesses need real-time information to operate, and batch processing is not practical. However, batch methods can be efficient and convenient in some situations.

For example, batch processing can be used for large amounts of data that must be processed on a routine schedule, such as weekly paychecks, daily credit card transaction updates, or closing stock data that must be calculated and published in the following day's news media. The main advantages of batch methods are:

- Tasks can be planned and run on a predetermined schedule, without user involvement.

- Batch programs that require major network resources can run at times when costs, and impact on other traffic, will be lowest.

- A batch method is well-suited to address security, audit, and privacy concerns, because it runs in a relatively controlled environment.

Real-World Examples

Figure 10-21 shows a familiar **point-of-sale** (POS) terminal in a supermarket chain. The diagram in Figure 10-22 on the next page shows how that POS terminal might trigger a series of online and batch processing events. Notice that the system uses online processing to handle data entry and inventory updates, while reports and accounting entries are performed in a batch. Why would any company choose a mix of online and batch processing? The answer is that it makes good business sense. Consider the following scenario in a typical retail store:

- During business hours, a salesperson enters a sale on a POS terminal, which is part of an online system that handles daily sales transactions and maintains an up-to-date inventory file.

- When the salesperson enters the transaction, online processing occurs. The system performs calculations, updates the inventory file, and produces output on the POS terminal in the form of a screen display and a printed receipt. At the same time, each sales transaction creates input data for day-end batch processing.

ATM QUERY PROCESS

Step 1: Customer enters his or her account number and requests an account balance

Step 2: Retrieves current account balance

Step 3: Verifies bank account number and displays balance on ATM screen

FIGURE 10-20 When a customer requests a balance, the ATM system verifies the account number, submits the query, retrieves the current balance, and displays the balance on the ATM screen.
© Cengage Learning 2014

FIGURE 10-21 Retail point-of-sale terminals provide customer sales support and transaction processing capability.
© Karlheinz Schindler/dpa/Landov

POINT OF SALE (POS) PROCESSING

FIGURE 10-22 Many retailers use a combination of online and batch processing. When a salesperson enters the sale on the POS terminal, the online system retrieves data from the item file, updates the quantity in stock, and produces a sales transaction record. At the end of the day, a batch processing program produces a daily sales report and updates the accounting system.

© Cengage Learning 2014

- When the store closes, the system uses the sales transactions to produce the daily sales report, perform the related accounting entries, and analyze the data to identify slow or fast-moving items, sales trends, and related issues — such as store discounts for the next day.

Which method is better, online or batch processing? The answer is neither — they are totally different, but can work well together. In this scenario, an online system handles point-of-sale processing, which must be done as it occurs, while a batch method provides routine, overnight processing and marketing analysis. Online processing allows the data to be entered and validated immediately, so the information always is up to date. However, a heavy volume of online transactions can be expensive for smaller firms, and data backup and recovery also adds to IT costs. In contrast, when used properly, batch processing can be cost-effective and less vulnerable to system disruption.

CASE IN POINT 10.3: R/WAY TRUCKING COMPANY

You are the new IT manager at R/Way, a small but rapidly growing trucking company headquartered in Cleveland, Ohio. The company slogan is "Ship It R/Way — State-of-the-Art in Trucking and Customer Service." R/Way's information system currently consists of a file server and three workstations where freight clerks enter data, track shipments, and prepare freight bills. To perform their work, the clerks obtain data from the server and use database and spreadsheet programs stored on their PCs to process the data.

Unfortunately, your predecessor did not design a relational database. Instead, data is stored in several files, including one for shippers, one for customers, and one for shipments. The system worked well for several years, but cannot handle current volume or support online links for R/Way shippers and customers. The company president is willing to make changes, but he is reluctant to spend money on major IT improvements unless you can convince him that they are necessary.

What would you recommend and why?

NETWORK MODELS

A network allows the sharing of hardware, software, and data resources in order to reduce expenses and provide more capability to users. When planning a network design, you must consider network terms and concepts, including the OSI model, network modeling tools, network topology, network protocols, and wireless networks, which are covered in this section. Other important issues, such as network performance and security, are covered in Chapter 12, Managing Systems Support and Security.

The OSI Model

Based on the discussion of system architecture earlier in this chapter, you already understand basic network terms such as client, server, LAN, WAN, client/server architecture, tiers, middleware, and cloud computing.

Before you study network topology, you should be aware of the **OSI (Open Systems Interconnection) model**, which describes how data moves from an application on one computer to an application on another networked computer. The OSI model consists of seven layers, and each layer performs a specific function.

The OSI model provides physical design standards that assure seamless network connectivity, regardless of the specific hardware environment. If you took a networking course, you probably studied the OSI model in detail. As an IT professional, if your tasks include network installation, configuration, and maintenance, you will need additional resources and information about the OSI model.

Network Topology

The way a network is configured is called the **network topology**. Topology can refer to a physical or a logical view of the network. For example, **physical topology** describes the actual network cabling and connections, while **logical topology** describes the way the components interact. It is important to understand the distinction, because a specific physical topology might be able to support more than one logical topology. For example, it is not uncommon to run cabling in a certain pattern because of physical installation and cost issues, but to use a different pattern for the logical topology.

The workstations in Figure 10-23 are arranged in a circular shape, but that might or might not reflect the network topology. The examples shown in Figures 10-24 to 10-28 on pages 426 to 428 represent a logical topology, as seen by network users, who do not know or care about the physical cabling pattern.

LAN and WAN networks typically are arranged in four patterns: hierarchical, bus, ring, and star. The concepts are the same regardless of the size of the network, but the physical implementation is different for a large-scale WAN that spans an entire business enterprise compared with a small LAN in a single department. The four topologies are described in the following sections.

HIERARCHICAL NETWORK In a **hierarchical network**, as shown in Figure 10-24 on the next page, one or more powerful servers control the entire network. Departmental servers control lower levels of processing and network devices. An

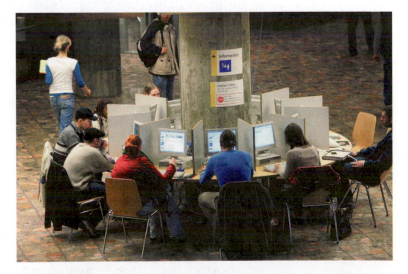

FIGURE 10-23   Although these workstations form a circle physically, the layout has no bearing on the network topology, which might be a bus, ring, star, or other logical design.

© Patrick Seeger/dpa /Landov

FIGURE 10-24 A hierarchical network with a single server that controls the network.
© Cengage Learning 2014

example of a hierarchical network might be a retail clothing chain, with a central computer that stores data about sales activity and inventory levels and local computers that handle store-level operations. The stores transmit data to the central computer, which analyzes sales trends, determines optimum stock levels, and coordinates a supply chain management system. In this situation, a hierarchical network might be used, because it mirrors the actual operational flow in the organization.

One disadvantage of a hierarchical network is that if a business adds additional processing levels, the network becomes more complex and expensive to operate and maintain. Hierarchical networks were often used in traditional mainframe-based systems, but are much less common today.

BUS NETWORK In a **bus network**, as shown in Figure 10-25, a single communication path connects the central server, departmental servers, workstations, and peripheral devices. Information is transmitted in either direction between networked devices, and all messages travel over the same central bus. Bus networks require less cabling than other topologies, because only a single cable is used. Devices can also be attached or detached from the network at any point without disturbing the rest of the network. In addition, a failure in one workstation on the network does not necessarily affect other workstations on the network.

One major disadvantage of a bus network is that if the central bus becomes damaged or defective, the entire network shuts down. Another disadvantage is that overall performance declines as more users and devices are added, because all message traffic must flow along the central bus. This does not occur in the treelike structure of a hierarchical network or the hub-and-spoke design of a star network, where network paths are more isolated and independent.

The bus network is one of the oldest LAN topologies, and is a simple way to connect multiple workstations. Before the proliferation of star networks, bus networks were very common. Today, the bus design is much less popular, but some firms have retained bus networks to avoid the expense of new wiring and hardware.

RING NETWORK Although ring networks are still around, they are somewhat outdated. IBM was a leader in ring network technology, and large companies who use IBM mainframe equipment still deploy the ring network design. A **ring network**, as shown in Figure 10-26, resembles a circle where the data flows in only one direction from one device to the next. In function, a ring network can be thought of as a bus network with the ends connected. One disadvantage of a ring network is that if a network device (such as a PC or a server) fails, the devices downstream from the failed device cannot communicate with the network.

STAR NETWORK Because of its speed and versatility, the star network is by far the most popular LAN topology today. A **star network** has a central networking device called a **switch**, which manages the network and acts as a communications conduit for all network traffic. In the past, a device known as a **hub** was used to connect star networks, but a switch offers advanced technology and much better performance. A hub or switch functions like a familiar multi-socket power strip, but with network devices such as servers, workstations, and printers plugged in rather than electrical appliances. The hub broadcasts network traffic, called **data frames**, to all connected devices. In contrast, a switch enhances network performance by sending traffic only to specific network devices that need to receive the data.

A star configuration, as shown in Figure 10-27 on the next page, provides a high degree of network control, because all traffic flows into and out of the switch. An inherent disadvantage of the star design is that the entire network is dependent on the switch. However, in most large star networks, backup switches are available immediately in case of hardware failure.

MESH NETWORK In the **mesh network** shown in Figure 10-28 on the next page, each node connects to every other node. While this design is extremely reliable, it also is very expensive to install and maintain. A mesh network resembles the Internet in

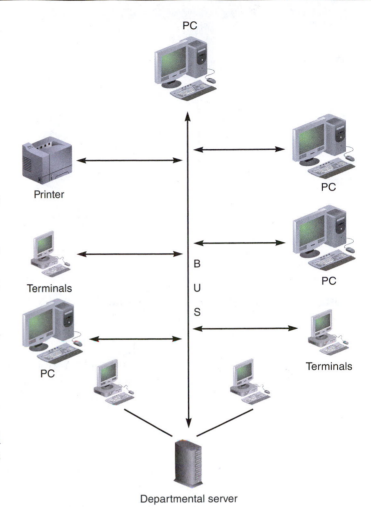

FIGURE 10-25   A bus network with all devices connected to a single communication path.

© Cengage Learning 2014

FIGURE 10-26   A ring network with a set of computers that send and receive data flowing in one direction.

© Cengage Learning 2014

FIGURE 10-27 A typical star network with a switch, departmental server, and connected workstations.

© Cengage Learning 2014

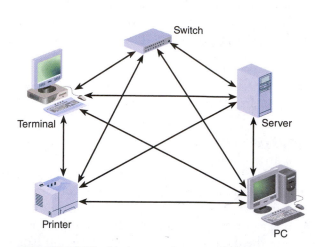

FIGURE 10-28 Mesh networks are used in situations where a high degree of redundancy is needed, such as military applications. The redundant design provides alternate data paths, but is expensive to install and maintain.

© Cengage Learning 2014

that a message can travel on more than one path. Originally developed for military applications, the primary advantage of a mesh network is redundancy, because multiple paths provide backup if communication problems arise or some nodes become inoperable.

Network Devices

Networks such as LANs or WANs can be interconnected using devices called routers. A **router** is a device that connects network segments, determines the most efficient data path, and guides the flow of data.

Using a router, any network topology can connect to a larger, dissimilar network, such as the Internet. This connection is called a **gateway**. The example in Figure 10-29 shows a star topology, where a switch connects nodes in the LAN and the router links

FIGURE 10-29 Routers can be used to connect LANs and WANs to other networks, such as the Internet.

© Cengage Learning 2014

the network to the Internet. A device called a **proxy server** provides Internet connectivity for internal LAN users. The vast majority of business networks use routers to integrate the overall network architecture.

Modeling Tools

As you translate a network model into a physical version of the system, you can use software tools, such as Microsoft Visio, which is a multipurpose drawing tool, to represent the physical structure and network components. Visio offers a wide variety of drawing types, styles, and downloadable templates, as shown in Figure 10-30.

WIRELESS NETWORKS

Although a wired LAN provides enormous flexibility, the cabling cost can be substantial, as well as the inevitable wiring changes that occur in a dynamic organization. Many companies find wireless technology to be an attractive alternative. A **wireless local area network**, or **WLAN**, is relatively inexpensive to install and is well-suited to

FIGURE 10-30   Visio offers many network templates that users can download free.
Screenshots used with permission from Microsoft.

workgroups and users who are not anchored to a specific desk or location. Most notebook computers are equipped with built-in wireless capability, and it is relatively simple to add this feature to existing desktop computers and workstations in order to set up a wireless network.

Like their wired counterparts, wireless networks have certain standards and topologies, which are discussed in the following sections.

Wireless Network Standards

Wireless networks are based on various standards and protocols that still are evolving. The most popular of these is called IEEE **802.11**, which is a family of standards developed by the **Institute of Electrical and Electronics Engineers (IEEE)** for wireless LANs.

Current wireless networks are based on variations of the original 802.11 standard. Several versions, or amendments, were intended to improve bandwidth, range, and security. The table in Figure 10-31 contains a brief comparison of the IEEE 802.11 amendments. Note that speed is measured in **Mbps (megabits per second)** or **Gbps (gigabits per second)**.

Early IEEE 802.11 standards had limited transmission capacity and were not popular. Later versions, such as **802.11g**, offered increased bandwidth and were widely accepted by the IT industry. The more recent **802.11n** uses **multiple input/multiple output (MIMO)** technology to boost performance. MIMO relies on multiple data paths, also called **multipath design**, to increase bandwidth and range. The latest proposed standards, 802.11ac and 802.11ad, are currently being tested. If wireless capacity continues to expand and security issues can be overcome, WLANs could replace wired networks in many situations. Wireless security is discussed in detail in Chapter 12, Managing Systems Support and Security.

Wireless Network Topologies

Like wired networks, wireless networks also can be arranged in different topologies. The two most common network topologies available for IEEE 802.11 WLANs are the Basic Service Set and the Extended Service Set Figure 10-32 shows simplified models of these topologies.

The **Basic Service Set (BSS)**, also called the **infrastructure mode**, is shown at the top of Figure 10-32. In this configuration, a central wireless device called an **access**

STANDARD	ADOPTED	SPEED	RANGE (Approx.)	NOTES
802.11b	1999	11 Mbps	100–200 feet	Early versions with major limitations, higher costs, and compatibility issues
802.11a	1999	54 Mbps	50–100 feet	
802.11g	2003	54 Mbps	50–100 feet	Widely adopted, works with 802.11b
802.11n	2009	100+ Mbps	Up to 150 feet	MIMO design, works with all prior standards
802.11ac	Pending	6 Gbps (Est.)	Undetermined	Multi-user MIMO, plus higher density — the ac and ad standards could power a total wireless environment for home and/or office use
802.11ad	Pending	6 Gbps (Est.)	Undetermined	

FIGURE 10-31 IEEE Wi-Fi standards and characteristics.

point or **wireless access point (WAP)**, is used to serve all wireless clients. The access point is similar to a hub in the LAN star topology, except it provides network services to wireless clients instead of wired clients. Because access points use a single communications medium, the air, they broadcast all traffic to all clients, just as a hub would do in a wired network. Typically, the access point itself is connected to a wired network, so wireless clients can access the wired network.

The second wireless topology is the **Extended Service Set (ESS)**, as shown at the bottom of Figure 10-32. An Extended Service Set is made up of two or more Basic Service Set networks. Thus, using an ESS topology, wireless access can be expanded over a larger area. Each access point provides wireless services over a limited range. As a client moves away from one access point and closer to another, a process called **roaming** automatically allows the client to associate with the stronger access point, allowing for undisrupted service.

Wireless Trends

Wireless technology has brought explosive change to the IT industry, and will continue to affect businesses, individuals, and society. Even in the ever-changing world of IT, it would be difficult to find a more dynamic area than wireless technology.

With the growing popularity of 802.11, many firms offer networking products, services, and information. One of the most significant groups is the **Wi-Fi Alliance**, which maintains a Web site at *www.wi-fi.org*. According to the site, the Alliance is a non-profit international association formed in 1999 to certify interoperability of wireless network products based on IEEE 802.11 specifications. Products that meet the requirements are certified as **Wi-Fi (wireless fidelity)** compatible. Currently the Wi-Fi Alliance has over 500 member companies from around the world, and over 9,000 products have received Wi-Fi certification. The stated goal of the Wi-Fi Alliance is to enhance the user experience through product interoperability.

Even though they have many advantages, wireless networks also have limitations and disadvantages. For example, devices that use the 2.4 GHz band can pick up interference from appliances such as microwave ovens and cordless telephones that use the same band. More important, wireless networks pose major security concerns because wireless transmissions are much more susceptible to interception and intrusion than wired networks. These issues are discussed in detail in Chapter 12, Managing Systems Support and Security.

Basic Service Set

Extended Service Set

FIGURE 10-32 Notice that the user in the upper screen has moved out of the BSS coverage area, and cannot communicate. In the lower screen, the user roams into another ESS coverage area, and the transition is seamless.

© Cengage Learning 2014

In addition to Wi-Fi, another form of wireless transmission called **Bluetooth** is very popular for short-distance wireless communication that does not require high power. Examples of Bluetooth devices include wireless keyboards, mice, printers, cell phone headsets, and digital cameras, among others. People with Bluetooth-equipped phones or PDAs can even beam information to each other and exchange digital notes.

Although the expansion of Wi-Fi has been dramatic, future technology promises even greater wireless speed, range, and compatibility. For example, in addition to 802.11 protocols for LANs, IEEE is working on **802.16** standards, sometimes called **WiMAX**, which are broadband wireless communications protocols for **MANs** (**metropolitan area networks**).

CASE IN POINT 10.4:   SPIDER IT SERVICES

Spider IT Services specializes in custom network design and installation. Firms hire Spider to do an overall analysis of their network needs, including a detailed cost-benefit study. Recently, a problem arose. One of Spider's clients complained that the relatively new network was too slow and lacked sufficient capacity. Reviewing the case, Spider's top management realized that the rapidly growing client had simply outgrown the network much earlier than anticipated.

Could this problem have been avoided? Note that IBM, in the article shown in Figure 10-15 on page 417, commented that performance can "degrade exponentially" in certain kinds of network situations. Consider the IBM article and other material in this chapter, and offer your views.

SYSTEMS DESIGN COMPLETION

System architecture marks the end of the systems design phase of the SDLC. Recall that back in the systems analysis phase, all functional primitives were identified and documented with process descriptions. The objective then was to identify the system's functions and determine *what* each logical module would do, without attempting to determine *how* that function would be carried out. Moving from analysis to design tasks, the development process continued with consideration of output and user interface design, data design, and system architecture issues. Now, based on a clear definition of system requirements and design, software applications can be developed, documented, and tested as part of the systems implementation phase of the SDLC, which is described in Chapter 11, Managing System Implementation.

Developers must also consider system management and support tools that can monitor system performance, deal with fault management, handle backup, and provide for disaster recovery. These topics are covered in detail in Chapter 12, Managing Systems Support and Security.

The final activities in the systems design phase are preparing a system design specification, obtaining user approval, and delivering a presentation to management.

System Design Specification

The **system design specification** is a document that presents the complete design for the new information system, along with detailed costs, staffing, and scheduling for completing the next SDLC phase — systems implementation.

The system design specification is the baseline against which the operational system will be measured. Unlike the system requirements document, which is written for users to understand, the system design specification is oriented toward the programmers who will use it to create the necessary programs. Some sections of the system requirements document are repeated in the system design specification, such as process descriptions, data dictionary entries, and data flow diagrams.

The system design specification varies in length, so you must organize it carefully and number all pages in sequence. You should include a cover page, a detailed table of contents, and an index. The contents of the system design specification depend on company standards and the complexity of the system. A typical system design specification typically includes the following sections.

1. *Management Summary.* This is a brief overview of the project for company managers and executives. It outlines the development efforts to date, provides a current status report, summarizes project costs, reviews the benefits of the new system, presents the systems implementation schedule, and highlights any issues that management will need to address.

2. *System Components.* This section contains the complete design for the new system, including the user interface, outputs, inputs, files, databases, and network specifications. You should include source documents, report and screen layouts, DFDs, and all other relevant documentation. You also should include the requirements for all support processing, such as backup and recovery, start-up processing, and file retention. If the purchase of a software package is part of the strategy, you must include any interface information required between the package and the system you are developing. If you use a CASE design tool, you can print design diagrams and most other documentation directly from the tool.

3. *System Environment.* This section describes the constraints, or conditions, affecting the system, including any requirements that involve operations, hardware, systems software, or security. Examples of operational constraints include transaction volumes that must be supported, data storage requirements, processing schedules, reporting deadlines, and online response times.

4. *Implementation Requirements.* In this section, you specify start-up processing, initial data entry or acquisition, user training requirements, and software test plans.

5. *Time and Cost Estimates.* This section provides detailed schedules, cost estimates, and staffing requirements for the systems development phase and revised projections for the remainder of the SDLC. You also present total costs-to-date for the project and compare those costs with your prior estimates.

6. *Additional Material.* Other material can be included at the end of the system design specification. In this section, you might insert documents from earlier phases if they would be helpful to readers.

User Approval

Users must review and approve the interface design, report and menu designs, data entry screens, source documents, and other areas of the system that affect them. The review and approval process continues throughout the systems design phase. When you complete the design for a report, you should meet with users to review the prototype, adjust the design if necessary, and obtain written approval. Chapter 8 contains guidelines and suggestions about report design.

Securing approvals from users throughout the design phase is very important. That approach ensures that you do not have a major task of obtaining approvals at the end, it keeps the users involved with the system's development, and it gives you feedback about whether or not you are on target. Some sections of the system design specification might not interest users, but anything that does affect them should be approved as early as possible.

Other IT department members also need to review the system design specification. IT management will be concerned with staffing, costs, hardware and systems software requirements, network impact, and the effect on the operating environment when the new system is added. The programming team will want to get ready for its role, and the operations group will be interested in processing support, report distribution, network loads, integration with other systems, and any hardware or software issues for which they need to prepare. You must be a good communicator to keep people up to date, obtain their input and suggestions, and obtain necessary approvals.

When the system design specification is complete, you distribute the document to a target group of users, IT department personnel, and company management. You should distribute the document at least one week before your presentation to allow the recipients enough time to review the material.

Presentations

TOOLKIT TIME

The Communication Tools in Part A of the Systems Analyst's Toolkit can help you develop better reports and presentations. To learn more about these tools, turn to Part A of the four-part Toolkit that follows Chapter 12.

Usually, you will give several presentations at the end of the systems design phase. The presentations give you an opportunity to explain the system, answer questions, consider comments, and secure final approval. Part A of the Systems Analyst's Toolkit can provide valuable guidelines and tips about oral presentations.

The first presentation is to the systems analysts, programmers, and technical support staff members who will be involved in future project phases or operational support for the system. Because of the audience, the presentation is technically oriented.

Your next presentation is to department managers and users from departments affected by the system. As in the first presentation, your primary objective is to obtain support and approval for the systems design. This is not a technical presentation; it is aimed at user interaction with the system and management's interest in budgets, schedules, staffing, and impact on the production environment.

The final presentation is delivered to management. By the time you give this presentation, you should have obtained all necessary approvals from prior presentations, and you should have the support of users and the IT department. Just like the management presentation at the end of the systems analysis phase, this presentation has a key objective: to obtain management's approval and support for the next development step — systems implementation — including a solid commitment for financial and other resources needed.

Based on the presentation and the data you submitted, management might reach one of three decisions: proceed with systems development, perform additional work on the systems design phase, or terminate the project.

A QUESTION OF ETHICS

© faberfoto_it/iStockphoto

The new accounting system is operational, but feedback from users has been negative. The most common complaint is that the system is not user-friendly. Some people in the IT department think that more user training would solve the problem. However, Sam, the IT manager, is opposed to a fresh round of training. "Let's just set up the network to monitor the users' keystrokes and mouse clicks, and see what the patterns are," he suggested. "We can analyze the data and come up with tips and suggestions that would make the system easier to use."

Your initial reaction is that Sam is wrong, for two reasons. First, you believe that monitoring would not be an effective method to learn what users really want. In your view, that should have been done in the system requirements phase. Second, you are bothered by an ethical question: Even though the proposed monitoring would involve company business, the company network, and company time, you feel that many users would resent the unannounced monitoring, and might feel that their performance or other computing activities were being appraised without their knowledge.

Sam has asked to you to write up a recommendation. What will you say about the ethical question that troubles you?

CHAPTER SUMMARY

An information system combines hardware, software, data, procedures, and people into a system architecture. The architecture translates the system's logical design into a physical structure that includes hardware, software, and processing methods. The software consists of application programs, also called applications, that handle the input, manage the processing logic, and provide the required output.

Before selecting an architecture, the analyst must consider enterprise resource planning, initial cost and TCO, scalability, Web integration, legacy interface requirements, processing options, security issues, and corporate portals.

Enterprise resource planning (ERP) establishes an enterprise-wide strategy for IT resources and specific standards for data, processing, network, and user interface design. Companies can extend ERP systems to suppliers and customers in a process called supply chain management. A systems analyst must assess initial cost and TCO and ensure that the design is scalable. Scalability means that a system can be expanded, modified, or downsized easily to meet business needs. The analyst also must consider if the system will be Web-centric and follow Internet design protocols, and if it must interface with existing systems, called legacy systems. System security is an important concern throughout the design process, especially for e-commerce applications that involve credit card and personal data. Processing options affect system design and resources required. The planned architecture can include a corporate portal which is an entrance to a multifunction Web site. Corporate portals can provide access for customers, employees, suppliers, and others.

An architecture requires servers and clients. Servers are computers that supply data, processing services, or other support to one or more computers called clients. In mainframe architecture, the server performs all processing, and terminals communicate with the centralized system. Clients can be connected in distributed systems to form local area networks (LANs) or wide area networks (WANs).

Client/server architecture divides processing between one or more clients and a central server. In a typical client/server system, the client handles the entire user interface, including data entry, data query, and screen presentation logic. The server stores the data and provides data access and database management functions. Application logic is divided in some manner between the server and the clients. In a typical client/server interaction, the client submits a request for information from the server, which carries out the operation and responds to the client. Compared to file server designs, client/server systems are more scalable and flexible.

A fat, or thick, client design places all or most of the application processing logic at the client. A thin client design places all or most of the processing logic at the server. Thin client designs provide better performance, because program code resides on the server, near the data. In contrast, a fat client handles more of the processing, and must access and update the data more often. Compared with maintaining a central server, fat client TCO also is higher, because of initial hardware and software requirements and the ongoing expense of maintaining and updating remote client computers. The fat client design is simpler to develop, because the architecture resembles traditional file server designs where all processing is performed at the client.

Client/server designs can be two-tier or three-tier (also called n-tier). In a two-tier design, the user interface resides on the client, all data resides on the server, and the application logic can run either on the server or on the client, or be divided between the client and the server. In a three-tier design, the user interface runs on the client and the data is stored on the server, just as with a two-tier design. A three-tier design also has a middle layer between the client and server that processes the client requests and translates them into data access commands that can be understood and carried out by the server. The middle layer is called an application server, because it provides the application logic, or business logic. Middleware is software that connects dissimilar applications and enables them to communicate and pass data. In planning the system design, a systems analyst also must consider cost-benefit and performance issues.

The Internet has had an enormous impact on system architecture. In implementing a design, an analyst should consider e-commerce architecture, the availability of packaged solutions, and service providers. The analyst also should understand the concepts of cloud computing and Web 2.0, which are shaping the future of Internet computing. Cloud computing uses a cloud symbol to represent the Internet. The cloud, which is transparent to users, provides a hardware-independent environment where remote servers handle all processing and computing functions, and the Internet itself replaces traditional networks. Web 2.0 refers to a new generation of the Web that will encourage people to collaborate, interact, and share information more dynamically. Web 2.0 is fueling the explosive growth of social networking and group-based communications.

The most prevalent processing method today is online processing. Users interact directly with online systems that continuously process their transactions when and where they occur and continuously update files and databases. In contrast, batch systems process transactions in groups and execute them on a predetermined schedule. Many online systems also use batch processing to perform routine tasks, such as handling reports and accounting entries.

Networks allow the sharing of hardware, software, and data resources in order to reduce expenses and provide more capability to users. The network is represented by a seven-layer model called the OSI (Open Systems Interconnection) model.

The way a network is configured is called the network topology. Networks typically are arranged in five patterns: hierarchical, bus, ring, star, and mesh. A single mainframe computer usually controls a hierarchical network, a bus network connects workstations in a single-line communication path, a ring network connects workstations in a circular communication path, a star network connects workstations to a central computer or networking device called a switch, and a mesh network connects every network node to every other node. Wireless networks, or WLANs, based on IEEE 802.11 standards, have seen explosive growth, especially in situations where the flexibility of wireless is important. The IEEE 802.11n standard uses MIMO, or multipath technology, which has increased wireless network speed and range. WLANs have two major topologies: BSS and, ESS. Although wireless networks are very popular, they do have some limitations and disadvantages, including interference and security concerns.

The system design specification presents the complete systems design for an information system and is the basis for the presentations that complete the systems design phase. Following the presentations, the project either progresses to the systems development phase, requires additional systems design work, or is terminated.

Key Terms

Chapter Exercises

Questions

1. This chapter begins with an architecture checklist. If you had to rank the items, from most important to least important, what would your list look like? Explain your answer.
2. What is enterprise resource planning (ERP)? What is supply chain management (SCM)?
3. Suppose you had a client who never used a network. Explain, in everyday terms, the role of network servers and clients.
4. Describe client/server architecture, including fat and thin clients, client/server tiers, and middleware.
5. Trace the history of system architecture, with particular emphasis on the impact of the personal computer and the Internet. Be sure to include examples.
6. Is batch processing still relevant? Why or why not?
7. Explain the difference between a LAN and a WAN.
8. Define the term topology, and draw a sketch of each wired and wireless network topology.
9. Explain the main difference between the BSS and ESS wireless topologies. To what kind of wireless topology do the 802.16 standards apply?
10. List the sections of a system design specification, and describe the contents.

Discussion Topics

1. Information technology has advanced dramatically in recent years. At the same time, enormous changes in the business world have occurred as companies reflect global competition and more pressure for quality, speed, and customer service. Did the new technology inspire the business changes, or was it the other way around?
2. E-commerce has seen explosive growth in recent years. What are the most important reasons for this trend? Will it continue? Why or why not?
3. This chapter describes guidelines that a systems analyst can use when considering an architecture. In your view, are all the items of equal weight and importance, or should some be ranked higher? Justify your position.
4. One manager states, "When a new system is proposed, I want a written report, not an oral presentation, which is like a sales pitch. I only want to see the facts about costs, benefits, and schedules." Do you agree with that point of view?

Projects

1. Visit the IT department at your school or a local company to learn about the network they use. Describe the network and draw a sketch of the configuration.
2. Prepare a 10-minute talk explaining Web 2.0 and cloud computing to a college class. Using the text and your own Internet research, briefly describe the five most important points you will include in your presentation.
3. Perform research on the Internet to identify a service provider that offers Web-based business solutions, and write a brief memo describing the firm and its services.
4. Perform research on the Internet to learn about trends in wireless networking, and typical costs involved in the installation of a wireless LAN.

Apply Your Knowledge

This section contains four mini-cases. Each case describes a situation, explains your role, and requires you to apply what you learned in the chapter.

1 Green Design

After several years as a successful architectural firm in Southern California, Green Design decided to expand by adding two new business ventures: a civil engineering projects group, and a group for commercial building projects. As a senior systems analyst, you have been asked to study the situation and make recommendations.

Tasks

1. Should Green Design adopt ERP? Why or why not? Provide specific reasons.
2. Is the experience of other companies relevant? Use the Internet to locate a software platform that may be useful to Green Design. Give a summary of ERP solutions you find for architectural and engineering firms.
3. Should Green Design use separate portals for employees, customers, and suppliers?
4. Before selecting software and hardware for the new system, how should Green Design evaluate initial cost and total cost of ownership? What would be the main components?

2 Passing Lane

Passing Lane is a small trucking company headquartered in Portland, Oregon. Passing Lane's information system consists of a file server and three workstations where freight clerks enter data, track shipments, and prepare freight bills. To perform their work, the clerks obtain data from the server and use database and spreadsheet programs stored on stand-alone PCs to process the data. At your meeting yesterday, Passing lane's president approved your recommendation to create a relational database to handle operations and provide links for the company's shippers and customers.

Tasks

1. Review the concept of supply chain management. Although Passing Lane offers services rather than products, could the SCM concept apply to the design of the new system? Why or why not?
2. What would be the advantages of selecting an Web-based architecture for Passing Lane's system?
3. Since the firm is growing rapidly, what design features should be included in the new system to ensure it can grow with the company.
4. Given that Passing Lane currently uses computers for managing their operations, what design considerations should be given to legacy systems? Explain your answer.

3 **Nothing But Net**

Nothing But Net is an IT consulting firm that specializes in network architectural design. As a newly hired systems analyst, you have been asked to explain the advantages and disadvantages of a variety of networking concepts. Your answers will be incorporated into a FAQ section of the new marketing brochure.

Tasks

1. Should an organization choose a new system based on client/server architecture? Why or why not?
2. Explain the pros and cons of thick or thin client characteristics.
3. What is the difference between physical and logical topology? Provide examples.
4. Will mobile devices replace desktop system units and traditional laptop computers? How would networks have to change if that were to happen?

4 **Alice's Restaurant Supply**

Alice's Restaurant Supply offers a line of specialty food products to institutional customers and restaurant chains. The firm prides itself on using only the finest ingredients and preparation methods. The owner, Alice Burns, hired you as an IT consultant to help her plan the system architecture for a new WLAN that will connect employee computers to the wired network. She asked you to start with the following questions:

Tasks

1. What wireless standards could be implemented in the new system? What are the pros and cons of each standard?
2. Choose a wireless standard to implement in Alice's Restaurant Supply, and explain your choice.
3. Suppose that microwave ovens and cordless telephones are used extensively in some parts of the facility. Would that affect your IEEE 802.11 amendment choice? What standards would *not* be a good choice in this type of environment?
4. Suppose that the new WLAN will also provide roaming services for employees who must use portable computers and tablets in many warehouse locations. Which wireless topology would be the best choice? Explain your answer.

Case Studies

Each chapter includes a Chapter Case, a Continuing Case, a Capstone Case, and an Online Case Simulation. You can learn more about the Online Case Simulation in the MIS CourseMate Features section.

Chapter Case: Precision Consulting

Background

Precision Consulting has helped many clients plan, design, and implement e-commerce solutions. As a newly hired systems analyst, you will be expected to work with other team members on e-commerce projects. You realize that have a lot to learn, and you decide to learn as much as you can about the e-commerce issues and solutions.

Tasks

1. Perform research to learn how much consumers are projected to spend on Internet purchases during the next three years, and describe the results. Does the estimate seem reasonable? Why or why not?
2. Many of Precision's clients are start-up firms that must fight hard to attract investment capital, and some traditional lenders are skeptical of new Web-based firms. Perform research to determine the mortality rate of new retail firms that use the Web as their primary marketing channel, and describe the results of your research.
3. Some IT professionals predict that traditional brick and mortar companies will greatly expand their Internet marketing efforts, making it even harder for new online firms to compete. Perform research to find out more about the topic and describe the results.
4. Suppose you were asked to draft an e-commerce sales brochure for Precision Consulting. List all the services in which potential customers might be interested.

Continuing Case: Personal Trainer, Inc.

Personal Trainer, Inc. owns and operates fitness centers in a dozen Midwestern cities. The centers have done well, and the company is planning an international expansion by opening a new "supercenter" in the Toronto area. Personal Trainer's president, Cassia Umi, hired an IT consultant, Susan Park, to help develop an information system for the new facility. During the project, Susan will work closely with Gray Lewis, who will manage the new operation.

Background

Susan and Gray finished their work on user interface, input, and output design. They developed a user-centered design that would be flexible and easy to learn. Now Susan turned her attention to the architecture for the new system.

Susan wanted to consider their own organization and culture, enterprise resource planning, total cost of ownership, scalability, Web integration, legacy systems, processing methods, security issues, and corporate portal. She also needed to select a network plan, or topology, that would dictate the physical cabling and network connections, or consider a wireless network. When all these tasks were completed, she would submit a system design specification for approval.

(continues)

Continuing Case: Personal Trainer, Inc.

Tasks

1. What would be the advantages of selecting an Internet-based architecture for the Personal Trainer's system?

2. If Personal Trainer wants to increase its Internet marketing efforts, what advice could you offer? Perform research to find out more about the topic of Web-based marketing before you answer Gray.

3. What software and hardware infrastructure will be necessary to ensure Personal Trainer can process point of sale transactions?

4. Prepare an outline for a system design specification and describe the contents of each section.

Capstone Case: New Century Wellness Group

New Century Wellness Group offers a holistic approach to healthcare with an emphasis on preventive medicine as well as traditional medical care. In your role as an IT consultant, you will help New Century develop a new information system.

Background

The New Century partners accepted your interface, output, input, and data designs and your recommendation to install a server and desktop computer clients on a local area network. At this point, you review your notes and plan the architecture for the New Century system.

New Century Wellness Group has four primary care physicians, one nurse practitioner (NP), four physical therapists, one registered nutritionist, eight nurses, and eight support staff. Each of the physicians, NP, therapists, nutritionist and support staff has their own workstations. The nurses work from one of three nurse stations that should have at least three computers at each station. Each nurse station will have a high-volume network laser printer and a scanner attached to one workstation. The checkin/checkout area will have an impact printer for multipart forms and a network laser printer. The network will include an online backup service, Internet access via a cable connection with a local cable company.

The partners want you to ensure the physical network is scalable, and able to handle the electronic medical record phase after the business support system is implemented. The electronic medical record phase will require a computer or thin client to be installed in each exam room and procedure room. They will also use portable computers and tablets to access patient information as the providers move from room to room around the clinic.

The hardware requirements are only part of the final installation plan which you must develop. You should start by reviewing the DFDs and object-oriented diagrams that you prepared in the systems analysis phase, and the ERDs and table designs that you created in the systems design phase. Then, review the system architecture checklist at the beginning of this chapter. With this information, you should be able to prepare a system design specification.

Tasks

1. Draw a simple floor plan for New Century Wellness group and include the placement of all network nodes including the placement of a server, and network equipment. How many ports will your switch need to accommodate?

2. Given this information, what physical and logical topologies would you recommend for New Century? Explain your answer.

3. What would be the benefits of using a wireless network? Are there any drawbacks?

4. Using the information you just prepared, as well as other information you developed for in previous chapters, prepare a system design specification that includes sections on the management summary, system components, system environment, implementation requirements, and time and cost estimates.

CASE Tool Workshop

Systems analysts use CASE tools to help them plan, build, and maintain information systems. To learn more about CASE tools, turn to Part B of the Toolkit that follows Chapter 12. You can complete these tasks with the Visible Analyst® CASE tool, which is available with this textbook, or a similar tool.

Background

Suppose you work as a computer lab assistant at your school. The lab supervisor wants to install a CASE tool on the network, but realizes there might be licensing issues.

Tasks

1. Visit the Web site for Visible Analyst® or another CASE tool, and investigate licensing options. Are network installations limited by the number of workstations, the number of users at any one time, or other constraints? Write a brief report with your findings.

2. The lab supervisor also told you that several computer science instructors want to assign team projects, where students would collaborate using a Web-based CASE tools that can run on mobile devices as well as lab workstations. She wants you to do research and determine whether such tools exist. Go online, see what you can find, and report back to her.

MIS CourseMate Features

If you have an MIS CourseMate access code, you can reinforce and extend your learning with premium content created for this textbook. For example, you can launch interactive Video Learning Sessions to help you understand systems development concepts and practice your skills. In addition, you can use MindTap Reader, which is a full, interactive, digital e-book.

MIS CourseMate also offers many learning features within each chapter, including an Online Case Simulation, a Critical Thinking Challenge, Video Learning Session Tasks, and a set of Learn It Online activities. To log on to the MIS CourseMate site at **www.cengagebrain.com**, you must create a student account and register this book.

Online Case Simulation: SCR Associates

Session 10: System Architecture

Overview

The SCR Associates case study is a Web-based simulation that allows you to practice your skills in a real-world environment. The firm offers IT consulting, solutions and training. SCR plans to open a new high-tech training center, and needs to develop a Training Information Management System (TIMS) to support the center. You are a newly hired systems analyst reporting to Jesse Baker, systems group manager, and will help her develop the system.

The case study takes you to the SCR Web site, where you receive e-mail and voice mail messages from Jesse, obtain information from SCR's resource libraries, and perform various tasks. Jesse has high standards, but seems very fair. She made it clear that she expects your work to be accurate, thorough, and professional.

Before You Begin

To prepare for this work session, you should review the following topics:

- ERP, TCO, and network topology
- The sections of a system design specification

How Do I Use the Online Case Simulation?

- Read the preview, and review the Chapter 1 background material if necessary.
- Visit the MIS CourseMate Web site at **www.cengagebrain.com**, locate the **SCR Case Simulation**, and click the **intranet** link. Enter your name and the password **sad10e**.
- When the opening screen displays, select this session. Then check your e-mail and voice mail, and start to work on your task list.

Preview: Session 10

Your supervisor, Jesse Baker, wants you to be familiar with the main issues that a systems analyst should consider when planning an architecture, including corporate organization and culture, enterprise resource planning, initial costs and TCO, scalability, Web integration, legacy interface requirements, processing options, security, and corporate portal issues.

Critical Thinking Challenge

In addition to technical ability, IT professionals need critical thinking skills. This feature can help you practice perception, organization, analysis, problem-solving, and decision-making skills that will be valuable in the workplace. You can visit **www.criticalthinking.org** to learn more about critical thinking and why it is so important.

Background

The IT team at Game Technology is working on an overall architecture for the new C3 system. They solicited RFPs from several hardware vendors, and decided to work with Network Illusions, a well-known local firm. Your job is to help analyze the server test results, and to draw network diagrams when requested.

The Network Illusions sales rep recommended a Model DX server for the C3 network, and submitted the following data, which shows projected network response times for various numbers of Game Technology users:

Projected Data: Server Model DX	Number of Users				
	10	20	30	40	50
Response Time (sec)	.01	.015	.02	.025	.03

Practice Tasks

Visit the MIS CourseMate Web site at **www.cengagebrain.com.** Then navigate to the resources for this chapter and locate the **Critical Thinking Challenge** feature. You will complete two Practice Tasks, using what you learned in the chapter. Then you can check your answers to be sure you're ready for the Challenge Tasks.

Challenge Tasks

After you complete the Practice Tasks, you learn about new developments at Game Technology.

Although the spec was for a Model DX server, Network Illusions delivered a newer model, called the DX+. The vendor sales rep said that performance would be the same or better, but the IT team decided to run a series of response time tests. To continue, navigate to the **Critical Thinking Challenge** feature for this chapter, select the **Challenge Tasks,** and follow the instructions.

Video Learning Sessions

Video Learning Sessions can help you understand systems development concepts and practice your skills. In this scenario, you will help design a Video Learning Session for this chapter.

Before You Begin

Review the chapter and list the main topics. Which ones did you find difficult to understand, and why? Can you think of other ways to explain the topics?

© craftvision/iStockph

Training Tasks

Suppose the IT training manager wants to encourage team members to watch the Video Learning Sessions. She wants you to submit a proposal for a new session that would explain the key topics in this chapter.

1. Which topics would you choose?
2. What specific skills or concepts would you include in the session?
3. How would you present the material?
4. Describe at least three graphic images that you would include in the video session.

Learn It Online

In each chapter, you can use this feature to apply your knowledge and practice your skills. The exercises include Chapter Reinforcement Questions, Flash Cards, Practice Tests, and various games, such as *Who Wants To Be a Computer Genius?*, *Wheel of Terms,* and the *Crossword Puzzle Challenge.*

PHASE **4** SYSTEMS IMPLEMENTATION

DELIVERABLE
A functioning information system

TOOLKIT SUPPORT
Primary tools: Communications and CASE tools

GOT MIS COURSEMATE?
One Video Learning Session explains structure charts

As the Dilbert cartoon suggests, successful systems implementation requires effective methods, a capable team, and management support. You will learn more about these topics in the systems implementation phase.

Systems implementation is the fourth of five phases in the systems development life cycle. In the previous phase, systems design, you created a physical model of the system. Now you will implement that design. Your tasks will include application development, documentation, testing, training, data conversion, and system changeover. The deliverable for this phase is a completely functioning information system.

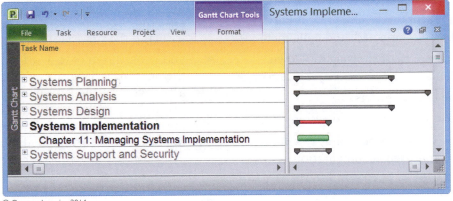

© Cengage Learning 2014

CHAPTER 11

Managing Systems Implementation

Chapter 11 describes the systems implementation phase of the SDLC. This chapter describes application development, installation, and evaluation.

INTRODUCTION

OBJECTIVES

When you finish this chapter, you will be able to:

- Explain the importance of software quality assurance and software engineering
- Describe application development using structured, object-oriented, and agile methods
- Draw a structure chart showing top-down design, modular design, cohesion, and coupling
- Explain the coding process
- Explain unit, integration, and system testing
- Differentiate between program, system, operations, and user documentation
- List the main steps in system installation and evaluation
- Develop training plans for various user groups, compare in-house and vendor training options, and describe effective training techniques
- Describe data conversion and changeover methods
- Explain post-implementation evaluation and the final report to management

Managing systems implementation involves application development, testing, documentation, training, data conversion, system changeover, and post-implementation evaluation of the results.

During systems implementation, the system design specification serves as a blueprint for constructing the new system. The initial task is application development, which requires systems analysts and programmers to work together to construct the necessary programs and code modules. Before a changeover, the system must be tested and documented carefully, users must be trained, and existing data must be converted. After the new system is operational, a formal evaluation of the results takes place as part of a final report to management.

If you have MIS CourseMate, you can view a Video Learning Session that explains how to use a structure chart to show program modules and their relationships.

PREVIEW CASE: Mountain View College Bookstore

Background: Wendy Lee, manager of college services at Mountain View College, wants a new information system that will improve efficiency and customer service at the three college bookstores.

In this part of the case, Tina Allen (systems analyst) and David Conroe (student intern) are talking about implementation tasks for the new system.

Participants:	Wendy, Tina, and David
Location:	Wendy Lee's office, Monday morning, February 10, 2014
Project status:	The system design specification was approved, and Tina and David are ready to implement the new bookstore information system.
Discussion topics:	Implementation tasks, including quality assurance, structure charts, testing, training, data conversion process, system changeover, and post-implementation evaluation

Tina:	Good morning, Wendy. We're ready to start the implementation process, and I'd like to go over our plans. David will be assisting me, so I asked him to join us.
Wendy:	*I'm glad you did. I met David during the interviews several months ago.*
David:	Hi, Wendy, good to see you again. What's next?
Tina:	Let's talk about quality assurance. We'll also discuss various implementation options, including agile methods, but we'll continue with a structured approach for now.
Wendy:	*Sounds good. What are the major tasks on your list?*
Tina:	Well, the biggest task is to translate the design into program code and produce a functioning system. We'll develop structure charts that the programmers can use as blueprints, and David will help me coordinate with the programmers.
David:	It will be great to see all the design work finally turn into a functioning system.
Tina:	It sure will. Anyway, we'll proceed to do several types of testing, and we'll document everything we do. When we're ready, we'll put the new system into what's called a test environment until we're ready to go online with the operational environment.
Wendy:	*What about training?*
Tina:	We'll consider several kinds of training — from vendors, or we might do our own.
Wendy:	*Then what?*
Tina:	The final steps will be data conversion and system changeover. After the new system is up and running, we'll schedule a formal evaluation and submit a final report. Here's a task list to get us started:

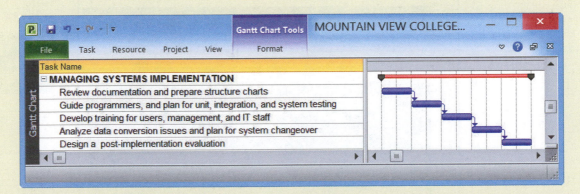

FIGURE 11-1   Typical systems implementation task list.

© Cengage Learning 2014

SOFTWARE QUALITY ASSURANCE

In today's competitive business environment, companies are intensely concerned with the quality of their products and services. A successful organization must improve quality in every area, including its information systems. Top management must provide the leadership, encouragement, and support needed for high-quality IT resources.

No matter how carefully a system is designed and implemented, problems can occur. Rigorous testing can detect errors during implementation, but it is much less expensive to correct mistakes earlier in the development process. The main objective of **quality assurance** is to avoid problems or to identify them as soon as possible. Poor quality can result from inaccurate requirements, design problems, coding errors, faulty documentation, and ineffective testing.

To improve the finished product, software systems developers should consider software engineering and internationally recognized quality standards.

Software Engineering

Because quality is so important, you can use an approach called software engineering to manage and improve the quality of the finished system. **Software engineering** is a software development process that stresses solid design, accurate documentation, and careful testing.

The Web site for the Software Engineering Institute (SEI) at Carnegie Mellon University is shown in Figure 11-2. SEI is a leader in software engineering and provides quality standards and suggested procedures for software developers and systems analysts. SEI's primary objective is to find better, faster, and less-expensive methods of software development. To achieve that goal, SEI designed a set of software development standards called the **Capability Maturity Model (CMM)**®, which has been used successfully by thousands of organizations around the globe. The purpose of the model was to improve software quality, reduce development time, and cut costs. More recently, SEI established a new model, called **Capability Maturity Model Integration (CMMI®)**, that integrates software and systems development into a much larger framework called **process improvement**. The CMMI® regards software as part

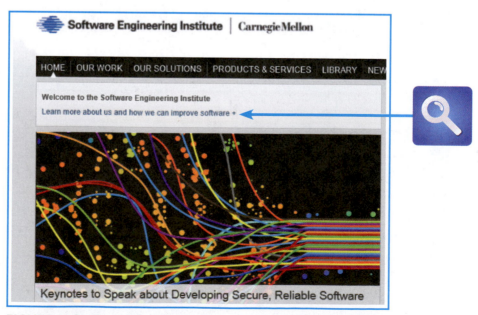

FIGURE 11-2 The Software Engineering Institute represents the cutting edge of software design and development technology.

© 2012 Carnegie Mellon University

of a larger quality improvement process, rather than as an end in itself. The CMMI® tracks an organization's processes, using five maturity levels, from Level 1, which is referred to as unpredictable, poorly controlled, and reactive, to Level 5, in which the optimal result is process improvement. The five maturity levels are shown in Figure 11-3.

International Organization for Standardization (ISO)

What do cars, tools, water, and toys have in common? Along with thousands of other products and services, they are all covered by ISO standards.

You learned in Chapter 9 that the International Organization for Standardization (ISO) is a worldwide body that establishes quality standards for products and services, as shown in Figure 11-4. ISO standards include everything from

FIGURE 11-3 The CMMI® includes five maturity levels, from Level 1, which is referred to as unpredictable, poorly controlled, and reactive, to Level 5, in which the optimal result is process improvement.

© 2012 TutorialsPoint.COM

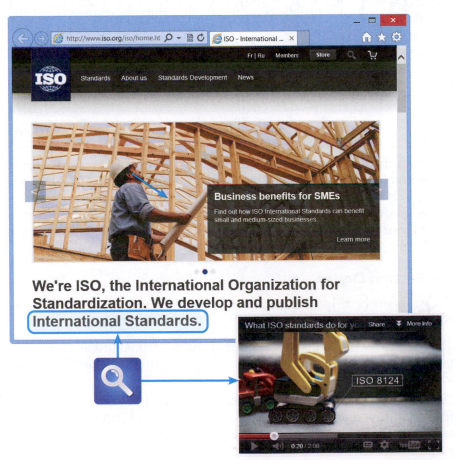

FIGURE 11-4 The International Organization for Standardization (ISO) is an international body that establishes standards for many products and services, including software development. ISO states that standards, which provide product quality, compatibility, and safety, often are taken for granted, and noticed only when they are absent.

© ISO.org

FIGURE 11-5 ISO standards include internationally recognized symbols.
© bytedust/Shutterstock.com

internationally recognized symbols, such as those shown in Figure 11-5, to the ISBN numbering system that identifies this textbook. In addition, ISO seeks to offer a global consensus of what constitutes good management practices — practices that can help firms deliver consistently high-quality products and services.

Because software is so important to a company's success, many firms seek assurance that software systems, either purchased or developed in-house, will meet rigid quality standards. In 2004, ISO updated a set of guidelines called **ISO 9000-3:2004,** which provided a quality assurance framework for developing and maintaining software. According to ISO, a revision of this standard will be released in 2013.

A company can specify ISO standards when it purchases software from a supplier or use ISO guidelines for in-house software development to ensure that the final result measures up to ISO standards. ISO requires a specific development plan, which outlines a step-by-step process for transforming user requirements into a finished product. ISO standards can be quite detailed. For example, ISO requires that a software supplier document all testing and maintain records of test results. If problems are found, they must be resolved, and any modules affected must be retested. Additionally, software and hardware specifications of all test equipment must be documented and included in the test records.

OVERVIEW OF APPLICATION DEVELOPMENT

Application development is the process of constructing the programs and code modules that serve as the building blocks of the information system. In Chapter 1, you learned that structured analysis, object-oriented (O-O) analysis, and agile methods are three popular development options. Regardless of the method, the objective is to translate the design into program and code modules that will function properly. Because systems implementation usually is very labor-intensive, developers often use project management tools and techniques to control schedules and budgets.

Review the System Design

At this point, it might be helpful to review the tasks involved in the creation of the system design.

- In Chapter 4, you learned about requirements modeling and how to use functional decomposition diagrams (FDDs) to break complex business operations down into smaller units, or functions.

- In Chapter 5, you learned about structured data and process modeling, and you created data flow diagrams (DFDs). You also developed process descriptions for functional primitive processes that documented the business logic and processing requirements.

- In Chapter 6, you developed an object-oriented model of the new system that included use case diagrams, class diagrams, sequence diagrams, state transition diagrams, and activity diagrams.

- In Chapter 7, you selected a development strategy.
- In Chapter 8, you designed the user interface.
- In Chapter 9, you worked with data design issues, analyzed relationships between system entities, and constructed entity-relationship diagrams (ERDs).
- In Chapter 10, you considered an overall system architecture.

Taken together, this set of tasks produced an overall design and a plan for physical implementation.

Application Development Tasks

If you used traditional structured or object-oriented (O-O) methods, you now are ready to translate the design into a functioning application. If you selected an agile development method, you will plan the project, lay the groundwork, assemble the team, and prepare to interact with the customers.

TRADITIONAL METHODS Building a new system requires careful planning. After an overall strategy is established, individual modules must be designed, coded, tested, and documented. A **module** consists of related program code organized into small units that are easy to understand and maintain. After the modules are developed and tested individually, more testing takes place, along with thorough documentation of the entire system, as shown in Figure 11-6.

When you create program modules using structured or object-oriented methods, you start by reviewing documentation from prior SDLC phases and creating a set of program designs. If you built a documentation file early in the development process and updated it regularly, you now have a valuable repository of information. The centerpiece of your documentation is the system design specification, accompanied by diagrams, source documents, screen layouts, report designs, data dictionary entries, and user comments. If you used a CASE tool during the systems analysis and design process, your job will be much easier. At this point, coding and testing tasks begin. Although programmers typically perform the actual coding, IT managers usually assign systems analysts to work with them as a team.

AGILE METHODS If you decided to use an agile approach, intense communication and collaboration will now begin between the IT team and the users or customers. The objective is to create the system through an iterative process of planning, designing, coding, and testing. Agile projects use various models, including the spiral model, or the Extreme Programming (XP) example shown in Figure 11-7 on the next page. Agile development and XP are discussed in detail later in this chapter.

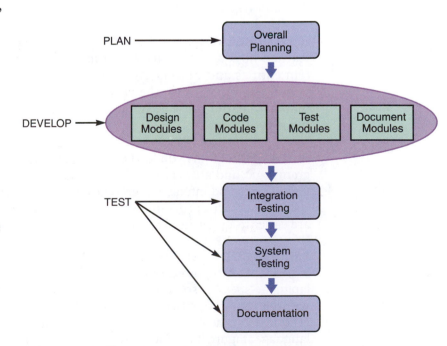

FIGURE 11-6 The main steps in application development.
© Cengage Learning 2014

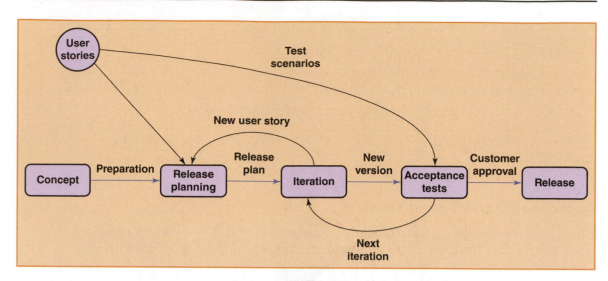

FIGURE 11-7   Simplified model of an Extreme Programming (XP) project. Note the emphasis on iteration and testing.
© Cengage Learning 2014

Systems Development Tools

Each systems development approach has its own set of tools that has worked well for that method. For example, structured development relies heavily on DFDs and structure charts; object-oriented methods use a variety of diagrams, including use case, class, sequence, and transition state diagrams; and agile methods tend to use spiral or other iterative models such as the example in Figure 11-7.

System developers also can use multipurpose tools to help them translate the system logic into properly functioning program modules. These generic tools include entity-relationship diagrams, flowcharts, pseudocode, decision tables, and decision trees.

ENTITY-RELATIONSHIP DIAGRAMS   During data design, in Chapter 9, you learned how to use entity-relationship diagrams to show the interaction among system entities and objects. An ERD is a useful tool regardless of which methodology you are using, because the various relationships (one-to-one, one-to-many, and many-to-many) must be understood and implemented in the application development process.

FLOWCHARTS   As you learned in Chapter 5, flowcharts can be used to describe program logic, and are very useful in visualizing a modular design. A **flowchart** represents logical rules and interaction graphically, using a series of symbols connected by arrows. Using flowcharts, programmers can break large systems into subsystems and modules that are easier to understand and code.

PSEUDOCODE   Pseudocode is a technique for representing program logic. Pseudocode is similar to structured English, which was explained in Chapter 5. Pseudocode is not language-specific, so you can use it to describe a software module in plain English without requiring strict syntax rules. Using pseudocode, a systems analyst or a programmer can describe program actions that can be implemented in any programming language. Figure 11-8 illustrates an example of pseudocode that documents a sales promotion policy.

SAMPLE OF A SALES PROMOTION POLICY

- Preferred customers who order more than $1,000 are entitled to a 5% discount, and an additional 5% discount if they used our charge card.

- Preferred customers who do not order more than $1,000 receive a $25 bonus coupon.

- All other customers receive a $5 bonus coupon.

PSEUDOCODE VERSION OF THE SALES PROMOTION POLICY

```
IF customer is a preferred customer, and
        IF customer orders more than $1,000 then
                Apply a 5% discount, and
                IF customer uses our charge card, then
                        Apply an additional 5% discount
        ELSE
                Award a $25 bonus coupon
ELSE
        Award a $5 bonus coupon
```

FIGURE 11-8   Sample of a sales promotion policy with logical rules, and a pseudocode version of the policy. Notice the alignment and indentation of the logic statements.

© Cengage Learning 2014

DECISION TABLES AND DECISION TREES   As you learned in Chapter 5, decision tables and decision trees can be used to model business logic for an information system. In addition to being used as modeling tools, analysts and programmers can use decision tables and decision trees during system development, as they develop code modules that implement the logical rules. Figure 11-9 shows an example of a decision tree that documents the sales promotion policy shown in Figure 11-8. Notice that the decision tree accurately reflects the sales promotion policy, which has three separate conditions, and four possible outcomes.

Project Management

Regardless of whether structured analysis, object-oriented design, or agile methods are used, even a modest-sized project might have hundreds or even thousands of modules. For this reason, application development can become quite complex and difficult to

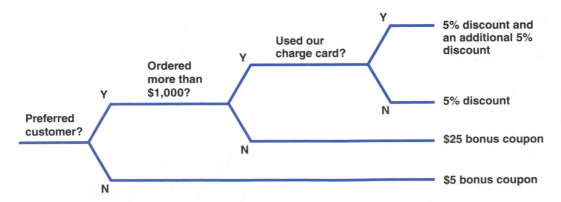

FIGURE 11-9   Sample decision tree that reflects the sales promotion policy in Figure 11-8. Like a decision table, a decision tree shows the action to be taken based on certain conditions.

© Cengage Learning 2014

manage. At this stage, project management is especially important. Users and managers are looking forward to the new system, and it is very important to set realistic schedules, meet project deadlines, control costs, and maintain quality. To achieve these goals, the systems analyst or project manager should use project management tools and techniques similar to those described in Chapter 3 to monitor and control the development effort.

The following sections describe the application development process. Structured development techniques and tools are discussed first, followed by object-oriented and agile development methods.

Video Learning Session
Structure Charts

If you have an MIS CourseMate access code, you can launch interactive Video Learning Sessions to help you understand systems development concepts and practice your skills. You can watch the sessions on your computer or mobile device, and pause, rewind, or replay a video at any time. To log on to the MIS CourseMate site at **www.cengagebrain.com**, you must create a student account and then register this book.

This session is about structure charts. You'll learn what a structure chart is and how you can use a structure chart to show program modules and their relationships.

© craftvision/iStockphoto

STRUCTURED APPLICATION DEVELOPMENT

Structured application development usually involves a **top-down approach**, which proceeds from a general design to a detailed structure. After a systems analyst documents the system's requirements, he or she breaks the system down into subsystems and modules in a process called **partitioning**. This approach also is called **modular design** and is similar to constructing a leveled set of DFDs. By assigning modules to different programmers, several development areas can proceed at the same time. As explained in Chapter 3, you can use project management software to monitor work on each module, forecast overall development time, estimate required human and technical resources, and calculate a critical path for the project.

Because all the modules must work together properly, an analyst must proceed carefully, with constant input from programmers and IT management to achieve a sound, well-integrated structure. The analyst also must ensure that integration capability is built into each design and thoroughly tested.

Structure Charts

Structure charts show the program modules and the relationships among them. A **structure chart** consists of rectangles that represent the program modules, with arrows and other symbols that provide additional information. Typically, a higher-level module, called a **control module**, directs lower-level modules, called **subordinate modules**. In a structure chart, symbols represent various actions or conditions. Structure chart symbols represent modules, data couples, control couples, conditions, and loops.

MODULE A rectangle represents a module, as shown in Figure 11-10. Vertical lines at the edges of a rectangle indicate that module 1.3 is a library module. A **library module** is reusable code and can be invoked from more than one point in the chart.

DATA COUPLE An arrow with an empty circle represents a data couple. A **data couple** shows data that one module passes to another. In the data couple example shown in Figure 11-11, the LOOK UP CUSTOMER NAME module exchanges data with the MAINTAIN CUSTOMER DATA module.

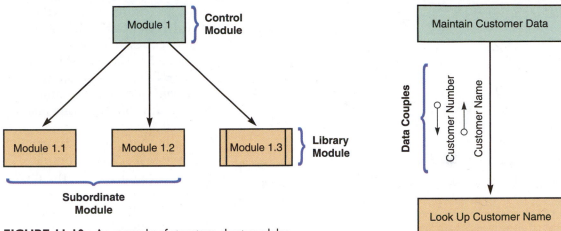

FIGURE 11-10 An example of structure chart modules.

© Cengage Learning 2014

FIGURE 11-11 An example of a structure chart data.

© Cengage Learning 2014

CONTROL COUPLE An arrow with a filled circle represents a control couple. A **control couple** shows a message, also called a **status flag**, which one module sends to another. In the example shown in Figure 11-12, the UPDATE CUSTOMER FILE module sends an ACCOUNT OVERDUE flag back to the MAINTAIN CUSTOMER DATA module. A module uses a flag to signal a specific condition or action to another module.

CONDITION A line with a diamond on one end represents a condition. A **condition** line indicates that a control module determines which subordinate modules will be invoked, depending on a specific condition. In the example shown in Figure 11-13, SORT INVENTORY PARTS is a control module with a condition line that triggers one of the three subordinate modules.

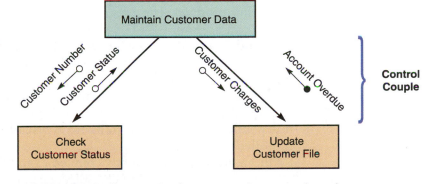

FIGURE 11-12 An example of a structure chart control couple.

© Cengage Learning 2014

LOOP A curved arrow represents a loop. A **loop** indicates that one or more modules are repeated. In the example shown in Figure 11-14 on the next page, the GET STUDENT GRADES and CALCULATE GPA modules are repeated.

Cohesion and Coupling

Cohesion and coupling are important tools for evaluating the overall design. As explained in the following sections, it is desirable to have modules that are highly cohesive and loosely coupled.

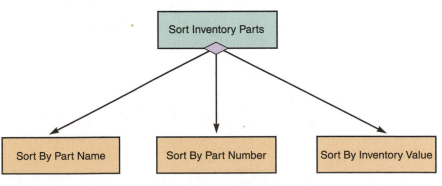

FIGURE 11-13 The diagram shows a control module that triggers three subordinate modules.

© Cengage Learning 2014

Cohesion measures a module's scope and processing characteristics. A module that performs a single function or task has a high degree of cohesion, which is desirable. Because it focuses on a single task, a cohesive module is much easier to code and

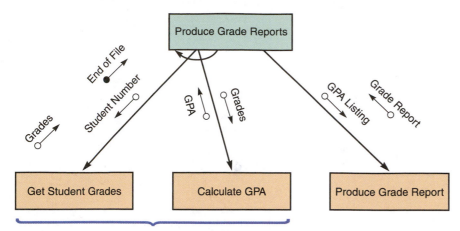

The curved arrow indicates that these modules are repeated.

FIGURE 11-14 The diagram shows a structure chart loop with two repeating modules.

© Cengage Learning 2014

reuse. For example, a module named VERIFY CUSTOMER NUMBER is more cohesive than a module named CALCULATE AND PRINT STATEMENTS. If you notice the word *and* in a module name, you know that more than one task is involved.

If a module must perform multiple tasks, more complex coding is required and the module will be more difficult to create and maintain. If you need to make a module more cohesive, you can split it into separate units, each with a single function. For example, by splitting the module CHECK CUSTOMER NUMBER and CREDIT LIMIT in Figure 11-15 into two separate modules, CHECK CUSTOMER NUMBER and CHECK CUSTOMER CREDIT LIMIT, cohesion is greatly improved.

Coupling describes the degree of interdependence among modules. Modules that are independent are **loosely coupled**, which is desirable. Loosely coupled modules are easier to maintain and modify, because the logic in one module does not affect other modules. If a programmer needs to update a loosely coupled module, he or she can accomplish the task in a single location. If modules are **tightly coupled**, one module is linked to internal logic contained in another module. For example, Module A might refer to an internal variable contained in Module B. In that case, a logic error in the Module B will affect the processing in Module A. For that reason, passing a status flag down as a message from a control module is generally regarded as poor design. It is better to have subordinate modules handle processing tasks as independently as possible, to avoid a cascade effect of logic errors in the control module.

In Figure 11-16, the tightly coupled example on the left shows that the subordinate module CALCULATE CURRENT CHARGES depends on a status flag sent down from the control module UPDATE CUSTOMER BALANCE. It would be preferable to have the modules loosely coupled and logically independent. In the example on the right, a status flag is not needed because the subordinate module APPLY DISCOUNT handles discount processing independently. Any logic errors are confined to a single location: the APPLY DISCOUNT module.

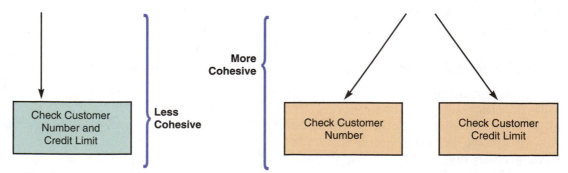

FIGURE 11-15 Two examples of cohesion. Notice that the single module on the left is less cohesive than the two modules on the right.

© Cengage Learning 2014

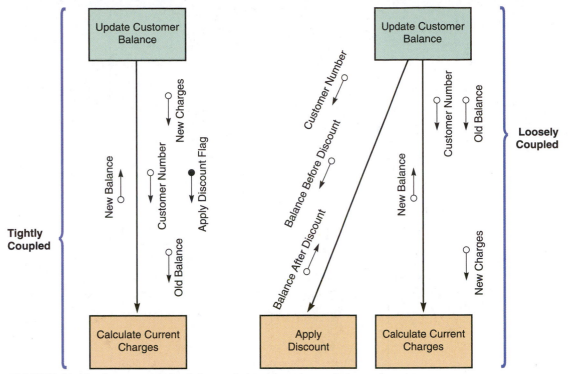

FIGURE 11-16   An example of tightly coupled and loosely coupled structure charts.

© Cengage Learning 2014

Drawing a Structure Chart

If you used a structured analysis method, your structure charts will be based on the DFDs you created during data and process modeling.

Typically, you follow four steps when you create a structure chart. You review DFDs to identify the processes and methods, identify the program modules and determine control-subordinate relationships, add symbols for couples and loops, and analyze the structure chart to ensure that it is consistent with your system documentation.

STEP 1: REVIEW THE DFDS Your first step is to review all DFDs for accuracy and completeness, especially if changes have occurred since the systems analysis phase. If object models also were developed, you should analyze them to identify the objects, the methods that each object must perform, and the relationships among the objects. A method is similar to a functional primitive, and requires code to implement the necessary actions.

STEP 2: IDENTIFY MODULES AND RELATIONSHIPS Working from the logical model, you transform functional primitives or object methods into program modules. When analyzing a set of DFDs, remember that each DFD level represents a processing level. If you are using DFDs, you would work your way down from the context diagram to the lower-level diagrams, identifying control modules and subordinate modules, until you reach functional primitives. If more cohesion is desired, you can divide processes into smaller modules that handle a single task. Figure 11-17 on the next page shows a structure chart based on the order system shown in Figures 5-16, 5-17, and 5-18 on pages 196–198. Notice how the three-level structure chart relates to the three DFD levels.

STEP 3: ADD COUPLES, LOOPS, AND CONDITIONS Next, you add couples, loops, and conditions to the structure chart. If you are working with DFDs, you can review the data flows and the data dictionary to identify the data elements that pass from one

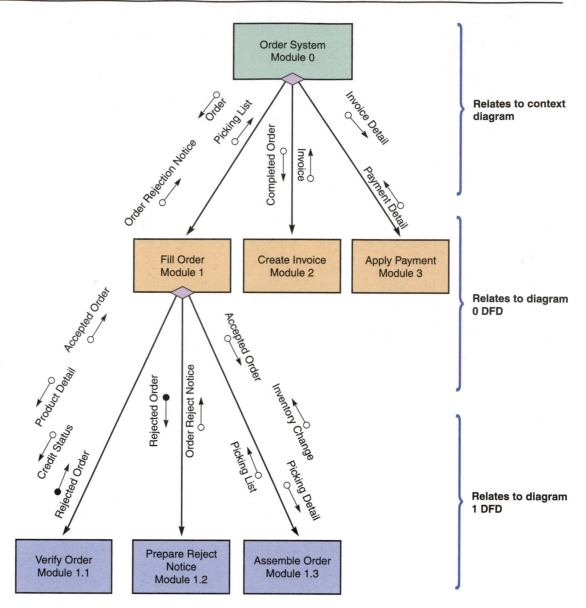

FIGURE 11-17 A structure chart based on the order system DFDs on pages 196–198. The three-level structure chart relates to the three DFD levels.

© Cengage Learning 2014

module to another. In addition to adding the data couples, you add control couples where a module is sending a control parameter, or flag, to another module. You also add loops and condition lines that indicate repetitive or alternative processing steps, as shown in Figure 11-17. If you also developed an object model, you can review the class diagrams and object relationship diagrams to be sure that you understand the interaction among the objects.

STEP 4: ANALYZE THE STRUCTURE CHART AND THE DATA DICTIONARY At this point, the structure chart is ready for careful analysis. You should check each process, data element, or object method to ensure that the chart reflects all previous documentation and that the logic is correct. You also should determine that modules are strongly cohesive and loosely coupled. Often, you must draw several versions of the chart. Some CASE tools can help you analyze the chart and identify problem areas.

OBJECT-ORIENTED APPLICATION DEVELOPMENT

When you studied the object-oriented methods described in Chapter 6, you learned that O-O analysis makes it easier to translate an object model directly into an object-oriented programming language. This process is called **object-oriented development**, or **OOD**. Although many structured design concepts also apply to object-oriented methodology, there are some differences.

Characteristics of Object-Oriented Application Development

When implementing a structured design, a structure chart is used to describe the interaction between program modules, as explained earlier. In contrast, when implementing an object-oriented design, relationships between objects already exist. Because object interaction is defined during the O-O analysis process, the application's structure is represented by the object model itself.

As Chapter 6 explains, objects contain both data and program logic, called methods. Individual object instances belong to classes of objects with similar characteristics. The relationship and interaction among classes are described using a class diagram, such as the one shown in Figure 11-18. A class diagram includes the class **attributes**, which describe the characteristics of objects in the class,

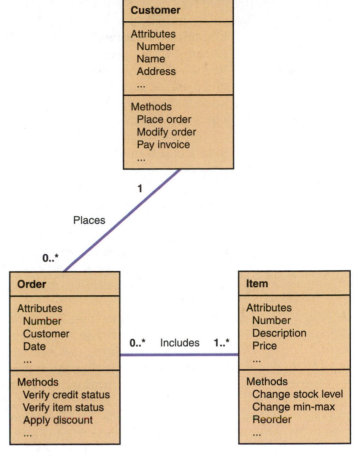

FIGURE 11-18 A simplified class diagram for a customer order processing system.
© Cengage Learning 2014

and **methods**, which represent program logic. For example, the CUSTOMER class describes customer objects. CUSTOMER attributes include NUMBER, NAME, ADDRESS, and so on. Methods for the CUSTOMER class include PLACE ORDER, MODIFY ORDER, and PAY INVOICE, among others. The CUSTOMER class can exchange messages with the ORDER class.

In addition to class diagrams, programmers get an overview of object interaction by using object relationship diagrams that were developed during the O-O analysis process. For example, Figure 11-19 shows an object relationship diagram for a fitness center. Notice that the model shows the objects and how they interact to perform business functions and transactions.

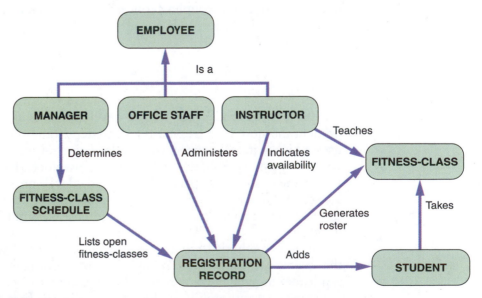

FIGURE 11-19 An object-relationship diagram for a fitness center.
© Cengage Learning 2014

Properly implemented, object-oriented development can speed up projects, reduce costs, and improve overall quality. However, these results are not always achieved. Organizations sometimes have unrealistic expectations, and do not spend enough time learning about, preparing for, and implementing the OOD process. For example, no one would build a bridge without a analysis of needs, supporting data, and a detailed blueprint — and the bridge would not be opened for traffic until it had been carefully inspected and checked to ensure that all specifications were met. O-O software developers sometimes forget that the basic rules of architecture also apply to their projects.

In summary, to secure the potential benefits of object-oriented development, systems analysts must carefully analyze, design, implement, test, and document their O-O projects.

Implementation of Object-Oriented Designs

When a programmer translates an object-oriented design into an application, he or she analyzes the classes, attributes, methods, and messages that are documented in the object model. During this process, the programmer makes necessary revisions and updates to class diagrams, sequence diagrams, state transition diagrams, and activity diagrams.

The programmer's main objective is to translate object methods into program code modules and determine what event or message will trigger the execution of each module. To accomplish the task, the programmer analyzes sequence diagrams and state transition diagrams that show the events and messages that trigger changes to an object. O-O applications are called event-driven, because each event, transaction, or message triggers a corresponding action. The programmer can represent the program steps in pseudocode initially, or use CASE tools and code generators to create object-oriented code directly from the object model.

Object-Oriented Cohesion and Coupling

The principles of cohesion and coupling also apply to object-oriented application development. Classes should be as loosely coupled (independent of other classes) as possible. In addition, an object's methods also should be loosely coupled (independent of other methods) and highly cohesive (perform closely related actions). By following these principles, classes and objects are easier to understand and edit. O-O programmers who ignore cohesion and coupling concepts may end up creating a web of code that is difficult to maintain. When code is scattered in various places, editing becomes complicated and expensive.

AGILE APPLICATION DEVELOPMENT

As you learned in Chapter 1, agile development is a distinctly different systems development method. It shares many of the steps found in traditional development, but uses a highly iterative process. The development team is in constant communication with the primary user, who is called the **customer**, shaping and forming the system to match the customer's specifications. Agile development is aptly named because it is based on a quick and nimble development process that easily adapts to change. Agile development focuses on small teams, intense communication, and rapid development iterations.

As agile methods become more popular, many software firms are offering packages that teams can use to manage and document the agile process. For example, Serena is a leader in agile development solutions. On its Web site, shown in Figure 11-20, a video uses an automobile analogy to describe the firm's four-step approach to agile development.

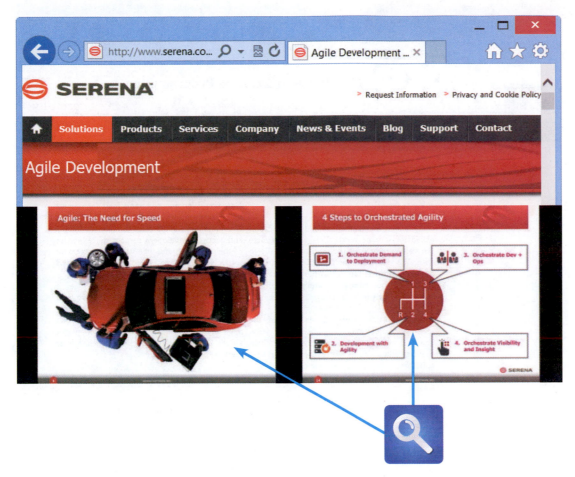

FIGURE 11-20   Serena's video clip uses an automobile analogy to describe the firm's four-step approach to agile development, which it calls *Orchestrated Agility*.

© 2012 Serena Software Inc.

You also learned in Chapter 1 about Extreme Programming (XP), which is one of the newest agile methods. XP is an iterative approach, as shown in Figure 11-21 on the next page, where a team of users and developers immerse themselves in systems development. XP supporters emphasize values such as simplicity, communication, feedback, respect, and courage. Success requires strong commitment to the process, corporate support, and dedicated team members. The following section describes a typical XP project.

An Extreme Programming (XP) Example

Suppose that a customer has requested a sales tracking system. The first step in the XP process, like any other development method, would be to define the system requirements. The customer begins by meeting with programmers and providing user stories. A **user story** is a short, simple requirements definition. Programmers review user stories to determine the project's requirements, priorities, and scope. Here are three user story examples:

- *As the sales manager, I want to identify fast or slow moving items so I can manage our inventory more effectively.*

- *As a store manager, I need enough lead time to replenish my stock so I don't run out of hot items.*

- *As a sales representative, I want to offer the best selection of fast selling items and clear out the old stock that is not moving.*

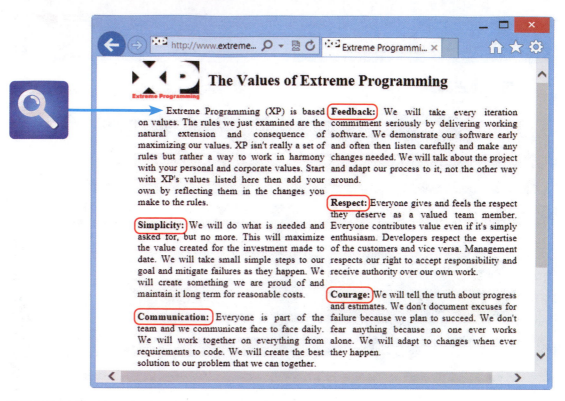

The Values of Extreme Programming

Extreme Programming (XP) is based on values. The rules we just examined are the natural extension and consequence of maximizing our values. XP isn't really a set of rules but rather a way to work in harmony with your personal and corporate values. Start with XP's values listed here then add your own by reflecting them in the changes you make to the rules.

Simplicity: We will do what is needed and asked for, but no more. This will maximize the value created for the investment made to date. We will take small simple steps to our goal and mitigate failures as they happen. We will create something we are proud of and maintain it long term for reasonable costs.

Communication: Everyone is part of the team and we communicate face to face daily. We will work together on everything from requirements to code. We will create the best solution to our problem that we can together.

Feedback: We will take every iteration commitment seriously by delivering working software. We demonstrate our software early and often then listen carefully and make any changes needed. We will talk about the project and adapt our process to it, not the other way around.

Respect: Everyone gives and feels the respect they deserve as a valued team member. Everyone contributes value even if it's simply enthusiasm. Developers respect the expertise of the customers and vice versa. Management respects our right to accept responsibility and receive authority over our own work.

Courage: We will tell the truth about progress and estimates. We don't document excuses for failure because we plan to succeed. We don't fear anything because no one ever works alone. We will adapt to changes when ever they happen.

FIGURE 11-21   Extreme programming relies on the core values shown here. Notice that users are invited to start with these values, and add their own.

© 2009 Don Wells

User stories do not deal with technical details and are so short that they are often written on index cards. Each user story is given a priority by the customer, so the requirements can be ranked. In addition, programmers assign a score to each user story that indicates the estimated difficulty of implementation. This information helps the team form a plan and assign its resources. Projects are often composed of many user stories, from which programmers can estimate the scope, time requirements, and difficulty of the project. In addition to the user stories, frequent face-to-face meetings with customers provide a higher level of detail as the project progresses.

The team must also develop a **release plan,** which specifies when user stories will be implemented and the timing of the releases. Releases are relatively frequent, and each system release is like a prototype that can be tested and modified as needed.

User stories are implemented in a series of iteration cycles. An **iteration cycle** includes planning, designing, coding, and testing of one or more features based on user stories. At the beginning of each iteration cycle, which is often two weeks long, the team holds an **iteration planning meeting** to break down the user stories into specific tasks that are assigned to team members. As new user stories or features are added, the team reviews and modifies the release plan.

As with any development process, success is determined by the customer's approval. The programming team regularly meets with the customer, who tests prototype releases as they become available. This process usually results in additional user stories, and changes are implemented in the next iteration cycle. As the project's code changes during each iteration, obsolete code is removed and remaining code is restructured to keep the system up to date. The iteration cycles continue until all user stories have been implemented, tested, and accepted.

Extreme Programming uses an interesting concept called parallel programming. In **parallel programming,** two programmers work on the same task on the same computer; one drives (programs) while the other navigates (watches). The onlooker examines the code strategically to see the *forest* while the driver is concerned with the individual *trees* immediately in front of him or her. The two discuss their ideas continuously throughout the process.

Another important concept in XP is that unit tests are designed *before* code is written. This **test-driven design** focuses on end results from the beginning and prevents programmers from straying from their goals. Because of the magnitude and intensity of the multicycle process, agile testing relies heavily on automated testing methods and software.

Programmers can use popular agile-friendly languages such as Python, Ruby, and Perl. However, agile methods do not require a specific programming language, and programmers also use various object-oriented languages such as Java, C++, and C#.

The Future of Agile Development

Agile methodology is becoming very popular for software projects. Its supporters boast that it speeds up software development and delivers precisely what the customer wants, when the customer wants it, while fostering teamwork and empowering employees. However, there are drawbacks to this adaptive rather than predictive method. Critics of agile development often claim that because it focuses on quick iterations and fast releases, it lacks discipline and produces systems of questionable quality. In addition, agile methodology may not work as well for larger projects because of their complexity and the lack of focus on a well-defined end product.

Before implementing agile development, the proposed system and development methods should be examined carefully. As experienced IT professionals know, a one-size-fits-all solution does not exist. For more information on agile methods, refer to the discussion of systems development methods that begins on page 21 in Chapter 1.

CODING

Coding is the process of turning program logic into specific instructions that the computer system can execute. Working from a specific design, a programmer uses a programming language to transform program logic into code statements. An individual programmer might create a small program, while larger programs typically are divided into modules that several individuals or groups can work on simultaneously.

Programming Environments

Each IT department has its own programming environment and standards. Visual Basic, Python, Ruby, and SQL are examples of commonly used programming languages, and many commercial packages use a proprietary set of commands. As the trend toward Internet-based applications continues, HTML/XML, Java, and other Web-centric languages will be used extensively.

To simplify the integration of system components and reduce code development time, many programmers use an **integrated development environment (IDE).** IDEs can make it easier to program interactive software products by providing built-in tools and advanced features, such as real-time error detection, syntax hints, highlighted code, class browsers, and version control. As you learned in Chapter 7, IBM WebSphere and Microsoft .NET are popular IDEs. In addition to these commercial packages,

TOOLKIT TIME

The CASE tools in Part B of the Systems Analyst's Toolkit can help you understand IDEs. To learn more about these tools, turn to Part B of the four-part Toolkit that follows Chapter 12.

programmers can use open-source IDEs such as Java-based NetBeans IDE and Eclipse. You can learn more about IDEs in Part B of the Systems Analyst's Toolkit.

Generating Code

You learned in earlier chapters that systems analysts use application generators, report writers, screen generators, fourth-generation languages, and other CASE tools that produce code directly from program design specifications. Some commercial applications can generate editable program code directly from macros, keystrokes, or mouse actions.

TESTING THE SYSTEM

After coding, a programmer must test each program to make sure it functions correctly. Later, programs are tested in groups, and finally the development team must test the entire system. The first step is to compile the program using a CASE tool or a language compiler. This process detects **syntax errors**, which are language grammar errors. The programmer corrects the errors until the program executes properly.

Next, the programmer desk checks the program. **Desk checking** is the process of reviewing the program code to spot **logic errors**, which produce incorrect results. This process can be performed by the person who wrote the program or by other programmers. Many organizations require a more formal type of desk checking called a **structured walkthrough**, or **code review**.

Typically, a group of three to five IT staff members participate in code review. The group usually consists of project team members and might include other programmers and analysts who did not work on the project. The objective is to have a peer group identify errors, apply quality standards, and verify that the program meets the requirements of the system design specification. Errors found during a structured walkthrough are easier to fix while coding is still in the developmental stages.

In addition to analyzing logic and program code, the project team usually holds a session with users called a **design walkthrough**, to review the interface with a cross-section of people who will work with the new system and ensure that all necessary features have been included. This is a continuation of the modeling and prototyping effort that began early in the systems development process.

The next step in application development is to initiate a sequence of unit testing, integration testing, and system testing, as shown in Figure 11-22.

Unit Testing

The testing of an individual program or module is called **unit testing**. The objective is to identify and eliminate execution errors that could cause the program to terminate abnormally, and logic errors that could have been missed during desk checking.

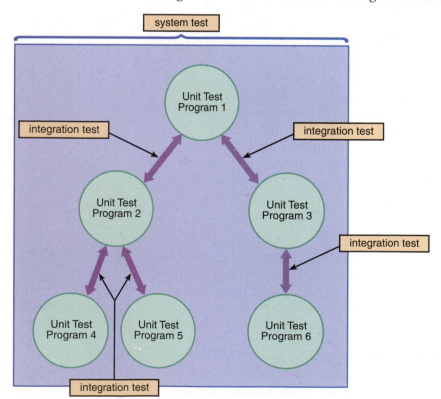

FIGURE 11-22 The first step in testing is unit testing, followed by integration testing, and then system testing.

Test data should contain both correct data and erroneous data and should test all possible situations that could occur. For example, for a field that allows a range of numeric values, the test data should contain minimum values, maximum values, values outside the acceptable range, and alphanumeric characters. During testing, programmers can use software tools to determine the location and potential causes of program errors.

During unit testing, programmers must test programs that interact with other programs and files individually, before they are integrated into the system. This requires a technique called stub testing. In **stub testing**, the programmer simulates each program outcome or result and displays a message to indicate whether or not the program executed successfully. Each stub represents an entry or exit point that will be linked later to another program or data file.

To obtain an independent analysis, someone other than the programmer who wrote the program usually creates the test data and reviews the results. Systems analysts frequently create test data during the systems design phase as part of an overall test plan. A **test plan** consists of detailed procedures that specify how and when the testing will be performed, who will participate, and what test data will be used. A comprehensive test plan should include scenarios for every possible situation the program could encounter.

Regardless of who creates the test plan, the project manager or a designated analyst also reviews the final test results. Some organizations also require users to approve final unit test results.

Integration Testing

Testing two or more programs that depend on each other is called **integration testing**, or **link testing**. For example, consider an information system with a program that checks and validates customer credit status, and a separate program that updates data in the customer master file. The output from the validation program becomes input to the master file update program. Testing the programs independently does not guarantee that the data passed between them is correct. Only by performing integration testing for this pair of programs can you make sure that the programs work together properly. Figure 11-22 shows integration testing for several groups of programs. Notice that a program can have membership in two or more groups.

Systems analysts usually develop the data they use in integration testing. As is the case with all forms of testing, integration test data must consider both normal and unusual situations. For example, integration testing might include passing typical records between two programs, followed by blank records, to simulate an unusual event or an operational problem. You should use test data that simulates actual conditions because you are testing the interface that links the programs. A testing sequence should not move to the integration test stage unless it has performed properly in all unit tests.

System Testing

After completing integration testing, you must perform **system testing**, which involves the entire information system, as shown in Figure 11-22 on page 466. A system test includes all typical processing situations and is intended to assure users, developers, and managers that the program meets all specifications and that all necessary features have been included.

During a system test, users enter data, including samples of actual, or live, data, perform queries, and produce reports to simulate actual operating conditions. All processing options and outputs are verified by users and the IT project development team to ensure that the system functions correctly. Commercial software packages must undergo system testing similar to that of in-house developed systems, although unit and integration testing usually are not performed. Regardless of how the system was developed, system testing has the following major objectives:

- Perform a final test of all programs

- Verify that the system will handle all input data properly, both valid and invalid

- Ensure that the IT staff has the documentation and instructions needed to operate the system properly and that backup and restart capabilities of the system are adequate (the details of creating this sort of documentation are discussed later in this chapter)

- Demonstrate that users can interact with the system successfully

- Verify that all system components are integrated properly and that actual processing situations will be handled correctly

- Confirm that the information system can handle predicted volumes of data in a timely and efficient manner

Successful completion of system testing is the key to user and management approval, which is why system tests sometimes are called **acceptance tests**. Final acceptance tests, however, are performed during systems installation and evaluation, which is described later in this chapter.

How much testing is necessary? The answer depends on the situation and requires good judgment and input from other IT staff members, users, and management, as shown in Figure 11-23. Unfortunately, IT project managers often are pressured to finish testing quickly and hand the system over to users. Common reasons for premature or rushed testing are demands from users, tight systems development budgets, and demands from top management to finish projects early. Those pressures hinder the testing process and often have detrimental effects on the final product.

You should regard thorough testing as a cost-effective means of providing a quality product. Every error caught during testing eliminates potential expenses and operational problems.

FIGURE 11-23 System testing requires good judgment and input from other IT staff members, users, and IT management.

© Dmitriy Shironosov/Shutterstock.com

No system, however, is 100% error-free. Often, errors go undetected until the system becomes operational. Errors that affect the integrity or accuracy of data must be corrected immediately. Minor errors, such as typographical errors in screen titles, can be corrected later.

Some users want a system that is a completely finished product, while others realize that minor changes can be treated as maintenance items after the system is operational. In the final analysis, you must decide whether or not to postpone system installation if problems are discovered. If conflicting views exist, management will decide whether or not to install the system after a full discussion of the options.

CASE IN POINT 11.2:   WebTest, Inc.

As a new systems analyst, you suspect that testing Web-based systems probably involves a different set of tools and techniques, compared to testing traditional LAN-based systems. Because you've always wanted to run your own IT company, you have decided to launch a start-up firm called WebTest, Inc., that would offer consulting services specifically aimed at testing the performance, integrity, efficiency, and security of Internet-based systems.

Your idea is to identify and purchase various Web site testing tools that currently are available, then use these tools as a Web site testing consultant. No one in your area offers this type of consulting service, so you have high hopes.

Now, you need to perform Internet research to learn more about Web testing software that is available. Review the Internet Resources Tools section, which is Part D of the Systems Analyst's Toolkit that follows Chapter 12, and use a search engine to develop a list of at least four products that you might want to use. For each product, write up a brief description of its overall purpose, its features and benefits, its cost, and how it would fit into your business game plan.

DOCUMENTATION

Documentation describes an information system and helps the users, managers, and IT staff who must interact with it. Accurate documentation can reduce system downtime, cut costs, and speed up maintenance tasks. Figure 11-24 on the next page shows an example of software that can automate the documentation process and help software developers generate accurate, comprehensive reference material.

Documentation is essential for successful system operation and maintenance. In addition to supporting a system's users, accurate documentation is essential for IT staff members who must modify the system, add a new feature, or perform maintenance. Documentation includes program documentation, system documentation, operations documentation, and user documentation.

Program Documentation

Program documentation describes the inputs, outputs, and processing logic for all program modules. The program documentation process starts in the systems analysis phase and continues during systems implementation. Systems analysts prepare overall documentation, such as process descriptions and report layouts, early in the SDLC. This documentation guides programmers, who construct modules that are well supported by internal and external comments and descriptions that can be understood and maintained easily. A systems analyst usually verifies that program documentation is complete and accurate.

System developers also use **defect tracking software**, sometimes called **bug tracking software**, to document and track program defects, code changes, and replacement code, called **patches**.

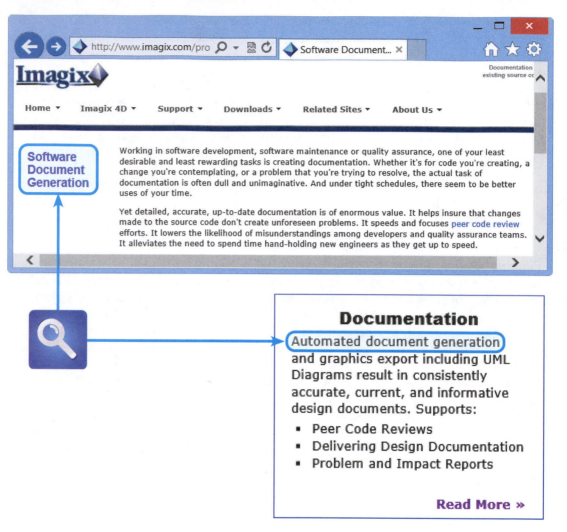

FIGURE 11-24   In addition to CASE tools, software such as Imagix can automate the task of software documentation.

© 2012 Imagix Corp.

System Documentation

System documentation describes the system's functions and how they are implemented. System documentation includes data dictionary entries, data flow diagrams, object models, screen layouts, source documents, and the systems request that initiated the project. System documentation is necessary reference material for the programmers and analysts who must support and maintain the system.

Most of the system documentation is prepared during the systems analysis and systems design phases. During the systems implementation phase, an analyst must review prior documentation to verify that it is complete, accurate, and up to date, including any changes made during the implementation process. For example, if a screen or report has been modified, the analyst must update the documentation. Updates to the system documentation should be made in a timely manner to prevent oversights.

Operations Documentation

If the information system environment involves a minicomputer, a mainframe, or centralized servers, the analyst must prepare documentation for the IT group that supports centralized operations. A mainframe installation might require the scheduling of batch jobs and the distribution of printed reports. In this type of environment, the IT operations staff serves as the first point of contact when users experience problems with the system.

Operations documentation contains all the information needed for processing and distributing online and printed output. Typical operations documentation includes the following information:

- Program, systems analyst, programmer, and system identification
- Scheduling information for printed output, such as report run frequency and deadlines
- Input files and where they originate; and output files and destinations
- E-mail and report distribution lists
- Special forms required, including online forms
- Error and informational messages to operators and restart procedures
- Special instructions, such as security requirements

Operations documentation should be clear, concise, and available online if possible. If the IT department has an operations group, you should review the documentation with them, early and often, to identify any problems. If you keep the operations group informed at every phase of the SDLC, you can develop operations documentation as you go along.

User Documentation

User documentation consists of instructions and information to users who will interact with the system and includes user manuals, Help screens, and tutorials. Programmers or systems analysts usually create program documentation and system documentation. To produce effective and clear user documentation — and hence have a successful project — you need someone with expert skills in this area doing the development, just as you need someone with expert skills developing the software. The skill set required to develop documentation usually is not the same as that to develop a system. This is particularly true as you move into the world of online documentation, which needs to coordinate with print documentation and intranet and Internet information. Technical writing requires specialized skills, and competent technical writers are valuable members of the IT team.

Just as you cannot throw a system together in several days, you cannot add documentation at the end. That is a common misconception and often proves fatal to a project. While that has always been true of software user documentation, this is an even more critical issue now that online Help and context-sensitive Help so often are needed. Context-sensitive Help is part of the program. You must put coded callouts in the text that link to the correct page of information in the documentation. To try to go back and add this after the fact would take a great deal of time; depending on the project size, it could take months! Additionally, it could introduce other coding errors — and it all has to be tested as well.

Systems analysts usually are responsible for preparing documentation to help users learn the system. In larger companies, a technical support team that includes technical writers might assist in the preparation of user documentation and training materials. Regardless of the delivery method, user documentation must be clear, understandable, and readily accessible to users at all levels.

User documentation includes the following:

- A system overview that clearly describes all major system features, capabilities, and limitations
- Description of source document content, preparation, processing, and samples
- Overview of menu and data entry screen options, contents, and processing instructions

- Examples of reports that are produced regularly or available at the user's request, including samples

- Security and audit trail information

- Explanation of responsibility for specific input, output, or processing requirements

- Procedures for requesting changes and reporting problems

- Examples of exceptions and error situations

- Frequently asked questions (FAQs)

- Explanation of how to get help and procedures for updating the user manual

Most users prefer **online documentation**, which provides immediate Help when they have questions or encounter problems. Many users are accustomed to context-sensitive help screens, hints and tips, hypertext, on-screen demos, and other user-friendly features commonly found in popular software packages; they expect the same kind of support for in-house developed software.

If the system will include online documentation, that fact needs to be identified as one of the system requirements. If the documentation will be created by someone other than the analysts who are developing the system, that person or group needs to be involved as early as possible to become familiar with the software and begin developing the required documentation and support material. In addition, system developers must determine whether the documentation will be available from within the program, or as a separate entity in the form of a tutorial, slide presentation, reference manual, or Web site. If necessary, links should be created within the program that will take the user to the appropriate documentation.

Effective online documentation is an important productivity tool because it empowers users and reduces the time that IT staff members must spend in providing telephone, e-mail, or face-to-face assistance. Interactive tutorials are especially popular with users who like to learn by doing, and visual impact is very important. For example, Adobe currently offers a series of videos called *Duane's World*, shown in Figure 11-25. The star of the series is Duane Nickulls. In addition to being an Adobe expert, he describes himself as a professional musician and an extreme athlete. The videos are an excellent example of cutting edge tutorial methods.

In addition to program-based assistance, the Internet offers an entirely new level of comprehensive, immediate support. Many programs include links to Web sites, intranet sites, and Internet-based technical support. For example, the Cisco Systems site shown in Figure 11-26 offers a wide range of support services and social media links that allow Cisco users to collaborate and share their knowledge.

Although online documentation is essential, written documentation material also is valuable, especially in training users and for reference purposes. A sample page from a user manual is shown in Figure 11-27 on page 474. Systems analysts or technical writers usually prepare the manual, but many companies invite users to review the material and participate in the development process.

No matter what form of user documentation your system will require, you must keep in mind that it can take a good deal of time to develop. The time between finishing software coding and the time when a complete package — including documentation — can be released to users is entirely dependent on how well the documentation is thought out in advance. If the completion of your project includes providing user documentation, this issue needs to be addressed from the very beginning of the project. Determining what the user documentation requirements are and ascertaining who will complete the documents is critical to a timely release of the project.

Neglecting user documentation issues until after all the program is complete often leads to one of two things: (1) The documentation will be thrown together quickly

FIGURE 11-25   Adobe uses a series of eye-catching videos called *Duane's World*, complete with rock music and foreign travel, to describe technology solutions.

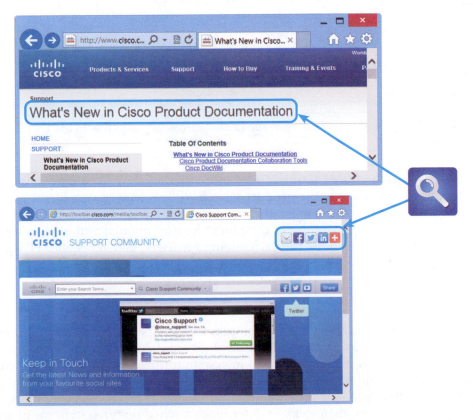

FIGURE 11-26   The new Cisco Support Community invites users to contribute valuable experience and documentation using social media.

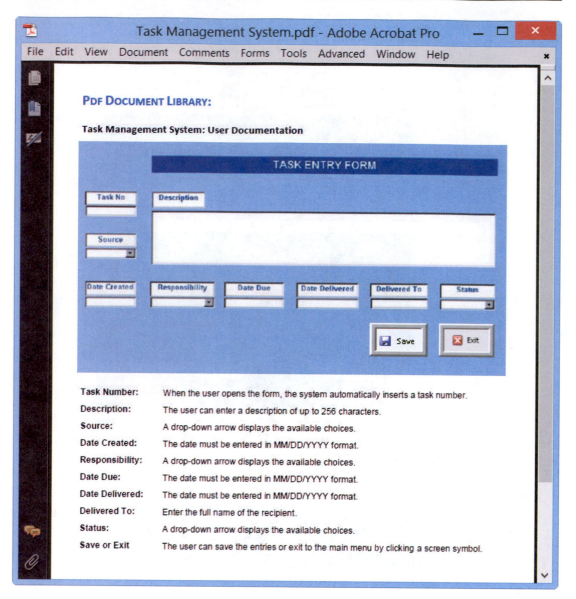

FIGURE 11-27 A sample page from a user manual. The instructions explain how to add a new task to the system.

© Cengage Learning 2014

just to get it out the door on time, and it more than likely will be inadequate; or (2) it will be done correctly, and the product release will be delayed considerably.

User training typically is scheduled when the system is installed; the training sessions offer an ideal opportunity to distribute the user manual and explain the procedures for updating it in the future. Training for users, managers, and IT staff is described later in this chapter.

MANAGEMENT APPROVAL

After system testing is complete, you present the results to management. You should describe the test results, update the status of all required documentation, and summarize input from users who participated in system testing. You also must provide detailed time schedules, cost estimates, and staffing requirements for making the system fully operational. If system testing produced no technical, economical, or operational problems, management determines a schedule for system installation and evaluation.

SYSTEM INSTALLATION AND EVALUATION

The following sections describe system installation and evaluation tasks that are performed for every information systems project, whether you develop the application in-house or purchase it as a commercial package.

The new system now is ready to go to work. Your earlier design activities produced the overall architecture and processing strategy, and you consulted users at every stage of development. You developed and tested programs individually, in groups, and as a complete system. You prepared the necessary documentation and checked it for accuracy, including support material for IT staff and users. Now, you will carry out the remaining steps in systems implementation:

- Prepare a separate operational and test environment
- Provide training for users, managers, and IT staff
- Perform data conversion and system changeover
- Carry out a post-implementation evaluation of the system
- Present a final report to management

OPERATIONAL AND TEST ENVIRONMENTS

You learned earlier that an environment, or platform, is a specific combination of hardware and software. The environment for the actual system operation is called the **operational environment** or **production environment**. The environment that analysts and programmers use to develop and maintain programs is called the **test environment**. A separate test environment is necessary to maintain system security and integrity and protect the operational environment. Typically, the test environment resides on a limited-access workstation or server located in the IT department.

Access to the operational environment is limited to users and must strictly be controlled. Systems analysts and programmers should not have access to the operational environment except to correct a system problem or to make authorized modifications or enhancements. Otherwise, IT department members have no reason to access the day-to-day operational system.

The test environment for an information system contains copies of all programs, procedures, and test data files. Before making any changes to an operational system, you must verify them in the test environment and obtain user approval. Figure 11-28 shows the differences between test environments and operational environments.

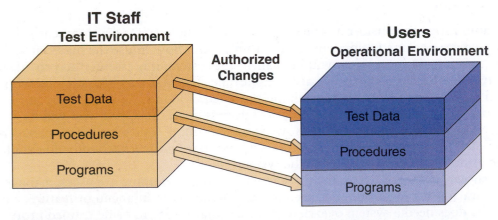

FIGURE 11-28 The test environment versus the operational environment. Notice that access to the test environment is limited to IT staff, while the operational environment is restricted to users.

© Cengage Learning 2014

FIGURE 11-29   In any situation, training must fit the needs of users and help them carry out their job functions.
© Marcin Balcerzak/Shutterstock.com

An effective testing process is essential, whether you are examining an information system or a batch of computer chips. Every experienced systems analyst can tell you a story about an apparently innocent program change that was introduced without being tested properly. In those stories, the innocent change invariably ends up causing some unexpected and unwanted changes to the program. After any modification, you should repeat the same acceptance tests you ran when the system was developed. By restricting access to the operational area and performing all tests in a separate environment, you can protect the system and avoid problems that could damage data or interrupt operations.

The operational environment includes hardware and software configurations and settings, system utilities, telecommunications resources, and any other components that might affect system performance. Because network capability is critically important in a client/server environment, you must verify connectivity, specifications, and performance before installing any applications. You should check all communications features in the test environment carefully, and then check them again after loading the applications into the operational environment. Your documentation should identify all network specifications and settings, including technical and operational requirements for communications hardware and software. If you have to build or upgrade network resources to support the new system, you must test the platform rigorously before system installation begins.

TRAINING

No system can be successful without proper training, whether it involves software, hardware, or manufacturing, as shown in Figure 11-29. A successful information system requires training for users, managers, and IT staff members. The entire systems development effort can depend on whether or not people understand the system and know how to use it effectively.

Training Plan

You should start to consider a **training plan** early in the systems development process. As you create documentation, you should think about how to use the material in future training sessions. When you implement the system, it is essential to provide the right training for the right people at the right time. The first step is to identify who should receive training and what training is needed. You must look carefully at the organization, how the system will support business operations, and who will be involved or affected. Figure 11-30 shows specific training topics for users, managers, and IT staff. Notice that each group needs a mix of general background and detailed information to understand and use the system.

As shown in Figure 11-30, the three main groups for training are users, managers, and IT staff. A manager does not need to understand every submenu or feature, but he or she does need a system overview to ensure that users are being trained properly and are using the system correctly. Similarly, users need to know how to perform their day-to-day job functions, but do not need to know how the company allocates system operational charges among user departments. IT staff people probably need the most

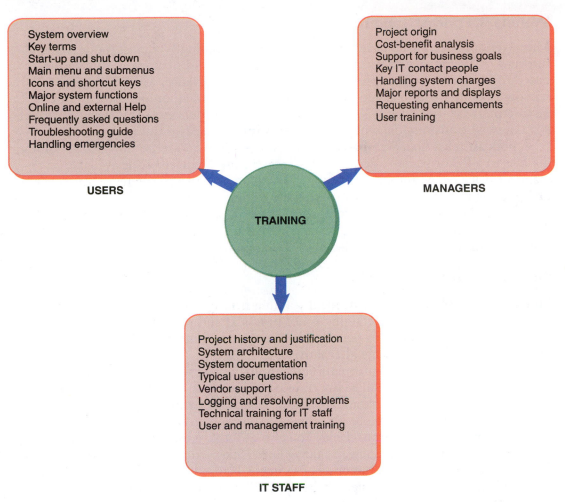

FIGURE 11-30 Examples of training topics for three different groups. Users, managers, and IT staff members have different training needs.
© Cengage Learning 2014

information. To support the new system, they must have a clear understanding of how the system functions, how it supports business requirements, and the skills that users need to operate the system and perform their tasks.

After you identify the objectives, you must determine how the company will provide training. The main choices are to obtain training from vendors, outside training firms, or use IT staff and other in-house resources.

Vendor Training

If the system includes the purchase of software or hardware, then vendor-supplied training is one of the features you should include in the RFPs (requests for proposal) and RFQs (requests for quotation) that you send to potential vendors.

Many hardware and software vendors offer training programs free or at a nominal cost for the products they sell. In other cases, the company might negotiate the price for training, depending on their relationship with the vendor and the prospect of future purchases. The training usually is conducted at the vendor's site by experienced trainers who provide valuable hands-on experience. If a large number of people need training, you might be able to arrange classes at your location.

Vendor training often gives the best return on your training dollars because it is focused on products that the vendor developed. The scope of vendor training, however, usually is limited to a standard version of the vendor's software or hardware. You might have to supplement the training in-house, especially if your IT staff customized the package.

Webinars, Podcasts, and Tutorials

Many vendors offer Web-based training options, including Webinars, podcasts, and tutorials. A **Webinar**, which combines the words Web and seminar, is an Internet-based training session that provides an interactive experience. Most Webinars are scheduled events with a group of preregistered users and an online presenter or instructor. A pre-recorded Webinar session also can be delivered as a **Webcast**, which is a one-way transmission, whenever a user wants or needs training support.

A **podcast** refers to a Web-based broadcast that allows a user to download multimedia files to a PC or portable device. Podcasts can be prescheduled, made available on demand, or delivered as automatic updates, depending on a user's preference. An advantage of a podcast is that subscribers can access the recorded material anywhere, anytime.

A **tutorial** is a series of online interactive lessons that present material and provide a dialog with users. Tutorials can be developed by software vendors, or by a company's IT team. A tutorial example is included in the in-house training section.

Outside Training Resources

You also can look into an independent training firm to provide in-house hardware or software training. If vendor training is not practical and your organization does not have the internal resources to perform the training, you might find that outside training consultants are a desirable alternative.

The rapid expansion of information technology has produced tremendous growth in the computer-training field. Many training consultants, institutes, and firms are available that provide either standardized or customized training packages.

If you decide to investigate outside training resources, you can contact a training provider and obtain references from clients. You also can seek assistance from nonprofit sources with an interest in training, including universities, industry associations, and information management organizations. For example, Figure 11-31 shows the Web site for Western Illinois University's Center for the Application of Information Technologies (CAIT), which describes a variety of IT education and training resources.

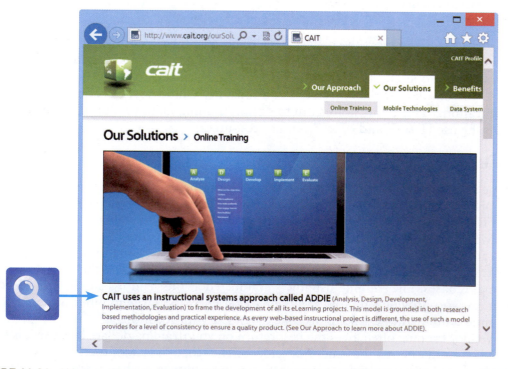

FIGURE 11-31 Western Illinois University's Center for the Application of Information Technologies (CAIT) helps organizations design, develop, and deploy information technology education and training.

Training Tips

The IT staff and user departments often share responsibility for developing and conducting training programs for internally developed software. If your organization has a service desk, the staff might be able to handle user training.

Multimedia is an effective training method. Presentation software, such as Microsoft PowerPoint, Apache OpenOffice Impress, or Corel Presentations, allows you to design training sessions that combine slides, animation, and sound. You also can use programs that capture actual keystrokes and mouse actions, and then replay the screens as a demonstration for users. If your firm has a media or graphic arts group, they can help you prepare training aids such as videotapes, charts, and other instructional materials. When developing a training program, you should keep the following guidelines in mind.

FIGURE 11-32 Users must be trained on the new system. Training sessions might be one-on-one or group situations such as the one shown here. Many vendors provide product training as part of an overall service to customers.
© Chris Schmidt/iStockphoto

- *Train people in groups, with separate training programs for distinct groups.* Group training, as shown in Figure 11-32, makes the most efficient use of time and training facilities. In addition, if the group is small, trainees can learn from the questions and problems of others. A training program must address the job interests and skills of a wide range of participants. For example, IT staff personnel and users require very different information. Problems often arise when some participants have technical backgrounds and others do not. A single program will not meet everyone's needs.

- *Select the most effective place to conduct the training.* Training employees at your company's location offers several advantages. Employees incur no travel expense, they can respond to local emergencies that require immediate attention, and training can take place in the actual environment where the system will operate. You can encounter some disadvantages, however. Employees who are distracted by telephone calls and other duties will not get the full benefit of the training. In addition, using the organization's computer facilities for training can disrupt normal operations and limit the amount of actual hands-on training.

- *Provide for learning by hearing, seeing, and doing.* Some people learn best from lectures, discussions, and question-and-answer sessions. Others learn best from viewing demonstrations or from reading documentation and other material. Most people learn best from hands-on experience. You should provide training that supports each type of learning.

- *Rely on previous trainees.* After one group of users has been trained, they can assist others. Users often learn more quickly from coworkers who share common experience and job responsibilities. Using a **train-the-trainer** strategy, you can select knowledgeable users who then conduct sessions for others. When utilizing train-the-trainer techniques, the initial training must include not only the use of the application or system, but some instruction on how to present the materials effectively.

Interactive Training

Usually, a relationship exists between training methods and costs. Training an airline pilot in a state-of-the-art simulator is quite different from helping corporate users learn a new inventory system. Obviously, training budgets are business decisions, and IT staff sometimes has to work with the resources that are available, rather than the resources they wish they had. Most people prefer hands-on training. However, other less-expensive methods can be used, including training manuals, printed handouts, and online materials. Even the user documentation like that shown in Figure 11-27 on page 474 can be valuable, if users know how to find and use it.

If you are launching a new system and you lack the resources to develop formal training materials, you can design a series of dialog boxes that respond with Help information and suggestions whenever users select various menu topics. A good user interface also includes helpful error messages and hints, as discussed in Chapter 8. However, the most effective training is interactive, self-paced, and multimedia-based. Online training and video tutorials are discussed in the following sections.

ONLINE TRAINING Regardless of the instructional method, training lessons should include step-by-step instructions for using the features of the information system. Training materials should resemble actual screens, and tasks should be typical of a user's daily work — the more realistic, the better. For example, Figure 11-33 shows a sample tutorial lesson for a sales prospect management system. In Lesson 1, the user learned how to enter and exit the system. In Lesson 2, the user learns how to add a sales prospect and return to the main menu.

More sophisticated tutorials might offer interactive sessions where users can perform practice tasks and view feedback. Online training materials also should include a reference section that summarizes all options and commands, lists all possible error messages, and what actions the user should take when a problem arises.

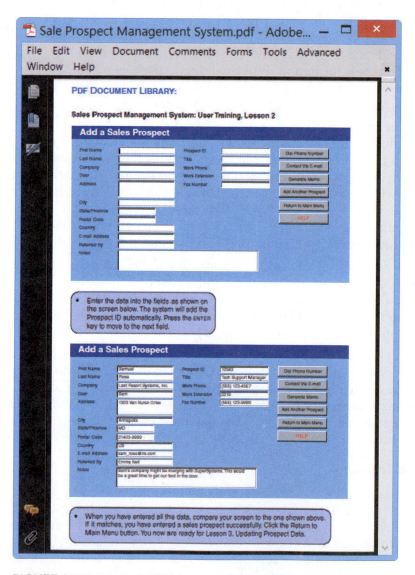

FIGURE 11-33   A sample lesson in an online tutorial.
© Cengage Learning 2014

VIDEO TUTORIALS You don't have to be a professional video developer to create effective training tutorials. For example, the Video Learning Sessions for this textbook were initially created as classroom teaching tools. Later, they were polished, edited, and transformed into streaming videos.

Suppose you want to develop a tutorial that shows how to create a structure chart, but you have no budget for special multimedia software. You have Windows 8 or Windows 7, and Office 2010, so you could start by creating a set of slides with screen text and graphic images. Then, you could add a live-motion screen capture and an audio narration. Finally, you could import the media into Windows Movie Maker where you can edit, save, and publish your training movie. Figure 11-34 shows a step-by-step plan for creating a video tutorial.

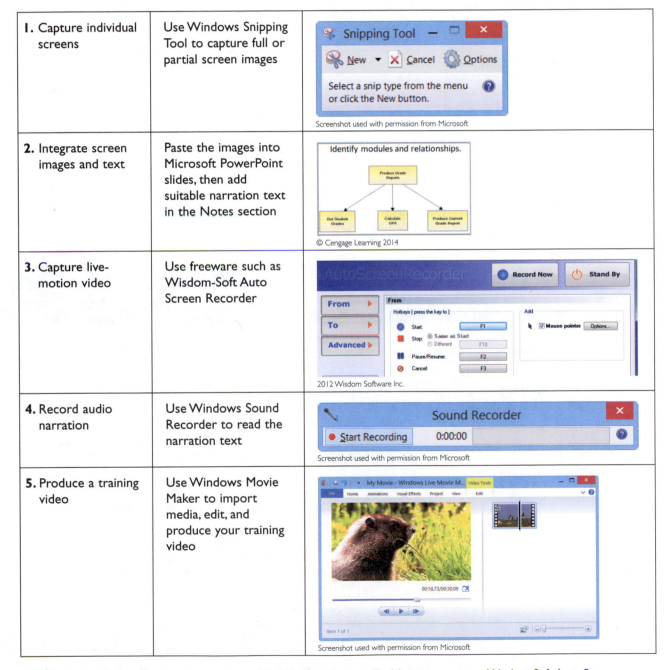

1. Capture individual screens	Use Windows Snipping Tool to capture full or partial screen images	
2. Integrate screen images and text	Paste the images into Microsoft PowerPoint slides, then add suitable narration text in the Notes section	
3. Capture live-motion video	Use freeware such as Wisdom-Soft Auto Screen Recorder	
4. Record audio narration	Use Windows Sound Recorder to read the narration text	
5. Produce a training video	Use Windows Movie Maker to import media, edit, and produce your training video	

FIGURE 11-34 You can use free software such as Windows Snipping Tool for image capture, Wisdom-Soft Auto Screen Recorder for live-motion video, and Windows Sound Recorder for audio narration. After you create the media, you can import the material into Windows Live Movie Maker.

Figure 11-35 shows a video training session design. The topic is the same Task Management System shown in Figure 11-27 on page 474. There, the focus was on effective documentation. Here, the goal is self-paced, interactive training for users. Figure 11-35 shows a screen design with instructions to the video developer, and a

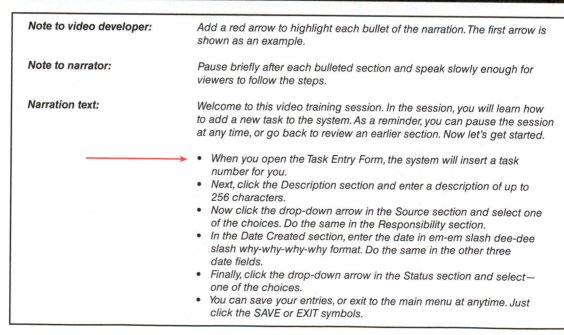

Note to video developer:	Add a red arrow to highlight each bullet of the narration. The first arrow is shown as an example.
Note to narrator:	Pause briefly after each bulleted section and speak slowly enough for viewers to follow the steps.
Narration text:	Welcome to this video training session. In the session, you will learn how to add a new task to the system. As a reminder, you can pause the session at any time, or go back to review an earlier section. Now let's get started.

- When you open the Task Entry Form, the system will insert a task number for you.
- Next, click the Description section and enter a description of up to 256 characters.
- Now click the drop-down arrow in the Source section and select one of the choices. Do the same in the Responsibility section.
- In the Date Created section, enter the date in em-em slash dee-dee slash why-why-why-why format. Do the same in the other three date fields.
- Finally, click the drop-down arrow in the Status section and select one of the choices.
- You can save your entries, or exit to the main menu at anytime. Just click the SAVE or EXIT symbols.

FIGURE 11-35 A sample video tutorial might include images, narration text, and notes to the video developer and narrator.

script with instructions to the narrator. At the end of the production process, these materials will be transformed into an integrated multimedia presentation.

In addition to shareware and built-in software, you can use a video editing application such as Camtasia, which offers a user-friendly interface. Figure 11-36 shows a Camtasia screen, where the user has imported a streaming video clip, several images, and a narration track at the bottom, which shows the sound waves that were recorded. Now the user can crop, split, and extend the video and audio tracks, and can add various special effects. Although it is not expensive, Camtasia is very powerful. You might be surprised to know that this tool was used in creating some of the Video Learning Sessions for this book. The screen in Figure 11-36 was captured as a live video clip. Do you recognize it?

When training is complete, many organizations conduct a full-scale test, or **simulation**, which is a dress rehearsal for users and IT support staff. Organizations include all procedures, such as those that they execute only at the end of a month, quarter, or year, in the simulation. As questions or problems arise, the participants consult the system documentation, help screens, or each other to determine appropriate answers or actions. This full-scale test provides valuable experience and builds confidence for everyone involved with the new system.

FIGURE 11-36 Camtasia is a moderately-priced video editing tool that can produce professional-quality training videos. In this example, a live video clip explains how to create a structure chart using the Visible Analyst® CASE tool. Notice the narration track at the bottom, which shows the sound waves that were recorded.

DATA CONVERSION

Data conversion is an important part of the system installation process. During **data conversion**, existing data is loaded into the new system. Depending on the system, data conversion can be done before, during, or after the operational environment is complete. You should develop a data conversion plan as early as possible, and the conversion process should be tested when the test environment is developed.

Data Conversion Strategies

When a new system replaces an existing system, you should automate the data conversion process, if possible. The old system might be capable of **exporting** data in an acceptable format for the new system or in a standard format, such as ASCII or ODBC. **ODBC (Open Database Connectivity)** is an industry-standard protocol that allows DBMSs from various vendors to interact and exchange data. Most database vendors provide ODBC drivers, which are a form of middleware. As you learned in Chapter 10, middleware connects dissimilar applications and enables them to communicate.

If a standard format is not available, you must develop a program to extract the data and convert it to an acceptable format. Data conversion is more difficult when the new system replaces a manual system, because all data must be entered manually unless it can be scanned. Even when you can automate data conversion, a new system often requires additional data items, which might require manual entry.

Data Conversion Security and Controls

You should maintain strict input controls during the conversion process, when data is extremely vulnerable. You must ensure that all system control measures are in place and operational to protect data from unauthorized access and to help prevent erroneous input.

Even with careful data conversion and input controls, some errors will occur. For example, duplicate customer records or inconsistent part numbers might have been tolerated by the old system, but will cause the new system to crash. Most organizations require that users verify all data, correct all errors, and supply every missing data item during conversion. Although the process can be time-consuming and expensive, it is essential that the new system be loaded with accurate, error-free data.

FIGURE 11-37   The four system changeover methods.

© Cengage Learning 2014

SYSTEM CHANGEOVER

System changeover is the process of putting the new information system online and retiring the old system. Changeover can be rapid or slow, depending on the method. The four changeover methods are direct cutover, parallel operation, pilot operation, and phased operation. Direct cutover is similar to throwing a switch that instantly changes over from the old system to the new. Parallel operation requires that both systems run simultaneously for a specified period, which is the slowest method. The other methods, pilot and phased operation, fall somewhere between direct cutover and parallel operation. Figure 11-37 illustrates the four system changeover methods.

Some observers feel that powerful cloud backup and parallel processing will reduce concerns about this mission-critical procedure. However, the prudent systems analyst should be on the safe side, and rely on traditional methods — at least for now.

Direct Cutover

The **direct cutover** approach causes the changeover from the old system to the new system to occur immediately when the new system becomes operational. Direct cutover usually is the least expensive changeover method because the IT group has to operate and maintain only one system at a time.

Direct cutover, however, involves more risk than other changeover methods. Regardless of how thoroughly and carefully you conduct testing and training, some difficulties can arise when the system goes into operation. Problems can result from data situations that were not tested or anticipated or from errors caused by users or operators. A system also can encounter difficulties because live data typically occurs in much larger volumes than test data.

Although initial implementation problems are a concern with all four changeover methods, they are most significant when the direct cutover approach is used. Detecting minor errors also is more difficult with direct cutover because users cannot verify current output by comparing it to output from the old system. Major errors can cause a system process to terminate abnormally, and with the direct cutover method, you cannot revert to the old system as a backup option.

Companies often choose the direct cutover method for implementing commercial software packages because they feel that commercial packages involve less risk of total system failure. Commercial software is certainly not risk-free, but the software vendor usually maintains an extensive knowledge base and can supply reliable, prompt fixes for most problems.

For systems developed in-house, most organizations use direct cutover only for noncritical situations. Direct cutover might be the only choice, however, if the operating environment cannot support both the old and new systems or if the old and new systems are incompatible.

Timing is very important when using a direct cutover strategy. Most systems operate on weekly, monthly, quarterly, and yearly cycles. For example, consider a payroll system that produces output on a weekly basis. Some employees are paid twice a month, however, so the system also operates semimonthly. Monthly, quarterly, and annual reports also require the system to produce output at the end of every month, quarter, and year. When a cyclical information system is implemented in the middle of any cycle, complete processing for the full cycle requires information from both the old and the new systems. To minimize the need to require information from two different systems, cyclical information systems usually are converted using the direct cutover method at the beginning of a quarter, calendar year, or fiscal year.

Parallel Operation

The **parallel operation** changeover method requires that both the old and the new information systems operate fully for a specified period. Data is input into both systems, and output generated by the new system is compared with the equivalent output from the old system. When users, management, and the IT group are satisfied that the new system operates correctly, the old system is terminated.

The most obvious advantage of parallel operation is lower risk. If the new system does not work correctly, the company can use the old system as a backup until appropriate changes are made. It is much easier to verify that the new system is working properly under parallel operation than under direct cutover, because the output from both systems is compared and verified during parallel operation.

Parallel operation, however, does have some disadvantages. First, it is the most costly changeover method. Because both the old and the new systems are in full operation, the company pays for both systems during the parallel period. Users must work in both systems and the company might need temporary employees to handle the extra workload. In addition, running both systems might place a burden on the operating environment and cause processing delays.

Parallel operation is not practical if the old and new systems are incompatible technically, or if the operating environment cannot support both systems. Parallel operation also is inappropriate when the two systems perform different functions or if the new system involves a new method of business operations. For example, until a company installs data scanners in a factory, it is impractical to launch a new production tracking system that requires such technology.

Pilot Operation

The **pilot operation** changeover method involves implementing the complete new system at a selected location of the company. A new sales reporting system, for instance, might be implemented in only one branch office, or a new payroll system might be installed in only one department. In these examples, the group that uses the new system first is called the **pilot site**. During pilot operation, the old system continues to operate for the entire organization, including the pilot site. After the system proves successful at the pilot site, it is implemented in the rest of the organization, usually using the direct cutover method. Therefore, pilot operation is a combination of parallel operation and direct cutover methods.

Restricting the implementation to a pilot site reduces the risk of system failure, compared with a direct cutover method. Operating both systems for only the pilot site is less expensive than a parallel operation for the entire company. In addition, if you later use a parallel approach to complete the implementation, the changeover period can be much shorter if the system proves successful at the pilot site.

Phased Operation

The **phased operation** changeover method allows you to implement the new system in stages, or modules. For example, instead of implementing a new manufacturing system all at once, you first might install the materials management subsystem, then the production control subsystem, then the job cost subsystem, and so on. You can implement each subsystem by using any of the other three changeover methods.

Analysts sometimes confuse phased and pilot operation methods. Both methods combine direct cutover and parallel operation to reduce risks and costs. With phased operation, however, you give a part of the system to all users, while pilot operation provides the entire system, but to only some users.

One advantage of a phased approach is that the risk of errors or failures is limited to the implemented module only. For instance, if a new production control subsystem fails to operate properly, that failure might not affect the new purchasing subsystem or the existing shop floor control subsystem.

Phased operation is less expensive than full parallel operation because you have to work with only one part of the system at a time. A phased approach is not possible, however, if the system cannot be separated easily into logical modules or segments. In addition, if the system involves a large number of separate phases, phased operation can cost more than a pilot approach.

Figure 11-38 shows that each changeover method has risk and cost factors. As a systems analyst, you must weigh the advantages and disadvantages of each method and recommend the best choice in a given situation. The final changeover decision will be based on input from the IT staff, users, and management — and the choice must reflect the nature of the business and the degree of acceptable risk.

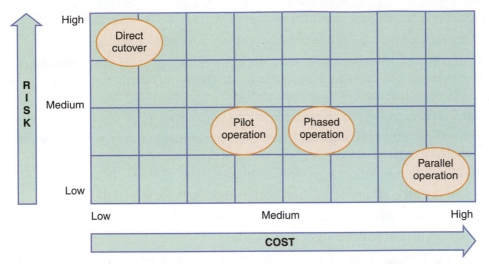

FIGURE 11-38   Relative risk and cost characteristics of the four changeover methods.

© Cengage Learning 2014

CASE IN POINT 11.3:   GLOBAL COOLING

You are a systems analyst at Global Cooling, a leading manufacturer of air conditioning units. You are leading a team that is developing a new production scheduling system. The project is now in the application development stage. Unit testing has been completed, and you are in the final stages of integration testing. Your supervisor, Ella Pham, is eager to implement the new application ahead of schedule and asked if you could trim system testing from two weeks to three days, and use a direct cutover method instead of the parallel changeover method that originally was planned. Write a brief memo expressing your views.

POST-IMPLEMENTATION TASKS

Once the new system is operational, you must perform two additional tasks: Prepare a post-implementation evaluation and deliver a final report to management.

Post-Implementation Evaluation

A **post-implementation evaluation** assesses the overall quality of the information system. The evaluation verifies that the new system meets specified requirements, complies with user objectives, and produces the anticipated benefits. In addition, by providing feedback to the development team, the evaluation also helps improve IT development practices for future projects.

A post-implementation evaluation should examine all aspects of the development effort and the end product — the developed information system. A typical evaluation includes feedback for the following areas:

- Accuracy, completeness, and timeliness of information system output
- User satisfaction
- System reliability and maintainability
- Adequacy of system controls and security measures
- Hardware efficiency and platform performance
- Effectiveness of database implementation
- Performance of the IT team
- Completeness and quality of documentation

- Quality and effectiveness of training
- Accuracy of cost-benefit estimates and development schedules

You can apply the same fact-finding techniques in a post-implementation evaluation that you used to determine the system requirements during the systems analysis phase. When evaluating a system, you should:

- Interview members of management and key users
- Observe users and computer operations personnel actually working with the new information system
- Read all documentation and training materials
- Examine all source documents, output reports, and screen displays
- Use questionnaires to gather information and opinions from a large number of users
- Analyze maintenance and help desk logs

Figure 11-39 shows the first page of a sample user evaluation form for the new information system where users evaluate 18 separate elements on a numerical scale, so the results can be tabulated easily. Following that section, the form provides space for open-ended comments and suggestions.

Whenever possible, people who were not directly involved in developing the system should conduct the post-implementation evaluation. IT staff and users usually perform the evaluation, although some firms use an internal audit group or independent auditors to ensure the accuracy and completeness of the evaluation.

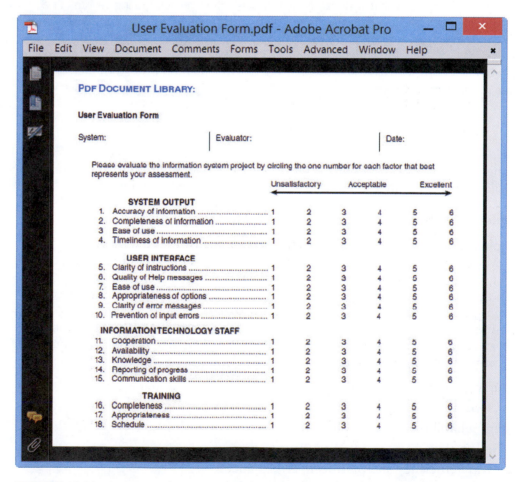

FIGURE 11-39 Sample user evaluation form. The numerical scale allows easy tabulation of results. Following this section, the form provides space for open-ended comments and suggestions.

When should post-implementation evaluation occur? Is it better to wait until the new system has been in operation for one month, six months, one year, or longer? Users can forget details of the developmental effort if too much time elapses before the evaluation. After several months or a year, for instance, users might not remember whether they learned a procedure through training, from user documentation, or by experimenting with the system on their own.

Users also might forget their impressions of IT team members over time. An important purpose of the post-implementation evaluation is to improve the quality of IT department functions, including interaction with users, training, and documentation. Consequently, the evaluation team should perform the assessment while users are able to recall specific incidents, successes, and problems so they can offer suggestions for improvement. Post-implementation evaluation primarily is concerned with assessing the quality of the new system. If the team performs the evaluation too soon after implementation, users will not have enough time to learn the new system and appreciate its strengths and weaknesses. Although many IT professionals recommend conducting the evaluation after at least six months of system operation, pressure to finish the project sooner usually results in an earlier evaluation in order to allow the IT department to move on to other tasks.

Ideally, conducting a post-implementation evaluation should be standard practice for all information systems projects. Sometimes, evaluations are skipped because users are eager to work with the new system, or because IT staff members have more pressing priorities. In some organizations, management might not recognize the importance and benefits of a post-implementation evaluation. The evaluations are extremely important, however, because they enable the development team and the IT department to learn what worked and what did not work. Otherwise, developers might commit the same errors in another system.

CASE IN POINT 11.4:   YORKTOWN INDUSTRIES

Cindy Winslow liked her new job as lead systems analyst at Yorktown Industries. She was pleased that her development team completed the new human resources system ahead of schedule and under budget. Cindy looked forward to receiving the post-implementation evaluation because she was confident that both the system and the development team would receive high marks from users and managers.

After the system operated for one month, Cindy received a call from her supervisor, Ted Haines. Ted told her that she would have to handle the evaluation, even though she headed the development effort. Cindy told Ted that she did not feel comfortable evaluating her own team's work. She explained that someone who was not involved in its development should do an independent evaluation. Ted responded that he had full confidence in Cindy's ability to be objective. He explained that no one else was available and he needed the evaluation quickly so he could move forward with the next stage in the corporate development plan.

Cindy was troubled about the situation and she called you, a professional acquaintance, for your advice. What would you tell her and why?

Final Report to Management

At the end of each SDLC phase, you submit a report to management, and the systems implementation phase is no exception. Your report should include the following:

- Final versions of all system documentation
- Planned modifications and enhancements to the system that have been identified
- Recap of all systems development costs and schedules
- Comparison of actual costs and schedules to the original estimates
- Post-implementation evaluation, if it has been performed

TOOLKIT TIME

The Communication tools in Part A of the Systems Analyst's Toolkit can help you develop better reports and presentations. To learn more about these tools, turn to Part A of the four-part Toolkit that follows Chapter 12.

The final report to management marks the end of systems development work. In the next chapter, you will study the role of a systems analyst during systems operation, security, and support, which is the final phase of the SDLC.

A QUESTION OF ETHICS

faberfoto_it/iStockphoto

Your friend Jill is handling the testing for the new accounting system, and right now she is very upset about the most recent results. "It seems like every time we fix one thing, another issue pops up! After ten days of testing and adjusting, we are meeting over 90% of the goals and benchmarks. If we're looking for perfection, we'll never make the implementation deadline for the new system, and the users will be all over us. Not to mention top management's reaction to a delay. I'm sure we can resolve some of these issues after the system becomes operational."

How would you respond to Jill? Are ethical issues involved? What are your responsibilities, as an employee, as an IT professional, and as a friend?

CHAPTER SUMMARY

The systems implementation phase consists of application development, testing, installation, and evaluation of the new system. During application development, analysts determine the overall design strategy and work with programmers to complete design, coding, testing, and documentation. Quality assurance is essential during the implementation phase. Many companies utilize software engineering concepts and quality standards established by the International Organization for Standardization (ISO).

Each systems development approach has its own set of tools. For example, structured development relies heavily on DFDs and structure charts. A structure chart consists of symbols that represent program modules, data couples, control couples, conditions, and loops. Object-oriented methods use a variety of diagrams, including use case, class, sequence, and transition state diagrams. Agile methods tend to use a spiral or other iterative model.

System developers also can use more generic tools to help them translate the system logic into properly functioning program modules. These tools include entity-relationship diagrams, flowcharts, pseudocode, decision tables, and decision trees.

If an agile development approach is used, then the customer creates user stories that describe required features and priority levels. In agile methodology, new system releases are made after many iterations and each is test-driven carefully by the customer.

Cohesion measures a module's scope and processing characteristics. A module that performs a single function or task has a high degree of cohesion, which is desirable. Coupling measures relationships and interdependence among modules. Modules that are relatively independent are loosely coupled, which is desirable. Cohesion and coupling concepts are used in structured development, but also are applicable to object-oriented development.

Typically, you follow four steps when you create a structure chart. You review DFDs and object models to identify the processes and methods, identify the program modules and determine control-subordinate relationships, add symbols for couples and loops, and analyze the structure chart to ensure that it is consistent with your system documentation.

Programmers perform desk checking, code review, and unit testing tasks during application development. Systems analysts design the initial test plans, which include test steps and test data for integration testing and system testing. Integration testing is necessary for programs that interact. The final step is system testing for the completed system. System testing includes users in the testing process.

In addition to system documentation, analysts and technical writers also prepare operations documentation and user documentation. Operations documentation provides instructions and information to the IT operations group. User documentation consists of instructions and information for users who interact with the system and includes user manuals, help screens, and tutorials.

During the installation process, you establish an operational, or production, environment for the new information system that is completely separate from the test environment. The operational environment contains live data and is accessible only by authorized users. All future changes to the system must be verified in the test environment before they are applied to the operational environment.

Everyone who interacts with the new information system should receive training appropriate to his or her role and skills. The IT department usually is responsible for training. Software or hardware vendors or professional training organizations also can provide training. When you develop a training program, remember the following guidelines: Train people in groups; utilize people already trained to help train others; develop separate programs for distinct employee groups; and provide for learning by using discussions, demonstrations, documentation, training manuals, tutorials, Webinars, and podcasts. Users learn better with interactive, self-paced training methods.

Data conversion often is necessary when installing a new information system. When a new system replaces a computerized system, you should automate the data conversion process if possible. The old system might be capable of exporting data in a format that the new system can use, or you might have to extract the data and convert it to an acceptable format. Data conversion from a manual system often requires labor-intensive data entry or scanning. Even when data conversion can be automated, a new system often requires additional data items, which might require manual entry. Strict input controls are important during the conversion process to protect data integrity and quality. Typically, data is verified, corrected, and updated during the conversion process.

System changeover is the process of putting the new system into operation. Four changeover methods exist: direct cutover, parallel operation, pilot operation, and phased operation. With direct cutover, the old system stops and the new system starts simultaneously; direct cutover is the least expensive, but the riskiest changeover method. With parallel operation, users operate both the old and new information systems for some period of time; parallel operation is the most expensive and least risky of the changeover methods. Pilot operation and phased operation represent compromises between direct cutover and parallel operation; both methods are less risky than direct cutover and less costly than parallel operation. With pilot operation, a specified group within the organization uses the new system for a period of time, while the old system continues to operate for the rest of the users. After the system proves successful at the pilot site, it is implemented throughout the organization. With phased operation, you implement the system in the entire organization, but only one module at a time, until the entire system is operational.

A post-implementation evaluation assesses and reports on the quality of the new system and the work done by the project team. Although it is best if people who were not involved in the systems development effort perform the evaluation, that is not always possible. The evaluation should be conducted early so users have a fresh recollection of the development effort, but not before users have experience using the new system.

The final report to management includes the final system documentation, describes any future system enhancements that already have been identified, and details the project costs. The report represents the end of the development effort and the beginning of the new system's operational life.

Key Terms

acceptance tests *468*

application development *452*

attributes *461*

bug tracking software *469*

Capability Maturity Model (CMM)® *450*

Capability Maturity Model Integration
   (CMMI)® *450*

code review *466*

coding *465*

cohesion *457*

condition *457*

control couple *457*

control module *456*

coupling *458*

customer *462*

data conversion *484*

data couple *456*

defect tracking software *469*

design walkthrough *466*

desk checking *466*

direct cutover *485*

documentation *469*

exporting *484*

flowchart *454*

integrated development environment
   (IDE) *465*

integration testing *467*

ISO 90003:2004 *452*

iteration cycle *464*

iteration planning meeting *464*

library module *456*

link testing *467*

logic errors *466*

loop *457*

loosely coupled *458*

methods *461*

modular design *456*

module *456*

object-oriented development (OOD) *461*

ODBC (Open Database Connectivity) *484*

online documentation *472*

operational environment *475*

operations documentation *471*

parallel operation *485*

parallel programming *465*

partitioning *456*

patches *469*

phased operation *486*

pilot operation *486*

pilot site *486*

podcast *478*

post-implementation evaluation *487*

process improvement *450*

production environment *475*

program documentation *469*

pseudocode *454*

quality assurance *450*

release plan *464*

simulation *483*

software engineering *450*

status flag *457*

structure chart *456*

structured walkthrough *466*

stub testing *467*

subordinate modules *456*

syntax errors *466*

system changeover *484*

system documentation *470*

system testing *468*

test data *467*

test-driven design *465*

test environment *475*

test plan *467*

tightly coupled *458*

top-down approach *456*

training plan *476*

train-the-trainer *479*

tutorial *478*

unit testing *466*

user documentation *471*

user story *463*

Webcast *478*

Webinar *478*

Chapter Exercises

Questions

1. List and describe the main tasks that are performed during systems implementation.
2. What is ISO, and why is it important to a systems developer?
3. What are the most significant differences among structured, object-oriented, and agile methods? What do they have in common?
4. Define a structure chart in language that a non-IT person would understand easily. Also provide a step-by-step description of how to create a structure chart.
5. What is cohesion? What is the difference between close coupling and loose coupling?
6. Describe three main types of testing and the order in which they are performed.
7. What is *Camtasia* and why would you use it? What is the *Windows Snipping Tool* and why would you use it?
8. What is the difference between an operational environment and a test environment?
9. List and describe the four main system changeover methods. Which one generally is the least expensive? Which is the safest? Explain your answers.
10. Why is a post-implementation evaluation important? Who should conduct it, and why?

Discussion Topics

1. Your supervisor said that "Integration testing is a waste of time. If each program is tested adequately, integration testing isn't needed. Instead, we should move on to system testing as soon as possible. If modules don't interact properly, we'll handle it then." Do you agree or disagree with this comment? Explain your answer.
2. Suppose you are a systems analyst developing a detailed test plan. Explain the testing strategies you will use in your plan. Will you use live or simulated data?
3. Use the Internet to locate an example of training for a software or hardware product. Write a brief summary of the training, the product, the type of training offered, and the cost of training (if available). Discuss your findings with the class.
4. Suppose that you designed a tutorial to train a person in the use of specific software or hardware, such as a Web browser. What specific information would you want to know about the recipient of the training? How would that information affect the design of the training material?

Projects

1. In this chapter, you learned about the importance of testing. Design a generic test plan that describes the testing for an imaginary system.
2. Design a generic post-implementation evaluation form. The form should consist of questions that you could use to evaluate any information system. The form should evaluate the training received and any problems associated with the program.
3. Create a one-page questionnaire to distribute to users in a post-implementation evaluation of a recent information system project. Include at least 10 questions that cover the important information you want to obtain.
4. Using the material in this chapter and your own Internet research, prepare a presentation on the pros and cons of agile development methods.

Apply Your Knowledge

This section contains four mini-cases. Each case describes a situation, explains your role, and requires you to apply what you learned in the chapter.

1 Rachel's Day Off Swimwear

Rachel's Day Off Swimwear is a successful chain of high end swimsuit boutiques. In the last six months, the firm added several new lines and opened a dozen new stores. The downside is that the company has outgrown its accounting software. The original accounting system was a package from Peachtree Software, which ran on a stand-alone PC and later on a network. Now, the firm is ready to install a new accounting package that can support current and future operations. You have been asked to implement the new system, which is called *Sage 50*.

Tasks

1. Who should receive training on the new software, and what topics should the training cover?
2. Go online and investigate the *Sage 50* product to learn whether it can import and upload existing data.
3. What changeover strategy would you suggest for the new accounting system? Explain your answer.
4. When should a post-implementation evaluation be conducted? Explain your answer.

2 Flying Fish Trucking

Flying Fish specializes in shipping fresh seafood up and down the coast. To improve service, the company wants to develop an in-house application called S^3 (Super Shipping System). When S^3 is operational, shippers and consignees will be able to track their shipments in real time, from departure point to destination.

Tasks

1. What types of documentation are needed for this application?
2. During application development, the IT staff will develop a structure chart. What steps should they follow?
3. What suggestions do you have for help screens and online tutorials?
4. What types of testing should be performed? What types of test data should be used?

3 **Sydney's Logistics**

Sydney's Logistics is a growing business that specializes in providing business services that many small firms do not have the expertise, the space or the resources to handle on their own. These services include warehouse receiving and storage, intermodal systems, and ISO-certified packaging, among others. Sydney's recently redesigned its computer system to reduce costs and achieve faster, more accurate information about its operations. At this point, the new system is ready for implementation. Two systems analysts will plan a modular design, and several and several programmers will code the modules.

Tasks

1. What issues should the systems analysts and programmers discuss before they proceed?
2. As a systems analyst on this project, how would you describe your primary responsibilities, and how could you contribute to the quality of the finished product?
3. As a programmer, how would you describe your primary responsibilities, and how could you contribute to the quality of the finished product?
4. Will the use of structure charts be beneficial during this stage of development? Discuss the advantages of structure charts compared with flowcharts and pseudocode.

 Victorian Creations

Victorian Creations specializes in the reproduction of furniture from the Victorian era. Recently the company updated its payroll software as an in-house development project. Users and IT staff members have completed comprehensive training sessions. The system has been operational for about six weeks, and no major problems have occurred. You are responsible for the post-implementation evaluation.

Tasks

1. What are some techniques you might use to obtain an accurate evaluation?
2. What are some specific questions you would include in a questionnaire? Who should receive the questionnaire?
3. Are there general guidelines that apply to the timing of a post-implementation evaluation? What are they?
4. Is this the best time to schedule a post-implementation evaluation? Why or why not? Are there other options? What are they?

Case Studies

Each chapter includes a Chapter Case, a Continuing Case, a Capstone Case, and an Online Case Simulation. You can learn more about the Online Case Simulation in the MIS CourseMate Features section.

Chapter Case: White Diamond Glass

White Diamond Glass produces handmade decorative glass in its upstate New York factory, and sells its wares to a global market. The company still is an industry leader, but sales have leveled off. Some managers believe that IT glitches are the problem.

Background

Last year, White Diamond rushed to implement a new Web-based system to boost sales. Unfortunately, the online system was not tested thoroughly and experienced start-up problems. For example, customers complained about order mix-ups and overcharges for deliveries. You are a new system analyst, and your supervisor asked you to investigate the problems.

Tasks

1. Based on what you know about e-commerce, how would you have tested a new Web-based system?
2. Should ISO standards have been considered? Explain your answer.
3. What should White Diamond do in the future to avoid similar problems when developing new systems?
4. Three months after the system changeover, you perform a post-implementation evaluation. Prepare three evaluation forms for the new information system: one for users, one for managers, and one for the IT operations staff.

Continuing Case: Personal Trainer, Inc.

Personal Trainer, Inc. owns and operates fitness centers in a dozen Midwestern cities. The centers have done well, and the company is planning an international expansion by opening a new "supercenter" in the Toronto area. Personal Trainer's president, Cassia Umi, hired an IT consultant, Susan Park, to help develop an information system for the new facility. During the project, Susan will work closely with Gray Lewis, who will manage the new operation.

Background

Susan finished work on system architecture issues, and her system design specification was approved. Now she is ready to address system implementation tasks, including quality assurance, structure charts, testing, training, data conversion, system changeover, and post-implementation evaluation.

Tasks

1. Plan the testing required for the system. You should consider unit, integration, and system testing in your test plan and determine who should participate in the testing.
2. You have asked Gray Lewis to contribute to the user manual for the new system. He suggested that you include a section of frequently asked questions (FAQs), which you also could include in the online documentation. Prepare 10 FAQs and answers for use in the printed user manual and context-sensitive Help screens.

Continuing Case: Personal Trainer, Inc.

3. Suggest a changeover method for the new billing system and provide specific reasons to support your choice. If you recommend phased operation, specify the order in which you would implement the modules. If your recommendation is for pilot operation, specify the department or area you would select as the pilot site and justify your choice.

4. Should the associates perform a post-implementation evaluation? If an assessment is done, who should perform it? What options are available and which would you recommend?

Capstone Case: New Century Wellness Group

New Century Wellness Group offers a holistic approach to healthcare with an emphasis on preventive medicine as well as traditional medical care. In your role as an IT consultant, you will help New Century develop a new information system.

Background

You completed the systems design for the business support system at New Century Wellness Group. The network will include a server, 27 workstations, and five network printers. The partners at the clinic have approved the design specification, and you hired two programmers, Bill Miller and Celia Goldring, to assist you with the programming and testing of the new system. You now are ready to finish the software development and begin installation, testing, and evaluation of the new system. Before you begin, you should review the DFDs, object-oriented diagrams, ERDs, and table designs that you prepared during systems analysis and systems design.

Tasks

1. What application development methods will you use? Explain your answer. What development tools will help your team finish the business support system and how will you use them?

2. Prepare a structure chart that shows the main program functions for the New Century system.

3. Develop a testing plan for the new system that addresses unit, integration, and system testing. Design the test data, and explain the design.

4. Identify the specific groups who will need training on the new system. For each group, describe the type of training you recommend and list the topics to be covered.

CASE Tool Workshop

Systems analysts use CASE tools to help them plan, build, and maintain information systems. To learn more about CASE tools, turn to Part B of the Toolkit that follows Chapter 12. You can complete these tasks with the Visible Analyst® CASE tool, which is available with this textbook, or a similar tool.

Background

Suppose you work for an IT consulting firm. One of the firm's clients is interested in using a CASE tool for in-house systems development. A brief presentation for the client will be held next week, and you will handle the section on structure charts. To prepare, you will need to review what you know about structure charts, and practice some basic skills.

Tasks

1. Launch the Visible Analyst® CASE tool, or a similar tool, and then visit the Help section for structure charts. Look for a description of the symbol set, and the definitions for data couples, control couples, and modules. Write a brief summary of what you found, or create a short slide presentation with the results.
2. Study Figure 11-12 on page 457, which is a simple example of a control couple. Use the CASE tool to create a structure chart that resembles the figure.

MIS CourseMate Features

If you have an MIS CourseMate access code, you can reinforce and extend your learning with premium content created for this textbook. For example, you can launch interactive Video Learning Sessions to help you understand systems development concepts and practice your skills. In addition, you can use MindTap Reader, which is a full, interactive, digital e-book.

MIS CourseMate also offers many learning features within each chapter, including an Online Case Simulation, a Critical Thinking Challenge, Video Learning Session Tasks, and a set of Learn It Online activities. To log on to the MIS CourseMate site at **www.cengagebrain.com**, you must create a student account and register this book.

Online Case Simulation: SCR Associates

Session 11: Managing Systems Implementation

Overview

The SCR Associates case study is a Web-based simulation that allows you to practice your skills in a real-world environment. The firm offers IT consulting, solutions and training. SCR plans to open a new high-tech training center, and needs to develop a Training Information Management System (TIMS) to support the center. You are a newly hired systems analyst reporting to Jesse Baker, systems group manager, and will help her develop the system.

The case study takes you to the SCR Web site, where you receive e-mail and voice mail messages from Jesse, obtain information from SCR's resource libraries, and perform various tasks. Jesse has high standards, but seems very fair. She made it clear that she expects your work to be accurate, thorough, and professional.

Before You Begin

To prepare for this work session, you should review the following topics:

- Data modules, conditions, couples, and loops
- Cohesion and coupling

How Do I Use the Online Case Simulation?

- Read the preview, and review the Chapter 1 background material if necessary.
- Visit the MIS CourseMate Web site at **www.cengagebrain.com**, locate the **SCR Case Simulation**, and click the **intranet** link. Enter your name and the password **sad10e**.
- When the opening screen displays, select this session. Then check your e-mail and voice mail, and start to work on your task list.

Preview: Session 11

You assisted your supervisor, Jesse Baker, in planning an architecture for the new TIMS system. Now she wants you to work on system implementation tasks and issues. Specifically, she wants you to develop a structure chart, testing and training plans, implementation guidelines, and a post-implementation review.

Critical Thinking Challenge

In addition to technical ability, IT professionals need critical thinking skills. This feature can help you practice perception, organization, analysis, problem-solving, and decision-making skills that will be valuable in the workplace. You can visit **www.criticalthinking.org** to learn more about critical thinking and why it is so important.

Background

The IT team at Game Technology is working on implementation strategies for the new Customer Contact Care system (C^3). You will help prepare a structure chart and create a video tutorial about changeover methods. Before you start, you plan to review Chapter 11 of your textbook.

First, you will work on the structure chart. You know that the system will rate contacts to identify the best sales prospects. The tasks are performed by a control module called Followup, which has three subordinate modules: List Contacts, Rate Contacts, and Produce Reports. Here are some details about the modules, data, and control couples. Study the table carefully and decide how to handle each of the data or control couples.

From	Data/Control Couple	To	Comments
Followup	Request Contact Data	List Contacts	Loop
List Contacts	Contact data	Followup	
Followup	Contact data	Rate Contacts	
Rale Contacts	Ratings	Followup	
Followup	Contact Data	Produce Reports	
List Contacts	End of File	Followup	Control Couple

You also need to work on the video tutorial. The team prepared the first two slides, shown here:

What is a Changeover Method?

?

Which Method Is Best For:
- A mission-critical accounting system
- A franchise operation with 500 locations
- A records archive system for five-year old data

© Cengage Learning 2014

Practice Tasks

Visit the MIS CourseMate Web site at **www.cengagebrain.com**. Then navigate to the resources for this chapter and locate the **Critical Thinking Challenge** feature. You will complete two Practice Tasks, using what you learned in the chapter. Then you can check your answers to be sure you're ready for the Challenge Tasks.

Challenge Tasks

After you complete the Practice Tasks, you learn about new developments at Game Technology.

You just found out that the structure chart needs a change. Also, you need to add another slide. To continue, navigate to the **Critical Thinking Challenge** feature for this chapter, select the **Challenge Tasks**, and follow the instructions.

Video Learning Sessions

The Video Learning Session in this chapter explains structure charts and how to use them.

Before You Begin

To prepare for the tasks, you should review the following topics:

- Data modules, conditions, couples, and loops
- Cohesion and coupling

© craftvision/iStockphoto

How to Watch a Session

Go to the Management Information Systems CourseMate Web site at **www.cengagebrain.com**. Then navigate to the resources for this book, locate the **Video Learning Sessions**, and select a session. You can watch the session on your computer or mobile device, and pause, rewind, or replay a video at any time.

Practice Tasks

After each session, visit the **Your Turn** feature to perform the tasks and check your answers.

Training Tasks

Suppose the IT training manager wants to encourage team members to watch the Video Learning Sessions. To spark interest, she plans to post a set of VLS previews, which you will prepare. Each preview must include an overview of the session, a description of the main topics, and one or more screen examples from the video. To get you started, she provided a task list:

1. Select a Video Learning Session from this chapter. Launch the video and note the title, objectives, and total running time. Include this information in your preview.
2. Run though the session and find a segment that does a good job of explaining a specific skill or concept.
3. In the segment you selected, choose one or more specific screens and capture each screen image with the Windows Snipping Tool. To do this in Windows 7 or Windows Vista, click **Start**, and then type **Snipping Tool**. In Windows 8, you can display the **Start** menu, and then type **Snipping Tool**.
4. Paste the screen image into your preview and explain how it would help a viewer understand the topic. Also add your comments about the video, and why it would be important to an IT professional. Your preview should be well-organized and readable.

Learn It Online

In each chapter, you can use this feature to apply your knowledge and practice your skills. The exercises include Chapter Reinforcement Questions, Flash Cards, Practice Tests, and various games, such as *Who Wants To Be a Computer Genius?*, *Wheel of Terms*, and the *Crossword Puzzle Challenge*.

PHASE **5** — SYSTEMS SUPPORT AND SECURITY

DELIVERABLE
An operational system that is properly maintained, supported, and secured

TOOLKIT SUPPORT
Communications, CASE, and financial analysis tools

As the Dilbert cartoon suggests, users want prompt support, but they might not always receive it. Unhappy users do not bode well for system success. You will learn more about effective user support in this phase.

Systems support and security is the final phase in the systems development life cycle. In the previous phase, systems implementation, you delivered a functioning system. Now, you will support and maintain the system, handle security issues, protect the integrity of the system and its data, and be alert to any signs of obsolescence. The deliverable for this phase is an operational system that is properly maintained, supported, and secured.

CHAPTER 12

Managing Systems Support and Security

Chapter 12 describes systems support and security tasks that continue throughout the useful life of the system. In addition to user support, this chapter discusses maintenance, security, backup and disaster recovery, performance measurement, and system obsolescence.

INTRODUCTION

OBJECTIVES

When you finish this chapter, you will be able to:

- Explain the systems support and security phase
- Describe user support activities, including user training and service desks
- Define the four types of maintenance
- Explain various techniques for managing systems maintenance and support
- Describe techniques for measuring, managing, and planning system performance
- Explain risk management concepts
- Assess system security at six levels: physical security, network security, application security, file security, user security, and procedural security
- Describe backup and disaster recovery
- List factors indicating that a system has reached the end of its useful life
- Assess future challenges and opportunities for IT professionals
- Develop a strategic plan for career advancement and strong IT credentials

Managing systems support and security involves three main concerns: user expectations, system performance, and security requirements.

A systems analyst is like an internal consultant who provides guidance, support, and training. Successful systems often need the most support because users want to learn the features, try all the capabilities, and discover how the system can help them perform their tasks. In most organizations, more than half of all IT department effort goes into supporting existing systems.

This chapter begins with a discussion of systems support, including user training and service desks. You will study the four main types of maintenance: corrective, adaptive, perfective, and preventive. You also will learn how the IT group uses maintenance teams, configuration management, and maintenance releases, and you will examine system performance issues and maintenance tools. You will analyze the security system at each of the six security levels: physical security, network security, application security, file security, user security, and procedural security. You will also learn about data backup and recovery issues. Finally, you will learn how to recognize system obsolescence, and about some of the challenges and opportunities you are likely to face as an IT professional.

PREVIEW CASE: Mountain View College Bookstore

Background: Wendy Lee, manager of college services at Mountain View College, wants a new information system that will improve efficiency and customer service at the three college bookstores.

In this part of the case, Tina Allen (systems analyst) and David Conroe (student intern) are talking about operation, support, and security issues for the new system.

Participants:	Tina and David
Location:	Tina's office, Friday afternoon, March 28, 2014
Project status:	Tina and David successfully implemented the bookstore information system. Now they will discuss strategies for supporting, maintaining, and securing the new system.
Discussion topics:	Support activities, training, maintenance, techniques for managing systems operation, enhancing system performance and security, and detecting system obsolescence

Tina: Well, we finally made it. The system is up and running and the users seem satisfied. Now we focus on supporting the system and ensuring that it delivers its full potential, and is properly secured and protected.

David: *How do we do that?*

Tina: First, we need to set up specific procedures for handling system support and maintenance. We'll set up a service desk that will offer user training, answer technical questions, and enhance user productivity.

David: *Sounds good. I'll set up a training package for new users who missed the initial training sessions.*

Tina: That's fine. You also should learn about the four types of maintenance. Users typically ask for help that requires corrective maintenance to fix problems or adaptive maintenance to add new features. As IT staff, we will be responsible for perfective maintenance, which makes the system more efficient, and preventive maintenance to avoid problems.

David: *Anything else for us to do?*

Tina: Yes, we'll need a system for managing maintenance requests from users. Also, we'll need to handle configuration management, maintenance releases, and version control. These tools will help us keep the system current and reduce unnecessary maintenance costs.

David: *What about keeping tabs on system performance issues?*

Tina: That's important, along with capacity planning to be sure the system can handle future growth.

David: *What about system security?*

Tina: Good question. We'll look at physical security, network security, application security, file security, user security, and procedural security. We'll also look at backup and disaster recovery issues.

David: *Sounds like we'll be busy for quite a while.*

Tina: Well, that depends on the system itself and user expectations. Every system has a useful life, including this one. We'll try to get a good return on our investment, but we'll also watch for signs of obsolescence. Here are some tasks we can work on:

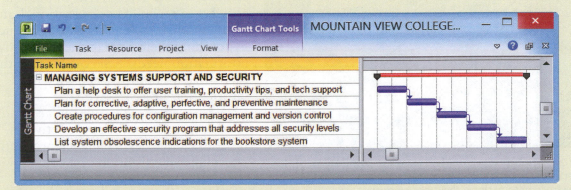

FIGURE 12-1   Typical systems support and security task list.
© Cengage Learning 2014

OVERVIEW

The systems support and security phase begins when a system becomes operational and continues until the system reaches the end of its useful life. Throughout the development process, the objective has been to create an information system that is efficient, easy to use, and affordable. After delivering the system, the IT team focuses on support and maintenance tasks.

The first part of this chapter covers four main topics. You will learn how to provide user support, maintain the system, manage the maintenance process, and handle system performance issues.

USER SUPPORT

Companies provide user support in many forms, including user training and a service desk to provide technical support and assistance.

User Training

In Chapter 11, you learned about initial training that is performed when a new system is introduced. Additionally, new employees must be trained on the company's information systems. For example, a firm that produces electronic assemblies must train its new employees, as shown in Figure 12-2.

If significant changes take place in the existing system or if a new version is released, the IT department might develop a **user training package**. Depending on the nature of the changes, the package could include online support via e-mail, a special Web site, a revision to the user guide, a training manual supplement, or formal training sessions. Training users about system changes is similar to initial training. The main objective is to show users how the system can help them perform their jobs.

Service Desks

As systems and data structures become more complex, users need constant support and guidance. To make data more accessible and to empower users, many IT departments create service desks. A **service desk**, also called a **help desk** or **information center (IC)**, is a centralized resource staffed by IT professionals who provide users with the support they need to do their jobs. A service desk has three main objectives: (1) Show people how to use system resources more effectively, (2) provide answers to technical or operational questions, and (3) make users more productive by teaching them how to meet their own information needs. A service desk is the first place users turn when they need information or assistance.

A service desk does not replace traditional IT maintenance and support activities. Instead, service desks enhance productivity and improve utilization of a company's information resources.

Service desk representatives need strong interpersonal and technical skills plus a solid

FIGURE 12-2 Whether a company is training manufacturing technicians, data entry personnel, or customer service representatives, employees need high-quality instruction to perform their jobs efficiently.
© iStockPhoto/fatihhoca

understanding of the business because they interact with users in many departments. A service desk should document carefully all inquiries, support tasks, and activity levels. The information can identify trends and common problems and can help build a technical support knowledge base.

A service desk can boost its productivity by using **remote control software**, which allows IT staff to take over a user's workstation and provide support and troubleshooting. Popular examples of remote control software include GoToMyPC by Citrix, LogMeIn Pro by LogMeIn, and PC Now by WebEx, among many others.

During a typical day, the service desk staff members shown in Figure 12-3 might have to perform the following tasks:

FIGURE 12-3   A service desk, also called a help desk or an information center, provides support to system users, so that users hopefully will not have the experience shown in the Dilbert® example on page 503.

© Shutterstock/Konstantin Chagin

- Show a user how to create a data query or report that displays specific business information

- Resolve network access or password problems

- Demonstrate an advanced feature of a system or a commercial package

- Help a user recover damaged data

- Offer tips for better operation

- Explain an undocumented software feature

- Show a user how to use Web conferencing

- Explain how to access the company's intranet or the Internet

- Assist a user in developing a simple database to track time spent on various projects

- Answer questions about software licensing and upgrades

- Provide information about system specifications and the cost of new hardware or software

- Recommend a system solution that integrates data from different locations to solve a business problem

- Provide hardware support by installing or reconfiguring devices such as scanners, printers, network cards, wireless devices, optical drives, backup devices, and multimedia systems

- Show users how to maintain data consistency and integrity among a desktop computer, a notebook computer, and a handheld computer or smartphone

- Troubleshoot software issues via remote control utilities

In addition to functioning as a valuable link between IT staff and users, the service desk is a central contact point for all IT maintenance activities. The service desk is where users report system problems, ask for maintenance, or submit new systems requests. A service desk can utilize many types of automated support, just as outside vendors do, including e-mail responses, on-demand fax capability, an online knowledge base, frequently asked questions (FAQs), discussion groups, bulletin boards, and automated voice mail. Many vendors now provide a live chat feature for online visitors.

Outsourcing Issues

As you learned in Chapter 7, many firms outsource various aspects of application development. This trend also includes outsourcing IT support and service desks. As with most business decisions, outsourcing has pros and cons. Typically, the main reason for outsourcing is cost reduction. Offshore call centers can trim expenses and free up valuable human resources for product development.

However, firms have learned that if tech support quality goes down, customers are likely to notice and might shop elsewhere. Critical factors might include phone wait times, support staff performance, and online support tools. The real question is whether a company can achieve the desired savings without endangering its reputation and customer base. Risks can be limited, but only if a firm takes an active role in managing and monitoring support quality and consistency.

MAINTENANCE TASKS

TOOLKIT TIME

The Financial Analysis tools in Part C of the Systems Analyst's Toolkit can help you analyze and manage maintenance costs, and determine when a system is reaching the end of its useful life. To learn more about these tools, turn to Part C of the four-part Toolkit that follows Chapter 12.

The systems support and security phase is an important component of TCO (total cost of ownership) because ongoing maintenance expenses can determine the economic life of a system.

Figure 12-4 shows a typical pattern of operational and maintenance expenses during the useful life of a system. **Operational costs** include items such as supplies, equipment rental, and software leases. Notice that the lower area shown in Figure 12-4 represents fixed operational expenses, while the upper area represents maintenance expenses.

Maintenance expenses vary significantly during the system's operational life and include spending to support maintenance activities. **Maintenance activities** include changing programs, procedures, or documentation to ensure correct system performance; adapting the system to changing requirements; and making the system operate more efficiently. Those needs are met by corrective, adaptive, perfective, and preventive maintenance.

Although some overlap exists, four types of maintenance tasks can be identified, as shown by the examples in Figure 12-5. **Corrective maintenance** is performed to fix

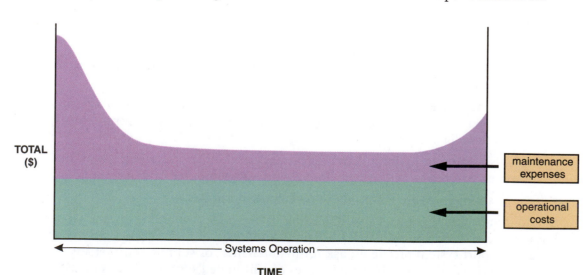

FIGURE 12-4 The total cost of operating an information system includes operational and maintenance costs. Operational costs (green) are relatively constant, while maintenance costs (purple) vary over time.
© Cengage Learning 2014

Examples of Maintenance Tasks

Corrective Maintenance
- Diagnose and fix logic errors
- Replace defective network cabling
- Restore proper configuration settings
- Debug program code
- Update drivers
- Utilize remote control software for problem diagnosis and resolution

Adaptive Maintenance
- Add online capability
- Add support for mobile devices
- Add new data entry field to input screen
- Install links to Web site
- Create employee portal

Perfective Maintenance
- Upgrade or replace outdated hardware
- Write macros to handle repetitive tasks
- Compress system files
- Optimize user desktop settings
- Upgrade wireless network capability
- Install more powerful network server

Preventive Maintenance
- Install new antivirus software
- Develop standard backup schedule, including off-site and cloud-based strategies
- Implement regular defragmentation process
- Analyze problem report for patterns
- Tighten all cable connections
- Develop user guide covering confidentiality rules and unauthorized use of company IT resources

FIGURE 12-5 Corrective maintenance fixes errors and problems. Adaptive maintenance provides enhancements to a system. Perfective maintenance improves a system's efficiency, reliability, or maintainability. Preventive maintenance avoids future problems.

© Cengage Learning 2014

errors, **adaptive maintenance** adds new capability and enhancements, **perfective mainte-nance** improves efficiency, and **preventive maintenance** reduces the possibility of future system failure. Some analysts use the term *maintenance* to describe only corrective maintenance that fixes problems. It is helpful, however, to view the maintenance con-cept more broadly and identify the different types of tasks.

Maintenance expenses usually are high when a system is implemented because problems must be detected, investigated, and resolved by corrective maintenance. Once the system becomes stable, costs usually remain low and involve minor adaptive maintenance. Eventually, both adaptive and perfective maintenance activities increase in a dynamic business environment.

Near the end of a system's useful life, adaptive and corrective maintenance expenses increase rapidly, but perfective maintenance typically decreases when it becomes clear that the company plans to replace the system. Figure 12-6 on the next page shows the typical patterns for each of the four classifications of maintenance activities over a system's life span.

Corrective Maintenance

Corrective maintenance diagnoses and corrects errors in an operational system. To avoid introducing new problems, all maintenance work requires careful analysis before making changes. The best maintenance approach is a scaled-down version of

	Immediately After Implementation	Early Operational Life	Middle Operational Life	Later Operational Life
Corrective Maintenance	High	Low	Low	High
Adaptive Maintenance (Minor Enhancements)	None	Medium	Medium	Medium
Adaptive Maintenance (Major Enhancements)	None	None	Medium to High	Medium to High
Perfective Maintenance	Low	Low to Medium	Medium	Low
Preventive Maintenance	Low	Medium	Medium	Low

FIGURE 12-6 Information systems maintenance depends on the type of maintenance and the age of the system.
© Cengage Learning 2014

the SDLC itself, where investigation, analysis, design, and testing are performed before implementing any solution. Recall that in Chapter 11 you learned about the difference between a test environment and an operational environment. Any maintenance work that could affect the system must be performed first in the test environment, and then migrated to the operational system.

IT support staff respond to errors in various ways, depending on the nature and severity of the problem. Most organizations have standard procedures for minor errors, such as an incorrect report title or an improper format for a data element. In a typical procedure, a user submits a systems request that is evaluated, prioritized, and scheduled by the system administrator or the systems review committee. If the request is approved, the maintenance team designs, tests, documents, and implements a solution.

As you learned in Chapter 2, many organizations use a standard online form for systems requests. In smaller firms, the process might be an informal e-mail message. For more serious situations, such as incorrect report totals or inconsistent data, a user submits a systems request with supporting evidence. Those requests receive a high priority and a maintenance team begins work on the problem immediately.

The worst-case situation is a system failure. If an emergency occurs, the maintenance team bypasses the initial steps and tries to correct the problem immediately. This often requires a **patch**, which is a specially written software module that provides temporary repairs so operations can resume. Meanwhile, a written systems request is prepared by a user or a member of the IT department and added to the maintenance log. When the system is operational again, the maintenance team determines the cause, analyzes the problem, and designs a permanent solution. The IT response team updates the test data files, thoroughly tests the system, and prepares full documentation. Regardless of how the priorities are set, a standard ranking method can be helpful. For example, Figure 12-7 shows a three-level framework for IT support potential impact.

PRIORITY	IMPACT	TIME FRAME
Level 1	Significant impact on IT operations, security, or business activity that requires immediate attention.	Implement patch as soon as possible.
Level 2	Some impact on IT operations, security, or business activity. Requires prompt attention, but operations can continue.	Patch as necessary and begin implementation prior to next release.
Level 3	Little or no impact on current IT operations, security, or business activity.	Implement in the next release.

FIGURE 12-7 This three-level ranking framework for IT support considers potential impact and response urgency.
© Cengage Learning 2014

The process of managing system support is described in more detail starting on page 512, including an overview of maintenance tasks and a procedural flowchart, which is shown in Figure 12-10 on page 515.

Adaptive Maintenance

Adaptive maintenance adds enhancements to an operational system and makes the system easier to use. An **enhancement** is a new feature or capability. The need for adaptive maintenance usually arises from business environment changes such as new products or services, new manufacturing technology, or support for a new Web-based operation.

The procedure for minor adaptive maintenance is similar to routine corrective maintenance. A user submits a systems request that is evaluated and prioritized by the systems review committee. A maintenance team then analyzes, designs, tests, and implements the enhancement. Although the procedures for the two types of maintenance are alike, adaptive maintenance requires more IT department resources than minor corrective maintenance.

A major adaptive maintenance project is like a small-scale SDLC project because the development procedure is similar. Adaptive maintenance can be more difficult than new systems development because the enhancements must work within the constraints of an existing system.

Perfective Maintenance

Perfective maintenance involves changing an operational system to make it more efficient, reliable, or maintainable. Requests for corrective and adaptive maintenance normally come from users, while the IT department usually initiates perfective maintenance.

During system operation, changes in user activity or data patterns can cause a decline in efficiency, and perfective maintenance might be needed to restore performance. When users are concerned about performance, you should determine if a perfective maintenance project could improve response time and system efficiency.

Perfective maintenance also can improve system reliability. For example, input problems might cause a program to terminate abnormally. By modifying the data entry process, you can highlight errors and notify the users that they must enter proper data. When a system is easier to maintain, support is less costly and less risky. In many cases, you can simplify a complex program to improve maintainability.

In many organizations, perfective maintenance is not performed frequently enough. Companies with limited resources often consider new systems development, adaptive maintenance, and corrective maintenance more important than perfective maintenance. Managers and users constantly request new projects, so few resources are available for perfective maintenance work. As a practical matter, perfective maintenance can be performed as part of another project. For example, if a new function must be added to a program, you can include perfective maintenance in the adaptive maintenance project.

Perfective maintenance usually is cost effective during the middle of the system's operational life. Early in systems operation, perfective maintenance usually is not needed. Later, perfective maintenance might be necessary, but have a high cost. Perfective maintenance is less important if the company plans to discontinue the system.

When performing perfective maintenance, analysts often use a technique called software reengineering. **Software reengineering** uses analytical techniques to identify potential quality and performance improvements in an information system. In that sense, software reengineering is similar to business process reengineering, which seeks to simplify operations, reduce costs, and improve quality — as you learned in Chapter 1.

FIGURE 12-8 Regardless of the type of system, high-quality maintenance must be performed by trained professionals.

DoD photo by Airman Charlie Whetstine, U.S. Navy

Programs that need a large number of maintenance changes usually are good candidates for reengineering. The more a program changes, the more likely it is to become inefficient and difficult to maintain. Detailed records of maintenance work can identify systems with a history of frequent corrective, adaptive, or perfective maintenance.

Preventive Maintenance

To avoid problems, preventive maintenance requires analysis of areas where trouble is likely to occur. Like perfective maintenance, the IT department normally initiates preventive maintenance. Preventive maintenance often results in increased user satisfaction, decreased downtime, and reduced TCO. Preventive maintenance competes for IT resources along with other projects, and sometimes does not receive the high priority that it deserves.

Regardless of the type of maintenance, computer systems must be supported by trained professionals, just as the aircraft shown in Figure 12-8 must be serviced by skilled technicians. In both cases, the quality of the maintenance will directly affect the organization's success.

CASE IN POINT 12.1: OUTBACK OUTSOURCING, INC.

You are a systems analyst at Outback Outsourcing, a firm that handles payroll processing for many large companies. Outback Outsourcing uses a combination of payroll package programs and in-house developed software to deliver custom-made payroll solutions for its clients. Lately, users have flooded you with requests for more new features and Web-based capability to meet customer expectations. Your boss, the IT manager, comes to you with a question. She wants to know when to stop trying to enhance the old software and develop a totally new version better suited to the new marketplace. How would you answer her?

MAINTENANCE MANAGEMENT

System maintenance requires effective management, quality assurance, and cost control. To achieve these goals, companies use various strategies, such as a maintenance team, a maintenance management program, a configuration management process, and a maintenance release procedure. In addition, firms use version control and baselines to track system releases and analyze the system's life cycle. These concepts are described in the following sections.

The Maintenance Team

A **maintenance team** includes a system administrator and one or more systems analysts and programmers. The system administrator should have solid technical expertise, and experience in troubleshooting and configuring operating systems and hardware. Successful analysts need a strong IT background, solid analytical abilities, good communication skills, and an overall understanding of business operations.

SYSTEM ADMINISTRATOR   A **system administrator** manages computer and network systems. A system administrator must work well under pressure, have good organizational and communication skills, and be able to understand and resolve complex issues in a limited time frame. In most organizations, a system administrator has primary responsibility for the operation, configuration, and security of one or more systems. The system administrator is responsible for routine maintenance, and usually is authorized to take preventive action to avoid an immediate emergency, such as a server crash, network outage, security incident, or hardware failure.

Systems administration is a vital function, and various professional associations, such as SAGE, which is shown in Figure 12-9, offer a wide variety of technical information and support for system administrators. Notice that SAGE members subscribe to a code of ethics that includes professionalism, integrity, privacy, and social responsibility, among other topics.

SYSTEMS ANALYSTS   Systems analysts assigned to a maintenance team are like skilled detectives who investigate and rapidly locate the source of a problem by using analysis and synthesis skills. *Analysis* means examining the whole in order to learn about the individual elements, while *synthesis* involves studying the parts to understand the overall system. In addition to strong technical skills, an analyst must have a solid grasp of business operations and functions. Analysts also need effective interpersonal and communications skills, and they must be creative, energetic, and eager for new knowledge.

PROGRAMMERS   In a small organization, a programmer might be expected to handle a wide variety of tasks, but in larger firms, programming work tends to be more specialized. For example, typical job titles include an **applications programmer**, who works on new systems development and maintenance; a **systems**

We as professional System Administrators do hereby commit ourselves to the highest standards of ethical and professional conduct, and agree to be guided by this code of ethics, and encourage every System Administrator to do the same.

Professionalism I will maintain professional conduct in the workplace and will not allow personal feelings or beliefs to cause me to treat people unfairly or unprofessionally.

Personal Integrity I will be honest in my professional dealings and forthcoming about my competence and the impact of my mistakes. I will seek assistance from others when required.

I will avoid conflicts of interest and biases whenever possible. When my advice is sought, if I have a conflict of interest or bias, I will declare it if appropriate, and recuse myself if necessary.

Privacy I will access private information on computer systems only when it is necessary in the course of my technical duties. I will maintain and protect the confidentiality of any information to which I may have access, regardless of the method by which I came into knowledge of it.

Laws and Policies I will educate myself and others on relevant laws, regulations, and policies regarding the performance of my duties.

THE SYSTEM ADMINISTRATORS' CODE OF ETHICS

Communication I will communicate with management, users, and colleagues about computer matters of mutual interest. I will strive to listen to and understand the needs of all parties.

System Integrity I will strive to ensure the necessary integrity, reliability, and availability of the systems for which I am responsible.

I will design and maintain each system in a manner to support the purpose of the system to the organization.

Education I will continue to update and enhance my technical knowledge and other work-related skills. I will share my knowledge and experience with others.

Responsibility to Computing Community I will cooperate with the larger computing community to maintain the integrity of network and computing resources.

Social Responsibility As an informed professional, I will encourage the writing and adoption of relevant policies and laws consistent with these ethical principles.

Ethical Responsibility I will strive to build and maintain a safe, healthy, and productive workplace.

I will do my best to make decisions consistent with the safety, privacy, and well-being of my community and the public, and to disclose promptly factors that might pose unexamined risks or dangers.

I will accept and offer honest criticism of technical work as appropriate and will credit properly the contributions of others.

I will lead by example, maintaining a high ethical standard and degree of professionalism in the performance of all my duties. I will support colleagues and co-workers in following this code of ethics.

FIGURE 12-9 SAGE seeks to establish standards of professional excellence, improve the technical skills of its members, and promote a comprehensive code of ethics.

© 2012 The USENIX Association

programmer, who concentrates on operating system software and utilities; and a **database programmer,** who focuses on creating and supporting large-scale database systems. Many IT departments also use a job title of **programmer/analyst** to designate positions that require a combination of systems analysis and programming skills.

ORGANIZATIONAL ISSUES   IT managers often divide systems analysts and programmers into two groups: One group performs new system development, and the other group handles maintenance. Some organizations use a more flexible approach and assign IT staff members to various projects as they occur. By integrating development and support work, the people developing the system assume responsibility for maintaining it. Because the team is familiar with the project, additional training or expense is unnecessary, and members are likely to have a sense of ownership from the onset.

Unfortunately, many analysts feel that maintenance is less interesting and creative than developing new systems. In addition, an analyst might find it challenging to troubleshoot and support someone else's work that might have been poorly documented and organized.

Some organizations that have separate maintenance and new systems groups rotate people from one assignment to the other. When analysts learn different skills, the organization is more versatile and people can shift to meet changing business needs. For instance, systems analysts working on maintenance projects learn why it is important to design easily maintainable systems. Similarly, analysts working on new systems get a better appreciation of the development process and the design compromises necessary to meet business objectives.

One disadvantage of rotation is that it increases overhead because time is lost when people move from one job to another. When systems analysts constantly shift between maintenance and new development, they have less opportunity to become highly skilled at any one job.

Newly hired and recently promoted IT staff members often are assigned to maintenance projects because their managers believe that the opportunity to study existing systems and documentation is a valuable experience. In addition, the mini-SDLC used in many adaptive maintenance projects is good training for the full-scale systems development life cycle. For a new systems analyst, however, maintenance work might be more difficult than systems development, and it might make sense to assign a new person to a development team where experienced analysts are available to provide training and guidance.

CASE IN POINT 12.2: BRIGHTSIDE INSURANCE, INC.

As IT manager at Brightside Insurance Company, you organized your IT staff into two separate groups — one team for maintenance projects and the other team for new systems work. That arrangement worked well in your last position at another company. Brightside, however, previously made systems assignments with no particular pattern.

At first, the systems analysts in your group did not comment about the team approach. Now, several of your best analysts have indicated that they enjoyed the mix of work and would not want to be assigned to a maintenance team. Before a problem develops, you have decided to rethink your organizational strategy. Should you go back to the way things were done previously at Brightside? Why or why not? Do other options exist? What are they?

Maintenance Requests

Typically, maintenance requests involve a series of steps, as shown in Figure 12-10. After a user submits a request, a system administrator determines whether immediate action is needed and whether the request is under a prescribed cost limit. In nonemergency requests that exceed the cost limit, a systems review committee assesses the request and either approves it, with a priority, or rejects it. The system administrator notifies affected users of the outcome.

Users submit most requests for corrective and adaptive maintenance when the system is not performing properly, or if they want new features. IT staff members usually initiate requests for perfective and preventive maintenance. To keep a complete maintenance log, all work must be covered by a specific request that users submit in writing or by e-mail.

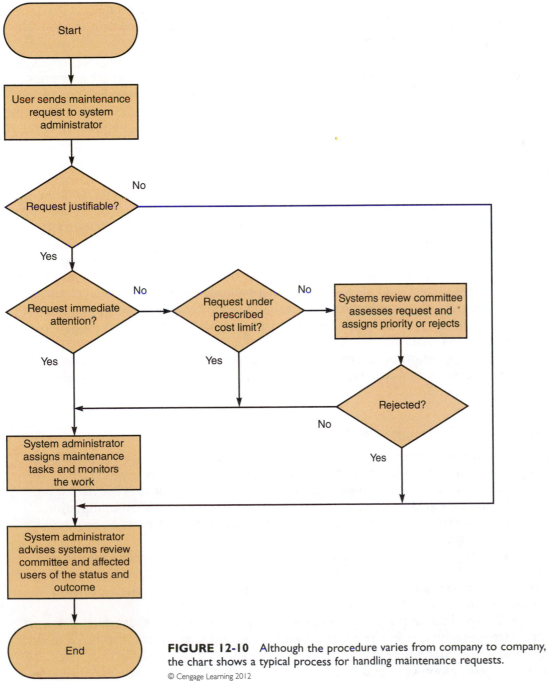

FIGURE 12-10 Although the procedure varies from company to company, the chart shows a typical process for handling maintenance requests.
© Cengage Learning 2012

INITIAL DETERMINATION   When a user submits a maintenance request, the system administrator makes an initial determination. If the request is justifiable and involves a severe problem that requires immediate attention, the system administrator takes action at once. In justifiable, but noncritical, situations, the administrator determines whether the request can be performed within a preauthorized cost level. If so, he or she assigns the maintenance tasks and monitors the work.

THE SYSTEMS REVIEW COMMITTEE   When a request exceeds a predetermined cost level or involves a major configuration change, the systems review committee either approves it and assigns a priority, or rejects it.

TASK COMPLETION   The system administrator usually is responsible for assigning maintenance tasks to individuals or to a maintenance team. Depending on the situation and the company's policy, the system administrator might consider rotating assignments among the IT staff or limiting maintenance tasks to certain individuals or teams, as explained in the previous section.

USER NOTIFICATION   Users who initiate maintenance requests expect a prompt response, especially if the situation directly affects their work. Even when corrective action cannot occur immediately, users appreciate feedback from the system administrator and should be kept informed of any decisions or actions that could affect them.

Establishing Priorities

In many companies, the systems review committee separates maintenance and new development requests when setting priorities. In other organizations, all requests are considered together, and the most important project gets top priority, whether it is maintenance or new development.

Some IT managers believe that evaluating all projects together leads to the best possible decisions because maintenance and new development require similar IT department resources. In IT departments where maintenance and new development are not integrated, it might be better to evaluate requests separately. Another advantage of a separate approach is that maintenance is more likely to receive a proportional share of IT department resources.

The most important objective is to have a procedure that balances new development and necessary maintenance work to provide the best support for business requirements and priorities.

Configuration Management

Configuration management (CM), sometimes referred to as **change control (CC)**, is a process for controlling changes in system requirements during software development. Configuration management also is an important tool for managing system changes and costs after a system becomes operational. Most companies establish a specific process that describes how system changes must be requested and documented.

As enterprise-wide information systems grow more complex, configuration management becomes critical. Industry standards have emerged, and many vendors offer configuration management software and techniques, as shown in Figure 12-11.

CM is especially important if a system has multiple versions that run in different hardware and software environments. Configuration management also helps to organize and handle documentation. An operational system has extensive documentation that covers development, modification, and maintenance for all versions of the installed system. Most documentation material, including the initial systems request, project management data, end-of-phase reports, data dictionary, and the IT operations and user manuals, is stored in the IT department.

Keeping track of all documentation and ensuring that updates are distributed properly are important aspects of configuration management.

About CM Crossroads

Founded in 1998 by Patrick Egan as a destination for discussions among the users of CCC/Harvest from PLATINUM technology **CM Crossroads** today is the web's most comprehensive developer community and resource center focused on configuration management and application lifecycle management. Over 200,000 unique visitors review resources at CM Crossroads each month viewing over 20,000 pages each day. CM Crossroads offers interactive discussion forums, a broad range of original articles and newsletters, a career search center and Jobs Board and an extensive library of resources in the CM Yellow Pages. CM Crossroads hosts the Configuration Management Body of Knowledge and is the publisher of the Configuration Management Journal.

The goal of CM Crossroads is to provide members with information and resources about the tools they use in a free and open format. Like a crossroads on the information highway, CM Crossroads represents a nexus at the center of the configuration management community where many paths may intersect and continue on. It is a place where configuration management professionals can begin their search for information and resources and return often to hear about the latest developments with their product of choice.

FIGURE 12-11 CM Crossroads provides a source of information and resources for configuration management professionals.
© 1998–2011 CMC Media, Inc.

Maintenance Releases

Keeping track of maintenance changes and updates can be difficult, especially for a complex system. When a **maintenance release methodology** is used, all noncritical changes are held until they can be implemented at the same time. Each change is documented and installed as a new version of the system called a **maintenance release**.

For an in-house developed system, the time between releases usually depends on the level of maintenance activity. A new release to correct a critical error, however, might be implemented immediately rather than saved for the next scheduled release.

When a release method is used, a numbering pattern distinguishes the different releases. In a typical system, the initial version of the system is 1.0, and the release that includes the first set of maintenance changes is version 1.1. A change, for example, from version 1.4 to 1.5 indicates relatively minor enhancements, while whole number changes, such as from version 1.0 to 2.0 or from version 3.4 to 4.0, indicate a significant upgrade.

The release methodology offers several advantages, especially if two teams perform maintenance work on the same system. When a release methodology is used, all changes are tested together before a new system version is released. This approach results in fewer versions, less expense, and less interruption for users. Using a release methodology also reduces the documentation burden because all changes are coordinated and become effective simultaneously.

A release methodology also has some potential disadvantages. Users expect a rapid response to their problems and requests, but with a release methodology, new features or upgrades are available less often. Even when changes would improve system efficiency or user productivity, the potential savings must wait until the next release, which might increase operational costs.

Commercial software suppliers also provide maintenance releases, often called **service packs**, as shown in Figure 12-12 on the next page. As Microsoft explains, a service pack contains all the fixes and enhancements that have been made available since the last program version or service pack.

Version Control

Version control is the process of tracking system releases, or versions. When a new version of a system is installed, the prior release is **archived**, or stored. If a new version causes a system to fail, a company can reinstall the prior version to restore operations. In addition to tracking system versions, the IT staff is responsible for configuring systems that have several modules at various release stages. For example, an accounting system might have a one-year-old accounts receivable module that must interface with a brand-new payroll module.

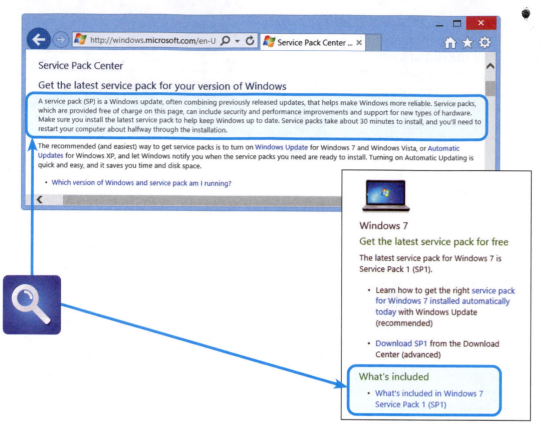

FIGURE 12-12 A Microsoft service pack provides access to up-to-date drivers, tools, security patches, and customer-requested product changes.

Screenshots used with permission from Microsoft.

Most firms use commercial applications to handle version control for complex systems, such as ERP. Serena Software's PVCS Version Manager, which is shown in Figure 12-13, is a popular example. Serena, a longtime provider of version control solutions, states that PVCS Version Manager can help meet compliance, documentation, and traceability requirements in regulated industries. Serena also mentions that the product uses a "snapshot" technique to capture development effort at any given point in time.

Baselines

A **baseline** is a formal reference point that measures system characteristics at a specific time. Systems analysts use baselines as yardsticks to document features and performance during the systems development process. The three types of baselines are functional, allocated, and product.

The **functional baseline** is the configuration of the system documented at the beginning of the project. It consists of all the necessary system requirements and design constraints.

The **allocated baseline** documents the system at the end of the design phase and identifies any changes since the functional baseline. The allocated baseline includes testing and verification of all system requirements and features.

The **product baseline** describes the system at the beginning of system operation. The product baseline incorporates any changes made since the allocated baseline and includes the results of performance and acceptance tests for the operational system.

FIGURE 12-13 The more complex the system, the more important the task of version control. Commercial software packages, such as this example from Serena Software, can help companies maintain controls and reduce costs.

© 2012 Serena Software Inc.

SYSTEM PERFORMANCE MANAGEMENT

Years ago, when most firms used a central computer for processing data, it was relatively simple to manage a system and measure its efficiency. Today, companies use complex networks and client/server systems to support business needs. A user at a client workstation often interacts with an information system that depends on other clients, servers, networks, and data located throughout the company. Rather than a single computer, it is the integration of all those components that determines the system's capability and performance. In many situations, IT managers use automated software and CASE tools to manage complex systems.

To ensure satisfactory support for business operations, the IT department must manage system faults and interruptions, measure system performance and workload, and anticipate future needs. The following sections discuss these topics.

Fault Management

No matter how well it is designed, every system will experience some problems, such as hardware failures, software errors, user mistakes, and power outages. A system administrator must detect and resolve operational problems as quickly as possible. That task, often called **fault management**, includes monitoring the system for signs of trouble, logging all system failures, diagnosing the problem, and applying corrective action.

The more complex the system, the more difficult it can be to analyze symptoms and isolate a cause. In addition to addressing the immediate problem, it is important to evaluate performance patterns and trends. Windows 8 and Windows 7 include a built-in fault management feature called Resource Monitor, which is shown in Figure 12-14 on the next page. Resource Monitor can evaluate CPU, memory, disk, and network activity in real time, and save the data in a log file. In addition to automated notification, fault management software can identify underlying causes, speed up response time, and reduce service outages.

Although system administrators must deal with system faults and interruptions as they arise, the best strategy is to prevent problems by monitoring system performance and workload.

FIGURE 12-14 Windows Resource Monitor displays CPU, memory, disk, and network activity in real time.
Screenshot used with permission from Microsoft.

Performance and Workload Measurement

In e-business, slow performance can be as devastating as no performance at all. Network delays and application bottlenecks affect customer satisfaction, user productivity, and business results. In fact, many IT managers believe that network delays do more damage than actual stoppages because they occur more frequently and are difficult to predict, detect, and prevent. Customers expect reliable, fast response 24 hours a day, seven days a week. To support that level of service, companies use performance management software, which is available from many vendors, including Cisco, Sun, and HP, among others.

To measure system performance, many firms use **benchmark testing**, which uses a set of standard tests to evaluate system performance and capacity. In addition to benchmark testing, performance measurements, called **metrics**, can monitor the number of transactions processed in a given time period, the number of records accessed, and the volume of online data. Network performance metrics include response time, bandwidth, throughput, and turnaround time, among others.

RESPONSE TIME   **Response time** is the overall time between a request for system activity and the delivery of the response. In the typical online environment, response time is measured from the instant the user presses the ENTER key or clicks a mouse button until the requested screen display appears or printed output is ready. Response time is affected by the system design, capabilities, and processing methods. If the request involves network or Internet access, response time is affected by data communication factors.

Online users expect an immediate response, and they are frustrated by any apparent lag or delay. Of all performance measurements, response time is the one that users notice and complain about most.

BANDWIDTH AND THROUGHPUT   Bandwidth and throughput are closely related terms, and many analysts use them interchangeably. **Bandwidth** describes the amount of data that the system can transfer in a fixed time period. Bandwidth requirements are expressed in bits per second. Depending on the system, you might measure bandwidth in **Kbps (kilobits per second)**, **Mbps (megabits per second)**, or **Gbps (gigabits per second)**. Analyzing bandwidth is similar to forecasting the hourly number of vehicles that will use a highway in order to determine the number of lanes required.

Throughput measures actual system performance under specific circumstances and is affected by network loads and hardware efficiency. Throughput, like bandwidth, is expressed as a data transfer rate, such as Kbps, Mbps, or Gbps. Just as traffic jams delay highway traffic, throughput limitations can slow system performance and response time. That is especially true with graphics-intensive systems and Web-based systems that are subject to Internet-related conditions.

In addition to the performance metrics explained in the previous section, system administrators measure many other performance characteristics. Although no standard set of metrics exists, several typical examples are:

- Arrivals — The number of items that appear on a device during a given observation time.
- Busy — The time that a given resource is unavailable.
- Completions — The number of arrivals that are processed during a given observation period.
- Queue length — The number of requests pending for a service.
- Service time — The time it takes to process a given task once it reaches the front of the queue.
- Think time — The time it takes an application user to issue another request.
- Utilization — How much of a given resource was required to complete a task.
- Wait time — The time that requests must wait for a resource to become available.

The Computer Measurement Group (CMG®) maintains a site, shown in Figure 12-15, that provides support and assistance for IT professionals concerned with performance evaluation and capacity planning.

TURNAROUND TIME   **Turnaround time** applies to centralized batch processing operations, such as customer billing or credit card statement processing. Turnaround time measures the time between submitting a request for information and the fulfillment of the request. Turnaround time also can be used to measure the quality of IT support or services by measuring the time from a user request for help to the resolution of the problem.

The IT department often measures response time, bandwidth, throughput, and turnaround time to evaluate system performance both before and after changes to the system or business information requirements. Performance data also is used for cost-benefit analyses of proposed maintenance and to evaluate systems that are nearing the end of their economically useful lives.

Finally, management uses current performance and workload data as input for the capacity planning process.

FIGURE 12-15 The Computer Measurement Group is a nonprofit organization that primarily is concerned with performance evaluation and capacity management.

Capacity Planning

Capacity planning is a process that monitors current activity and performance levels, anticipates future activity, and forecasts the resources needed to provide desired levels of service.

As the first step in capacity planning, you develop a current model based on the system's present workload and performance specifications. Then you project demand and user requirements over a one- to three-year time period and analyze the model to see what is needed to maintain satisfactory performance and meet requirements. To assist you in the process, you can use a technique called what-if analysis.

What-if analysis allows you to vary one or more elements in a model in order to measure the effect on other elements. For example, you might use what-if analysis to answer questions such as: How will response time be affected if we add more PC workstations to the network? Will our client/server system be able to handle the growth in sales from the new Web site? What will be the effect on server throughput if we add more memory?

Powerful spreadsheet tools also can assist you in performing what-if analysis. For example, Microsoft Excel contains a feature called Goal Seek that determines what changes are necessary in one value to produce a specific result for another value. In the example shown in Figure 12-16, a capacity planning worksheet indicates that the system can handle 3,840 Web-based orders per day, at 22.5 seconds each. The user wants to know the effect on processing time if the number of transactions increases to 9,000. As the Goal Seek solution in the bottom figure shows, order processing will have to be perfwormed in 9.6 seconds to achieve that goal.

FIGURE 12-16 In this Goal Seek example, the user wants to know the effect on processing time if the number of daily transactions increases from 3,840 to 9,000.

When you plan capacity, you need detailed information about the number of transactions; the daily, weekly, or monthly transaction patterns; the number of queries; and the number, type, and size of all generated reports. If the system involves a LAN, you need to estimate network traffic levels to determine whether or not the existing hardware and software can handle the load. If the system uses a client/server design, you need to examine performance and connectivity specifications for each platform.

Most important, you need an accurate forecast of future business activities. If new business functions or requirements are predicted, you should develop contingency plans based on input from users and management. The main objective is to ensure that the system meets all future demands and provides effective support for business operations. Some firms handle their own capacity planning, while others purchase software and services from companies such as TeamQuest, shown in Figure 12-17.

System Maintenance Tools

You can use automated tools that provide valuable assistance during the operation and support phase. Many CASE tools include system evaluation and maintenance features, including the following examples:

- Performance monitor that provides data on program execution times
- Program analyzer that scans source code, provides data element cross-reference information, and helps evaluate the impact of a program change
- Interactive debugging analyzer that locates the source of a programming error
- Reengineering tools
- Automated documentation
- Network activity monitor
- Workload forecasting tool

In addition to CASE tools, you also can use spreadsheet and presentation software to calculate trends, perform what-if analyses, and create attractive charts and graphs to display the results. Information technology planning is an essential part of the business planning process, and you probably will deliver presentations to management. You can review Part A of the Systems Analyst's Toolkit for more information on using spreadsheet and presentation software to help you communicate effectively.

🔧 TOOLKIT TIME

The CASE tools in Part B of the Systems Analyst's Toolkit can help you document business functions and processes, develop graphical models, and provide an overall framework for information system development. To learn more about these tools, turn to Part B of the four-part Toolkit that follows Chapter 12.

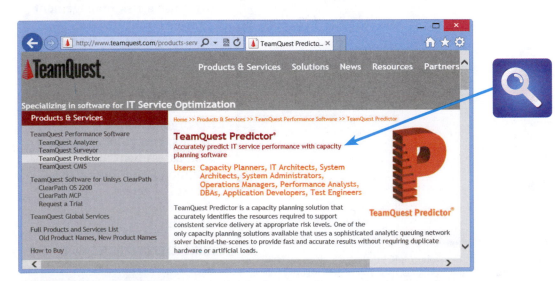

FIGURE 12-17 TeamQuest is an example of a firm that offers capacity planning software and services.

FIGURE 12-18   System security must provide information confidentiality, integrity, and availability.

© Cengage Learning 2014

SYSTEM SECURITY OVERVIEW

Security is a vital part of every information system. **Security** protects the system, and keeps it safe, free from danger, and reliable. In a global environment that includes many types of threats and attacks, security is more important than ever. This section includes a discussion of system security concepts, risk management, and common attacks against the system.

System Security Concepts

The **CIA triangle** in Figure 12-18 shows the three main elements of system security: confidentiality, integrity, and availability. **Confidentiality** protects information from unauthorized disclosure and safeguards privacy. **Integrity** prevents unauthorized users from creating, modifying, or deleting information. **Availability** ensures that authorized users have timely and reliable access to necessary information. The first step in managing IT security is to develop a **security policy** based on these three elements. Although it is beyond the scope of this chapter, the Microsoft Management Console (MMC) shown in Figure 12-19 is a portal to a broad array of built-in security tools and techniques.

FIGURE 12-19   The Microsoft Management Console (MMC) includes built-in security tools, such as password and lock-out policies, audit policies, user rights, and security configurations, among others.

Screenshot used with permission from Microsoft.

Risk Management

In the real world, *absolute* security is not a realistic goal. Instead, managers must balance the value of the assets being protected, potential risks to the organization, and security costs. For example, it might not be worth installing an expensive video camera monitoring system to protect an empty warehouse. To achieve the best results, most firms use a **risk management** approach that involves constant attention to three interactive tasks: risk identification, risk assessment, and risk control, as shown in Figure 12-20.

Risk identification analyzes the organization's assets, threats, and vulnerabilities. **Risk assessment** measures risk likelihood and impact. **Risk control** develops safeguards that reduce risks and their impact.

RISK IDENTIFICATION   The first step in risk identification is to list and classify business assets. An **asset** might include company hardware, software, data, networks, people, or procedures. For each asset, a risk manager rates the impact of an attack and analyzes possible threats. A **threat** is an internal or external entity that could endanger an asset. For example, threat categories might include natural disasters, software attacks, or theft, as shown in Figure 12-21.

Next, the risk manager identifies vulnerabilities and how they might be exploited. A **vulnerability** is a security weakness or soft spot, and an **exploit** is an attack that takes advantage of a vulnerability. To identify vulnerabilities, a risk manager might ask questions like these: *Could hackers break through the proxy server? Could employees retrieve sensitive files without proper authorization? Could people enter the computer room and sabotage our servers?* Each vulnerability is rated and assigned a value. The output of risk identification is a list of assets, vulnerabilities, and ratings.

RISK ASSESSMENT In IT security terms, a **risk** is the impact of an attack multiplied by the likelihood of a vulnerability being exploited. For example, an impact value of 2 and a vulnerability rating of 10 would produce a risk of 20. On the other hand, an impact value of 5 and a vulnerability rating of 5 would produce a risk of 25. When risks are calculated and prioritized, **critical risks** will head the list. Although ratings can be subjective, the overall process provides a consistent approach and framework.

Risk Management

FIGURE 12-20 Risk management requires continuous risk identification, assessment, and control.

© Cengage Learning 2014

Threat Categories and Examples

THREAT CATEGORY	EXAMPLE
Extortion	Hacker steals trade secrets and threatens to release them if not paid.
Hardware and software failures	Router stops functioning, or software causes the application server to crash.
Human error or failure	Employee accidentally deletes a file.
Natural disasters	Flood destroys company building and networked systems.
Service failure	Electricity is disrupted and brings the entire system down for hours.
Software attack	A group plants destructive software, a virus, or a worm into a company network.
Technical obsolescence	Outdated software is slow, difficult to use, and vulnerable to attacks.
Theft of physical or intellectual property	Physical server is stolen, intellectual property is stolen or used without permission; may be physical or electronic.
Trespass and espionage	Employee enters unlocked server room and views the payroll data on a forbidden system.
Vandalism	Attacker defaces Web site logo, or destroys CEO's hard drive physically or electronically.

FIGURE 12-21 System threats can be grouped into several broad categories. Note the examples provided for each category.

© Cengage Learning 2014

RISK CONTROL After risks are identified and assessed, they must be controlled. Control measures might include the following examples: *We could place a firewall on the proxy server; We could assign permissions to sensitive files; We could install biometric devices to guard the computer room.* Typically, management chooses one of four risk control strategies: avoidance, mitigation, transference, or acceptance. **Avoidance** eliminates the risk by adding protective safeguards. For example, to prevent unauthorized access to LAN computers, a secure firewall might be installed. **Mitigation** reduces the impact of a risk by careful planning and preparation. For example, a company can prepare a disaster recovery plan in case a natural disaster occurs. **Transference** shifts the risk to another asset or party, such as an insurance company. **Acceptance** means that nothing is done. Companies usually accept a risk only when the protection clearly is not worth the expense.

The risk management process is iterative — risks constantly are identified, assessed, and controlled. To be effective, risk managers need a combination of business knowledge, IT skills, and experience with security tools and techniques.

Attacker Profiles and Attacks

An **attack** is a hostile act that targets the system, or the company itself. Thus, an attack might be launched by a disgruntled employee, or a hacker who is 10,000 miles away. Attackers break into a system to cause damage, steal information, or gain recognition, among other reasons. Attackers can be grouped into categories, as shown in Figure 12-22, while Figure 12-23 describes some common types of attacks.

The following sections discuss how companies combat security threats and challenges by using a multilevel strategy.

SECURITY LEVELS

To provide system security, you must consider six separate but interrelated levels: physical security, network security, application security, file security, user security, and procedural security. Like the chain shown in Figure 12-24 on page 528, system

Attacker Characteristics

ATTACKER	DESCRIPTION	SKILL SET
Cyberterrorist	Attacks to advance political, social, or ideological goals.	High
Employee	Uses unauthorized information or privileges to break into computer systems, steal information, or cause damage.	Varies
Hacker	Uses advanced skills to attack computer systems with malicious intent (black hat) or to expose flaws and improve security (white hat).	High
Hacktivist	Attacks to further a social or political cause; often involves shutting down or defacing Web sites.	Varies
Script kiddie	Inexperienced or juvenile hacker who uses readily available malicious software to disrupt or damage computer systems, and gain recognition.	Low
Spy	Non-employee who breaks into computer systems to steal information and sell it.	High

FIGURE 12-22 IT security professionals have coined labels for various types of attackers.
© Cengage Learning 2014

Types of Attacks and Examples

ATTACK	EXAMPLES
Back door	Attacker finds vulnerability in software package and exploits it.
Denial of service or distributed denial of service	One or more computers send a stream of connection requests to disable a Web server.
Dumpster diving	Attacker scours the trash for valuable information that can be used to compromise the system.
Mail bombing	Enormous volumes of e-mail are sent to a target address.
Malicious code	Attacker sends infected e-mail to the target system. Attackers may use viruses, worms, Trojan horses, keystroke loggers, spyware, or scripts to destroy data, bog down systems, spy on users, or assume control of infected systems.
Man in the middle	The attacker intercepts traffic and poses as the recipient, sending the data to the legitimate recipient but only after reading the traffic or modifying it.
Password cracking	Hacker attempts to discover a password to gain entry into a secured system. This can be a dictionary attack, where numerous words are tried, or a brute force attack, where every combination of characters is attempted.
Phishing	False DNS (Domain Name Server) information steers the user to the attacker's Web site. Attackers trick users into thinking they are visiting a legitimate site, such as a bank site, then attempt to obtain bank account numbers, usernames, and passwords.
Privilege escalation	Employee tricks a computer into raising his or her account to the administrator level.
Sniffing	Network traffic is intercepted and scanned for valuable information.
Social engineering	An attacker calls the service desk posing as a legitimate user and requests that his or her password be changed.
Spam	Unwanted, useless e-mail is sent continuously to business e-mail accounts, wasting time and decreasing productivity.
Spoofing	IP address is forged to match a trusted host, and similar content may be displayed to simulate the real site for unlawful purposes.

FIGURE 12-23 Attacks can take many forms, as this table shows. IT security managers must be able to detect these attacks and respond with suitable countermeasures.

© Cengage Learning 2014

security is only as strong as the weakest link. The following sections describe these security levels, and the issues that must be addressed. Top management often makes the final strategic and budget decisions regarding security, but systems analysts should understand the overall picture in order to make informed recommendations.

Physical Security

The first level of system security concerns the physical environment, including IT resources and people throughout the company. Special attention must be paid to

Security Levels

FIGURE 12-24 Each security link has a specific focus, and the overall chain is only as strong as the weakest link.

© Cengage Learning 2014

critical equipment located in operations centers, where servers, network hardware, and related equipment operate. Large companies usually have a dedicated room built specifically for IT operations. Smaller firms might use an office or storage area. Regardless of its size and shape, an operations center requires special protection from unwanted intrusion. In addition to centrally located equipment, all computers on the network must be secure because each server or workstation can be a potential access point. Physical access to a computer represents an entry point into the system and must be controlled and protected.

OPERATIONS CENTER SECURITY Perimeter security is essential in any room or area where computer equipment is operated or maintained. Physical access must be controlled tightly, and each entrance must be equipped with a suitable security device. All access doors should have internal hinges and electromagnetic locks that are equipped with a battery backup system to provide standby power in the event of a power outage. When the battery power is exhausted, the doors should fail in a closed position, but it should be possible for someone locked inside the room to open the door with an emergency release.

To enhance security, many companies are installing **biometric scanning systems**, which map an individual's facial features, fingerprints, handprint, or eye characteristics, as shown in Figure 12-25. These high-tech authentication systems replace magnetic identification badges, which can be lost, stolen, or altered.

Video cameras and motion sensors can be used to monitor computer room security and provide documentation of all physical activity in the area. A motion sensor uses infrared technology to detect movement, and can be configured to provide audible or silent alarms, and to send e-mail messages when one is triggered. Other types of sensors can monitor temperature and humidity in the computer room. Motion sensor alarms can be activated at times when there is no expected activity in the computer room, and authorized technicians should have codes to enable or disable the alarms.

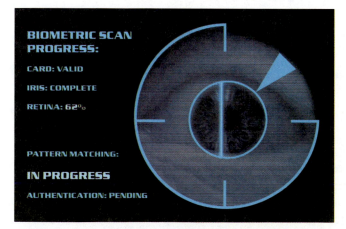

BIOMETRIC SCAN PROGRESS:

CARD: VALID

IRIS: COMPLETE

RETINA: 62%

PATTERN MATCHING:

IN PROGRESS

AUTHENTICATION: PENDING

FIGURE 12-25 Companies use biometric scanning to analyze the features of the eye's iris, which has more than 200 points that can be measured and used for comparison.

© Andy Piatt/Shutterstock

SERVERS AND DESKTOP COMPUTERS If possible, server and desktop computer cases should be equipped with locks. This simple, but important, precaution might prevent an intruder from modifying the hardware configuration of a server, damaging the equipment, or removing a disk drive. Server racks should be locked to avoid the unauthorized placement and retrieval of keystroke loggers. A **keystroke logger** is a device that can be inserted between a keyboard and a computer. Typically, the device resembles an ordinary cable plug, so it does not call attention to itself. The device can record everything that is typed into the keyboard, including passwords, while the system continues to function normally. Keystroke loggers can be used legitimately to monitor, back up, and restore a system, but if placed by an intruder, a keystroke logger represents a serious security threat.

In addition to hardware devices, keystroke logging software also exists. A keystroke logging program can be disguised as legitimate software and downloaded from the Internet or a company network. The program remains invisible to the user as it records keystrokes and uploads the information to whoever installed the program. Such malicious software can be removed by antivirus and antispyware software, discussed later in the Application Security section.

Tamper-evident cases should be used where possible. A tamper-evident case is designed to show any attempt to open or unlock the case. In the event that a computer case has been opened, an indicator LED remains lit until it is cleared with a password. Tamper-evident cases do not prevent intrusion, but a security breach is more likely to be noticed. Many servers now are offered with tamper-evident cases as part of their standard configuration.

Monitor screen savers that hide the screen and require special passwords to clear should be used on any server or workstation that is left unattended. Locking the screen after a period of inactivity is another safeguard. Microsoft Windows 7 and Windows 8 allow an administrator to include this feature in security policies. Also, you can use a **BIOS-level password**, also called a **boot-level password** or a **power-on password**, that must be entered before the computer can be started. A boot-level password can prevent an unauthorized person from booting a computer by using a CD-ROM or USB device.

Finally, companies must consider electric power issues. In mission-critical systems, large-scale backup power sources are essential to continue business operations. In other cases, computer systems and network devices should be plugged into an **uninterruptible power supply (UPS)** that includes battery backup with suitable capacity. The UPS should be able to handle short-term operations in order to permit an orderly backup and system shutdown.

PORTABLE COMPUTERS When assessing physical security issues, be sure to consider additional security provisions for notebook, laptop, and tablet computers. Because of their small size and high value, these computers are tempting targets for thieves and industrial spies. Although the following suggestions are intended as a checklist for notebook computer security, many of them also apply to desktop workstations.

- Select an operating system, such as Windows 8, that allows secure logons, BIOS-level passwords, and strong firewall protection. You can also select hardware that allows you to require BIOS-level passwords. Also, log on and work with a user account that has limited privileges rather than an administrator account, and mask the administrator account by giving it a different name that would be hard for a casual intruder to guess.

- Mark or engrave the computer's case with the company name and address, or attach a tamper-proof asset ID tag. Many hardware vendors allow corporate customers to add an asset ID tag in the BIOS. For example, after powering up, you might see the message: *Property of SCR Associates – Company Use Only.* These measures might not discourage a professional thief, but might deter a casual thief, or at least make your computer relatively less desirable because it would be more difficult to use or resell. Security experts also recommend that you use a generic carrying case, such as an attaché case, rather than a custom carrying case that calls attention to itself and its contents. Also be sure to complete and submit all manufacturer registration cards.

- Consider devices that have a built-in fingerprint reader, such as the laptop fingerprint scanner shown in Figure 12-26 on the next page.

FIGURE 12-26   Some notebook computers feature a fingerprint reader, which is a small metallic sensor located near the keyboard or display.

© MadTatyana/Shutterstock

- Many notebook computers have a **Universal Security Slot (USS)** that can be fastened to a cable lock or laptop alarm. Again, while these precautions might not deter professional thieves, they might discourage and deter casual thieves.

- Back up all vital data before using the notebook computer outside the office. Also, instead of using your computer's hard drive, save and transport highly sensitive data on removable media, such as a flash memory device.

- Use tracking software that directs your laptop periodically to contact a security tracking center. If your notebook is stolen, the call-in identifies the computer and its physical location. Armed with this information, the security tracking center can alert law enforcement agencies and communications providers. As shown in Figure 12-27, Absolute Software sells a product called LoJack for Laptops, which offers call-in service, as well as a remote data erase capability. Some versions of the product even provide a payment if the firm does not recover your stolen laptop.

- While traveling, try to be alert to potential high-risk situations, where a thief, or thieves, might attempt to distract your attention and snatch your computer. These situations often occur in crowded, noisy places like airport baggage claim areas, rental car counters, and security checkpoints. Also, when traveling by car, store your computer in a trunk or lockable compartment where it will not be visible.

- Establish stringent password protection policies that require minimum length and complexity, and set a limit on how many times an invalid password can be entered before the system locks itself down. In some situations, you might want to establish file encryption policies to protect extremely sensitive files.

CASE IN POINT 12.3: OUTER BANKS COUNTY

Outer Banks County is a 200-square-mile area in coastal North Carolina, and you are the IT manager. The county has about a hundred office employees who perform clerical tasks in various departments. A recent budget crisis has resulted in a wage and hiring freeze, and morale has declined. The county manager has asked you to install some type of keystroke logger to monitor employees and determine whether they are fully productive. After your conversation, you wonder whether there might be some potential privacy and security issues involved.

For example, does an employer have a duty to notify its employees that it is monitoring them? Should the employer notify them even if not required to do so? From a human resources viewpoint, what would be the best way to approach this issue? Also, does a potential security issue exist? If an unauthorized person gained possession of the keystroke log, he or she might be able to uncover passwords and other sensitive data.

What are your conclusions? Are these issues important, and how would you respond to the county manager's recommendation? Before you answer, you should go on the Internet and learn more about keystroke loggers generally, and specific products that currently are available.

Network Security

A **network** is defined as two or more devices that are connected for the purpose of sending, receiving, and sharing data, which is called network traffic. In order to connect to a network, a computer must have a **network interface,** which is a combination of hardware and software that allows the computer to interact with the network. To provide security for network traffic, data can be encrypted, which refers to a process of encoding the data so it cannot be accessed without authorization.

ENCRYPTING NETWORK TRAFFIC   Network traffic can be intercepted and possibly altered, redirected, or recorded. For example, if an **unencrypted,** or **plain text,** password or credit card number is transmitted over a network connection, it can be stolen. When the traffic is encrypted, it still is visible, but its content and purpose are masked.

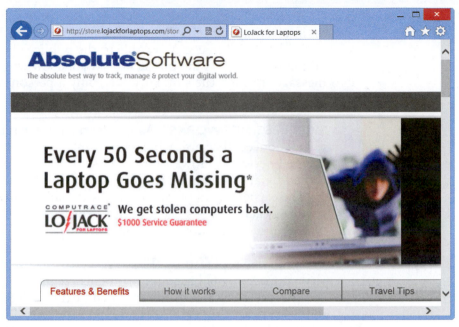

FIGURE 12-27   Many students use LoJack on their notebook computers. The product offers automated call-in identification and remote data erase capability.

©2012 Absolute Software Corporation

Figure 12-28 shows an example of encrypted traffic compared to plain text traffic. In the upper screen, the user has logged on using a password of *sad10e.* Notice that anyone who gains access to this data easily could learn the user's password. In the lower screen, the user has logged on to a secure site, such as an online bank account, and used a password, but the encryption process has made it impossible to decipher the keystrokes.

Two commonly used encryption techniques are private key encryption and public key encryption. **Private key encryption** is symmetric because a single key is used to encrypt and decrypt information. While this method is simple and fast, it poses a fundamental problem. To use symmetric encryption, both the sender and receiver must possess the same key beforehand, or it must be sent along with the message, which increases the risk of interception and disclosure.

In contrast, **public key encryption (PKE)** is asymmetric, because each user has a pair of keys: a public key and a private key. Public keys are used to encrypt messages. Users can share their public keys freely, while keeping their private keys tightly guarded. Any message encrypted with a user's public key can only be decrypted with that user's private key. This method is commonly used in secure online shopping systems.

the user logged on and entered a password of *sad10e,* which is visible in the unencrypted version

the user logged on to a secure site that uses encryption, and the password is unintelligible

FIGURE 12-28   The upper screen shows an example of unencrypted text, which contains a visible password. In the lower screen, the encrypted text cannot be read.

© Cengage Learning 2014

A recent Wikipedia article at wikipedia.org/wiki/Public-key_cryptography uses an interesting analogy. The article suggests that PKE is similar to a locked mailbox with a mail slot that is accessible to the public. The mailbox's location (street address) represents the public key. Anyone knowing the street address can drop a message through the slot. However, only a person with a key can open the box and read the message.

WIRELESS NETWORKS   As you learned in Chapter 10, wireless network security is a vital concern because wireless transmission is much more vulnerable than traffic on a wired network. However, if wireless traffic is encrypted, any data that is intercepted by an unintended recipient will be useless to the intruder.

The earliest form of wireless security, called **Wired Equivalent Privacy (WEP)**, required each wireless client to use a special, preshared key. Although this method was used by many home and small office networks, it provided relatively weak protection.

WEP was replaced by **Wi-Fi Protected Access (WPA)**, which offered major security improvements based on protocols created by the Wi-Fi Alliance. The most recent wireless security enhancement, called **WPA2**, further strengthens the level of wireless protection. WPA2 is an extension of WPA based on a full implementation of the **IEEE 802.11i** standard. According to the WiFi Alliance, the WPA2 standard became mandatory for all new devices seeking Wi-Fi certification after 2006. WPA2 is compatible with WPA, so companies easily can migrate to the new security standard.

PRIVATE NETWORKS   It is not always practical to secure all network traffic. Unfortunately, encrypting traffic increases the burden on a network, and can decrease network performance significantly. In situations where network speed is essential, such as a Web server linked to a database server, many firms use a private network to connect the computers. A **private network** is a dedicated connection, similar to a leased telephone line. Each computer on the private network must have a dedicated interface to the network, and no interface on the network should connect to any point outside the network. In this configuration, unencrypted traffic safely can be transmitted because it is not visible, and cannot be intercepted from outside the network.

VIRTUAL PRIVATE NETWORKS   Private networks work well with a limited number of computers, but if a company wants to establish secure connections for a larger group, it can create a virtual private network (VPN). A **virtual private network (VPN)** uses a public network, such as the Internet or a company intranet, to connect remote users securely. Instead of using a dedicated connection, a VPN allows remote clients to use a special key exchange that must be authenticated by the VPN. Once authentication is complete, a secure network connection, called a **tunnel**, is established between the client and the access point of the local intranet. All traffic is encrypted through the VPN tunnel, which provides an additional level of encryption and security. As more companies allow employees to work from home, a VPN can provide acceptable levels of security and reliability.

PORTS AND SERVICES   A **port**, which is identified by a number, is used to route incoming traffic to the correct application on a computer. In TCP/IP networks, such as the Internet, all traffic received by a computer contains a destination port. Because the destination port determines where the traffic will be routed, the computer sorts the traffic by port number, which is included in the transmitted data. An analogy might be a large apartment building with multiple mailboxes. Each mailbox has the same street address, but a different box number. Port security is critically important because an attacker could use an open port to gain access to the system.

A **service** is an application that monitors, or listens on, a particular port. For example, a typical e-mail application listens on port 25. Any traffic received by that port is routed to the e-mail application. Services play an important role in computer security, and they can be affected by port scans and denial-of-service attacks.

- Port scans. **Port scans** attempt to detect the services running on a computer by trying to connect to various ports and recording the ports on which a connection was accepted. For example, the result of an open port 25 would indicate that a mail server is running. Port scans can be used to draw an accurate map of a network, and pinpoint possible weaknesses.

- Denial of service. A **denial of service (DoS)** attack occurs when an attacking computer makes repeated requests to a service or services running on certain ports. Because the target computer has to respond to each request, it can become bogged down and fail to respond to legitimate requests. A much more devastating attack based on this method is called a **distributed denial of service (DDoS)** attack. This attack involves multiple attacking computers that can synchronize DOS attacks and immobilize a server, as shown in Figure 12-29. The seriousness of a DOS attack is evident in the National Cyber Alert System tip shown in Figure 12-30 on the next page.

FIREWALLS   A **firewall** is the main line of defense between a local network, or intranet, and the Internet. A firewall must have at least one network interface with the Internet, and at least one network interface with a local network or intranet. Firewall software examines all network traffic sent to and from each network interface. Preset rules establish certain conditions that determine whether the firewall will allow the traffic to pass. When a matching rule is found, the firewall automatically accepts, rejects, or drops the traffic. When a firewall rejects traffic, it sends a reply indicating that the traffic is not permissible. When a firewall drops traffic, no reply is sent. Firewalls can be configured to detect and respond to denial-of-service attacks, port scans, and other suspicious activity.

Figure 12-31 on the next page shows a basic set of firewall rules for a company that has a Web server and a mail server. In this example, the firewall would accept public Web server traffic only on ports 80 and 443, and public mail server traffic only on port 25. The firewall would allow private LAN traffic to any destination and port.

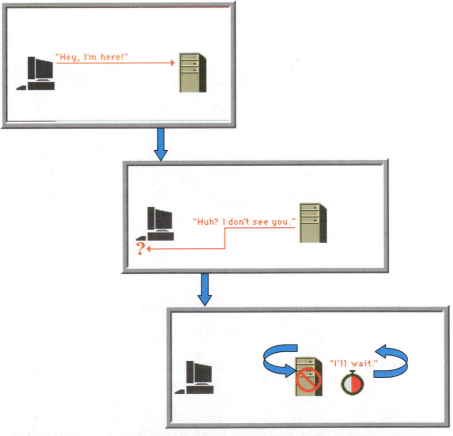

FIGURE 12-29   In a denial of service attack, an attacker sends numerous authentication requests with false return addresses. The server tries unsuccessfully to send authentication approval, and eventually is disabled by the flood of requests.

© Cengage Learning 2014

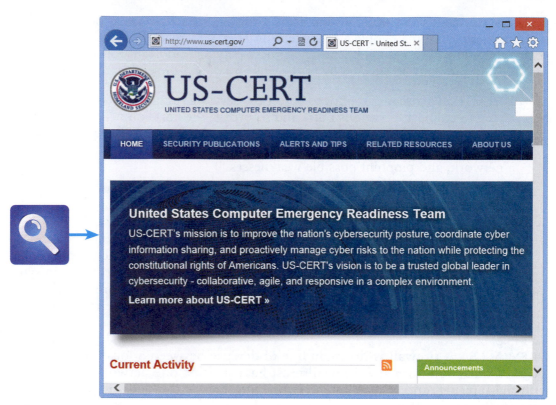

FIGURE 12-30 The United State Computer Emergency Readiness Team (US-CERT) is a key player in the battle against cybersecurity threats. Note the agency's difficult mission: to protect the nation while also protecting the constitutional rights of Americans.
Courtesy of US-CERT

RULE	INTERFACE	SOURCE	DESTINATION	PORT	ACTION
1	Public	Any	Web Server	80	Accept
2	Public	Any	Web Server	443	Accept
3	Public	Any	Web Server	Any	Reject
4	Public	Any	Mail Server	25	Accept
5	Public	Any	Mail Server	Any	Reject
6	Public	Any	Any	Any	Drop
7	Private	LAN	Any	Any	Accept

FIGURE 12-31 Examples of rules that determine whether the firewall will allow traffic to pass.
© Cengage Learning 2014

NETWORK INTRUSION DETECTION Suppose an intruder attempts to gain access to the system. Obviously, an intrusion alarm should be sounded when certain activity or known attack patterns are detected. A **network intrusion detection system (NIDS)** is like a burglar alarm that goes off when it detects a configuration violation. The NIDS also can alert the administrator when it detects suspicious network traffic patterns. A NIDS requires fine-tuning to detect the difference between legitimate network traffic and an attack. It is also important that a NIDS be placed on a switch or other network device that can monitor all network traffic. Although a NIDS requires some administrative overhead, it can be very helpful in documenting the efforts of attackers and analyzing network performance.

Application Security

In addition to securing the computer room and shielding network traffic, it is necessary to protect all server-based applications. To do so, you must analyze the application's functions, identify possible security concerns, and carefully study all available documentation. Application security requires an understanding of services, hardening, application permissions, input validation techniques, software patches and updates, and software logs.

SERVICES   In the network security section, you learned that a service is an application that monitors, or listens, on a particular port. You can determine which services are running by using a port scan utility. If a particular application is not needed, it should be disabled. This will improve system security, performance, and reliability. An unnecessary or improperly configured service could create a vulnerability called a **security hole**. For example, if a loosely configured FTP (File Transfer Protocol) service is available to a hacker, he or she might be able to upload destructive code to the server.

HARDENING   The **hardening** process makes a system more secure by removing unnecessary accounts, services, and features. Hardening is necessary because the default configuration of some software packages might create a vulnerability. For example, initial software settings might include relatively weak account permissions or file sharing controls. Hardening can be done manually or by using a configuration template, which speeds up the process in a large organization.

Hardening also includes additional protection such as antivirus and antispyware software. These programs can detect and remove **malware**, which is hostile software designed to infiltrate, damage, or deny service to a computer system. Malware includes worms, Trojan horses, keystroke loggers, and spyware, among others.

APPLICATION PERMISSIONS   Typically, an application is configured to be run only by users who have specific rights. For example, an **administrator account**, or **superuser account**, allows essentially unrestricted access. Other users might be allowed to enter data, but not to modify or delete existing data. To prevent unauthorized or destructive changes, the application should be configured so that nonprivileged users can access the program, but cannot make changes to built-in functions or configurations. **User rights**, also called **permissions**, are discussed in more detail in the file security section.

INPUT VALIDATION   As you learned in Chapter 8, when designing the user interface, input validation can safeguard data integrity and security. For example, if an application requires a number from *1* to *10*, what happens if an alphabetic character or the number *31* is entered? If the application is designed properly, it will respond with an appropriate error message. Chapter 8 also explained data entry and validation checks, which are important techniques that can improve data integrity and quality. Failure to validate input data can result in output errors, increased maintenance expense, and erratic system behavior.

PATCHES AND UPDATES   In an operational system, security holes or vulnerabilities might be discovered at any time. Patches can be used to repair these holes, reduce vulnerability, and update the system. Like any other new software, patches must be tested carefully. Before applying a patch, an effort should be made to determine the risks of *not* applying the patch, and the possibility that the patch might affect other areas of the system.

Many firms purchase software packages called **third-party software**. Patches released by third-party software vendors usually are safe, but any patch must be reviewed carefully before it is applied. Because researching and applying patches is time consuming and expensive, many software vendors offer an **automatic update service** that enables an application to contact the vendor's server and check for a needed patch or update. Depending on the configuration, available patches can be downloaded and installed without human intervention, or might require approval by IT managers. Although it is convenient, automatic updating carries substantial risks, and should be used only if changes can readily be undone if unexpected results or problems develop.

SOFTWARE LOGS   Operating systems and applications typically maintain a **log** that documents all events, including dates, times, and other specific information. Logs can be important in understanding past attacks and preventing future intrusions. For example, a pattern of login errors might reveal the details of an intrusion attempt. A log also can include system error messages, login histories, file manipulation, and other information that could help track down unauthorized use. Software logs should be monitored constantly to determine if misuse or wrongdoing has occurred. As explained in the network security section, a network intrusion detection system (NIDS) can alert a system administrator whenever suspicious events occur. Windows Event Viewer, shown in Figure 12-32, is an example of a built-in software log.

File Security

Computer configuration settings, users' personal information, and other sensitive data are stored in files. The safety and protection of these files is a vital element in any computer security program, and a systems analyst needs to consider the importance of encryption, or encoding files to make them unreadable by unauthorized users, and permissions, which can be assigned to individual users or to user groups.

ENCRYPTION   As you learned in the section on network security, **encryption** scrambles the contents of a file or document to protect it from unauthorized access.

FIGURE 12-32 Windows Event Viewer can log application usage, security settings, and system changes.

Screenshot used with permission from Microsoft.

All corporate data must be protected, but encryption is especially important for sensitive material such as personnel or financial records. You can encrypt data easily using the Professional editions of Windows 8 and Windows 7. In addition, Windows 8 offers a feature called BitLocker, which provides additional encryption options. To learn more about these terms, visit www.lockergnome.com and search for the term *efs*.

PERMISSIONS File security is based on establishing a set of permissions, which describe the rights a user has to a particular file or directory on a server. The most common permissions are read, write, and execute. Typical examples of permissions include the following:

- Read a file — The user can read the contents of the file.
- Write a file — The user can change the contents of the file.
- Execute a file — The user can run the file, if it is a program.
- Read a directory — The user can list the contents of the directory.
- Write a directory — The user can add and remove files in the directory.

When assigning file permissions, a system administrator should ensure that each user has only the minimum permissions necessary to perform his or her work — not more. In some firms, the system administrator has broad discretion in assigning these levels; in other companies, an appropriate level of management approval is required for any permissions above a standard user level. In any case, a well-documented and enforced permissions policy is necessary to promote file security and reduce system vulnerability.

USER GROUPS Individual users who need to collaborate and share files often request a higher level of permissions that would enable any of them to change file content. A better approach, from a system administrator's viewpoint, might be to create a user group, add specific users, and assign file permissions to the group, rather than to the individuals. Many firms use this approach because it allows a user's rights to be determined by his or her work responsibilities, rather than by job title or rank. If a person is transferred, he or she leaves certain groups and joins others that reflect current job duties.

User Security

User security involves the identification of system users and consideration of user-related security issues. Regardless of other security precautions and features, security ultimately depends on system users and their habits, practices, and willingness to support security goals. Unfortunately, many system break-ins begin with a user account that is compromised in some way. Typically, an intruder accesses the system using the compromised account, and may attempt a **privilege escalation attack**, which is an unauthorized attempt to increase permission levels.

User security requires identity management, comprehensive password protection, defenses against social engineering, an effective means of overcoming user resistance, and consideration of new technologies. These topics are discussed in the following sections.

IDENTITY MANAGEMENT **Identity management** refers to controls and procedures necessary to identify legitimate users and system components. An identity management strategy must balance technology, security, privacy, cost, and user productivity. Identity management is an evolving technology that is being pursued intensively by corporations, IT associations, and governments.

The Burton Group, a leading IT security consultant, has described identity management as a "set of electronic records that represent ... people, machines, devices, applications, and services." This definition suggests that not just users, but also each component in a system, must have a verifiable identity that is based on unique characteristics. For example, user authentication might be based on a combination of a password, a Social Security number, an employee number, a job title, and a physical location.

Because of the devastating consequences of intrusion, IT managers are giving top priority to identity management strategies and solutions.

PASSWORD PROTECTION   As the section on physical security points out, a secure system must have a password policy that requires minimum length, complexity, and a limit on invalid login attempts. Although passwords are a key element in any security program, users often choose passwords that are easy to recall, and they sometimes resent having to remember complex passwords. Even so, IT managers should insist on passwords that have a minimum length, require a combination of case-sensitive letters and numbers, and must be changed periodically. Unfortunately, any password can be compromised if a user writes it down and stores it in an easily accessible location such as a desk, a bulletin board, or under the keyboard.

Several years ago, a hacker made headlines by gaining access to the e-mail account of a political candidate. The intruder signed on as the candidate, requested a new password, guessed the answers to the security questions, and was able to enter the account. These actions were totally illegal, and constituted a serious felony under federal law.

SOCIAL ENGINEERING   Even if users are protecting and securing their passwords, an intruder might attempt to gain unauthorized access to a system using a tactic called **social engineering**. In a social engineering attack, an intruder uses social interaction to gain access to a computer system. For example, the intruder might pretend to be a new employee, an outside technician, or a journalist. Through a series of questions, the intruder tries to obtain the information that he or she needs to compromise the system. A common ploy is for the attacker to contact several people in the same organization, and use some information from one source to gain credibility and entry to another source.

An intruder also might contact a service desk and say: "Hi. This is Anna Dressler from accounting. I seem to have forgotten my password. Could you give me a new one?" Although this request might be legitimate, it also might be an attacker trying to access the system. A password never should be given based solely on this telephone call. The user should be required to provide further information to validate his or her identity, such as a Social Security number, employee ID, telephone extension, and company e-mail address.

One highly publicized form of social engineering is called **pretexting**, which is a method of obtaining personal information under false pretenses. Pretexting, which is described in the Federal Trade Commission statement shown in Figure 12-33, is a very real threat. The best way to combat social engineering attacks is with employee education, more training, and a high level of awareness during day-to-day operations.

USER RESISTANCE   Many users, including some senior managers, dislike tight security measures because they can be inconvenient and time consuming. Systems analysts should remind users that the company owes the best possible security to its customers, who have entrusted personal information to the firm; to its employees, who also have personal information stored in company files; and to its shareholders, who expect the company to have a suitable, effective, and comprehensive security program that will safeguard company assets and resources. When users understand this overall commitment to security and feel that they are part of it, they are more

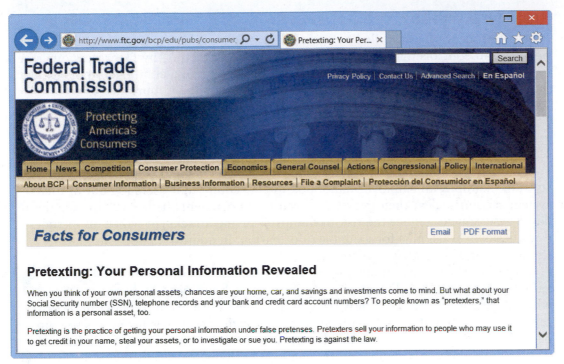

FIGURE 12-33 As the Federal Trade Commission points out, pretexting involves obtaining your personal information under false pretenses.

Courtesy of the Federal Trade Commission

likely to choose better passwords, be more alert to security issues, and contribute to the overall success of the company's security program.

NEW TECHNOLOGIES   In addition to traditional measures and biometric devices, technology can enhance security and prevent unauthorized access. For example, the **security token** shown in Figure 12-34 is a physical device that authenticates a legitimate user. Some firms provide employees with security tokens that generate a numeric validation code, which the employee enters in addition to his or her normal password.

Unfortunately, new technology sometimes creates new risks. For example, a powerful search application can scan all the files, documents, e-mails, chats, and stored Web pages on a user's computer. Although this might provide a convenient way for users to locate and retrieve their data, it also can make it easier for an intruder to obtain private information, especially in a multiuser environment, because the program can recall and display almost anything stored on the computer. Also, if an intruder uses the term *password* in a search, the program might be able to find password reminders that are stored anywhere on the computer. To increase privacy for multiuser computers, each user should have a separate account, with individual usernames and passwords.

Business and personal users also should use caution when they consider cloud-based storage and services. In this environment, where the technology changes rapidly, the best bet is to work with well-established vendors, who can provide significant cloud security experience and safeguards.

FIGURE 12-34 Security tokens, which come in various forms, can provide an additional level of security.

© Shutterstock/Lim Yong Hian

Procedural Security

Procedural security, also called **operational security**, is concerned with managerial policies and controls that ensure secure operations. In fact, many IT professionals believe that security depends more on managerial issues than technology. Management must work to establish a corporate culture that stresses the importance of security to the firm and its people. Procedural security defines how particular tasks are to be performed, from large-scale data backups to everyday tasks such as storing e-mails or forms. Other procedures might spell out how to update firewall software or how security personnel should treat suspected attackers.

All employees should understand that they have a personal responsibility for security. For example, an employee handbook might require that users log out of their system accounts, clear their desks, and secure all documents before leaving for the day. These policies reduce the risk of **dumpster diving** attacks, in which an intruder raids desks or trash bins for valuable information. In addition, paper shredders should be used to destroy sensitive documents.

Procedural security also includes safeguarding certain procedures that would be valuable to an attacker. The most common approach is a *need-to-know* concept, where access is limited to employees who need the information to perform security-related tasks. Many firms also apply a set of classification levels for access to company documents. For example, highly sensitive technical documents might be available only to the IT support team, while user-related materials would be available to most company employees. If classification levels are used, they should be identified clearly and enforced consistently.

CASE IN POINT 12.4: CHAIN LINK CONSULTING, INC.

Chain Link Consulting is an IT consulting firm that specializes in system security issues. The company's president has asked you to help her put together a presentation to a group of potential clients at a trade show meeting next month. First, she wants you to review system security issues, considering all six security levels. Then she wants you to come up with a list of ways that Chain Link could test a client's security practices, in order to get a real-world assessment of vulnerability.

To make matters more interesting, she told you it was OK to be creative in your recommendations, but not to propose any action that would be illegal or unethical. For example, it would be OK to pose as a job applicant with false references to see if they were being checked, but it would not be appropriate to pick a lock and enter the computer room.

Your report is due tomorrow. What will you suggest?

Procedural security must be supported by upper management and fully explained to all employees. The organization must provide training to explain the procedures and issue reminders from time to time that will make security issues a priority.

BACKUP AND RECOVERY

Every system must provide for data backup and recovery. **Backup** refers to copying data at prescribed intervals, or continuously. **Recovery** involves restoring the data and restarting the system after an interruption. An overall backup and recovery plan that prepares for a potential disaster is called a **disaster recovery plan**.

The tragic events of September 11, 2001, and increased concern about global terrorism have led many companies to upgrade their backup and disaster recovery plans.

Heightened focus on disaster recovery has spawned a whole new industry, which includes new tools and strategies. Many IT professionals feel that terrorism concerns have raised security awareness throughout the corporate world. Although they are separate topics, backup and disaster recovery issues usually are intertwined. The following sections cover these topics in more detail.

Backup Policies

The cornerstone of business data protection is a **backup policy**, which contains detailed instructions and procedures. An effective backup policy can help a firm continue business operations and survive a catastrophe. The backup policy should specify backup media, backup types, and retention periods.

BACKUP MEDIA   Backup media can include tape, hard drives, optical storage, and online storage. Physical backups must be carefully identified and stored in a secure location. **Offsiting** refers to the practice of storing backup media away from the main business location, in order to mitigate the risk of a catastrophic disaster such as a flood, fire, or earthquake. Even if the operating system includes a backup utility, many system administrators prefer to use specialized third-party software that offers more options and better controls for large-scale operations.

In addition to on-site data storage, cloud-based storage is growing rapidly. Many companies use online backup and retrieval services offered by vendors such as Rocky Mountain Software and IBM. For a small- or medium-sized firm, this option can be cost effective and reliable.

BACKUP TYPES   Backups can be full, differential, incremental, or continuous. A **full backup** is a complete backup of every file on the system. Frequent full backups are time consuming and redundant if most files are unchanged since the last full backup. Instead of performing a full backup, another option is to perform a **differential backup**, which is faster because it backs up *only* the files that are new or changed since the last full backup. To restore the data to its original state, you restore the last full backup, and then restore the last differential backup. Many IT managers believe that a combination of full and differential backups is the best option because it uses the least amount of storage space and is simple.

The fastest method, called an **incremental backup**, only includes recent files that never have been backed up by any method. This approach, however, requires multiple steps to restore the data — one for each incremental backup.

Most large systems use **continuous backup**, which is a real-time streaming method that records all system activity as it occurs. This method requires expensive hardware, software, and substantial network capacity. However, system restoration is rapid and effective because data is being captured in real time, as it occurs. Continuous backup often uses a **RAID (redundant array of independent disks)** system that mirrors the data. RAID systems are called **fault tolerant** because a failure of any one disk does not disable the system. Compared to one large drive, a RAID design offers better performance, greater capacity, and improved reliability. When installed on a server, a RAID array of multiple drives appears to the computer as a single logical drive. Figure 12-35 on the next page shows a comparison of various backup methods.

RETENTION PERIODS   Backups are stored for a specific **retention period** after which they are either destroyed or the backup media is reused. Retention periods can be a specific number of months or years, depending on legal requirements and company policy. Stored media must be secured, protected, and inventoried periodically.

Comparison of Backup Methods

BACKUP TYPE	CHARACTERISTICS	PROS AND CONS	TYPICAL FREQUENCY
Full	Backs up all files.	Slowest backup time and requires the most storage space. Rapid recovery because all files are restored in a single step.	Monthly or weekly.
Differential	Only backs up files that are new or changed since the last full backup.	Faster than a full backup and requires less storage space. All data can be restored in just two steps by using the last full backup and the last differential backup.	Weekly or daily.
Incremental	Only backs up files that are new or changed since the last backup of any kind.	Fastest backup and requires the least storage space because it only saves files that have never been backed up. However, requires many restore steps — one for each incremental backup.	Daily or more often.
Continuous	Real-time, streaming method that records all system activity.	Very expensive hardware, software, and network capacity. Recovery is very fast because system can be restored to just before an interruption.	Usually only used by large firms and network-based systems.

FIGURE 12-35   Comparison of full, differential, incremental, and continuous backup methods.
© Cengage Learning 2014

Business Continuity Issues

Global concern about terrorism has raised awareness levels and increased top management support for a business continuity strategy in the event of an emergency. A disaster recovery plan describes actions to be taken, specifies key individuals and rescue authorities to be notified, and spells out the role of employees in evacuation, mitigation, and recovery efforts. The disaster recovery plan should be accompanied by a **test plan**, which can simulate various levels of emergencies and record the responses, which can be analyzed and improved as necessary.

After personnel are safe, damage to company assets should be mitigated. The plan might require shutting down systems to prevent further data loss, or moving physical assets to a secure location. Afterward, the plan should focus on resuming business operations, including the salvaging or replacement of equipment and the recovery of backup data. The main objective of a disaster recovery plan is to restore business operations to pre-disaster levels.

Disaster recovery plans are often part of a larger **business continuity plan (BCP)**, which goes beyond a recovery plan, and defines how critical business functions can continue in the event of a major disruption. Some BCPs specify the use of a hot site. A **hot site** is an alternate IT location, anywhere in the world, that can support critical systems in the event of a power outage, system crash, or physical catastrophe. A hot site requires **data replication**, which means that any transaction on the primary system must be mirrored on the hot site. If the primary system becomes unavailable, the hot site will have the latest data and can function seamlessly, with no downtime.

Although hot sites are attractive backup solutions, they are very expensive. However, a hot site provides the best insurance against major business interruptions. In addition to hot sites, business insurance can be important in a worst-case scenario. Although expensive, business insurance can offset the financial impact of system failure and business interruption.

SYSTEM OBSOLESCENCE

At some point, every system becomes obsolete. For example, you might not remember punched cards, but they represented the cutting edge of data management back in the 1960s. Data was stored by punching holes at various positions, and was retrieved by machines that could sense the presence or absence of a punched hole. Most full-size cards stored only 80 characters, or bytes, so more than 12,000 cards would be needed to store a megabyte. Punched cards were even used as checks and utility bills. Today, this technology is obsolete.

Constantly changing technology means that every system has a limited economic life span. Analysts and managers can anticipate system obsolescence in several ways and it never should come as a complete surprise.

A system becomes obsolete when it no longer supports user needs, or when the platform becomes outmoded. The most common reason for discontinuing a system is that it has reached the end of its economically useful life, as indicated by the following signs:

- The system's maintenance history indicates that adaptive and corrective maintenance are increasing steadily.

- Operational costs or execution times are increasing rapidly, and routine perfective maintenance does not reverse or slow the trend.

- A software package is available that provides the same or additional services faster, better, and less expensively than the current system.

- New technology offers a way to perform the same or additional functions more efficiently.

- Maintenance changes or additions are difficult and expensive to perform.

- Users request significant new features to support business requirements.

Systems operation and support continue until a replacement system is installed. Toward the end of a system's operational life, users are unlikely to submit new requests for adaptive maintenance because they are looking forward to the new release. Similarly, the IT staff usually does not perform much perfective or preventive maintenance because the system will not be around long enough to justify the cost. A system in its final stages requires corrective maintenance only to keep the system operational.

User satisfaction typically determines the life span of a system. The critical success factor for any system is whether or not it helps users achieve their operational and business goals. As an IT staff member, you should expect to receive input from users and managers throughout the systems development process. You should investigate and document all negative feedback because it can be the first signal of system obsolescence.

At some point in a system's operational life, maintenance costs start to increase, users begin to ask for more features and capability, new systems requests are submitted, and the SDLC begins again.

FUTURE CHALLENGES AND OPPORTUNITIES

The only thing that is certain about the future is continuous change. Change itself is neither good nor bad — the real issue is how people and companies deal with the challenges and opportunities that are bound to occur.

No one would start a complex journey without a map and a plan. To navigate the future of information technology, companies require strategic plans, which were discussed in Chapter 2. An individual also needs a plan to reach to a specific goal or destination. This section discusses trends and predictions that will affect all IT professionals. To prepare for the challenges ahead, individuals will need to plan and develop their knowledge, skills, and credentials.

Trends and Predictions

Navigating an IT career can be compared to sailing a small boat in difficult seas. Even if you are a very good captain, you will be subjected to forces and circumstances that are beyond your control. What you *can* do is to understand these forces and try to prepare for them. Figure 12-36 describes some winds of change that include globalization, technology integration, cloud computing, and the workplace of the future.

In addition to the trends described in Figure 12-36, most firms will face economic, social, and political uncertainty. Many IT experts believe that in this environment, the top priorities will be the safety and security of corporate operations, environmental issues, and bottom-line TCO. Gartner Inc. is a leading consulting firm that is well-known for its predictions. Here are some examples of what Gartner sees on its radar for the next few years:

- The financial impact of cybercrime will grow at a compound rate of 10 percent per year.

- Mobile application development using smartphones and tablets will outnumber PC-based software by a four-to-one ratio.

- The prices for most cloud services will include a global energy surcharge.

- One of every two e-mail users will rely primarily on a browser, tablet or mobile client, instead of a desktop client.

- Half of all companies will make proof of independent security testing a precondition for using any type of cloud service.

- Twenty percent of Asia-sourced hardware consumed in the U.S. will shift to the Americas.

Gartner also predicted that large enterprises will require suppliers to certify their green credentials and sourcing policies. One issue might relate to the explosion of data storage and server farms, such as the one shown in Figure 12-37 on page 546. For example, in a 2011 press release, Google stated that it continuously uses enough electricity to power 200,000 homes, but the company also said that it makes the planet greener because people save energy by performing tasks online. Google also predicted that by 2013, more than 30 percent of its energy needs would be met with renewable sources.

Strategic Planning for IT Professionals

An IT professional should think of himself or herself as a business corporation that has certain assets, potential liabilities, and specific goals. Individuals, like companies, must have a strategic plan. The starting point is to formulate an answer to the following career planning question: What do I want to be doing three, five, or ten years from now?

TREND	DESCRIPTION	IMPACT ON IT GENERALLY	IMPACT ON FUTURE SYSTEMS ANALYSTS
Globalization	New kinds of corporations will be globally integrated, driven by the Internet, and free of traditional trade barriers.	Language skills will be extremely important. Technology will open new opportunities for developing countries to compete more effectively. Knowledge workers will communicate and collaborate across borders and boundaries.	Systems analysts will be directly affected by global trends. They will probably work for more firms in their careers, be exposed to more information, need more technical skills, and see greater change than at any time in history.
Technology Integration	Powered by an enormous increase in computing power, new IT models will include networks with smart, interconnected devices such as communication systems, automobiles, entertainment, highway infrastructure, and power grids.	New technology will drive major changes in how personal and business services are provided. Firms will compete in a global marketplace that will reward innovation, creativity, and positive societal outcomes.	The systems analyst will need a mix of business savvy and technical skills. He or she will have a unique opportunity to work at the intersection of business operations and IT. Synergy between technology growth and globalization will create jobs and opportunities for people with the right skills.
Cloud Computing	Cloud computing is a new model for delivering business and IT services. It will have a profound impact on business strategies, including product innovation, marketing, customer relationships, and social media.	The full potential of cloud computing will be realized by firms that can integrate cloud-based infrastructure, services, servers, data access, and a secure environment. Creativity and innovation will be rewarded, and competition will be intense.	Like any new technology, systems development for cloud-based applications will be a challenge for some, and an opportunity for others. Regardless of the development method or platform, an analyst will need business savvy and technical know-how to help an organization take full advantage of the cloud.
The Workplace: Critical Thinking Creativity Adaptability	In the face of worldwide competition and enormous technology change, firms will stress innovation, vision, and the ability to adapt rapidly. The ability to think critically will be vital.	Successful IT workers must be able to innovate, analyze, communicate effectively, and "think outside the box." The winners will be those who can adapt to change and embrace new technology and new ways of doing business.	Students preparing for the workplace of tomorrow will need a strong skill set. Systems analysts will be expected to bring communications, modeling, problem-solving, decision-making, and critical thinking skills to the workplace — and to be aware of ethical issues that might affect them.

FIGURE 12-36 Major trends and their impact on IT generally and on future systems analysts.

© Cengage Learning 2014

Working backward from your long-term goals, you can develop intermediate milestones and begin to manage your career just as you would manage an IT project. You can even use the project management tools described in Chapter 3 to construct a Gantt chart or a PERT/CPM chart using months (or years) as time units. Once the plan is developed, you would monitor it regularly to see whether you were still on schedule.

FIGURE 12-37 The rapid growth of data centers and server farms has increased energy consumption significantly and raised environmental concerns.
© Shutterstock/Oleksiy Mark

Planning a career is not unlike planting a tree that takes several years to reach a certain height. Once you know the desired height and the annual growth rate, you can determine when you must plant the tree. Similarly, if you want to possess a particular educational credential two years from now, and the credential takes two years to earn, then you need to start on it immediately if you want to adhere to your planned track.

IT Credentials and Certification

In recent years, technical credentials and certification have become extremely important to IT employers and employees. In a broad sense, **credentials** include formal degrees, diplomas, or certificates granted by learning institutions to show that a certain level of education has been achieved successfully. The term **certification** also has a special meaning that relates to specific hardware and software skills that can be measured and verified by examination. For example, a person might have a two- or four-year degree in Information Systems and possess a CompTIA A+ certification, which attests to the person's computer hardware knowledge and skills. Many IT industry leaders offer certification, including Microsoft, Cisco, Novell, Oracle, and Sun Microsystems.

Critical Thinking Skills

In additional to technical skills, IT professionals must have **soft skills**, such as communications, interpersonal, and perceptive abilities. IT professionals also need critical thinking skills to succeed in the workplace.

Our digital society is inundated with massive amounts of data. Data mining, clever algorithms, and technical innovation are important, but the most valuable asset is an employee who can solve problems. The IT community has become interested in **critical thinking skills** that can help a person find, organize, analyze, and use the information he or she needs on the job. Many employers now seek critical thinkers who can locate data, identify important facts, and apply their knowledge in real-world decisions.

Many training courses exist for technical skills, but how do you develop your critical thinking skills? The best answer is to practice by performing tasks that resemble actual workplace tasks. As a future systems analyst, you already have an advantage — you know how to develop models, organize data, and recognize patterns. You can also complete the *Critical Thinking Challenge* exercises at the end of each chapter. These exercises require critical thinking skills, and can help you learn, practice, and apply skills that you can take to the workplace.

IT professionals also should be aware that the **Educational Testing Service (ETS)** provides assessment and certification of critical thinking skills, as shown in Figure 12-38. The scenario-based iSkills® test measures perception, organization, analysis, problem solving, and decision making. Just as with hardware or software skills, formal certification is valuable in the job marketplace, but the greatest value is in learning the skills and using them to achieve your career goals.

FIGURE 12-38   Employers like to hire people who can think logically and effectively. The Educational Testing Service (ETS) measures critical thinking skills using an interactive test with realistic scenarios, and will provide certificates to students who are proficient.

© 2012 by Educational Testing Service

Many instructors find that individual and team-based exercises can strengthen critical thinking skills. Examples include games, puzzles, brainstorming, creative problem-solving, decision tables, working with ethical questions, Boolean logic, Venn diagrams, and using cause-and-effect tools such as Pareto charts, X-Y diagrams, and fishbone diagrams, all of which can be found in this textbook.

A QUESTION OF ETHICS

© faberfoto_it/iStockphoto

Jamie just completed a routine security audit on the company's information systems, and she found several areas of vulnerability. For example, file permissions have not been updated in some time, no comprehensive password policy exists, and network traffic is not fully encrypted. She noted these areas, among others, in a report to Tamika, her supervisor. The report included specific recommendations to fix the problems.

Tamika responded by saying that budgets are tight right now, and she could not approve Jamie's requests to resolve these issues. As an IT professional, Jamie is very uncomfortable with the risk level, but she has been unable to sway Tamika. When Jamie discussed the situation with her friend, Ethan, he said, "Why worry about it? If it's good enough for Tamika, it should be good enough for you."

What do you think of Ethan's advice, and why? Is this an ethical question? If Jamie still is uncomfortable, what are her options?

CHAPTER SUMMARY

Systems support and security cover the period from the implementation of an information system until the system no longer is used. A systems analyst's primary involvement with an operational system is to manage and solve user support requests.

Corrective maintenance includes changes to correct errors. Adaptive maintenance satisfies new systems requirements, and perfective maintenance makes the system more efficient. Adaptive and perfective maintenance changes often are called enhancements. Preventive maintenance is performed to avoid future problems.

The typical maintenance process resembles a miniature version of the systems development life cycle. A systems request for maintenance work is submitted and evaluated. If it is accepted, the request is prioritized and scheduled for the IT group. The maintenance team then follows a logical progression of investigation, analysis, design, development, testing, and implementation.

Corrective maintenance projects occur when a user or an IT staff member reports a problem. Standard maintenance procedures usually are followed for relatively minor errors, but work often begins immediately when users report significant errors.

In contrast to corrective maintenance, adaptive, perfective, and preventive maintenance projects always follow the organization's standard maintenance procedures. Adaptive maintenance projects occur in response to user requests for improvements to meet changes in the business or operating environments. The IT staff usually initiates perfective maintenance projects to improve performance or maintainability. Automated program restructuring and reengineering are forms of perfective maintenance. In order to avoid future problems, IT staff perform preventive maintenance, which involves analysis of areas where trouble is likely to occur.

A maintenance team consists of one or more systems analysts and programmers. Systems analysts need the same talents and abilities for maintenance work as they use when developing a new system. Many IT departments are organized into separate new development and maintenance groups where staff members are rotated from one group to the other.

Configuration management is necessary to handle maintenance requests, to manage different versions of the information system, and to distribute documentation changes. Maintenance changes can be implemented as they are completed or a release methodology can be used in which all noncritical maintenance changes are collected and implemented simultaneously. A release methodology usually is cost effective and advantageous for users because they do not have to work with a constantly changing system. Systems analysts use functional, allocated, and product baselines as formal reference points to measure system characteristics at a specific time.

System performance measurements include response time, bandwidth, throughput, and turnaround time. Capacity management uses those measurements to forecast what is needed to provide future levels of service and support. Also, CASE tools that include system evaluation and maintenance features can be used during the systems operation, security, and support phase.

Security is a vital part of every computer system. System security is dependent upon a comprehensive security policy that defines how organizational assets are to be protected and how attacks are to be responded to.

Risk management creates a workable security policy by identifying, analyzing, anticipating, and reducing risks to an acceptable level. Because information systems face a wide array of threats and attacks, six separate but interrelated security levels should be analyzed: physical security, network security, application security, file security, user security, and procedural security. Physical security concerns the physical environment, including critical equipment located in a computer room, as well as safeguards for servers and desktops throughout the company. Network security involves encryption techniques, as well as private networks and other protective measures, especially where wireless transmissions are concerned. Application security requires an understanding of services, hardening, application permissions, input validation techniques, software patches and updates, and software logs. File security involves the use of encryption and permissions, which can be assigned to individual users or to user groups. User security involves identity management techniques, a comprehensive password protection policy, an awareness of social engineering risks, and an effective means of overcoming user resistance. Procedural security involves managerial controls and policies that ensure secure operations.

Data backup and recovery issues include backup media, backup schedules, and retention periods, as well as backup designs such as RAID and Web-based backups.

All information systems eventually become obsolete. The end of a system's economic life usually is signaled by rapidly increasing maintenance or operating costs, the availability of new software or hardware, or new requirements that cannot be achieved easily by the existing system. When a certain point is reached, an information system must be replaced, and the entire systems development life cycle begins again.

Many IT experts predict intense competition in the future, along with economic, political, and social uncertainty. Facing these challenges, top IT priorities will be the safety and security of corporate operations, environmental concerns, and bottom-line TCO.

An IT professional should have a strategic career plan that includes long-term goals and intermediate milestones. An important element of a personal strategic plan is the acquisition of IT credentials and certifications that document specific knowledge and skills. Many IT industry leaders offer certification. In addition to technical ability, other skills, such as critical thinking skills, also are extremely valuable.

Key Terms

acceptance 526

adaptive maintenance 509

administrator account 535

allocated baseline 518

applications programmer 513

archived 517

asset 524

attack 526

automatic update service 535

availability 524

avoidance 526

backup 540

backup media 541

backup policy 541

bandwidth 520

baseline 518

benchmark testing 520

biometric scanning systems 528

BIOS-level password 529

boot-level password 529

business continuity plan (BCP) 542

capacity planning 521

certification 546

change control (CC) 516

CIA triangle 524

confidentiality 524

configuration management (CM) 516

continuous backup 541

corrective maintenance 509

credentials 546

critical risk 525

critical thinking skills 546

database programmer 514

data replication 542

denial of service (DOS) 533

differential backup 541

disaster recovery plan 540

distributed denial of service (DDOS) 533

dumpster diving 540

Educational Testing Service (ETS) 546

encryption 536

enhancement 511

exploit 525

fault management 519

fault tolerant 541

firewall 533

full backup 541

functional baseline 518

Gbps (gigabits per second) 520

hardening 535

help desk 506

hot site 542

identity management 537

IEEE 802.11i 532

incremental backup 541

information center (IC) 506

integrity 524

Kbps (kilobits per second) 520

keystroke logger 528

log 536

maintenance activities 508

maintenance expenses 508

maintenance release 517

maintenance release methodology 517

maintenance team 512

malware 535

Mbps (megabits per second) 520

metrics 520

mitigation 526

network 531

network interface 531

network intrusion detection system (NIDS) 534

offsiting 541

operational costs 508

operational security 540

patch 510

perfective maintenance 509

permissions 535

plain text 531

port 532

port scan 533

power-on password 529

pretexting 538

preventive maintenance 531

private key encryption 532

private network 532

privilege escalation attack 537

procedural security 540

product baseline 518

programmer/analyst 514

public key encryption (PKE) 531

RAID (redundant array of independent disks) 541

recovery 540

remote control software 507

response time 520

retention period 541

risk 525

risk assessment 524

risk control 524

risk identification 524

risk management 524

security 524

security hole 535

security policy 524

security token 539

service 533

service desk 506

service packs 517

social engineering 538

soft skills 546

software reengineering 511

superuser account 535

system administrator 513

systems programmer 513

tamper-evident cases 529

test plan 542

third-party software 535

threat 525

throughput 520

transference 526

tunnel 532

turnaround time 521

unencrypted 531

uninterruptible power supply (UPS) 529

Universal Security Slot (USS) 530

user rights 535

user training package 506

version control 517

virtual private network (VPN) 532

vulnerability 525

what-if analysis 522

Wi-Fi Protected Access (WPA) 532

Wired Equivalent Privacy (WEP) 532

WPA2 532

Chapter Exercises

Questions

1. Describe four types of system maintenance and provide two examples of each type.
2. As an IT manager, would you assign newly hired systems analysts to maintenance projects? Why or why not?
3. What is configuration management and why is it important?
4. Define the term *what-if analysis*. How could you use a spreadsheet in capacity planning?
5. What is a release methodology? Why is version control important?
6. Define the following terms: *response time*, *bandwidth*, *throughput*, and *turnaround time*. How are the terms related?
7. What are some key issues that you must address when considering data backup and recovery?
8. Explain the concept of risk management, including risk identification, assessment, and control.
9. What are the six security levels? Provide examples of threat categories, attacker profiles, and types of attacks.
10. Provide an example of technical obsolescence, and explain how it can be a threat to an information system.

Discussion Topics

1. Assume that your company uses a release methodology for its sales system. The current version is 5.5. Decide whether each of the following changes would justify a version 6.0 release, or be included in a version 5.6 update: (a) Add a new report, (b) add a Web interface, (c) add data validation checks, (d) add an interface to the marketing system, and (e) change the user interface.
2. The four types of IT system maintenance also apply to other industries. Suppose you were in charge of aircraft maintenance for a small airline. What would be a specific example of each type of maintenance?
3. An IT manager assigns programmers and systems analysts to maintenance projects if they have less than two years of experience or if they received an average or lower rating in their last performance evaluation. Do you agree with this practice?
4. What are the most important IT security issues facing companies today? Have these changed in the last five years, and will they continue to change? How should companies prepare themselves for security threats and problems in the future?

Projects

1. Using the Internet, locate a software package designed to automate version control. List the key features and describe your findings in a brief memo.
2. Develop a process for managing change requests and design a form to handle a generic change request. The process should include a contingency plan for changes that must be resolved immediately.
3. Visit the IT department at your school or at a local company and find out whether performance measurements are used. Write a brief report describing your findings.
4. Explain how to use the Goal Seek feature in Microsoft Excel, and create a worksheet that demonstrates this feature.

Apply Your Knowledge

This section contains four mini-cases. Each case describes a situation, explains your role, and requires you to apply what you learned in the chapter.

1 Floor Candy

Floor Candy is a small firm that manufactures high-quality rugs and carpets. Using special software, the company can translate a customer sketch into an attractive custom design. Three years ago, the IT staff developed a Web-based order system. The system has performed well, and most maintenance has involved correcting minor errors. Now the company would like to add more features, including menu-driven design tools, and a more customer-friendly interface.

Tasks

1. What types of maintenance has the IT staff performed? What types of maintenance will they perform if new features are added?
2. If new features are added, what methodology should the IT staff use to add the functions and enhancements?
3. What IT security measures should the firm adopt? Prepare a security checklist, and be sure to consider all six security levels.
4. Even though the new system is only three years old, the marketplace changes constantly. In three more years, should Floor Candy consider replacing the new system? What factors and information should guide that decision?

2 Paperback Press

Paperback Press specializes in reprinting classic literature. Three years ago, the company implemented a new system to track inventory and signal when books need to be reprinted. The new system was well received by users, and inventory problems have decreased significantly. Since the inventory system became operational, however, users have requested increased functionality and changes in screen forms and reports. You have been called in as a consultant to help the company make some decisions about system maintenance.

Tasks

1. Should Paperback Press have a specific process to manage future changes and enhancements? What should it be?
2. If new features are added, what methodology should the IT staff use to add functions and enhancements?
3. Suppose that you had to assign specific IT staff members to maintain the inventory control system. How would you accomplish the task? Describe your strategy in a brief memo.
4. What should Paperback Press watch for to detect possible obsolescence in the future? Develop a checklist with specific examples that management could use.

3   Budget Travel

Budget Travel provides business travel arrangements through 12 metropolitan offices. A key selling point is the firm's client management database, which includes preferences such as airline seating choices, favorite rental cars, and hotel options. Budget Travel purchased the client management software as an off-the-shelf vendor package and modified the program to meet the company's needs. The package has been operational for one year and has performed well. Budget Travel now wants to expand its operation by adding six more locations. Management has asked you to help the company plan what will be needed in IT support for the business expansion.

Tasks

1. What capacity planning issues should the company consider?
2. What performance and workload measurement issues should the company consider at this time?
3. Should the company establish a system baseline before the integration of the six new sites? Explain your answer.
4. As an IT consultant, you should learn as much as you can about the client's business, including the impact of the Internet on the travel agency business. Research this issue online, and decide what strengths, weaknesses, opportunities, and threats exist for Budget Travel.

4   Sherwood Associates

Sherwood Associates is an IT consulting firm that develops new systems and maintains older systems for its clients. Sherwood recently was hired to address security concerns regarding an existing system that was developed by another firm. The client is concerned about the security of customer information. They recently terminated several employees for poor performance, and they are worried that confidential data might have been compromised. Also, after an extensive audit, several laptops seem to be missing.

Tasks

1. What IT security measures should the firm adopt? Prepare a security checklist, and be sure to consider all six security levels.
2. What physical security measures can be implemented to safeguard equipment?
3. How would you suggest that mobile devices be secured?
4. How can the firm keep its data secure?

Case Studies

Each chapter includes a Chapter Case, a Continuing Case, a Capstone Case, and an Online Case Simulation. You can learn more about the Online Case Simulation in the MIS CourseMate Features section.

Chapter Case: Best of the Best! (BoB)

Best of the Best! uses the name BoB in its advertising. As the firm's slogan points out, the quality is the same, no matter how you look at it. BoB imports and sells gourmet coffees, cheeses, and specialty foods from around the world. BoB operates 12 retail stores in large malls, and also sells to online customers.

Background

About a month ago, BoB implemented a new point-of-sale (POS) system at all locations. Using a client/server design, the workstations in the firm's 12 retail stores are networked to a server at the main office. Sales reps in the stores use the system to record sales transactions, manage customer accounts, and to print various daily, weekly, and monthly reports.

When the new sales system was installed, the IT development team conducted extensive training for the sales staff, and set up a support desk. The IT team also prepared a user manual and distributed copies to all sales and office staff.

Store managers have reported that sales-people do not like the new system and find it very confusing. When an IT support person visited the stores to investigate the problem, she discovered that the new people were having problems with the interface, and could not understand the user manual. They said that it was unclear, very hard to read, and did not use familiar terms. When she asked for examples of confusing instructions, the sales staff showed her the following examples:

- Obtaining the authorization of the store manager on Form RBK-23 is required before the system can activate a customer charge account.
- Care should be exercised to ensure that the BACKSPACE key is not pressed when the key on the numeric keypad with a left-facing arrow is the appropriate choice to accomplish nondestructive backspacing.
- To prevent report generation interruption, the existence of sufficient paper stock should be verified before any option that requires printing is selected. If not, the option must be reselected.
- The F2 key should be pressed in the event that a display of valid merchandise codes is required. That same key terminates the display.

Tasks

1. What should BoB have done to avoid this situation?
2. Should the sales support staff ask the IT department to rewrite the user manual as a maintenance project, or should they request more training for sales staff? Can you offer any other suggestions?
3. Rewrite the user manual instructions so they are clear and understandable, and use the guidelines in Communications Tools found in Part A of the Systems Analyst's Toolkit. What steps would you take to test the new version?
4. In the process of rewriting the user manual instructions, you discover that some of the instructions were not changed to reflect system maintenance and upgrade activities. A request form on the firm's intranet, for example, has replaced Form RBK-23. BoB also has phased out printed reports in favor of online reports, with a menu-driven interface. Rewrite the user manual instructions to reflect the changes.

Continuing Case: Personal Trainer, Inc.

Personal Trainer, Inc. owns and operates fitness centers in a dozen Midwestern cities. The centers have done well, and the company is planning an international expansion by opening a new "supercenter" in the Toronto area. Personal Trainer's president, Cassia Umi, hired an IT consultant, Susan Park, to help develop an information system for the new facility. During the project, Susan will work closely with Gray Lewis, who will manage the new operation.

Background

System changeover and data conversion were successful for the new Personal Trainer system. The post-implementation evaluation indicated that users were pleased with the system. The evaluation also confirmed that the system was operating properly. Several users commented, however, that system response seemed slow. Susan Park, the project consultant, wants to meet with you to discuss operation, maintenance, and security issues affecting the new system.

Tasks

1. What might be causing the slow response time? Prepare a brief memo explaining system performance and workload measurement, using nontechnical language that Personal Trainer users can understand easily.
2. What could be causing the network slowdowns at Personal Trainer? If a problem does exist, which performance and workload measures would you monitor to pinpoint the problem?
3. At the end of the systems analysis phase, you studied the economic feasibility of the system and estimated the future costs and benefits. Now that the system is operational, should those costs and benefits be monitored? Why or why not?
4. You decide to prepare a security checklist for Personal Trainer. Prepare a list of security issues that the firm should evaluate and monitor. Be sure to organize the items into categories that match the six security levels.

Capstone Case: New Century Wellness Group

New Century Wellness Group offers a holistic approach to healthcare with an emphasis on preventive medicine as well as traditional medical care. In your role as an IT consultant, you will help New Century develop a new information system.

Background

You implemented the new system at New Century Wellness Group successfully, and the staff has used the system for nearly four months. Overall, New Century is pleased with the improvements in efficiency, office productivity, and patient satisfaction.

Some problems have surfaced, however. The office staff members call you almost daily to request assistance and suggest changes in certain reports and forms. You try to be helpful, but now you are busy with other clients. Actually, your contract with New Century required you to provide support only during the first three months of operation, but you want to encourage them to begin working on Phase Two of the computer upgrade project. Anita Davenport, New Century's office manager, reported that the system seems to slow down at certain times during the day, making it difficult for the staff to keep up with its workload. Also, you are increasingly are concerned about system security. A recent article in the local newspaper described an incident where a disgruntled former employee was planning to break into a computer system and destroy or alter data.

Tasks

1. What might be causing the slow response time? Prepare a brief memo explaining system performance and workload measurement, using nontechnical language that New Century users can understand easily.

(continued)

2. New Century's partners asked you to provide ongoing maintenance for the new system. In order to avoid any misunderstanding, you want to provide a brief description of the various types of maintenance. Prepare a brief memo that does this, and include at least two realistic examples of each type of maintenance.

3. Although the system has been operational for a short time, users already have submitted several requests for enhancements and noncritical changes. Should New Century use a maintenance release methodology to handle the requests? Why or why not?

4. What are the main security issues that New Century should address? Prepare a memo that lists the primary concerns and offers a specific recommendation for dealing with each issue.

CASE Tool Workshop

Systems analysts use CASE tools to help them plan, build, and maintain information systems. To learn more about CASE tools, turn to Part B of the Toolkit that follows Chapter 12. You can complete these tasks with the Visible Analyst® CASE tool, which is available with this textbook, or a similar tool.

Background

Suppose that you are evaluating various CASE tools, and you want to learn more about built-in security and performance enhancement issues.

Tasks

1. Using the Help feature, determine what security features are available in Visible Analyst®, or another CASE tool. Describe what you found in a brief memo, and include screen shots if possible.

2. Can Visible Analyst®, or another CASE tool, enhance system performance by speeding up access to stored data? If so, how would that be accomplished?

MIS CourseMate Features

If you have an MIS CourseMate access code, you can reinforce and extend your learning with premium content created for this textbook. For example, you can launch interactive Video Learning Sessions to help you understand systems development concepts and practice your skills. In addition, you can use MindTap Reader, which is a full, interactive, digital e-book.

MIS CourseMate also offers many learning features within each chapter, including an Online Case Simulation, a Critical Thinking Challenge, Video Learning Session Tasks, and a set of Learn It Online activities. To log on to the MIS CourseMate site at **www.cengagebrain.com**, you must create a student account and register this book.

Online Case Simulation: SCR Associates

Session 12: Managing Systems Support and Security

Overview

The SCR Associates case study is a Web-based simulation that allows you to practice your skills in a real-world environment. The firm offers IT consulting, solutions, and training. SCR plans to open a new high-tech training center, and needs to develop a Training Information Management System (TIMS) to support the center. You are a newly hired systems analyst reporting to Jesse Baker, systems group manager, and will help her develop the system.

The case study takes you to the SCR Web site, where you receive e-mail and voice mail messages from Jesse, obtain information from SCR's resource libraries, and perform various tasks. Jesse has high standards, but seems very fair. She made it clear that she expects your work to be accurate, thorough, and professional.

Before You Begin

To prepare for this work session, you should review the following topics:

- Service desks
- Version control, configuration management, and capacity planning
- System security

How Do I Use the Online Case Simulation?

- Read the preview, and review the Chapter 1 background material, if necessary.
- Visit the MIS CourseMate Web site at **www.cengagebrain.com**, locate the **SCR Case Simulation**, and click the **intranet** link. Enter your name and the password **sad10e**.
- When the opening screen displays, select this session. Then check your e-mail and voice mail, and start to work on your task list.

Preview: Session 12

You assisted your supervisor, Jesse Baker, in various implementation tasks, and the TIMS system is up and running. Now she wants you to focus on system operation, support, and security tasks. Specifically, she wants you to work on a service desk, version control, configuration management, capacity planning, and system security issues. She also wants you to create a checklist that will help SCR know when the TIMS system is reaching the end of its useful life.

Critical Thinking Challenge

In addition to technical ability, IT professionals need critical thinking skills. This feature can help you practice perception, organization, analysis, problem-solving, and decision-making skills that will be valuable in the workplace. You can visit **www.criticalthinking.org** to learn more about critical thinking and why it is so important.

Background

Your team leader wants to develop a standard method for rating and ranking maintenance requests for the new C^3 system. The idea is to develop some type of grid that could suggest priorities based on the type of maintenance requested and the potential impact on operations. When you review your notes from your systems analysis textbook, you realize that you used a similar approach when you created a risk matrix in Chapter 3, developed an evaluation model in Chapter 7, and selected a changeover method in Chapter 11.

The team leader also wants to test IT security levels with a simulated attack, something like a fire drill. The planned exercise would include realistic threats that will allow the team to evaluate responses and security procedures.

Practice Tasks

Visit the MIS CourseMate Web site at **www.cengagebrain.com**. Then navigate to the resources for this chapter and locate the **Critical Thinking Challenge** feature. You will complete two Practice Tasks, using what you learned in the chapter. Then you can check your answers to be sure you're ready for the Challenge Tasks.

Challenge Tasks

After you complete the Practice Tasks, you learn about new developments at Game Technology.

Your initial design was good, but the team leader wants you to try another approach. She put these questions to you: "Should corrective maintenance get a higher priority than other types of maintenance? Why or why not? Should cost-benefit issues be considered? If so, how would this be done?" Also, your security plan was good, but did not go far enough. The team leader wants you to include at least five more types of attacks, with examples and suggested responses.

To continue, navigate to the **Critical Thinking Challenge** feature for this chapter, select the **Challenge Tasks, and** follow the instructions.

Video Learning Sessions

Video Learning Sessions can help you understand systems development concepts and practice your skills. In this scenario, you will help design a Video Learning Session for this chapter.

Before You Begin

Review the chapter and list the main topics. Which ones did you find difficult to understand, and why? Can you think of other ways to explain the topics?

© craftvision/iStockphoto

Training Tasks

Suppose the IT training manager wants to encourage team members to watch the Video Learning Sessions. She wants you to submit a proposal for a new session that would explain the key topics in this chapter.

1. Which topics would you choose?
2. What specific skills or concepts would you include in the session?
3. How would you present the material?
4. Describe at least three graphic images that you would include in the video session.

Learn It Online

In each chapter, you can use this feature to apply your knowledge and practice your skills. The exercises include Chapter Reinforcement Questions, Flash Cards, Practice Tests, and various games, such as *Who Wants To Be a Computer Genius?*, *Wheel of Terms*, and the *Crossword Puzzle Challenge*.

THE SYSTEMS ANALYST'S TOOLKIT

Can you figure out what Dilbert's boss is talking about? He is using jargon that makes no sense. Worse yet, he is providing no leadership. Hopefully, when you complete the Systems Analyst's Toolkit, you will do a much better job!

The Systems Analyst's Toolkit presents a valuable set of skills and knowledge that you can use throughout the systems development process.

Part A discusses communication tools that can help you write clearly, speak effectively, and deliver powerful presentations.

Part B describes CASE tools that you can use to design, construct, and document an information system.

Part C demonstrates financial analysis tools you can use to measure project feasibility, develop accurate cost-benefit estimates, and make sound decisions. If you have MIS CourseMate, you can view three Video Learning Sessions that explain these financial analysis tools.

Part D describes Internet resource tools that you can use to locate information, obtain reference material, and monitor IT trends and developments.

© Cengage Learning 2014

PART **A**

Communication Tools

In **Part A** of the Systems Analyst's Toolkit, you will learn about written and oral communication skills that you will need to use as a systems analyst.

INTRODUCTION

OBJECTIVES

When you finish this part of the Toolkit, you will be able to:

- List overall guidelines for successful communications
- Write effective letters, memos, and e-mail messages
- Measure the readability of written material
- Organize and prepare written reports that are required during systems development
- Follow guidelines for effective oral communication
- Plan, develop, and deliver a successful presentation
- Use effective speaking techniques to achieve your objectives
- Manage and strengthen your communication skills

A successful systems analyst must have good written and oral communication skills to perform his or her job effectively. Never underestimate the importance of effective communication, whether you are using a memo, e-mail, an oral presentation, or a social networking site to convey your ideas. The following guidelines will help you prepare and deliver effective presentations. Remember, however, that nothing increases your ability to communicate better than practicing these skills.

PREVIEW CASE: Mountain View College Bookstore

Background: Wendy Lee, manager of college services at Mountain View College, wants a new information system that will improve efficiency and customer service at the three college bookstores.

In this part of the case, Tina Allen (systems analyst) and David Conroe (student intern) are talking about communication tools and techniques.

Participants: Tina and David
Location: Mountain View College Cafeteria, at the beginning of the bookstore
                       information system project
Discussion topics: Guidelines for successful oral and written communications

Tina: David, before we start the project for Wendy, let's talk about written and oral communication tools and techniques. We'll be using these throughout the systems development process.

David: *Fine with me. I've always enjoyed my English and writing courses.*

Tina: Well, everything you learned in school certainly applies in the workplace. The basic principles of good communications apply everywhere. But in a business environment there are some additional issues to keep in mind.

David: *Such as?*

Tina: For example, you will be preparing documents, presentations, and training material for users. In each situation, you have to consider the audience very carefully, including their technical knowledge, organizational level, and experience. You'll need to adjust your approach based on those factors, and be aware of the readability of your written work. Also, you'll be using e-mail as a primary communications tool.

David: *I understand. Are there any special ground rules for using e-mail?*

Tina: Well, e-mail can be more casual than typical business writing — but not *too* casual. We'll talk about that, along with ways to maximize your online effectiveness using software such as Microsoft Outlook. Also, we'll go over some guidelines for preparing presentations.

David: *Sounds good to me. When do we start?*

Tina: Right now. Here's a task list to get us under way:

FIGURE TK A-1   Typical communication tasks.
© Cengage Learning 2014

SUCCESSFUL COMMUNICATION STRATEGIES

Successful communication does not just happen. Usually, it is the result of a specific strategy that includes careful planning, hard work, and practice. To be a successful communicator, you must consider five related questions about yourself, your audience, and your objectives: why, who, what, when, and how. You also must consider the cultural context of your communication. Above all, you must know your subject and have confidence in yourself.

Why, Who, What, When, and How

The **why, who, what, when, and how of communications** are important questions that you must answer before you communicate. These five questions are described in the following section.

WHY Know *why* you are communicating, and what you want to accomplish. Ask yourself the question, "Is this communication necessary, and what specific results am I seeking?" Your entire communication strategy depends on the results that you need.

WHO Know *who* your targets are. Chapter 1 describes how information needs of users depend on their organizational and knowledge levels. When communicating with management, for example, sometimes a fine line exists between saying enough and saying too much. Each situation is different, so you must use good judgment and be alert for input from your audience.

WHAT Know *what* is expected of you and when to go into detail. This is directly related to knowing who your targets are and the organizational and knowledge levels of your audience. For example, a vice president might expect less detail and more focus on how a project supports the company's strategic business goals. You must design your communications just as carefully as your systems project. For example, will the recipients expect you to address a specific issue or topic? Will they expect cost estimates or charts? Design your communications based on the answers to those questions.

WHEN Know *when* to speak and *when* to remain silent and let others continue the discussion. To be an effective speaker, you must be a good listener — and use audience feedback to adjust your presentation. Good timing is an essential part of every presentation. Your delivery must be paced properly — too fast and you will lose your audience; too slow and they might become bored.

HOW Know *how* to communicate effectively. You can strengthen your communication skills by using Toolkit suggestions, reflecting upon your own experiences, and observing successful and unsuccessful techniques used by others.

Cultural Context

Communication strategy is affected by the cultural context in which the communication takes place, as shown in Figure TK A-2. Cultural factors can include geography,

FIGURE TK A-2 Every communication takes place within an overall cultural context.
© Cengage Learning 2014

background, educational level, and societal differences, among others. These differences must be considered when asking and answering the *why, who, what, when,* and *how* questions.

In addition to these factors, you learned in Chapter 1 that corporate culture is very important. A **corporate culture** includes the beliefs, rules, traditions, values, and attitudes that define a company and influence its way of doing business. To be successful, a systems analyst must understand, and work within this culture. For example, if you speak to a group in a company that encourages a highly participative style, you might want to solicit feedback, invite audience comments, or conduct a poll during your presentation. Similarly, if the organization or group is very formal, or very informal, you might want to adjust your style accordingly.

Know Your Subject

No matter how well you plan your communication, you must know your subject inside and out. Your credibility and effectiveness will depend on whether others believe you and support your views. No one can know everything, so it is important to adopt a specific preparation strategy. For example, before a presentation, consider what others expect you to know and what questions they will ask. No matter how well you prepare, however, you will not have an answer for every question. Remember that it is better to say, "I don't know, but I'll find out and get back to you," rather than to guess.

WRITTEN COMMUNICATIONS

Good writing is important because others often judge you by your writing. If you make a mistake while speaking, your audience probably will forget it. Your written errors, however, might stay around for a long time. Grammatical, typographical, and spelling errors distract readers from your message. Your written communications will include e-mail messages, memos, letters, workgroup communications, and formal reports.

Writing Style and Readability

If you have not taken a writing course, you should consider doing so. If you have a choice of courses, select one that focuses on business writing or technical writing. Any writing class, however, is worth the effort. Most bookstores and libraries have excellent books on effective communications, and many Internet sites offer writing guidelines, tips, and grammar rules. As you prepare written documents, keep in mind the following suggestions:

1. Know your audience. If you are writing for nontechnical readers, use terms that readers will understand.
2. Use the **active voice** whenever possible. For example, the active voice sentence "Tom designed the system," is better than, "The system was designed by Tom," which is an example of the **passive voice**.
3. Keep your writing clear, concise, and well-organized. Each paragraph should present a single topic or idea.
4. Use an appropriate style. For example, use a conversational tone in informal documents and a business tone in formal documents.
5. Use lists. If a topic has many subtopics, a list can organize the material and make it easier to understand.
6. Use short, easy-to-understand words. Your objective is not to impress your audience with the size of your vocabulary.

7. Avoid repeating the same word too often. Use a thesaurus to locate synonyms for frequently repeated words. Many word processing programs include a thesaurus and other tools to help you write better.

8. Check your spelling. You can use the spell checker in your word processing program to check your spelling, but remember that a **spell checker** is a tool that identifies only words that do not appear in the program's dictionary. For example, a spell checker will not identify instances when you use the word *their*, instead of the word *there*.

9. Check your grammar. Most word processing programs include a **grammar checker**, which is a tool that can detect usage problems and offer suggestions. When you use a grammar checker, you can set various options to match the level and style of the writing and to highlight or ignore certain types of usage. For example, you can set the grammar checker in Microsoft Word to check grammar rules only, or you can configure it to check writing style, as shown in Figure TK A-3, including gender-specific words, sentence fragments, and passive sentences.

10. Review your work carefully. Then double-check it for spelling, grammatical, and typographical mistakes. If possible, ask a colleague to proofread your work and suggest improvements.

All writers must consider **readability**, which analyzes ease of comprehension by measuring specific characteristics of syllables, words, and sentences. Two popular readability tools are the Flesch Reading Ease Score and the Flesch-Kincaid Grade Level Score.

The **Flesch Reading Ease score** measures the average sentence length and the average number of syllables per word and rates the text on a 100-point scale using the formula shown in Figure TK A-4. With this tool, the higher the score, the easier it is to understand. Microsoft suggests that for most standard documents, you should aim for a score of 60–70.

The **Flesch-Kincaid Grade Level score** uses the same variables, but in a different formula that produces a rating keyed to a U.S. grade-school level. For example, a score of 8.0 would indicate material easily understood by a person at an eighth-grade reading level. With this tool, Microsoft suggests that for most standard documents, you should aim for a score of 7.0 to 8.0.

E-Mail, Memos, and Letters

Because e-mail will be your primary tool for written communication, it is important to use it properly and effectively. E-mail usually is less formal than other written correspondence, but you still must follow the rules of good grammar, correct spelling, and clear writing.

Although many authors use a more conversational style for e-mail, you should remember that e-mail messages often are forwarded to other recipients or groups, and so

FIGURE TK A-3 You can set the grammar checker in Microsoft Word to check grammar rules only, or you can configure it to check your writing style.

Screenshot used with permission from Microsoft.

you must consider the users to whom it might be distributed. If you regularly exchange messages with a specific group of users, most e-mail programs allow you to create a distribution list that includes the members and their e-mail addresses. For example, Figure TK A-5 shows how to use Microsoft Outlook to send an e-mail to a six-person systems development team. Now that e-mail has become the standard method of business communication, it is important that all users know how to use e-mail properly, professionally, and courteously. This topic is discussed in the following section.

Although e-mail is the main form of internal communication, internal memos and announcements still are important, and external communications often require letters printed on company letterhead. Most companies use a standard format, or template, for internal memos and external letters. If your company stores those on a network, you can download and use the templates. If you want to create your own designs, you can use a word processor to create templates with specific layouts, fonts, and margin settings. A **template** gives your work a consistent look and makes your job easier. Most word processing programs also provide a feature that allows you to design your memos as forms and fill in the blanks as you work.

Social Media at Work

Social media is seeing explosive growth, which is certain to continue. This section focuses on just one aspect of this trend: social media in the office. It would be difficult to cite a communication method with greater potential

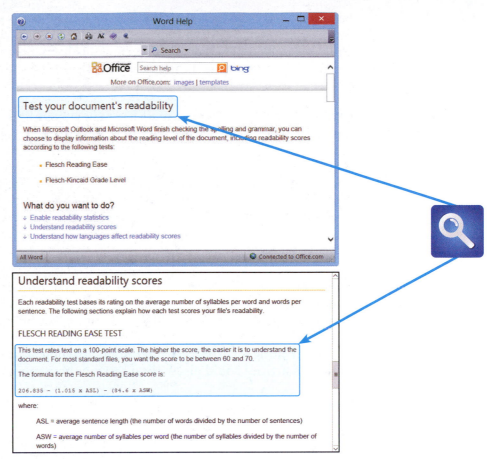

FIGURE TK A-4 Two popular readability measurement tools are the Flesch Reading Ease Score and the Flesch-Kincaid Grade Level Score.
Screenshots used with permission from Microsoft.

FIGURE TK A-5 Microsoft Outlook allows users to create distribution lists for sending e-mail messages.
Screenshots used with permission from Microsoft.

benefits – and dangers – than the volatile mix of social networking and modern business settings. Many employees use social networking to advance their careers. Unfortunately, others have been reprimanded or worse for saying too much, or to the wrong people, or at the wrong time. An IT professional should consider the following issues:

THE BACKDROP   Corporations are racing to embrace social media in their marketing plans. They have learned that they can create excitement, call attention to their products, and reach out to a young, active, socially aware market. In the corporate world, social media-driven event marketing has become a specialty unto itself, as you can see from visiting the Pepsi, NASCAR, or NFL sites, many of which sport multiple logos and links to Twitter and Facebook, among others. These trends are healthy, from an IT viewpoint, because they demonstrate that technology and creativity have an important role in corporate strategy, and that is good news for systems analysts.

ADVANTAGES   IT professionals can use social media to network with others, find out about new technology, meet colleagues, discuss career issues, and maintain a Web-based presence that would have been impossible just a few years ago. A person can gain credibility by sharing information and technical tips, posting how-to videos, or documenting an especially interesting assignment or challenge. However, any one of these activities could also have disastrous consequences.

RISKS   Drivers who are stopped for speeding often say "I didn't know I was going that fast." Similarly, employees who misuse social media usually plead ignorance. But there is a better way: know the rules, observe the rules, and when in doubt — don't!

Most firms have social media policies that govern workplace behavior. Some prohibit personal communications on company time or with company resources. Others use a case-by-case approach. Rather than guess at your company's policy, you should find out exactly what is the policy and make sure you understand it clearly.

THREE WAYS TO GET FIRED   You must be absolutely sure that your message content is appropriate, and in no way violates your company's confidentiality policy. One way to get fired quickly is to brag about a new marketing strategy before it has been publicly announced. Another way is to be somewhere or do something that might degrade your company's image, especially if your employer can be identified by your nametag, uniform, or location. Perhaps the quickest way to get fired is to launch an angry verbal attack on your fellow employees or managers.

OTHER ISSUES   You should use a "need to know" approach, so you direct your messages to those who have a legitimate interest, and are people you trust. Avoid blanket messaging and broadcasting. Also think about whether the content is appropriate for the site you are using. For example, a funny joke might be out of place on LinkedIn, but OK on Twitter. Your minute-to-minute experience at a rock concert might interest some people, but you might not want to send it to your entire contact list or your followers.

The bottom line is that social networking, instant messaging, and cell-phone texting are popular because they allow informal, interactive, and immediate communication. While these can be valuable collaboration tools, users should exercise good judgment and common sense, just as they would in any form of interpersonal contact. No one will remember all your excellent messages. They will, however, never forget the inappropriate ones.

Netiquette

Netiquette combines the words *Internet* and *etiquette*. With the explosive growth of social networking, netiquette is more important than ever. If you follow the guidelines in the preceding section, you can avoid major problems. But you should set your sights higher than that. An IT professional should have strong communication skills, and use good manners, proper style, and lots of common sense.

On the Web, you can find many sources of information about netiquette. For example, the NetManners.com site shown in Figure TK A-6 offers many guidelines, tips, and links. The site also reminds viewers of the comment made many years ago by Dale Carnegie, a famous educator and authority on interpersonal relations. Mr. Carnegie said that others evaluate us based on "what we do, how we look, what we say, and how we say it."

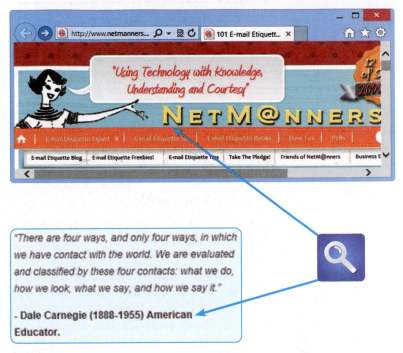

"There are four ways, and only four ways, in which we have contact with the world. We are evaluated and classified by these four contacts: what we do, how we look, what we say, and how we say it."

- Dale Carnegie (1888-1955) American Educator.

FIGURE TK A-6 This site offers netiquette guidelines, tips, and links.
© 2000–2012 NetM@nners.com

All e-mail users should be aware of some simple rules, most of which are nothing more than good manners and common sense. For example, an excellent starting point is to avoid sending material that is personal or confidential, because your messages might be forwarded by others and distributed more widely than you intended. Another important rule is never to send or reply to an e-mail when you are tired or upset. Instead, you can write a draft if you want to, but save the unsent message so you can review it later.

Here are some common rules and tips:

- Always fill in the subject field with a brief description of the contents.
- Be brief — in most cases, less is more.
- Be professional. Remember, if it has your name on it, it reflects on you personally and that often is how people will view your messages.
- Be sure to check your spelling.
- Don't forward jokes or chain letters without the permission of the recipient.
- Don't overuse humor or sarcasm that might work in a face-to-face situation, but not in an e-mail context.
- Don't type in all caps — it is like YELLING! It is also hard to read.
- Don't use colored fonts, background, or images in business e-mail messages.
- Don't use the return receipt request feature unless there is a valid business reason to do so.
- If you have large attachment files, try to zip or compress them before sending.
- If you send a message to a group of people, especially if they don't know each other, use a blind copy (Bcc) for all of the recipients in order to shield the addresses from the entire group.
- Never give out personal contact information of others without their specific permission to do so.
- Never include personal information unless you are 100% sure of your recipient and no other means of communication would provide better privacy and security.

- Remember that there are copyright laws. You do not have an unrestricted right to do whatever you please with someone else's e-mail message to you. Laws against discrimination and defamation can also apply to e-mail messages.

- When replying, don't include all the earlier messages unless there is a reason to do so.

In addition to these guidelines, it is important to follow company policy regarding communications at work. Many firms restrict personal communications that involve company time or equipment, and courts have upheld an employer's right to limit or monitor such communications.

Workgroup Software

Many companies use **workgroup software**, often called **groupware**, because it enhances employee productivity and teamwork. In addition to basic e-mail, workgroup software enables users to manage and share their calendars, task lists, schedules, contact lists, and documents. Popular examples of workgroup software include Microsoft Outlook and Novell's GroupWise, which is shown in Figure TK A-7.

Google Docs, which is shown in Figure TK A-8, offers free, Web-based collaboration. Using this application, a team can work on centrally stored documents instead of e-mailing drafts back and forth. Teams also can use powerful multiauthoring software, such as Adobe Acrobat, to add revisions, notes, and comments to PDF documents.

Reports

You must prepare many reports during systems development, including the preliminary investigation report, the system requirements document at the end of the systems analysis phase, the system design specification at the end of the system design phase, and the final report to management when the system goes into operation. You also might submit other reports, such as status reports, activity reports, proposals, and departmental business plans. You will create your reports as electronic documents, so you can attach them to e-mails.

When you create a report that will be delivered electronically, like the one shown in Figure TK A-9 on page 572, you should use the same high standards that apply to traditional printed materials. Notice that Microsoft Word provides many pre-made templates that you might be able to use for your report. Once you create a Word document, it is simple to transform it in to Adobe PDF format, which offers several advantages. For example, PDF files are:

- Very flexible. You can work with pages as modules, and combine or extract them to create custom versions of your documents.

FIGURE TK A-7 Workgroup software, such as Novell's GroupWise, allows a user to collaborate with others by sharing documents and folders.

© 2012 Novell

- Totally compatible. The PDF format travels well, and can be used and interchanged among virtually all devices, operating systems, applications, and hardware platforms.

- More secure. Unlike Microsoft Word, a PDF document can't readily be changed without leaving some trace, and the PDF format does not permit executable code, such as macros, to be embedded. However, no document is 100% secure. The PDF format might not deter a professional thief or intruder, but it can help with day-to-day office security concerns. Also, while the PDF format is not totally immune to malware and virus attacks, it is regarded as more resistant to these threats, compared to Word.

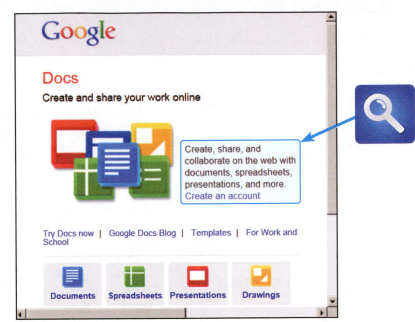

FIGURE TK A-8 An employee team can use Google Docs to work on centrally stored documents.
© 2012 Google

Whether you create the report using Microsoft Word, Adobe Acrobat, or some other program, your work must be professional, well-organized, and well-written. Experienced systems analysts know that when you put your name on a document, readers will see your work as a reflection of your personal skills and abilities. Also, for better or worse, the document will probably be around for a long time to come. With those thoughts in mind, you might want to review the written communication guidelines that appear on pages 566 to 567.

Although most reports are delivered electronically, in some cases you must prepare printed versions. For example, suppose you had to submit a written system requirements document. You probably would create various sections, including an introduction, an executive summary, findings, recommendations, time and cost estimates, expected benefits, and an appendix containing relevant data.

INTRODUCTION   The introduction usually includes a title page, table of contents, and brief description of the proposal. The title page should be clean and neat and contain the name of the proposal, the subject, the date, and the names of the development team members. If the project already has a recognized name or acronym, you should use it. Also, you can include a table of contents when the report is long or includes many exhibits. Many word processing programs include a tool that can generate a table of contents automatically.

EXECUTIVE SUMMARY   The executive summary is used to summarize the entire project, including your recommendations, in several paragraphs. Generally, the executive summary should not exceed 200 words or one page.

FINDINGS   Use the findings section to describe the major conclusions that you or the team reached during the systems analysis phase. You can make the findings section detailed or summarized, depending on the project. You must explain the logical design of the new system in a way that nontechnical managers can understand clearly. With a management audience, the most important task is to explain how the proposed system supports the company's business needs.

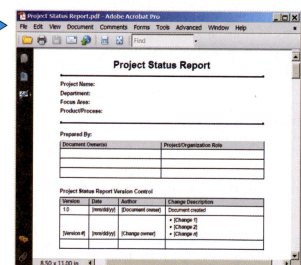

FIGURE TK-A-9   You can start with a Microsoft Word report template, and then transform it into Adobe PDF format.

Screenshots used with permission from Microsoft and Adobe Systems Incorporated.

RECOMMENDATIONS   The recommendations section presents the best system alternative, with a brief explanation that should mention economic, technical, operational, and schedule feasibility.

COSTS AND BENEFITS   In the costs and benefits section, you should list the advantages, disadvantages, costs, and benefits of each major system alternative. You should include a clear description of the financial analysis techniques you used. You might want to apply one or more of the financial analysis tools described in Part C of the Systems Analyst's Toolkit. You can use tables or graphs to support and clarify your alternatives when necessary.

APPENDIX   When you have a large number of supporting documents such as questionnaires or sampling results, you should put those items in an appendix located at the end of the document. Make sure you include only relevant information, and provide references for interested readers.

ORAL COMMUNICATIONS

An **oral presentation** is required at the end of the preliminary investigation and again at the conclusion of the systems analysis phase. You might need to give more than one presentation in some situations to present technical material to members of the IT department or to present an overview for top managers. When preparing an oral presentation, you should perform six important tasks: Define the audience, define the objectives for your presentation, organize the presentation, define any technical terms you will use, prepare your presentation aids, and practice your delivery.

Define the Audience

Before you develop a detailed plan for a management presentation, you must define the audience. Senior managers often prefer an executive summary rather than a detailed presentation, but that is not always the case, especially in smaller companies where top management is more involved in day-to-day activities. If you consider the expectations of your audience and design your presentation accordingly, you will improve your chances of success.

Define the Objectives

When you communicate, you should focus on your objectives. In the management presentation for the systems analysis phase, your goals are the following:

- Inform management of the status of the current system
- Describe your findings concerning the current system problems
- Explain the alternative solutions that you developed
- Provide detailed cost and time estimates for the alternative solutions
- Recommend the best alternative and explain the reasons for your selection

Organize the Presentation

Plan your presentation in three stages: the introduction, the information, and the summary. First, you should introduce yourself and describe your objectives. During the presentation, make sure that you discuss topics in a logical order. You should be as specific as possible when presenting facts — your listeners want to hear your views about what is wrong, how it can be fixed, how much it will cost, and when the objectives can be accomplished. In your summary, briefly review the main points, and then ask for questions.

Define Any Technical Terms

You should avoid specialized or technical terminology whenever possible. If your audience might be unfamiliar with a term that you plan to use, either define the term or find another way to say it so they will understand your material.

Prepare Presentation Aids

Much of what people learn is acquired visually, so you should use helpful, appropriate visual aids to help the audience follow the logic of your presentation and hold their attention. Visual aids also can direct audience attention away from you, which is helpful if you are nervous when you give the presentation. You can use a visual aid with an outline of topics that will help you stay on track. You can enhance the effect of your presentation with visual aids that use various media and software, as explained in the following sections.

VISUAL AIDS Visual aids can help you display a graphical summary of performance trends, a series of cost-benefit examples, or a bulleted list of important points. You can use whiteboards, flip charts, overhead transparencies, slides, films, and videotapes to enhance your presentation. When preparing your visual aids, make sure that the content is clear, readable, and easy to understand. Verify ahead of time that the audience can see the visual material from anywhere in the room. Remember that equipment can fail unexpectedly, so be prepared with an alternate plan.

PRESENTATION SOFTWARE With a computer and a projection system, you can use **presentation software**, such as Microsoft PowerPoint, to create a multimedia slide show. As shown in Figure TK A-10 on the next page, Microsoft offers free tutorials with advanced tips and techniques that can improve your presentations. The lower screen shows a Microsoft PowerPoint training video.

Preparing an effective slide presentation requires time and effort, and personal experience is the best teacher. There is no universal agreement about how to prepare a slide show, and many sources of information exist. Some overall guidelines include the following:

- Your first step (and perhaps the most important) is to prepare an overall outline that will be the foundation of your presentation. You should focus on the content and structure of your presentation before you consider visual issues.

FIGURE TK A-10   Microsoft PowerPoint offers many free online tutorials that demonstrate the full potential of the software.

Screenshots used with permission from Microsoft

- Remember that a fine line exists between providing too little information and too much.

- Display one topic per slide, and try to follow the rule often called the **7 by 7 rule**: no more than seven items per slide, and no more than seven words per item. Some presenters believe that a **6 by 6 rule** is even more effective.

- When displaying a list of items, consider using a series of slides to add each point sequentially, especially if you want to focus attention on the item being discussed.

- Use bullets rather than numbers, unless you are showing a specific sequence or order.

- Choose easily readable fonts. Use sans serif styles, such as **Arial**, for all body text. If you do use a serif style (such as Times Roman), apply it only in titles.

- Use appropriate point sizes for titles and body text. Your goal is to prepare slides that are readable and visually attractive.

Although point size selection depends on individual judgment and experience, here are some suggestions to get you started: For titles, try either 40- or 36-point fonts; for body text, 32- or 24-point fonts usually work well.

- Select special effects carefully — too many graphics, colors, sounds, or other special effects will distract your audience.

- You can include tables or graphics, but keep them simple and easy to understand. Also, you can use a special effect, such as boldface, italic, underlining, or a different color, to highlight an important word or phrase.

- Strive for a consistent look and feel among your slides, and position visual elements in the same place on each slide. You should use a master template to ensure uniformity and conform to company-wide standards that might apply, such as a copyright notice, a confidentiality statement, or placement of the company name and logo. Choose colors carefully, and keep them consistent. Usually, light letters on a dark background are easiest to read. Presentation software normally has predefined color palettes that provide background and text colors that ensure readability. Use these palettes as a guideline for selecting colors when possible.

- Be sure to check spelling and grammar!

- During the presentation, do *not* read your slides to the audience! They can read the slides on their own. Your slide presentation is an outline that provides structure and emphasis — it is not the presentation itself.

- It is important to deliver a presentation that can be viewed easily from anywhere in the room. When setting up, consider the size of the room, the number of people attending, the size and location of your visual aids, and the characteristics of any projection equipment you will be using.

Practice

The most important part of your preparation is practice. You should rehearse several times to ensure that the presentation flows smoothly and the timing is correct. Practicing will make you more comfortable and build your confidence.

Do not be tempted to write a script. If you read your presentation, you will be unable to interact with your audience and adjust your content based on their reactions. Instead, prepare an outline of your presentation and practice from the outline. Then, when you deliver the actual presentation, you will not have to struggle to remember the exact words you planned to say, and you will be able to establish a good rapport with your audience.

The Presentation

When you deliver your presentation, the following pointers will help you succeed:

SELL YOURSELF AND YOUR CREDIBILITY As a presenter, you must sell yourself and your credibility. A brilliant presentation will not convince top managers to approve the system if they are not sold on the person who gave the presentation. On the other hand, projects often are approved on the basis of the presenter's knowledge, commitment, and enthusiasm.

Your presentation must show confidence about the subject and your recommendations. You should avoid any conflicts with the people attending the presentation. If you encounter criticism or hostility, remain calm and stay focused on the issues — not the person making the comments. You will have a successful presentation only if you know the material thoroughly, prepare properly, and sell yourself and your credibility.

CONTROL THE PRESENTATION During the presentation, you must control the discussion, maintain the pace of the presentation, and stay focused on the agenda — especially when answering questions. Although you might be more familiar with the subject material, you should not display a superior attitude toward your listeners. Maintain eye contact with the audience and use some humor, but do not make a joke at someone else's expense.

ANSWER QUESTIONS APPROPRIATELY Let your audience know whether you would prefer to take questions as you go along or have a question-and-answer session at the end. Sometimes the questions can be quite difficult. You must listen carefully and respond with a straightforward answer. Try to anticipate the questions your audience will ask so you can prepare your responses ahead of time.

When answering a difficult or confusing question, repeat the question in your own words to make sure that you understand it. For example, you can say, "If I understand your question, you are asking …" This will help avoid confusion and give you a moment to think on your feet. To make sure that you gave a clear answer, you can say, "Have I answered your question?" Allow follow-up questions when necessary.

USE EFFECTIVE SPEAKING TECHNIQUES The delivery of your presentation is just as important as its content. You can strengthen your delivery by speaking clearly and confidently and projecting a relaxed approach. You also must control the pace of your delivery. If you speak too fast, you will lose the audience, and if the pace is too slow, people will lose their concentration and the presentation will not be effective.

Many speakers are nervous when facing an audience. If this is a problem for you, keep the following suggestions in mind:

- Control your environment. If you are most nervous when the audience is looking at you, use visual aids to direct their attention away from you. If your hands are shaking, do not hold your notes. If you are delivering a computer-based presentation, it is a good idea to use a handheld wireless device to control the slides. Concentrate on using a strong, clear voice. If your nervousness distracts you, take a deep breath and remind yourself that you really do know your subject.

- Turn your nervousness to your advantage. Many people do their best work when they are under a little stress. Think of your nervousness as normal pressure.

- Avoid meaningless filler words and phrases. Using words and phrases such as *okay, all right, you know, like, um*, and *ah* are distracting and serve no purpose.

- Practice! Practice! Practice! Some people are naturally gifted speakers, but most people need lots of practice. You must work hard at practicing your presentation and building your confidence. Many schools offer speech or public speaking courses that are an excellent way of practicing your skills. It also can be advantageous to preview your presentation with one or more people and ask for input.

Online Presentations

In addition to face-to-face meetings, you might have to deliver an **online presentation**, possibly with two-way communication between you and the audience. You have several options. You might use PowerPoint 2010 to broadcast a live presentation, as shown in Figure TK A-11, and your online audience would see the slides in a Web browser. Your presentation also could include an audio narrative. If you want real-time participation, you might consider Cisco's WebEx, which is shown in Figure TK A-12, or a similar product. WebEx can handle live audio and video, and allows you to deliver a fully interactive Webinar. Microsoft also offers a robust Web-conferencing platform called Live Meeting, shown in Figure TK A-13, which supports presentations, group meetings, and collaboration.

FIGURE TK A-11   With PowerPoint 2010, you can broadcast a live presentation to a remote audience, who can view it in a Web browser.

Screenshot used with permission from Microsoft.

FIGURE TK A-12   Cisco's WebEx can handle live audio and video, and allows you deliver an interactive Webinar.

© 2012 Cisco

MANAGING YOUR COMMUNICATION SKILLS

More than ever, employees must rely on their personal skills and experience. In an uncertain world and a turbulent economy, individuals should think of themselves as profit-making companies, complete with assets, liabilities, strengths, and areas for development. In Chapter 2, you learned that a company must have a strategic plan, and the same is true for an individual. Armed with a plan to improve your communication skills, you are much more likely to reach your full potential.

Learn, Demo & Buy Microsoft® Live Meeting

Microsoft® Live Meeting is an easy-to-use and reliable web conferencing solution that lets you connect up to 1,250 attendees with just an Internet connection and web browser.

The service is fully hosted by Microsoft and includes a choice of several low, flat monthly subscription pricing options. Expert training and 24x7x365 live technical support is available for presenters and attendees joining at no extra charge. Get set up to host meetings in less than 24 hours.

FIGURE TK A-13 Microsoft Live Meeting supports presentations, group meetings, conferences, and collaboration.
Screenshot used with permission from Microsoft.

Communicating is like any other activity — the more you practice, the better you become. Many resources are available for students and IT professionals who want to improve their written and oral communication skills. For example, the Vocational Information Center site shown in Figure TK A-14 offers a wide range of free resources and links that can help you become a better writer, presenter, and public speaker. The Association for Computing Machinery (ACM) also offers many online courses and tutorials for members, including students and IT professionals.

Some people find it difficult to stand in front of a group and deliver a presentation or report. For many years, membership in Toastmasters, International has been a popular way to gain confidence, overcome stage fright, and develop public speaking

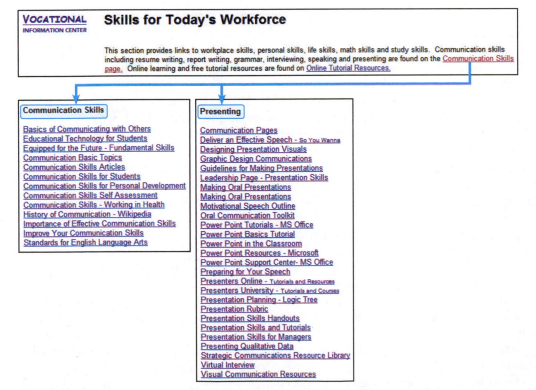

FIGURE TK A-14 The Vocational Information Center offers many online courses and tutorials on communications skills.
Vocational Information Center 1999–2008 ©

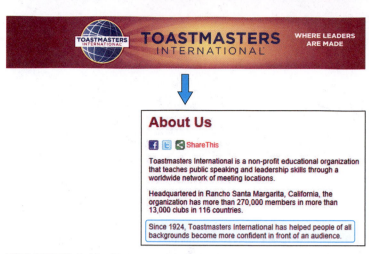

FIGURE TK A-15 Toastmasters International is famous for helping people become better public speakers.

© 2012 Toastmasters International

skills. As shown in Figure TK A-15, Toastmasters offers a friendly environment where members critique each speech in a positive manner, note the strengths, and offer suggestions about what might be improved. With more than 270,000 members in 116 countries, this organization offers an excellent way to develop better public speaking skills.

TOOLKIT SUMMARY

Your success as a systems analyst depends on your ability to communicate effectively. You must know why you are communicating, what you want to accomplish, who your targets are, what is expected of you, and when to go into detail. You must know your subject and how to use good written and oral communications techniques.

You will be judged by your written work, so it must be free of grammatical, spelling, and punctuation errors. You should write e-mail, letters, and memos clearly, and the writing style should match the situation. Many firms have standard formats for letters and memos, and you can use templates to achieve consistency.

Social media is extremely popular because it allows informal, interactive, and immediate communication. While social media can be a valuable collaboration tool, users should exercise good judgment and common sense, just as they would in any form of interpersonal contact. They must understand clearly any workplace policies and rules that affect the use of social media, both on and off the job.

Your writing must be clear and understandable. You can use readability measurement tools such as the Flesch Reading Ease score and the Flesch-Kincaid Grade Level score.

You will prepare various reports during systems development, and the format will vary depending on the nature of the report. Your reports should have a cover memo and might include an introduction, an executive summary, findings, recommendations, time and cost estimates, expected benefits, and a data section.

In addition to written communications, you must communicate effectively in person. You might have to deliver several presentations to different audiences at different times during the SDLC. Presentations are an important form of oral communication, and you should follow specific guidelines in preparing your presentation. You prepare by defining your audience, identifying your objectives, and organizing the presentation itself. You also need to define technical terms and prepare visual aids to help your audience understand the material. Most important, you must practice your delivery to gain confidence and strengthen your presentation skills. You may also want to deliver your presentation through an online venue.

When you develop slide presentations, you should follow the 6 by 6 rule or 7 by 7 rule and other guidelines that will make your slides easy to read and understand. You should select fonts and point sizes carefully, and strive for a consistent look and feel throughout the presentation. Special effects can be interesting, but do not overuse them.

When you give the presentation, you are selling your ideas and your credibility. You must control the discussion, build a good rapport with the audience, answer all questions clearly and directly, and try to use good speaking techniques. Again, the best way to become a better speaker is to practice.

Every IT professional should have a strategic plan to manage and improve written and oral communication skills. Many online resources offer courses, tutorials, and support to help you develop the skills you will need in the workplace.

Key Terms

6 by 6 rule *574*
7 by 7 rule *574*
active voice *565*
corporate culture *565*
Flesch-Kincaid Grade
  Level score *566*
Flesch Reading Ease score *566*

grammar checker *566*
groupware *570*
netiquette *569*
online presentation *576*
oral presentation *572*
passive voice *565*
presentation software *573*

readability *566*
spell checker *566*
template *567*
visual aids *573*
why, who, what, when, and
  how of communications *564*
workgroup software *570*

Toolkit Exercises

Review Questions

1. What is a corporate culture, and why is it important? Describe the culture at a business where you have been employed.
2. Mention five specific techniques you can use to improve your written documents.
3. What techniques can help e-mail communications? Provide specific examples.
4. Create a one-page document with at least five grammatical errors. Then run the Microsoft Word grammar checker and describe the results.
5. When preparing an oral presentation, what six tasks should you perform?
6. When you organize a presentation, what three stages do you plan?
7. Why are visual aids important? Give at least three examples of different types of visual aids, and explain how you would use each type in a presentation.
8. Based on your own experience, what tends to make a PowerPoint presentation stronger or weaker? Provide specific examples.
9. Name three specific strategies you can use if you get nervous during a presentation.
10. Why is practice so important when preparing a presentation? Provide a specific example from your own experience.

Discussion Topics

1. Most people agree that business e-mail can be more conversational than formal written documents, but even e-mail has its limits. As a manager, what guidance would you give people regarding e-mail style and usage?
2. Is it possible to overcommunicate? For example, in Chapter 4 you learned to avoid leading questions, which might suggest an answer. Can you think of other examples, like newspaper headlines, where "less is more"?
3. Many articles stress the importance of body language. Think of examples where you noticed a person's body language. Did it relate to something they were trying to communicate — or something they were trying *not* to communicate?
4. Should e-mail monitoring by an employer always be permissible, never permissible, or does the answer depend on specific factors? If so, what are they?

Projects

1. *The Elements of Style* by William Strunk, Jr. and E. B. White is a popular reference manual for proper English usage. The book identifies many words and phrases that are commonly misused, including *between* and *among*, *affect* and *effect*, *different from* and *different than*, *like* and *as*, and *infer* and *imply*. Review *The Elements of Style* or another source, and explain how these words should be used.
2. Using Microsoft PowerPoint or another program, prepare a presentation on "How to Prepare an Effective Slide Presentation." Assume that your audience is familiar with presentation software, but has no formal training.
3. As a training manual writer, choose a simple hardware or software task and write a two- or three-paragraph description of how to perform the task. Then use your word processing software to check the readability statistics. Try to keep the Flesch Reading Ease score above 60 and the Flesch-Kincaid Grade Level score to 8.0 or less.
4. View at least three examples of public speaking. You can investigate TV network news broadcasts, C-SPAN, or any other source. Describe each speaker's gestures, expressions, voice levels, inflections, timing, eye contact, and effectiveness.

PART B

CASE Tools

In **Part B** of the Systems Analyst's Toolkit, you will learn how CASE tools can help you perform systems development and maintenance tasks.

INTRODUCTION

OBJECTIVES

When you finish this part of the Toolkit, you will be able to:

- Explain CASE tools and the concept of a CASE environment

- Trace the history of CASE tools and their role in a fourth-generation environment

- Define CASE terms and concepts, including a repository, modeling tools, documentation tools, engineering tools, and construction tools

- Explain an integrated development environment (IDE) and application life cycle management (ALM) solutions

- Provide examples of CASE tool features

- Describe CASE tool trends, and how they relate to object-oriented analysis and agile methods

Computer-aided systems engineering (CASE), also called **computer-aided software engineering**, is a technique that uses powerful software, called **CASE tools**, to help system developers design and construct information systems. In this part of the Systems Analyst's Toolkit, you will learn about the history, characteristics, and features of CASE tools. You will see specific examples of CASE tools and how they are used in various development tasks. In addition, you will learn about integrated software development environments and application life cycle management.

PREVIEW CASE: Mountain View College Bookstore

Background: Wendy Lee, manager of college services at Mountain View College, wants a new information system that will improve efficiency and customer service at the three college bookstores.

In this part of the case, Tina Allen (systems analyst) and David Conroe (student intern) are talking about CASE tools and concepts.

Participants:	Tina and David
Location:	Tina's office, early in the systems planning phase
Discussion topics:	CASE tools, integrated development environments, CASE terms and concepts

Tina: David, before we get too far into the project, let's talk about CASE tools and concepts and how we can use them in the development process.

David: *Sure. I saw examples of CASE tools in my systems analysis course. CASE stands for computer-aided systems engineering, right?*

Tina: Yes. Some people say CASE stands for computer-aided *software* engineering instead of computer-aided *systems* engineering. There's really no difference. Either way, CASE tools are an integral part of the systems development process, and can be used with structured, object-oriented, or agile development methods.

David: *Will we use CASE tools on the bookstore project?*

Tina: Yes. We'll start by identifying and modeling business functions and processes. That information will become part of a central repository, which is a database that stores all the characteristics of the information system.

David: *Then what?*

Tina: We'll use CASE tools to draw various diagrams, including DFDs, UML diagrams, functional decomposition diagrams, and business process diagrams. You'll learn about these as we go along. We might also use CASE tools to generate program code, screens, and reports. Also, depending on the software environment we select, we might use an integrated development environment.

David: *What's that?*

Tina: An integrated development environment is like a built-in CASE tool that a vendor integrates into a software product.

David: *Anything else?*

Tina: Well, before we decide on a CASE tool, we'll take a look at several examples. Here's a task list to get us started:

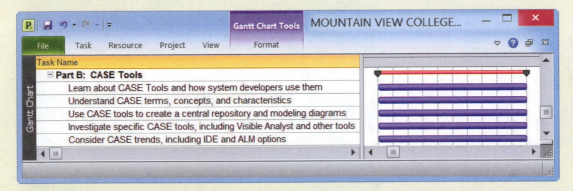

FIGURE TK B-1   Typical CASE tool tasks.

© Cengage Learning 2014

OVERVIEW OF CASE TOOLS

If you ask a carpenter for an example of a tool, the response might be a hammer, drill, or screwdriver. Put the same question to a chef, and the answer might be a measuring cup, knife, or spatula. Every type of work requires specific tools to do the job properly, and system development is no different. CASE tools can reduce costs, speed up development, and provide comprehensive documentation for future maintenance or enhancements.

The Carnegie Mellon Software Engineering Institute (SEI) is a leader in software engineering and development. SEI helps organizations improve their software capabilities and develop or acquire high quality software. As shown in Figure TK B-2, SEI focuses on overall architecture, system design, software development, tools, and methods.

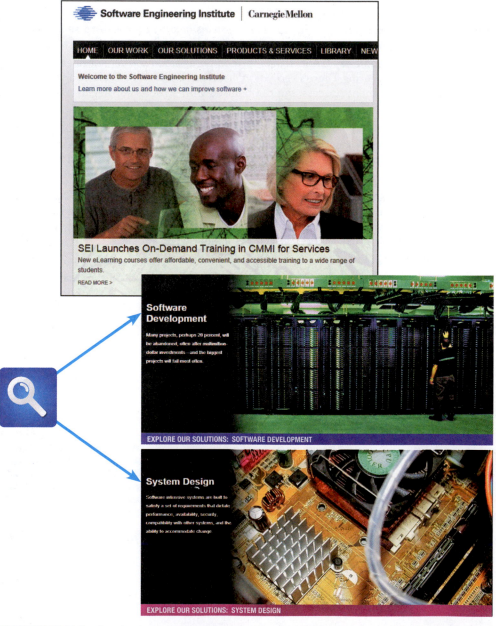

FIGURE TK B-2   As a leader in software standards and quality management, SEI offers cutting-edge software development and systems design tools.

CASE Tools History

As early as the 1960s, programmers used tools such as editors and code debuggers to write mainframe computer applications. Today, in our software-driven world, CASE tools have evolved into powerful resources that systems analysts need to build and maintain complex information systems.

Traditional code was written in **procedural programming languages** such as COBOL, which required a programmer to create a command for each processing step. In contrast, modern languages such as Visual Basic or Java are **non-procedural**, or **event-driven**, programming languages because instead of writing a series of instructions, a programmer defines the actions that the program must perform when certain events occur. Because non-procedural languages are **object-oriented programming languages (OOPL)**, they make it easier to implement an object-oriented system design, which you learned about in Chapter 6.

Another trend involves powerful programming languages called **fourth-generation languages (4GLs)** that are part of the **fourth-generation environment**, which was described in Chapter 7, Development Strategies. In a fourth-generation environment that includes modern CASE tools, system developers can deliver high quality software, shorten the timetable, and reduce expense.

The Marketplace for CASE Tools

The CASE tool marketplace includes a wide variety of vendors and products, and no one tool dominates the market. You can search the Web to locate CASE tool products and vendors, and even visit secondary sites such as Wikipedia to locate additional sources. Depending on their features, some CASE tools can cost thousands of dollars, while others are available as shareware, or even as freeware, as shown in Figure TK B-3.

You also can visit Microsoft's download center to sample various Express Editions, which are free, but limited, versions of software development tools, as shown in Figure TK B-4.

How do you select a CASE tool? The answer depends on the type of project, its size and scope, possible budgetary and time constraints, and the preferences and experience of the system development team. After you study the terms, concepts, and examples in this part of the Toolkit, you will be able to evaluate various products and make an informed decision. The first step in learning about CASE tools is to understand basic CASE terms and concepts.

FIGURE TK B-3 This site offers many free downloads, such as the UML modeling tool shown here.

© 1999–2011 by Visual Paradigm

FIGURE TK B-4   Microsoft offers free Express editions, which are trial versions of software development tools. The latest release, Visual Studio Express 2012, became available in September 2012.

Screenshots used with permission from Microsoft.

CASE Terms and Concepts

A typical CASE tool is actually a set of individual tools that share a repository of information. The important terms and concepts are explained in the following sections.

Repository

A **repository** is a database that serves as a central storage location for all information about the system being developed. Once a data element has been defined in the repository, it can be accessed and used by processes and other information systems. For example, your sales processing, accounts receivable, and shipping systems all might require data about customers. After the CUSTOMER data element is entered in the repository, all three systems can share a consistent, up-to-date definition.

When you define a data element in the repository, you can assign a data type and format, a range of acceptable values, and one or more aliases. An **alias** is an alternative name for a data element. The repository can be searched, and all instances of the data element will be listed. For example, Figure TK B-5 shows a Visible Analyst search for the data element named CUSTOMER NUMBER. As the screens show, you can search the entire repository, or among specific types of diagrams, and the results will show all instances of the data element.

Individual Tools

An integrated set of CASE tools can be used to model, document, engineer, and construct the information system, as explained in the following sections.

MODELING TOOLS Throughout the SDLC, system developers use modeling tools and diagrams to represent the system graphically. The textbook describes many examples, including Unified Modeling Language diagrams and functional decomposition diagrams (Chapter 4), data flow diagrams (Chapter 5), various object diagrams (Chapter 6),

FIGURE TK B-5   A Visible Analyst repository search for the data element named CUSTOMER NUMBER. The results will show all instances of the data element.

Screenshot used with permission from Visible Systems Corporation.

entity-relationship diagrams (Chapter 9), and structure charts (Chapter 10). Most popular CASE products offer these modeling tools, among others. One of the most important benefits of a **CASE environment** is that it provides an overall framework that allows a developer to create a series of graphical models based on data that has already been entered into a central repository.

DOCUMENTATION TOOLS The main source of system documentation is the repository, which was explained in the previous section. In most CASE software, the repository automatically identifies the new entries and adds them to the database. In addition to the repository itself, many CASE products provide tools that check automatically for inconsistent or incomplete information in forms, reports, and diagrams. This is especially important in large, complex systems.

ENGINEERING TOOLS Engineering tools include forward engineering and reverse engineering tools. **Forward engineering** means translating business processes and functions into applications. Some CASE tools allow you to build the system either by editing objects and code directly, or by modifying graphical representations such as DFDs and UML diagrams. As you learned in Chapter 1, CASE tools such as System Architect and Visible Analyst allow you to develop a business model that can be translated into information system components. **Reverse engineering** allows you to examine an existing application and break it down into a series of diagrams, structure charts, and source code. Using a reverse engineering CASE tool, an analyst can transform existing application source code into a working model of the system. This can be especially important when integrating new systems with legacy systems or systems that were developed in different environments. Figure TK B-6 shows an example of an Imagix reverse engineering tool.

CONSTRUCTION TOOLS A full-featured CASE tool can handle many program development tasks, such as generating application code, screens, and reports.

- An **application generator**, also called a **code generator**, allows you to develop computer programs rapidly by translating a logical model directly into code. As shown in Figure TK B-7, the Tangible Architect states that it easily can create .NET database applications. In this crowded CASE tool marketplace, other vendors offer products that can generate applications in languages such as C, C++, Java, and AgileC.

FIGURE TK B-6 Imagix claims that its reverse engineering tool can automate many expensive, time-consuming tasks.

© 2012 Imagix Corp..

FIGURE TK B-7 Tangible Architect includes a code generator that can create .NET database applications.
© Tangible Architect

- A **screen generator,** or **form painter,** is an interactive tool that helps you design a custom interface, create screen forms, and handle data entry format and procedures. The screen generator allows you to control how the screen will display captions, data fields, data, and other visual attributes. Modern CASE tools usually include a screen generator that interacts with the data dictionary. As shown in Figure TK B-8, Gillani Software's FourGen® CASE tool set includes a form painter and a screen code generator, along with many other powerful features.

- A **report generator,** also called a **report writer,** is a tool for designing formatted reports rapidly. Using a report generator, you can modify a report easily at any stage of the design process. When you are satisfied with the report layout, the report writer creates a report definition and program code that actually produces the report. You also can input sample field values to create a **mock-up report** for users to review and approve.

FIGURE TK B-8 Gillani's FourGen® CASE tools include a form painter and a screen code generator.
©2011 Gillani Inc..

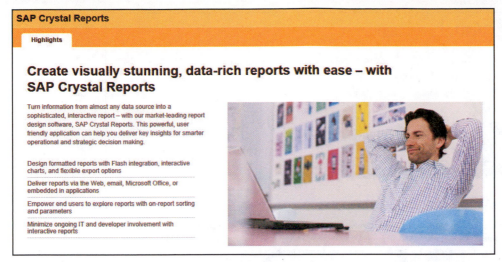

FIGURE TK B-9   SAP Crystal Reports is a popular report generator that can display business analytics and support decision-making.
© 2012 SAP AG.

SAP Crystal Reports, shown in Figure TK B-9, is a very popular report generator. According to SAP, Crystal Reports is a user-friendly, scalable tool that can display business analytics and support decision-making. **Business analytics**, which are discussed in Chapter 9, can measure past performance, help managers understand business trends, and monitor current operations.

DEVELOPMENT ENVIRONMENTS

A **development environment** refers to the mix of software tools, methods, and physical resources that an IT team uses to create an information system. Systems development is dynamic, and analysts should be aware of emerging trends, such as the integrated development environment (IDE), and various application life cycle management (ALM) solutions. These concepts are described in the following sections.

Integrated Development Environments

Although generic CASE tools can be used to plan and design any type of information system, it usually is easier to use an **integrated development environment (IDE)**, which uses built-in tools provided by the software vendor. For example, Oracle provides Oracle Designer, which is packaged with Oracle's application software. According to the company, Oracle Designer models business processes, data entities, and relationships — and easily can transform the models into applications. Other firms, such as SAP and Sybase, also offer IDE tools that make it easier to create applications based on their products.

Microsoft's Visual Studio is a well-known IDE. Visual Studio 2012 includes development tools specifically designed to support Microsoft's .NET application development strategy. In addition to these commercial packages, programmers can use open-source IDE software, such as Java-based NetBeans.

Application Life Cycle Management Environments

Many vendors of traditional IDEs, including Microsoft, now offer new **application life cycle management (ALM)** tools, as shown in Figure TK B-10. Although no standard definition exists, ALM generally refers to a start-to-finish approach to planning, designing, developing, deploying, managing, and maintaining an

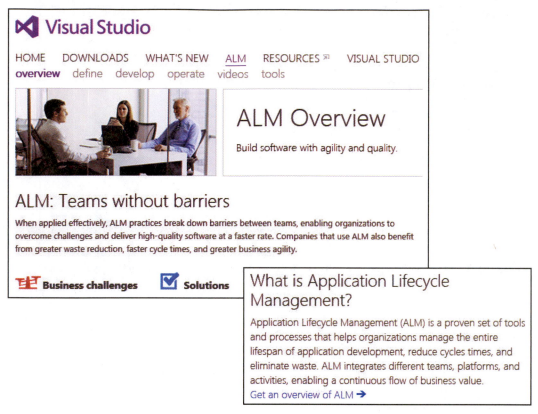

FIGURE TK B-10   Microsoft's Visual Studio 2012 stresses the benefits of ALM.
Screenshots used with permission from Microsoft.

information system. According to Microsoft, Visual Studio 2012 offers ALM tools and processes that can help an organization speed up systems development and reduce costs.

IBM also stresses the ALM concept, and uses the term **silo** to describe an isolated work environment. In the Redpaper® shown in Figure TK B-11 on the next page, authors Bruce Powel Douglass and Mats Gothe describe IBM's Rational Workbench® as an integrated solution. According to the authors, when developers operate in silos, effectiveness suffers. The authors also suggest that RationalWorkbench® offers a new approach that replaces what they call "one-size fits no one" development solutions. They state that the Rational Workbench® spans systems engineering, project management, software development, and quality management. The full text of the Redpaper is available at *www.ibm.com/redbooks*.

ALM trends are described in an interesting paper published by Gartner Consulting, as shown in Figure TK B-12 on the next page. Gartner views ALM as an emerging market, driven by new technology and corporate pressure for cost reduction, and predicts that silo development will give way to integrated ALM products in the future.

Pros and Cons of Integrated Development Tools

In a specific software environment, an integrated development tool is highly effective because it is built into the vendor's software package. The only possible disadvantage is that each IDE is different, and requires a learning curve and skills that might or might not be readily transferable. In contrast, non-specific CASE tools such as Visible Analyst or Rational System Architect can be used in any development environment. Given the dynamic changes in IT, a systems analyst should seek to learn as many development and CASE tools as possible.

Redpaper

Bruce Powel Douglass
Mats Gothe

IBM Rational Workbench for Systems and Software Engineering

An integrated solution for systems life cycle management

Without integration across the systems delivery life cycle, systems and software teams are left to operate in silos. When silos form, product delivery effectiveness suffers. In order to deliver smarter products that respond to changing market needs, it is necessary to allow systems and software engineering teams to work efficiently and to manage all the life cycle work products through collaboration. The IBM Rational Workbench for Systems and Software Engineering software, shown in Figure 1, provides this integrated systems life cycle management solution.

FIGURE TK B-11 Note IBM's reference to silos, and the emphasis on life cycle management.

© Copyright IBM Corporation 1994, 2012

LICENSED FOR DISTRIBUTION

Gartner.

Magic Quadrant for Application Life Cycle Management

These trends emphasize issues we have seen during the past five years that have been the basis for the adoption of integrated ALM products, rather than silos: agile teams, geographically distributed projects, complex processes or complex products. Although we are seeing more integrated ALM adoption, clients rarely start with a vision of massive enterprise deployment, and many of the products evaluated in this market are evolutions of siloed solutions. Consequently, we see initial deployments proving the concepts, then a move to viral adoption and broader build-out — for example, requirements management may be deployed first, then test management and the connection of requirements to test cases.

FIGURE TK B-12 Gartner views ALM as an emerging market, driven by new technology and corporate pressure for cost reduction.

© 2012 Gartner, Inc..

CASE TOOL EXAMPLES

You can choose from dozens of vendors and CASE tools that offer a wide range of functions, characteristics, and appearance. The following sections include examples of several popular CASE tools.

Visible Analyst

Visible Systems Corporation is an important player in the software development market. Visible offers tools for data and application modeling, code generation, and software configuration management.

The Visible Analyst® CASE tool can generate many types of models and diagrams. Figure TK B-13 shows two sample diagrams for a library system: an entity-relationship diagram and a data flow diagram. Both examples are integrated with the central data repository shown in Figure TK B-14 on the next page. The Library System repository stores all objects that appear in models, diagrams, and definitions. If a user requests a list of system data flows, the program displays the screen shown here. A central repository provides consistency, saves time, and reduces development costs.

Rational Software

IBM offers many systems development and modeling products, including a powerful tool called Rational System Architect, shown in Figure TK B-15 on the next page. IBM claims that the product stresses modeling and collaboration, and is a suite of tools that can align processes, information, and technologies. A trial version of the software can be downloaded from IBM's site.

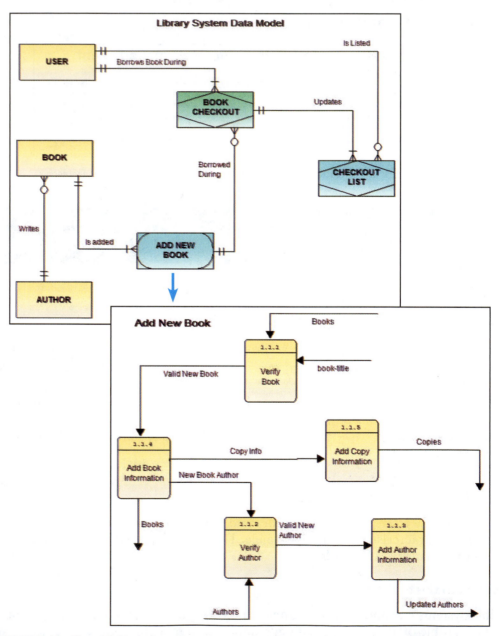

FIGURE TK B-13 These Visible Analyst diagrams integrate with a central data repository for the Library System.

FIGURE TK B-14 The repository for the Library System stores the objects that appear in models, diagrams, and definitions.

Screenshot used with permission from Visible Systems Corporation.

FIGURE TK B-15 IBM's Rational Systems Architect stresses collaboration and integration. Note the use of the term "silos," which was mentioned in the IBM Redpaper shown in Figure TK B-11 on page 591

© Copyright IBM Corporation 1994, 2012

CASE TOOL TRENDS

Traditional CASE software evolved from simple utilities, such as code editors, to powerful multipurpose tools that can help you envision, plan, and build an entire information system. The evolution of CASE software will continue, as developers seek even more powerful tools that can model complex business processes and integrate with customer and supplier systems.

Just as modern spacecraft could not have been built without specialized, high-technology tools, future software will be planned, constructed, and maintained with a new generation of CASE tools. The following sections discuss CASE tool trends and method-specific tools.

New Products and Features

CASE tool vendors constantly offer more features and greater flexibility. One example is a framework to help transform business processes into an information system. A **framework** organizes and documents system development tasks. For example, the **Zachman Framework** shown in Figure TK B-16 arranges traditional fact-finding questions into a useful matrix. The vertical axis shows five development stages and stakeholder roles, while the horizontal axis displays six essential fact-finding questions.

In each of the 30 "cells," Visible Analyst® suggests specific tools, diagrams, and methods to document the development process. Perhaps the most powerful feature is that all the data is integrated and stored automatically in a central repository, which can easily be viewed and updated.

As software becomes more powerful and complex, the lines between traditional CASE tools and other modeling tools continue to blur. For example, Microsoft Visio can model networks, business processes, and many types of special diagrams. Visio offers a variety of online tutorials and training, as shown in Figure TK B-17 on the next page.

Another trend is the increasing use of integrated development environments. Chapter 11 explains how an IDE can simplify the integration of system components and reduce code development time. An IDE typically includes built-in tools such as real-time error detection, syntax hints, highlighted code, class browsers, and version control. In addition to IBM's WebSphere and Microsoft's .NET, programmers can use open-source IDEs such as Java-based NetBeans IDE and Eclipse.

Method-Specific CASE Tools

As Chapter 11 explains, each systems development approach has a set of tools that has worked especially well for that method. For example, structured development relies heavily on DFDs and structure charts. Object-oriented methods use a variety of diagrams, such as use case, class, sequence, and transition state diagrams. Agile methods tend to use spiral or other iterative models. Chapter 1 describes several method-specific

FIGURE TK B-16   The Zachman Framework provides an easy-to-follow matrix that helps system developers work on specific areas, and then integrate the results into an overall model.

modeling tools. In addition to these tools, system developers also use multi-purpose tools to help them translate the system logic into properly functioning program modules. These generic tools include entity-relationship diagrams, flowcharts, pseudocode, decision tables, and decision trees.

Structured analysis is a traditional approach that is time-tested and easy to understand. Structured modeling tools are described in detail in Chapter 5, Data and Process Modeling. However, as Chapter 1 points out, **object-oriented analysis and design** (OOAD) is very popular. Widespread use of object-oriented languages has spurred interest in O-O CASE and UML-based modeling tools, which provide seamless development from planning to actual coding. Other O-O features include modular design and reusable code, which can reduce costs and speed up development. Object-oriented analysis and design tools and techniques are described in Chapter 6, Object Modeling.

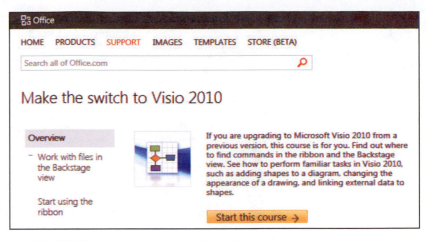

FIGURE TK B-17   Microsoft Visio offers self-paced online tutorials, complete with a self-assessment feature.
Screenshot used with permission from Microsoft..

The most recent trend is the popularity of agile methods. Chapter 11 includes a detailed description of an agile project, including the iterative cycles and the intense contact between developers and users. According to Scott W. Ambler, a well-known IT consultant, agile developers use a wide range of modeling tools, including CASE tools. However, many agile teams find that simple whiteboard sketching works best for them, as shown in Figure TK B-18.

Although it is difficult to predict the future, it seems clear that CASE tools will continue to evolve and become more powerful. At the same time, system developers will sometimes choose simpler, low-tech methods and techniques as modeling tools.

TOOLKIT SUMMARY

CASE stands for computer-aided systems engineering. CASE tools are software programs that system developers use to help them design and construct information systems. CASE tools can reduce costs, speed up development, and provide comprehensive documentation that can be used for future maintenance or enhancements.

Older systems used program code that was written in procedural languages such as COBOL, which required a programmer to create code statements for each processing step. Modern languages such as C++ and Java are non-procedural, or event-driven, languages because a programmer defines the actions that the program must perform when certain events occur.

Non-procedural languages, called 4GLs, are object-oriented programming languages (OOPL). 4GLs are important components of a fourth-generation environment that allows system developers to develop accurate prototypes, cut development time, and reduce expense.

A repository is a database that serves as a central storage location for all information about the system being developed. Once a data element has been defined in the repository, it can be accessed and used by processes and other information systems. An alias is an alternative name for a data element. The repository can be searched, and all instances of the data element will be listed.

An integrated set of CASE tools can be used to model, document, engineer, and construct the information system. Modeling tools represent the system graphically by

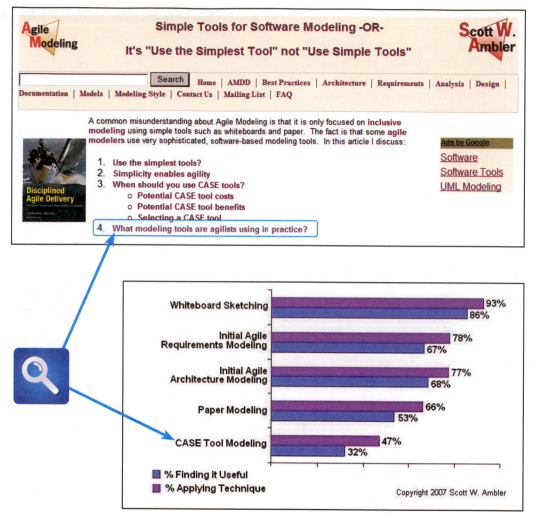

FIGURE TK B-18   Scott Ambler's survey indicates that although many Agile developers use CASE tool modeling, the technique is not especially popular.

© 2001–2012 Scott W. Ambler

using various types of diagrams, including data flow diagrams (DFDs), Unified Modeling Language (UML) diagrams, functional decomposition diagrams, structure charts, and network diagrams.

The main source of system documentation is the repository, which identifies new elements and adds them to the database. Additional documentation is provided by tools that check automatically for inconsistent or incomplete information in forms, reports, and diagrams.

Forward engineering means translating business processes and functions into applications. Reverse engineering allows you to examine an existing application and break it down into a series of diagrams, structure charts, and, in some cases, source code.

A CASE tool can handle many program development tasks, such as generating application code, screens, and reports.

An integrated development environment (IDE) uses a built-in CASE tool that a software vendor includes to make it easier to plan, construct, and maintain a specific software product. Examples of IDEs include Oracle Designer and Microsoft Visual Studio.

Many vendors, including IBM and Microsoft, are calling attention to application life cycle management (ALM) concepts and tools. ALM refers to a start-to-finish approach to planning, designing, developing, deploying, managing, and maintaining an information system.

Two trends seem clear: CASE tool vendors will continue to include powerful new features, and the popularity of object-oriented tools will continue to grow.

Key Terms

Toolkit Exercises

Review Questions

1. Define CASE, CASE tools, and a CASE environment.
2. Explain the difference between procedural and non-procedural languages.
3. Describe 4GLs and their characteristics.
4. Define a repository, and explain its role in the systems development process.
5. What are forward and reverse engineering tools, and how are they used?
6. Provide an example of an application generator and a screen generator.
7. How is a report generator used, and what is a mock-up report?
8. Explain the concept of an integrated development environment and provide two examples of IDEs.
9. Explain the concept of an application life cycle management environment and provide two examples of ALMs.
10. What is the emerging role of object-oriented analysis and design methods? Agile methods?

Discussion Topics

1. Would a systems analyst be better off in a position where he or she works with an IDE, or where generic CASE tools are used? Explain your answer.
2. Visit the Web sites for Rational System Architect and Visible Analyst. If you could choose only one of these products, which one would you select, and why?
3. If you were a programmer, would you prefer to work with procedural or non-procedural languages? Explain your reasons.
4. Some analysts believe that if the trend toward more powerful CASE tools continues, many tedious development tasks might be performed automatically. Is there a limit to the capabilities of future CASE software? Could a complete information system be designed by describing a business operation and specifying certain inputs and outputs? Explain your answer.

Projects

1. Search the Internet for a simple, user-friendly CASE tool that you would recommend for your school's computer lab. Visit the vendor's site and learn all you can about the product. Write a brief report that describes your experience.
2. Visit *www.visual-paradigm.com*. Locate and download the Community Edition, which is free, or a 30-day trial edition. Experiment with the program and write a brief report that describes your experience.
3. Search the Internet and locate an example of a screen generator. Visit the vendor's site and learn all you can about the product. Write a brief report that describes your experience.
4. Go to the site shown in Figure TK B-8 on page 588 and learn more about Gillani's FourGen CASE Tools. Write a brief report summarizing your findings.

PART C

Financial Analysis Tools

In **Part C** of the Systems Analyst's Toolkit, you will learn how to use financial analysis tools during planning, analysis, design, implementation, support, and securing an information system.

INTRODUCTION

OBJECTIVES

When you finish this part of the Toolkit, you will be able to:

- Define economic feasibility
- Classify costs and benefits into various categories, including tangible or intangible, direct or indirect, fixed or variable, and developmental or operational
- Understand chargeback methods and how they are used
- Use payback analysis to calculate the length of time that it takes for a project to pay for itself
- Use return on investment analysis to measure a project's profitability
- Use present value analysis to determine the value of a future project measured in current dollars

Part C of the Systems Analyst's Toolkit shows you how to use various tools to calculate a project's costs and benefits. As a systems analyst, you need to know how to calculate costs and benefits when you conduct preliminary investigations, evaluate IT projects, and make recommendations to management.

Financial analysis tools are important throughout the systems development life cycle. For example, in Chapter 2, you learn that economic feasibility depends on a comparison of costs and benefits. A project is economically feasible if the future benefits outweigh the estimated costs of developing or acquiring the new system. In Chapter 7, when you analyze development strategies, you apply financial analysis tools and techniques as you examine various options. Then, as Chapter 12 explains, you use these tools again to recognize the end of a system's useful life.

If you have MIS CourseMate, you can view three Video Learning Sessions that explain how to use financial analysis tools, including payback analysis, return on investment (ROI), and net present value (NPV).

PREVIEW CASE: Mountain View College Bookstore

Background: Wendy Lee, manager of college services at Mountain View College, wants a new information system that will improve efficiency and customer service at the three college bookstores.

In this part of the case, Tina Allen (systems analyst) and David Conroe (student intern) are talking about financial analysis tools and techniques.

Participants:	Tina and David
Location:	Mountain View College Cafeteria, during the systems planning phase
Discussion topics:	Economic feasibility, chargeback methods, cost-benefit classification, payback analysis, return on investment analysis, and net present value analysis

Tina: Hi, David. Before we go any further with the preliminary investigation, I wanted to meet with you to discuss financial analysis tools and techniques and how we will apply them.

David: *Fine with me. Where do we start?*

Tina: Well, because economic feasibility depends on a project's costs and benefits, the first step is to classify those costs and benefits into specific categories. For example, costs can be tangible or intangible, direct or indirect, fixed or variable, and developmental or operational.

David: *Okay, I understand. What do we do after we classify everything?*

Tina: Then we use one or more financial analysis tools: payback analysis, return on investment analysis, and net present value analysis. We'll learn how to use them to evaluate the system and compare alternatives. We'll also talk about chargeback methods.

David: *What are they?*

Tina: A chargeback method is just a way to allocate costs for an IT system. We'll have to talk to Wendy about that. Meanwhile, here's a task list we can work on:

FIGURE TK C-1 Typical financial analysis tasks.

© Cengage Learning 2014

DESCRIBING COSTS AND BENEFITS

As a systems analyst, you must review a project's costs and benefits at the end of each SDLC phase so management can decide whether or not to continue the project. Before you can use the economic analysis tools described in this section of the Toolkit, you must learn how to identify and classify all costs and benefits.

As you learned in Chapter 2, **economic feasibility** means that the projected benefits of the proposed system outweigh the projected costs. When you determine economic feasibility, you must consider the project's benefits compared to the project's **total cost of ownership** (TCO), which includes ongoing support and maintenance costs, as well as acquisition costs.

Figure TK C-2 shows Hewlett-Packard's free TCO analysis tool. HP urges visitors to take the *TCO Challenge*, and points to studies showing that the majority of total IT costs occur *after* the purchase, and that nearly half the costs lie outside the IT department's budget. HP also cites a study that shows a staggering TCO of $21,000 for a $2,000 PC when all costs are considered over a five-year period. HP noted that the most significant cost factor is user support, including peer-to-peer assistance that rarely is documented or measured.

Cost-benefit analysis tools also are available from various vendors and organizations, including the Infotech site shown in Figure TK C-3. Infotech's free TCO calculator provides a three-year planning horizon and graphical output.

Figure TK C-4 shows a cost-benefit tool that focuses on technology evaluation. The vendor, New Venture Tools, is supported by the European Union, and is intended to help European entrepreneurs with online technology, training, and IT support.

Cost Classifications

Costs can be classified as tangible or intangible, direct or indirect, fixed or variable, and developmental or operational. **Tangible costs** are costs for which you can assign a specific dollar value. Examples of tangible costs include employee salaries, hardware and software purchases, and office supplies. Tangible costs also include the interest charges that firms must pay when they need to borrow money for working capital or to finance new projects. In times of high interest rates, these costs can be significant and must be considered.

FIGURE TK C-2   HP invites visitors to try a free *TCO Challenge* in order to improve TCO and return on investment (ROI).

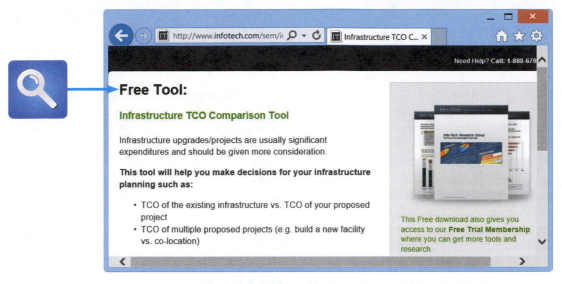

FIGURE TK C-3   Infotech offers a free TCO comparison tool that can be used in infrastructure planning.
© 1997–2012 Info-Tech Research Group

FIGURE TK C-4   New Venture Tools, which is part of an EU-supported project, includes a cost-benefit analysis tool to aid IT planning and decision-making.
© 2001 URENIO Research Unit

In contrast, **intangible costs** are costs whose dollar value cannot be calculated easily. The cost of customer dissatisfaction, lower employee morale, and reduced information availability are examples of intangible costs.

If the analyst examines an intangible item carefully, however, it sometimes is possible to estimate a dollar value. For example, users might dislike a system because it is difficult to learn. Their dissatisfaction is an intangible cost, but if it translates into an increase in errors that must be corrected, you probably could assign a tangible dollar cost. You should try to work with tangible costs whenever possible.

Direct costs are costs that can be associated with the development of a specific system. Examples of direct costs include the salaries of project team members and the purchase of hardware that is used only for the new system. In contrast, **indirect costs,** or **overhead expenses,** cannot be attributed to the development of a particular information system. The salaries of network administrators, copy machine rentals, and insurance expenses are examples of indirect costs.

Fixed costs are costs that are relatively constant and do not depend on a level of activity or effort. Many fixed costs recur regularly, such as salaries and hardware rental charges. **Variable costs** are costs that vary depending on the level of activity. The costs of printer paper, supplies, and telephone line charges are examples of variable costs.

Developmental costs are incurred only once, at the time the system is developed or acquired. Those costs might include salaries of people involved in systems development, software purchases, initial user training, and the purchase of necessary hardware or furniture. **Operational costs** are incurred after the system is implemented and continue while the system is in use. Examples of operational costs include system maintenance, ongoing training, annual software license fees, and communications expense.

Some costs apply to more than one category of expenses. For example, overtime pay for clerical staff during the systems analysis phase would be classified as developmental, variable, and direct. A monthly fee for maintaining the company's Web site would be regarded as operational, fixed, and indirect.

Managing Information Systems Costs and Charges

Management wants to know how much an information system costs, so it is important for the systems analyst to understand direct costs, indirect costs, and methods of allocating IT charges within the company.

Direct costs usually are easier to identify and predict than indirect costs. For example, the salaries of project team members and the purchase of hardware, software, and supplies for the new system are direct costs. After a new information system goes into operation, other direct costs might include the lease of system-specific hardware or software.

Many IT department costs cannot be attributed directly to a specific information system or user group. Those indirect costs can include general hardware and software acquisition expenses; facility maintenance, air conditioning, security, rent, insurance, and general supplies; and the salaries of operations, technical support, and information center personnel.

A **chargeback method** is a technique that uses accounting entries to allocate the indirect costs of running the IT department. Most organizations adopt one of four chargeback methods: no charge, a fixed charge, a variable charge based on resource usage, or a variable charge based on volume.

1. **No charge method.** Some organizations treat information systems department indirect expenses as a necessary cost of doing business, and IT services are seen as benefiting the entire company. Thus, indirect IT department costs are treated as general organizational costs and are not charged to other departments. In this case, the information systems department is called a **cost center** because it generates accounting charges with no offsetting credits for IT services.

2. **Fixed charge method.** With this method, the indirect IT costs are divided among all the other departments in the form of a fixed monthly charge. The monthly charge might be the same for all departments or based on a relatively constant factor such as department size or number of workstations. By using a fixed charge approach, all indirect costs are charged to other departments, and the IT group is regarded as a profit center. A **profit center** is a department that is expected to break even or show a profit. Under the profit center concept, company departments purchase services from the IT department and receive accounting charges that represent the cost of providing the services.

3. **Variable charge method based on resource usage. Resource allocation** is the charging of indirect costs based on the resources used by an information system. The allocation might be based on connect time, server processing time, network resources required, printer use, or a combination of similar factors.

Connect time is the total time that a user is connected actively to a remote server — some Internet service providers use this as a basis for charges. In a client/server system, **server processing time** is the time that the server actually responds to client requests for processing. The amount a particular department is charged will vary from month to month, depending not only on that department's resource usage, but also on the total resource usage. The IT department is considered a profit center when an organization uses the resource allocation method.

4. **Variable charge method based on volume.** The indirect IT department costs are allocated to other departments based on user-oriented activity, such as the number of transactions or printing volume. As with the resource allocation method, a department's share of the costs varies from month to month, depending on the level of activity. In this case, the IT department is considered a profit center.

Benefit Classifications

In addition to classifying costs, you must classify the benefits that the company expects from a project. Like costs, benefits can be classified as tangible or intangible, fixed or variable, and direct or indirect. Another useful benefit classification relates to the nature of the benefit: positive benefits versus cost-avoidance benefits. **Positive benefits** increase revenues, improve services, or otherwise contribute to the organization as a direct result of the new information system. Examples of positive benefits include improved information availability, greater flexibility, faster service to customers, higher employee morale, and better inventory management.

In contrast, **cost-avoidance benefits** refer to expenses that would be necessary if the new system were not installed. Examples of cost-avoidance benefits include handling the work with current staff instead of hiring additional people, not having to replace existing hardware or software, and avoiding problems that otherwise would be faced with the current system. Cost-avoidance benefits are just as important as positive benefits, and you must consider both types when performing cost-benefit analysis.

COST-BENEFIT ANALYSIS

Cost-benefit analysis is the process of comparing the anticipated costs of an information system to the anticipated benefits. Cost-benefit analysis is performed throughout the SDLC to determine the economic feasibility of an information system project and to compare alternative solutions. Many cost-benefit analysis techniques exist. This section covers discussion of only the three most common methods: payback analysis, return on investment analysis, and present value analysis. Each of the approaches analyzes cost-benefit figures differently, but the objective is the same: to provide reliable information for making decisions.

© craftvision/iStockphoto

Video Learning Session
Payback Analysis

Video Learning Sessions can help you understand key concepts, practice your skills, and check your work. To access the sessions, visit the Management Information Systems CourseMate Web site at **www.cengagebrain.com** and navigate to the **Video Learning Sessions** for this book. This session is about payback analysis. You'll learn how to calculate the payback period for a project and how to use a spreadsheet to determine a project's payback period.

Payback Analysis

Payback analysis is the process of determining how long it takes an information system to pay for itself. The time it takes to recover the system's cost is called the **payback period**. To perform a payback analysis, you carry out the following steps:

1. Determine the initial development cost of the system.
2. Estimate annual benefits.
3. Determine annual operating costs.
4. Find the payback period by comparing total development and operating costs to the accumulated value of the benefits produced by the system.

When you plot the system costs over the potential life of the system, you typically see a curve such as the one shown in Figure TK C-5. After the system is operational, costs decrease rapidly and remain relatively low for a period of time. Eventually, as the system requires more maintenance, costs begin to increase. The period between the beginning of systems operation and the point when operational costs are rapidly increasing is called the **economically useful life** of the system.

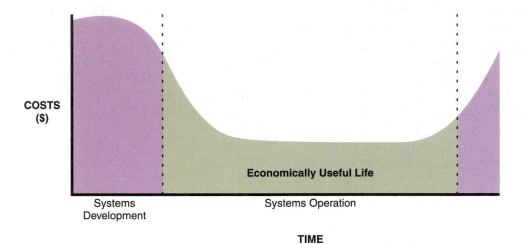

FIGURE TK C-5 The costs of a typical system vary over time. At the beginning, system costs are high due to initial development expense. Costs then drop during systems operation. Maintenance costs begin to increase until the system reaches the end of its economically useful life. The area between the two dashed lines shows the economically useful life of this system.

© Cengage Learning 2014

When you plot the benefits provided by an information system against time, the resulting curve usually resembles the one shown in the upper graph in Figure TK C-6. Benefits start to appear when the system becomes operational, might increase for a time, and then level off or start to decline.

When conducting a payback analysis, you calculate the time it takes for the accumulated benefits of an information system to equal the accumulated costs of developing and operating the system.

In the lower graph in Figure TK C-6, the cost and benefit curves are plotted together. The dashed line indicates the payback period. Notice that the payback period is not the point when current benefits equal current costs, where the two lines cross. Instead, the payback period compares accumulated costs and benefits. If you graph current costs and benefits, the payback period corresponds to the time at which the areas under the two curves are equal.

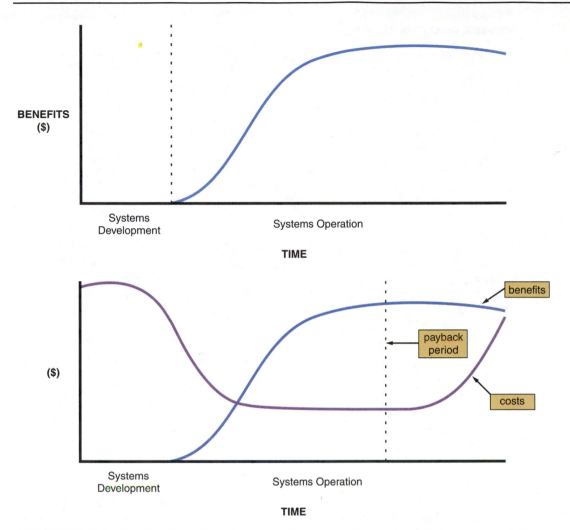

FIGURE TK C-6 Benefits of an information system change over time, as shown in the upper graph. The lower graph shows costs and benefits plotted on the same graph. The dashed line indicates the payback period, when accumulated benefits equal accumulated costs.

© Cengage Learning 2014

Figure TK C-7 on the next page contains two cost-benefit tables. The tables show the anticipated annual costs, cumulative costs, annual benefits, and cumulative benefits for two information systems projects. Year 0 (zero) corresponds to the year in which systems development begins. The development of Project A takes less than one year, so some benefits are realized in Year 0. Systems development for Project B requires more than one year, so the benefits do not begin until some time in Year 1.

In Project A, by the end of Year 4, the cumulative costs are $135,700, which slightly exceeds the $132,000 cumulative benefits. By the end of Year 5, however, the cumulative benefits of $171,000 far exceed the cumulative costs, which are $157,700. Therefore, at some point in time during Year 5, the accumulated costs and benefits are equal, and the payback period is established. In Project B, a similar situation exists. By the end of Year 4, Project B's cumulative costs are $191,000, which is greater than the cumulative benefits of $156,000. At some point during Year 5, cumulative benefits will exceed cumulative costs, and the system will have paid for itself.

If more specific information is available regarding the timing of costs and benefits during a year, you can calculate the payback period more precisely. Another approach is to create a chart that shows the exact point when cumulative benefits exceed cumulative costs, which is explained in the following section.

PAYBACK ANALYSIS EXAMPLES

PROJECT A:				
YEAR	COSTS	CUMULATIVE COSTS	BENEFITS	CUMULATIVE BENEFITS
0	60,000	60,000	3,000	3,000
1	17,000	77,000	28,000	31,000
2	18,500	95,500	31,000	62,000
3	19,200	114,700	34,000	96,000
4	21,000	135,700	36,000	132,000
5	22,000	157,700	39,000	171,000
6	23,300	181,000	42,000	213,000

PROJECT B:				
YEAR	COSTS	CUMULATIVE COSTS	BENEFITS	CUMULATIVE BENEFITS
0	80,000	80,000	——	——
1	40,000	120,000	6,000	6,000
2	25,000	145,000	26,000	32,000
3	22,000	167,000	54,000	86,000
4	24,000	191,000	70,000	156,000
5	26,500	217,500	82,000	238,000
6	30,000	247,500	92,000	330,000

FIGURE TK C-7 Payback analysis data for two information systems proposals: Project A and Project B.
© Cengage Learning 2014

Some managers are critical of payback analysis because it places all the emphasis on early costs and benefits and ignores the benefits received after the payback period. Even if the benefits for Project B in Year 6 soared as high as $500,000, the payback period for that project still occurs during the fifth year of operation. In defense of payback analysis, the earlier cost and benefit predictions usually are more certain. In general, the further out in time that you extend your projections, the more unsure your forecast will be. Thus, payback analysis uses the most reliable of your cost and benefit estimates.

Payback analysis rarely is used to compare or rank projects because later benefits are ignored. You would never decide that Project A is better than Project B simply because the payback period for A is less than that for B; considering all the costs and all the benefits when comparing projects makes more sense.

Even with its drawbacks, payback analysis is popular. Many business organizations establish a minimum payback period for approved projects. If company policy requires a project to begin paying for itself within three years, then neither project in Figure TK C-7 would be approved, though both are economically feasible because total benefits exceed total costs.

Using a Spreadsheet to Compute Payback Analysis

You can use a spreadsheet to record and calculate accumulated costs and benefits, as shown in Figure TK C-8. The first step is to design the worksheet and label the rows and columns. After entering the cost and benefit data for each year, you enter the formulas. For payback analysis, you will need a formula to display cumulative totals, year by year. For example, the first year in the cumulative costs column is the same as Year 0 costs, so the formula in cell C6 is =B6. The cumulative cost total for the

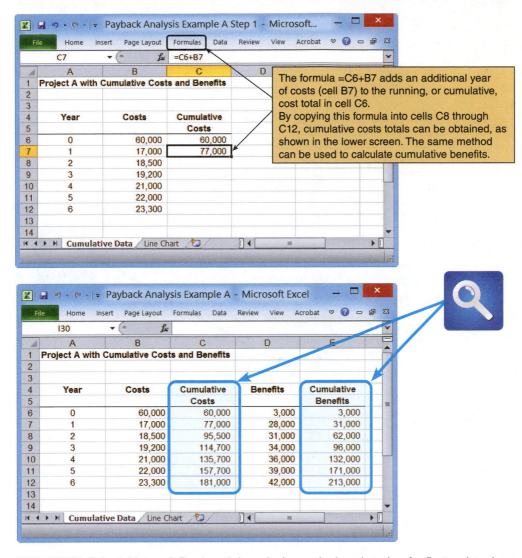

FIGURE TK C-8 A Microsoft Excel worksheet displays payback analysis data for Project A in the upper screen. When cumulative cost and benefit formulas are entered, the finished worksheet in the lower screen appears.

© Cengage Learning 2014

second year is Year 0 cumulative total + Year 1 costs, so the formula for cell C7 is =C6+B7, and so on. The first worksheet shows the initial layout and the second worksheet shows the finished spreadsheet.

After you verify that the spreadsheet operates properly, you can create a line chart that displays the cumulative costs, benefits, and payback period, which is identified by the intersection of the cost and benefit lines, as shown in Figure TK C-9 on the next page.

Video Learning Session
Return on Investment

Video Learning Sessions can help you understand key concepts, practice your skills, and check your work. To access the sessions, visit the Management Information Systems CourseMate Web site at **www.cengagebrain.com** and navigate to the **Video Learning Sessions** for this book. This session is about return on investment (ROI) analysis. You'll learn how to calculate ROI for a project and how to use a spreadsheet to determine a project's return on investment.

© craftvision/iStockphoto

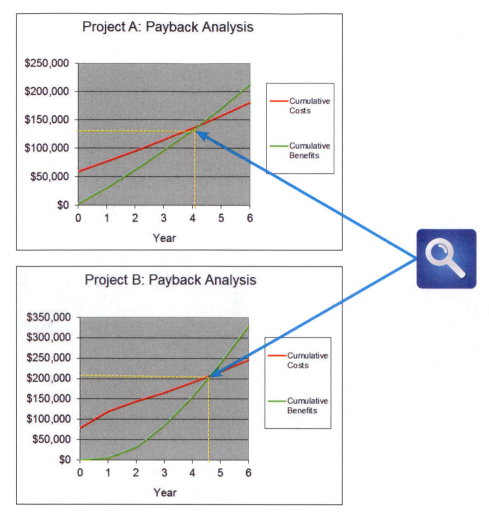

FIGURE TK C-9   Microsoft Excel can be used to show the payback period by creating a chart of cumulative costs and benefits. Note that Project A has a shorter payback period than Project B.

© Cengage Learning 2014

Return on Investment Analysis

Return on investment (ROI) is a percentage rate that measures profitability by comparing the total net benefits (the return) received from a project to the total costs (the investment) of the project. ROI is calculated as follows:

ROI = (total benefits − total costs) / total costs

Return on investment analysis considers costs and benefits over a longer time span than payback analysis. ROI calculations usually are based on total costs and benefits for a period of five to seven years. For example, Figure TK C-10 shows the ROI calculations for Project A and Project B. The ROI for Project A is 17.7%, and the ROI for Project B is 33.3%.

In many organizations, projects must meet or exceed a minimum ROI. This minimum ROI can be an estimate of the return the organization would receive from investing its money in other investment opportunities such as treasury bonds, or it can be a higher rate that the company requires for all new projects. If a company requires a minimum ROI of 15%, for example, then both Projects A and B would meet the criterion.

You also can use ROI for ranking projects. If Projects A and B represent two different proposed solutions for a single information systems project, then the solution represented by Project B is better than the Project A solution. If Projects A and B represent two different information systems projects, and if the organization has sufficient resources to pursue only one of the two projects, then Project B is the better choice.

Critics of return on investment analysis raise two points. First, ROI measures the overall rate of return for the total period, and annual return rates can vary considerably. Two projects with the same ROI might not be equally desirable if the benefits of one project occur significantly earlier than the benefits of the other project. The second criticism is that the ROI technique ignores the timing of the costs and benefits. This concept is called the time value of money, and is explained in the section on the present value analysis method.

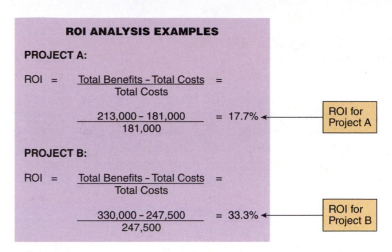

FIGURE TK C-10 Return on investment analysis for Project A and Project B shown in Figure TK C-7 on page 608.
© Cengage Learning 2014

Using a Spreadsheet to Compute ROI

You also can use spreadsheet programs to calculate the ROI. To do so for Project A, first set up the worksheet and enter the cost and benefit data. You can use cumulative columns (as you did in payback analysis) but you also will need two overall totals (one for costs and one for benefits), as shown in Figure TK C-11.

The last step is to add a formula to calculate the ROI percentage rate, which is displayed in cell E13 in Figure TK C-11. As stated previously, the ROI calculation is total benefits minus total costs, divided by total costs. Therefore, the formula that displays the ROI percentage in cell E13 is = (E11–C11)/C11.

A major advantage of using a spreadsheet is if your data changes, you can modify your worksheet and calculate a new result instantly.

You also can use pre-built templates instead of starting from scratch. For example, if you have MIS CourseMate, you can visit the online Forms Library and download Excel templates for ROI and NPV analysis.

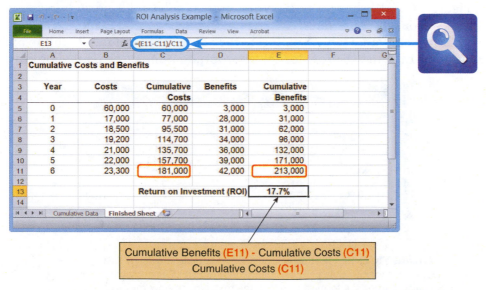

FIGURE TK C-11 Sample ROI worksheet. Notice that cell E13 contains the ROI formula.
© Cengage Learning 2014

Video Learning Session
Present Value Analysis

Video Learning Sessions can help you understand key concepts, practice your skills, and check your work. To access the sessions, visit the Management Information Systems CourseMate Web site at **www.cengagebrain.com** and navigate to the **Video Learning Sessions** for this book. This session is about present value analysis. You'll learn how to calculate net present value (NPV) for a project and how to use a spreadsheet to determine a project's net present value.

© craftvision/iStockphoto

Present Value Analysis

A dollar you have today is worth more than a dollar you do not receive until one year from today. If you have the dollar now, you can invest it and it will grow in value. For example, would you rather have $100 right now or a year from now? The answer should be obvious. If you receive the $100 now, you can invest it in a mutual fund that has an annual return of 8%. One year from now, you will have $108 instead of $100.

You might decide to approach ROI from a different direction. For example, instead of asking, "How much will my $100 be worth a year from now?" you can ask, "How much do I need to invest today, at 8%, in order to have $100 a year from now?" This concept is known as the **time value of money**, as shown in Figure TK C-12, and it is the basis of the technique called **present value analysis**.

The **present value** of a future dollar is the amount of money that, when invested today at a specified interest rate, grows to exactly one dollar at a certain point in the future. The specified interest rate is called the discount rate. In present value analysis, a company uses a discount rate that represents the rate of return if the money is put into relatively risk-free investments, such as bonds, instead of being invested in the project.

Most companies require a rate of return that is higher than the discount rate because of the degree of risk in any project compared with investing in a bond. Companies often reject projects that seem attractive because the risk is not worth the potential reward.

To help you perform present value analysis, adjustment factors for various interest rates and numbers of years are calculated and printed in tables called **present value tables**. Figure TK C-12 shows a portion of a present value table, including values for 10 years at various discount rates.

To use a present value table, you locate the value in the column with the appropriate discount rate and the row for the appropriate number of years. For example,

PERIODS	6%	8%	10%	12%	14%
1	0.943	0.926	0.909	0.893	0.877
2	0.890	0.857	0.826	0.797	0.769
3	0.840	0.794	0.751	0.712	0.675
4	0.792	0.735	0.683	0.636	0.592
5	0.747	0.681	0.621	0.567	0.519
6	0.705	0.630	0.564	0.507	0.456
7	0.665	0.583	0.513	0.452	0.400
8	0.627	0.540	0.467	0.404	0.351
9	0.592	0.500	0.424	0.361	0.308
10	0.558	0.463	0.386	0.322	0.270

FIGURE TK C-12 Portion of a present value table showing adjustment factors for various time periods and discount rates. Values in the table are calculated using the formula shown in the text. Notice how the factors decrease as time and percentages increase.

© Cengage Learning 2014

to calculate the present value of $1 at 12% for five years, you look down the 12% column in Figure TK C-12 until you reach the row representing five years. The table value is 0.567. To determine what the present value of $3,000 will be in five years with a discount rate of 12%, multiply the present value factor from the table by the dollar amount; that is, PV = $3,000 × 0.567 = $1,701.

Many finance and accounting books contain comprehensive present value tables, or you can obtain this information on the Internet, as shown in Figure TK C-13.

To perform present value analysis, you must time-adjust the cost and benefit figures. First, you multiply each of the projected benefits and costs by the proper present value factor, which depends on when the cost will be incurred or the benefit will be received. The second step is to sum all the time-adjusted benefits and time-adjusted costs. Then, you calculate the **net present value (NPV)** of the project, which is the total present value of the benefits minus the total present value of the costs. Figure TK C-14 on the next page shows the calculation of net present value for two sample projects.

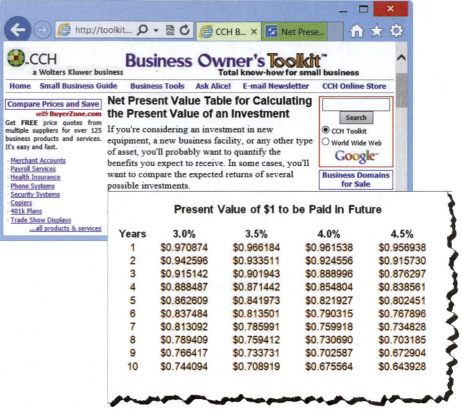

FIGURE TK C-13 The CCH Business Owner's Toolkit offers a small business guide, and a wide range of financial tools, including this present value table.
© 1995–2007, CCH Incorporated

In theory, any project with a positive NPV is economically feasible because the project will produce a larger return than would be achieved by investing the same amount of money in a discount rate investment. Remember that risks are associated with any project, however, and management typically insists on a substantially higher return for high-risk projects. For example, both projects in Figure TK C-15 on page 615 have positive net present values and appear economically worthwhile.

Suppose, however, that you knew one of the projects had a 90% probability of achieving its goals, while the other project had only a 70% chance. To be attractive, the project with the higher risk would have to offer a corresponding higher reward. Chapter 3 explains how project managers evaluate risks. Figure 3-33 on page 112 shows a matrix that includes various combinations of risk probability and impact.

Net present value also can be used to compare and rank projects. All things being equal, the project with the highest net present value is the best investment. Figure TK C-14 shows that Project B is a better investment than Project A because it has a higher net present value.

Present value analysis provides solutions to the shortcomings of payback analysis and return on investment analysis. Unlike payback analysis, present value analysis considers all the costs and benefits, and not just the earlier values. In addition, present value analysis takes into account the timing of costs and benefits, so their values can be adjusted by the discount rate that provides a common yardstick and recognizes the time value of money. Even so, companies often use all three methods to get more input for making decisions. Sometimes a project will score higher on one method of analysis and lower on another.

NET PRESENT VALUE EXAMPLES

PROJECT A:

	Year 0	Year 1	Year 2	Year 3	Year 4	Year 5	Year 6	Total
Benefits:	3,000	28,000	31,000	34,000	36,000	39,000	42,000	
Present Value Factor (12%):	1.000	0.893	0.797	0.712	0.636	0.567	0.507	
Present Value:	3,000	25,004	24,707	24,208	22,896	22,113	21,294	143,222
Costs:	60,000	17,000	18,500	19,200	21,000	22,000	23,300	
Present Value Factor (12%):	1.000	0.893	0.797	0.712	0.636	0.567	0.507	
Present Value:	60,000	15,181	14,745	13,670	13,356	12,474	11,813	141,239
Net Present Value:								**1,983** ← net present value of Project A

PROJECT B:

	Year 0	Year 1	Year 2	Year 3	Year 4	Year 5	Year 6	Total
Benefits:	——	6,000	26,000	54,000	70,000	82,000	92,000	
Present Value Factor (12%):	——	0.893	0.797	0.712	0.636	0.567	0.507	
Present Value:	——	5,358	20,722	38,448	44,520	46,494	46,644	202,186
Costs:	80,000	40,000	25,000	22,000	24,000	26,500	30,000	
Present Value Factor (12%):	1.000	0.893	0.797	0.712	0.636	0.567	0.507	
Present Value:	80,000	35,720	19,925	15,664	15,264	15,026	15,210	196,809
Net Present Value:								**5,377** ← net present value of Project B

FIGURE TK C-14   Net present value analysis for Project A and Project B. The tables use discount factors from external sources, such as the CCH site shown in Figure TK C-13 on the previous page.
© Cengage Learning 2014

Using a Spreadsheet to Calculate Present Value

There are two ways to calculate present value using a spreadsheet program such as Microsoft Excel. You can enter the discount adjustment factors from an external table, and use a simple formula to apply the factors. However, many analysts find it easier to use a built-in NPV formula that handles the calculations. The two methods are described in the following sections. The example shows costs and benefits for a proposed information system with a one-year development period, a three-year useful life, and a 6% discount rate.

USING EXTERNAL FACTORS   The first method is to create a spreadsheet similar to Figure TK C-15. Starting with the estimated benefits, you would enter adjustment factors in cells C5, D5, and E5. Then you would create formulas in cells C6, D6, and E6 that multiply the three factors times the dollar amounts for each year, with a total shown in column F. You would do the same thing for the estimated costs. Finally, when you subtract total costs from total benefits, the net present value for the proposed system displays in cell F12.

FIGURE TK C-15 The top screen shows how to use discount factors to calculate present value in a Microsoft Excel spreadsheet. In this case, the present value of benefits is $79,160. The bottom screen shows an example of the NPV function, which is a menu-driven formula that is built into Excel. The slight difference between the values is because Excel uses more decimal places.

© Cengage Learning 2014

USING A BUILT-IN FORMULA The second method, which is shown in the bottom screen in Figure TK C-15, uses a built-in spreadsheet function to calculate present value. You enter the amounts, the discount rate, and number of time periods, and the program does the rest. Using this approach, you perform four steps, starting with the benefits.

1. First, create a spreadsheet similar to the upper screen in Figure TK C-15, but do not enter any factors or formulas — just the year-by-year cost and benefit amounts.

2. Next, select cell F6, and click the Function button on the formula bar. Select the NPV function, and you will see a dialog box similar to the bottom of Figure TK C-15. You are using a 6% discount rate, so enter .06 in the Rate box.

3. Now enter the three benefit amounts: 20,000 for Value1, 30,000 for Value2, and 40,000 for Value3 and click the OK button (not shown in the figure).

4. At this point, a present value appears in cell F6. Now follow the same method to enter the cost amounts. When you subtract the PV of costs from the PV of benefits, the result is the net present value, or NPV. Notice there is a slight difference in the two methods because Excel uses more decimal places. The difference is not significant.

TOOLKIT SUMMARY

As a systems analyst, you must be concerned with economic feasibility throughout the SDLC, and especially during the systems planning and systems analysis phases. A project is economically feasible if the anticipated benefits exceed the expected costs. When you review a project, you work with various feasibility and cost analysis tools.

You must classify project costs as tangible or intangible, direct or indirect, fixed or variable, and developmental or operational. Tangible costs are those that have a specific dollar value, whereas intangible costs involve items that are difficult to measure in dollar terms, such as employee dissatisfaction. Direct costs can be associated with a particular information system, while indirect costs refer to overhead expenses that cannot be allocated to a specific project. Fixed costs remain the same regardless of activity levels, while variable costs are affected by the degree of system activity. Developmental costs are one-time systems development expenses, while operational costs continue during the systems operation and use phase.

Every company must decide how to charge or allocate information systems costs and the chargeback method. Common chargeback approaches are no charge, a fixed charge, a variable charge based on resource usage, or a variable charge based on volume.

Some companies use a no charge approach because IT services benefit the overall organization. This method treats the IT group for accounting purposes as a cost center that offers services without charge. In contrast, if management imposes charges on other departments, the IT department is regarded as a profit center that sells services that otherwise would have to be purchased from outside the company.

You also must classify system benefits. Many benefit categories are similar to costs: tangible or intangible, fixed or variable, and direct or indirect. Benefits also can be classified as positive benefits that result in direct dollar savings or cost-avoidance benefits that allow the firm to avoid costs that they would otherwise have incurred.

Cost-benefit analysis involves three common approaches: payback analysis, return on investment (ROI) analysis, and present value analysis. You can use spreadsheet programs to help you work with those tools.

Payback analysis determines the time it takes for a system to pay for itself, which is called the payback period. In payback analysis, you compare total development and operating costs to total benefits. The payback period is the point at which accumulated benefits equal accumulated costs. A disadvantage of this method is that payback analysis analyzes only costs and benefits incurred at the beginning of a system's useful life.

Return on investment (ROI) analysis measures a system by comparing total net benefits (the return) to total costs (the investment). The result is a percentage figure that represents a rate of return that the system offers as a potential investment. Many organizations set a minimum ROI that all projects must match or exceed and use ROI to rank several projects. Although ROI provides additional information compared with payback analysis, ROI expresses only an overall average rate of return that might not be accurate for a given time period. Also, ROI does not recognize the time value of money.

Present value analysis adjusts the value of future costs and benefits to account for the time value of money. By measuring all future costs and benefits in current dollars, you can compare systems more accurately and consistently. Present value analysis uses mathematical factors that you can derive or look up in published tables. You also can use a spreadsheet function to calculate present value. Many companies use present value analysis to evaluate and rank projects.

Key Terms

chargeback method *604*

connect time *605*

cost center *604*

cost-avoidance benefits *605*

cost-benefit analysis *605*

developmental costs *604*

direct costs *603*

economic feasibility *602*

economically useful life *606*

fixed charge method *604*

fixed costs *604*

indirect costs *603*

intangible costs *603*

net present value (NPV) *613*

no charge method *604*

operational costs *604*

overhead expenses *603*

payback analysis *606*

payback period *606*

positive benefits *605*

present value *612*

present value analysis *612*

present value tables *612*

profit center *604*

resource allocation *604*

return on investment (ROI) *610*

server processing time *605*

tangible costs *602*

time value of money *612*

total cost of ownership (TCO) *602*

variable charge method based on resource usage *604*

variable charge method based on volume *605*

variable costs *604*

Toolkit Exercises

Questions

1. How do you know if a project is economically feasible? Why is TCO important?
2. Describe each cost classification and include two examples.
3. What are four chargeback methods? In your view, is one more "fair" than another?
4. Describe each benefit classification, and include two examples.
5. What formula do you use to calculate the payback period?
6. What formula do you use to calculate ROI?
7. Would the formulas in questions 5 and 6 also apply to heavy equipment, such as a bulldozer? Why or why not?
8. Define the term *present value*, and provide an example.
9. What is the meaning of the phrase, *time value of money*?
10. Why is it difficult to assign a dollar figure to an intangible cost? Can it ever be done? Explain your answer, and provide an example.

Discussion Topics

1. Suppose your supervisor asks you to inflate the benefit figures for an IT proposal in order to raise the priority of his or her favorite project. Would this be ethical? Does internal cost-benefit analysis affect company shareholders? Why or why not?
2. In this Toolkit Part, you learned how to use payback analysis, ROI, and NPV to assess IT projects. Could these tools also be used in your personal life? Give an example of how you might use each one to help you make a financial decision.
3. Is there a role for intuition in the decision-making process, or should all judgments be made strictly on the numbers? Explain your answer.
4. The time value of money can be an important factor when analyzing a project's NPV. Is the time value of money just as important in periods of low inflation as it is in periods of high inflation? Explain your answer.

Projects

1. Suppose you are studying two hardware lease proposals. Option 1 costs $4,000, but requires that the entire amount be paid in advance. Option 2 costs $5,000, but the payments can be made $1,000 now and $1,000 per year for the next four years. If you do an NPV analysis assuming a 14% discount rate, which proposal is less expensive? What happens if you use an 8% rate?
2. Assume the following facts:
   - A project will cost $45,000 to develop.
   - When the system becomes operational after a one-year development period, operational costs will be $9,000 during each year of the system's five-year useful life.
   - The system will produce benefits of $30,000 in the first year of operation, and this figure will increase by a compound 10% each year.

   What is the payback period for this project?
3. Using the same facts as in Project 2, what is the ROI for this project?
4. Using the same facts as in Project 2, what is the NPV for this project?

PART D

Internet Resource Tools

In **Part D** of the Systems Analyst's Toolkit, you will learn about Internet resource tools that can help you perform your duties and achieve your personal and professional goals.

INTRODUCTION

OBJECTIVES

When you finish this part of the Toolkit, you will be able to:

- Describe the characteristics of the Internet and the World Wide Web

- Plan an Internet search strategy, review your information requirements, use the proper search tools and techniques, evaluate the results, and consider copyright and data integrity issues

- Use search engines, subject directories, and the invisible Web to locate the information you require

- Demonstrate advanced search techniques, including Boolean logic and Venn diagrams

- Describe Internet communication channels, including social networking, forums, newsletters, blogs, podcasts, RSS feeds, Webinars, mailing lists, Web-based discussion groups, chat rooms, instant messaging, and text messaging

- Provide examples of IT community resources of value to a systems analyst

- Explain the benefits and disadvantages of online learning opportunities

The Internet offers a wealth of information about every conceivable subject. Without a good road map, however, it is easy to become overwhelmed by the sheer volume of material. Part D of the Systems Analyst's Toolkit will describe various Internet resources, assist you in formulating an effective information-gathering strategy, and explain Internet resource tools and techniques that you can use to access the information you need.

PREVIEW CASE: Mountain View College Bookstore

Background: Wendy Lee, manager of college services at Mountain View College, wants a new information system that will improve efficiency and customer service at the three college bookstores.

In this part of the case, Tina Allen (systems analyst) and David Conroe (student intern) are talking about Internet resource tools.

Participants: Tina and David
Location: Mountain View College Cafeteria, near the end of the systems analysis
                       phase
Discussion topics: Internet resource tools

Tina:	Hi, David. Did you get a chance to try that new search engine?
David:	*I sure did. First, I formulated an Internet search strategy, as you suggested, and then I did a search using the logical operators that we talked about. I liked the way the search engine organized the results for me. I also followed your suggestions about checking out the quality of the results.*
Tina:	Sounds good. But remember — sometimes it might be better not to start your search with a search engine.
David:	*Why not?*
Tina:	Well, the Internet is a huge place. In some situations, you might want to get a broad overview of a topic before plunging into a specific search. If so, you might want to use a subject directory like Yahoo! or the Librarians' Index to the Internet. Another important resource is called the invisible Web, which is a collection of searchable databases that usually are not accessed by search engines.
David:	*Okay. What about using other communication channels like social networking sites, forums, newsletters, blogs, podcasts, RSS feeds, Webinars, mailing lists, Web-based discussion groups, chat rooms, instant messaging, and text messaging?*
Tina:	They all are important ways to get online information. Also remember that the IT community has many resources that can help you locate information, keep up with IT developments, and advance your career with knowledge and training.
David:	*It seems like the more I know about the Internet, the more I have to learn.*
Tina:	I feel the same way. Let's see what else we can learn about Internet resource tools. Here's a task list to get us started:

FIGURE TK D-1   Typical Internet resource tasks.

© Cengage Learning 2014

OVERVIEW

As a systems analyst, you rely on your knowledge, skills, and experience. Fortunately, you have access to the Internet, where an enormous storehouse of information is available to you at little or no cost. The **Internet** is a worldwide network that integrates many thousands of other networks, which in turn link millions of government, business, educational, and personal users around the globe. The Internet can assist you with technical problems and can help you advance your career by offering access to training, education, and communication with other IT professionals.

The Internet allows you to visit the **World Wide Web**, usually referred to as the **Web**, which contains billions of text and multimedia documents called **Web pages**. A collection of related Web pages is called a **Web site** and is stored on a computer called a **Web server**. A **Web browser**, or **browser**, is a software program that allows you to access and display Web pages that are delivered to you by a Web server. Microsoft Internet Explorer, Mozilla Firefox, Google Chrome, and Apple Safari are popular browsers that offer powerful graphic interfaces to help you navigate the Web.

This Toolkit Part begins with a step-by-step plan for Internet research, followed by a summary of search basics and a detailed discussion of search engines, subject directories, and the invisible Web. Internet communications tools are covered next, including social networking, forums, newsletters, blogs, podcasts, RSS feeds, Webinars, mailing lists, Web-based discussion groups, chat rooms, and instant messaging. The last section presents valuable online resources available within the IT community.

PLANNING AN INTERNET RESEARCH STRATEGY

An Internet research strategy is necessary to avoid frustration and wasted time. A pilot or ship captain would not begin a journey without knowing the destination. Similarly, you can use a four-step plan to navigate efficiently and confidently toward your objectives:

Step 1. Review your information requirements.

Step 2. Use the proper search tools and techniques.

Step 3. Evaluate the results.

Step 4. Consider copyright and data integrity issues.

Over time, you will gain experience and develop your own preferences for using the Internet. You should remember that each research situation is unique, and several tools and techniques might be necessary to achieve the results you seek.

Step 1. Review Your Information Requirements

The first step to finding information online is to make sure you really understand what you are seeking. You need to think about the topic to ensure that you are casting an appropriate net. For example, a supervisor might ask you to help decide between two specific CASE products. Your initial inclination might be to find a review of various CASE applications. Upon reflection, however, you realize it would be more useful to understand CASE tools in a general sense before comparing specific products. Therefore, you decide to start with a more generalized search instead of going directly to vendor sites.

Step 2. Use the Proper Search Tools and Techniques

Once you feel that you understand the information required, it is time to pick an initial tool. At this point, you face some choices. Should you use search engines or subject directories? Should you seek commercial sites, IT publications, professional associations, forums, or other areas to explore? What about social networking?

As you gain experience, you will be able to handle a wide range of Internet tools and resources. As with most skills, the more you use them, the more expertise you acquire. In time, you probably will develop your own list of favorite tools and resources.

Step 3. Evaluate the Results

By definition, the Internet is essentially open and unregulated. On the plus side, a huge diversity of information is available. The quality of content, however, varies greatly. Unlike published journals or textbooks, almost anyone can post content on the Web. This means that the searcher must review the information very carefully. Questions to ask when accessing content include the following:

SOURCE Is the author identifiable? Does the author have expertise on the subject? You might need to trace back through Web site addresses or URLs to find biographical information, or do a separate search on the author's name.

ACCURACY Does the information come from a commercial source that is offering its own solution? Is it from an association with an inherent bias? Often, it is very difficult to find completely objective information. Identifying biases and finding information from a variety of sources are ways to address this problem.

SCOPE Is the information specific enough? If not, you should narrow and refine your search and seek additional resources until you locate the information you need. When you use a search engine, one way to do this is to perform a **subsearch** using the results of the initial search as a starting point.

CURRENCY How old is the information? Is the topic static or dynamic? In the IT world, technology changes very quickly. If you locate information that appears to be out of date, you might seek more recent data to ensure that your results are valid.

LOOK AND FEEL Is the information easy to access and navigate? If the site is designed in a logical manner and offers value-added links to worthwhile pages and resources, do not be overly concerned with style — some excellent material is created by authors and producers who focus on content, not design.

If you find the content useful, be sure to credit the source properly when you use it. You must observe legal and ethical standards when you deal with Internet material. To learn more about proper citation and to view specific examples of how to cite electronic material, you can visit the excellent collection of resources at *www.are searchguide.com*.

Step 4. Consider Copyright and Data Integrity Issues

Before you copy or download your search results, you must ensure that you legally can use the material, and that the content is safe and free of threats.

The first issue involves copyright law. Many people regard the Web as a public domain, but in reality, it is more like a book or a CD. In other words, you might own a CD, but you do not own the material on that CD — you only possess a license to use the content in certain ways. On the Web, you should look for copyright notices and restrictions. If in doubt, you might have to contact the copyright holder to seek permission.

The second issue involves data integrity. It is important to protect your network and computer system from any unwanted viruses or **malware,** which is malicious software that might jeopardize your security or privacy. Unlike intellectual content, which is easy to evaluate, it is impossible for you to determine the integrity and validity of the internal file structure and format without a virus detection tool. As

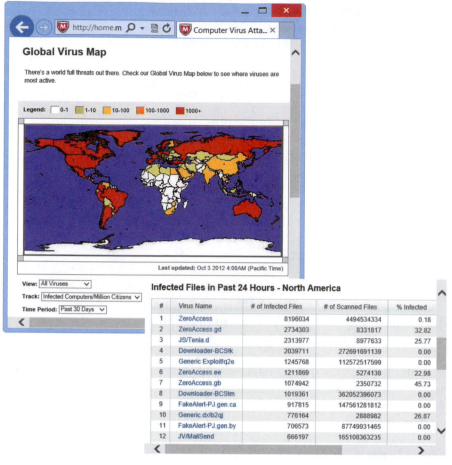

FIGURE TK D-2 McAfee's site shows how many computers and files are infected at any given time.
© 2003–2012 McAfee, Inc.

Figure TK D-2 shows, many thousands of viruses are identified each day. Viruses and other intrusions cost businesses many millions of dollars in lost data and additional effort. Without proper protection, you run the risk of not only corrupting your own files or hard drive but also bringing your entire company network down.

If the information is legally usable and safe, you can save it to your hard drive or network, depending on the content and purpose. The information you find may be in one of many formats, including word-processing documents, spreadsheets, and databases; Adobe PDF files; and multimedia material with file extensions such as .jpg, .mp3, .flv, and .mov.

You can download files directly to your hard drive from many Web sites. If this option is not offered explicitly, you can try right-clicking a link or embedded object to display a list of choices that includes downloading the selected information.

The following sections discuss search engines, subject directories, the invisible Web, and other Internet tools in more detail.

SEARCH BASICS

As you journey on the Internet, you will use various navigation tools and techniques. To reach your destination, you must know how to use search engines, subject directories, and a collection of searchable databases called the invisible Web.

A **search engine** is an application that uses keywords and phrases to locate information on the Internet. **Meta-search engines** are tools that can apply multiple search engines simultaneously. For most people, search engines are the workhorses of information gathering. Search engines employ a variety of approaches to gathering information, and although they are extremely valuable, users should be aware of potential problems. For example, search results can be affected if the search engine permits commercial users to achieve higher priority based on payment of fees. Also, search engines access only a portion of the Internet.

A **subject directory** or **topic directory** is a Web site that allows you to find information by using a hierarchy, starting with a general heading and proceeding to more specific topics. A subject directory is an excellent starting point when you want an overview of a topic before proceeding to specific Web sites. Typically, a subject directory is created by an editorial staff that visits, evaluates, and organizes the sites into various categories and subcategories.

The **invisible Web**, also called the **deep Web** or **hidden Web**, refers to a vast collection of documents, databases, and Web pages that are usually not detected by search engines, but can be accessed using other tools and techniques. The invisible Web is a huge information storehouse, many times larger than the searchable Web, and includes thousands of university, scientific, and government libraries.

The following sections cover search engines, subject directories, and the invisible Web in more detail.

SEARCH ENGINES

A search engine often is the best starting point for gathering information. A well-planned search will narrow the range of content to a manageable level and will allow you to explore the choices or execute a subsearch within the focused results. As with any tool, it is important to understand the intended use and limitations of a search engine before applying it to a task.

Although many search engines exist, the market is dominated by Google, as shown in Figure TK D-3. Google's appeal includes a robust package of features that users can access easily, and Google works hard to make its users feel like family members. However, when a single firm dominates a market, there is a risk that the firm's name can become a generic verb, such as *"You can Google it."*

FIGURE TK D-3 The chart shows the dominant market share enjoyed by Google.
Chart ©Cengage Learning 2014; Data from www.netmarketshare.com

Search Engine Concepts

Search engines use a specialized computer program called a **spider** or **crawler** that travels from site to site **indexing**, or cataloging, the contents of the pages based on **keywords**. The results are compiled into a database, so what you are searching is not the Web itself, but the contents of the search engine's database.

No single search engine can catalog the shifting contents of the Web, and even the most powerful engines do not cover all Web content. If a particular site is not widely linked, or its author does not submit it to major search engines, then the material is invisible to them. Also, any site that requires a visitor to type in data, such as a name, cannot be accessed by search engines.

Although search engine indexes are incomplete and often dated, they are capable of delivering an overwhelming number of results, or **hits**. The *real* issue is quality versus quantity. When comparing search engines, it is important to know the company's policy toward allowing commercial sites to boost their ranking in a **pay for performance** arrangement. Links that are subsidized by companies are called **sponsored links**.

Not all search engines work the same way. By understanding the underlying algorithms, or specific rules, that drive these information engines, it is possible to better target your search. For example, some sites, like Google, rank their pages by analyzing the number of other sites that link to that page. Other search engines organize results differently. For example, Ask.com uses an interesting approach called ExpertRank™ technology, which ranks a site based on the number of authoritative sites that reference it, not just based on general popularity. You usually can determine an engine's approach by clicking the *About* tab or link on the search site.

INDEXED SEARCH ENGINES Google, Yahoo!, and Bing are **indexed search engines** that organize and rank the results of a search. Although they have much in common, each tool has its own search algorithms, features, and user interface.

META-SEARCH ENGINES One of the most popular meta-search engines is Dogpile, which collects search results from Google, Yahoo!, Bing, and several others. Because each search engine uses its own method of searching, each returns a different set of results. According to the company, Dogpile reviews all the results, decides which are most relevant, and eliminates duplicates. In promoting its product, Dogpile's colorful analogy is that *"You get the best from the big dogs without all the mess."*

Another powerful meta-search engine is ixquick, which sorts search results based on how many search engines agree on the result. A five-star rating means that five separate search engines ranked the result in their top 10. Ixquick also includes a worldwide telephone directory and a video search tool that can access more than 18 million hours of video.

Search Techniques

Consider the following suggestions when you begin a search:

- Refine your topic. Unless you limit the scope of your search, you might be overwhelmed by the number of results. If you are looking for general information on a broad topic, consider a subject directory site.

- Translate your question into an effective search query. Searches are executed on keywords. You will improve your success if you pick the proper keywords. Try to find unique words or phrases and avoid those with multiple uses. For example, a search for the term *hard drive* might produce information about a computer hardware device or a difficult auto trip. Also consider using advanced search techniques, which are described in the following section.

- Review the search results and evaluate the quality of the results. If the search needs refinement or additional material, you can either use the site's advanced search techniques or select a different Internet resource altogether.

- It is important to organize the results of your search so you can recognize and revisit important sites. Some search engines offer a personalized search history, which you can review and edit for this purpose. Many people find that the easiest solution is to create favorites or bookmarks in their browser for sites visited in important searches, using a set of folders and subfolders. If you do this, you can wait until you start the search, or you can create your filing system ahead of time.

To be effective, you should understand the mechanics of the search engine, use proper spelling, find unique phrases, and experiment with a variety of approaches. If you are consistently returning too many results, try using topic-specific terms and advanced search techniques. Conversely, if too few results are returned, eliminate the least important terms or concepts, broaden your subject, or use more general vocabulary when you select terms.

Online Tutorials

When you learn a skill, it usually helps to get some tips and pointers from an expert. Many years ago, in a predigital era, librarians were an essential source of guidance for researchers. As the Internet evolved, so did librarians, so it is not surprising that libraries offer valuable advice about Internet-based research.

The table in Figure TK D-4 shows several examples of library-oriented tutorials. The screen at the bottom of the figure shows a tutorial from the Teaching Library at the University of California, Berkeley. According to the site, this is one of the most

Source	Notes	URL
Colorado State University Libraries	Multi-media style with many examples	www.lib.colostate.edu/tutorials/boolean.html
Edison State College Libraries	Uses animation to explain basic concepts	www.edison.edu/library/researchskills/Unit4/4boolean.php
Louisiana State University Libraries	Good coverage of the deep Web	www.lib.lsu.edu/instruction/deepweb/deepweb-print.html
Ohio State University Library	Several videos, including one on using Google	www.liblearn.osu.edu/tutor/
Purdue University Libraries	Comprehensive coverage plus brief *two-minute tips*	www.lib.purdue.edu/rguides/tutorials.html
University of California Berkley	According to the site, this is one of the most popular tutorials on web search skills	www.lib.berkeley.edu/TeachingLib/Guides/Internet/About.htm

© Cengage Learning 2014

FIGURE TK D-4 Six examples of free, online tutorials offered by college and university libraries. In the screen at the bottom, notice the "How to use" section, which mentions a table of contents and a glossary.

© 2012 The Regents of the University of California

heavily used and linked-to tutorials on Web search skills, and has been translated into dozens of languages. The University allows noncommercial use of these materials, which it calls *Research-Quality Web Searching*.

Advanced Search Techniques

Many search engines offer powerful **advanced search** features that allow you to refine and control the type of information returned from searches. These features can include the option to search within returned results and the ability to search within specific areas, such as forums. Perhaps the most powerful advanced feature is the option to use Boolean logic.

Boolean logic is a system named after British mathematician George Boole and refers to the relationships among search terms. You can use various combinations of the **logical operators** OR, AND, and NOT to improve your search success greatly. Figure TK D-5 illustrates the use of the operators with search terms. The graphics shown in the figure are called Venn diagrams. A **Venn diagram** uses circular symbols to illustrate Boolean logic. Venn diagrams are named after John Venn, a nineteenth-century scholar who devised a scheme for visualizing logical relationships. In the sample diagrams, the shaded area indicates the results of the search.

LOGICAL OPERATORS	EXAMPLE	VENN DIAGRAM (SHADED AREA INDICATES RETURNED RESULTS)
A **or** B	Baseball **or** Football	Baseball ⬤⬤ Football
A **and** B	Baseball **and** Football	Baseball ◯⬤◯ Football
A **not** B	Internet **not** Web	Internet ⬤◯ Web
A **or** B **or** C	Colorado **or** Mining **or** Gold	Colorado ⬤⬤ Mining / Gold
A **and** B **and** C	Colorado **and** Mining **and** Gold	Colorado ◯◯ Mining / Gold
A **and** B **not** C	Colorado **and** Mining **not** Gold	Colorado ◯⬤◯ Mining / Gold

FIGURE TK D-5 Examples of logical operators OR, AND, and NOT. The shaded area represents the returned results. OR is the most inclusive term, returning results if any of the terms appear; AND requires all keywords to appear; and NOT excludes results even if they are found in the same document.

© Cengage Learning 2014

To learn more about how logical operators work, consider the following diagrams:

OR The first diagram at the top of Figure TK D-5 shows that the **OR** term will retrieve all results containing either term. Notice that the shaded area includes both circles. The OR operator can be used when you need a wide search net.

AND The second diagram in Figure TK D-5 shows that the **AND** term will retrieve only those results in which all terms linked by the AND operator are present. Notice that the shaded area includes only the overlapping portion of the two circles. The more terms or concepts combined in an AND search, the fewer pages will be returned. The AND operator often is used to narrow a set of search results.

NOT The third diagram in Figure TK D-5 shows how the NOT operator can be used to exclude certain records. In this diagram, consider the closely related terms, Internet and Web. It is likely that these terms both appear in many Web pages. The **NOT** operator will strip out the results containing the unwanted term. For example, the search string, Internet NOT Web, will return only those pages with the term, Internet. You should use the NOT operator carefully, because the term you want to exclude may be intertwined with the term you seek in many documents that would be useful to you.

The last three diagrams in Figure TK D-5 illustrate other combinations of logical operators where three search terms are involved.

USING PHRASES Suppose you want to find sites that sell board games that require players to use strategy, such as Monopoly®. In your search, you could specify both terms, *strategy* AND *game*, but your results probably would include many documents that describe game strategies used in various sports, which is not what you are seeking. A better approach might be to search using the phrase "strategy game" enclosed in quotes. A **phrase** is more specific than an AND operator because it specifies an exact placement of terms. In this example, the phrase "strategy game" will not retrieve any documents unless they contain that exact phrase.

The implementation of Boolean logic varies by search engine. Some engines require the use of full Boolean searching using the complete operators (OR, AND, NOT) in the search window. Others use implied Boolean logic with keyword searching. In **implied Boolean logic,** symbols are used to represent Boolean operators, such as a plus sign (+) for AND, and a minus sign (-) for NOT. If two search terms are entered in the search window with a space between them, some search engines may assume an OR; others assume an AND. You need to consult the site's Help files to understand the underlying rules.

USING FILL-IN FORMS Most search engines provide an advanced search feature that offers a fill-in form similar to the Google example shown in Figure TK D-6. Many users find it easier to fill in a form than to work with Boolean operators. The examples in Figure TK D-6 on the next page include sample search terms, and on its site, Google offers many more advanced search samples and tips. Notice that the Google site also offers advanced search tips.

Search Checklist

Many people find it helpful to prepare for an Internet search by using a checklist similar to the following:

- Does the topic have any unique words, phrases, or acronyms? If so, use these terms in the search.
- Do any of the search terms have other spellings or names? If so, include these with an OR operator in the search.

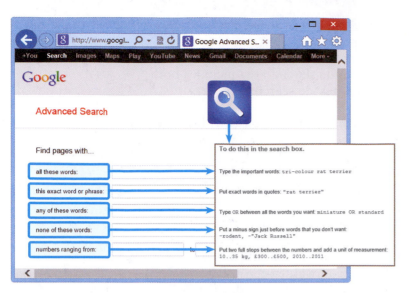

FIGURE TK D-6 These five examples show how to use Google's fill-in form to perform an advanced search. On its site, Google offers many more advanced search samples and tips.

Courtesty of Google

- Are certain additional words or phrases likely to appear in any Web document? If so, consider adding an AND operator to narrow the search.

- Is there any unrelated material that my search terms might pick up? If so, consider using the NOT operator to exclude these documents.

- Are any organizations, publications, or institutions likely to have an interest in my topic? If so, try to locate their Web sites and then conduct a further search using the site indexes and databases available on the site.

- Is the search returning results too numerous to examine? If so, keep adding additional terms to narrow the search and reduce the number of hits until a reasonable number is achieved.

SUBJECT DIRECTORIES

A subject directory collects and organizes Web sites in a top-down format, based on subjects and topics. An analogy might be a corporate organization chart, where you could go to the top person for an overview, then visit with lower-level employees to obtain specific information about their areas.

A subject directory is an excellent tool when you want general information about a topic before plunging into an array of specific Web sites. Yahoo! offers a popular subject directory that serves as a **portal**, or entrance to other Internet resources. Other academic and professional directories target the specific needs of researchers and users who concentrate on particular subjects. Many subject directories are reviewed by human experts, rather than computer robots, to ensure relevance and quality of links.

A Subject Directory Example

Subject directories organize information into various categories and provide an overall framework for finding information. For example, suppose you wanted to use the Yahoo! Directory to learn more about communications and networking magazines. First, you would navigate to the Yahoo! directory site at *dir.yahoo .com*. The first screen, which is shown at the top of Figure TK D-7, contains a list of main topics, one of which is *Computer & Internet*. When you click this item, you would see a display similar to the second screen in Figure TK D-7, which shows various subtopics, including *Communications and Networking*. As you continue, you would click the *Magazines* link shown in the third screen, and you would see a list of publications that you could explore, some of which appear in the bottom screen.

In addition to Yahoo!, other popular subject directories include About.com and an organization called ipl2, which was the result of a merger between the Internet Public Library (IPL) and the Librarians' Internet Index (LII). The new entity, which has a Web site at *ipl2.org*, offers a free question-and-answer service staffed by volunteers who are professional librarians and library science graduate students.

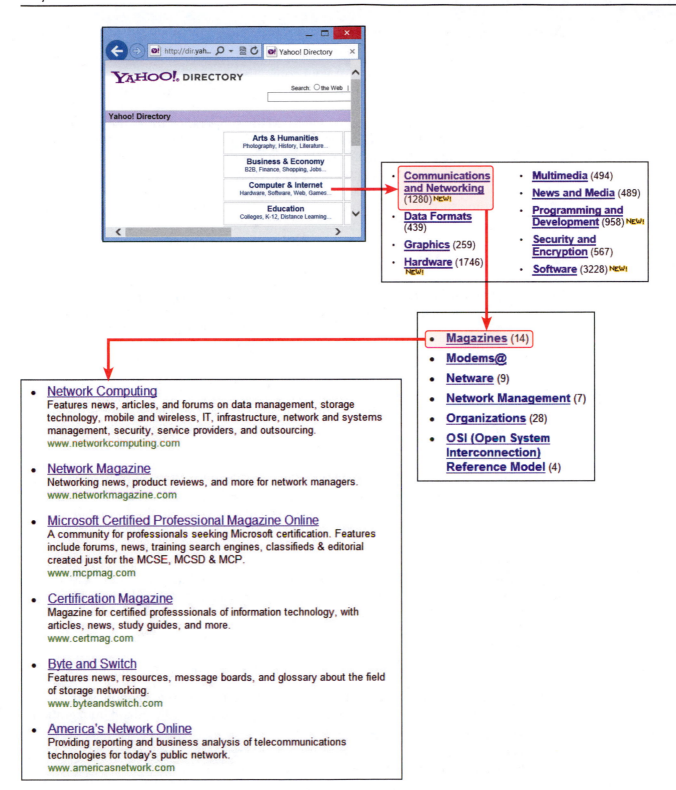

FIGURE TK D-7 Using a search directory is quite different from using a search engine, and can be faster and more efficient. In the example shown, the user visited the Yahoo! Directory, clicked the Computer & Internet category, and then selected the Communications and Networking topic. Next, the user requested a list of magazines, which are displayed in the last panel.

Advantages and Disadvantages of Subject Directories

The main advantage of a subject directory is that it provides an overview when you are not sure of the size and scope of your topic. Later, when you have a better understanding of your subject, you can use a search engine to seek additional information and examples.

Subject directories also have shortcomings. Many subject directories use human expertise to formulate the subject organization and determine the placement of links. This process involves subjective decisions that might affect the quality of search results. Some subject directories are updated continually; others might not be current. Also, unlike a search engine, a subject directory forces you to work your way through a series of levels, rather than using specific words and phrases to locate directly the material you seek.

THE INVISIBLE WEB

Everyone is familiar with what is called the **visible Web**, which refers to Web sites that are indexed by the major search engines and are publicly accessible. As discussed earlier, much more information is available on the Internet that is not indexed. This valuable information source includes numerous text, graphics, and data files stored in collections that are unreachable by search engines.

The invisible Web includes searchable databases that contain an enormous amount of information in university and government libraries, as well as thousands of specialized databases that are maintained by institutions and organizations around the world.

Much of the invisible Web is open to the public, but some databases are password protected. Many sites allow guest access, but some areas can be accessed only by members of a specific group.

In an article in the *Journal of Electronic Publishing*, author Michael K. Bergman compared Internet searching to dragging a net across the surface of the ocean. He stated that "While a great deal may be caught in the net, there is still a wealth of information that is deep, and therefore, missed. The reason is simple: Most of the Web's information is buried far down on dynamically generated sites, and standard search engines never find it." Mr. Bergman pointed out that traditional search engines create their indices by spidering, or crawling, through many millions of Web pages. He pointed out that "To be discovered, the page must be static and linked to other pages.... Because traditional search engine crawlers cannot probe beneath the surface, the deep Web has heretofore been hidden."

Invisible Web Examples

A few examples of information on the invisible Web include the following:

- Specialized topic databases: subject-specific collections of information, such as corporate financial filings and reports, genealogy records, or Ellis Island immigration data
- Hardware and software vendors: searchable technical support databases for large sites such as Microsoft's or Oracle's knowledge bases
- Publications: databases of published and archived articles
- Libraries: searchable catalogs for thousands of libraries, including the Library of Congress and numerous university and institutional libraries
- Government databases: census data, statutes, patents, copyrights, and trademarks
- Auction sites: searchable listings of items, bidders, and sellers
- Locators: telephone numbers, addresses, and e-mail addresses
- Career opportunities: job listings and résumé postings

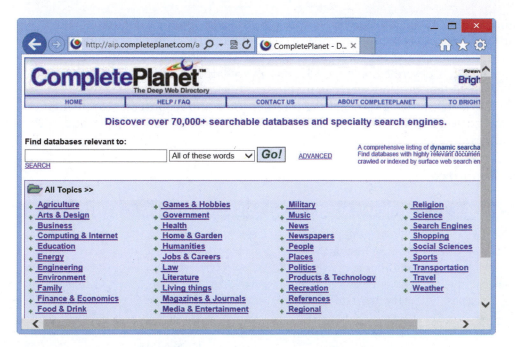

FIGURE TK D-8 The CompletePlanet site is organized by topics, and has links to many searchable databases whose contents cannot be indexed by traditional search engines.
© 2000–2010. BrightPlanet Corp.

Navigation Tools for the Invisible Web

You can access the invisible Web in several ways. One approach is to use a search engine to locate a portal, or entrance, to a searchable database by including the word, *database*, as a required search term. For example, if you are searching for information about printer drivers, you could specify "printer drivers" AND database. The additional term will narrow the search results and increase the likelihood of finding searchable collections of printer drivers.

You also can access the invisible Web by using specialized portals that list and organize searchable databases. An example of an invisible Web portal is CompletePlanet.com, which is shown in Figure TK D-8. CompletePlanet.com claims to access over 70,000 invisible Web databases that are frequently overlooked by traditional searching, and also offers a special search tool called the Deep Query Manager™.

If you spend a significant amount of time searching the invisible Web, you might want to use special navigation software to assist you. For example, EndNote is an application offered by Thomson Reuters, as shown in Figure TK D-9. EndNote uses a special information transfer method that allows a user to connect directly to hundreds of government and university databases on the invisible Web.

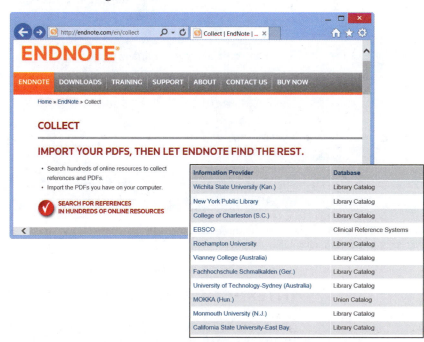

FIGURE TK D-9 Many researchers use Endnote, which allows you to connect directly to hundreds of government and university databases. The inset panel shows a small sample of the available sites and resources.
© 2012 Thomson Reuters

Another way to navigate the invisible Web is to use a **proprietary database;** your school or local library probably subscribes to several. Popular examples include EBSCOhost, ProQuest, and IEEE's Xplore. Also, the Association for Computing Machinery, which is described on page 642, has a very large IT database that is open to its members, including students who can join for a modest fee.

Figure TK D-10 shows a recap of the Internet tools and resources: search engines, subject directories, and the invisible Web. Notice that each has advantages and disadvantages.

Recap of Internet Search Resources

RESOURCE	POSSIBLE USES	ADVANTAGES	DISADVANTAGES	NOTES
Search Engines	Good initial starting point, especially if you have an overall understanding of the topic. Search engines can lead you to important government, professional, or commercial sites.	Flexibility. You can choose from many different engines with various features. Some allow newsgroup access as well. Meta-search engines can return and rank results from multiple sources. Advanced search techniques can be used.	Frequently produces information overload. Can return many irrelevant or out-of-date links. Without a refined search, it is impossible to examine results carefully. Some sites allow companies to improve their hits by "pay for performance."	You can improve search effectiveness significantly by using advanced search techniques based on logical operators.
Subject Directories	Good way to get a broad overview of a topic before accessing specific sites.	With a subject directory, you can maintain broader focus and perspective, and work from the general to the specific without getting lost in a maze of Web sites.	Material is organized by human intervention; quality, currency, and accuracy might vary.	Once you work your way through the various levels, you might be able to bookmark the resource for more direct future access.
Invisible Web	Information from nonindexed databases and searchable directories such as company financial reports, library holdings, industry reports, and government information.	Very diverse resource. Many more pages on the Web are non-indexed rather than indexed.	Can be difficult to access unless you know where to look. Navigating a searchable database can be more difficult than using a traditional search engine, because no common interface exists.	Portal sites are available to help you navigate the invisible Web. You can use a general search engine to locate searchable databases by searching a subject term and the word *database*.

FIGURE TK D-10 A recap of the three main Internet search resources: search engines, subject directories, and the invisible Web. Notice that each option has advantages and disadvantages.

© Cengage Learning 2014

INTERNET COMMUNICATION CHANNELS

Suppose that you are asked to analyze your organization's virus protection requirements. As part of your research, you would want to learn about relevant news, developments, and the latest virus threats. You also might want to suggest several specific products. Assume that you performed your research using a search engine. Now you want to check your conclusions by getting feedback from other IT professionals. You can consider using social networking sites, forums, newsletters, blogs, podcasts, Webcasts, RSS feeds, Webinars, mailing lists, Web-based discussion groups, chat rooms, and instant messaging.

Social Networking

Social networking sites such as Facebook, Twitter, and LinkedIn have gained enormous popularity in recent years. Many people use these communication channels along with more traditional choices, such as e-mail, blogs, chat rooms, and instant messaging. As a systems analyst, social networking allows you to connect to an extended family of personal and professional contacts, with unlimited opportunities.

Forums

Most people are familiar with bulletin boards they see at school, at work, and in their communities. Using thumbtacks or tape, people post information and read what others have posted. A **forum**, or **newsgroup**, is the electronic equivalent of the everyday bulletin board. Forums offer online discussions that address every conceivable subject and interest area. A forum can put you in touch with the knowledge, experience, and opinions of a large online community.

Yahoo! and Google allow users to join thousands of groups, and to create new ones if they wish. The Google site in Figure TK D-11 shows Google Groups, which offers a user-friendly interface and many social media features.

Because of its dominant role in the search engine market, Google users have another benefit: in addition to recent content, they can search literally millions of postings that go back many years.

To understand how forums work, consider the following example. In your research on virus protection, which was mentioned in the previous section, assume that you have narrowed the product choices down to two. You are having trouble, however, differentiating between them and would like feedback from current users. You might want to visit individual product sites for user testimonials, but you would be unlikely to find a negative opinion on a vendor's site. You also could poll your professional colleagues, but you want to survey a variety of users that goes beyond your limited circle.

At this point, you might decide to tap into an appropriate newsgroup and see if there have been any postings that are relevant to you. Some forums are moderated, in which articles are sent to a person who approves them before they are posted for the group. Before you post, you should read the FAQ files associated with each newsgroup. The term **FAQs** stands for **frequently asked questions**. FAQs are a common method of providing guidance on questions that users are likely

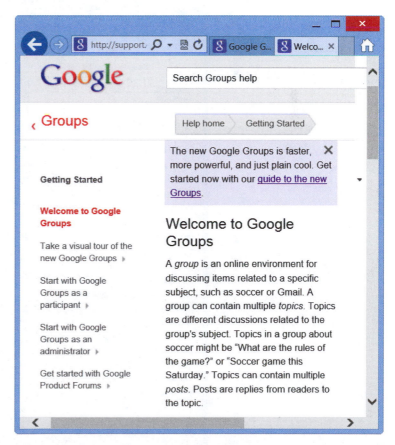

FIGURE TK D-11   Google Groups allows you to participate in numerous discussion groups on every imaginable topic, and to create new groups.
Courtesy of Google

to ask. In many cases, FAQs describe the particular **netiquette**, or Web guidelines for protocol and courtesy, that exist on a particular newsgroup or site. You can learn more about netiquette in Part A of the Systems Analyst's Toolkit.

As you gain experience, you might decide to subscribe to forums that address topics of interest to you.

Newsletters, Blogs, Podcasts, and Webcasts

Newsletters are a convenient way to keep current on topics of interest. Many online magazines and other groups offer free e-mail newsletters to subscribers interested in specific topics. For example, as shown in Figure TK D-12, *InfoWorld* readers can access a wide range of newsletters, blogs, and podcasts.

A **blog** is a Web-based log, or journal. Computer-related blogs can provide valuable information for a systems analyst. Also, many vendors offer Web-based training options, including podcasts. A **podcast**, sometimes called a **Webcast**, refers to online material that can be delivered as a streaming download to users, who can receive multimedia files and open them on a computer or download them to an iPod®, iPad®, smartphone, or other portable player. Podcasts can be prescheduled, made available on demand, or delivered as automatic updates, depending on a user's preference. An advantage of a podcast is that users, called subscribers, can access the material anywhere, anytime.

RSS Feeds

The term **RSS** stands for **Really Simple Syndication**. RSS is a format for publishing frequently updated content to users who subscribe to an RSS download, also called a feed, an **RSS feed,** or a **Web feed**. Web publishers such as Yahoo!, Google, CNN, MSNBC, and many other newspapers, magazines, vendors, and blogs use RSS feeds to distribute news and updates to subscribers, who can read the content with software called an **RSS reader**, a **feed reader,** or an **aggregator**.

Figure TK D-13 shows how Yahoo! uses RSS feeds to publish news items, and a sample of the wide variety of available topics. Many main headings, such as *Computers and Internet*, also contain a lengthy list of subtopics. In addition, Yahoo! allows you to create a custom RSS feed by typing a term or phrase

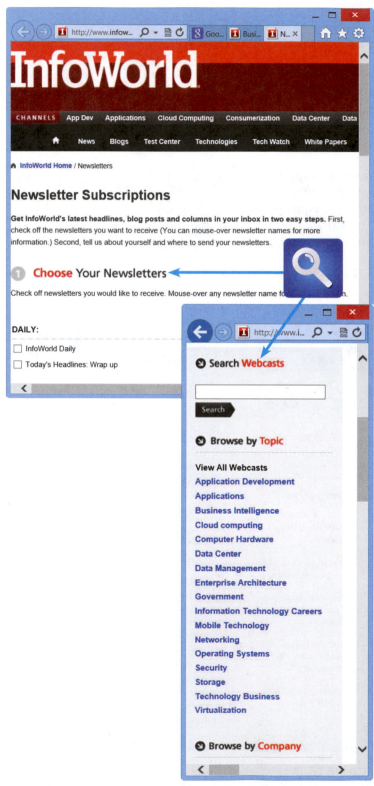

FIGURE TK D-12 InfoWorld offers free newsletters, Webcasts, and other valuable online resources.

into a search box. For example, if you were especially interested in news updates about Cisco routers, you could create a Yahoo! feed that would capture and download all articles on that topic. Yahoo! feeds make it easy for an IT professional to stay well informed on topics of interest. However, notice the important caution regarding the use of the content. Yahoo! states that the feeds are free for individuals and nonprofit organizations for noncommercial use, but that proper attribution is required.

Webinars

A **Webinar**, which combines the words *Web* and *seminar*, is an Internet-based training session that provides an interactive experience. Most Webinars are scheduled events with a group of preregistered users and an online presenter or instructor. A prerecorded Webinar session also can be delivered as a Webcast.

Mailing Lists

A **mailing list**, also called a **listserv**, is similar to a newsgroup in that it provides a forum for people who want to exchange information about specific topics. Like a newsgroup, users can post messages and view postings made by others. Instead of a bulletin board approach, however, a mailing list uses e-mail to communicate with users. A computer called a **list server** directs e-mail to people who subscribe to, or join, the mailing list.

What kind of content does the Yahoo! Directory offer via RSS?
The Yahoo! Directory is a human-created and maintained library of web sites organized into categories and subcategories. Yahoo! editors review these sites for potential inclusion in the Directory, and to evaluate the best place to list them.

The Yahoo! Directory is now offering the following feeds in RSS format. The feeds are free of charge to individuals and nonprofit organizations for non-commercial use. Attribution (included in each feed) is required.

| Arts |
| Arts > Literature |
| Arts > Performing Arts |
| Arts > Photography |
| Arts > U.S. History |
| Business and Economy |
| Business and Economy > Business to Business |
| Business and Economy > Shopping and Services |
| Computers and Internet |
| Computers > Video Games |
| Computers > Viruses & Worms |
| Computers > Weblogs |
| Education |
| Entertainment |
| Entertainment > Actors and Actresses |
| Entertainment > Celebrity Galleries |
| Entertainment > Movies |

FIGURE TK D-13 Yahoo! uses RSS feeds to publish news about a wide variety of topics, some of which are shown here. The Yahoo! site also allows you to create a customized feed by entering a search term or phrase.
© 2012 Yahoo! Inc.

When a person subscribes to a list, he or she can receive e-mail messages as they are posted. Subscribers also can access a collection of messages called a **digest**. Many mailing lists maintain Web sites where users can search message archives.

A systems analyst would be interested in mailing lists that focus on information technology. To locate IT-related mailing lists, you can visit the Web sites of professional organizations, and you can try adding the phrase *mailing list or listserv* to your search topic. Also, as shown in Figure TK D-14 on the next page, you can visit Web sites such as *lsoft.com* and *tile.net* that organize mailing lists by name and subject.

Web-Based Discussion Groups

Another online communication resource is called a **Web-based discussion group**, which is an online community that combines features of mailing lists and forums. Web-based discussion groups can be accessed through portals, such as Yahoo! or Google, or by visiting vendor sites, such as Cisco, IBM, or Apple. Group members can receive messages either individually or in digest form like a mailing list, and they can browse messages stored on the group's Web site. In addition to text messages, group Web sites often include membership lists and contact information, photo galleries, and links of interest to members.

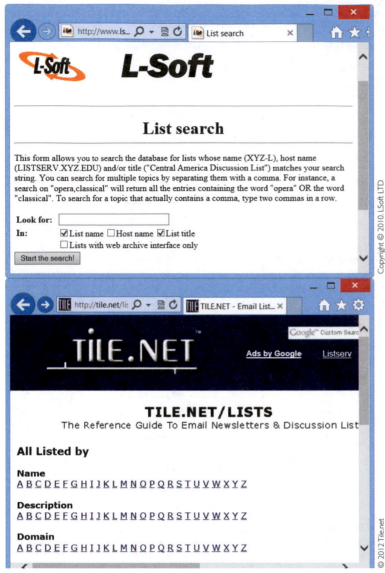

FIGURE TK D-14   Lsoft.com and tile.net are examples of Web sites that organize mailing lists by name and subject.

Suppose you crossed an excellent technical support site with a great social network. What would you get? The answer might be Microsoft Community, which is shown in Figure TK D-15.

Web-based discussion groups are popular because they offer a convenient and free meeting place with a graphical interface that makes it easy for users to access information and exchange messages.

Chat Rooms

A **chat room**, also called a **channel,** is an online meeting place where users can interact and converse in real time. The chat room concept originated with **IRC**, which stands for **Internet Relay Chat**. IRC is a multichannel system supported by servers that enable conversations, group or individual, on a worldwide basis. You can learn more about IRC at the Web site *www.irc.org*, and you can follow links to see a list of available IRC channels that might be of interest to you.

Instant Messaging and Text Messaging

Instant messaging (IM) allows online users to exchange messages immediately, even while they are working in another program or application. Users are alerted that other members of their group are available online, and users can send and receive messages or enter into a chat with other users.

Although instant messaging began as a popular feature in home-oriented services such as AOL and Yahoo!, it has become an important business communications tool, and many firms use enterprise-wide IM tools such as Microsoft Lync. Corporate use of IM, however, raises serious security and privacy concerns because it is relatively uncontrolled. Also, certain industries such as banking and health care must observe legal regulations that govern all their communications, including IM, which must be logged and documented. Corporate security can be compromised by unauthorized instant messaging and exchange of files. Also, applications such as Skype and other computer-based voice and video channels add a burden to network bandwidth and efficiency. To combat these threats, firms such as Blue Coat offer software that can manage instant messaging and provide necessary security and controls.

Many people use **text messaging**, or **texting**, to send brief written messages from one mobile phone or wireless device to another. Users can also send text messages from a computer to a handheld device. The popularity of IM and texting has given rise to hundreds of abbreviations that reduce message size and speed up the communication process. Some well-known examples include HTH (*hope that helps*), IDK (*I don't know*), IMHO (*in my humble opinion*), JSYK (*just so you know*), LOL (*laugh*

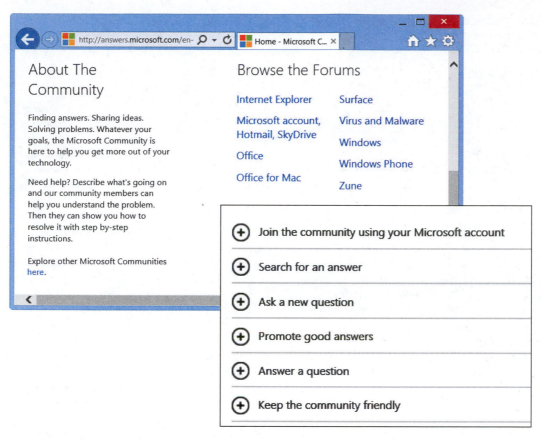

FIGURE TK D-15   The Microsoft Community site offers technical forums, searchable knowledge bases, and an opportunity to meet, interact, and share your views with colleagues and people with similar interests.

Screenshot used with permission from Microsoft.

out loud), MIRL (*meet in real life*), and TYIA (*thank you in advance*). Abbreviations like these are especially important to Twitter users, who are limited to 140 characters in each message.

Figure TK D-16 on the next page shows a recap of online IT channels that can assist a systems analyst in online research and communication: social networking sites, forums, newsletters, mailing lists, RSS feeds, Web-based discussion groups, chat rooms, and instant messaging. Notice that each resource has advantages and disadvantages.

INFORMATION TECHNOLOGY COMMUNITY RESOURCES

If you were asked to check a stock price or research the weather in a distant city for a business trip, you probably would not use a search engine. Instead, you would visit a favorite site you use regularly to access specific information. Similarly, when you require IT information, you can access a huge assortment of sites and resources that can be called the **information technology (IT) community**. This vast collection includes many sites that IT professionals can use to research specific questions or obtain background information. As a systems analyst, you are a member of this community. Like most communities, it offers you resources and support, including answers to technical questions, updates on new products and services, and information about training opportunities. The IT community includes numerous publications and online magazines, searchable databases, Web-based discussion groups, and mailing lists.

Four important components of the IT community are corporate resources, government resources, professional resources, and online learning resources, which are described in the following sections.

Recap of Internet Communication Channels

RESOURCE	POSSIBLE USES	ADVANTAGES	DISADVANTAGES	NOTES
Social Networking Sites	Communicating with others who share similar interests.	Opens up new resources that can help you personally and professionally.	Your network can become too large and impersonal. Too much activity can be distracting.	Extremely convenient, popular, and no subscription fees.
Forums	Answers to technical questions, advice, and support.	Can find information on every conceivable subject — good place to exchange views with other analysts.	Cumbersome to search through message threads. Need to assess quality of information carefully.	Some major search engines allow newsgroup access.
Newsletters, Blogs, and Podcasts	Good way to follow trends and developments regarding specific IT topics.	Most newsletters, blogs, and podcasts are free to users who can subscribe to specific topics.	Not interactive, and the amount of information can be overwhelming. Difficult to filter irrelevant items.	Some newsletters, blogs, and podcasts are published daily; others weekly or monthly.
RSS Feeds	Provide news and updates for readers of online newspapers, magazines, and blogs.	Convenient way to keep posted on virtually any topic of interest.	Unless topics are specific, the volume of information might be difficult to sift through.	Rapid growth is expected to continue as more users discover this valuable resource.
Webinars	Internet-based training that can provide an interactive experience.	Users can plan, schedule, and pre-register for online sessions.	Only available when scheduled — otherwise not interactive.	Very popular technique because of convenience and cost-effectiveness.
Mailing Lists	Members can exchange information with others about specific topic of interest.	Messages arrive by e-mail, rather than in the form of bulletin board postings.	Amount of material might be difficult to read and analyze.	Some mailing lists, or listservs, allow members to search archived messages.
Web Discussion Groups	Members form a Web-based community regarding topics of common interest.	Combine many convenient features of forums and mailing lists.	Although free, these groups usually must be accessed through a Web portal.	Web discussion groups offer a mix of features and convenience.
Chat Rooms	Online meeting places where users can interact and converse.	Many IT chat rooms attract professionals who are willing to help each other solve problems.	Discussions take place in real time, which might not be convenient. Dialog might be unfocused and irrelevant to your needs.	Many large vendors, such as Microsoft, offer technical chat rooms.
Instant Messaging and Text Messaging	Users can exchange messages immediately, either online or by cell phone.	Highly efficient means of real-time communication on topics of interest. Good way to collaborate on team projects.	Can be distracting to a busy user, and sheer volume of nonessential messages can be a problem.	IM and text messaging have moved beyond the personal desktop and are acceptable business communication tools.

FIGURE TK D-16 A recap of Internet communication channels that can assist a systems analyst in online research and communication. Notice that each option has advantages and disadvantages.

Corporate Resources

Corporate resources can provide general IT knowledge and background, as well as help solve specific business challenges. It is very important to evaluate corporate content carefully, because some sites are developed by companies with an interest in selling you a specific solution or product.

If you are looking for help on a software application, it is a good idea to start by reviewing the software documentation. In many cases, technical support is included free of charge for a specific period of time. If you are working with an application with expired technical support, the software provider's Web site will describe support options that are available to you, including various fees and charges. Common problems often are addressed in the FAQ section.

An important corporate resource to systems analysts is their own internal company Web site or intranet. An intranet must be easy to access and provide access to valuable information. Companies increasingly are using intranets as a means of sharing information and working toward common solutions. Intranets can contain company policies and procedures, lessons-learned files, and financial information. They also enable employees to access and update their personal benefit information. In many organizations, the intranet is reducing the volume of paper memos and reports by serving as an enterprise-wide library and clearinghouse.

Government Resources

The IT needs of the federal government are enormous. Not surprisingly, a number of excellent federal IT resources are available on the Internet. Many sites offer comprehensive, nonbiased information and valuable advice for IT professionals. For example, recent U.S. General Accounting Office (GAO) reports on the IT industry have covered everything from an analysis of the information security practices to a framework for assessing IT investments. Additionally, government sites can provide information on federal, state, and local business policies and regulations. The General Services Administration (GSA) site depicted in Figure TK D-17 is a good source for federal policies and regulations, especially for firms that do business with the government.

Personal and Professional Resources

Most individuals have friends, acquaintances, and other people who they know or would like to meet. Whether the communication channel involves e-mail, chats, forums, or social networking, the goal is to expand contacts and opportunities. Some observers have compared social networks to small virtual communities or neighborhoods, where people can meet and share information. Their objectives might be personal, or might relate to technical matters, career topics, or professional growth.

In addition to social networking, a systems analyst can consider membership in one or more IT-related

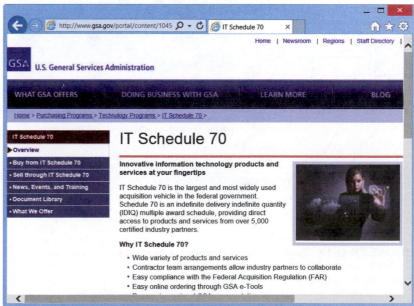

FIGURE TK D-17 The GSA site contains information about federal IT policies, news, and related links. The screen shows a sample from the IT Regulations, Guidelines, and Laws section.

FIGURE TK D-18 The ACM site is one of many resources that a systems analyst can use to keep up with current issues, trends, and opportunities.
© 2012 ACM

FIGURE TK D-19 Students should explore the Modern Analyst site, which includes forums about many topics covered in this textbook. This would be a good place to connect with others and share information.
© 2006-2011 by Modern Analyst Media LLC

associations. Many organizations focus on a specific topic such as project management, software engineering, or information security. Membership in some associations is free or relatively inexpensive, and employers often subsidize professional memberships that are directly related to a person's job duties. The links provided by these sites often are quite useful. Professional organizations, such as the **Information Technology Association of America (ITAA)** or the **Association for Computing Machinery (ACM)**, which is shown in Figure TK D-18, also sponsor seminars and training. Many associations offer electronic newsletters that relate to your area of interest and are delivered to you by e-mail on a periodic basis.

Systems analysts also should be aware of the Modern Analyst site shown in Figure TK D-19. Notice that the forums include many topics covered in this textbook. This site would be an excellent source of information, and a place to connect with others.

Online Learning Resources

It is difficult to keep up with the constantly changing IT landscape. Targeted professional development is a way for IT workers to remain focused and current in their chosen areas. In the past, this goal often meant attending lengthy and expensive off-site training courses. Advances in bandwidth and processing power have made online learning an increasingly attractive option for many IT professionals.

Online learning, also referred to as **e-learning**, is a term that refers to the delivery of educational or training content over the public Internet or an intranet. You can locate learning opportunities by searching the Web or through various professional associations. Many schools and colleges have seen a tremendous increase in demand for online learning and have increased their course offerings accordingly.

Online learning can take many forms, ranging from individual self-paced instruction with little or no instructor involvement, to interactive, instructor-led groups with streaming audio and video capability. When choosing an online learning method, your learning goals and the quality of the content are the most important considerations. You need to think about your personal learning preferences. For example, you might learn better in a collaborative environment rather than working alone. If that is the case, consider options that include an interactive peer community. The following are some advantages and disadvantages that apply to the use of online resources:

BENEFITS OF ONLINE LEARNING   Benefits of online learning include the following:

- Convenient. You can participate in training when and where you want.

- Economical. Online learning options generally are less expensive than traditional face-to-face learning.

- Customizable. Generally, you can tailor the learning experience to your interests and needs.

DISADVANTAGES OF ONLINE LEARNING   Disadvantages of online learning include the following:

- Interaction. Although online learning can be highly collaborative, it lacks the face-to-face component that some learners find necessary. Additionally, you are less likely to receive the focused feedback that you would get when participating in traditional classroom training.

- Interface. Although bandwidth and computing power have increased greatly in recent years, the interface in an online learning experience might be a limitation. For example, you might experience slower processing performance, especially if the training uses interactive video, audio, or high-resolution graphics.

- Suitability. Online learning might not be the best option, particularly if the content is complicated and unfamiliar to you.

Figure TK D-20 shows a recap of online IT resources, including possible uses, advantages, and disadvantages.

Recap of Online IT Resources

RESOURCE	POSSIBLE USES	ADVANTAGES	DISADVANTAGES	NOTES
Corporate Resources	Specific technical hardware or software help, training opportunities.	First stop for troubleshooting proprietary software or hardware.	Very often an agenda is associated with the site — for example, advocating a particular product or service.	Vendor sites contain valuable specific product or solution information (check the site's FAQs). Many offer newsletters for interested visitors.
Government Resources	Information on IT regulations.	Wide variety of general topics, from congressional studies to industry-relevant government regulations.	Not all information can be accessed via the Web — sometimes sites refer to a document number for ordering. Information tends to be general and not always relevant.	Suggested sites: Library of Congress, General Accounting Office, Government Computer News.

Continues

RESOURCE	POSSIBLE USES	ADVANTAGES	DISADVANTAGES	NOTES
Personal and Professional Resources	A combination of social networking, access to professional sites, and membership in IT organizations can expand personal and professional resources related to IT ethics, technical issues, and career opportunities.	Social networking is fun because it involves person-to-person contact. IT industry-related sites often provide valuable links and information on training opportunities.	Social networking is not a precise tool for specific issues. Conversely, many IT sites are too specialized to be of general interest.	Some IT sites can serve as portals to a collection of online resources.
Online Learning Resources	An IT professional needs to stay current in a constantly changing technology environment. Online learning can provide job-specific skills and support for career advancement.	Convenient, economical, and customizable. You can participate in training when and where you want, and online learning options are generally less expensive than traditional face-to-face learning.	Online learning lacks the face-to-face component that some learners find necessary. Learners are less likely to receive focused feedback. Also, the interface in an online learning experience might be a limitation. Online learning might not be the best option if the content is complicated and unfamiliar.	When considering online learning, you must know your personal learning style. You should examine the entire range of options, from individual self-paced instruction with little or no instructor involvement, to inter-active, instructor-led classes.

FIGURE TK D-20   A recap of online resources that a systems analyst can use to keep up with current issues and trends in IT. Notice that each option has advantages and disadvantages.

© Cengage Learning 2014

TOOLKIT SUMMARY

The Internet is a worldwide network that integrates many thousands of other networks, which in turn link millions of government, business, educational, and personal users around the globe. The Internet can assist you in your daily work by helping you solve technical problems and in the ongoing development of your career by providing access to training and professional education.

The Internet allows access to the World Wide Web, usually called the Web, which refers to the global collection of electronic documents stored on the Internet. These documents are referred to as Web pages, which are organized and stored on individual Web sites.

An Internet research strategy should use a four-step approach: review your information requirements, use the proper search tools and techniques, evaluate the results, and consider copyright and data integrity issues. Many people find it helpful to prepare for an Internet search by using a checklist to identify key terms, phrases, and characteristics of the topic.

The primary research tools include search engines, subject directories, and a collection of searchable database resources called the invisible Web. A search engine uses keywords and phrases to locate information on the Internet and list the results of the search. Users should be aware that results can be affected if the search engine permits commercial users to achieve higher priority based on payment of fees. Also, search engines access only a portion of the Internet. Meta-search engines are tools that can apply multiple search engines simultaneously.

A subject directory is a Web site that allows you to access topics by using a hierarchy, starting with general headings and proceeding to more specific topics. A subject directory is an excellent starting point when you want an overview of a particular topic before proceeding to specific Web sites.

The invisible Web, or hidden Web, describes numerous text, graphics, and data files stored in collections that are unreachable by search engines.

Many analysts use social networking as a primary online tool to expand personal and professional contacts and communication. Other Internet tools that might be of value to a systems analyst are forums, newsletters, blogs, podcasts, RSS feeds, Webinars, mailing lists, Web-based discussion groups, chat rooms, and instant messaging. Forums, or newsgroups, are online discussion groups that address every conceivable subject and interest area. Newsletters are published by numerous commercial and nonprofit groups that offer membership subscriptions to users who are interested in specific topics. A mailing list, or listserv, allows subscribing members to post and receive messages forwarded to them by a list server. A Web-based discussion group, usually accessed through a portal such as Yahoo!, combines features of forums and mailing lists for its members. A chat room is an online meeting place where users can interact and converse in real time. Instant messaging allows online users to exchange messages immediately, even while they are working in another program or application.

When an IT professional needs to research a topic or seek background information, he or she can turn to an assortment of sites and resources called the information technology (IT) community. The IT community includes corporate, government, professional, and online learning resources.

Professional development through online learning is a way for IT workers to remain current in their chosen areas. Online learning refers to the delivery of educational or training content over the Internet or an intranet. Online learning is convenient, economical, and customizable. Some disadvantages, however, include a lack of face-to-face interaction, limitations of the interface, and the fact that not everyone works well with this type of training.

Key Terms

Toolkit Exercises

Questions

1. Are the Internet and the World Wide Web one and the same? Why or why not?

2. How do search engines differ from subject directories? Is one approach better than the other? Why or why not?

3. What is the invisible Web, and how large is it?

4. How would you plan an Internet research strategy?

5. How would you assess the *quality* of Internet research results?

6. What are sponsored links? Could they affect the quality of your search results? How?

7. What is Boolean logic? Provide three examples using everyday terms.

8. What do Venn diagrams display, and why is the information valuable?

9. Describe social networking, forums, newsletters, blogs, podcasts, RSS feeds, Webinars, mailing lists, Web-based discussion groups, chat rooms, and instant messaging. How can these tools be used in Internet research?

10. What is the information technology community, and what resources does it offer?

Discussion Topics

1. The textbook explains that some companies pay to obtain a higher ranking when search results are displayed. Is this good, is it bad, or does it not matter to you as a user? Explain your position.

2. Some people rely heavily on social networking, instant messaging, and texting to communicate with friends and business colleagues. Others find these methods distracting. Do you use social networking, instant messaging, or texting? Why or why not?

3. Could Boolean logic and Venn diagrams be useful in everyday life? How might they be used?

4. The Internet has affected many aspects of our society. What are the most important benefits of the Internet, and what problems has it created?

Projects

1. Use a search engine and enter the following words: *presidential candidates in 2016*. Run the search and notice how many results appear. Now place quotation marks around the phrase and run the search again. Explain the difference in the results.

2. Will the search phrase *commercial television* return the same results as the phrase *television commercial*? Experiment with a search engine, and explain the results you obtain.

3. Use the Yahoo! subject directory to identify two dictionaries of technical terms. Begin with the subject *Computer & Internet*, and then follow the appropriate links until you obtain results. Describe the results of your research. What other research strategies could you use for this task?

4. Perform research on the Web to learn more about RSS feeds. Then write a practical, step-by-step guide for users who want to set up RSS feeds at their workstations.

INDEX

associative entity An entity that has its own set of attributes and characteristics. Associative entities are used to link between many-to-many (M:N) relationships. 361

ATM. *See* automated teller machine (ATM)

attack A hostile act that targets an information system, or an organization itself. 526

attribute A single characteristic or fact about an entity. An attribute, or field, is the smallest piece of data that has meaning within an information system. For example, a Social Security number or company name could be examples of an attribute. In object-oriented analysis, an attribute is part of a class diagram that describes the characteristics of objects in the class. Also known as a data element. 226, 229–230, 356, 461

audience, defining for oral presentation, 572

audit fields Special fields within data records to provide additional control or security information. Typical audit fields include the date the record was created or modified, the name of the user who performed the action, and the number of times the record has been accessed. 390

audit log files Audit log files record details of all accesses and changes to a file or database and can be used to recover changes made since the last backup. 390

audit trail An audit trail records the source of each data item and when it entered a system. In addition to recording the original source, an audit trail must show how and when data is accessed or changed, and by whom. All these actions must be logged in an audit trail file and monitored carefully. 301, 330

authorization zone Part of a form that contains any required signatures. 320

automated facsimile A system that allows a customer to request a fax using e-mail, the company Web site, or a telephone. The response is transmitted in a matter of seconds back to the user's fax machine. 327

automated teller machine (ATM), 327, 329, 422–423

automatic update service Enables an application to contact the vendor's server and check for a needed patch. 535–536

availability One of the three main elements of system security: confidentiality, integrity, and availability (CIA). Availability ensures that authorized users have timely and reliable access to necessary information. 524

avoidance One of four risk control strategies. In avoidance, the risk is eliminated by adding protective safeguards. 526

back door attack, 527

backup The process of saving a series of file or data copies to be retained for a specified period of time. Data can be backed up continuously, or at prescribed intervals. 540–543

backup media Data storage options, including tape, hard drives, optical storage, and online storage. 541

backup policy A backup policy contains detailed instructions and procedures for all backups. 541

balancing A process used to maintain consistency among an entire series of diagrams, including input and output data flows, data definition, and process descriptions. 192, 194–196

bandwidth The amount of data that the system can handle in a fixed time period. Bandwidth requirements are expressed in bits per second (bps). 419, 520

baseline A formal reference point that measures system characteristics at a specific time. Systems analysts use baselines as yardsticks to document features and performance during the systems development process. 518

Basic Service Set (BSS) A wireless network configuration in which a central wireless device called an access point is used to serve all wireless clients; also called infrastructure mode. 430–431

batch A group of data, usually inputted into an information system at the same time. 328

batch control A total used to verify batch input. Batch controls might check data items such as record counts and numeric field totals. For example, before entering a batch of orders, a user might calculate the total number of orders and the sum of all the order quantities. When the batch of orders is entered, the order system also calculates the same two totals. If the system totals do not match the input totals, then a data entry error has occurred. 318

batch input A process where data entry is performed on a specified time schedule, such as daily, weekly, monthly, or longer. For example, batch input occurs when a payroll department collects time cards at the end of the week and enters the data as a batch. 328

batch processing, 423

B2B (business-to-business) A commercial exchange (e.g. products or services) between businesses, typically enabled by the Internet or electronic means. 9, 10

B2C (business-to-consumer) A commercial exchange (e.g. products or services) between businesses and consumers conducted over the Internet. 9

BCP. *See* business continuity plan (BCP)

benchmark A benchmark measures the time a package takes to process a certain number of transactions. 279–280

benchmark testing Benchmark testing is used by companies to measure system performance. 279

benefit analysis. *See* cost-benefit analysis

Bergman, Michael K. 632

best-case estimate The most optimistic outcome is called the best-case estimate. 96

Bigazi Modeler, 242–243

binary digit The smallest unit of data is one binary digit, called a bit. 388

binary storage format A format that offers efficient storage of numeric data. For example, when you specify numeric data types using Microsoft Access, you can choose from a variety of storage formats, including integer and long integer, among others. 388

Bing, 626

biometric devices Devices that identify a person by a retina scan or by mapping a facial pattern. 56

biometric scanning systems Mapping an individual's facial features, handprint, or eye characteristics for identification purposes. 528

BIOS-level password A password that must be entered before the computer can be started. It prevents an unauthorized person from booting a computer by using a USB device or a CD-ROM. Also called a power-on password or a boot-level password. 529

bit The smallest unit of data is one binary digit, called a bit. 388

BitLocker (Windows 8), 537

black box A metaphor for a process or action that produces results in a non-transparent or non-observable manner. In data flow diagrams, a process appears as a black box where the inputs, outputs, and general function of the process are known, but the underlying details are not shown. 181–182, 231–232

black hole A process is said to be a "black hole" if it has no output. 183

block sequence code Code that uses blocks of numbers for different classifications. 382

blog A Web-based log, or journal. 326, 636, 640

Bluetooth A form of wireless transmission very popular for short-distance wireless communication that does not require high power. 330, 432

body zone The main part of the form. It usually takes up at least half of the space on the form and contains captions and areas for entering variable data. 320

Boehm, Barry, 26

Boeing, 15

Boole, George, 628

Boolean logic A system named after British mathematician George Boole and refers to the relationships among search terms. 628–629

boot-level password A password that must be entered before the computer can be started. It prevents an unauthorized person from booting a computer by using a USB device or a CD-ROM. Also called a BIOS-level password or a boot-level password. 529

bottom-up technique A bottom-up technique analyzes a large, complex project as a series of individual tasks, called project tasks. 93

BPM. *See* business process model (BPM)

BPMN. *See* business process modeling notation (BPMN)

BPO. *See* business process outsourcing (BPO)

brainstorming A fact-finding technique for gaining information, through the use of a small group discussion of a specific problem, opportunity, or issue. 159–160

Brooks, Frederick, Jr. 113

Brooks' Law This interesting concept was stated by Frederick Brooks, Jr. an IBM engineer, who observed that adding manpower to a late software project only makes it later. 115

browser A Web browser, or browser, is a software program that allows you to access and display Web pages that are delivered to you by a Web server. 622

BSS. *See* Basic Service Set (BSS)

bug tracking software System developers use defect tracking software, sometimes called bug tracking software, to document and track program defects, code changes, and replacement code, called patches. 469

build or buy Choice between developing in-house software and purchasing software, often called a build or buy, or make or buy, decision. 266–268

Burton Group, 538

bus network In a bus network, a single communication path connects the mainframe computer, server, workstations, and peripheral devices. Information is transmitted in either direction from any workstation to another workstation, and any message can be directed to a specific device. 426–427

business, 9–13
　B2B, 9, 10
　B2C, 9
　continuity, 542–543
　future, 10–13
　information systems, 14–17
　Internet model, 9
　modeling business operations, 13–14

business analytics Using software to measure past performance to help managers understand business trends and monitor current operations. 589

business case Refers to the reasons, or justification, for a proposal. 48, 54–55

business continuity plan (BCP) A plan that defines how critical business functions can continue in the event of a major disruption. 542–543

business information system, 14–17

business logic Business logic determines how a system handles data and produces useful information. Business logic, also called business rules, reflect the operational requirements of the business. Examples include adding the proper amount of sales tax to invoices, calculating customer balances and finance charges, and determining whether a customer is eligible for a volume-based discount. 181, 415

business model A business model graphically represents business functions that consist of business processes, such as sales, accounting, and purchasing. 19